Childhood
Psychopathology

a developmental approach

Childhood Psychopathology

a developmental approach

IRWIN J. KNOPF

Emory University

PRENTICE–HALL, INC., ENGLEWOOD CLIFFS, N.J. 07632

ABC4018

Library of Congress Cataloging in Publication Data

Knopf, Irwin J. (date).
  Childhood psychopathology.

  Bibliography: p.
  Includes index.
  1. Child psychopathology. I. Title. [DNLM:
1. Psychopathology—In infancy and childhood.
2. Mental disorders—In infancy and childhood.
WS350 K72e]
RJ499.K57   618.9′28′907   78–10101
ISBN 0–13–130336–8

© 1979 by Prentice-Hall, Inc., Englewood Cliffs, N.J. 07632

Printed in the United States of America

10 9 8 7 6 5 4 3 2 1

Editorial/production supervision by Marina Harrison
Cover design by Judy Knopf
Manufacturing buyer: Phil Galea

PRENTICE-HALL INTERNATIONAL, INC., *London*
PRENTICE-HALL OF AUSTRALIA PTY. LIMITED, *Sydney*
PRENTICE-HALL OF CANADA, LTD., *Toronto*
PRENTICE-HALL OF INDIA PRIVATE LIMITED, *New Delhi*
PRENTICE-HALL OF JAPAN, INC., *Tokyo*
PRENTICE-HALL OF SOUTHEAST ASIA PTE. LTD., *Singapore*
WHITEHALL BOOKS LIMITED, *Wellington, New Zealand*

DEDICATED TO BOBBIE

Contents

PART III   Clinical Syndromes

PART IV   Future Considerations

Preface

Throughout its history, the field of psychopathology has been concerned almost exclusively with disorders of the adult years while little, if any, attention has been directed toward childhood psychopathology. One only needs to examine the traditional college course offerings and the many published textbooks in the area for ample support of this observation. And yet, the primary emphasis on adult aberrations is understandable since it reflects the relative availability of clinical and research findings on these populations.

However, our society's recent fascination with youth has stimulated the strong need to identify quick and easy child rearing formulae and to establish special child-centered programs that promote normal development. Deviant behavioral patterns of youngsters, especially disruptive ones, have become matters of public concern because they have become too difficult to manage through society's existing institutions. Problems arising from mental retardation, learning disabilities, drug abuse, delinquency, and changing sexual mores, among others, cry out for social action. In turn, these issues have generated interest in the creation of programs of prevention, early identification, and remediation. The relatively new child sub-specialists in the fields of medicine, psychology, education, social work, and nursing have responded to this challenge by training a growing number of professionals who are prepared to study and work with abnormal behaviors in children. Their efforts already have furthered our understanding of the causes, treatment, and management of many childhood disorders. But we merely have explored the tip of the iceberg with so much more to be discovered!

This heightened public interest and the growing involvement of students in child-oriented professional careers are sufficient reasons for writing a textbook devoted entirely to childhood psychopathology. However, in the final analysis, my long time enthusiasm and fascination with the field became the dominant motivational force. My intention was to bring together in a single presentation as much as is currently known about childhood psychopathology without strict allegiance to either a particular theoretical viewpoint or a single source of data. Because too often our current knowledge is inconsistent and incomplete, I approached the writing with a conceptual openness and with the freedom to include the best available information from both the clinical and research literatures. However, extensiveness in reporting without direction and interpretation runs the risk of poor pedagogy, especially for beginning students. Consequently, I have tried to go beyond a compilation of what is currently known to include critical evaluations and limitations in our knowledge, interpretations of the accumulated data, and inferences about future directions.

As a scientist, I have a penchant for quantitative data that are obtained under controlled conditions. As a practicing clinician, I also have acquired a healthy respect for the contributions that even a single, but carefully observed, case can make. I believe that investigative endeavors can be sharpened appreciably by sound clinical insights, and that effective clinical work can be enhanced by a solid grasp of research methodology. Therefore, the book draws from the empirical, experimental, and clinical findings to provide students with a blend of information that hopefully will further their interest in both research and practice. In addition, excerpts from clinical cases and samples of research studies are included to illustrate various abnormal conditions, different treatment approaches, and methodological issues and problems.

Equally important to the substance and organization of the book is its emphasis on development which involves sequential and orderly changes over time in the organism's structure and function, and which is affected by the complex interplay of biological and socio-psychological factors. Behavior cannot be viewed as a static event that occurs simply "out of the blue". Instead, behavior can be understood more reasonably as a dynamic occurrence that has been influenced by prior conditions that interact in complex ways. Moreover, all behaviors lead to some consequences that, in turn, may trigger off other responses. In order to increase the student's appreciation of the dynamic and multi-dimensional nature of behavior in the growing child, a developmental perspective is taken as a major theme that is reflected in specific chapters as well as generally throughout the book. I also have tried (albeit imperfectly) to organize the chapters dealing with the various clinical syndromes within a broad developmental outline. While this developmental progression provides the student with an age perspective by which frequent and common abnormal behaviors may be viewed, the developmental progression should not be regarded as fixed or distinct time periods in which other forms of psychopathology cannot occur.

The book consists of fourteen chapters that are divided into four parts. The four chapters of Part I deal with introductory material and the basic issues of: Childhood Psychopathology: Past and Present; The Nature of Psychopathology; Normal Personality Development; and Conceptual Models of Psychopathology. Part II covers methods of assessment and treatment in two chapters, while Part III consists of seven chapters dealing with the full range of clinical syndromes from infancy through late adolescence and the college years. These clinical chapters discuss the behaviors manifested (symptoms), factors associated with the clinical picture, differential diagnostic problems, incidence estimates, etiological considerations (genetic, biological, and psychological), and the most frequently used and promising treatment approaches for each disorder. The final part of the book consists of a single chapter dealing with outcome implications and prevention.

Childhood Psychopathology was written as a comprehensive but beginning text primarily for undergraduates majoring in psychology, education, or sociology, or for those who are preparing for child-oriented careers in these areas or in medicine, dentistry, nursing, social work, counseling, juvenile justice or corrections. Although a specific undergraduate course of this type is not yet commonplace, I am persuaded that the situation will change rapidly over the next several years. Childhood psychopathology is simply too important, too alive and productive, and too relevant to college students to be omitted much longer from the usual course offerings. Until the change occurs at the college level, the book also should be useful to beginning graduate and professional students in a variety of child related programs as both a source of study and reference.

Completing an undertaking of this magnitude could not have been possible without the help, advice, and encouragement from so many giving people. I want to express my deep feelings of affection and gratitude to my wife, Bobbie, whose unfaltering love, understanding, and friendship for more than twenty-seven years have been a significant influence and a source of strength in my life. Her collaboration on this project was evident in so many ways, but especially in her genuine willingness to read the entire manuscript almost as many times as I did, and in her professional appraisal of the book's organization, contents, and readability. I also am proud of and grateful to our children, David, Bill and Randy for their encouragement and assistance with the manuscript, and particularly to our daughter, Judy, for her artistic talents in creating the cover for the book. I have been fortunate to be associated with helpful colleagues and loyal and dedicated graduate students who helped search the literature, evaluated various chapters, and checked the accuracy of references. I am grateful for their efforts and particularly those of Dr. Philip H. Dreyer, Nancy Hayim, June Kaufman, Richard Rosenberg, and Andrew Schiff. I also am indebted to the many anonymous reviewers whose criticisms and suggestions improved the manuscript, and to Jeffrey Bogart, John Isley, and Marina Harrison for their confidence and technical assistance. Finally, I owe a debt of gratitude to Margaret Madgett and Marcia Rice for their secretarial expertise and care with which they prepared the many drafts and the final manuscript.

Childhood
Psychopathology

a developmental approach

PART 1 Basic Issues

Childhood Psychopathology

past and present

1

PROLOGUE

Tommy W., a four-year-old only child, was referred for psychological evaluation because of his peculiar motor patterns and his slow emotional and social development. For more than a year his parents had been reluctant to take this step in spite of repeated urgings by their pediatrician who recognized that the boy was suffering from some serious psychological disorder. On the other hand, Mr. and Mrs. W. believed, since Tommy had been born prematurely, one day soon he would have a sudden spurt of growth that would bring his developmental level up to normal.

Mrs. W. had had some difficulty conceiving, but her pregnancy had been uneventful. Tommy weighed slightly over four pounds at birth, and he was placed in an incubator for about two weeks before he could be taken home. He slept in short bursts, but for the first few months he cried much of the time he was awake. He was bottle fed and would take only several ounces at a single feeding, prompting mother to feed him at frequent intervals. During this time she first noticed that he was unresponsive to being picked up and to being held by her or his father. His unresponsiveness to social stimuli continued, although he did show an early interest in toys. His motor development was slow in that he didn't stand until fourteen months or walk unaided until twenty months. Tommy spoke his first word on his first birthday, but within the next six months he spoke only two or three short sentences that were difficult to understand. At about age two, Tommy stopped speaking except for saying his own name and making funny vocal noises to himself.

Because of his unresponsiveness to people and his slow language development, Mr. and Mrs. W. thought Tommy might be hard of hearing, but medical tests revealed no auditory defect. He was toilet trained before his second birthday, but by the age of three, he began soiling his pants and smearing feces on the walls and on the furniture. At about this time, he also began to rock back and forth while sitting, to whirl on his toes in little circles, and to bang his head against the wall at bedtime. He engaged in these strange motor patterns for long periods while he vocalized incomprehensible sounds to himself. His disinterest in people continued, although he was fascinated and content when playing with his toys.

On examination, Tommy appeared to be frail, thin, and small for his age. He was neatly attired and tidy but he seemed to have a glazed and vacuous look on his face. He took the psychologist's hand and went with him to the play room without any show of concern about separating from his mother. During the evaluation session, Tommy spent much of the time either whirling or sitting in a corner rocking and banging his head against the wall. He rejected the examiner's overtures but became interested in playing with blocks. Except for his apparent interest and preference for inanimate objects, he was virtually unapproachable. During the several subsequent sessions, his peculiar motor patterns persisted. However, he did evidence interest in the play room and a need to rearrange the furniture and toys as he had previously left them. Each time he entered the playroom and found it changed, he screamed, whirled, and rocked for a short while and then went about putting everything back to the way it was before. Tommy was later diagnosed as a psychotic child (see Chapter 8) who required immediate and prolonged professional care.

One would think that the strange and peculiar behaviors of children like Tommy were always matters of public fascination and importance. But until recent years, abnormal behavior of children have been virtually ignored. Instead the possessed, the lunatic, or the mentally ill adult have captured the spotlight from the beginning of human history.

The reasons for the almost exclusive emphasis on adult abnormalities can be traced to the way Western civilization differentiated the responsibilities of adults and children, to the high mortality rate of children in ancient and medieval times, and to the failure of those early societies to distinguish childhood as separate and different from adult life.

Adults always have been expected to meet certain social and economic obligations for themselves, and, as society developed, for others as well (family and community). Since abnormal conditions often impair one's ability to meet these obligations, the afflicted adult can be a potential source of danger, an economic liability, and a community management problem. In severe instances, the community is forced to take some remedial action to preserve its own integrity. Past societies have dealt with the problem of afflicted adults by methods designed to either persuade or brutally torture the afflicted people in order to drive off the evil spirit. These societies have tried to isolate them through institutionalization (prisons or asylums) or to treat the sickness. Currently, we deal with the problem by more humane public provisions of free or low-cost treatment and hospitalization, and through public welfare and family subsistence programs.

In contrast, contemporary society views children as minors who are dependent on adults for their care and well being. Since society believes that children need supervision, it assigns this responsibility to the family and holds parents accountable for any disruption, danger, or economic loss their children create. Rarely, and only when parents fail to adequately manage their children, does the community become involved. Under these cultural guidelines, the problems of disordered adults are handled by the adults themselves or by the community, whereas those of children much more consistently are considered the responsibilities of the family. In addition, while society regards adults as more stable, more resistant to change, and more fixed in their behavioral patterns, it tends to view children as growing and everchanging organisms until they reach maturity (adulthood). Although this optimistic outlook regarding human development has important implications for prevention programs, it has been obscured for too long by the focus on the immediate problems of the abnormal adult, as well as by the common "do nothing, wait and see" attitude parents (such as Mr. and Mrs. W.) have readily adopted for their children.

Children have not always been viewed in this light, and many of our current ideas about them are of relative recent vintage. Therefore, we will begin with an historical review that traces the evolution of the ideas and forces that have led to the scientific inquiry of childhood psychopathology. This approach not only will enable us to show how and where childhood psychopathology began, but also will provide a broader context with which to view the field's present and future directions.

The Discovery of Childhood

Prior to the Seventeenth Century

While it may be difficult for us to conceive of a world without children as we know them today, our ancient ancestors perceived children as little adults or *homunculi* (little men) without personalities of their own (Aries, 1962). In all likelihood, this perception was attributable to the extremely high incidence of infant mortality and to the short life expectancy for everyone in those days. Under environmental conditions that argued against survival, it was safer and surely less painful for adults to remain aloof from and uninvolved with their young children.

Evidence that the medieval world lacked awareness of the unique state of childhood was creatively drawn by Aries (1962, recommended for fascinating reading) from paintings, sculpture, figures on tombstones, diaries, and autobiographies. Except for later characterizations of the Infant Jesus, art forms rarely portrayed children as anything other than miniature adults. Children dressed as adults without any distinguishing feature other than the quality of clothes differentiating social classes. Similarly, there were no special play activities, games, or literature for children, or any particular topic, including sexual matters, that could not be openly discussed in their presence. Even the word "child" was not used in the restricted way we use it now, since it referred to a state of dependence in adults who were of lower and of more submissive rank to others. Childhood was neither of interest nor of significance to the medieval world, because it was such a brief period that passed quickly for those few who survived. Although children of all ages mingled freely with adults, they were viewed as weaker and more fragile, and as economic pawns of their elders who arranged marriage contracts for them that often were consummated by the age of twelve (Brown, 1939). School life and apprenticeships began for the privileged after infancy (age six) in a setting where the young and the old were intermingled, and where strict discipline maintained by corporal punishment (the birch stick) and, in rare cases, by imprisonment was the rule. And in medieval times, the family existed solely in a formal sense for the transmission of life, property, and names.

Beyond the Seventeenth Century

According to Aries (1962) changes began to appear in the seventeenth century, initially in the upper socioeconomic classes, when adults more openly expressed affection and amusement in response to the child's endearing qualities of simplicity, humor, and tenderness. Themes of childhood emerged in family portraits showing parents coddling, holding hands with, and playing with their children, and in characterizations of groups of boys and girls at play. Notice was also taken of childhood jargon and of childrens' games and play activities. As adults became more openly attached to and interested in children, they began to stress the need to understand them in order to correct their behavior, to develop their reasoning ability, and to turn

them into "good Christians." Aries noted that the ideas about morality changed, too, as the concept of the "innocence" of the child surfaced in sharp contrast to the notion of immodesty held in previous times. For example, the sexual ribaldries of adults were no longer permitted for children. Instead, children were taught to exercise control over the social behaviors that now were considered indecent. For some, this shift in morality carried over to the kinds of material children were allowed to read, giving rise to the appearance of a separate literature for children and adults. But most important, the innocence of children and the idea of childhood was affirmed by the Church in the seventeenth century as it introduced the first communion ceremony, which has since become an important religious festival of childhood.

The family, which originated in the fifteenth century, changed from a contract that legitimized marriage for the transmission of property to heirs to a more meaningful relationship between parents and children. Children became an integral part of everyday life and their parents showed an increasing concern for their education, career, and future welfare. The emergence of childhood and parental involvement also was linked with the more religious notion that children were the living images of their parents, an inspiring belief that further enhanced the family bond.

Education turned from mere instruction in basic skills to a larger concern for the physical, mental, and spiritual welfare of the student. Two opposing views of education emerged: one favoring a protective and coddling approach; the other representing a more moralizing and an authoritarian attitude. However, both views recognized the weakness of children and the fact that they were developing organisms who needed special instruction and moral training. In fact, by the eighteenth century, Rousseau, the father of modern educational philosophy, underscored the idea of childhood when he wrote:

We expect to find the man in the child without thinking of what the child is before he is a man. . . . Childhood has ways of seeing, thinking, feeling peculiar to itself; nothing is more absurd than to wish to substitute ours in their place (Brown, 1939, p. 11).

Largely through the writings of such philosophers as Locke and Pestalozzi, children were seen as unformed and malleable in character with inclinations for evil and virtue that could be checked and shaped through the influence of parents and teachers (Strickland, 1970). More than a century later, Horace Mann promoted this idea in America as he successfully fought for compulsory schooling on the grounds that early education and conscientious parenting together would result in the development of worthy citizens.

At last after so many centuries of indifference, ignorance, and neglect, childhood was recognized as a valuable and distinct period of life. But this struggle for recognition was paralleled by a much more stormy battle that raged for as many years centering about who controls children, who holds the ultimate responsibility for what children may do and what is done to them, and who has the final say about matters concerning their life and death? As we shall see in the next section, the issue of who has the authority to direct the child's activities has aroused bitter controversy among

parents, the Church, and the State throughout history.

The Control of Children

It may seem sinister to suggest, but nonetheless it is true, that the perennial struggle for the control of children stemmed from their special value as a labor force, as a source of military strength in defending or extending the State, and as spiritual recruits for increasing the influence of the Church. As rich resources leading to economic, political, or religious gains, children have been exploited and abused for centuries without regard for their person or welfare. However, with the discovery of childhood, there has been an increasing trend for some group to intercede on behalf of children when they have been abused excessively.

Children as a Labor Force

In primitive times when the concept of paternity was unknown, children were closely linked to their mothers who were their obvious source of survival. However, just as soon as possible, youngsters were put to work, first as aides to women and later as either hunters or tillers of the soil to provide food for themselves and others. In ancient Sparta, children (both boys and girls) were wards of the state. A council of elders held the authority to decide whether they would live or die (Brown, 1939). Similarly, initially the children of Thebes were taken care of by public funds, although they were required to repay the debt through work just as soon as they were able. As Christianity emerged and grew, parents became the supreme authority of children until the sixteenth century, when the Church issued strict injunctions regulating children and when the State (for example, England) tried to take control by legislating an apprenticeship system and compulsory military training. The battle between the Church and the State also was evident in the field of education, as both forces tried to exert its influence on the developing child through directives concerning what should and should not be taught. But for the most part, children were under the primary control of parents who, in turn, were strongly influenced by the Church. For almost the next three centuries, children were subjected to oppressive and punitive living conditions in which parents sold them or bonded them out for economic purposes, and restrained their evil impulses by the fear of God's wrath and severe punishment.

During the Industrial Revolution children became an obvious and lucrative source of cheap labor to be exploited by the pecuniary interests of business and the state. In the nineteenth century, children were the victims of the indentured service associated with apprenticeships and the factory system that required them to work as many as fourteen hours a day in unhealthy and unsafe settings (Brown, 1939). A number of states enacted legislation in response to these abusive labor practices by limiting women and children to a ten-hour work day, while a law passed earlier in England prohibited children under twelve years of age from either working at night or working more than twelve hours a day. Late in the nineteenth century, the Society for the Prevention of Cruelty to Children was founded in the United States and in England to protect the rights of children and to eliminate the cruel and inhumane treatment inflicted on them. In addition, various welfare agencies formed for serving the interest of children (such as the Children's Aid Society) and were influential in the passage of laws requiring compulsory school attendance for working children. In 1912, the Federal Children's Bureau was established, thus extending the State's jurisdiction and responsibility for the welfare of children to the areas of child labor, child health and recreation, child education, and the care of the atypical child. The Wages and Hours Bill of 1938 prohibited the employment of children under sixteen years of age in hazardous occupations (manufacturing and mining). Since the early part of the twentieth century, mechanization, labor unions, and the economic need to find enough jobs for adults all have contributed significantly to the declining use of child labor in our society.

Child Abuse

As we have seen, children often were abused, severely treated, brutally punished, and immorally exploited up to the end of the nineteenth century in many different ways by various people or institutions who held absolute authority over their fate. Under the law, children were put to death for stealing a loaf of bread, or imprisoned for other trivial offenses where they became the prey of hardened and seasoned criminals (Wilkerson, 1973). In the nineteenth century, judicial reform occurred when Illinois and Colorado established separate juvenile courts to provide children with less harsh treatment and to deal with the special problem of juvenile delinquency. Unfortunately, this new view of justice for children was not fully realized, since the correctional and remedial personnel and facilities needed to implement an effective program simply were not made available. Even today, the existence of separate courts and detention facilities for children have done little to reduce the incidence of juvenile delinquency or to decrease the recidivism rate for these youngsters (see Chapter 12).

Child abuse was first noted as a contemporary problem and concern in 1946, and later named the "Battered Child Syndrome" in 1961 (Shepherd, 1973). The term refers to regular physical assaults on the child by the parents (usually one) with fists, sticks, hot irons, cigarettes, or other harmful objects that often result in lacerations, burns, broken bones, internal bleeding, and sometimes death. In a broader context, child abuse also includes children who are sexually molested or who are seriously neglected and deprived of the necessary ingredients for survival. In 1959, the United Nations Assembly adopted a declaration affirming its belief that human rights belong to children as well as adults, and stating their resolve to enact more effective child abuse laws and to improve juvenile courts and child welfare services (Coughlin, 1973). Even more recent recognition of this problem (which some experts say was much more serious one hundred years ago) has resulted in many states enacting legislation requiring physicians to report instances of child abuse, and in Congress enacting the 1974 Child Abuse and Prevention Act, which allocated eighty-five million dollars to treat these youngsters and their parents ("The Battered Children," 1977).

Child abusers tend to be suspicious of others, socially isolated, and have low frustration tolerance. They are not easily identified by their sex, economic status, race, or religious preference. Their most frequently shared characteristic, however, is that they have a history of being battered or neglected as children. In addition to the problem of identification, the problem of ac-

cumulating the evidence necessary to prove child abuse is extremely difficult, since parents may take their battered children to different hospitals to avoid detection, and because the police are prevented by law from intruding into family affairs unless there are ample grounds for suspicion. Doctors also are placed in the difficult position of interpreting their medical findings on the basis of indirect evidence and of challenging the parent's account of the injury.

In this country, the courts have held two different views concerning the boundaries of parental discipline. One view makes the parent the sole arbiter in punishing the child as long as the punishment "does not result in disfigurement or permanent injury, or is not inflicted maliciously." The other position states that "the parent has a right to punish a child within the bounds of moderation and reason so long as he does it for the welfare of the child; but that if he exceeds due moderation, he becomes criminally liable" (Shepherd, 1973, p. 177). Under either interpretation of the law, clearly the interests of the State are more potent than those of the parents in protecting the welfare of children. The fact that child abuse or neglect now ranks fifth as the leading cause of death for young children in the United States (following accidents, cancer, congenital abnormalities, and pneumonia) is sufficient justification for the intrusion of society on the individual rights of abusive parents.

In addition to the issue of the physical abuse and neglect of the child, contemporary society faces a number of other controversial questions about the rights of children. The heated arguments about abortion that pit the rights of the mother against the rights of the unborn child, the compulsory school-attendance requirement for all children, the legitimacy of children born by artificial insemination, and the total disregard of children's rights to consent to or turn down medical procedures such as surgery and drug use are only some of the difficult issues that will require resolution in the future.

Child Welfare

Child welfare is a social and legislative movement that began in the latter part of the nineteenth century as a response to excessive child abuse. The movement has produced a good deal of regulative legislation and has brought about the creation of specialized agencies for the purpose of protecting children. During this century, laws have been enacted dealing with almost every aspect of child welfare including mandatory immunization, care of the physically and mentally handicapped child (to be discussed later in this chapter under Mental Retardation), the protection and care of homeless and neglected children, and the medical inspection of children before they begin school. Maternal and baby clinics, community health centers, playgrounds and parks for recreation, compulsory education, and free school lunches to stave off malnutrition are among the facilities and programs developed and publically funded to provide every child with at least the minimum ingredients for normal physical and emotional development. While these laws and programs primarily have been intended for the benefit and welfare of children abused and neglected by parents who have been ignorant, incompetent, or unavailable (through death, desertion, or the like), they have, at the same time, given to the State (at all levels of government), and not to parents, the supreme authority to act on the behalf of children. The way future generations of children develop may very well

rest on the final outcome of this struggle for control.

The Emergence of Childhood Psychopathology as a Field

Up to this point, we have been concerned with a general account of the past status and, to some extent, the present status of children. We now turn to the consideration of those more specific but divergent forces that have contributed to the development of child psychopathology as an area of scientific inquiry and clinical practice. Obviously, the emergence of this field has neither a clearly fixed beginning nor a single antecedent condition. Many factors have interacted collectively in some unique way, although the task of tracing these factors and assessing their relative impact is especially difficult since it requires the sorting out of events that occurred within a relatively brief time span. We have organized the material included in this section with respect to what now appears to be the major factors that have led to the emergence of the field, and we have recognized the possibility that later historians, with a better time perspective, may choose to interpret the past in a different light with different emphases.

Early Views of Adult Psychopathology

The history of ideas concerning the cause of psychopathology has been tied largely to adult conditions and behaviors that have aroused public attention from the beginning of recorded time. The oldest view, *demonology,* assumed that abnormal behaviors were attributable to evil spirits that inhabited objects, animals, and people (Zilboorg and Henry, 1941). Early Greek civilization embellished this view by suggesting that the gods had the dual power of causing and curing possession. During the "Dark Ages," demonology was revitalized and used by the Church to investigate and eliminate witchcraft. Throughout these years, the underlying philosophy for treating demonology remained the same, although the specific methods employed changed. Demons were either mollified or removed, although a decided preference for punitive methods was evident.

The organic disease view, first introduced by Hippocrates who spoke of humors and corresponding personality temperaments, became viable and dominant in the eighteenth century when significant advances occurred in the fields of anatomy, physiology, neurology, chemistry, and general medicine (Zilboorg and Henry, 1941). These advances made possible the demonstration of organic pathology as the basis of many physical ailments and buoyed the expectation that abnormal behavior would have a similar cause. Early in the twentieth century, the discovery of a specific organic etiology (syphilitic infection) for a disorder known as General Paresis provided the confirmation for the previously assumed causal link between brain pathology and psychopathology. Gall's theory of phrenology further emphasized the brain as the principal organ underlying personality aberrations by proposing that character traits were localized in some thirty-seven different areas of the brain and that psychopathology was tied to the overdevelopment of these areas.

An even more respected influence (or at least a less controversial one) was Wilhelm Griesinger, a German psychiatrist, who held a similar view about the disease of the brain and abnormal behavior. Griesinger is credited with writing the first modern textbook in psychiatry and for emphasizing the organic viewpoint as an exclusive cause of mental illness. However, Emil Kraepelin (1856–1926), a follower of Griesinger, played the singularly important role in perpetuating the organic view (Zilboorg and Henry, 1941). Kraepelin not only recognized the significance of brain pathology in abnormal behavior, but he also developed a classification system that is the disease basis of the one largely used today. Kraepelin observed that certain groups of symptoms in hospitalized patients occurred together often enough to be considered specific types of mental diseases. Each type was regarded as distinct and followed its own fixed course. His early classification focused on two prominent types of mental diseases which he called *manic-depressive psychosis* and *dementia praecox* (now known as *schizophrenia*). He brought together the excited and euphoric symptoms of mania with the melancholic and despondent states of depression and noted that these different mood symptoms generally succeeded each other in the same individual. He suggested that the cause of manic-depression was an irregularity of metabolic functioning attributable to some kind of hereditary defect. Dementia praecox was caused by malfunctioning sex glands that produced an unhealthy chemical state that adversely affected the central nervous system.

During the nineteenth century, pychiatry contributed little to child psychopathology with a few notable exceptions. Benjamin Rush, the founder of American psychiatry, Esquirol, who was associated with the hospital reform movement in France, and Griesinger all made isolated references to specific forms of childhood disorders in their more extensive writing on adult psychopathology (Rie, 1971, pp. 3–50). In addition, Harms (1967) noted that there were at least three books published during this period which were primarily devoted to the mental disorders of children. However, there were few facilities and programs designed especially for disordered children except in the area of mental retardation.

Mental Retardation

The first childhood disorder to arouse public attention was mental retardation which was seen in ancient Greece and Rome where it was treated with contempt and persecution. With the rise of Christianity, the public attitude shifted from disdain to pity. During the Dark Ages the mentally retarded either served as fools (jesters) for the amusement of others or they were abandoned to fend for themselves (Rosen, Clark, and Kivitz, 1976). The Renaissance provided a period of enlightenment and an impetus for the scientific inquiry into mental retardation. For example, in 1672 Sir Thomas Willis labeled the condition as *feeblemindedness* and gave the first detailed description of its varying degrees. The terms *mental deficiency* and *mental retardation,* both referring to the same condition, were introduced in the 1920s and 1950s respectively (Potter, 1972).

But the first real stirrings of sustained interest in treating mental retardation occurred dramatically at the close of the eighteenth century with Jean Itard's valiant attempt to educate the Wild Boy of Aveyron who was discovered by peasants as he ran naked through a forest in the south of France (Lane, 1976). Victor, as he was later named by Itard, quickly became the object of considerable curiosity, fear, and a determined hunt that finally resulted in his capture. He was put on display in the village square, but he soon escaped only to return to the village two years later. Standing almost alone in his conviction that Victor

was educable and that his strange and retarded development was the result of prolonged sensory deprivation and isolation from human contact, Itard undertook the enormous task of bringing up the boy (who was then about seventeen years old) "to a civilized state." After five laborious years of intensive tutoring, Itard abandoned the project because Victor remained mute and showed little progress. However, the publicity surrounding the case stimulated a good deal of interest in the possibility of training the mentally retarded. Although a few schools for the retarded already had been founded, additional ones in Europe and in America were established following Itard's celebrated experiment (Rosen *et al.,* 1976).

Itard's work in mental retardation was carried forth first in Europe and then in the United States by Edward Seguin (1812–1880), who became a leader in educating both the legislature and the public about the problems of this disorder (Rie, 1971). Seguin shared Itard's belief that retardates were educable and could be cured by physiological training of sensory functions, especially perception. However, the optimistic outlook of Itard and Seguin about mental retardation soon gave way to pessimism as professional workers and the public were influenced by a renewed interest in Mendelian genetics and the findings of pedigree studies suggesting that mental retardation was an inherited disease leading to delinquency and crime. This pessimistic climate made it possible not only to enact eugenic laws that permitted sterilization of retardates, but also to justify their isolation in prisons and pauper homes (Rosen *et al.,* 1976). Although newer and more specialized facilities (residential schools) began to appear during the early part of the twentieth century, segregation of the mentally retarded persisted. Many of these institutions, still in existence today, were constructed in remote geographical areas as a way of protecting the public. However, their inaccessible location also created a real deterrent for parents to maintain close ties with their institutionalized youngsters.

During the course of this century, considerable progress has taken place in the area of mental retardation. This can be attributed to the influence of multiple factors. Some of these factors, such as the development of intelligence tests, the founding of child-guidance clinics, and the emergence of child psychology as a field of study, will be discussed in later sections of this chapter. Other factors, such as advances in genetics, improved pre- and post-natal care, better health and nutrition for mothers and infants, and the development of training programs for educational specialists, that have led to more effective prevention, assessment, and treatment of the mentally retarded will be included in Chapters 10 and 14. However, we need to acknowledge the special and influential role that parents have played in successfully pressuring for facilities and programs. Parents and other interested citizens founded the National Association of Parents and Friends of Mentally Retarded Children in 1950, which later became the National Association for Retarded Citizens (Blain, 1975). The Association serves as an advocate for mentally retarded citizens at the national, state, and local levels, and it is involved in such varied activities as sponsoring research, mounting educational programs aimed at the general public, providing the documentation necessary for the preparation of new legislation, and delivering direct management and training services. The Association also worked with other groups under the sponsorship of President John F. Kennedy to bring about the President's Panel on Mental Retardation in 1962, which later called for new legal concepts, research, prevention, facilities, and emphasis on the home and local care of retardates. These efforts led to the passage of the Mental Retardation Facilities and Community Mental Health Centers Construction Act in 1963, which funded new facilities and programs (Blain, 1975).

However, unlike the early interest shown in mental retardation, most of the major forces that influenced the field of child psychopathology did not emerge until the latter part of the nineteenth century or the first two decades of this century. Many of these developments occurred concurrently, suggesting a zeitgeist that was conducive to ferment and change, and an interaction that promoted progress. Which of these parallel forces made others possible or which is most important are questions we cannot readily answer. We simply can note surface relationships when they are apparent and encourage the readers to make their own judgments about the matter of significance.

Intelligence Tests

As an outgrowth of interest in mental retardation, the mental testing movement began in 1904 with the creation of a commission by the French Minister of Education to assure the best training possible for all retarded children and to construct a test that would identify feebleminded youngsters (Goodenough, 1949; Anastasi, 1965). A psychologist by the name of Alfred Binet was asked to develop the measuring device. He completed it in 1905 with the aid of his collaborator, Theophile Simon. In the 1908 and 1911 revisions of the scale, Binet introduced the concept of *mental age* by grouping test items according to the chronological age at which children usually answered them correctly. Children whose test performance (mental age) matched their chronological age were average. Those who exceeded their chronological age were considered brighter than average, whereas those with a mental age lower than their chronological age were below average in intelligence. In this way, Binet found a procedure that provided a frame of reference (relative to the chronological norms) for the interpretation of his test of intelligence. A year later William Stern improved on Binet's idea by suggesting the *intelligence quotient* (now better known as the IQ) to express the relationship between the child's mental age and chronological age in quantitative terms. In this country Lewis Terman and associates restandardized and modified the original Binet-Simon scales, and they popularized the IQ in a new test version called the *Stanford-Binet Intelligence Scale,* which was published in 1916. The new test and its subsequent revisions became the most widely used individual intelligence test for children until the Wechsler scales appeared (see Chapter 5).

During World War I, it became necessary to construct new tests of intelligence to help the military select mentally able servicemen from a large number of illiterate recruits (Anastasi, 1965). The new tests were designed with economy in mind, since they could be administered to groups of people (group intelligence tests) by a proctor as contrasted to the Binet-type scales where one person at a time is tested by a trained psychologist. In addition, the test items were completely nonverbal (performance tests), and therefore independent of the academic skills in which the illiterate subjects were deficient. In the course of time, test constructors and users became increasingly aware of factors other than in-

telligence that could influence IQ scores. These factors included education, culture, the skill of the examiner, and so forth. In addition, they gave more attention to the important issues of reliability, validity, and standardization procedures, as well as other problems and limitations of tests.

Public acceptance of mental tests encouraged the development of newer measuring devices purporting to assess academic achievement, personality, special aptitudes, abilities, interests, and brain damage. As school attendance became mandatory and the period of education was lengthened for children, the need for some of these tests became more apparent as increasing numbers of youngsters came to the attention of school authorities for emotional and academic problems. The availability of intelligence and other psychological tests opened the way for the more objective and accurate assessment of children's abilities, the more effective preparation of remedial programs, and the empirical investigation of many important research questions associated with the intellect, personality, and social functioning of children and adults.

Child Study Movement and Psychoanalysis

Late in the nineteenth century, child psychology came into being as a field of scientific inquiry mainly because of the pioneering efforts of G. Stanley Hall in this country and the development of several research techniques to systematically observe the child's behavior (Dennis, 1949). Although it is no longer in use as a research tool because of problems of observer error and reliability, the baby biography was an early scientific method of studying the child and was the basis for the development of more adequate techniques. G. Stanley Hall ushered in the child-study movement by methodologically improving the questionnaire as a method of obtaining information about children. He sent large numbers of questionnaires to parents, teachers, and children as a way of accumulating data about child development in such diverse areas as motor abilities, fears, dreams, appetites, prayers, and emotional expressions (Watson, 1959). Hall's intense interest in learning about children marked the beginning of the scientific study of the child *per se* in America, and it represented the conviction that this area of study was important to psychology's goal of understanding human behavior. Moreover, the child-study movement was essential in bringing about the field of child psychopathology, since it provided the necessary developmental norms by which abnormality could be judged and it generated the basic data for a better understanding of how abnormal behaviors occur.

Hall (1844–1924) was a man of great stature and influence as a psychologist, educator, and university president. He not only made advances in his own research, but also he trained other psychologists who made significant advances in the area of intelligence testing and in the study of normal child development. The most important step for the field of child psychopathology occurred in 1909, when Hall invited Sigmund Freud to Clark University to receive an honorary degree and to lecture on his theory of psychoanalysis. Freud's theory already had achieved considerable attention and recognition in Europe, but his trip to America introduced his theory here and marked the beginning of its unprecedented popularity and influence in the realm of adult and child psychopathology. However, to put Freud's contribution in historical

perspective we need to begin with the events that made his work possible.

In an era (from the eighteenth century on) when psychopathology was predominantly viewed as an organic disease, a new line of thinking emerged that proposed psychological factors as the cause of abnormal behavior and that almost exclusively focused on the frustrations and emotional conflicts of early childhood and daily living as the bases of mental illness.

Curiously enough, the beginnings of this development can be traced to the highly dramatic work of Anton Mesmer (1734–1815), a physician who was eventually banned from practicing in France and denounced as a charlatan. He died in obscurity in Switzerland (Zilboorg *et al.*, 1941; Deutsch, 1949; Mora, 1967). Mesmer believed that the stars influenced people through magnetic forces, and that an imbalance of magnetic forces within an individual could cause illness. Therefore, he reasoned that magnetic powers could be used to cure his patients. Mesmer was a flamboyant showman with a bag of props and staging know-how equal to the skills of a P. T. Barnum or a Cecil B. DeMille. He sat his patients around a large tub that had iron rods protruding from it and in which he put various chemicals. He darkened the room, played appropriate music, and made his appearance dressed in a purple robe with a wand in his hand which he used to touch each person and affect a dramatic cure. Mesmer called his magnetic power *animal magnetism,* and erroneously attributed his treatment successes to it rather than to the effect of suggestion or hypnosis or both. In 1784, the French Academy of Science appointed a distinguished committee to investigate the curative powers of magnetism. However, their investigation failed to confirm that animal magnetism was responsible for Mesmer's results. The importance of Mesmer's contributions lies in the fact that he unknowingly focused attention on psychological processes (hypnosis and suggestion) as potent variables in the acquisition and elimination of abnormal behaviors, and that his work stimulated others to develop it further.

At about the same time, two French physicians, Liebeault (1823–1904) and Bernheim (1837–1919) were impressed with the curative effects of suggestion after successfully using mesmerism to treat their rather unsophisticated peasant patients. Further study led them to observe that hypnosis could remove many of the physical symptoms found in hysterical patients and it could induce these symptoms in perfectly normal individuals. Thus, they concluded that hysteria and hypnosis were closely related and that hysteria was a form of self-hypnosis (Zilboorg *et al,* 1941; Deutsch, 1949).

Their view was refuted initially by Jean Charcot (1825–1893), who was then head of Salpetriere, a mental hospital in France. However, Charcot could not provide adequate evidence to support his organic (microscopic lesions from trauma) view of hysteria or successfully challenge the evidence of Bernheim and Liebeault for theirs. Charcot not only accepted his defeat gracefully, but he used his influence to facilitate the study of the role of psychological factors in the production of mental illness.

Soon thereafter, Charcot brought to Salpetriere a young scientist by the name of Pierre Janet (1859–1947), who described a phenomenon called *dissociation,* which he claimed was central to hysteria. Janet believed that the normal personality consisted of systems of organized ideas and actions that interacted with each other. He used dissociation to describe a separation

among the systems of the personality, and the isolation of certain systems from the rest of the personality. The distinguishing characteristic of this isolation was amnesia, a failure of the hysterical patient to remember relationships between critical events and systems of ideas. This was exemplified in the case of Irene, a young woman who periodically went into a sleepy state and then re-enacted the upsetting scene of her mother's death. After Irene completed this re-enactment, she returned to her prior normal state and carried on with whatever she was doing without any apparent effects and without memory of what transpired during the dissociated state. In viewing the process of dissociation, Janet called attention to the power of the personality to block out unpleasant events and experiences.

During this period, a young neurologist by the name of Sigmund Freud (1856–1939) began to collaborate with a more senior physician, Joseph Breuer (1842–1925) who used hypnosis successfully in the removal of hysterical symptoms. As he treated one of his hysterical patients, Breuer noted a peculiar periodic state in which the patient appeared confused and mumbled thoughts that were not readily understandable. He called this condition *absence,* and he found that the patient could reveal the fantasies that were present during her period of absence while under hypnosis. Breuer subsequently introduced into his hypnotic sessions encouragement for the patient to talk freely about her problems and to fully express the emotional states associated with them. This procedure permitted the patient to release emotional tensions and to uncover the difficulties that gave rise to her hysterical symptoms.

Breuer and Freud noted, however, that the patient could not see the relationship between her problems and her hysterical symptoms, although it was readily apparent to both of them. This led them to discover the *unconscious* and to ascribe to it a most important role in the determination of behavior (Freud and Breuer, 1959). Their continued work permitted observations that highlighted certain difficulties and limitations in their procedures. They found that symptom removal cures under hypnosis lasted only a relatively short period of time (a few months) before other hysterical symptoms (symptom substitution) appeared in the patient.

The discovery that not all of his patients could be hypnotized led Freud to conclude that these patients could not be permanently cured through hypnosis alone. Instead, Freud began to use a method he later called *free association,* which did away with the induction of an hypnotic trance. He encouraged the patient to relax and to say anything and everything that came to mind without conscious direction, censure, or regard for logic. In effect, free association opened the door to past unconscious memories that troubled the patient and caused hysterical symptoms. The technique proved to be more than a method for releasing suppressed emotions and for revealing unconscious problems; it led Freud to other significant discoveries.

Freud observed that his patients could not comply consistently with the rules of free association. This led him to formulate defense mechanisms and the ideas of resistance and repression (banishment of unacceptable impulses to the unconscious) which protect the personality from unbearable and unacceptable thoughts and impulses. Freud also sought to identify those impulses that were so discrepant with societal standards and so repugnant to the individual that they fell under the rule of repression, and yet were so strong that they would seek expression even through a neurotic illness. Because of the Victorian attitude toward sex and Freud's observation that many of his female patients used neurotic behavior to avoid sexual relationships, he concluded that the strangulation of sexual impulses was the basic source of neuroses.

By the beginning of the twentieth century, Freud had formulated many of the basic ingredients of his psychoanalytic theory in which he emphasized the importance of early childhood experiences for later personality development. He focused on the sexual drive as the basic source of anxiety and neuroses and described stages of development in which problems of dealing with sexuality at various ages had implications for later personal adjustment and the formation of neuroses. Although we shall present a more detailed discussion of Freud's psychoanalytic theory in Chapters 3 and 4, we should note that Freud continued to refine and elaborate his theory up to the time of his death.

What we must underscore in the context of this historical account is that psychoanalytic theory greatly influenced the fields of child psychology and child psychopathology through its emphasis on the critical role of early-childhood experiences for both normal and abnormal personality development. Freud established the significance of past experiences for the understanding of present behavior and promoted the importance of childhood beyond what Hall could have hoped for, when he brought Freud to this country. Although Freud constructed psychoanalysis as a theory and a treatment method intended primarily for neurotic adults, he demonstrated in the famous case of Little Hans that the notions he inferred from adult patients about infantile sexuality and psycho-sexual stages of development in particular were directly revealed in the child (Freud, 1959). Little Hans, a five year old boy suffering from a horse phobia, was treated for it by his father under Freud's supervision. The father provided Freud with detailed information about the boy's past history and current behaviors from which Freud was able to confirm some aspects of his theory as well as to formulate the nature of Hans' unconscious conflicts. In Hans, Freud found evidence of sexuality as early as age two, castration anxiety at age three, and sexual desires toward mother accompanied by fear and hostility toward father between the ages of four and five. In addition, Freud showed that psychoanalysis could be effectively used in treating a phobic reaction (intense fear) in a young child.

Now that we have presented Freud's contribution to the study of child psychopathology, we need to return to the child-study movement and discuss other significant developments that occurred about this time. One of the major contributors to the field of learning and child psychology was Ivan Pavlov (1849–1936), a Russian physiologist who developed the experimental method of classical conditioning (Pavlov, 1928). Although Pavlov's work influenced the scientific inquiry on learning at all levels of human development, its major impact on child psychology was to provide an experimental procedure that made infants and young children suitable subjects for psychological study. Pavlov showed that learning can occur if a previously neutral stimulus is paired successively with a stimulus already known to elicit the response in question. His experiments showed that hungry dogs learned to salivate to the sound of a bell alone after repeated pairings of the sound and food were presented in close

temporal order. In 1920, Watson and Rayner (1920) used the Pavlovian paradigm to demonstrate the acquisition of a fear response in an eleven-month-old boy named Albert. Prior observations of Albert indicated that he was not afraid of a white rat but that he showed fear of loud noises. The experimenters, therefore, arranged repeated presentations of a white rat followed closely by a loud noise until Albert evidenced a fear reaction to the presentation of the rat alone.

In this country, John B. Watson (1878–1958) introduced *behaviorism* in 1913 as a reaction against psychology's chief interest at that time in studying consciousness, and in its use of methods that were designed to provide information about what was going on inside the individual (Watson, 1913). Watson adopted the view that psychology as a science need only concern itself with behaviors that can be directly observed and measured. Through the analysis of stimulus-response (S-R) connections, the more complex forms of human behavior eventually can be understood. He argued for an environmentalistic position in which environmental forces play a dominant role in influencing and shaping personality, and he intended for child psychology to be the focus of his behaviorism (White, 1970). He established an infant laboratory, and, on the basis of his research on emotional conditioning, he wrote a book dealing with the psychological care of infants that greatly influenced child care and training practices (Watson, 1928). Watson's own words best convey his position and the optimism he held for it in determining the course of development:

Give me a dozen healthy infants, well-formed, and my own specialized world to bring up in, and I'll guarantee to take any one at random and train him to be any type of specialist. I might select—doctor, lawyer, artist, merchant—chief, yes, even beggar-man and thief, regardless of his talents, penchants, tendencies, abilities, vocation and race of his ancestors. . . . Please note that when this experiment is made I am allowed to specify the way the children are brought up and the type of world they have to live in (Watson, 1925, p. 82).

Watson's behaviorism was carried forth by B. F. Skinner, whose work in operant conditioning provided another important experimental paradigm for learning. His systematic research primarily with pidgeons not only has contributed significantly to the understanding and prediction of human behavior, but also it has had enormous application to education and the treatment of abnormal conditions. Skinner's operant conditioning involves the strengthening of a stimulus-response bond by reinforcing (rewarding) the response when it occurs, and by making the reinforcement contingent on the emission of the proper response. It is the procedure that we use to teach a dog a new trick, or a child to do his or her homework; and it is, like Watson's behaviorism, totally focused on the discovery of principles that govern behavior and unconcerned with what goes on inside the organism.

With the addition of the experimental method to the earlier research techniques of baby biographies and the Hall-type questionnaires, it became possible to study a wider range of factors in children of various ages, including abilities, achievement, interests, emotional reactions, drawings, and cognitive processes. Much of this literature contributed new knowledge about children's abilities and the orderly changes in their behavior that come with maturity. The founding of university-sponsored nursery schools in the 1920s permitted longitudinal behavioral studies that extended over peri-

ods of months and sometimes years. Developmental norms and the role of maturation with respect to the child's readiness to learn was highlighted in the 1930s and 1940s in the observational research of Arnold Gesell (1880–1961), a student of Hall (Gesell, 1928; Dennis, 1935; Gesell, Thompson, and Amatruda, 1938). Although not very clearly articulated, the view of human development as a sequential process of maturational stages characterized by the accumulation of normative data vis-a-vis its potential for the adjustment of the child seemed to prevail until the 1950s (White, 1970).

Mental Hygiene Movement and Child Guidance Clinics

At the turn of the twentieth century, the most important figure in American psychiatry was Adolph Meyer (1866–1950), who exerted influence not as a theoretician but as a teacher and an integrator of information. Meyer, a Swiss psychiatrist, came to this country in 1893 to work as a pathologist in a state hospital (Lief, 1948). Impressed with the almost impossible task of examining pathological tissues without life-history information, Meyer pressed for a program that would carefully study the patient's full life course. He accumulated large amounts of data that led him to emphasize psychological processes and variables, since autopsies performed on the mental patients he studied rarely demonstrated organic pathology. He became interested in the antecedent conditions of mental illness, and he saw the importance of gathering statistical data about childhood disorders. One of Meyer's students, Leo Kanner, later became the founder of child psychiatry in the United States. With the cooperation of the departments of pediatrics and psychiatry at Johns Hopkins University Medical

School, Kanner formed a clinic where he and his students evaluated and treated a wide variety of abnormal conditions in children. He accumulated basic data on the incidence of various childhood abnormalities and was the first to identify and describe a psychotic syndrome which he called *early infantile autism* (Chapter 8).

Meyer viewed psychopathology as faulty reactions of a psychobiological organism (the mind and the body) that can be understood only through a careful and chronological analysis of the individual's past history and corrected through the acquisition of new reactions (habits). He preferred the concept of *reaction type* to the prevailing psychiatric assumption of disease and favored *forms of unsuccessful adjustment* to the legal and popular term "insanity." Perhaps most important for the field of child psychopathology was his interest in prevention and his willingness to lend his influence and support to the mental-hygiene movement, a project started by a former mental patient by the name of Clifford Beers.

Beers, a graduate of Yale University, became obsessed with the fear that he, too, would be a victim of epilepsy soon after his older brother evidenced the disease. Beers became depressed and attempted suicide, and he was hospitalized in several mental institutions for about three years. In 1908, after he had recovered in the home of an attendant, Beers wrote *A Mind That Found Itself*, in which he described his own experiences as a mental patient and the cruel and horrible treatment he and others received in the institutions (Beers, 1908). Beers successfully aroused the interest and concern of some highly influential citizens and professionals. Together with Meyers and others, Beers organized the National Committee for Mental Hygiene in 1909. Intended as an organization to encourage the prevention and early identification of mental illness, to dissipate the public's pervasive attitudes of fear about it, and to improve the prevailing conditions in mental hospitals, the National Committee exerted considerable influence. It was a guiding force in establishing the first training program for psychiatric social workers at Smith College in 1918, and in accumulating information about community needs that led to public interest in developing facilities that would treat children's disorders.

Lightner Witmer established the first psychological clinic for children in 1896 at the University of Pennsylvania. Although interested in school-age children who were educationally retarded and/or handicapped, Witmer did not ignore those with emotional or nonacademic problems. Two years later, Illinois and Colorado created separate juvenile courts to deal with the special problems of juvenile delinquency and to provide legal consideration for juvenile offenders apart from adults. Experience with the juvenile court led to the conclusion that delinquent children frequently evidenced abnormal behaviors that were modifiable. In 1909, William Healy founded the first child-guidance clinic in Chicago (named the Juvenile Psychopathic Institute) as a clinical treatment facility for delinquent youths. Aided by the pressure exerted by the National Committee for Mental Hygiene, other child-guidance clinics were established to handle a broader range of psychological disorders in children (Kanner, 1972). In 1921, Thom founded the prototype of the modern child-guidance clinic in Boston. Staffed by a multidisciplined team consisting of a psychiatrist, a psychologist, and a social worker, the clinic treated the undesirable habits of preschoolers in order to minimize their risk of later developing more serious difficulties. Intervention was broadened beyond the exclusive focus on the child to include work with parents, siblings, teachers, and others who may have contributed to the child's problem.

Later Developments

As we have seen, progress for the mentally retarded and handicapped child was fostered by the emergence of psychological tests to measure intelligence and other abilities, and by the research on normal child development. In addition, parent groups awakened the public to the special needs of impaired and disordered children by advocating community and legislative involvement. Although started in 1914, teacher training programs for special education achieved substantial growth and effective quality after World War II, providing competent professionals in the areas of mental retardation, social and emotional maladjustment, sensory and speech deficits, and learning disabilities.

The need to train other child specialists was dramatized by the mental hygiene movement and the burgeoning of child-guidance clinics throughout the United States. Psychiatric social workers functioned as the primary clinic contact for parents, families, and schools, and as the professional member of the clinic team who interpreted information to and worked therapeutically with the child's parents (most often mother). In addition to these traditional functions, today social workers assume the role of child therapist, family therapist, and liason with other agencies in the community. Guidance clinics became a fertile training resource for social workers, psychiatrists, and psychologists. Child psychiatrists assumed the role of principal child therapists and medical administrators, while psychologists functioned mainly as mental testers, diagnostic evaluators, and researchers. But with the rapid development of clinical psychology following World War II, the roles and functions of psychologists in child clinics broadened to include psychotherapy, behavior therapy, family, school, and other agency consultation, diagnosis, training, research, and administration. At this point in time, it is recognized that no discipline is equipped with the necessary skills and experience to deal effectively with all facets of child psychopathology, although many perform similar and overlapping functions.

Psychoanalysis continued to dominate the field as Freud's student, Melanie Klein, and his daughter, Anna Freud, introduced modifications in the 1920s making his theory and treatment method more applicable to children. Klein replaced free association with play techniques (see Chapter 6) on the grounds that play was a natural activity of children and that it revealed the same sources of anxiety and unconscious conflicts as words did for adults. Anna Freud used play, especially drawings, as well as dreams to understand and treat children's problems, and she elaborated on her father's notions of the ego and its defensive functions. Then, in 1950, Erik Erikson's book, *Childhood and Society,* made an enormous impact on the field as he analyzed the human life cycle and identity in terms of a *psychosocial* stage theory as contrasted to Freud's psychosexual states of development (see Chapter 3) (Erikson, 1950).

Pediatric medicine became interested in the psychological aspects of child care largely as a result of the influences of psychoanalytic theory, the mental testing movement, normative data from child psychology, and Watson's environmental view of learning. Pediatricians who were thrust into the position of giving advice about child-rearing practices now could offer suggestions that were based on the important psychological ingredients of development. In 1945, Benjamin Spock, a pediatrician, published a manual entitled *Baby and Child Care* that rapidly became the bible for millions of parents who found answers to virtually all of their questions about child rearing (Spock, 1968).

Unbelievable growth and diversification have characterized the field of psychology over the last three to four decades. With some exceptions, prior to World War II, psychology was concerned with its own advancement as a science and the seeking of data that would be useful for the understanding and predicting of human behavior. After the war, formal doctoral programs in clinical psychology were established combining didactic course work, research requirements, and supervised clinical experience. Within recent years, specialty training in child clinical psychology has been offered in many university graduate programs. In addition, the science-practice orientation is very much evident in the field of child psychology where job opportunities within education, pediatrics, juvenile corrections, and early child-care programs are quite commonplace.

Research, training, and service programs aimed at benefitting the health and welfare of children were stimulated especially by federal funds during the 1960s. Presidents Kennedy and Johnson and their administrations were involved significantly in the problem of mental retardation and in supporting special programs for the culturally disadvantaged. The creation of the National Institute of Child Health and Human Development in 1963 acknowledged our national commitment to promote activities that would enhance the quality of life for all children. Recent legislation [1] amending the Education of the Handicapped Act provides for financial aid to the states for the education of handicapped children. These amendments are intended to assure free and appropriate public education for *all* handicapped children and to guarantee their rights for maximal educational opportunities. In addition, the law requires the assessment of school programs designed to meet these special needs. The legislation is inclusive with respect to the definition of handicapped children and assures professional attention to the education and remediation of so many heretofore neglected youngsters. However, for funding purposes, each state may not count more than 12 percent of the number of its children aged five through seventeen years as handicapped.

Although still in its infancy, the field of psychopathology is currently flourishing with exciting ideas, more adequately controlled and systematic research, more graduate and professional training programs, and more service facilities and programs than were thought possible some twenty or thirty years ago. In a relatively brief period of time and in spite of meager and stormy beginnings, the study of developmental psychopathology has made great strides in understanding and treating abnormal behaviors of children. But as we shall see, there is much more to learn and much more to be done. We hope the remaining chapters will challenge some to con-

[1] PL 94–142 was enacted November 28, 1975 (Federal Register, 1976, 41, No. 230)

tribute their own research and to add new insights and directions to the field.

Summary

Interest in the study of child psychopathology is of recent vintage. Prior to the seventeenth century, children were thought of as little adults without personalities of their own, and without distinctive clothes, play activities, literature, schools, or propriety about topics of discourse. Following the discovery of childhood as a period of life separate from adulthood, children became the object of controversy among parents, the Church, and the State for their control. This struggle was considered in the historical context of children as a labor force, the problem of child abuse, and the child welfare movement.

No fixed beginning can be established for the emergence of the field of child psychopathology, although many divergent forces occurring late in the nineteenth century and in the first several decades of the twentieth century were influential in bringing it about. Except for the area of mental retardation, the early ideas about adult psychopathology and the field of psychiatry took little notice of childhood disorders. The impact of past and recent developments in mental retardation, intelligence tests and other psychological tests, child psychology, psychoanalysis, the mental-hygiene movement, and child-guidance clinics was discussed. Later developments, especially in the training of educational specialists, social workers, child psychiatrists, and clinical and child clinical psychologists were noted as important contributors to the current status of the field.

REFERENCES

ANASTASI, A. (Ed.). *Individual Differences*. New York: Wiley, 1965.

ARIES, P. *Centuries of Childhood* (trans. by Robert Baldick). New York: Vintage Books (Random House), 1962.

"The Battered Children." *Newsweek*, October 10, 1977, pp. 112–115.

BEERS, C. W. *A Mind That Found Itself*. New York: Longmans, Green, 1908.

BLAIN, D. "Twenty-five Years of Hospital and Community Psychiatry: 1945–1970," *Hospital and Community Psychiatry*, 1975, *26*, 605–609.

BROWN, F. J. *The Sociology of Childhood*. Englewood Cliffs, New Jersey: Prentice-Hall, 1939.

COUGHLIN, B. J. "United Nations Declaration of the Rights of the Child." In A. E. Wilkerson (Ed.), *The Rights of Children*. Philadelphia: Temple University Press, 1973, pp. 3–23.

DENNIS, W. "The Effect of Restricted Practice Upon the Reaching, Sitting, and Standing of Two Infants." *Journal of Genetic Psychology*, 1935, *47*, 17–32.

DENNIS, W. "Historical Beginnings of Child Psychology." *Psychological Bulletin*, 1949, *46*, 224–235.

DEUTSCH, A. *The Mentally Ill in America*. New York: Columbia University Press, 1949.

ERIKSON, E. H. *Childhood and Society*. New York: Norton, 1950.

FREUD, S. Analysis of a Phobia in a Five-Year-Old Boy. In *Collected Papers* (Vol. III) (trans. by Alix and James Strachey). New York: Basic Books, Inc., 1959.

FREUD, S., and J. BREUER. On the Psychical Mechanisms of Hysterical Phenomena. In *Collected Papers* (Vol. 1) (trans. by Joan Rivière). New York: Basic Books, Inc., 1959.

GESELL, A. *Infancy and Human Growth*. New York: Macmillan, 1928.

GESSELL, A., THOMPSON, H. and C. S. AMATRUDA. *The Psychology of Early Growth*. New York: Macmillan, 1938.

GOODENOUGH, F. L. *Mental Testing: Its History, Principles, and Applications*. New York: Holt, Rinehart, and Winston, 1949.

HARMS, E. *Origins of Modern Psychiatry*. Springfield, Illinois: Charles C. Thomas, 1967.

KANNER, L. *Child Psychiatry* (4th ed.). Springfield, Illinois: Charles C. Thomas, 1972.

LANE, H. *The Wild Boy of Aveyron*. Cambridge, Massachusetts: Harvard University Press, 1976.

LIEF, A. *The Commonsense Psychiatry of Dr. Adolf Meyer*. New York: McGraw-Hill, 1948.

MORA, G. "History of Psychiatry." In A. M. Freedman and H. I. Kaplan (Eds.), *Comprehensive Textbook of Psychiatry*. Baltimore: Williams and Wilkins, 1967, pp. 2–34.

PAVLOV, I. P. *Lectures on Conditioned Reflexes*. New York: Liveright, 1928.

POTTER, H. W. "Mental Retardation in Historical Perspective." In S. I. Harrison and J. F. McDermott (Eds.). *Childhood Psychopathology: An Anthology of Basic Readings*. New York: International Universities Press, 1972, pp. 733–743.

RIE, H. E. "Historical Perspective of Concepts of Child Psychopathology." In H. E. Rie (Ed.), *Perspectives in Child Psychopathology*. Chicago: Aldine-Atherton, 1971, pp. 3–50.

ROSEN, M., CLARK, G. R. and M. S. KIVITZ (Eds.). *The History of Mental Retardation: Collected Papers* (Vol. 1). Baltimore: University Park Press, 1976, pp. XIII–XXIV.

SHEPHERD, R. E., Jr. "The Abused Child and the Law." In A. E. Wilkerson (Ed.). *The rights of children*. Philadelphia: Temple University Press, 1973, pp. 174–189.

SPOCK, B. *Baby and Child Care* (new rev. ed.). New York: Pocket Books, 1968.

STRICKLAND, C. E. "American Attitudes Toward Children." In E. Blishen (Ed.) *Encyclopedia of Education* (Vol. II). New York: Macmillan, 1970, pp. 77–92.

WATSON, J. B. *Behaviorism*. New York: Norton, 1925.

WATSON, J. B. *Psychological Care of Infant and Child*. New York: Norton, 1928.

WATSON, J. B. "Psychology as the Behaviorist Views It." *Psychological Review*, 1913, *20*, 158–177.

WATSON, J. B. and R. RAYNER. "Conditioned Emotional Reaction." *Journal of Experimental Psychology*, 1920, *3*, 1–4.

WATSON, R. I. *Psychology of the Child: Personal, Social and Disturbed Child Development*. New York: Wiley, 1959.

WHITE, S. H. "The Learning Theory Tradition and Child Psychology. In P. H. Mussen (Ed.), *Carmichael's Manual of Child Psychology* (Vol. 1) (3rd ed.). New York: Wiley, 1970, pp. 657–701.

WILKERSON, A. E. (Ed.). *The Rights of Children.* Philadelphia: Temple University Press, 1973.

ZILBOORG, G. and G. W. HENRY. *History of Medical P·ychology.* New York: Norton, 1941.

The Nature of Psychopathology

2

PROLOGUE

Martin, a nine year old caucasian boy, was referred for psychological evaluation because of his poor performance in school, surly and hostile behavior in school and at home, several recent thefts, frequent lying, bed wetting for the last three years, and his inability to get along with peers, parents, siblings, or teachers. The youngest of three boys, his brothers were three and six years older than he. Mother had separated and divorced when Martin was about six years old, and a year later she married a man who was ten years her senior and who had not been married before. Martin's stepfather was an electrician who worked long hours to provide a good income for his family. He had high expectations for his stepsons and was extremely critical of them when they failed to measure up to his standards. Mother, too, was demanding. In addition, she was high strung, easily upset, a meticulous housekeeper, and a woman who had doubts about her ability to cope with her sons, her husband, and her home responsibilities.

Martin's brothers seemed to get along well at home and were excellent students in school. They excelled in athletics and were a great source of pride to their parents. Martin began first grade doing well but, when his mother and father divorced, his school performance fell off and he began wetting his bed at night. Martin's mother and his brothers were very critical of him, tending to pick on Martin and use him as a scapegoat for their own pent up frustration and anger. Martin's academic difficulties continued, and he had to repeat the second grade. His stepfather soon added another critical voice, and Martin reacted by striking back with anger. He fought with his brothers, talked back to his mother, and fabricated stories to avoid doing what his parents asked of him. At school, he began to bully and fight younger boys and take some of their belongings and hide them. Teachers noted that he seemed to enjoy tormenting other children, but they could not find any effective way to stop his aggression. Shortly before he was referred for evaluation, Martin stole a neighbor's bicycle and some money from his mother's purse. He rode around until long past dinner time when he was expected home. He returned the bike to the neighbor's garage, and then entered the back door of his house, only to be greeted by a set of worried but very angry parents. The next day, his parents decided that Martin needed professional help.

What prompted Martin's parents to seek the assistance of a psychologist? Was it primarily their concern about his theft of the bike and money, or was it a reaction to a combination of Martin's prior behaviors and his most recent actions as worrisome indications of a serious problem? Whichever reason prompted them, their choice rested on some vague and implicit notion about what constitutes abnormal behavior. Although there is no single definition that we would agree upon at this point, or, for that matter, that would completely satisfy most professional workers, we need to define the domain of abnormal behavior in order to have a common basis for further study. In addition, we need to grapple with the issues and problems surrounding the classification of children's disorders to better understand what groupings have been proposed, how the various categories are used, and how reliable they are. Finally, as important background information, we need to consider the scope of the problem, the procedures used to measure the frequency of abnormal conditions, and the sources of error associated with these measures.

What Is Psychopathological Behavior?

Martin's case illustrates that psychopathology may be easier to recognize than to define, because psychopathology involves a number of important dimensions that are given differential weight in arriving at a decision. His mother and stepfather had the opportunity to evaluate Martin's behavior continually in light of his previous personality, its appropriateness to his life circumstances, and its effect on him and others. They may have seen his academic decline and bedwetting at age six as a temporary but understandable response to the stress of his parents' separation and divorce. But the persistence of these behaviors along with the appearance of hostile and then antisocial acts suggested that his condition had not only worsened, but that it was also seriously affecting the lives of others. Martin's mother and stepfather recognized his psychopathology, but they based their recognition on multiple and vague criteria that were not generally applicable. Therefore, we must delineate a set of criteria for psychopathological behavior that is generalizable beyond the single case and is comprehensive and explicit.

Abnormal behavior may be thought of as deviant in the sense that it deviates statistically from the normal, the usual, the most common or typical reaction found in the majority of the population. But this criterion is limited since it implies that normality would include behaviors that are most common, and exclude those that deviate from the norm but that society may regard as superior, such as the behavior of the extremely bright child or the gifted athlete. Moreover, this standard would require that we consider within the bounds of normality the common practice of drinking and drug abuse found among high schoolers, even though society views these behaviors as deviant and undesirable. The fact that research indicates that few children go through life completely free of behavioral and adjustment difficulties implies by statistical standards that such behaviors as temper tantrums, fears, overactivity, bedwetting, lying, and stealing are normal (Werry and Quay, 1971; Johnson, Wahl, Martin, and Johansson, 1973). Yet factors other than mere occurrence, such as persistence, age of onset, or the appearance of a combination of some of these behaviors (as evidenced by Martin) may override statistical considerations in differentiating normal from abnormal.

In addition to these limitations, the statistical criterion as it now stands is too broad and vague in that it defines normal behavior in terms of what the majority does but not in terms relative to a more specific or meaningful frame of reference. However, the next two sections will deal with statistical criteria that take note of cultural values and changes in behavior that occur with development.

Cultural Norms

From the beginning of civilization, people have always noted certain behaviors that were sufficiently distinctive to be labeled abnormal. Some of these behaviors appear to be universal, since they can be found in similar forms all over the world. In fact, studies have shown that such psychopathological behaviors as hallucinations, delusions, phobias, and sexual deviations are evident across different cultures (Copeland, 1968; Al-Issa, 1969; Dohrenwend and Dohrenwend, 1974). At the same time, differences among cultures have also been reported in both the incidence of abnormal behaviors and in the specific ways they are expressed. Although suicide and alcoholism are well known universal phenomena, suicide is rare among Muslims and compulsive drinking is unusual among Jews and Chinese-Americans (Bazzoui and Al-Issa, 1966; Kleinmuntz, 1974). The specific content of a disordered behavior, such as a delusion, also is influenced by cultural factors. A delusion of persecution in Africa may take the form of a fixed belief that some large, wild, and dangerous animal is out there for the sole purpose of stalking and destroying the deluded person. In this country, the delusional content might focus on the belief that the person is under the electronic surveillance of foreign agents who plan to seize and murder him. Therefore, a distinction must be made between the basic characteristics of abnormal behavior that are constant in all cultures, and those features that vary because of cultural differences. In general, behaviors that reduce, interfere with, or disrupt the individual's personal and social adjustment are considered abnormal in all societies. However, the specific form these disruptive behaviors take, the explanation given for them, and their frequency of occurrence vary from culture to culture. The processes and functions underlying human behavior (normal and abnormal) are the same in all societies, while the specific behavioral expressions are influenced largely by one's culture. Obviously, then, what is regarded as abnormal by one culture may very well be normal in another.

The first of our criterion of psychopathological behavior, the *cultural norm,* recognizes that every culture establishes approved standards and expectations for the behavior of its members. Cultural norms change from time to time, but usually there is a "lag" between the introduction of the change and its widespread acceptance by the culture. Typically, cultural norms are more specific and restrictive in their prohibitions in contrast to the greater flexibility allowed for their sanctions. Moreover, there is usually more latitude and leeway given to children in terms of what they may and may not do. For example, our culture prohibits certain aggressive acts for adults, such as physical assault and stealing, while similar aggressive responses are subtly permitted for children in that they may fight, attack each other, and take things that don't belong to them without great penalty. In addition, cultural norms provide standards of behavior that are situationally defined. For the adolescent, nudity is permissible in the privacy of his or her home or even in the less than private locker room at the school gym, but it is certainly prohibited when shopping or going to class. In this way, society identifies certain behavior patterns and situations as acceptable.

Developmental Norms

Knowledge of the developmental process is essential in making decisions about whether a child's behavior is normal or abnormal, although statistical averages (as we have already noted) have their limitations for defining abnormality. We know that most children are toilet trained before the age of three. By this standard, Martin's bedwetting deviates significantly from developmental norms, since he has been enuretic for the last three years. Of course, if Martin were younger (let us say four years old), then the deviation would be less extreme and more difficult to categorize as abnormal. In general, the greater the deviation from developmental norms, the higher the agreement will be with regard to the abnormality of the behavior.

But not all developmental deviations reflect abnormality in the sense of impaired or insufficient progress. Some children walk unaided at an earlier age than the norm, or have vocabularies and linguistic skills that far exceed the average. Most, but not all, instances of rapid or early development are looked upon as positive indications of exceptional abilities. It is at the slow end of the continuum where developmental deviations have their major significance as a negative criterion of abnormality.

Frequency, Intensity, and Duration

For discussion purposes, let us consider the question: Is the behavior of pulling hair from one's head abnormal? While many might respond affirmatively, others might ask for additional information before answering. If pulling hair occurred only once, or at the most twice, the answer might change to a firm "no." If, however, pulling hair was a frequent event, the answer would be "yes." Therefore, *frequency* is an important dimension in defining abnormal behaviors. In this regard, we should note that the absence or rarity of a response may be just as significant as high frequency. Martin's infrequent expression of warm and positive feelings is as indicative of abnormality as is his excessive lying or his frequent bedwetting.

Another characteristic useful in determining whether a behavior is abnormal is *intensity* or *degree*. If pulling hair merely involved the removal of a single strand of hair rather than large clumps, the behavior would be within normal limits. However, when behaviors are evident in extremes of intensity or degree, they generally fall outside of the bounds of normality and inside the range of abnormality.

Similarly, we need to include the dimension of *duration* to aid in distinguishing normal from abnormal behavior. Martin's lying and stealing take on greater significance if they are manifest over a long rather than a brief time span. The greater the persistence of deviant behaviors, the more likely they are to be considered as falling within the domain of abnormality.

Intellectual and Cognitive Functioning as a Criterion

In the management of everyday affairs, we expect that normal people will function well within their intellectual capabilities, even though most people do not operate at maximum efficiency most of the time. A healthy fourteen year old of superior intelligence who couldn't remember his name, address, or whereabouts would strike most of us as odd and abnormal.

Cognitive malfunctioning is apparent when a disparity exists between ability and actual performance in such areas as attention, comprehension, judgment, learning, memory, thinking, and perception. The larger the difference between a person's capabilities and actual performance, the greater is the likelihood of abnormal behavior. Children of average or higher intelligence who are extremely distractible, unable to carry out simple instructions, or unable to learn the difference between friend and foe, and those who cannot recall important, recent, or past events illustrate cognitive impairment indicative of abnormal behavior.

For the most part, normal thought processes tend to be logical, coherent, organized, and appropriate to the situation. Gross disruption and impairment of these patterns and peculiar content, known as a *thought disorder,* usually are good indicators of abnormal behavior. Wouldn't you think there

was something radically wrong with an eleven-year-old boy who responded characteristically to simple questions such as "How are you today?" with "My God! The world is coming to an end. The weasel stole all of the bees . . . no more honey . . . no more money. The heck with you, you S.O.B. What do you have against fried flies?"

A particularly important instance of cognitive dysfunction is in the child's *perception of reality.* During normal development we learn to move about unimpaired in our environment by interpreting external cues. We learn that distant objects look smaller than nearer ones and to correct our perception when these cues are incorrect, such as when viewing things that are submerged in water. With practice and success experiences, our confidence in these perceptions of physical objects and space increases. From time to time we check our impressions with those of others, especially when in doubt. Misperceptions or *hallucinations* occur when a person sees, hears, or smells something that is not present in the external world of reality. Hallucinatory experiences may involve any of the senses, although visual and auditory misperceptions are the most frequently noted. Beliefs that are based on false premises are known as *delusions,* which are faulty perceptions or incorrect appraisals of reality or the actual behavior of others.

The ramblings of a five-year-old child about his or her imaginary playmate may be normal, but similar behavior in a teenager would be properly labeled as abnormal. The belief that the moon dangerously pollutes the atmosphere because it is made of blue cheese is distinctly abnormal in a college graduate, although it may be within normal limits for a gullible retardate who was spoofed by an older sibling. Thus, in order to be useful as a criterion of abnormal behavior, cognitive dysfunction must be considered in light of intellectual potential, developmental norms, frequency, duration, and degree of impairment.

Emotional Expression and Control as a Criterion

Some of the most vivid illustrations of abnormal behavior come from the emotional area of human functioning. Scenes of wild, explosive, and unpredictable emotional expressions are often used to describe the behavior of those considered abnormal. Extremes or sudden fluctuations of moods, infantile, inappropriate, or lack of emotional expression, and irrational but persistent fears are some of the emotional signs of personal instability. "A proper emotional development prepares the individual to appreciate the pleasurable aspects of emotion and to cope adaptively with the unpleasant. The well-rounded personality is not flat or wholly intellectual but expressive and emotionally responsive in a disciplined manner" (Nash, 1970, p. 306).

During the course of development, children learn to alter the way they express emotions. Infants show fear by crying, while teenagers may respond by avoiding or withdrawing from the feared stimuli. Children also learn to size up the situation in terms of what emotion is appropriate and what manner is acceptable for its expression. With maturity, people are expected to increase the degree of control they exercise over their feelings. Thus, over time youngsters may show required changes in the expression of anger from frantic temper tantrums to direct physical attack to verbal expression of anger, and so forth.

Deviations in emotional expression and control are varied and numerous. Emotional behavior can be *inappropriate* to the situation as in the show of elation over the news of the death of a loved one, or *insufficient* or *exaggerated* as reflected in either indifference or a prolonged grief reaction to a broken engagement. There may be either too little or too much control exercised over emotional responsivity as seen in impulsive acting-out behavior or in emotional constriction and inhibition. In addition, emotional regression or the use of emotional expressions evident in an earlier period of development may indicate abnormal behavior. Temper tantrums in a twelve year old who had since learned to express anger verbally is a sign of emotional regression and emotional immaturity. Here again, the greater the deviation from normal developmental patterns, the greater is the likelihood that the behavior would be regarded as abnormal.

Sometimes *personal discomfort* is considered a useful criterion of abnormal behavior, because it is often (but not necessarily always) a byproduct of such a state. Worry, anxiety, fears, and despondent feelings often become pervasive and all-consuming to the point where some, if not many, areas of functioning are affected adversely. When personal discomfort in any form is enduring and sufficiently troublesome to interfere with normal functioning, it can be considered abnormal. However, we must keep in mind that not all abnormal emotional behaviors are painful or uncomfortable. Seriously regressed psychotics may show silly emotional responses and a readiness to inflict pain on others or themselves without any apparent sign of personal distress. Those in prolonged states of euphoria (even if inappropriate) appear to be ecstatically happy. Sexual deviants and drug users apparently derive a great deal of pleasure from their abnormal behaviors.

Coping in Interpersonal Relations as a Criterion

It is well recognized that humans are not solitary creatures but social animals who require relationships with others for their well being. To function adequately in society, a person must acquire the capacity to interact with others on friendly and co-operative terms and maintain relationships of mutual respect, agreement, and responsibility. Because this is such an important area of human function, deviations from the expected patterns, especially those in which the rights of others are offended or violated, are considered abnormal. Typically, disruptions in a person's ability to cope with interpersonal relationships are associated with or lead to impaired functioning in many areas. Difficulties in interpersonal relations, such as social withdrawal and isolation, suspiciousness, fear, hatred of others, and uncooperativeness are behaviors that make almost any facet of life difficult to manage.

But not all deviant interpersonal relations justifiably fall within the domain of abnormal behavior. Rudeness, insensitivity, deceit, and infidelity are among the behaviors that are socially deviant, but not in and of themselves abnormal. Similarly, criminal acts of murder, rape, and theft, while deviant, cannot be classed as abnormal without further qualifications.

What then are the necessary additional considerations? If the behavior is committed by a person who is rational and otherwise shows no signs of cognitive impairment, then we think of the act, albeit vulgar, immoral, or criminal, as outside the domain of abnormality. If, however, the behavior is performed by a person whose judgment, thinking, memory, or perception is disturbed, then we consider the behavior ab-

normal. Emotional dysfunction is another factor that helps differentiate abnormal social behaviors from other kinds of deviant interactions. When emotional instability is present along with deviant interpersonal behavior, the social interaction is more likely to be abnormal than criminal. Therefore, in order to use interpersonal deviancy as a criterion of abnormal behavior, it is necessary to apply it in conjunction with the other criteria of cognitive and emotional dysfunction.

In summary, there is no single criterion for defining abnormal behaviors. However, for our purposes, we define *abnormal behaviors* as those that persistently deviate from cultural and developmental norms in either extremes of frequency and intensity, and that are evidenced by impairment in one or more of the following areas of human functioning: intellectual and cognitive, emotional expression and control, and interpersonal relationships.

How Is Psychopathology Classified?

In the field of behavior disorders, a classification system arranges those individuals exhibiting abnormal behavior into diagnostic groupings according to certain common characteristics. From the very beginning, classification has been influenced greatly by a disease view of psychopathological behavior. This influence dates back to the contributions of Hippocrates, although the major impetus came in the nineteenth century when Emil Kraepelin undertook the careful compilation of clinical records and histories of hospitalized patients. Based on these data, he constructed a classification system that was essentially a descriptive one, in which all of his observations and clinical findings were used as diagnostic criteria. The data included symptoms and clusters of symptoms, etiology when known, physiological changes, and observations about the course and outcome.

In addition to Kraepelin, several others have contributed to present-day classification of abnormal behavior. Eugen Bleuler (1857–1939), who worked extensively with the disorder known as *dementia praecox,* or schizophrenia, brought about significant changes both in the name and the concept of that disorder. Bleuler's lucid description of schizophrenia and its subcategories not only replaced the Kraepelinian view of the disorder but also significantly modified its classification up to the present. Adolph Meyer (1866–1950) argued against the Kraepelinian bias that focused on the study of symptomatology, and especially against the inclination to view symptoms as signs of specific brain lesions. He took a broader approach claiming that abnormal behaviors were faulty life adaptations produced by many factors such as psychological, social, physiological, and constitutional, and not exclusively brain pathology. He introduced the concept of *reaction types* as a substitute for the narrowly conceived disease entities, and he emphasized the total individual as a psychobiological organism constantly called upon to adapt to a social environment (Meyer, 1948; Muncie, 1948).

Because no single system of classifying abnormal behavior had been adopted as the official standard in the field, diversity tended to prevail. Clinicians either modified existing systems or constructed their own to meet their special needs and those of the clinical facilities in which they worked. The result was "a polyglot of diagnostic labels and systems, effectively blocking communication and the collection of medical statistics" (*Diagnostic and Statistical Manual,* 1965, p. V). This state of confusion triggered off several attempts to establish a standard nomenclature that would be nationally accepted and used.

Adult Classification Systems (DSM–I, DSM–II, DSM–III)

In 1927, the New York Academy of Medicine moved to establish a standard nomenclature of disease that would be nationally accepted. The first edition entitled *Standard Classified Nomenclature of Disease* was published in 1933 and was followed by two revisions, the last of which appeared in 1942. During World War II, however, psychiatrists found this system to be inadequate, since it dealt effectively with only ten percent of the total cases seen. Following the war, the American Psychiatric Association undertook a revision of the Standard system. Based on material received from the Army and Veterans Administration, ideas from psychiatric training programs, suggestions from their own members, and data from the literature, they drafted a proposed revision. They revised it again and finally published it in 1951 as the *Diagnostic and Statistical Manual* (DSM–I). Curiously enough, the manual virtually ignored childhood disorders *per se* except for the inclusion of a few conditions that it listed with adult syndromes, in a manner somewhat reminiscent of the way children were viewed before childhood was discovered. In 1968, a second revision was published, known as DSM–II, which consisted of ten major categories. For the first time one of these categories was devoted exclusively to children ("Behavior Disorders of Childhood and Adolescence") and included the following subcategories: Behavior disorders, hyperkinetic reaction, withdrawing reaction, overanxious reaction, runaway reaction, unsocialized aggressive

TABLE 2–1 Summary of DSM–III Categories

Diagnostic and Statistical Manual *of Mental Disorders* *Diagnostic Categories*	Pervasive Developmental Disorders Attention Deficit Disorder Specific Developmental Disorders
A. Organic Mental Disorders	Stereotyped Movement Disorders
B. Drug Use Disorders	Speech Disorders Not Elsewhere Classified
C. Schizophrenic Disorders	Conduct Disorders
D. Paranoid Disorders	Eating Disorders
E. Affective Disorders	Anxiety Disorders
F. Psychoses Not Elsewhere Classified	Disorders Characteristic of Late Adolescence
G. Anxiety Disorders	Other Disorders of Childhood or Adolescence
H. Factitious Disorders	N. Reactive Disorders Not Elsewhere Classified
I. Somatoform Disorders	O. Disorders of Impulse Control Not Elsewhere
J. Dissociative Disorders	Classified
K. Personality Disorders	P. Sleep Disorders
L. Psychosexual Disorders	Q. Other Disorders and Conditions
Gender Identity or Role Disorders	Unspecified Mental Disorder (Not Psychotic)
Paraphilias	Psychic Factors in Physical Condition
Psychosexual Dysfunctions	No Mental Disorder
M. Disorders Usually Arising in Childhood or	Conditions Not Attributable to Known Mental
Adolescence (see Table 2–2)	Disorder
Mental Retardation	Administrative Categories

reaction, group delinquent reaction, and other reaction. In addition, another major category, transient situational disturbances, dealt with special symptoms most commonly found in children. These additions, albeit far from adequate, represented a substantial shift in the recognition given to child psychopathology by the American Psychiatric Association.

DSM–III is the latest and most radical revision not only in its attempt to be both specific and inclusive but also in its rather extensive provisions for childhood disorders [*DSM–III: Diagnostic and Statistical Manual of Mental Disorder* (3rd ed.), 4–15–77 draft]. This classification system consists of seventeen major categories summarized in Table 2–1. It also provides operational criteria that specify the clinical phenomena needed to justify the diagnosis, and a multiaxial framework that gives the diagnostician additional categories on which to code the patient. There are five axes: two dealing with other categories of mental

disorders; one for designating nonmental medical disorders; one for rating the severity of psychosocial stressors; and one characterizing the highest level of adaptive functioning the patient achieved within the last year.

The major category devoted to child psychopathology is more extensive and inclusive than what appeared in the previous two editions. It is designated as "Disorders Usually Arising in Childhood or Adolescence" and each of its subcategories is summarized in Table 2–2. Psychosexual disorders, particularly gender disturbances that occur during childhood and adolescence are not included in this section, although they are covered in the adult part. Surprisingly, this major category sets no age limit separating childhood from adolescence, and, in fact, includes subcategories that may be appropriate for the college years (Identity and Emancipation Disorder) or for older adults if the present condition dates back to early childhood (Attention Deficit Dis-

TABLE 2–2   Summary Description of DSM–III's Category on Childhood Disorders

---

Disorders Usually Arising in Childhood or Adolescence

The disorders in this section usually arise and are evident in childhood or adolescence, although no arbitrary age limit is used to define childhood or adolescence. The diagnoses in this section may apply to adults if they experienced the condition since childhood and no adult category applies. Childhood conditions resembling adult disorders that may not be continuous with these adult conditions have been given different names. A severity rating of functional impairment is made for conduct disorders. The multiaxial framework should be used whenever possible.

1. Mental Retardation

Three essential features must be present: (1) significant subaverage general intellectual functioning, (2) concurrent deficits in adaptive behavior, and (3) onset before the age of eighteen. The diagnosis is made regardless of the nature of the etiological factors, although a known biological cause should be coded on Axis III. When mental retardation develops after age eighteen, it is designated as a dementia and is coded within the organic mental disorders section. There are four subtypes of mental retardation reflecting the degree of intellectual impairment. These are labeled as mild, moderate, severe, or profound depending on an IQ criterion.

2. Pervasive Developmental Disorders

These disorders are characterized by distortions in the timing, rate, and sequence of many basic psychological functions, and they differ from specific developmental disorders in two ways: (1) the specifics show a delay in time or rate of specific discrete functions while the pervasives evidence a marked distortion of the timing, rate, and sequence of many general psychological functions that profoundly distort social and interpersonal development; and (2) the specifics appear as if they are passing through an earlier normal developmental stage, while the pervasives manifest severe qualitative abnormalities that are not normal for any stage of development. Pervasive development disorders were previously labeled atypical children, symbiotic psychotic children, and childhood schizophrenia.

A. Infantile Autism

The essential features of this syndrome include lack of responsiveness to other human beings, gross impairment in communicative skills, and bizarre responses to various aspects of the environment. All features develop within the first forty-two months of age. The operational criteria of infantile autism are as follows: (1) onset usually prior to thirty months but up to forty-two months, (2) lack of responsiveness to other human beings, (3) self-isolation, (4) gross deficits in language development, (5) if speech is present, peculiar speech patterns, and (6) peculiar interest or attachments to animate or inanimate objects.

B. Early Childhood Psychosis

Profound disturbance in emotional relationships with people and a multiplicity of bizarre characteristics developing during infancy or early childhood are the essential features. Early childhood psychosis is diagnosed by the following operational criteria: (1) gross and sustained impaired emotional relationships, (2) bizarre beliefs or preoccupations, (3) four of the eight associated features (acute and illogical anxiety, disturbed affect, resistance to environmental change, peculiar motility, speech abnormalities, language disturbances, abnormal sensory and perceptual experiences, self-mutilation), and (4) onset during infancy or early childhood.

C. Pervasive Development Disorder of Childhood, Residual State

This category is intended to meet the following operational criteria: (1) the patient's condition once was diagnosed as a pervasive developmental disorder, (2) the current clinical picture does not meet the criteria for either infantile autism or early childhood psychosis, and (3) the patient is still manifesting symptoms caused by the original disorder.

D. *Unspecified Pervasive Developmental Disorders*

3. *Attention Deficit Disorders*

This category includes two separate disorders characterized by developmentally inappropriate short attention and poor concentration.

A. *Attention Deficit Disorder with Hyperactivity*

The operational criteria for this disorder are as follows: (1) excessive general hyperactivity or motor restlessness for age, (2) difficulty sustaining attention, (3) impulsive behavior as evidenced in at least two of the following: sloppy work but with effort to perform, frequent calling out of turn or making inappropriate sounds in class, frequent interruption of or intrusion into activities of other children, difficulty waiting for one's turn, poor frustration tolerance, fighting with children brought on by low frustration tolerance, and (4) duration of condition at least one year.

B. *Attention Deficit Disorder Without Hyperactivity*

Children with this disorder manifest, for their age, an impairment in the ability to concentrate, difficulty in completing tasks, and conspicuous lack of organization or forethought as they move from one activity to another. They exhibit difficulty sustaining attention and focusing attention but without hyperactivity. The diagnosis should not be made before the age of four. Specific developmental disorders are common and should be coded on Axis II. Impaired academic performance often is present. The operational criteria for this disorder is similar to those described in (A) except for the hyperactivity and motor component.

4. *Specific Developmental Disorders* (Axis II)

These disorders are coded on Axis II and are diagnosed only when there is a delay in development that is *not* an essential criterion for another disorder. The coding carries no etiological implications and should be made on the basis of the individual's current level of functioning without regard to its origin.

A. *Specific Reading Disorder*

The essential feature of this disorder is a serious impairment in the development of reading skills not explicable in terms of mental age or inadequate schooling. The impairment should be determined by a performance on a standardized reading test and it should be significantly less than predicted on the basis of the child's chronological age and a full-scale IQ obtained from an individually administered intelligence test.

B. *Specific Arithmetical Disorder*

The essential feature of this disorder is a serious impairment of arithmetic skills not explicable in terms of mental age or inadequate schooling. The diagnosis should be established by performance on standardized tests of arithmetic achievement significantly below that which would be expected on the basis of the child's chronological age and full-scale IQ on an individually administered intelligence test.

C. *Developmental Language Disorder*

Delayed language disorder is separated into two types:

1. *Expressive type* is characterized by an impairment in the encoding or production of language while the understanding or decoding skills remain relatively intact. The operational criteria include a defect or delay in the production of language, and the absence of hearing impairment, general retardation, trauma, or seizures that could explain the defect.

2. *Receptive type* involves both the comprehension and production of language such that language acquisition is severely impaired. The deficit must be present from the first year of life and there must be an absence of general mental retardation or other more pervasive disorder that could explain the language disability in order for the diagnosis to be made.

D. *Developmental Articulation Disorder*

The essential feature of this disorder is defective articulation of the later acquired speech sounds occurring in the absence of other language impairment or physical or intellectual disorders.

E. *Coordination Disorder*

This involves a serious impairment in the development of motor coordination in the absence of mental retardation or any neurological disorder that would account for the motor coordination problems.

F. *Enuresis*

Primary Enuresis is characterized by persistent involuntary voiding of urine by day or night that is considered abnormal for the age of individual. The frequency should be at least one such event per month after the child has reached the age of five.

Secondary Enuresis is differentiated from primary by the second operational criteria that states that the frequency should be at least one such event per month after a period of urinary continence lasting at least one year.

G. *Encopresis*

This disorder consists of a persistent voluntary or involuntary passage of feces of normal or near normal consistency in places deemed inappropriate for that purpose by the individual's own sociocultural setting. This should occur at a frequency of at least one such event per month for a period after the child has reached the age of five.

H. *Mixed Specific Developmental Disorders*

This category should be used when the patient manifests more than one specific developmental disorder, none of which is predominant.

I. *Other Specific Developmental Disorders*

This category is used when there is a serious impairment in a specific area of development that is not covered by the categories specified.

J. *Unspecified Specific Developmental Disorders*

5. *Stereotyped Movement Disorders*

A. *Motor Tic Disorder*

This disorder involves purposeless, involuntary movements that are frequent, rapid, spasmodic and repetitive, and that occur in the absence of an established neurological etiology. The disorder's duration should be for at least one month, and no verbal tics are present for the diagnosis to be made.

B. *Motor-Verbal Tic Disorder* (Gilles de la Tourette Syndrome)

Individuals with this disorder suffer from motor and verbal tics and from sudden vocalizations. Other operational criteria include age of onset between two and fifteen years, multiple involuntary motor and verbal tics, and symptoms that wax and wane.

C. *Unspecified Tic Disorder*

D. *Other Stereotyped Movement Disorders*

This category is intended for conditions such as head banging, rocking, repetitive hand movements consisting of quick rhythmical small hand rotations, or repetitive voluntary movements involving the fingers or arms. They are distinguishable from tics in that they consist of voluntary movements and are not spasmodic. Children with these disorders are not distressed by the same symptoms as those with tics.

6. *Speech Disorders Not Elsewhere Classified*

A. *Stuttering*

This disorder consists of persistent repetitions or prolongations of sounds, syllables, or words; or persistent, unusual hesitations and pauses that disrupt the rhythmic flow of speech. It occurs in the absence of mental retardation as the cause of the speech impairment.

B. *Elective Mutism*

This disorder is characterized by a pervasive and persistent refusal to speak in social or school situations, though the children are able and willing to speak to selected persons, usually family or peers. The diagnosis is made only when the refusal to speak is not symptomatic of any other disorder listed and when there is evidence of normal intellectual functions.

7. Conduct Disorders

These disorders involve repetitive and persistent patterns of misconduct such as delinquency, destructiveness, or other violations of the rights of others beyond the ordinary mischief and pranks of children and adolescents.

A. Undersocialized Conduct Disorder. Aggressive Type

The operational criteria include (1) a persistent lack of concern for the feelings of others; (2) a pattern of antisocial behavior of at least four months' duration with at least one of the following: assault, defiance and defiant disobedience, destructiveness, cruelty, and vindictiveness; (3) failure to develop peer friendship patterns; and (4) behavioral difficulties at school.

B. Undersocialized Conduct Disorder. Unaggressive Type

These children (1) fail to form social bonds and develop a pattern of normal attachment to others; (2) lack bold or openly aggressive behavior, unless with those who are younger and weaker than they; (3) show five or more of the following behaviors for at least four months: stealing, lying, lack of friends, superficial friendliness for self-seeking purposes, whining and temper tantrums, repetitive running away from home overnight, repetitive staying out late at night, chronic disobedience, complaining that "nobody likes me or nobody cares about me," and poor frustration tolerance.

C. Socialized Conduct Disorder

This disorder is defined operationally by the following criteria: (1) involvement over at least a four months' period in a pattern of antisocial behavior involving either group fighting, petty thievery, minor vandalism, or other more serious delinquent or antisocial activity, such as group stealing, burglary, larceny, or assault, (2) evidence of some dependable and lasting attachments and age-appropriate relationships with some persons, whether companions, family members, or others, and (3) the presence of impairment in social relationships in the family and in school, as well as impairment in age-appropriate responsibilities at home and school.

8. Eating Disorders

A. Anorexia Nervosa

The essential features of this disorder are excessive behaviors directed toward losing weight, peculiar patterns of handling food, weight loss, intense fear of gaining weight, disturbance about body image, and in women, amenorrhea.

B. Bulimia

This disorder is characterized by an episodic pattern of binge eating (rapid consumption of a large amount of food in a discrete period of time, usually less than two hours), accompanied by an awareness of the disordered eating pattern and a fear of not being able to voluntarily stop eating, and depressive moods and self-deprecating thoughts. Bulimic patients must have at least three of the following symptoms: rapid consumption of food during a binge; consumption of high caloric food during a binge; inconspicuous eating during a binge; the termination of binge eating by abdominal pain, sleep, social interruption, or self-induced vomiting; repeated attempts to lose weight by severely restrictive diets or self-induced vomiting; an eating pattern of alternate binges and fasts; and use of cathartics for weight control.

C. Pica

This disorder involves the persistent eating of non-nutritional substances for at least one month.

D. Ruminati (Merycism)

The essential features are regurgitation of food with failure to thrive, or weight loss developing after a period of normal functioning.

9. Anxiety Disorders of Childhood or Adolescence

A. Separation Anxiety Disorder

Exaggerated distress of at least one month duration at separation from parents, home, or other familial surroundings that is not accounted for by any other mental disorder.

B. *Shyness Disorder*

This disorder involves the persistent shrinking from familiarity or contact with all strangers to the extent that it interferes with peer functioning. The child must be at least two and a half years of age and the shyness must be present for at least three months. These children usually have warm and satisfying relations with family members.

C. *Overanxious Disorder*

This disorder is characterized by anxiety for at least three months evidenced by persistent worrying about future events but not focused on a specific situation or object and not attributable to a recent psychosocial stressor. The anxiety is not symptomatic of another disorder and at least one of the following symptoms of anxiety also must be present: concern with competence, difficulty falling asleep, somatic complaints with no medical basis, and frequent frightening dreams.

10. *Disorders Characteristic of Late Adolescence*

A. *Emancipation Disorder of Adolescence or Early Adult Life*

The essential feature is symptomatic expression of a conflict over independence following the recent growth of independence from parental control or supervision. The condition is not secondary to any other mental disorder, and it must be manifested by two or more of the following symptoms: difficulty making independent decisions, increased dependence on parental advice, unwarranted concern about parental possessiveness, adoption of values deliberately in opposition to parents, rapid development of markedly dependent peer relationships, and homesickness.

B. *Identity Disorder*

Distress over an inability to reconcile aspects of the self into a relatively coherent and acceptable sense of self, not secondary to another mental disorder with onset not prior to an age of fourteen.

C. *Specific Academic or Work Inhibition*

The predominant clinical feature is severe distress interfering significantly with any of the following academic or work tasks and manifested by anxiety related to examinations or other tests; inability to write papers or prepare reports or to perform in studio arts activities, or by difficulty in concentration on studies or work, or avoidance of studying or work which does not seem to be under the conscious control of the individual. The previous academic or work functioning should have been at least adequate, and the individual should have intellectual and academic or work skills that are adequate, and the condition is not caused by any other mental disorder.

11. *Other Disorders of Childhood or Adolescence*

A. *Oppositional Disorder*

Pervasive opposition to all authority regardless of self-interest occurring after the age of two through the age of eighteen. There is a continual argumentativeness and an unwillingness to respond to reasonable persuasion, which is not accounted for by a conduct disorder, an adjustment disorder, or a pervasive developmental disorder.

B. *Academic Underachievement Disorder*

Failure to achieve in most school tasks despite adequate intellectual capacity, a supportive and encouraging social environment, and apparent effort. The failure occurs in the absence of a demonstrable specific learning disability and is caused by emotional conflict not clearly associated with any other mental disorder.

Reprinted with permission of American Psychiatric Association. From Diagnostic and Statistical Manual of Medical Disorders, 3rd ed., Draft Version, Task Force on Nomenclature and Statistics, 4/5/77.

order). Childhood disorders resembling those seen in the adult but that may not lead to their adult counterpart are given separate subcategories in this section. In addition, there are many diagnoses offered elsewhere in the manual such as phobias and adjustment disorders that can be applied to children.

The final draft of DSM–III, due to be published sometime in 1979 or 1980, is clearly more comprehensive and explicit in diagnostic criteria and categories than the previous editions. Although it is too early to judge, DSM–III gives every indication of being significantly more reliable and valid than any classification system that has yet to appear. In addition, DSM–III should reassure those concerned with the tendency of classification systems to neglect the "whole" individual. While the very nature of any sort of classification is to highlight some features and ignore others, with its multiaxial orientation, DSM–III minimizes this problem by looking at children and adults from many perspectives.

Child Classification Systems

Although the need for a uniform classification system for children and adolescence had been noted for years (Group for the Advancement of Psychiatry, 1957), it was not until 1966 that the Committee on Child Psychiatry of the Group for the Advancement of Psychiatry (GAP) completed and published their proposed system (Group for the Advancement of Psychiatry, 1966). At the time of publication, there were at least twenty three other child classification systems in use, illustrating the diversity and diagnostic confusion that has characterized the field.

The GAP system consists of ten major categories ordered (although poorly) along the dimension of prognosis, and ranging from healthy responses to the most severe disorders. A summary of these categories and the subcategories noted for each are included in Table 2–3. Embracing the psychosomatic, developmental, and psychosocial views, the system can best be characterized as a clinical descriptive one that can be used by clinicians of varying backgrounds. The category, Healthy Responses, has never been used in any system but is included here to minimize the practice of clinicians to exaggerate minor childhood problems into pathological ones for classification purposes. For example, the new category gives the clinician the opportunity to categorize bedwetting in a two-year old as a healthy response rather than calling it abnormal. Another new category, Developmental Deviations, deals with deviations in maturational rate, or sequence, or personality development that are frequently noted in children but that are not adequately classified under other systems.

In 1969, The World Health Organization (WHO) published a multiaxial classification system for childhood disorders (Rutter *et al.,* 1969). This system includes the following four axes: (1) clinical psychiatric syndrome, (2) intellectual level (IQ), (3) associated etiological biological factors, and (4) any associated etiological psychosocial factors. Thus, a psychotic child (1) who is severely retarded (2) and who has epilepsy (3) would be coded on three of the four axes. The advantage of classifying children on various relevant dimensions offered by the WHO system is now available in the new multiaxial look of DSM–III.

A statistical technique, known as *factor analysis,* has been used empirically to isolate clusters of characteristics observed in children that then become the major categories of the classification system. The effec-

TABLE 2–3   Psychopathological Disorders in Childhood Proposed Classification

---

1. *Healthy Responses*

This category assesses the positive strengths of the child and tries to avoid the diagnosis of healthy states by the exclusion of pathology. The criteria for assessment are the intellectual, social, emotional, personal, adaptive, and psychosocial functioning of the child in relation to developmental and situational crises.

Healthy responses:
1. Developmental crisis
2. Situational crisis
3. Other responses

2. *Reactive Disorders*

This category is based on disorders in which behavior and/or symptoms are the result of situational factors. These disturbances must be of a pathological degree so as to distinguish them from the healthy responses to a situational crisis.

3. *Developmental Disorders*

These are disorders in personality development that may be beyond the range of normal variation in that they occur at a time, in a sequence, or in a degree not expected for a given age level or stage in development.

Developmental Deviations:
1. Deviations in maturational patterns
2. Deviations in specific dimensions of development
3. Motor
4. Sensory
5. Speech
6. Cognitive functions
7. Social development
8. Psychosexual
9. Affective
10. Integrative
11. Other developmental deviation

4. *Psychoneurotic Disorders*

These disorders are based on unconscious conflicts over the handling of sexual and aggressive impulses that remain active and unresolved, though removed from awareness by the mechanism of repression. Marked personality disorganization or decompensation, or the gross disturbance of reality testing is not seen. Because of their internalized character, these disorders tend toward chronicity, with a self-perpetuating or repetitive nature. Subcategories are based on specific syndromes.

Psychoneurotic Disorders:
1. Anxiety type
2. Phobic type
3. Conversion type
4. Dissociative type
5. Obsessive-compulsive type
6. Depressive type
7. Other psychoneurotic disorder

5. *Personality Disorders*

These disorders are characterized by chronic or fixed pathological trends, representing traits that have become ingrained in the personality structure. In most but not all such disorders, these trends or traits are not perceived by the child as a source of intrapsychic distress or anxiety. In making this classification, the total personality picture must be considered and not just the presence of a single behavior or symptom.

Personality Disorders
   1. Compulsive personality
   2. Hysterical
   3. Anxious
   4. Overly dependent
   5. Oppositional
   6. Overly inhibited
   7. Overly independent
   8. Isolated
   9. Mistrustful
Tension-discharge disorders:
   1. Impulse-ridden personality
   2. Neurotic personality disorder
Sociosyntonic personality disorders:
   1. Sexual deviation
   2. Other personality disorder

6. *Psychotic Disorder*

These disorders are characterized by marked, pervasive deviations from the behavior that is expected for the child's age. They are revealed in severe and continued impairment of emotional relationships with persons; loss of speech or failure in its development; disturbances in sensory perception; bizarre or stereotyped behavior and motility patterns; marked resistance to change in environment or routine; outbursts of intense and unpredictable panic; absence of a sense of personal identity; and blunted, uneven, or fragmented intellectual development. Major categories are based on the developmental period with subcategories in each period for the listing of a specific syndrome, if known.

Psychotic Disorders:
   1. Psychoses of infancy and early childhood
      a. Early infantile autism
      b. Interactional psychotic disorder
      c. Other psychosis of infancy and early childhood
   2. Psychoses of later childhood
      a. Schizophreniform psychotic disorder
      b. Other psychosis of later childhood
   3. Psychoses of adolescence
      a. Acute confusional state
      b. Schizophrenic disorder, adult type
      c. Other psychosis of adolescence

7. *Psychophysiologic Disorders*

These disorders are characterized by a significant interaction between somatic and psychological components. They may be precipitated and perpetuated by psychological or social stimuli of stressful nature. These disorders ordinarily involve those organ systems innervated by the autonomic nervous system.

Psychophysiologic Disorders:
   1. Skin
   2. Musculoskeletal
   3. Respiratory
   4. Cardiovascular
   5. Hemic and lymphatic
   6. Gastrointestinal
   7. Genitourinary
   8. Endocrine
   9. Of nervous system
   10. Of organs of special sense
   11. Other psychophysiologic disorders

8. *Brain Syndromes*

These disorders are characterized by impairment of orientation, judgment, discrimina-

tion, learning, memory, and other cognitive functions, as well as by frequent labile affect. They are basically caused by diffuse impairment of brain tissue function. Personality disturbances of a psychotic, neurotic, or behavioral nature also may be present.
   Brain Syndromes:
     1. Acute
     2. Chronic

 9. *Mental Retardation*

10. *Other Disorders*
   This category is for disorders that cannot be classified by the above definitions or for disorders we will describe in the future.

Reprinted by permission from *Psychological Disorders in Childhood: A Proposed Classification,* Group for the Advancement of Psychiatry, 419 Park Avenue South, New York, N.Y. 10016.

tiveness of this statistical approach rests on the nature and character of the items on which each child is rated, since the final cluster of symptoms is derived from these initial data. Consequently, factor analytic classifications differ from one investigator to another, because the original variables under study and the items used to measure them are likely to be divergent. An example of a factor analytic classification scheme is the one proposed by Achenbach (1966), who found two general clusters which he called *internalizing* and *externalizing* or *personality problems* and *conduct problems.* In addition to the general clusters, the system also includes specific symptom clusters that are either subsumed by the general clusters or peculiar to certain developmental periods. Some of the *internalizing* symptoms include phobias, insomnia, stomach-aches, and seclusiveness, while *externalizing* symptoms include destructiveness, stealing, and running away. These factorial data have been replicated with new samples of children and have been used to show that *externalizing* boys were independently rated as more impulsive and aggressive, while *internalizing* boys were considered more passive, more inclined to stay longer in psychotherapy, and to improve with treatment (Achenbach and

Lewis, 1971). Several other studies using these two general clusters with children from clinics and schools indicate relationships that support the validity of these categories (Achenbach, 1974).

The best known and most widely used psychoanalytic approach to classification is Anna Freud's "Developmental Profile" (Freud, 1965). Essentially, the profile is a diagnostic tool based on the developmental sequence proposed by psychoanalytic theory. It is used as a standard with which to compare the development of a given child. Freud rejected the heavy reliance on symptom description as the basis of diagnosing children's disorders and favored instead a more thorough assessment of the child's personality structure, functioning, and development, detailed in her developmental profile. However, she gave no objective criteria to aid the clinician in completing each part of the profile or indications of how information on the separate variables should be integrated and synthesized. Unfortunately, the profile has spawned little research and even less evaluative data, since the publications to date have, for the most part, been clinically descriptive of a single case.

Other and more specific classification schemes have been used for research purposes, especially in instances where investigators are concerned with studying one or relatively few psychopathological conditions. Usually these miniature systems specify a set of diagnostic criteria that are more behavioral and more amenable to the careful selection of clinical populations for study than is possible with the more traditional and global systems. For example, the DeMyer-Churchill system (DeMyer, Churchill, Pontius, and Gilkey, 1971) provides a set of criteria to distinguish psychotic children (see Chapter 8) into subgroups that are not included in DSM–III, GAP, or other systems previously described. Similarly, a checklist prepared by Rimland (1971) to differentiate one group of psychotic children from other groups (discussed in Chapter 8) is still popular with researchers studying childhood psychoses.

Reliability of Classification

From the time of Kraepelin to the present, the classification of abnormal behavior has had as its principal goals the understanding of etiology, the prediction of the course and outcome, and the appropriate selection of treatment for the various abnormal conditions. To a large extent, the usefulness of a classification scheme depends on the degree of consistency or agreement achieved in categorizing abnormal behavior. If little agreement is obtained, then the system has very limited pragmatic value in meeting the purpose for which it was constructed. The issue we raise is the important matter of reliability, which we shall now consider.

The Reliability of Classification

The reliability that we speak of may be one of three types:

1. *Observer agreement*—a measure of agreement of categorization by two or more observers.

2. *Consistency agreement*—a measure of agreement on categories over time, such as between the initial and final diagnosis.

3. *Frequency agreement*—a measure of agreement between two or more random samples of the same population with regard to the frequency of cases falling into each diagnostic category (Zubin, 1967).

Most studies of reliability have been, in fact, concerned with observer agreement, and have been based on the adult categories specified in DSM–I. We should also note that the data obtained from many of these studies, especially the earlier ones, are difficult to interpret because of their methodological shortcomings. These shortcomings involve (1) very small and unrepresentative samples of patients, (2) lack of control for rater differences in training and experience, and (3) dearth of information about patients on which ratings were based (Beck, 1962). More carefully designed studies have shown consistently that agreement is high when the classification is restricted to a few major categories that are grossly distinct from each other. However, reliability estimates sharply decline when a greater number and more specific diagnostic categories are included (Hunt, Witson, and Hunt, 1953; Schmidt and Fonda, 1956; Kreitman, Sainsbury, Morrisey, Towers, and Scrivener, 1961; Sandifer, Pettus, and Quade, 1964).

In general, *consistency of diagnosis over time* as a reliability measure yields even lower estimates than that obtained from studies of observer agreement (Zubin, 1967). However, this finding may be more indicative of the dramatic changes that can take place in the symptoms of a patient from one period of time to another than of poor rater reliability. This is particularly true of those patients who, after a brief period of hospitalization, show a decrease in agitated and anxiety generated behavior because they are now in a more secure and protected environment. In addition, the increased use of drugs to treat patients and to make them more manageable has tended to bring about symptom changes over time.

Illustrative of the third measure of reliability, *frequency agreement,* is a study involving 538 women who were admitted to a large midwestern psychiatric hospital for the first time (Pasamanick, Dinitz, and Lefton, 1959). The patients were assigned to one of three autonomously operated wards on the basis of bed availability. There were no differences among the patients on the three wards with respect to marital status, age, education, urban-rural residence, or type of admission (voluntary or involuntary). Three different psychiatrists were placed in charge of each ward. In this way, a situation was constructed that provided each psychiatrist with equal access to patient information from other professional workers, and with the "same type" of patient to diagnose. The results showed marked discrepancies among the samples with respect to the frequency that the three major diagnostic categories were used. In this connection, Zubin noted that of four studies he reviewed (including Pasamanick *et al.*), only one showed agreement among samples. He concluded, "In general, the results of comparative studies of random samples with regard to distribution of diagnoses do not yield a consistent picture regarding reliability" (Zubin, 1967, p. 388).

Interest in assessing the reliability of the classification of children's disorders is recent, primarily because there was no single system that could be used uniformly until the appearance of the GAP proposal. Since its publication, the GAP scheme has been the subject of several investigations. One study found that two of the GAP categories accounted for seventy five percent of the 200 cases sampled (Personality Disorder and Psychotic Disorder). Six other categories were used sparingly (from about four to eight percent), while the two new categories (Healthy Responses and Developmental Deviation) practically were not used at all (Sabot, Peck, and Raskin, 1969). Another study attempted to determine the effectiveness of the GAP system over a twelve month period (Bemporad, Pfeiffer, and Bloom, 1970). In contrast, the new categories were found to be useful for this sample of 310 children in that they accounted for almost twenty four percent of the cases. Moreover, the distribution of the cases among the GAP categories between these two studies differed markedly in almost all instances. It is difficult to resolve the large discrepancies between these two studies, because the second study did not describe the patients used with respect to socioeconomic level, race, age, educational level, and family structure. It is entirely possible that some of the differences in the findings were attributable to the substantial differences in the population sampled.

The most extensive study to date involved the diagnosis by twenty experienced child psychiatrists of forty four cases (case histories and diagnoses) submitted by member of the GAP subcommittee (Freeman, 1971). The results indicated that four categories (Reactive Disorders, Neurotic Disorders, Personality Disorders, and Psychotic Disorders) accounted for eighty three percent of the diagnoses, while the remaining categories accounted for only seventeen percent of the diagnoses. The two new categories (Healthy Responses and Developmental Deviation) were rarely used, once again raising the question of their value in a classification system. The reliability of the four frequently used categories was between sixty one and seventy two percent. There was no evidence that diagnostic agreement is higher for any specific age group. Data were also gathered to obtain a consistency over time measure of reliability by requiring the twenty clinicians to rediagnose a sample of selected cases some three months later. The clinicians placed eighty six out of a total of 120 diagnoses in the same category as before, yielding a seventy two percent agreement estimate. This figure is even more impressive in light of the fact that three cases accounted for twenty six of the thirty four disagreements recorded, and that three cases were responsible for low agreement even in the initial ratings. These findings reflect fairly high reliability for the four categories used most frequently, and a decrease in reliability when more specific subcategories are employed.

No data are available as yet with which to evaluate the reliability of the other classification systems discussed earlier.

Evaluation of Classification

Evidently the reliability of psychiatric classification is low except when diagnosis is restricted to a few broad categories. Although much of this evidence comes from studies using an out-dated system primarily intended for adults, similar inferences seem to be supported by data involving children and a classification scheme for child psychopathology (GAP). Diagnostic accuracy becomes increasingly more difficult as more categories are used and finer discriminations are required. The validity question, that is, how well diagnosis meets its goals, is extremely difficult to answer, since the goals of classification are so numerous and diverse.

In addition, DSM–II has been seriously criticized on other grounds. It has been regarded as unscientific in that it was finalized by a majority vote of selected psychiatrists rather than firmly rooted in careful empirical study. Perhaps more damaging is the confounding of etiology, symptoms, and outcome as the bases for diagnosis. Commenting on this diversity of principles, Draguns and Phillips stated, "This confusion not only makes for conceptual inelegance; it implies an ever continuing process of diagnosis terminated only at the point of patient's death. Ultimately, this orientation makes diagnosis intrinsically uncertain and unknowable" (Draguns and Phillips, 1971, p. 5). The use of behavioral description as the basic data for classification has been suggested as an alternative (Zigler and Phillips, 1961). Both etiology and prognosis would be treated as correlates of the particular class to which their relationship is known, but not as inherent attributes of the various categories. It can be argued that the present classification system is even inadequate as a descriptive scheme, because the principle of symptom appearance is not applied consistently to all categories, and the symptoms presumed to be associated with each category are not clearly specified. The system simply fails to delineate the criteria for making assignments to any given category.

Another major criticism is that classification implies separate and mutually exclusive entities. Yet there is considerable overlapping in symptomatology among the categories. For example, it has been found that the symptom of depression occurred in sixty-five percent of patients diagnosed as manic-depressive, in fifty-eight percent of those diagnosed as psychoneurotic, and in thirty-one percent of those diagnosed as character disorders (Zigler and Phillips, 1961). Moreover, in actual practice, only one or two symptoms may be used to determine the diagnosis, although a particular entity often is characterized by many symptoms. The weight given to one or several symptoms for inclusion or exclusion in a diagnostic category is, in fact, left to the judgment of the clinician (Lorr, Klett, and McNair, 1963). It has been estimated that about five percent of the disagreement in diagnosis is attributable to the inconsistent behavior of the patient, 32.5 percent to the inconsistent behavior of the diagnostician, and 62.5 percent to the inadequacy of the classification system (Ward *et al.,* 1962). If this appraisal is correct, then diagnostic reliability can be increased to some extent by reducing those disagreements introduced by the clinician. Improvement in the clinicians' training in the uniform use of the classification scheme as the basis for diagnostic decisions would go a long way in minimizing this source of error. However, the problems inherent in classification strongly suggest that primary attention must be directed to the development of changes in the system itself.

The issue of attaching psychiatric labels to children has aroused controversy between those who see potential danger in it, and those who see its advantage in early intervention. Diagnostic labels, especially ones that reflect serious disorders, may stick to the child over the years and possibly influence later evaluations even when they are no longer appropriate. Labeling may stigmatize and set the child apart from peers, and it may encourage others to look for the child to behave in a way commensurate with the label. Unfortunately, diagnostic categories appear real and valid to many, although we now know that they lack the precision and reliability to warrant such confidence. For these reasons and to protect children from future abuses, many clinicians are reluctant to fix a diagnostic label to children who evidence abnormal behaviors, if in the future there is a chance that others might have access to the diagnosis. On the other hand, it can be argued that diagnostic labels need not be abused or misinterpreted if the clinician exercises care in the evaluation and good judgment about who has access to it. The diagnosis should serve as the basis of a treatment plan and should be helpful in later evaluations of the child as a basis for comparison and as a measure of the child's progress.

For the present, DSM–III and to a lesser extent the GAP proposal enjoy official status and widespread use throughout the country. Within the limitations already noted, classification brings uniformity to the ordering of psychopathology and continues to serve an important communication function among professionals. While it is necessary to be aware of its shortcomings, it would be premature to ignore or completely reject the current system. Meehl supported this position when he remarked, "There is a sufficient amount of etiological and prognostic homogeneity among patients belonging to a given diagnostic group, so that the assignment of a patient to his group has probability implications which it is clinically unsound to ignore" (Meehl, 1959, p. 103). More recently, it has been argued that classification is essential for research and fundamental to the clinician in organizing the multi-faceted aspects of mental disorders (Shakow, 1968). Over the years, classification has increased our knowledge of psychopathology, and further important insights should be forthcoming with increased efforts to improve both the system and the process. We are drawn to the conclusion that the student must be familiar with the diagnostic categories presently used, because they represent handles that systematically open the storehouse of available knowledge in the field. In addition, they stress the orderly and careful accumulation of observations so necessary for making diagnostic decisions.

Scope and Measurement of Psychopathology

Measures

Statistical data about the occurrence of abnormal behavior may be arrived at in three different ways: incidence, prevalence, and expectancy. *Incidence* refers to the total number of *new* cases of a disorder that occurs within a specified population and a period of time. *Prevalence* is a more extensive measure in that it refers to the total number of cases (old and new) present in a given population during a specified time interval.

The major difference between incidence and prevalence measures is that the latter reflects both incidence and duration. For example, if we interpret as incidence data the often cited statistic that over one-half of all hospital beds are occupied by the mentally ill, we would conclude erroneously that there are more people who evidence abnormal behavior than is actually the case. However, if we understand this finding as prevalence data, we recognize the fact that the internment for mental disorders is much longer than the time required for other hospitalized conditions. Therefore, the statistic should not be taken to mean that one-half of all new hospital admissions each year consists of mentally ill people, but rather that mental patients occupy half of

the beds available because their hospital stay is relatively long (Kramer, 1957; Malzberg, 1963).

The probability that a person will fall into a specific category of abnormal behavior sometime during his or her lifetime is an *expectancy* measure. Although informative, an expectancy measure is biased since it does not take into account the individual's age when the question is asked concerning the chances of becoming mentally ill. The longer one lives, the greater number of years available in which the probabilities of abnormal behavior apply. Therefore, it is more useful to ask what is one's risk of a behavior disorder *if one lives* to a certain age. In this way, the risk is expressed as a conditional probability, not as a joint probability of both living to such an age and becoming mentally ill. For example, the probability of living to the age of ninety and being mentally ill is less than the chances of having a behavior disorder given that one does live to the age of ninety.

Sources of Error in Measurement

Unfortunately, all of these measures are subject to several sources of error that make it difficult to estimate the extent of the problem in any definitive way. Typically, frequency figures of abnormal behavior come from public and private clinics and hospital census records. These data do not include instances of abnormal behaviors that are tolerated or go unrecognized within some subcultures of our society. For example, school phobias (fear of and refusal to go to school) are more likely to go unnoticed in a low socio-economic urban area than in an upper-middle-class urban neighborhood because truancy is implicitly sanctioned in that subculture. In addition, the measures do not reflect the number of less severe cases that are handled within the confines of the family, or those cases that are masked by physical symptoms such as asthma. There is a strong tendency for some parents to postpone as long as possible the professional attention needed by their disturbed children. For that matter, some professionals tend to shy away from using diagnostic labels connoting severe abnormal conditions to reduce the danger that the diagnosis will adversely affect how others react to the child in the future. Moreover, official statistics are not adjusted in terms of the availability of services and facilities. Therefore, they do not include those cases that are unadmitted because facilities either are nonexistent or unavailable because of overcrowded conditions. A more serious source of error is the great diversity among professionals and institutions with regard to the definition and classification of abnormal behavior. Therefore, all of these measures are affected in an unsystematic way by the variability of the diagnostic labels used to categorize abnormal behaviors.

Scope of the Problem

In spite of these limitations, we do know that the United States faces a sizable and serious problem. The 1970 census indicated that we are a nation of young people with approximately fifty million of our citizens classified as minors (twenty six percent of the total population) and with one-half of this figure under the age of ten. Several separate estimates give cause for concern in that they reflect that up to ten percent of all school age children require professional attention for abnormal behaviors, and that children now constitute about thirty four percent of the total population served by outpatient mental-health centers as compared to twenty-seven percent in 1967 (Bower, 1969; *Crisis in Child Mental Health: Challenge for the 1970's,* 1970; Garmezy, 1975). Since 1973, the number and rate of hospital admissions (adjusted for birth rate) among children under eighteen years of age has been declining. However, it is too early to tell if this is a reliable trend or nothing more than yearly fluctuations like those noted in the previous four years (Taube and Meyer, 1975). In all probability, the decrease in hospital admissions represents a significant shift away from mental hospitals to a more extensive use of relatively new community facilities such as community mental-health centers. Of the children under eighteen years of age admitted to state and county mental hospitals in 1973, one percent was under five years of age, seven percent were between five and nine years, thirty percent were between ten and fifteen years, and sixty three percent were between fifteen and seventeen years old. However, the age at which children most frequently are referred for professional attention is between ten and fourteen years (Redick, 1973).

It has been known for a long time that boys outnumber girls in practically every diagnostic category of abnormal behavior, although as yet no satisfactory explanation for this finding is available. In some instances, the male-female ratio is as high as 5:1 (Gilbert, 1957; Morse, Cutler, and Fink, 1964; Redick, 1973). Equally puzzling is the fact that this relationship tends to hold until late adolescence. However, it dissipates in adulthood to the point where females may even exceed males in those abnormal conditions where unequal sex distributions are found. For hospitalized children, the boys exceed girls in every age group, but especially between the ages of five and nine years (Taube & Meyer, 1975).

Although the magnitude of aberrant behaviors in children is greater than we would wish, we can look to the future with optimism knowing that the field now provides formal training for its professional workers. Moreover, the encouraging advances in knowledge obtained through research make it more reasonable than ever before to expect that abnormal behaviors of children will be identified earlier, treated more effectively, and, to a greater extent, prevented.

Summary

In this chapter we defined abnormal behavior in terms of the following criteria:

1. Cultural Norm: the established standards and expectations approved by the culture for the behavior of its members.
2. Developmental Norm: The expectations based on our knowledge of the developmental process.
3. Intellectual and Cognitive Functioning: an apparent disparity between ability and actual performance in attention, comprehension, judgment, learning, memory, thinking, and perception.
4. Emotional Expression and Control: an insufficient or an exaggerated emotional reaction, inappropriate emotional expression, infantile emotional reactions, moods of despondency, extreme elation, sudden fluctuation, or too little or too much emotional control.
5. Coping in Interpersonal Relations: disruptions in or inability to cope with interpersonal relations, social withdrawal, isolation, suspiciousness, fear and hatred of others, and uncooperativeness. This criterion must be used in conjunction with the other criteria of cognitive and emotional dysfunction.

We also argued that the characteristics of *frequency, intensity* or *degree,* and *duration* are necessary in applying the above criteria in defining the domain of abnormal behavior.

We presented summaries of the new psychiatric classification system (DSM–III) and the GAP proposal for the classification of children's disorders. In addition, we considered the WHO multiaxial classification for childhood disorders, Achenbach's factor analytic system, Anna Freud's developmental profile, and other miniature schemes for research purposes.

We discussed measures of reliability and research findings. In general, reliability of classification is fairly high when few and broad categories are used, but it declines sharply when a greater number and more specific categories are included. We reviewed major criticisms and problems inherent in the classification system, although we concluded that classification brings order and uniformity to psychopathology and serves an important communication function among professionals.

We also considered the problems associated with estimating the frequency of occurrence of abnormal behavior, and we defined incidence, prevalence, and expectancy measures. All of these measures are affected by the variability of the diagnostic labels used to categorize abnormal behavior, by the availability of service facilities, by instances that are either tolerated or unrecognized within some subcultures of our society, and by the inclination of families to deny or ignore the problem. We presented some overall estimates of the scope of the problem.

Epilogue

The follow-up story on Martin is disappointing. During the three years he was seen at the Clinic, Martin had several different therapists in both individual and group psychotherapy. An abnormal EEG was uncovered, which together with his acting out behavior suggested potential benefit from chemotherapy. He was given two anticonvulsant drugs for almost a year and a half, although no behavioral improvements were noted. Soon thereafter, Martin was placed on a trial dose of an amphetamine which, according to the therapist, produced positive behavioral results. However, his mother and teachers observed no improvement in his behavior. Finally, medication and psychotherapy were discontinued because the family became pessimistic over Martin's prospect for improvement and the clinic's effectiveness in treating' him. Possibly the absence of a careful diagnostic work-up and the failure to arrive at a diagnosis for Martin were significant factors in the clinic's ineffectiveness in structuring an appropriate treatment plan for Martin and his family.

REFERENCES

ACHENBACH, T. M. "The Classification of Children's Psychiatric Symptoms: A Factor-Analytic Study." *Psychological Monographs*, 1966, *80*: (Whole No. 615), 1–37.

ACHENBACH, T. M. *Developmental Psychopathology*. New York: Ronald Press, 1974.

ACHENBACH, T. M. and M. LEWIS. "A Proposed Model for Clinical Research and Its Application to Encopresis and Enuresis." *Journal of the American Academy of Child Psychiatry*, 1971, *10*, 535–554.

AL-ISSA, I. "Problems in the Cross-Cultural Study of Schizophrenia." *Journal of Psychology*, 1969, *71*, 143–151.

BAZZOUI, W. and I. AL-ISSA. "Psychiatry in Iraq." *British Journal of Psychiatry*, 1966, *112*, 827–832.

BECK, A. T. "Reliability of Psychiatric Diagnoses. I. A Critique of Systematic Studies." *American Journal of Psychiatry*, 1962, *119*, 210–216.

BEMPORAD, J., PFEIFFER, C., and W. BLOOM. "Twelve Months Experiences with the GAP Classification of Childhood Disorders." *American Journal of Psychiatry*, 1970, *127*, 658–664.

BOWER, E. M. *The Early Identification of Emotionally Handicapped Children in School* (2nd ed.). Springfield, Illinois: Thomas, 1969.

COPELAND, J. "Aspects of Mental Illness in West African Students." *Social Psychiatry*, 1968, *3*, 7–13.

Crisis in Child Mental Health: Challenge for the 1970's. Report of the Joint Commission on Mental Health of Children. New York: Harper and Row, 1970.

DeMYER, M. K., CHURCHILL, D. W., PONTIUS, W., and K. M. GILKEY. "A Comparison of Five Diagnostic Systems for Childhood Schizophrenia and Infantile Autism." *Journal of Autism and Childhood Schizophrenia*, 1971, *1*, 175–189.

Diagnostic and Statistical Manual. American Psychiatric Association. Washington, D.C.: Special Printing, 1965.

DSM–III: Diagnostic and Statistical Manual of Mental Disorders (3rd ed.). The Task Force on Nomenclature and Statistics of the American Psychiatric Association. New York: The American Psychiatric Association, 4/15/77 (draft).

DOHRENWEND, B. P. and B. S. DOHRENWEND. "Social and Cultural Influences on Psychopathology. *Annual Review of Psychology,* 1974, *25,* 417–452.

DRAGUNS, J. G. and L. PHILLIPS. *Psychiatric Classification and Diagnosis: An Overview and Critique.* Morristown, New Jersey: General Learning Press, 1971.

FREEMAN, M. "A Reliability Study of Psychiatric Diagnosis in Childhood and Adolescence." *Journal of Child Psychology and Psychiatry and Allied Disciplines,* 1971, *12*: (1) , 43–54.

FREUD, A. *Normality and Pathology in Childhood.* New York: International Universities Press, 1965.

GARMEZY, N. "The experimental study of children vulnerable to psychopathology." In A. Davids (Ed.), *Child Personality and Psychopathology: Current Trends,* Vol. 2. New York: Wiley, 1975.

GILBERT, G. M. "A Survey of Referral Problems in Metropolitan Child Guidance Centers. *Journal of Clinical Psychology,* 1957, *13,* 37–42.

Group for the Advancement of Psychiatry, Committee on Child Psychiatry: The Diagnostic Process in Child Psychiatry. GAP report No. 38, August, 1957.

Group for the Advancement of Psychiatry, Committee on Child Psychiatry: Psychopathological Disorders in Childhood: Theoretical Considerations and a Proposed Classification. GAP report No. 62, June 1966.

HUNT, W. A., WITSON, C. L., and E. B. HUNT. In P. H. Hoch and J. Zubin (Eds.), *Current Problems in Psychiatric Diagnosis.* New York: Gruen and Stratton, 1953.

JOHNSON, S., WAHL, G., MARTIN, W., and S. JOHANSSON. "How Deviant Is the Normal Child? A Behavioral Analysis of the Preschool Child and His Family." In R. Rubin, J. Brady and J. Henderson (Eds.), *Advances in Behavior Therapy:* Proceedings of the Association for Advancement of Behavior Therapy, 1969–73, Vol. 4. New York: Academic Press, 1973.

KLEINMUNTZ, B. *Essentials of Abnormal Psychology.* New York: Harper and Row, 1974, p. 389.

KRAMER, M. A. "A Discussion of the Concepts of Incidence and Prevalence as Related to Epidemiologic Studies of Mental Disorder. *American Journal of Public Health,* 1957, *47,* 826–840.

KREITMAN, N., SAINSBURY, P., MORRISEY, J., TOWERS, J., and J. SCRIVENER. "The Reliability of Psychiatric Assessment: An Analysis." *Journal of Mental Science,* 1961, *197,* 887–908.

LORR, M., KLETT, C. J., and D. M. McNAIR. *Syndromes of Psychosis.* New York: MacMillan, 1963.

MALZBERG, B. "Mental Disorders in the United States." In A. Deutsch and H. Fishman (Eds.), *Encyclopedia of Mental Health* (6 vols.) . New York: Franklin Watts, 1963.

MEEHL, P. E. "Some Ruminations on the Validation of Clinical Procedures." *Canadian Journal of Psychology,* 1959, *13,* 102–128.

MEYER, A. *The Commonsense Psychiatry of Doctor Adolph Meyer* (A. Lief, Ed.) . New York: McGraw-Hill, 1948.

MORSE, W. C., CUTLER, R. L., and A. H. FINK. *Public School Classes for the Emotionally Handicapped: A Research Analysis.* Washington, D.C.: Council for Exceptional Children, 1964.

MUNCIE, W. *Psychobiology and Psychiatry* (2nd ed.) . St. Louis: Mosby, 1948.

NASH, J. *Developmental Psychology: A Psychobiological Approach.* Englewood Cliffs, New Jersey: Prentice-Hall, 1970, p. 306.

PASAMANICK, B., DINITZ, S., and M. LEFTON. Psychiatric Orientation and Its Relation to Diagnosis and Treatment in a Mental Hospital. *American Journal of Psychiatry*, 1959, *116*, 127–132.

REDICK, R. *Utilization of Psychiatric Facilities by Persons Under Eighteen Years of age. United States, 1971.* Statistical Note 90. Department of Health, Education, and Welfare, 1973.

RIMLAND, B. "The Differentiation of Childhood Psychoses: An Analysis of Checklists for 2,218 Psychotic Children." *Journal of Autism and Childhood Schizophrenia*, 1971, *2*, 161–174.

RUTTER, M., LEBOVICI, S., EISENBERG, L., SNEVNEVSKIJ, A. V., SADOUN, R., BROOKE, E., and T. Y. LIN. "A Triaxial Classification of Mental Disorders in Childhood." *Journal of Child Psychology and Psychiatry*, 1969, *10*, 41–61.

SABOT, L. M., PECK, R., and J. RASKIN. "The Waiting Room Society." *Archives of General Psychiatry*, 1969, *21*, 25–32.

SANDIFER, M. G., Jr., PETTUS, C., and D. QUADE. "A Study of Psychiatric Diagnosis." *Journal of Nervous and Mental Disease*, 1964, *139*, 350–356.

SCHMIDT, H. W. and C. P. FONDA. "The Reliability of Psychiatric Diagnosis." *Journal of Abnormal and Social Psychology*, 1956, *52*, 262–267.

SHAKOW, D. "The Role of Classification in the Development of the Science of Psychopathology with Particular Reference to Research. In M. M. Katz, J. O. Cole, and W. E. Barton (Eds.), *The Role and Methodology of Classification in Psychiatry and Psychopathology*. Public Health Service Publication No. 1584. U.S. Department of Health, Education, and Welfare, Public Health Service, 1968, pp. 116–143.

TAUBE, C. A., and N. G. MEYER. *Children and State Mental Hospitals*. DHEW Statistical Note 115. Publication No. (ADM) 75–158. Rockville, Maryland: U.S. Department of Health, Education, and Welfare, 1975.

WARD, C. H., BECK, A. T., MENDELSON, M., MOCK, J. E., and J. K. ERBAUGH. "The Psychiatric Nomenclature: Reasons for Diagnostic Disagreement." *Archives of General Psychiatry*, 1962, *7*, 198–205.

WERRY, J. S. and H. C. QUAY. "The Prevalence of Behavior Symptoms in Younger Elementary School Children. *American Journal of Orthopsychiatry*, 1971, *41*, 136–143.

ZIGLER, E. and L. PHILLIPS. "Social Competence and Outcome in Psychiatric Disorder." *Journal of Abnormal and Social Psychology*, 1961, *63*, 264–271.

ZUBIN, J. "Classification of the Behavior Disorders." *Annual Review of Psychology*, 1967, *18*, 373–406.

Normal Personality Development

3

PROLOGUE

There was a CHILD WENT FORTH EVERY DAY,
And the first object he looked upon and received with wonder or pity or love
or dread, that object he became,
And that object became part of him for the day or a certain part of the day
. . . or for many years or stretching cycles of years.

The early lilacs became part of this child,
And grass, and white and red morning glories, and white and red clover, and
the song of the phoebe-bird,
And the March-born lambs, and the sow's pink-faint litter, and the mare's foal,
and the cow's calf, and the noisy brood of the barnyard, or by the mire
of the pondside . . . and the fish suspending themselves so curiously
below there . . . and the beautiful curious liquid . . . and the water-
plants with their graceful flat heads . . . all became part of him.

. . . . His own parents . . . he that propelled the fatherstuff at night, and
fathered him . . . and she that conceived him in her womb and birthed
him . . . they gave this child more of themselves than that,
They gave him afterward every day . . . they and of them became part of him.

. . . . These became part of that child who went forth every day, and who now
goes and will always go forth every day.
And these became of him or her that peruses them now.

(WHITMAN, 1959, pp. 138–139)

The cry of new life sets off the exhilarating mixture of feelings of parental duty, dreams, aspirations, fears, and uncertainties. The miracle of the child is unparalleled by any other single human event. Nowhere in the animal kingdom does the newborn go forth with as much attention from so many, and for such a prolonged period of time. Whitman's view of the child as profoundly influenced and moulded by environmental forces gives little credit to hereditary factors or to the interactionist position so widely accepted today. Nevertheless, poetic license permits Whitman to capture an important set of conditions that take on maximum significance once the child is born.

In our society, we favor the growing child showing above average physical, mental, emotional, or social development, and we become distraught when the child displays almost any feature that is below average. In fact, the only deviance in children we find acceptable is that of exceptionality; all else brings unhappiness, disappointment, problems, and even misery. Low birth weight (say of four pounds two ounces) not only is regarded as below average, but also as abnormal (premature), whereas an eight pound two ounce baby (while above average) may be considered healthy and robust. But there is a point at which above average characteristics become abnormal, as illustrated in obesity, hyperactivity, and the unusually rapid growth of giantism. Since either extreme may be abnormal, how can we hope to recognize deviance without some basic understanding of normal development? Almost all parents experience some anxiety about their child's normality (especially their first born) with respect to eating or sleep patterns, motor and physical growth trends, language progress, socialization, and cognitive performance.[1] In the absence of developmental norms, there is no tangible way of either measuring or assessing the progress of children as they grow and mature. It is commonplace for parents to seek this sort of normative data from their pediatricians, and from others

who either have children or have experience with them. As students interested in abnormal behaviors of children, we, too, must have a good grasp of what constitutes normal development, factors affecting it, and its methodological and interpretative limitations.

In this chapter, we try to provide a framework of normal personality development from which developmental psychopathology can be understood better. Obviously, we cannot hope to present in one chapter either the breadth or the details ordinarily included in a single course or in a text devoted exclusively to this topic. Nevertheless, we have attempted to sort out some of the essential aspects of normal development to enhance our appreciation of children as they mature from infancy through adolescence. For our purpose, therefore, we shall consider the basic principles of development, some of the major variables influencing its course, and the theoretical positions that are currently prominent.

Principles of Development

Data about child behavior and growth has made it possible to discern certain orderly patterns that follow a set of general principles by which human development can be understood. The most widely accepted principles deal with the direction and progression of physical growth and motor development.

Directional Principles

There are two principles concerned with the directional flow of physical development. These state that growth and motor development generally proceed from the head to the tail (*cephalocaudal*) and from

[1] A detailed presentation of these developmental norms can be found in Gesell, Ilg, Ames, and Rodell, 1974.

the central axis to the periphery *(proximodistal)* of the human body. Both growth principles are manifest in prenatal and postnatal development. The head of the human fetus develops initially, while the lower portions form later on. Similarly, the central axis of the human fetus develops before the limb buds form from which the hands, fingers, and toes subsequently appear. Postnatally, cephalocaudal growth is illustrated in the disproportionate size of the infant's head in relation to the torso and the even smaller legs. In fact, the newborn's head approximates the size of the adult, whereas the torso and especially the legs are expected to grow a great deal more before they reach adult proportions. In addition, the infant's head is functionally more mature than the torso and extremities in that the mouth, eyes, and ears are functional before grasping appears, and prior to the use of the legs and feet. The proximodistal growth and motor development for the infant can be seen in the development of hand use. First the baby uses the hand (reaching) as a whole unit through gross movements of the arm up to the shoulder. Months later, the baby gains control of fingers or can make oppositional movements of thumb and finger in picking up things.

Principles of Progression

Like directional patterns, two principles have been identified to describe the progression of development. The first states that progress occurs in patterns from the general to the specific (sometimes called the principle of *differentiation*), or from the simple to the complex. Newborns have undifferentiated reactions to painful stimuli since their behavior is gross and general rather than specific. The pain of being pricked accidentally by a pin will elicit a generalized reaction; babies will cry, kick, and vigorously move their arms, but months later their reaction will be noticeably more specific in the sense that they probably will cry and try to avoid the painful pin prick.

The second principle *(asynchronous growth)* states that different parts and subsystems of the human organism develop at different rates and times, and that the various parts of a person do not grow equally or all at once. In a way, this has been implicit in what has been discussed thus far. The head, in both size and function, develops earlier than the lower and more peripheral regions. Asynchronous growth occurs prenatally and postnatally in spurts that have implications for what can be expected of children during different periods of development. For example, adolescence is a period in our culture in which there is a tremendous growth spurt that levels off in the beginning of adulthood. Development of both primary and secondary sexual characteristics occurs rapidly during this period, although almost no changes in these characteristics take place between late infancy and puberty.

Self-Emergence and Independence

This general principle deals with personality and social development. It describes the child's progress from an undifferentiated and almost totally dependent organism to a distinctive and independent self. In contrast to physical and motor development, personal growth and social growth are much more difficult to measure and more likely to stir controversy. Nevertheless, the principle holds if one looks at the overall development of the child from infancy through adolescence.

At birth, babies do not know their names

or have any observable awareness of who they are as separate and intact organisms. They learn about their own bodies and the world around them through sensory and motor exploration, while they develop a self-concept gradually through their interactions with the environment. Coincidentally, as their competency to cope without assistance increases, they are more inclined to and able to think and act on their own. They can be expected to exhibit increased self-control and regulation of their feelings and behavior as they become more familiar with the contingencies of given situations and the consequences of their responses. In broad perspective, the helpless, dependent, emotionally volatile, and undifferentiated self of the infant matures over time into a more independent, emotionally controlled, responsible, and distinctive self as he or she reaches adulthood.

Maturation and Readiness

Maturation refers to physical alterations in size, and "qualitative changes in tissues or in anatomical and physiological organization" (Stone and Church, 1973, p. 191). With respect to child development, maturation is extremely important in that these physiological transformations make it possible for new behaviors to emerge, that is, the child is biologically *ready* to acquire a new behavior without a great deal of practice or preparation. For instance, maturation must occur before a child can walk, although a child's readiness to walk will not in and of itself result in locomotion unless the opportunity is provided. Studies have shown that either deprivation of or extensive practice in walking prior to maturational readiness will not appreciably affect the age at which the child walks (McGraw, 1935; Dennis and Dennis, 1940).

Similarly, only when babies reach a particular stage of maturation are they able to bring bladder and bowel sphincters under control. Fastidious or eager parents who begin toilet training before these changes occur are likely to engage in a losing battle with their child and precipitate unnecessary anxiety and conflict for all parties concerned. Understanding of and knowledge about maturation can go a long way in minimizing needless parent-child strife and in increasing the child's chances of successful acquisition of new behaviors.

Factors Affecting Development

Development is an active process that consists of "two essential components: the notion of a system possessing a definite structure and a definite set of pre-existing capacities; and the notion of a sequential set of changes in the system, yielding relatively permanent but novel increments not only in its structure but in its mode of operation as well" (Nage, 1957, p. 17). Thus we think of development as involving sequential and orderly changes over time in the organism's structure and function. Research has shown that the factors affecting development are multitudinous, ranging from the biological, which includes heredity, congenital factors, maturation, temperament, prenatal and postnatal care, drugs, and nutrition, to the sociopsychological, emphasizing race, social class, cultural context, family, school, peer relationships, early neonatal experiences—especially the effect of mother and father, and the learning potential of the newborn. Obviously, the space limitations of this section preclude an exhaustive discussion of these factors. However, for our purposes, we will focus on *heredity, temperament,* the *multidirec-*

tional effects of the parent-child interaction, the *school,* and *peer relations* as they influence later personality development.

Nature-Nurture

Interest in the role of heredity versus environment as determinants of human structure and function has been unabated since the early days of psychology as a science. While past inquiry emphasized the relative contributions of either nature or nurture, this approach has been replaced by an interactional one in which the potential impact of each factor varies on a continuum, allowing for greater or lesser interplay of the other factor in determining behavior (Anastasi, 1958; Cohen, 1976). For example, the causal effects of genetic factors may be so extensive as to produce a debilitating and irreversible condition such as Down's Syndrome (a form of mental retardation we will discuss in Chapter 10) and to significantly limit the opportunity of environmental forces to influence the developmental outcome. On the other hand, the potential effect of an inherited allergy, such as hay fever, is less extensive, since there is ample opportunity for environmental conditions (reducing the amount of pollen) to control the outcome.

Similarly, there are two categories of environmental factors—organic accidents and cultural heritage—that represent continua ranging from direct to indirect in their impact on development (Anastasi, 1958). Such birth complications as prolonged delivery, the use of forceps, or breech delivery may seriously impair the baby's oxygen supply (anoxia), leading to the destruction of brain cells and the direct consequence of mental retardation. In contrast, less direct influence on intellectual development may occur in children who have acquired sensory defects

(visual or auditory) and for whom educational opportunities and enrichment may be restricted by their organic impairment. Similarly, the potential impact of cultural heritage can vary from minimal to maximal in that a variable such as race may so severely restrict both the individual's motivation and social chances to achieve as to negate the influence of other genetic attributes.

In this interactional context, heredity may be thought of as providing the basic biological organization by which the organism's physical structure and personality can develop. We know that genetic factors can determine exclusively such physical characteristics as eye color, skin pigmentation, texture and color of hair, baldness, color blindness, and blood type. We know, too, that heredity accounts for other human characteristics that are more or less affected by experience, such as height, intelligence, and temperament, and it accounts for areas of genetic predisposition that are only manifested in the presence of certain noxious environmental conditions, e.g., the mental disorder known as schizophrenia (Rosenthal, 1970). Therefore, it is important to keep in mind that people are uniquely different in both their genetic make-up (except for monozygotic twins) and in their environmental experiences, making it unlikely that they will develop in the same way or be capable of responding in the same manner to similar experiences (Cohen, 1976).

Temperament

Parents or anyone who has had the opportunity of observing babies at birth will attest to their differences in temperament. Indeed, research inquiries on the significance of temperament not only have identified specific infant reaction patterns that have consequences for personality development, but also have suggested relationships between temperament and childhood behavior disorders (Thomas and Chess, 1977). Based on the longitudinal studies undertaken by Thomas, Chess, and Birch over a twenty year period, the concept of temperament has come to refer to individual differences in inborn potentials for action characterized by particular behavioral styles and significantly affected by the interplay of environmental forces. These investigators established the following nine categories on which the infant's behavioral style or temperamental reactivity can be classified:

1. Activity level—the proportion of active to inactive periods.
2. Rhythmicity—regularity of biological functions of hunger, sleep and wakefulness, and excretion.
3. Approach and withdrawal to new situations and people.
4. Adaptability to new situations.
5. Threshold of responsiveness—the intensity of stimulation needed to evoke a discernible response.
6. Intensity of reaction—the energy of the response.
7. Quality of mood—the amount of pleasant, friendly, and joyful behavior versus unpleasant, unfriendly, and crying behavior.
8. Distractibility—the degree to which extraneous stimuli change behavior.
9. Attention span and persistence—time spent on an activity and the effect of distraction on activity.

Using ratings of these nine reactive patterns, the investigators showed that after the first ten years of life children were remarkably stable and consistent in temperamental reactivity (Thomas, Chess, and Birch, 1970). For example, a child rated positive on the approach and withdrawal category at one year of age approached strangers without fear and slept well in new surroundings, while at ten years the same child went to camp happily and loved to ski the first time. In addition, three temperamental constellations were factored out of the basic nine categories, each with its own characteristic style of relating to life situations (Thomas, Chess, and Birch, 1968; Thomas and Chess, 1977). The *difficult child* type included those children who evidenced irregularity in biological function, negative withdrawal responses to new stimuli, frequent and loud crying periods, slow adaptibility to change, and frustration resulting in frequent tantrums. In contrast, the *easy child* grouping was characterized by regularity, adaptability, smiling at strangers, accepting some frustration, positive approach responses to new stimuli, and predominant positive moods of mild to moderate intensity. Somewhere in between these two patterns was the third constellation, the *slow-to-warm-up child,* consisting of youngsters who showed initial negative responses of mild intensity to new stimuli that became positive if given time to warm up, slow adaptibility, and some irregularity in biological functioning.

While these groupings are broad and imprecise, it is significant that seventy percent of those children from the original population who later evidenced emotional problems and needed psychiatric attention were classified as *difficult,* but only eighteen percent were identified as *easy.* Moreover, *difficult* children represented ten percent of all the children sampled by these investigators (a figure that corresponds to other estimates of occurrence of abnormal behaviors in children), while forty percent fell into the *easy* category (Thomas and Chess, 1977). These findings suggest the possibilities that useful predictions about childhood psychopathology can be made from early temperament measures, and that disorders can be prevented through the early identification of high-risk children. In this context, Thomas and Chess (1977) emphasize "the goodness of fit" between the child and the environment. They posit that when there is a significant discrepancy between the child's temperamental dispositions and environmental demands, severe stress and psychopathological development are likely to occur.

Another view of temperament has been recently proposed by Buss and Plomin (1975), who suggest that individual differences are governed by four temperaments: *activity, emotionality, sociability,* and *impulsivity.* These are depicted as dimensions (each ranging from one extreme to the other). The potential to occupy some place on the dimension of each of the four temperaments is inherited, although the final form the initial inherited tendency takes depends on environmental influences. Every person represents some combination of the four temperaments that are the basic building blocks of personality. Buss and Plomin claim that the proposed nine temperaments of Thomas *et al.* have not been substantiated as truly inherited, and that if this criterion were applied, both views would identify similar temperaments.

Research on temperament has added to the understanding of individual differences, of the interplay of heredity and environment in the stability of reactive patterns over time, and of the early identification of probable psychopathology. But equally important, inquiry on temperament has called attention to the influence of temperamental reactivity on parental responses to the child. For too long, theorists have focused on the effect of first mother and now both mother and father as shapers of

the child's personality without fully appreciating the multidirectional components of parent-child interactions. As Buss and Plomin state:

The child is not merely the passive recipient of environmental shaping. Our theory assumes an interaction between the child and the forces that mold his personality. He is an initiator who in part makes his own environment. He is a reinforcer, selectively rewarding or punishing agents in his environment for the way they behave toward him. And he is a responder, who modifies the impact of the environment on his personality. This is a considerably more complex model of personality development than that of the child as a blank slate on which the environment writes. But we suggest that it is a truer picture of what actually happens (Buss and Plomin, 1975, p. 237).

Therefore, we now turn to a discussion of the multidirectional effects of parent-child interactions on later personality development by considering the child as a stimulus, the effect of mother, the effect of father, and the total interacting system.

The Child as a Stimulus

Richard Bell (1968) first emphasized the child as a stimulus in and an active component of the parent-child relationship. Bell examined the autonomy-control issue of child-rearing and found that active children elicit upper-limit control behavior from parents presumably as a means of reducing and redirecting the behaviors of the child that exceed parental limits. He noted, in contrast, that parents set lower-limit controls for lethargic children in order to stimulate their behavior up to parental expectations. Thus, Bell showed that the responses of young children can serve to modify the behaviors of adults. Thomas and Chess (1977) similarly observed that to a large extent parental responses are a function of the child's temperamental constellation, which determines the smoothness or turmoil of management routines. Mothers prefer children of the "easy child type," because these youngsters reassure them that they are adequate, healthy, and loving mothers, whereas "difficult" children tend to make mothers feel threatened, resentful, or anxious. The researchers also stress the uniqueness of the child and the potential danger involved in assuming that there is one child-care practice that is favorable for all types of children. They claim that the child who is unable to respond to the currently favored child-rearing practice is under severe stress and is at risk for the development of psychopathology.

Brazleton (1969) also emphasizes the uniqueness of the newborn baby by describing three types of infants (average, quiet, and active) and their development. He suggests that babies manifest unique qualities that are obvious from birth onward and that these qualities set the tone of parental reactions to the child. More specifically, parental reactions are a function of an interaction between their preconceived notions of child-rearing and the nature of the infant. Brazleton adopts the view that the neonate influences the environment as much as it affects him or her, and he advises new mothers to be aware of the special characteristics of their babies and to find individualized ways to respond to them.

Within recent years, the effect of the infant on its caretaker has been the subject of increasing systemmatic study for which several promising research strategies have been developed (Lewis and Rosenblum, 1974). One strategy, involving the manipulation of certain stimulus characteristics of the infant to determine their effects on the caregiver, has been used to experimentally produce visual defects and drug-induced bodily malformations in infant animals (Lindburg, 1969; Berkson, 1974). The findings indicated that the defective animals were either treated like younger animals or given additional help and attention by their mothers. Another research strategy consists of examining certain biological aspects of infants (sex, physical stature, arousal level) and assessing their impact on the caretaker. For example, Korner (1974) found that the aversive properties of crying behavior in early infancy was a good initiator of maternal attention, and that irritable babies received more maternal attention and stimulation than "good" ones. Korner also stressed the importance of maternal factors in establishing the affectional bond between mother and child, especially when a dyadic mismatch occurs, that is, when the mother is either unable or unwilling to respond to the infant's cues. For example, one mother who is afraid of spoiling her child may fail to provide the soothing he or she requires, while another mother who needs to cuddle her baby may be disappointed and ungratified if her child fails to respond to cuddling.

Other investigators prefer studying the interactive, dynamic, and changing dyad of mother-child relationships rather than strategies that focus on a single component of the system. For example, Brazleton and his associates (Brazleton, Koslowski, and Main, 1974) used detailed film studies to look at behavioral components of mother-child interactions. They arrived at five kinds of experiences mothers can provide for their babies. These include: (1) reducing interfering activity by soothing the child when he or she is irritable or by attending to the baby's discomforts; (2) encouraging the child to be more alert and receptive; (3) creating an atmosphere of expectancy for further interaction; (4) accelerating the child's attention to receive and send messages by smiling and vocalizing in response to the baby's efforts to do these things; and (5) allowing for reciprocity by being sensitive to the child's cues and giving him or her time to respond.

The Effects of Early Mothering

During infancy, the baby's mother (or anyone who assumes the role) becomes a powerful reinforcer, an influential stimulus, and an object of the baby's responses. She satisfies the infant's needs by feeding, comforting, or easing pain; she stimulates the child to respond through talking, moving, and playing; and she permits the child to explore by fingering her face, squeezing her nose, pulling her hair, or tugging at her beads. It is through these interactions that the infant becomes attached to mother as an important object of behavior and gains sufficient sensory stimulation and need gratification for the development of a healthy personality. Although Freud spoke of the importance of early mothering on later personality development, it was Margaret Ribble (among others) who tried to study its effects (Ribble, 1944). After carefully observing 600 infants, Ribble noted that sensory experiences (tactile, kinesthetic, and auditory stimulation) provided by the mother were critical for stable personality development, and that mother's failure to provide these vital sensory experiences would result in both biological and psychological damage to the child.

The significant experimental breakthrough came with the creative work of Harry Harlow and his associates, who undertook a number of studies in which infant monkeys were reared with two kinds of inanimate surrogate mothers: a wire-mesh one and one covered with terry-cloth material. Infant monkeys were separated from their mothers not more than twelve hours after birth and were reared and fed by either wire or cloth mothers. Regardless of their prior mothering experience, baby monkeys clearly preferred the cloth mother, and they spent more time clinging to her than to the wire mother (Harlow and Zimmerman, 1959). In addition, the monkeys with the cloth mother evidenced a sense of security that enabled them to explore a fear arousing stimulus, whereas the monkeys with the wire mother exhibited fear and avoidance in this situation. These findings emphasized tactile stimulation as a principal ingredient of the mother-child relationship.

But Harlow soon discovered that tactile stimulation was not the only important variable for normal development. Regardless of which surrogate mother the monkeys had, those raised in isolation from peers later showed abnormal behaviors that included aggressiveness, self-mutilation, withdrawal, social indifference, and inability to imitate heterosexual behavior (Harlow, 1962). Harlow concluded, "Since it is agemate or peer affection even more than maternal affection that is basic to the success or failure of a monkey's or human's subsequent social and sexual life (Harlow and Harlow, 1962), one can defend the position that the mother's primary personal-social function is to aid and abet the infant in making age-mate adjustment" (Harlow and Harlow, 1971, p. 205).

The infant's need for kinesthetic stimulation usually dispensed by mother in cuddling, rocking, and holding her baby while walking has only recently become the subject of experimental study. The available evidence indicates that monkeys who experience early maternal deprivation develop distinct stereotyped patterns of body-rocking (Berkson and Mason, 1964, pp. 635–652). In an effort to identify the specific aspects of maternal deprivation that leads to body-rocking, Mason (1968) compared two groups of rhesus monkeys raised with either a stationary or a mobile artificial mother. Infant monkeys tested at ten months showed typical body-rocking patterns when reared with a stationary mother, while those raised with mobile surrogates showed no such behavior. These findings support the view that rocking is a sensory need of infant monkeys and perhaps of humans. Additional evidence of the importance of vestibular stimulation (motion) in facilitating behavioral development comes from research with premature human infants. Those premature babies who were exposed systematically to motion achieved greater motor and auditory-visual responses than those who did not receive vestibular stimulation (Neal, 1970).

This line of investigation has helped us identify some of the specific variables associated with early mothering and their effects on later personality development. Another related line of investigation has focused on the effects of maternal deprivation. A study observing institutionalized infants who received different amounts of care and handling dramatically demonstrated the debilitating effects of maternal deprivation. A two-year follow-up indicated that the children who remained in the deprived institutional setting showed both profound intellectual and motor retardation, and a higher incidence of disease and mortality (Spitz, 1945). Spitz described a syndrome, called *anaclitic depression,* that he saw in some of the deprived children during the second half of their first year. "The children would lie or sit with wide open, ex-

pressionless eyes, frozen, immobile faces, and a far away expression as if in a daze, apparently not perceiving what went on in their environment" (Spitz and Wolf, 1946, p. 314). He believed that the debilitating effects (both physiological and psychological) of maternal deprivation could be arrested and reversed if mothering was resumed within three months, and if the deprivation didn't continue beyond the first year of the infant's life. The infant's response to maternal deprivation has been described as falling into three stages: *protest, despair,* and *detachment* from mother after the infant is reunited with mother (Bowlby, 1960). Later animal studies have confirmed both the protest and despair stages, but failed to corroborate the detachment stage (Seay, Hansen, and Harlow, 1962; Seay and Harlow, 1965; Spencer-Booth and Hinde, 1966; Kaufman and Rosenblum, 1967; Spencer-Booth and Hinde, 1971; Schlottman and Seay, 1972).

While the mother-child relationship traditionally has been viewed as unique and of critical importance to later personality development largely because mother typically has assumed the role of the primary caregiver, the work of Ribble and later Harlow and his associates has brought into sharper focus the more essential effects of early sensory experiences (rather than the mother *per se*) on the child's development. Moreover, the findings of Ainsworth (Ainsworth, 1967) indicate that infants could establish strong bonds with those who do not provide caretaking. This suggests that other persons may play an important role in the child's development. The popular idea that mother is the most important figure in the infant's life because she spends the most time with the infant is unsupported by research data, which show that the time spent in interacting is a poor predictor of the quality of the relationship between infant and parent. In fact, the most important factor is the *quality* of the relationship, as evidenced by the intact relationships found between working mothers and their children (Bossard and Boll, 1966). A minimal amount of interaction is necessary to allow attachment to form. Beyond that, it appears that the quality is unrelated to the degree of the interaction (Ainsworth, Bell, and Stayton, 1974). As for the infant's preference for mother or father, the data are mixed, with some studies showing that both parents are attachment figures for the child, while the majority show that mothers are preferred (Lamb, 1976a). However, data supporting this conclusion come from laboratory settings where the infant is under some stress, while in natural situations (stress-free) infants do not favor one parent over the other.

The Effect of Father

Until recently, the role of the father in child development has been obscured by the emphasis placed on the importance of mother-infant relationships, and by the assumption that father merely serves as an occasional mother substitute in nurturing the child before the age of three. However, the research data suggest that the early and strong father-infant bonding is qualitatively different than the mother-infant attachment (Lamb, 1976b). Although fathers spend less time with their infants, many (but not all) are responsive to their cues, enjoy interacting with them, and become early and enduring central figures in their social worlds.

In a well-controlled and informative study, Santrock (1972) set out to determine the effect of father absence on third and sixth graders' IQ and achievement scores.

The subject sample was sufficiently large to permit analysis of onset of father absence at birth to two, three to five, six to nine, ten to eleven, and twelve to thirteen years of age, as well as by type of absence, that is, death, divorce, desertion, separation, or presence of a stepfather. Subjects were Caucasian boys and girls who came from lower socioeconomic homes. Both IQ and achievement scores were most depressed for boys whose fathers died when the child was between the ages of six to nine, while the other forms of father absence had the most detrimental effect on cognitive development during the birth to two years for both girls and boys. Boys whose fathers were absent consistently scored lower than either father-absent girls or father-present boys. Moreover, when fathers who were absent because of divorce, separation, or desertion were replaced through remarriage during the first five years of the child's life, the effect on the cognitive development of boys was positive but not on girls. In addition, Hoffman (1971) studied the relationship of father absence to moral development in seventh-grade Caucasian boys and girls from low and middle socioeconomic level homes. He found clear evidence that father absence had a detrimental effect on conscience development in boys but not on girls.

Using measures of parent-child relations, internal-external locus of control, and self-concept, Moerk (1973) compared the test scores of the sons of imprisoned fathers and of divorced fathers with those of juvenile delinquents and normal youngsters. Profiles of sons of imprisoned fathers were more similar to those of juvenile delinquents and less similar to the normal controls than were the profiles of the sons of divorced fathers. Absence of father has also been linked with alcoholism in young men whose fathers were in the home until they were fifteen years of age, with hospitalized female alcoholics evidencing serious behavior problems, and with suicidal attempts and drug addiction in both males and females (Jacobs and Teicher, 1967; Oltman and Friedman, 1967; Rosenberg, 1969; Rathod and Thompson, 1971).

The importance of father for their daughters is illustrated in a rather elaborate study involving seventy-two adolescent first-born daughters (ages thirteen to seventeen) whose parents lived together or were divorced, or whose fathers had died (Hetherington, 1973). Noteworthy among the extensive findings were the indications that girls who had grown up without fathers felt insecure and apprehensive in relating to male peers and adults, although they expressed these feelings differently. Girls of divorced parents reported more heterosexual activity while those whose fathers had died tended to be more sexually inhibited. Higher self-esteem and positive feelings about father were noted more frequently for daughters whose fathers had died as compared to those whose parents were divorced.

Although considerably more data are needed to explicate the impact of the father on the personality development of the child, a number of trends from the available research have been noted (Radin, 1976; Parke and Sawin, 1977). Paternal nurturance seems to be more highly correlated with the cognitive competence of boys than of girls, and father absence *before the age of five* seems to be particularly damaging to the cognitive functioning of young boys. In addition, father absence in the early years hinders the mathematical skills of girls, and it is associated with a cognitive profile in college men that is more typical of females. For both sexes, authoritarian paternal behavior or intense paternal involvement in the problem solving activities of the child are related to reduced academic competence. Fathers do well at many of the traditional feminine tasks of child care, but, unlike mothers, they tend to provide more physical stimulation for their babies than verbal stimulation. Baby boys seem to benefit more than girls from interactions with their fathers not only cognitively but in social situations as well. In fact, as early as five months, baby boys show less fear of strangers or less apprehension on being left alone when fathers have taken care of them and played with them. Thus,

A father influences his children's mental development through many and diverse channels: through his genetic background, his manifest behavior with his offspring, the attitudes he holds about himself and his children, the behavior he models, his position in the family system, the material resources he is able to supply for his children, the influence he is able to exert on his wife's behavior, his ethnic heritage, and the vision he holds for his children. Finally, when he dies or separates from the family, the memories he leaves with his wife and children continue to exert an influence, perhaps equal to the impressions he made on the youngsters when he was physically present (Radin, 1976, p. 270).

The Total Interacting System—The Family

Thus far, we have discussed the three main characters in a one-child family unit primarily as single components of a complex interacting system, although we have considered each (the child, the mother, and the father) as influencing and being influenced by the behaviors of others. Figure 3–1 schematically depicts the multiple interplay that initially has the greatest impact on the child's personality and social de-

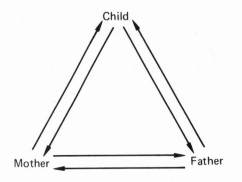

FIGURE 3–1 Schematic illustration of family multidirectional interaction system

velopment. As children grow older, the family's almost exclusive control of them and impact on them decrease and give way to other major sources of influence, such as the school and peer groups, although their ties to the family are never completely broken or abandoned (Cohen, 1976). Throughout a person's life, the family provides a sense of security, role differentiation, and group membership that not only facilitates adaptive and effective functioning within society but also serves to perpetuate itself through marriage and procreation. Unfortunately, our research technology has not as yet permitted adequate study of the multidirectional interplay of forces within a family unit other than to examine the effects of single or dyadic components on the child's development (as illustrated in the foregoing discussion).

One dyadic relationship, that of husband-wife, has been of interest not only because it changes to some extent when a child arrives, but also because the quality and nature of this relationship sets the tone of harmony or disharmony, cooperation or antagonism, consistency or inconsistency, and stability or instability for the family unit. According to Lidz:

A coalition between the parents is necessary not only to give unity of direction but also to provide each parent with the support essential for carrying out his or her cardinal functions. The wife, for example, can better delimit her erotic investment to maternal feelings when her wifely sexual needs are being satisfied by her husband. The tendency of small groups to divide up into dyads that create rivalries and jealousies is diminished markedly if the parents form a unity in relation to their children. The child's tendency to possess one or the other parent for himself alone—the essence of the Oedipal situation—is ˙overcome if the parental coalition is firm, frustrating the child's fantasies and redirecting him to the reality that requires repression of such wishes. If the parents form a coalition not only as parents but also as a married couple, the child is provided with adult models who treat one another as alter egos, each striving for the partner's satisfaction as well as for his own. The child then grows up valuing marriage as an institution that provides emotional gratification and security and, thus, gains a long-range goal to pursue (Lidz, 1970, p. 29).

Indeed, several different kinds of faulty parental coalitions have been described as occurring in families that evidence psychotic or other abnormal conditions (Lidz, Fleck, and Cornelison, 1965). For example, *chronic disharmony* between parents is a coalition that exerts undue pressure on the child to take sides with one of the two warring parents and that seriously impedes identification with either parent, since each is deprecated by the other. A *skewed parental coalition* is characterized by a severe abnormal disorder in one parent while the other passively submits and appeases the disturbed spouse to keep the marriage intact. Obviously, such a lopsided coalition requires extreme passivity on the part of the accommodating parent (leading one to wonder about his or her emotional stability), and it provides a family environment for children in which abnormal behaviors and unrealistic views of the world

ned.
oali-
in a
ther
their
ather
ment
e as
they
o pa-
lying
m be-
orce.
The failure of parents ~~~~~~~~~~~ effective coalition inevitably draws the child into the conflictual situation producing anxiety, insecurity, and role models that interfere with normal personality development.

The School

Apart from the family, no institution has a greater and more continuous impact on the child's social and personality development than our educational system. When we consider that children spend half of their waking lives for many years in the school, it is not surprising that it becomes the center for not only academic instruction but also for the acquisition of social skills and competence. Cohen (1976) likens the school to the family in its form and mode of operating (although not in content), since in both situations the child is placed into a relatively self-contained unit and is expected to be responsive to adult controls. However, entrance into school usually represents the child's first prolonged separation from the familiar and comforting family environs. In this new setting, demands are made to do things that are not always rewarding and greater independence is required.

What the child experiences, how the child perceives school, whether school will positively or negatively affect the child's motivation to learn, to persevere, to act independently, to cope with frustrations, and to acquire a sense of competence and self-worth will depend largely on teacher-pupil relationships. In our society, preschool, kindergarten, and first-grade teachers are likely to be women who perform functions that are similar to those customarily assumed by the mother (Mussen, Conger, and Kagan, 1974). They compliment and reward the child's desirable behaviors and reprimand undesirable behaviors; they may provide nurturance in the form of cookies and juice; and they help the child to get in or out of outer garments during the winter months or on rainy days. Teachers may also provide entertainment since they play games and read stories to children much like their mothers are apt to do. Yet, some writers have suggested that the early and continued exposure of children, especially boys, to women teachers may foster the attitude that school is more appropriate for girls than for boys. This attitude may in part account for the higher academic achievement of girls in the first several grades.

Perhaps more important than the teacher's sex is his or her personal characteristics and their effect on the child's academic and social progress. In general, children make their greatest social, emotional, and academic progress with teachers who are warm, flexible, encouraging of creative expression coupled with demanding greater responsibility, interested in their students, and authoritative in providing direction and guidance. In contrast,

. . . optimal academic and personal growth will not be stimulated in most students by the teacher who is either rigidly authoritarian, hostile, or unresponsive to student needs, or the one who is indecisive and uncertain, poorly trained, narcissistic, or preoccupied with his or her own anxieties and personal problems" (Mussen, Conger, and Kagan, 1974, p. 495).

Of course, not all children perceive and react to the same teacher in the same way, making it even more important for the teacher to possess those personal attributes of warmth, flexibility, and competence that would enable him or her to enhance the development of each student in the class. Teachers should appreciate and accept their students' individual differences and be aware that motivation to learn and the building of self-worth are facilitated by prior successes and drastically impaired by repeated failure.

Teachers of socioeconomically disadvantaged youngsters should recognize that their potential influence on these students may be even greater than that of teachers of middle-class children, since the culturally deprived child is likely to be more vulnerable to the stress of new situations as a result of earlier family experiences that have been deficient in nurturance and support (Yee, 1968). In addition, disadvantaged children as compared to middle-class youngsters often come from environments that poorly prepare them for the demands of the school. Often they lack the attention skills necessary in classroom and in laboratory situations (Whiteman and Deutsch, 1968; Knopf and Kirchner, 1974; Knopf and Mabel, 1975). These children also tend to be less motivated and less ambitious in their academic aspirations than their middle-class counterparts, and, to make matters worse, typically they attend schools that are overcrowded, physically deteriorated, and lacking in adequate resources (Mussen, Conger, and Kagan, 1974).

Peer Relations

As the child grows older, peer relations become increasingly important as a source of influence in social and personality development. The opportunity for peer interactions provides children with normative standards by which they can compare and to some extent modify their own feelings, thoughts, and actions. Peer groups begin to form early in middle childhood as the child extends his or her interpersonal ties beyond the immediate family (Mussen, Conger, and Kagan, 1974). Initially, these groups consist of informal and tenuous associations that over time evolve into more structured, stable, and cohesive organizations that sometimes involve special rituals and paraphenalia (such as the Scout groups for boys and girls).

The peer group is an alternative social unit to the family.

[It] is formed through a community of equals, where status and leadership patterns are defined through natural group processes; consequently, the peer group provides an exercise in communal formation where positions are earned (and subject to change) as a result of skill and democratic procedures, rather than imposed or assumed as a function of prior conditions and obligations (Cohen, 1976, p. 83).

Consequently, membership in a group affords social status and enhances self-esteem, whereas rejection from a group can have serious negative effects. Children can be cruel and insensitive so that a child's frailty or some other characteristic might be the basis for his or her exclusion from a peer group and the justification of the continued torment he or she receives from the group. Such a child is likely to feel angry, alienated, threatened, and devalued to the point where he or she is apt to avoid aca great impact on researchers, educators, and other child-care workers, and because ...ether they provide a broad but under-...ble perspective of the developing

...tic Theory

...d Freud. As noted in Chapter 1, ...theoretical contributions not only ...legitimacy to the study of children ...se, but also focused lasting attention on ...e critical role of the early years of child-hood in determining the person's basic character structure. In fact, Freud believed that essentially personality was formed by the end of the child's fifth year of life, and that, in the main, later growth involved an elaboration of the already established basic structure. Since our interest for now focuses on normal development, we shall deal with those aspects of Freud's psycho-analytic theory that bear directly on this subject, leaving for later consideration (Chapter 4) his theoretical contributions to psychopathology.

According to psychoanalytic theory, the personality consists of three major systems: the *id,* the *ego,* and the *superego.*[2] Although each component has its own functions, characteristics, and guiding principles, in the normal personality each interacts with the other components and together they operate in an integrated fashion. The id is the inherited and original energy system of the personality that is present at birth, and from which the ego and the superego are later energized and differ-entiated. The id represents the world of subjective reality, and its activities are governed by what Freud called the *pleasure*

... it is di......man development in th......action. New evidence shows th......pportunity to encounter individuals wh......quals, chil-dren do not learn effective com......ication skills, do not acquire the competencies needed to modulate their aggressive actions, have difficul-ties with sexual socialization, and are disad-vantaged with respect to the formation of moral values. Peer relations are not luxuries in human development, but necessities. In fact, one's com-petence in engagements with other children and one's centrality in the peer group are nearly as predictive of later difficulties in development as intellectual competence. I am persuaded by a variety of recent literature that poor peer re-lations in childhood are among the most power-ful predictors of later social and emotional mala-dies (Hartup, 1977, p. 1).

Theories of Normal Development

Having considered the basic principles by which development occurs and some of the important variables that influence its course, we turn now to a discussion of the three most viable and promising theoretical views of normal development: the *psycho-analytic,* the *cognitive-developmental,* and the *learning.* These views have been singled out for presentation because they have had

[2] Much of this section is based on the following of Freud's writings: Freud, 1922; Freud, 1959; Freud, 1957; Freud, 1933.

principle, that is, the seeking of pleasure and the avoidance of pain. It is entirely amoral, unaware of the demands of external or objective reality, and incapable of making judgments. Thus, Freud viewed the newborn infant as a pleasure-bound organism seeking immediate gratification of impulses without regard for or knowledge of objective reality, as evidenced by the crescendo cry of the baby who won't stop until he is fed and who seems oblivious to the fact that mother is preparing the food.

In seeking immediate gratification, the id largely functions by a primary process that includes motor actions or mental images of the desired object if it isn't immediately available (imagining and grabbing at the mother's breast when hungry). However, images alone cannot reduce tension states (mental images of food do not satisfy hunger); they must be augmented by a secondary process that permits the developing child to interact appropriately with the objective world of reality to satisfy its needs. In addition, the id's demands for immediate satisfaction are likely to lead the infant into dangerous conflicts with the external environment (such as the baby's getting hurt when reaching for a desired object or touching a hot burner), since the id is cut off from the external world and it knows nothing of ensuring the organism's survival. Finally, as the caregiver tries to foster self-control skills in the child by gradually withholding immediate and continuous gratification, the infant is forced to deal with the demands of the environment.

It is within this context that the ego develops to facilitate the aims of the id by the acquisition of skills enabling the child to achieve pleasure in ways that are within the bounds of objective reality. The ego emerges from the id as the component of the personality that is concerned with reason, the preservation of the organism, and the modification of the pleasure principle (but not its nullification). Guided by the *reality principle* (keeping experiences within external constraints), the ego employs the secondary process (thought processes that distinguish the subjective from the objective worlds of reality) to delay tension states until an appropriate object is found that satisfies the need. The ego also protects the child by making use of the sensations of anxiety as warning signals of danger that in turn prompt safer responses. As the executive of the personality, the ego controls cognitive and intellectual functioning and acts as a mediator between id impulses and the demands of reality, and between the id and the superego.

The superego is the last system of the personality to develop, and it is as unbending and unreasonable as its original source, the id. As the moral component of the personality, the superego represents the cultural past in the sense that it incorporates the traditional values of society and the more specific values of parents. It is recognized by its judicial functions (the conscience) in rendering judgments about right and wrong and in its strivings for perfection and the ideal. In trying to control the impulses of the id, the superego seeks to permanently block the id's gratification. This is in contrast to the ego's efforts to postpone gratification. The superego keeps a careful watch over the ego, attempts to direct it, and threatens to punish it for id gratification. When the ego and the superego are in complete agreement, there is little to distinguish them, but when the ego fails to block the impulses of the id, tensions flare up and the superego becomes visible as pangs of conscience.

In addition to the description of these

essential components of the personality, Freud's major contribution to human development was his view of infant sexuality and its connection to a temporal series of differentiated stages by which personality develops. Surprisingly, Freud formulated this aspect of psychoanalytic theory largely from observations of his adult patients who repeatedly evidenced childish traits and recalled early childhood experiences that seemed to be determinants of their current behaviors. He posited excessive frustration or indulgence of the child's needs as the two primary causes of disruption in the normal growth process, and he specified *fixation* and *regression* as ways by which growth either can be permanently halted at a particular stage of development or temporarily reverted to earlier forms of behavior. Freud also believed that all behaviors are determined by (unconscious) drives known as *instincts* that activate internal tensions and prompt actions that remove or lessen the tension. Instincts are the inborn energy states of the id that give rise to tension. They are reducible to the two fundamental ones of sexuality and aggression. Freud conceived of sexuality as broadly corresponding to pleasure-seeking activities and erogenous strivings for bodily satisfaction (and not strictly tied to genital satisfaction), while he regarded aggression as the need to destroy objects.

According to Freud, the sexual drive, which he characterized as libidinal energy and tension, develops through a time ordered series of stages that are associated with various erotic areas of the body. These stages constitute the sequential periods of growth that every child must pass through for the formation of normal personality. The child's failure to deal effectively with libidinal tension at each stage of psychosexual development leads to either fixation or regression and adjustment problems later in life.

The first stage, known as the *oral* period, occurs during the initial eighteen to twenty-four months of the infant's life in which stimulation of the erogenous zones of the lips and mouth by objects such as nipples, toys, and fingers provide pleasure and relieve libidinal tension.

During the second period, called the *anal* phase, the anus becomes the site of sexual stimulation and gratification. This stage extends from about eighteen months to approximately three years (roughly corresponding to the period of toilet training) during which time the child seems to derive sensual pleasure from both the retention and expulsion of fecal matter.

The *phallic* stage occurs between the third and fifth year of the child's life when the genitals become the primary focus of sexual excitation and pleasure. Soon thereafter, the child enters the *oedipal* period, when the libidinal source of gratification becomes an external object, that is, the opposite sex parent becomes the object of libidinal pleasure instead of the youngster's own genitals and body. The child views the parent of the same sex as an obstacle and as a source of interference with the sexual desire for the other parent. The child's wish to replace and eliminate the same-sex parent arouses guilt and fear of retaliation, as well as a sense of inadequacy to accomplish this tremendous feat. This period is conflictual and tumultuous for the child, but it is resolved through a process of identification with the same-sex parent (being like him or her).

The longest psychosexual stage of development, known as the *latency period*, begins at about age six and extends through preadolescence. It is a stage where sexual tensions and activities are dormant, where the child can recover from the turmoil of the oedipal phase, and where further identification with the same-sex parent occurs. The final period, the *genital stage,* takes place during adolescence at a time when the sexual drive is heightened and the opposite sex becomes the sexual object for those who have developed normally.

The psychosexual stages of development are significant not only as focuses of sensual pleasure but also as important sources of parent-child interactions in which enduring patterns are established for the gratification of the child's needs. During the early periods, the baby is exposed to adults who facilitate his or her pleasure-seeking activities and who gradually impose limits on them. According to Freud, the manner in which libidinal needs are satisfied or frustrated has important implications for the child's social development and for the formation of specific character traits. For example, Freud proposed bipolar personality traits that were associated with each stage of psychosexual development and believed that manifestations of either extreme of the trait reflected fixation (caused by indulgence or frustration) at that particular developmental level. Thus, an excessively indulged person fixated at the oral level would evidence traits of optimism, gullibility, and admiration, while the orally frustrated fixated person would show pessimism, suspiciousness, and envy (Maddi, 1972). In this way, Freud's theory described the means by which specific personality attributes are initially acquired, and more broadly suggested that the nature of the child's experiences during each stage of development determines the form that personality structure will take.

Erik Erikson. Erikson used a Freudian psychoanalytic orientation to fashion a view of personality development that has come to be more palatable than Freud's to most child-care workers. In contrast to Freud, Erikson placed greater emphasis on the ego than the id in personality development, stressed the importance of social and cultural influences beyond the mother-father-child triangle, and adopted a more optimistic view of human nature in which he saw components conducive to growth and not doom in every personal and social crisis (Erikson, 1963; Maier, 1965). He proposed eight stages of development that include the adult years, reflecting his belief that the individual constantly redevelops his or her personality in passing from one phase to the next. Moreover, he maintained that development follows a universal course and that each person must face and master a central problem at each stage of development. A person's successful resolution to each conflict contributes to ego strength, while failure results in a carry over of problems that impair attempts to resolve the new problems of later phases. Table 3–1 describes the major characteristics of both Freud's and Erikson's stages of development.

During phase 1 (first year of life) the infant is faced with the central problem of acquiring a sense of basic trust while overcoming basic distrust. Trust, the cornerstone of the personality, enables the infant to feel comfortable and to experience a minimum of fear in new situations, while distrust can lead to such serious consequences as the withdrawal reaction of a psychotic child. The quality of the maternal relationship is critical in determining the amount of trust the infant will derive.

Phase 2 coincides with Freud's anal stage. It is concerned with the conflict of autonomy versus self-doubt and shame. During this period, children discover that their behavior is self-determined and that they can function with a sense of autonomy, especially as they develop new motor skills.

TABLE 3–1 Freud's and Erikson's Stages of Development

Freud		Erikson	
Age	*Stage*	*Age*	*Stage*
Birth–1 year	Oral	Infancy	Trust versus Mistrust
1–3 years	Anal	Early Childhood	Autonomy versus Shame, Doubt
3–5 years	Phallic	Middle Childhood	Initiative versus Guilt
5–12 years	Latency	Late Childhood	Industry versus Inferiority
12–adult	Genital	Adolescence	Identity versus Role confusion
		Young Adulthood	Intimacy versus Isolation
		Middle Adulthood	Creativity versus Stagnation
		Maturity	Integrity versus Despair

... ubt ... joy ... ous. ... the ... con- ... sive ... cen- ... ex- ... ains ... hild ... ntal ... ages ... the ... rsus ... riod ... and ... pe-

riod when children make new conquests, master ambulatory skills, and reach out to expand their activities and abilities (Maier, 1965). Initiative is encouraged by parental behaviors that include both approval and regulation. Guilt occurs because the child develops a superego at this time, and because the oedipal relationship provides additional opportunity for guilt feelings.

Phase 4 (corresponding to Freud's latency period) focuses on the conflict of industry versus inferiority. Children during middle-childhood begin to gain recognition for their accomplishments. Usually they start formal schooling with a determination to master new skills. In the process, they begin to develop work habits that will be important later on. The danger of this stage is that the child may develop a sense of inadequacy and inferiority that comes from the child's previous level of lesser production and competence. During this period, children see their involvement with peers of the same sex as essential.

Beginning with adolescence, phase 5 is concerned with the conflict of identity versus role confusion. The occurrence of rapid physiological changes along with the challenge of impending tangible adult tasks create conflicts in adolescents about their role in the world. Teen-agers become overly concerned with their inability to settle on an occupational goal, while they readily "overidentify" with peer-group heroes. Some integration of past identification occurs during this phase, but, in the main, adolescents search for peer social values to guide their identity.

In phases 6, 7, and 8 Erikson emphasizes the fact that development continues beyond childhood and youth with the conflicts of intimacy versus isolation, generativity versus stagnation, and ego integrity versus despair. The crisis in phase 6 arises from the avoidance of intimacy because of fear of failure and ego loss, which may result in feelings of isolation. The hazardous undertaking of establishing a permanent relationship with a suitable spouse very well may be the battleground of this conflict. In phase 7, adults become primarily concerned with guiding the next generation by developing a strong marital union and by having children, while in the last phase adults need to learn to accept and adapt to the successes and failures of daily living and go forward without despair and unafraid of death. Erikson ties ego-integrity to basic trust when he comments, ". . . healthy children will not fear life, if their parents have integrity enough not to fear death" (Erikson, 1963, p. 269).

Cognitive-Developmental Theory

In contrast to psychoanalytic theory, the cognitive-developmental approach stresses the higher mental processes and intellectual factors as the basic ingredients and integrative threads of human development (Cohen, 1976). It does not compartmentalize development into discrete areas of experience, such as social, emotional, or intellectual, nor does it have any need to make assumptions about unconscious processes or major systems of the developing organism.

Jean Piaget. The work of Jean Piaget is voluminous, highly original, and couched in unfamiliar and difficult to understand constructs. But, unmistakably, it is one of the most influential works in child development. Piaget's theory stresses the universal nature of intellectual development and views development as an evolutionary process that is innate and fixed (Flavell, 1963; Maier, 1965; Tuddenham, 1966). Like Erikson, he holds to the assumption that development progresses through successive stages for all children, but that the rate of progress varies from child to child. Although he studied perception, moral attitudes, and motivation among other areas,

his overriding interest was intelligence or in pursuing the question, "How does knowledge develop and change?" (Tuddenham, 1966, p. 210).

Piaget's cognitive theory begins with the idea that motor action is the source from which mental operations develop, that is, early sensorimotor activities of infants markedly influence later cognitions. Infants begin life with innate reflexes, some of which are modifiable through experience and become the behavioral elements from which more complex and symbolic forms of cognitive behavior develop. Piaget's penchant for ordering a relationship (that is similar in form and structure) between biological and mental structure is illustrated by his assumption that a *schema* exists in the mind that corresponds to each innate reflex and later to each behavior sequence. Schema, a concept that is important to Piaget's theory, refers to the organization of all experiences of a particular kind into a cognitive structure that can change with learning.

Intelligence is the ability to adapt, and adaptation depends on the dual learning processes of *assimilation* and *accommodation*. Assimilation refers to the tendency to incorporate external reality into some meaningful structure (schema), while accommodation is "the process by which a schema *changes* so as to adapt better to the assimilated reality" (Tuddenham, 1966, p. 213). Piaget divides cognitive development into the following four stages that roughly correspond to age periods: the sensorimotor stage—birth to approximately two years; the preoperational stage—two to seven years; the stage of concrete operations —seven to eleven years; and the stage of formal operations—eleven to fifteen years and older (Tuddenham, 1966).

Piaget devotes more detailed analysis to the sensorimotor period than to any other, perhaps because of the opportunities he had to observe his own three children during this time. He divides this period into six substages beginning with the infant's use of reflexes and progressing to the acquired behavior patterns of voluntary movements and active exploration. The child progresses from a very self-centered existence to one that is object-centered. "During this period the various sensory spaces of vision, touch, and the rest, are coordinated into a single space and objects evolve from their separate sensory properties into *things* with multiple properties, permanence, and spatial relationships to other objects" (Tuddenham, 1966, p. 215). The introduction of the concept of object permanence is important as an explanatory base for the child's memory (mental images) of objects beyond his or her immediate sensory experiences with them.

Language acquisition and development highlight the preoperational stage and enable the child to shift from total reliance on motor activity to an increased use of symbolic activity (cognitive), ranging from problem solving to concerns dealing with the environment. Initially, the child is the center of the world, but through *decentering,* a time scale and a spatial world independent of the child begin to emerge. Two-year-old children have egocentric thoughts that are specific to the situation and reflective only of their point of view. Sometime around four years of age, children begin to view the world less subjectively as their perspective gradually widens. The child's reasoning is still distorted during this phase, since the child tends to attend to one essential feature of a problem while neglecting other important aspects. Piaget illustrates this by presenting a child with two identical elongated vases containing the same amount of water. If the water in one vase is poured into a short and broad

base jar, the child will insist that the amount of water in the vase is greater than what is in the jar. Piaget contends that the child has focused only on the height of the vase without attending to other dimensions in reaching the conclusion that the taller of the two vessels contains more water.

The stage of concrete operations ushers in the capacity to reason, albeit at a concrete level. For the first time, the child can produce a mental representation of a series of actions, such as tracing with paper and pencil the route the child travels to and from school. The child also recognizes the notion of conservation and sees volume, weight, length, and number as constant, even when minor changes in their external appearance are introduced (such as shifting water from one vase to a jar). The child learns to reason in relational terms and is able to discern that the concept of shorter or taller, for example, is relative to two or more objects and not absolute characteristics of each. In addition, the child learns to classify, number, and order things in relation to an organized whole, which leads to a notion of certainty about the world. During the last phase of intellectual development, the phase of formal operations, the adolescent is capable of thinking about all of the possible solutions to a problem by systematically exploring the possibilities and checking the effectiveness of each. Adolescents can think in hypothetical terms, and they are capable of forming abstractions and dealing with symbols. For Piaget, the capacity to formulate hypotheses and to handle logical relationships brings intellectual growth to its peak (Tuddenham, 1966).

Kohlberg — Moral Development. Another example of a cognitive-developmental theory is the one offered by Kohlberg dealing with moral development and involving the concepts of reason and judgment. Kohlberg's research is largely an outgrowth of the earlier work of Piaget, who viewed morality as a system of rules for conduct that the child forms from the influence of the child's parents and other significant adults, and the child's own experiences (Cohen, 1976).

According to Piaget, the interaction of individual growth factors and social experiences instrumental in the development of moral judgment may be distinguished by reference to four successive and invariant stages of emergence. These include a period of motor development, followed by an egocentric stage, leading to a period of cooperative effort, and, finally, terminating in the child's recognition of moral principle in the establishment of social order" (Cohen, 1976, pp. 177–178).

Although Piaget's view has been greeted with mildly favorable reactions, the work of Kohlberg is more complete and detailed and currently provides an important extension of the cognitive-developmental approach to the development of moral judgment. A descriptive summary of Kohlberg's three levels of moral judgment and its six stages of development is given in Table 3–2 (Kohlberg, 1967, p. 171).

TABLE 3–2 *   Kohlberg's Classification of Moral Judgment into Levels and Stages of Development

Basis of Moral Judgment Levels	*Stages of Development*
I Moral value resides in external, quasi-physical happenings, in bad acts, or in quasi-physical needs rather than in persons and standards.	Stage 1: Obedience and punishment orientation. Egocentric deference to superior power or prestige, or a trouble-avoiding set. Objective responsibility. Stage 2: Naively egoistic orientation. Right action is that instrumentally satisfying the self's needs and occasionally others'. Awareness of relativism of value to each actor's needs and perspective. Naive egalitarianism and orientation to exchange and reciprocity.
II Moral value resides in performing good or right roles, in maintaining the conventional order and the expectancies of others.	Stage 3: Good-boy orientation. Orientation to approval and to pleasing and helping others. Conformity to stereotypical images of majority of natural role behavior, and judgment by intentions. Stage 4: Authority- and social-order-maintaining orientation. Orientation to "doing duty" and to showing respect for authority and maintaining the given social order for its own sake. Regard for earned expectations of others.
III Moral value resides in conformity by the self to shared or sharable standards, rights, or duties.	Stage 5: Contractual legalistic orientation. Recognition of an arbitrary element or starting point in rules or expectations for the sake of agreement. Duty defined in terms of contract, general avoidance of violation of the will or rights of others, and majority will and welfare. Stage 6: Conscience or principle orientation. Orientation not only to actually ordained social rules but to principles of choice involving appeal to logical universality and consistency. Orientation to conscience as a directing agent and to mutual respect and trust.

* From Cohen, 1976, p. 181. Reprinted with permission of Macmillan Publishing Co., Inc. Copyright © 1976, Stewart Cohen.

Kohlberg's research evaluating moral judgment employs a set of stories, each containing a moral dilemma. The child is asked to make moral judgments concerning the behaviors of the characters in the story (Kohlberg, 1969). Some evidence suggests that Kohlberg's view of moral development involves a component of cognitive growth, since the stages he proposes correlate moderately well with IQ (Hoffman, 1970). Additional data are available that support his claim that all children go through the same successive stages of development (Kohlberg, 1969). However, other findings have raised serious questions about the validity of the developmental stages (Bandura, 1969a; Hoffman, 1970). These latter researchers are learning theorists who prefer to view development as continually changing and as a function of maturational growth and learning and not as a set of discrete and invariant stages. In general, stage theorists such as Freud, Erikson, Piaget, and Kohlberg hold a maturational view of development in which biological factors play a central role in the sequential and orderly unfolding of behavior. In contrast, learning theorists emphasize environmental conditions that give rise to the acquisition of behavior and those that maintain or produce changes in behavior (Cohen, 1976).

Learning Theory

The importance of learning in the developing child is difficult to exaggerate because its influence pervades almost every aspect of his or her functioning. It plays a role in eating, bowel and bladder control, language development, interpersonal relations, emotional expression, motivation, thinking, remembering, perceiving, motor skills, and in the formation of attitudes and values. Although limited by biological factors, *learning is the process by which environmental forces bring about lasting changes in behavior through practice.* For example, the child who is born deaf will be unable to learn normal speech patterns, and no amount of practice will enable the paraplegic to learn to run or play soccer. Learning results in long-lasting behavior change, as distinguished from temporary alterations that occur from fatigue, drugs, or adaptation. Practice or experience is essential to differentiate learning from the effects of physical maturation and biological factors, such as brain injury or damage. Changes in behavior that result from learning may be either desirable or undesirable, since the process of acquisition makes no distinction between good and bad behaviors.

There are many learning theories that attempt to account for human behavior, and not, as we might think, one single view that is followed by most psychologists. However, before we can discuss even a select sample of learning theories, we must become familiar with the basic concepts and the different kinds of learning.

Reinforcement. The concept of reinforcement is extremely important in a discussion of the learning process. If the occurrence or removal of an event or condition leads to the strengthening of a stimulus-response (S-R) connection or to the increased probability that a response will be emitted, the event or condition may be referred to as a *positive* or *negative reinforcer.* Positive reinforcement usually is thought of as a reward that either meets the biological requirements of the organisms (primary), such as food, water, or rest, or that meets the learned needs (secondary) of the individual, such as approval, recognition, or

TABLE 3–3 *   Characteristics of Reinforcement and Punishment

Positive Reinforcement	Negative Reinforcement	Punishment
1. Produced by instrumental behavior	1. Consists of the removal of unwanted consequences	1. Used to weaken behaviors, but frequently ineffective
2. Increases the probability of a particular instrumental response	2. Strengthens instrumental avoidance behavior	2. Consists of following instrumental responses by an unpleasant consequence, or removing one that is desired
3. Increases the intensity of a particular instrumental response	3. Strengthens instrumental escape behavior	3. Suppresses behavior, but does not necessarily weaken it
4. Sustains instrumental responses that have been learned	4. Increases the behavior that removes it	4. May instigate other instrumental responses that accomplish the same goal (being caught stealing during the day instigates stealing at night)
5. Elicits respondent emotional behaviors that induce approach behavior (enthusiasm, zest, encouragement, joy, excitement, pleasure)	5. Resembles positive reinforcement when instrumental responses remove certain aversive consequences (shortening a prison sentence by good behavior; receiving reduced work load as reward for good work)	5. May result in conditioned emotional responses (ulcers, chronic headache, resentment, and other psychosomatic processes; anger, hatred, fear, anxiety, distrust)
	6. Resembles punishment when instrumental responses simply prevent punishment (performing a job to avoid punishment by the boss, cleaning one's room to prevent mother's nagging)	6. May result in avoidance or escape behaviors (active avoidance; learning what to do to avoid the punishment; passive avoidance; learning what not to do to avoid or escape from the punishment)
		7. If mild, may stimulate alternative behaviors

Note: Reinforcement strengthens, punishment weakens. Strictly speaking, punishment cannot be avoided: An angry parent who is motivated to punish his child will administer the punishment in spite of the child's cries, protests, and pleadings. If punishment can be avoided or escaped, then we are dealing with negative reinforcement.

From Dicaprio, 1974, p. 144. Reprinted with permission of W. B. Saunders Co., Inc. Copyright © 1974, Nicholas S. Dicaprio.

affection. Negative reinforcement involves the removal of an unpleasant or aversive consequence that strengthens avoidance or escape behavior, as illustrated in the student who does an extra term paper to avoid failing the course. In contrast, *punishment* is a condition or event that is presented after a response occurs that will decrease the probability that the response will be emitted, that is, it will weaken the S-R association. Table 3–3 describes more fully the characteristics of positive and negative reinforcement and punishment. Under optimal conditions, punishment is the most effective way of eliminating an unwanted response. However, in real-life situations, punishment is rarely given with either sufficient intensity or suddenness to have more than transient effects. Just how effective punishment can be in eliminating behavior permanently is illustrated by the one trial learning of the child who gets burned by touching a hot burner of a stove, or by the child who is shocked by putting his or her finger into a light socket. In most human situations, punishment is not administered at maximum strength initially. Parents typically begin to correct their child's behavior by gentle verbal prods that may escalate into screams, exile, and eventually spanking without much success in curbing the unwanted behavior. If punishment is to be used, the most extreme form should be employed at the outset, but the ethical and moral problems involved keep most of us from doing what should be done when we choose to use punishment as a way of changing behavior.

In many instances, reinforcement is difficult to identify until after learning takes place. In this sense, it is not independent of learning, but it is inferred from it. We know that food, water, or the cessation of pain are reinforcers for hungry, thirsty, or hurting animals, although we often don't know in advance, especially when we deal with complex human behaviors, what specific reward will reinforce learning. For these instances, the work of Premack (1965) has been most useful. Premack notes that reinforcing stimuli (rewards) control responses, that is, food controls eating and water controls drinking in the sense that these responses are highly likely to occur in the presence of these stimuli. In contrast, a response to be reinforced such as social interaction for a withdrawn child will occur less frequently in the presence of people than eating will in the presence of food. According to Premack's Principle, the opportunity to engage in higher probability responses will reinforce lower probability responses. By observing a person's behavior, one can determine which behaviors are most likely to be emitted. Once having determined that these behaviors have a high probability of occurrence, then the opportunity to perform any of these preferred behaviors can be employed as reinforcers for wanted behaviors. Thus, the experimenter can gain control over the

low probability desired behavior by manipulating the subject's opportunity to perform preferred behaviors, such as permitting a child to watch TV only after homework is done. In this way, reinforcers can be independent of learning and identified in advance.

Kinds of Learning. There are numerous experimental paradigms (or arrangements) employed by psychologists to study the learning process, although for our purposes, we shall discuss only three major types: classical conditioning, operant conditioning, and imitation learning or modeling.

1. *Classical Conditioning:* First introduced by Ivan P. Pavlov, the Nobel Prize winning Russian physiologist, this paradigm involves the pairing of a previously neutral stimulus, the *conditioned stimulus* (CS), with a stimulus called the *unconditioned stimulus* (UCS) that consistently elicits a specific response, called the unconditioned response (UCR). The basic experimental paradigm is schematically illustrated in Figure 3–2. Pavlov showed that through successive temporal pairing of the CS (the onset of a light or the sound of a buzzer) with the UCS which serves as the reinforcer (the sight of meat powder), the CS comes to elicit a specific response of salivation, called the *conditioned response* (CR). Through this simple procedure Pavlov showed that a new stimulus-response connection could be established through learning. He also showed that a CR could be diminished and eventually eliminated from the animal's repertory in the absence of the UCS. The progressive weakening of a CR under these conditions is known as *extinction,* although there are special occasions referred to as *spontaneous recovery* when an extinguished CR reappears.

Another principle uncovered by Pavlov,

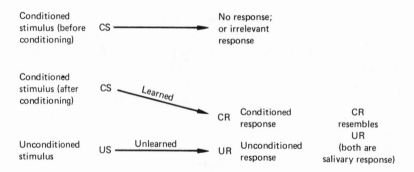

The association between the unconditioned stimulus and the unconditioned response exists at the start of the experiment and does not have to be learned. The association between the conditioned stimulus and the conditioned response is a learned one. It arises through the pairing of the conditioned and unconditioned stimuli followed by the unconditioned response (i.e., reinforcement). The conditioned response resembles the unconditioned one (though they need not be identical).

FIGURE 3–2   A diagram of classical conditioning (From *Introduction to Psychology,* 3rd ed., by Ernest R. Hilgard, copyright © 1962 by Harcourt Brace Jovanovich, Inc., reprinted with permission.)

stimulus generalization, provides an explanation for our ability to respond appropriately to new stimuli as long as they are similar to familiar ones. Generalization occurs when a similar stimulus but not identical to the original one elicits the same response. The closer the similarity to the original stimulus, the more completely will the new stimulus substitute for it. Thus, a child who has been scratched by a Persian cat will not only avoid Persian cats, but also other kinds of cats and to a lesser extent other four-legged furry animals. The effect of generalization can be reduced through a process known as *discrimination,* in which the association between a particular CS and a CR is reinforced through conditioning, while the CRs to similar CSs are eliminated through extinction. In this way, the organism learns to discriminate stimuli, and to respond to the appropriate one.

After a CS acquires the ability to elicit a CR, it may be successfully paired (this time serving as the UCS) with a new CS, which eventually will also elicit the same CR. This *higher order conditioning* is an important finding because it extends the

possibilities of learning through conditioning in our daily lives.

2. *Operant Conditioning:* Unlike the sequence of events in classical conditioning where the reinforcer is paired with the CS and is presented *before* the response is made, operant conditioning employs a different sequence of events wherein reinforcement is given *after* the organism makes the appropriate response. Because reinforcement is contingent on what the organism does, operant conditioning is sometimes referred to as *instrumental learning* (the response is instrumental in obtaining reinforcement). No such contingency exists in classical conditioning because the organism is reinforced (the UCS is presented) regardless of what response is given. However, responses that are classically conditioned are considered to be *elicited* and under direct stimulus control in that they are reflex-like and specific to the UCS, such as salivation to food, eyeblink to a puff of air to the eyelid, or leg flexion to an electric shock to the animal's hindlimb.

In contrast, operant responses are *emitted* in the sense that they are available in

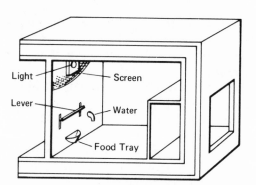

The diagram shows the interior arrangement of the box used in operant conditioning of the rat. The space behind the panel at the left contains additional apparatus. This box has been named a "Skinner-box" after its developer. (From Skinner, 1938)

FIGURE 3–3 (From Hilgard, 1962, p. 259. Reprinted with permission.)

the organism's response repertory, and they appear spontaneously rather than as a response to a specific stimulus. The stimulus situation in this kind of learning is nonspecific as in an operant chamber (sometimes called a Skinner box, referring to B. F. Skinner, a major contributor to our understanding of operant conditioning) shown in Figure 3–3, where the hungry animal must by chance make a bar-pressing response before it receives food as a reinforcer. In this way, the animal's behavior of bar pressing "operates" on the environment to produce the effect of obtaining food.

Much like everyday situations, operant conditioning can and does occur without the reinforcer following the responses every time (continuous reinforcement). In fact, experimental studies have used different schedules of *intermittent reinforcement* in which reinforcement may occur after a fixed number of nonreinforced responses, at fixed time intervals following the last reinforcement, after variable numbers of nonreinforced responses, or at variable time intervals between reinforcements. Many of the principles found with classical conditioning such as extinction, spontaneous recovery, and generalization apply equally as well to operant conditioning. In addition, novel or new responses that are not already available

in the organism's repertory can be learned through a procedure known as *shaping*. Initially, approximations of the wanted response is reinforced, followed by the reinforcement of responses that are increasingly similar to it, until only the appropriate response is reinforced. This is what the trainer of a marineland show is likely to do in teaching a porpoise to play basketball or retrieve a ball.

3. *Imitation Learning or Modeling:* Whereas reinforcement plays a central role in the two kinds of learning already discussed, reinforcement and overt practice is not necessary in imitation learning. This type of learning takes place by observing another person, or a *model,* make a response or a set of responses. Can you recall putting a piece of white chalk or a candy cigarette up to your lips, taking a deep breath, and then exhaling to imitate the adult cigarette smoker? Especially for the developing child, the opportunities for imitation learning are almost limitless in such obvious behaviors as emotional expressions, and in more subtle behaviors as attitudes toward others. The first time a four-year-old vocalizes anger by using a four letter word, the child probably is imitating someone (probably a family member) who had used the expression earlier and probably often.

Bandura (1969b; 1971) is one of the learning investigators who has stimulated interest in modeling. He maintains that exposure to various modeling situations may produce previously unexhibited behavior, inhibit or disinhibit responses, or serve as facilitators for existing responses. The retention and delayed reproduction of modeled behavior requires representational or symbolic mediation (Bandura, Grusec, and Menlove, 1966).

Examples of Learning Theory. The learning views of Dollard and Miller, Rotter, and Bandura (and their followers) have been selected as illustrations of learning theories that have generated considerable research. Although these approaches deal with the acquisition of both normal and abnormal behaviors, our discussion of them will focus on normal personality development leaving (as we have for the psychoanalytic view) for Chapter 4 what they and other learning theorists have to say about psychopathology.

1. *Dollard and Miller* (1950): Dollard and Miller introduced one of the earliest learning models of personality by attempting to translate psychoanalytic theory into a system (S-R) largely based on conditioning and drive-reduction postulates. They described four essential components of learning—*cue, response, drive,* and *reinforcement*—in which cues determine the nature of the responses (that is, what response will occur as well as when and where it will take place) and learning consists of the establishment of cue-response connections (S-R). S-R bonds are strengthened when the responses to the cues produce drive-reduction (reinforcement). According to this view, drive is a motivational state that impels or energizes the organism to respond (without specific direction). Any event or response that reduces the strength

of a drive is reinforcing, leading to an increased probability that the response will be repeated. Drives must be present in the organism in order for learning to occur whether they are primary (innate), such as hunger, thirst, sex, and pain, or secondary (acquired), such as fear, anxiety, or the need for money or achievement. Reward or reinforcement is also necessary for the maintenance of an S-R connection. Thus, for learning to take place, the organism must want something (drive), must notice something (cue), and must do something (response) that reduces the strength of the drive (reinforcement).

In this system, responses are thought of as arranged in a hierarchy (at first innate) with respect to their probability of occurrence to a particular cue. When a response is reinforced, its probability of recurring increases and its relative position within the hierarchy changes. Thus, the hierarchy of a child's responses at any given time is a function of previous learning. Responses may be extinguished in the absence of reinforcement, and they may generalize to similar stimuli or to different stimuli through labels or symbols (such as words designating a class of objects). Dollard and Miller also differentiate between instrumental responses and cue-producing responses, suggesting that the former are directly observable responses that accomplish drive reduction, while the latter usually occur within the individual (such as mental thoughts or images) to produce information that may be linked with instrumental responses.

The principle of reinforcement replaces Freud's concept of the pleasure principle, while their account of higher mental processes and description of learned drives and skills more clearly amplifies Freud's view of the ego. Conflict plays an important role in Dollard and Miller's theory, as it did in

Freud's as the underlying basis of neuroses (see Chapter 11). They define conflict as competing or opposing responses that tend to block or inhibit overt behavior (instrumental responses), leaving the drive unsatisfied and creating tensions that continue or increase. Most conflicts involve competition between drives and inhibitory emotional responses such as fear and guilt, so that those caught in a conflict are likely to experience the tensions of the unsatisfied drive, as well as the distress of the intense fear that prevents the occurrence of instrumental responses that would reduce the drive. Dollard and Miller agree with Freud's emphasis on early childhood experiences, noting that conflicts can and do occur early in life at a time when the young child is poorly equipped to deal with them. Inhibiting emotions (fear or guilt) often become associated with primary drives, forming the acquired basis of life-long tensions and the presence of fear or guilt when drives are present and even reduced. For example, the baby who responds to a drive state by crying (such as the discomfort of a soiled diaper) and who in turn is scolded or verbally reprimanded by a fastidious mother is not only thwarted in trying to satisfy the tension state but also learns to fear or feel guilty about the gratification of needs. Moreover, Dollard and Miller suggest that conflicts occurring before the child develops language are unconscious (outside the child's awareness and not accessible to the higher mental processes) and much more difficult to treat later on.

2. *Rotter's Social Learning Theory* (Rotter, Chance, and Phares, 1972): In 1954, Julian Rotter first described his particular approach to social learning in which he postulated the three basic theoretical concepts of *behavior potential* (B.P.), *expectancy* (E.), and *reinforcement* (R.V.) to account for human behavior in complex social situations. Rotter arranged these concepts in the seemingly simple equation of B.P. $= f$ (E. & R.V.) without making any mathematical assumptions about the relationship between expectancy and reinforcement value (although he favors a multiplicative one). The formula states that the probability of occurrence of a particular behavior in a specific situation (behavior potential) is a function of *both* the subjectively held probability (expectancy) that the behavior in question will be reinforced, and the value of the reinforcer (reinforcement value) to the responder (Rotter, Chance, and Phares, 1972). A fourth basic concept, the psychological situation, implicit in the formula, was used to reflect the stimulus complex to which the organism reacts and to acknowledge the selectivity of reactions to diverse kinds of stimulation.

Rotter thinks of behavior in broad terms as including any response made to a meaningful stimulus that is directly or indirectly measurable. He regards reinforcement (either internal or external) as any event that changes the potential for occurrence of a given behavior, while he thinks of reinforcement value as the relative preference for one of a number of reinforcements to occur if the probability of occurrence for all of them were equal. Rotter defines expectancy as the subjectively held probability that a specific or set of reinforcements will occur in a given situation or situations.

The developing child acquires a number of expectancies as he or she tries to satisfy need. The boy who repeatedly fails to get his father to play with him soon develops a generalized expectancy that he will be rejected by his father. If the boy's need to engage father in play is strong (reinforcement value), then he is likely to persist in his efforts, although the expectancy of achieving the goal is low. If, on the other hand, the boy's need for father is reduced, for example through interactions with another highly valued male figure such as a teacher or grandfather, his attempts to gain father's attention will fall off considerably. However, the boy carries the generalized expectancy into new situations, so that he is likely to expect rejection in a new encounter with an adult male. Only through subsequent interactions with this adult can the generalized expectancy be modified to more closely correspond to the adult's actual behavior, assuming that the reinforcement value of this adult is sufficiently high for the boy to pursue additional encounters.

3. *Bandura's Social Learning Theory:* Combining some innovative principles of imitation learning with the established procedures of operant conditioning, Bandura and Walters introduced a social-learning theory that attempted to more adequately (than other learning theorists) account for the acquisition of novel responses in children and adults (Bandura and Walters, 1963). They emphasized the importance of imitation (modeling) in the learning of both deviant and conforming behaviors, and they cited numerous examples where modeling occurs, such as sex-linked roles, vocational roles, child-rearing practices, and learning to perform specific acts such as lacing a shoe. Imitation learning may occur through direct modeling, or through symbolic modeling, although the mode of modeling will affect the rate and level of learning. Bandura describes imitation as an active process that is determined by four interrelated subprocesses: attention, retention, motoric reproduction, and incentive and motivation (Bandura, 1969b, pp. 213–262).

Attention is necessary since imitation would not be possible if the observer failed to attend to the model or failed to notice the distinctive characteristics of the model's behavior. Retention of the model's behavior or modeling situation is also necessary in order for the child to reproduce it without the continued presence of the external model. The process of motoric reproduction, although complex, must be available in order for the child to actually perform the modeled behavior. Finally, incentive and motivation must be present if overt performance of the modeled sequence is to occur. Here, Bandura distinguished between learning and the capacity to reproduce modeled behavior on the one hand, and its activation into overt performance on the other. A youngster may learn a modeled sequence and be capable of reproducing it but may not perform it either because of negative consequences or the absence of incentives. Behavior is maintained through direct reinforcement given to the individual or through vicarious reinforcement given to the model (but not to the observer), or through self-reinforcement in which the individual administers self-rewards or self-punishments.

Bandura and Walters used data from both field and laboratory studies to support the influence of modeling and patterns of reinforcement in the learning of prosocial and deviant aggressive, dependent, and sexual behaviors. For example, they showed that aggressive-punitive parents are likely to produce aggressive children, especially if the parents (models) are highly successful in controlling rewards. Moreover, frustrated children, who under ordinary conditions would respond with aggression, can be taught novel patterns, that is, they would exhibit unaggressive and inhibited behavior after observing the inhibited behavior of a model. Whether the aggressive behavior of the model was rewarded or punished also differentially affected the behavior of the children who were observers. Those who observed aggression rewarded showed more aggressive behavior than the children who observed punishment as a result of the model's aggressive behavior.

Research has also shown that positive reinforcement will increase the child's aggressive behavior, and that the effects of this reinforcement will transfer to new social situations. As expected, punishment tends to inhibit aggressive responses, although a great deal of punishment-training may lead to aggression directed to objects or persons who are not the punitive agent (displaced aggression). While there is less research evidence available about the effect of reinforcement on dependency and sexual behavior, Bandura and Walters propose that "reinforcement variables modify these classes of responses in much the same manner as they modify aggression" (Bandura and Walters, 1963, p. 160).

Summary

This chapter was primarily intended to provide a framework of normal personality development from which developmental psychopathology can be better understood. The basic principles of development, the major variables influencing its course, and the theoretical positions that have generated research were considered.

Human development follows a set of lawful and orderly general principles. Growth and motor development proceed from head to tail (cephalocaudal) and from the central axis to the periphery (proximodistal) of the human body. Moreover, development progresses from the general to the specific (differentiation), and at different rates at different times (asynchronous growth). All of these principles are evident prenatally and postnatally, and they apply to both structure and function. In the area of personality and social development, the child progresses from an undifferentiated and almost totally dependent organism to a distinct and independent self.

Maturation refers to the physical alterations in size, and qualitative changes in tissues or in anatomical and physiological organization. It is extremely important for child development, because these physiological transformations make the organism biologically ready to learn new behaviors. Without maturation, no amount of practice or preparation would be sufficient for certain new behaviors to emerge.

Development involves sequential and orderly changes over time in the organism's structure and function which is affected by many factors. The variables of heredity, temperament, the multidirectional effects of the parent-child interaction, the school, and peer relations were considered as they influence later personality development.

The final section of the chapter was devoted to a discussion of the three major theoretical views of personality development: the psychoanalytic, the cognitive-developmental, and the learning. These views were singled out because they have had a great impact on researchers, educators, and other child-care workers, and because collectively they provide a broad but understandable perspective of the developing child. The views of both Freud and Erikson were considered under psychoanalytic theory, those of Piaget and Kohlberg within the cognitive-developmental framework, and those of Dollard and Miller, Rotter, and Bandura as representative of learning theory. In explicating these views, emphasis was placed on normal development, leaving for later consideration the theoretical underpinnings of abnormal behavior.

REFERENCES

AINSWORTH, M. D. *Infancy in Uganda: Infant Care and Growth of Love.* Baltimore: Johns Hopkins Press, 1967.

AINSWORTH, M. D., BELL, S. M., and D. J. STAYTON. "Infant-Mother Attachment and Social Development: Socialization as a Product of Reciprocal Responsiveness to Signals. In M. Richards (Ed.), *The Integration of a Child into a Social World.* Cambridge, England: Cambridge University Press, 1974, pp. 99–135.

ANASTASI, A. "Heredity, Environment, and the Question of 'How?'" *Psychological Review*, 1958, *65*, 197–208.

BANDURA, A. "Social Learning of Moral Judgments." *Journal of Personality and Social Psychology*, 1969a, *11*, 275–279.

BANDURA, A. *Principles of Behavior Modification.* New York: Holt, Rinehart, and Winston, 1969b.

BANDURA, A. *Social Learning Theory.* Morristown, N.J.: General Learning Press, 1971.

BANDURA, A., GRUSEC, J. R., and F. L. MENLOVE. "Observational Learning as a Function of Symbolization and Incentive Set. *Child Development*, 1966, *37*, 499–506.

BANDURA, A., and R. H. WALTERS. *Social Learning and Personality Development.* New York: Holt, Rinehart, and Winston, 1963.

BELL, R. Q. "A Reinterpretation of the Direction of Effects in Studies of Socialization. *Psychological Review*, 1968, *75*, 81–95.

BERKSON, G. and W. A. MASON. "Stereotyped Behavior of Chimpanzees: Relation to General Arousal and Alternative Activities." *Perceptual and Motor Skills*, 1964, *19*, 635–652.

BERKSON, G. "Social Responses of Animals to Infants with Defects. In M. Lewis and L. A. Rosenblum (Eds.), *The Effect of the Infant on Its Caregiver.* New York: Wiley, 1974, pp. 233–250.

BOSSARD, J. H., and E. S. BOLL. *The Sociology of Child Development* (4th ed.). New York: Harper and Row, 1966.

BOWLBY, J. "Separation Anxiety." *International Journal of Psychoanalysis*, 1960, *41*, 89–113.

BRAZLETON, T. B. *Infants and Mothers: Differences in Development.* New York: Delacorte Press, 1969.

BRAZLETON, T. B., KOSLOWSKI, B., and M. MAIN. "The Origins of Reciprocity: The Early Mother-Infant Interaction." In M. Lewis and L. A. Rosenblum (Eds.), *The Effect of the Infant on its Caregiver.* New York: Wiley, 1974, pp. 49–76.

BUSS, A. H. and R. PLOMIN. *A Temperament Theory of Personality Development.* New York: Wiley, 1975.

COHEN, S. *Social and Personality Development in Children.* New York: Macmillan, 1976.

DENNIS, W. and M. G. DENNIS. "The Effect of Cradling Practices upon the Onset of Walking in Hopi Children." *Journal of Genetic Psychology*, 1940, *56*, 77–86.

DICAPRIO, N. S. *Personality Theories: Guides to Living.* Philadelphia: Saunders, 1974.

DOLLARD, J. and N. E. MILLER. *Personality and Psychotherapy.* New York: McGraw-Hill, 1950.

ERIKSON, E. H. *Childhood and Society* (2nd ed.). New York: Norton, 1963.

FLAVELL, H. H. *The Developmental Psychology of Jean Piaget.* Princeton, N.J.: Van Nostrand Reinhold, 1963.

FREUD, S. *Beyond the Pleasure Principle* (trans. by C. M. Hubback). London: International Psychoanalytic Press, 1922.

FREUD, S. *The Ego and the Id* (trans. by J. Riviere). London: Institute of Psychoanalysis and Hogarth Press, 1957.

FREUD, S. "Instincts and Their Vicissitudes" (trans. by J. Riviere). In *Collected Papers* (1st ed.) (Vol. 4). New York: Basic Books, Inc., 1959.

FREUD, S. *New Introductory Lectures to Psychoanalysis* (trans. by W. J. H. Sprott). New York: Norton, 1933.

GESELL, A., ILG, F. L., AMES, L. B., and J. L. RODELL. *Infant and Child in the Culture of Today* (rev. ed.). New York: Harper and Row, 1974.

HARLOW, H. F. "The Heterosexual Affectional System in Monkeys." *American Psychologist*, 1962, *17*, 1–9.

HARLOW, H. F. and M. K. HARLOW. "Psychopathology in Monkeys." In H. D. Kimmel (Ed.), *Experimental Psychopathology: Recent Research and Theory*. New York: Academic Press, 1971, pp. 203–229.

HARLOW, H. and R. ZIMMERMAN. "Affectional Responses in the Infant Monkey." *Science*, 1959, *130*, 421–432.

HARTUP, W. W. "Peer Interaction and Social Organization." In P. H. Mussen (Ed.), *Carmichael's Manual of Child Psychology* (3rd ed.) (Vol. 2). New York: Wiley, 1970, pp. 361–456.

HARTUP, W. W. "Peers, Play, and Pathology: A New Look at the Social Behavior of Children." *Newsletter, Society for Research in Child Development*, Fall, 1977, 1–3.

HETHERINGTON, E. M. "Girls Without Fathers." *Psychology Today*, 1973, 6:9, 47–52.

HILGARD, E. R. *Introduction of Psychology* (3rd ed.). New York: Harcourt Brace & Jovanovich, 1962.

HOFFMAN, M. "Moral Development." In P. Mussen (Ed.), *Carmichael's Manual of Child Psychology*. New York: Wiley, 1970, pp. 261–359.

HOFFMAN, M. L. "Father Absence and Conscience Development." *Developmental Psychology*, 1971, *4*, 400–406.

JACOBS, J. and J. D. TEICHER. "Broken Homes and Social Isolation in Attempted Suicides of Adolescents. *International Journal of Social Psychiatry*, 1967, *13*, 139–149.

KAUFMAN, I. C. and L. A. ROSENBLUM. "Depression in Infant Monkeys Separated from Their Mothers." *Science*, 1967, *155*, 1030–31.

KNOPF, I. J. and G. L. KIRCHNER. "Differences in the Vigilance Performance of Second-Grade Children as Related to Sex and Achievement." *Child Development*, 1974, *45*, 490–495.

KNOPF, I. J. and R. M. MABEL. "Vigilance Performance in Second Graders as a Function of Interstimulus Intervals, Socioeconomic Levels, and Reading." *Merrill-Palmer Quarterly of Behavior and Development*, 1975, *21*, 195–203.

KOHLBERG, L. "Stage and Sequence: The Cognitive-Developmental Approach to Socialization." In D. A. Goslin (Ed.), *Handbook of Socialization Theory and Research*. Chicago: Rand McNally, 1969, pp. 347–480.

KOHLBERG, L. "Moral and Religious Education and the Public Schools: A Developmental View." In T. Sizer (Ed.), *Religion and Public Education*. Boston: Houghton Mifflin, 1967, pp. 164–183.

KORNER, A. F. "The Effect of the Infant's State, Level of Arousal, Sex, and Ontogenetic Stage on the Caregiver." In M. Lewis and L. A. Rosenblum (Eds.),

The Effect of the Infant on its Caregiver. New York: Wiley, 1974, pp. 105–120.

LAMB, M. E. (Ed.), *The Role of the Father in Child Development.* New York: Wiley, 1976a.

LAMB, M. E. "The Role of the Father: An Overview." In M. E. Lamb (Ed.), *The Role of the Father in Child Development.* New York: Wiley, 1976b, pp. 1–61.

LEWIS, M. and L. A. ROSENBLUM (Eds.), *The Effect of the Infant on its Caregiver.* New York: Wiley, 1974.

LIDZ, T. "The Family as the Developmental Setting." In E. J. Anthony and C. Koupernik (Eds.), *The Child in His Family* (Vol. 1). New York: Wiley-Interscience, 1970, pp. 19–39.

LIDZ, T., FLECK, S., and A. CORNELISON. *Schizophrenia and the Family.* New York: International Universities Press, 1965.

LINDBURG, D. G. "Behavior of Infant Rhesus Monkeys with Thalidomide-Induced Malformations: A Pilot Study." *Psychonomic Science,* 1969, *15,* 55–56.

MADDI, S. R. *Personality Theories: A Comparative Analysis* (rev. ed.). Homewood, Illinois: Dorsey Press, 1972.

MAIER, H. *Three Theories of Child Development.* New York: Harper and Row, 1965.

MASON, W. A. *Early Social Deprivation in the Nonhuman Primates.* New York: The Rockefeller University Press and Russell Sage Foundation, 1968.

McGRAW, M. B. *Growth: A Study of Johnny and Jimmy.* New York: Appleton-Century-Crofts, 1935.

MOERK, E. L. "Like Father Like Son: Imprisonment of Fathers and the Psychological Adjustment of Sons." *Journal of Youth and Adolescence,* 1973, *2:*4, 303–312.

MUSSEN, P. H., CONGER, J. J., and J. KAGAN. *Child Development and Personality* (4th ed.). New York: Harper and Row, 1974.

NAGEL, E. "Determinism and Development." In D. B. Harris (Ed.), *The Concept of Development.* Minneapolis: University of Minnesota Press, 1957, pp. 15–24.

NEAL, M. V. "The Relationship Between a Regimen of Vestibular Stimulation and the Developmental Behavior of the Premature Infant." (Doctoral dissertation, New York University, 1970.) *Dissertation Abstracts International,* 1970, *30:*10-A, 4151.

OLTMAN, J. E., and S. FRIEDMAN. "Parental Deprivation in Psychiatric Conditions: III. In Personality Disorders and Other Conditions." *Diseases of the Nervous System,* 1967, *28,* 298–303.

PARKE, R. D., and D. B. SAWIN. "Fathering: It's a Major Role." *Psychology Today,* 1977, *11,* 109–113.

PREMACK, D. "Reinforcement Theory." In D. Levine (Ed.), *Nebraska Symposium on Motivation,* 1965, pp. 123–180.

RADIN, N. "The Role of the Father in Cognitive, Academic, and Intellectual Development." In M. E. Lamb (Ed.), *The Role of the Father in Child Development.* New York: Wiley, 1976, pp. 237–276.

RATHOD, N. H. and I. G. THOMSON. "Women Alcoholics." *Quarterly Journal of Studies of Alcohol,* 1971, *32,* 45–52.

RIBBLE, M. "Infantile Experience in Relation to Personality Development." In J. Mcv. Hunt (Ed.), *Personality and the behavior disorders.* New York: Ronald Press, 1944, pp. 621–651.

ROSENBERG, C. M. "Determinants of Psychiatric Illness in Young People. *British Journal of Psychiatry*, 1969, *115*, 907–915.

ROSENTHAL, D. *Genetic theory and abnormal behavior.* New York: McGraw-Hill, 1970.

ROTTER, J. B., CHANCE, J. E., and E. J. PHARES. *Applications of a Social Learning Theory of Personality.* New York: Holt, Rinehart, and Winston, 1972.

SANTROCK, J. W. "Relation of Type and Onset of Father Absence to Cognitive Development." *Child Development*, 1972, *43*, 455–469.

SCHLOTTMAN, R. S., and H. SEAY. "Mother-Infant Separation in the Java Monkey (Macaca Irus)." *Journal of Comparative and Physiological Psychology*, 1972, 79:2, 334–340.

SEAY, B., HANSEN, E., and H. HARLOW. "Mother-Infant Separation in Monkeys. *Journal of Child Psychology and Psychiatry*, 1962, *3*:3–4, 123–132.

SEAY, B., and H. HARLOW. "Maternal Separation in the Rhesus Monkey." *Journal of Nervous and Mental Disease*, 1965, *140*:6, 434–441.

SPENCER-BOOTH, Y. and R. A. HINDE. "Effects of Six Days Separation from Mother on 18- to 32-Week Old Rhesus Monkeys." *Animal Behavior*, 1971, *19*:1, 174–191.

SPENCER-BOOTH, Y., and R. A. HINDE. "The Effects of Separating Rhesus Monkey Infants from Their Mothers for Six Days." *Journal of Child Psychology and Psychiatry*, 1966, *7*, 179–197.

SPITZ, R. A. "Hospitalism: An Inquiry into the Genesis of Psychiatric Conditions in Early Childhood." In O. Fenichel et al. (Eds.), *The Psychoanalytic Study of the Child* (Vol. 1). New York: International Universities Press, 1945, pp. 53–64.

SPITZ, R. A. and K. M. WOLF. "Anaclitic Depression: An Inquiry into the Genesis of Psychiatric Conditions in Early Childhood." In O. Fenichel et al. (Eds.), *The Psychoanalytic Study of the Child* (Vol. II). New York: International Universities Press, 1946, pp. 313–342.

STONE, L. J. and J. CHURCH. *Childhood and Adolescence* (3rd ed.). New York: Random House, 1973.

THOMAS, A., and S. CHESS. *Temperament and Development.* New York: Brunner/Mazel, 1977.

THOMAS, A., CHESS, S., and H. BIRCH. "The Origin of Personality." *Scientific American*, 1970, *223*:2, 102–109.

THOMAS, A., CHESS, S., and H. BIRCH. *Temperament and Behavior Disorders in Children.* New York: New York University Press, 1968.

TUDDENHAM, R. D. "Jean Piaget and the World of the Child." *American Psychologist*, 1966, *21*, 207–217.

WHITEMAN, M. and M. DEUTSCH. "Social Disadvantage as Related to Intellective and Language Development." In M. Deutsch, I. Katz, and A. R. Jensen (Eds.), *Social Class, Race, and Psychological Development.* New York: Holt, Rinehart and Winston, 1968, pp. 86–114.

WHITMAN, W. *Leaves of Grass.* M. Cowley, (Ed.). New York: Viking Press, 1959, pp. 138–139.

YEE, A. H. "Source and Direction of Causal Influence in Teacher-Pupil Relationships." *Journal of Educational Psychology*, 1968, *59*, 275–282.

Conceptual Models of Psychopathology

4

PROLOGUE

Eric was a short, obese, somewhat effeminate fourteen-year-old who achieved poorly in school despite his above average intelligence test scores. In class, he was described as restless, distractible, inattentive, irritating to others, and disinterested. The victim of frequent physical and verbal attacks from his peers, Eric allowed himself to be bullied without ever fighting back. He had no friends and showed no interest in any activity outside of the home. He refused to participate in sports, to join clubs, to attend parties, or to venture out by himself once he returned home from school. Apart from fighting almost endlessly with his seventeen-year-old sister, Eric enjoyed helping his mother cook, clean, or perform any of her routine household chores. He liked to watch TV for hours on end while gorging himself on large quantities of candy, pretzels, potato chips, and soda pop.

Eric's parents were also short and obese. Father owned a small business that required long working days, which he used to justify his reluctance to assume any responsibilities at home. Consequently, he saw his role as a financial provider for the family, and his wife's as the manager of the home. Mother accepted her position as the key figure in the family with assertiveness, zeal, and an air of self-sacrifice. She was nurturant, indulging, and over-protective, especially to Eric, whom she treated as "her baby." She protected him from his sister whenever they fought, kept his poor school performance from father, and denied that Eric was obese, or that he had any social or personal problems.

Eric was born prematurely and kept in an incubator for two weeks before he could leave the hospital. He gained weight rapidly, slept well, and seemed to be a healthy and happy infant. He had no serious illnesses, accidents, brain injury, or surgery. His motor and language development were within normal limits. Everything went well until Eric enrolled in school at the age of six. His initial difficulty in separating himself from mother quickly turned into a full blown problem. He feigned illnesses to avoid going to school or created such disturbances in school that mother had to be called to take him home. After several months of these daily battles and sheer frustration, mother angrily insisted that he go to school and that he be kept there regardless of his acting-out behaviors. Through the cooperation of the principal and mother's persistent resolve, Eric's school refusal subsided. However, from that time on his academic performance was consistently below his capacities and his behavior was troublesome to both teachers and peers. After years of denying the problem and hoping for change, mother finally sought professional help because Eric's school and social problems had worsened.

Given these same descriptive facts, Eric's behaviors can be understood in a variety of ways, depending on our frame of reference or how we choose to conceptualize his difficulties. He could be thought of as possessed by supernatural forces, suffering from a disease, the product of heredity or his environment, or the combined result of internal and external factors. Because no single frame of reference has demonstrated validity in accounting for the full range of abnormal conditions, and because each conception charts different directions and consequences, we need to examine a sample of currently influential models. Although these models are not completely independent of each other, we have taken the liberty of grouping them into two broad and somewhat arbitrary categories to facilitate their exposition and understanding. First, we clarify what a model is, as well as its implications and consequences. Then, we select views within the *medical-disease models* and the *environmental models*.

The Nature of Conceptual Models

Definition

Conceptual models are frames of reference that provide a broad but cohesive way of understanding and explaining abnormal behaviors. Models make basic etiological assumptions that often have the ring of plausibility, but that seldom are completely verified by scientific evidence. These causal assumptions give rise to differential interpretations of the available data and lead to other assumptions and inferences as the model is elaborated and developed. Usually, models generate their own vocabularies and technical terms that reflect their particular orientation and emphasize their uniqueness. But as we shall see, the explanatory concepts of models tend to overlap in varying degrees, sometimes to the extent that they blur the models' boundaries as distinct frames of reference.

Implications and Consequences

While conceptual models generate useful research hypotheses, initially they encourage studies designed to either support or challenge the model. However, once a model achieves widespread acceptance, alternative positions become more peripheral and less influential, often regardless of their validity. All too often, the model may persist because of its plausibility and because its advocates maintain an almost unalterable faith in its premise, as with demonology, where proponents continue to believe in supernatural forces despite the absence of scientific support. Contemporary interest in witchcraft, demons, and the occult is reflected in the success of the TV show *Bewitched,* and books and subsequent movies such as *Rosemary's Baby, The Exorcist,* and the *Omen.* It also is evidenced in colloquialisms such as "I don't know what *possessed* me to do . . . ," or "I'd sell my *soul* if I could only have . . . ."

The adoption of a model not only increases the resistance to other views, but it also has a number of important consequences. These include: who is identified as abnormal, criteria used, treatment, kinds of institutional provisions, and public attitude toward those labeled abnormal. Perhaps an illustration will help our understanding of what a conceptual model is and of the consequences that follow its adoption.

Within recent years, frequent reports of unidentified flying objects (UFOs) have strengthened the belief that UFOs come from other planets in the solar system, even though no verifiable evidence exists to support this view. The fact is that people have always tried to find rational explanations for those inexplicable events they experience as a way of understanding themselves and their environment. That many have long believed that other planets are inhabited by some form of life was dramatically illustrated on a Sunday night in 1938 (Halloween), when approximately one million people became panic-stricken while listening to a radio broadcast of the Mercury Theatre. Orson Welles and a company of players dramatized a version of "The War of the Worlds" by H. G. Wells so realistically that many listeners became terrified and fled from the fictitious invading monsters from Mars (Cantrill, 1940).

The popular comic strips of Buck Rogers and Flash Gordon widely syndicated in those days, and more recent TV shows and movies such as *Space 1999, Star Trek, Star*

Wars, and *Close Encounters of the Third Kind* attest to the public's continued fascination with the idea that other planets are inhabited by some form of life. Science fiction of this sort has gained considerable credibility in the last several decades because it has been stimulated and reinforced by almost unbelievable technological advances, especially in space exploration. In addition, international tensions and conflicts have heightened our fears of being attacked by alien forces. Therefore, it is not surprising that many people believe that UFOs are space ships from other planets.

Let us suppose for a moment that this was the prevalent view in our society. Under these circumstances, we could reasonably conjecture certain highly probable consequences. Our country, and perhaps others, would be prompted to construct some sort of identification and warning systems in the interest of capturing one of the vessels to learn who and what sent it into our world, and the nature of its scientific technology. Special public funds would be allocated for a detection program and for a speed-up of our own space exploration efforts. Mobilization of national resources would be associated with a sharp rise in the number of reported sightings of UFOs along with growing public fears of infiltration. It is even possible to imagine that unexplained deaths, disappearances, epidemics, or mysterious happenings would be attributed to the evil acts of space creatures, particularly if these events were coupled with UFO sightings. If fear turned into panic, military control and rule would become more acceptable and, indeed, welcomed by many.

As far fetched as this UFO fantasy may seem, it does illustrate that once a conceptual model achieves widespread acceptance, it determines a number of important events regardless of the validity of its premise. The model assumed that UFOs were the vehicles of living creatures from outer space. The assumption set into motion a number of important actions because of its ring of plausibility and its concurrence with a long-standing popular belief. When augmented by enormous public fear and anxiety, the original premise became increasingly difficult to question and/or test. As acceptance increased, fewer tests of the model occurred, and scientific advances tended to focus on technological improvements within the system. In such cases, invariably the development of alternate conceptual models is retarded, sometimes for long periods of time.

Medical Disease Models

The primary explanatory model of abnormal behavior in our society is a medical one, complete with its own language, institutions, professional personnel, and types of remediation that reflect *disease* as its basic assumption. Both laymen and professionals widely use and accept such words as mental illness, mental health, and mental patient to describe the disorder, the institutionalized program, and the specific person who manifests abnormal behavior. Moreover, mental patients receive care in mental hospitals or clinics and services from a mental health "team," frequently led by a physician called a psychiatrist. Federal, state, and local governments continue to mount programs to "stamp out mental illness" by allocating funds to build institutions, train personnel, and support research within this medical-disease model. In our society, we hospitalize the mentally ill because we consider them "sick" and incapable of caring for themselves, in spite of the fact that no tangible disease has been demonstrated.

The disease model of psychopathology was adopted from physical medicine, where there is abundant evidence for the etiological link between organic pathology and physical symptoms. The model makes a leap of faith hoping that similar biophysical causes eventually will be connected to mental and behavioral symptoms. It assumes that the pathological process occurs *within* the organism, be it genetic, biophysical, or psychogenic in nature.

Genetic Model

From the time of Darwin and Galton, heredity has been acknowledged as an important determinant of both the biological and psychological make-up of people. The well-known nature-nurture controversy is as much a part of contemporary psychology as it was of psychology in the days of William James, although we have a better understanding of human genetics today than ever before. With regard to psychopathology, at least two positions have been posited: (1) the view that genetic factors are primary and sometimes exclusive determinants and that they are only minimally and superficially influenced by environmental forces; and (2) the more moderate notion that heredity disposes the person to act in certain ways but that these predispositions can be modified by learning and one's life experiences. However, in order to better understand these models, we need to digress a bit to consider some of the basic elements of genetics, and the research methods used to study the role of genetics in psychopathology.

Chromosomes and Genes. Chromosomes are long threadlike bodies that can be seen with the aid of an electron microscope in the nucleus of every human cell. Each cell contains twenty-three pairs or a total of forty-six chromosomes that can be studied by special techniques of photographic enlargements. Pictures of pairs of chromosomes are then arranged according to a prescribed order, known as *karyotype,* by which comparisons can be made with the karyotype of a standardized human cell. In this way chromosomal abnormalities can be identified.

All body cells reproduce by dividing into new cells with forty-six chromosomes in each. As the cell divides, each chromosome splits lengthwise down the middle, and each half moves to opposite sides of the cell. Later, when the cell divides down the center, each new cell is left with the same forty-six chromosomes that were included in the original cell. This process of body cell division is referred to as *mitosis.* In contrast, germ cells, which produce the sex cells (sperm and ova), undergo a different pattern of division in their final stage, known as *meiosis.* At this point, the number of chromosomes in each germ cell is reduced to twenty-three single chromosomes instead of twenty-three pairs. Thus, one member from each of the twenty-three pairs of chromosomes goes into either the new sperm or egg cell, and each parent contributes an equal number (twenty-three) of chromosomes to the fertilized ovum at the time of conception.

Genes are tiny bodies that are presumed to be arranged linearly by the thousands in each chromosome. They are thought to be the transmitters of heredity, although for many years little was actually known about them. As recently as 1953 the biochemical structure and the basis for its action was discovered (Watson and Crick, 1953), and not until 1969 was a single gene isolated (Shapiro et al., 1969). It now is known that genes are composed of a com-

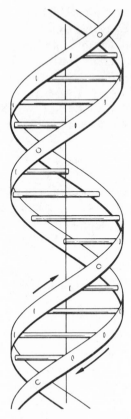

FIGURE 4–1 Diagrammatic representation of a double DNA molecule. The two ribbons symbolize the two phosphate-sugar chains, and the horizontal rods the pairs of bases holding the chains together. The vertical line marks the fiber axis. (From Watson and Crick, Molecular structure of nucleic acid, *Nature,* 171, 737–738, 1953. Reprinted with permission.)

plex chemical substance called *deoxyribonucleic acid* (DNA). Each DNA molecule consists of two chains (with five-carbon sugars) twisted around each other in the form of a helix that resembles a spiral ladder. The chains are linked by pairs of chemicals that appear much like rungs of the ladder. In every DNA molecule (see Figure 4–1) there are thousands of these chemical linkages or rungs. DNA has two primary functions, that of genetic replication from one generation to another and that of transferring information (genetic code). The coded information in a DNA molecule is transmitted to a single-stranded molecule known as *ribonucleic acid* (RNA) which then moves into the cytoplasm of the cell. Acting as a messenger, RNA initiates certain chemical reactions that eventually determine bodily structure and function.

Mendel's Laws of Genetic Transmission. Almost one hundred years before genes were experimentally confirmed, an Austrian monk by the name of Gregor Mendel hypothesized their existence through long and careful cross-fertilization studies of the garden pea. Working with red-flowering and white-flowering strains of peas, Mendel found that the offsprings were the same color in successive generations when plants of the same strain were paired, that is red with red, and white with white. He maintained that this inherited factor (later called a *gene*) was preserved and passed along from generation to generation unchanged. After he crossbred the two strains (red and white), he noted that the first offsprings were red. However, if he mated these offsprings, the next generation resulted in an average of three red to one white plant, suggesting that the inherited factor is evident in predictable proportions in such crossbreedings.

On the basis of studies of this sort, Mendel discovered the phenomena of dominance, recessiveness, and intermediate hybrid, and he formulated his now classic principles of genetic transmission. He said genes were found in pairs with each gene being either dominant or recessive. A gene is dominant when it determines the characteristic under the control of that pair of genes, whereas it is recessive when that characteristic will only be manifest if both genes of the pair are recessive. An intermediate hybrid refers to a compromise in the characteristic that may result from crossbreeding (a pink offspring from the pairing of red and white).

While much of Mendel's theorizing has been confirmed, geneticists recently have shown that human genetic transmission is more complex than his original view, and that there are many exceptions of Mendel's principles (Dobzhansky, 1962; Rosenthal, 1970, 1971). For many human characteristics, genes do not act on the basis of the simple dominant-recessive principles, but rather in numerous other ways. One gene of a pair may show only *partial dominance* over the other gene, in which case the manifest characteristic will be similar to the dominant version but less prominent or extreme than that produced by two dominant gene members of that pair. In addition, there are instances when a dominant gene fails to produce a trait 100 percent of the time, as one might expect. If the observable trait occurs less often and deviates from the perfect prediction generated from Mendelian principles, a condition known as *partial* or *incomplete penetrance* is said to exist. Moreover, many human traits are determined by complex combinations of gene pairs rather than by one pair. This is called *polygenic inheritance* and it is responsible for producing wide variations in a trait such as that often noted in the hair color or height of offsprings from the same set of parents.

Certainly, it would be easier to study the role of inheritance in determining abnormal behavior if human characteristics were as simple in their genetic features as those found by Mendel in his studies of the garden pea. However, heredity does not directly produce psychopathology in the sense that specific genes correspond to specific behavior abnormalities. Instead, genes should be thought of as providing the basic biological organization in which psychopathology can develop. Therefore, human genetics must concern itself with observable traits or *phenotypes* (the physical features and behavioral patterns of an individual), and it must be content for the present to make inferences about the genetic trait or *genotype* (the genetic potential of an individual) that may produce it.

Research Methods. Much of the early thinking about the role of heredity in abnormal behavior was stimulated by Darwin's theory of natural selection and by the work of his cousin, Francis Galton, who observed strong hereditary ties between the lineage of certain distinguished British families and some of the most intellectually outstanding Englishmen of that time. Even more celebrated and influential was Goddard's study of the Kallikak family (Goddard, 1912), which, like Galton's, used the *pedigree method* to show the role of heredity in determining abnormal behavior. Goddard studied the descendants of Martin Kallikak (a coded name for a soldier in the American Revolution War) who fathered children by two women, one mentally retarded and the other intellectually normal. Unwittingly, Kallikak had created a set of circumstances that was of potential scientific merit. The pairing of a normal father with both a normal and a mentally retarded mother made it possible to compare the offsprings from both unions with respect to the incidence of mental retardation and other abnormalities. Goddard traced the descendants from each union through suc-

cessive generations. He found that a large number of descendants of the retarded mother were feebleminded and manifested other forms of abnormal behavior, whereas all of the descendants of the normal mother were normal. Goddard used the data to support the conclusion that the observed abnormal behaviors were genetically transmitted by the retarded mother.

More explicitly, the pedigree method consists of tracing the incidence of a trait or phenotype in all family members over several generations in order to make inferences about the genotype and genetic principle involved. It is a naturalistic method in which data are dependent on selected and infrequent accidents of nature that are too unrepresentative of the general population to warrant firm conclusions. While pedigree studies are of limited value, they have the potential of uncovering tentative relationships that can be further explored by more rigorous and statistically adequate methods.

The *contingency* or *family-risk method* represents an improvement over pedigree studies because it uses large samples of relatives of index cases or probands (known carriers of the trait under investigation) to assess the degree to which the trait is related to blood ties, and to compare the incidence of the trait found in the experimental group with that noted in a sample drawn from the normal population. The greater the relationship between the trait and the closeness of blood ties (parents, siblings, and children as contrasted to uncles, nieces, and cousins), and the higher the incidence of the trait in the family group as compared to normal controls, the more convincing is the evidence for genetic transmission. Yet, caution must be exercised in drawing causal inferences from family-risk studies, because correlational data (the relationship between the incidence of a trait and heredity closeness) merely reflect a relationship between two variables and not cause and effect. It is quite possible that other unaccounted for variables, such as the environmental impact of being reared in a psychopathological home, may contribute significantly to the positive correlation obtained. Without proper control for environmental factors, the data from contingency studies cannot be regarded as unequivocal with respect to the influence of heredity on abnormal behavior.

The application of the essential ingredients of the contingency method to provide more precise genetic and potentially other controls is represented in the *twin study method*. This approach uses monozygotic (identical) twins who originate from the same fertilized ovum and have the same genotypes of genetic structure, and dizygotic (fraternal) twins who only have half of their genetic structure in common (much like ordinary siblings). A *concordance rate* is established by computing the percent of cases in which both members of a twin pair manifest the trait in question. When identical twins show a higher concordance rate for the trait than fraternal twins, we have presumptive evidence of a genetic influence. However, this is based on the assumption that identical twins and fraternal twins are exposed to the same environmental conditions, an assumption that has been seriously questioned and weakened with the observation that environmental influences are more similar for identical than for fraternal twins.

Although twin studies have been widely used and offer numerous advantages, the method is not without limitations. Mittler (1971) noted that errors of classifying are introduced that affect reliability, even when such sophisticated techniques are used as blood groupings and fingerprinting. More-

over, differences in identical twins that are assumed to be the result of environmental factors may be produced by gene mutations or chromosomal errors that occur during mitosis, or late in gestation. Finally, it should be emphasized that twin studies do not provide information about genetic transmission, but rather genetic influence that is inferred from concordance rates.

Adoption studies have been used as a control for the effect of environmental factors. One type of adoption study compares the incidence of a disorder in two groups of children who have been placed in presumably "normal" foster homes, but who differ in family genetics with regard to the disorder under study. More specifically, one group of children (the index cases) are the product of one biological parent who evidences the disorder, while the other group (the control cases) come from two biologically "normal" parents. If the incidence of the disorder is more common among the index cases than among the controls, then genetic transmission can be inferred. If, however, incidence rates are equal in both groups, the disorder can be attributed to factors other than genetics. While this method recognizes the importance of controlling for environmental influences, it nevertheless provides no certainty that the foster environment is "normal" or that one or more members of the foster family is not affected by some psychological disorder.

A more sophisticated adoption method is the *cross-fostering approach*. A group of children from biologically "normal" parents are placed in foster homes in which one or both of the adopted parents are affected by the disorder. They are compared with a group of children placed in "normal" foster homes whose (at least one) biological parents evidence the disorder. The incidence rates of the disorder found in the adoptees for each group are then used to reflect the relative potency of hereditary and environmental factors. This approach greatly reduces the confounding environmental factors found in most other methods.

More recently, researchers have favored the predictive studies involving the early identification of *high-risk* children (youngsters who have one biological parent manifesting the disorder but who have not themselves shown signs of the disturbance at the time of initial study) and *super high-risk* children (those with both biological parents affected by the disorder). This research strategy has been especially popular in studying schizophrenia (an adult psychotic condition) and includes the longitudinal assessment of the impact of environmental factors on children who are at risk for that disorder (Mednick and McNeill, 1968; Mednick, 1973; Hanson, Gottesman and Heston, 1976; Erlenmeyer-Kimling, 1976). This approach prospectively examines populations considered to be either *high-risk* or *super high-risk* to identify vulnerable persons at an early age in order to determine the characteristics that are associated with the development of the disorder and to establish preventive intervention.

Having reviewed the basic elements of human genetics and the research strategies that have been used, we can now return to the consideration of the two primary conceptual models: (1) the view that genetic factors are primary and exclusive determinants of abnormal behavior, and (2) the position that heredity predisposes the person to act in certain ways, but that these predispositions are modified by learning and one's life experiences.

Franz Kallman, a pioneer and significant contributor to the field of behavioral genetics, argues for the central role of heredity

in the development of various forms of abnormal behaviors.

. . . the importance of genetic elements in the organization of behavior patterns rests on the interdependence of organic structure and psychologic function throughout the life of the individual. There is no behavior without an organism, no organism without a genotype, and no physiologic adaptedness without continuous and integrated gene activity (Kallman, 1973, p. 25).

While crediting environmental forces as the coequal of heredity (after conception), Kallman downplayed its impact by restricting its effect to the limits established by the individual's genetic constitution. Whether it be through genetic transmission, enzymatic control, or mutative effects, it is a person's genetic composition and action that primarily determine whether normal or abnormal behaviors appear.

In contrast to this rather extreme view, there is a middle ground that seems more palatable to most behavioral scientists. One variant suggests that both inheritance and environment play an important explanatory role in accounting for individual differences found among people. Morphological differences in the form and structure of the organism's biological systems and in the psychological processes have a substantial hereditary basis.

Individual infants are endowed with far reaching anatomical distinctiveness; each has a distinctive endocrine system, and a highly distinctive nervous system; a highly distinctive brain. The same distinctiveness carries over into the sensory and biochemical realms, and into their individual psychologies. It is not surprising, therefore, that each individual upon reaching adulthood exhibits a distinctive pattern of likes and dislikes not only with respect to trivialities, but also with respect to what may be regarded the most important things in life (Williams, 1973, p. 35).

In this context, Williams calls attention to the importance of genetic factors, but also includes environmental influences. Accordingly, people are born with innate and distinctive biological characteristics that are modified by learning and everyday life experiences in different ways depending upon their genetic potentialities.

A· similar proposition is the view of genetic vulnerability in which psychopathology is manifested when innate biological characteristics interact with noxious environmental variables. Vulnerability is a predisposition that increases the risk of breakdown but doesn't assure its occurrence, unless the person lives in an unpleasant environment that prompts the learning of certain maladaptive behaviors (Mednick, Schulsinger, and Schulsinger, 1975, pp. 221–252). To a great extent, the idea of genetic vulnerability (also psychological and sociological vulnerability) has been bolstered by "risk" research, which encompasses both the predisposing factors that establish the person's adaptation threshold and the stress factors of life's experiences that combine with these inherited characteristics to produce abnormal behavior patterns (Garmezy, 1975, pp. 171–216).

At this point in time, few researchers in the field would deny the importance of the genetic-model and its great potential as an explanatory basis of psychopathology. However, the most reasonable position we can take is the one so clearly stated by Zubin.

We designate a disorder as genetic when we are still ignorant of its environmental parameters and vice versa. In most so-called genetic disorders, the hereditary component is necessary but not sufficient. It is the interaction of both hereditary and environmental factors that is both necessary and sufficient for producing a disorder (Zubin, 1972, p. 290).

The Biochemical Model

The biochemical model to some extent overlaps with the genetic model, where genes may be the precursors to the absence or excess of certain enzymes needed for normal mental functioning; where errors of metabolism are inherited; and where genetic vulnerability provides the basis for biochemical changes underlying abnormal behaviors (Kety, 1973, pp. 92–103; Zubin, 1969, pp. 281–309).

The search for biochemical agents as the etiological basis of mental illness, especially of schizophrenia, has had a long and elusive history. If virulent germs and toxins can cause physical diseases, it seems only reasonable to suppose that similar factors can cause diseases of the mind. In fact, much of the biochemical research on psychopathology can be characterized as a quest for a psychotoxic agent that is both necessary and sufficient to produce mental illness (Kety, 1969, pp. 155–171). Moreover, etiological research has tended to follow the various trends in medicine. For example, when bacteria were discovered to be the cause of some diseases, researchers suggested that bacteria in the person's intestinal flora produced a toxin that disrupted the central nervous system (Brill, 1969, pp. 114–154). When medical attention shifted to viruses, researchers sought a viral cause of mental illness. Similarly, the discovery of hereditary metabolic diseases prompted the search for some deficiency or aberration in biochemical pathways as the cause of abnormal behaviors (Kety, 1969, pp. 155–171). Recent advances in the fields of biochemistry and neuropharmacology have led to a number of hypotheses concerning the possible alterations in the metabolism of certain brain chemicals (neurochemicals). In the last ten years, considerable attention has focused on a particular group of naturally occurring neurochemical substances that are classified as *monoamines*. The three common ones that have been extensively studied are *serotonin, dopamine,* and *norepinephrine*. In order to understand the possible relationship of these compounds to psychopathological processes, it is necessary to discuss briefly their roles as *neurotransmitters* or mediators of neural communication in the central nervous system.

In the central nervous system, the basic functional unit is the *neuron* (nerve cell). Information is transferred in the brain through the interaction of neurons across specialized structures termed *synapses* (spaces between neurons) by chemical neurotransmitters such as dopamine (DA) and norepinephrine (NE) (Julien, 1975). This is schematically represented in Figures 4–2 and 4–3. Thus, any increase or decrease in action of these substances will affect neural communication, and ultimately behavior. Figure 4–2 illustrates the steps going from the synthesis of the neurotransmitter to its transmission. First, it is manufactured in the *cell body* of the neuron,[1] then transported down through the *axonal processes*,

and then packaged and stored in the axon *terminal* of the *presynaptic neuron* (the nerve cell actively releasing the neurotransmitter), where it is protected from destruction. Information is transmitted in a two-step process: (1) the *electrical stage* in which the information received by the presynaptic neuron (cell 1) is translated into an electrical nerve impulse that is carried down the axon to its terminal; and (2) the *chemical stage* in which upon reaching the terminal the nerve impulse causes the release of the neurotransmitter into the synaptic cleft, and on to an adjacent *postsynaptic* neuron (cell 2, the nerve cell receiving the information in the form of the neurotransmitter) (see Figure 4–3 which is an enlargement of the synaptic area shown in Figure 4–2). The transmitter activates specific sites termed *receptors* on the postsynaptic neuron, and then is released back into the synaptic cleft where it is either metabolized (degraded) or taken back up into the terminal of the presynaptic cell.

Recent advances in research techniques have made it possible to map pathways of neurons in the brain that are mediated by specific neurotransmitters (DA, NE, and serotonin), and have, therefore, changed the perspective regarding brain and behavior relations. Formerly, the focus was on the isolation of particular areas or loci in the brain controlling specific functions (such as eating, sleeping, and aggressive behaviors). The current emphasis is on identifying conduction systems (of neurons) as mediators of behavior.

Now that we have considered the function of the monoamines as neurotransmitters, let us examine some of the evidence linking these compounds to abnormal behavior, more specifically to schizophrenia, since recent research has focused its attention on this disorder. A current biochem-

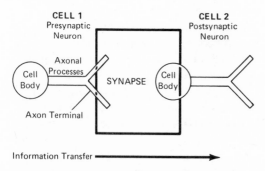

FIGURE 4–2   Neuronal communication

[1] According to Goldfarb and Wilk (1976) much of the synthesis occurs within the presynaptic terminal as well.

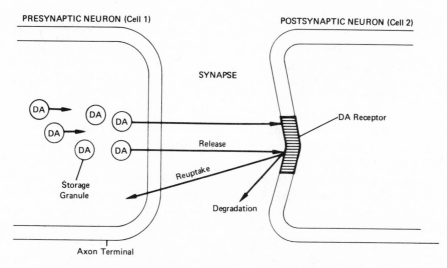

FIGURE 4–3 Synaptic transmission in the dopaminergic (DA) neuron

ical view suggests that this disorder results from an imbalance of monoamines, in particular NE and DA. The hypothesis has received substantial support from a variety of research findings that initially note a clinical resemblance between amphetamine psychosis and paranoid schizophrenia. Amphetamine, a central nervous system stimulant drug, when used at *high* doses with normal subjects for long periods of time, produces a behavioral syndrome that mimics schizophrenia and includes stereotypies, compulsive grooming, scanning, heightened fear and anxiety, suspiciousness, delusions, and hallucinations. In contrast, the administration of amphetamine in *low* doses (too low to produce psychotic symptoms in normals) to schizophrenic subjects exacerbates their symptoms (West, 1974; Snyder et al., 1974; Davis, 1974). It has also been shown that amphetamine acts at the biochemical level by enhancing the release and preventing the reuptake of DA and NE at the central nerve terminals (Groves & Rebec, 1976). These actions serve to in-

crease the amounts of DA and NE in the synapse, and thus ultimately to raise the activity of these neurotransmitters in the brain. Antipsychotic drugs such as chloropromazine and haloperidol used to treat schizophrenics or as antidotes to amphetamine psychosis act as DA and NE receptor blockers, which serve to diminish the effects of these neurotransmitters in the central nervous system (Snyder et al., 1974). Finally, elevated levels of DA or NE metabolites have been found in the urine of schizophrenic patients during periods of severe symptomatology (Arieti and Brody, 1974). Thus, based on the evidence of the biochemical model of amphetamine psychosis, along with pharmacological data strongly suggestive of disordered monoamine metabolism, in the case of schizophrenia, there is a strong link between biochemistry and behavior. In the area of childhood psychopathology, there are data associating altered monoamine levels in disorders such as hyperactivity and childhood psychosis (Ritvo, 1975; Coleman, 1973). For example, amphetamine (or a derivative) is used to effectively control hyperactive children, suggesting a similar neurochemical action as described for schizophrenia in adults.

The biochemistry of psychopathology is a highly complex and technical area of research fraught with methodological problems that are most difficult to resolve. It often rests on the questionable assumption that descriptive differences in peripheral measures (such as blood levels of monoamines) have etiological implications for underlying central brain mechanisms. Typical studies have attempted to correlate specific symptomatology with biological and/or physiological findings (Boulton, 1971), while ethical considerations have prevented more direct experimental approaches with humans. Research has also been hampered by poor diagnostic agreement about what constitutes a given disorder, and by subject variables that are contaminated by the consequences of mental illness, such as diet, prior treatment, long-term hospitalization, recent stressful experiences, and level of physical activity (Chassen, 1967; Kety, 1960, pp. 120–145; Klerman, 1971; Selye, 1974; Kety, 1969). In sum, any proposed relationship between biochemical changes in the metabolism of neurotransmitters of the brain and certain observable behaviors or subjective experiences requires, at least at this time, a "leap" from chemistry to behavior without sufficient direct evidence to make the journey valid (Mendels and Frazier, 1974).

Despite these methodological limitations and the promising indication that neurotransmitter aberrations in the central nervous system are associated with some of the more severe forms of abnormal behavior, the search for a causal biochemical factor continues. Yet, mental disorders are complex psychobiological phenomena that are no more likely to have a single cause than are such traits as weight, personality, and intelligence.

Neurophysiological Model

This model assumes that the etiology of abnormal behavior resides in brain pathology that is either inherited, congenital, or acquired. It maintains that normal cognitive and behavioral functioning depend on the anatomical and physiological integrity of the brain, and that defects, insults, or damage that violate this important organ provide the physical basis for disordered thinking and behavior. To a great extent, the model overlaps with both the genetic and biochemical views, since it acknowledges the crucial role of genetic transmission or aberrations, as well as metabolic and biochemical changes in affecting brain function. But, the neurophysiological model is broader and in some ways more general than the others, because it also includes a wider array of etiological agents such as congenital anomalies, acquired intrauterine aberrations or diseases, Rh incompatibilities, prenatal effects of X-irradiation and drugs, toxemias of pregnancy, premature births, and traumatic brain insults during or after birth. The relationship between any of these events and the emergence of abnormal behaviors is often correlational and not indicative of cause and effect. Even when a causal link is more evident, knowledge of the specific details bridging the aberrant brain structure or function to behaviors is, as yet, far from complete.

Research Methods. 1. Brain lesions produced by cooling, radiation, electrolysis, or chemical means, and the ablation of brain tissue have been used to study the effects of brain damage on behavior. For therapeutic purposes, lesions have been produced in humans (epilepsy), but, for obvious ethical reasons, creating lesions is precluded as an investigative tool. Thus, animals have been frequently used on the grounds that the data obtained would be applicable to humans. The general procedure involves the lesioning or excising of a specific brain area followed by an examination of the associated behavioral effects. Later, the animal is sacrificed, and a post-mortem study of the tissue (histology) is done to verify the lesion sites. For example, Nauta (1972) found that monkeys with bilateral lesions of the frontal lobes showed many of the perceptual and memory deficits noted in humans with similar areas of destruction.

2. Electrical stimulation of the human brain has been used as both a therapeutic measure and an investigative device to study brain mechanisms and functions in relation to abnormal behaviors (Delgado, 1969). By actually triggering seizures through the stimulation of appropriate brain areas, Delgado has been able to localize the sources of epileptic seizures. In addition, he uses the electrical implants to monitor brain activity as it correlates with human behavior. There are, of course, a number of ethical issues related to the use of electrical stimulation in humans: experimental control rather than therapy; destruction of tissue along the path of the implant; and the high intensity of stimulation used that is many orders of magnitude greater than that which would naturally occur in the brain. As Vaughan (1969) points out:

The sometimes dramatic effects of cortical stimulation in many have led many to impute to it a precision and specificity justified neither by the necessarily limited human observations nor by the more detailed parametric studies in experimental animals. Since the manifestations of cortical stimulation may be drastically modified by alterations in stimulus parameters or by prior stimulation, conclusions concerning the functional specificity of any brain region based primarily upon the results of stimulation must be viewed with caution. (Vaughan, 1969, p. 67).

3. The electroencephalogram (EEG) is an instrument used to record electrical activity of the brain by means of electrodes attached to the scalp. With the aid of EEG tracings, researchers have for more than fifty years tried to differentiate mental patients from normals and to obtain information about the reactivity of the central nervous system of disordered persons. Unfortunately, the EEG has not proved useful in diagnosing most psychiatric conditions, although it has been effective in identifying epilepsy and organic brain lesions, and in diagnosing those hyperactive children who respond well to stimulant medication (Goldstein and Sugarman, 1969; Satterfield, Cantwell, and Satterfield, 1974). However, the usefulness of the EEG as an analytic tool is limited by the lack of understanding of its cause and significance for *normal* brain function.

4. Increased technical sophistication has made it possible to use the EEG to measure cerebral responses evoked (*evoked potential*) by sensory stimulation, such as flashes of light, electric shock, or auditory clicks. These evoked responses have been found to be associated with a wide range of psychopathology, although very little specificity in the response characteristics has been evident thus far (Shagass and Straumanis, 1969.) The methodological problems of this approach include the difficulty in obtaining an adequate baseline by which to measure electrophysiological changes resulting from stimulus presentations, and the difficulty in removing all sources of extraneous electrical activity coming from ei-

ther the subject (muscle activity) or outside sources such as the equipment itself.

5. A relatively recent and complicated type of cortical response that has been associated with attention is called the *contingent negative variation* (CNV). It is marked by a slow rise in negative potential when the subject anticipates the presentation of a stimulus, but it is not evident when the subject is unaware that the stimulus will occur (Walter, 1975). The procedure consists of instructing the subject to perform a response (press a bar) when a particular stimulus such as an auditory click is presented (S2). However, prior to the presentation of S2, another stimulus (S1) such as a light flash is presented much like the arrangement found in classical conditioning. When S1 is presented, the subject's EEG tracings show a slow negative shift in potential until the S2 appears. In other words, the subject's brain surface becomes increasingly negative after S1 is presented, and this cortical response serves as an indication that the person is attentive and anticipating the presentation of S2. Thus, CNV can be thought of as reflecting a transitory state of increased arousal that is terminated after the response to the imperative stimulus (S2) is made (Beatty, 1975). The technique has revealed CNV differences in children with learning disabilities, and it is being used currently in the study of psychotic children to reveal impairment in the central nervous system that underlies such mental processes as attention, expectation, and motivation (Cohen, Offner, and Palmer, 1967; Small, DeMyer, and Milstein, 1971).

6. Peripheral measures of the autonomic nervous system also have been used to make inferences about mental activity. One such index, skin conductance (GSR), measures the change in skin resistance resulting from alterations in sweat-gland activity, which is thought to indicate arousal or emotionality. Mednick and Schulsinger (1968) looked at skin conductance in children of schizophrenic mothers and found that the skin conductance response is predictive of later schizophrenia. More recently, Venables (1977) reported some early results from an ongoing large-scale longitudinal study of approximately 1800 three-year-old children living in two representative communities on the island of Mauritius. This study differs from earlier high risk ones in that it includes children of various racial backgrounds, it defines risk as not based on genetic variables but determined *solely* by abnormal electrodermal responsivity. The initial assessment carried out in 1973 included behavioral observations of play and mother-child interactions, and psychophysiological measurements of skin conductance, EEG, and heart rate. Venables found two abnormal GSR groups, hyper- and hypo- responders, and he was able to identify some children who showed the same hyper- responsive pattern of skin conductance as that manifested by high-risk children who later became schizophrenic. Only time will tell whether the hyper- responders in Venables' sample will later develop psychopathology; but, for now, he believes that the skin conductance measure reflects the underlying neural impairment of attention found in schizophrenia.

At present, neurophysiological methods used to examine the etiology and course of psychopathology are hindered by problems of diagnostic inaccuracies, confounding effects of institutionalization and medication, and the incomplete understanding of the intricacies of the human brain. Indeed we probably are less knowledgeable about neurophysiological factors and their implications for abnormal behaviors than we are about the variables associated with either the genetic or biochemical models.

Psychoanalytic Model
(Intrapsychic Views)

Fashioned and modified over forty years by Sigmund Freud, the psychoanalytic model is perhaps the most complete of the medical models so far discussed. While it has attracted both ardent and unshakable supporters as well as severe critics, few would question its profound influence on the fields of personality and psychopathology. In its simplest form, Freud's theory rests on two essential assumptions: *psychic determinism* and *the unconscious.*

Freud believed that every human act, whether it is directly observable such as a smile or only noted through self-report such as a fantasy, occurs as a function of prior mental events and not as a matter of happenstance. Previous events and experiences (both internal and external of the organism) determine all facets of a person's behavior. Therefore, one of Freud's major tasks consisted of trying to find and then eliminate the psychic determinants of abnormal behaviors.

The other cornerstone of psychoanalytic thinking is the unconscious, an inference made early by Freud to explain the thoughts, wishes, memories, information, and experiences of which his neurotic patients were unaware (Hogan, 1976). He proposed that people banish (repress) unpleasant experiences and unacceptable feelings from consciousness because of their threatening nature. In addition, he suggested that the unconscious contains memories of pre-verbal infantile experiences and informally acquired information that are almost impossible to recover. Similar memory difficulties are encountered with repressed (emotionally charged) material, because the person has learned to use a variety of psychological defenses to prevent it from becoming conscious. Freud also proposed another level of accessibility, called the *preconscious,* to account for mental content that was presently unavailable to the person, but which could be readily brought into awareness. Recognizing the difficulty in obtaining direct evidence to demonstrate the unconscious (since we can only know about the material after it has been transformed into consciousness), he nevertheless argued for proof of its existence through inferences made from other behaviors such as slips of the tongue, misplacing of objects, jokes, neurotic symptoms, recurrent patterns that lead to negative consequences, or excessive protestations. He used the technique of free association as a way of uncovering unconscious material. He interpreted lateness and missed appointments as signs of unconscious resistance to treatment, and focused on the hidden (latent) content of dreams to understand the unconscious.

Anxiety plays a central role in Freud's theoretical view. It may arise from fear of the real dangers in the external world, fear of punishment for the expression of libidinal drives, and from feelings of guilt about acting in ways that are discrepant with the values of society and the family (Hogan, 1976). Anxiety, therefore, is a tension state determined by external factors that serves as a danger signal and as a motivator to reduce the tension through such acts as withdrawing from a dangerous situation, inhibiting an unacceptable impulse, or following a moralistic course. The responsibility for coping with anxiety resides with the ego, which utilizes a variety of defense mechanisms for this purpose. All people, both normal and abnormal, use defenses to reduce anxiety, although the abnormal personality relies heavily on a smaller repertoire of defenses than the healthy personality. Table 4–1 presents some of the major defense mechanisms described by Freud.

In his paper, "Neurosis and Psychosis"

TABLE 4–1 Defense Mechanisms and Their Descriptive Characteristics

Defense	*Description*
Repression:	The process by which the ego bars anxiety-producing memories, ideas, or perceptions from consciousness.
Denial:	Similar to repression, it is the unconscious act of simply denying the existence of painful facts or feelings. Denial enables the individual to avoid anxiety by refusing to admit the truth.
Reaction formation:	The process by which the ego substitutes actions and feelings directly opposite to those that might be produced by sexual or aggressive impulses. A reaction formation masks threatening feelings.
Displacement:	The transfer of instinctual emotions from one object to another. Displacement permits the release of tensions in a manner that is less anxiety producing, for example, by kicking the wall instead of one's mother.
Sublimation:	A way of expressing unacceptable impulses in an acceptable manner. Sublimation channels ego-threatening drives into constructive outlets such as art and science.
Rationalization:	The process of avoiding anxiety by finding justifiable excuses for doing something unacceptable. Rationalization helps the ego maintain self-respect.
Intellectualization:	Similar to rationalization, it is the process of concealing threatening feelings by discussing them in an abstract, intellectual manner.
Projection:	The unconscious act of blaming others or attributing one's faults to others. Projection frees the ego from taking responsibility for faulty actions or traits.
Regression:	A method of dealing with external or internal conflicts by retreating to an immature stage of development. A threatened individual will regress to behaviors that provided comfort in the past.

(Freud, 1959), Freud discussed the relationship between the ego and the id that gives rise to the abnormal behaviors characteristic of neurosis, and the failure of the ego to deal with the environment (the outer world) that results in the loss of reality and psychosis. More specifically, he viewed neurosis as arising from the ego's rejection (through repression) of the expression of an instinctual impulse. The repressed impulse persists in seeking expression until it finds a substitutive way of gratification (a symptom) that the ego is unable to control. However, this maneuver threatens the integrity of the ego, and the ego fights back against the symptom as it had previously struggled to prevent the expression of the original impulse. This intrapsychic conflict between the ego and the id represents the essential basis of the clinical manifestations

of a neurosis (a more extensive discussion of the psychoanalytic view of neurosis is presented in Chapter 11).

In contrast, Freud saw psychosis as originating in the ego's inability to cope with the demands of the outside world, and creating instead a world of its own, a world that is less threatening, more gratifying of primitive impulses, but quite removed from reality. In a psychosis, reality (the outer world) is replaced by the new world the ego has substituted for it.

Freud's view of human existence is a rather pessimistic one, full of tension and conflicts that at best only can be temporarily reduced and resolved (Hogan, 1976). Both past and present problems contribute to continued discomfort. Difficulties encountered in handling the various stages of psychosexual development lead to enduring personality traits and to immature and inappropriate sources of libidinal gratification that heighten anxiety and prevent attempts to find more mature ways of obtaining satisfaction. Weak ego development or an excessively strict superego, for example, also increase the likelihood of intrapsychic conflict requiring too much psychic energy to resolve and still deal effectively with reality. Present day-to-day living is hardly possible without tension and intrapsychic conflict. These arise from the organism's demand for instinctual gratification on the one hand, and society's many restrictions and prohibitions against libidinal satisfaction on the other. The struggle between the id seeking immediate gratification and the superego striving for moralistic and ideal behavior is ever present. Therefore, Freud believed that most people are somewhat neurotic and that psychological health is not the average state but rather an ideal one.

Despite the creative and insightful nature of Freud's thinking and the significant influence his contributions have had, psychoanalytic theory has not enjoyed empirical support. The theory's inclusiveness and generality along with its substantial number of interacting components make it impossible to test with the research methods presently available (Sarason, 1966). Apart from the matter of validity, the theory has more recently been criticized on the grounds that Freud was an antifeminist (reflecting the attitude of his time) who viewed women as morally and intellectually inferior to men (Hogan, 1976).

Other Intrapsychic Views

We noted earlier that some of Freud's followers voiced strong opposition to certain aspects of his psychoanalytic theory.

Eventually, this prompted them to develop positions of their own. Carl Jung, the first to break with Freud, constructed a complicated and somewhat mystical system. In it he rejected Freud's emphasis on sex as the primary source of libidinal energy, and his emphasis on the crucial role of the first five years in personality development (Jung, 1964). Jung proposed a distinction between extroverted and introverted personalities and introduced the concept of the collective unconscious which, in addition to the personal unconscious (storehouse of the individual's past experiences forgotten or repressed), he viewed as a storehouse of innate memories of human beings' shared experiences throughout history. He used the collective unconscious and the ideas that people everywhere share a common set of instincts as well as universal developmental patterns to account for the similarities found among people of different cultures.

Dissatisfied with Freud's attention to sexual instincts and his biological orientation, Alfred Adler stressed environmental and social forces as important determinants of behavior. He conceived of healthy people as social animals who were motivated by the need to meet their communal obligations, love others, and fulfill their work objectives. He attributed abnormal behaviors to inferiority feelings (inferiority complex) that arise from the person's real or imagined failure to achieve self-fulfillment and self-actualization. Harry Stack Sullivan, a more recent dissident, viewed disordered interpersonal relationships as the primary source of internalized anxiety which produced aberrant behaviors. Whatever modifications these or other dissenters introduced, they all assumed, as did Freud, that the etiological origin of abnormal behaviors stems from internal conflicts (intrapsychic) associated with early childhood experiences.

Critique of Medical Models

A major critic of the disease model, especially to the idea that biophysical defects cause mental disorders, has been Thomas Szasz (1960). He argued that a disease of the brain is a defect in the nervous system and should be labeled as such. Moreover, disease should not be used as a causal explanation for problems in living or for what beliefs a person embraces, be they political, religious, or delusional. Szasz noted that the term *mental illness* is widely accepted as referring to deviations from psychosocial, ethical, and legal norms, and that this connotes something quite different from a brain disease. Yet, these deviations are claimed (by the model) to be remediable through medical action, an illogical intervention to alleviate problems that are defined by nonmedical criteria. The disease concept of abnormal behaviors, according to Szasz, has outlived its usefulness, and it functions as a myth to obscure the real struggles of human existence and the conflicts in needs, values, and goals that are inherent in day-to-day living.

Other critics of the disease model prefer *failure of human adaptation* to mental illness, since empirical evidence is not readily available to support a disease concept (Draguns and Phillips, 1971). There have been relatively few diseases identified as the basis of abnormal behaviors (general paresis, phenylketonuria, Tay-Sachs disease are examples) despite almost a century of searching, and these usually have become part of the field of medicine and are excluded from the domain of psychology. While some of the more extreme and less frequent disorders of childhood may have their etiological origins in biophysical factors, it is doubtful that the disease model will prove fruitful in accounting for or dealing with the vast majority of abnormal behaviors found in children today.

Environmental Models

The basic reason for separately classifying medical-disease models and environmental models rests on the markedly different etiological assumptions made by each. Instead of searching for causal factors within the organism as the medical views are prone to do, the environmental models focus almost exclusively on *external* variables (sociocultural and psychological) as the primary determinants of abnormal behaviors. But, the consistency of these broad categories may appear marred by the persistence of some environmental models in considering aberrant behaviors as diseases in spite of the fact that the analogy of pathogens (between neurophysiological defects and problems in living) is faulty (Szasz, 1960).

Whether they ignore or acknowledge the innate and biological characteristics of the individual, researchers and theorists within the environmental camp believe in the potency of cultural mores, social systems, economic influences, and unique life experiences in shaping (through the learning process) personality patterns. In choosing another etiological orientation, they tend to explore different variables with different investigative tools and designs, and to look for remedial and preventive solutions that are primarily consonant with the very causal factors they emphasize. In the section that follows, we shall examine a sample of these views to provide a sense of what these models are like.

Sociocultural Models

These models emphasize the importance of culture and social systems as determinants of human behavior. They study the effect of such global and pervasive variables as the family, race, socio-economic levels, rural versus urban living, religious affiliation, and cultural attitudes on personality development, while often making inferences from correlational data. Sociocultural models tend to oversimplify complicated relationships, since they are prone to deal in broad generalities or in incomplete analysis of specific variables. Yet, there are few who would discount their contributions in highlighting the important role played by sociocultural factors in personality development.

Both Emile Durkheim, a French sociologist, and George H. Mead, an American philosopher, pioneered the view that society precedes the individual in the sense that people are born into a society that controls, molds, and gives form and meaning to their existence (Hogan, 1976). People do not create societies (although they may be instrumental in bringing about changes in them), but rather, cultures exist as greater and more powerful forces than humans. For example, this is evidenced by the predictable impact of social class on so many important aspects of human life, ranging from one's attire, physical appearance and mannerisms, language, how much and what kind of education one receives, the nature of child-rearing practices, type and adequacy of diet, and religious affiliation, to the standards governing one's moral, sexual, and interpersonal behaviors, among others. According to Durkheim, children internalize the social standards of a society in three stages of development: (1) learning to respect the social rules, (2) becoming a member of and identifying with several subgroups of that society (family, peer groups, religious group, a team, or a club), and (3) behaving independently in accordance with the society's rules.

Durkheim also introduced a concept, which he called *anomie,* to refer to a breakdown of a society's regulatory machinery, wherein the socially defined standards of conduct no longer serve as effective guidelines for behavior (Merton, 1964, pp. 213–242). Anomie occurs when (1) social norms are no longer commonly shared by members of the society, (2) there is a decline in the application of sanctions against violations of these standards, or (3) members of the society are not morally obligated to conform to them. It is manifest in periods of social disorganization and change, and when members of a society have limited access to valued goals as illustrated in the struggle of the poor to acquire material wealth. It also occurs when alternative social norms are simultaneously present, as in the case of subcultural groups living side by side, or during the acculturation of second generation Americans.

Anomie is associated with psychopathology in that it is a source of alienation and is characterized by anxiety, uncertainty, insecurity, lowered self-esteem, identity confusion, and a sense of impotence about acting in effective ways. There is evidence suggesting that alienation in our society is a growing problem that is closely related to personality disorganization, acts of violence, and a rising crime rate (Sager, 1968). During recent years, our society has seen a great deal of alienation, largely in adolescents who have attempted to resolve conflicts with their families and society through membership in a drug, school drop-out, or some other "antiestablishment" group. While new group membership may satisfy strong needs for acceptance—affiliation, security, and self-worth—it may also serve to reinforce behaviors that are maladaptive.

The anomie associated with acculturation is particularly noteworthy since American society has grown as a melting pot of cultures and since it is currently struggling to be more aware of the needs and problems of minority groups. *Acculturation* refers to the transition made by members of one culture as they assume membership in another culture. It involves the *stress* of forsaking one's heritage at the risk of damaging the integrity of the personalities involved (Lehmer, 1969). Similarly, although more subtle, acculturation takes place within a large and complex culture (such as ours) that includes many different subcultures. For example, middle-class Americans place a high value on achievement and competition, and they view as "culturally deprived" minority groups who don't share these values. They tend to disregard the values of minority subcultures and place their members in institutions that are structured to meet middle-class values. The Navajo child, whose subculture encourages cooperation and frowns on competition, or the black ghetto child, whose culture conveys the difficulty and futility of academic achievement, will not only perform poorly in middle-class public schools, but also will be pressed to attain standards that are not highly valued by their own subculture. Under these circumstances, the majority subculture threatens the survival of other subcultures which hold discrepant values. If minority children hold onto their heritage, they are likely to experience failure in school along with deprecation and alienation from the dominant society. If, on the other hand, they abandon their old cultural values for middle-class ones, they run the risk of alienation and rejection from their own subculture without being assured of membership in the new culture. Societies or individuals in transition from one culture to another increase the probability of behavioral disorders, because the traditional bonds of practices and values that hold families and communities together are disrupted (Wittkower and Fried, 1958).

Tangential but tempting evidence comes from studies of second-generation American children born to immigrant parents in which their conflict over the rejection of old-world cultural practices are described (Thomas and Znaniecki, 1958). Immigrant parents maintain their stability and security by holding onto their roots and old values, while their youngsters increase their instability by rejecting the old values as they struggle to obtain membership in a new culture. In studying the extent of the immigrant's alienation from the American culture and its relationship to abnormal behavior, research showed that persons living in areas isolated from their ethnic group had a higher rate of behavior disorders than people who were members of the dominant ethnic group (Durham, 1961).

While the sociocultural perspective calls attention to important variables affecting human behavior, it is limited by its almost total emphasis on environmental forces to the exclusion of the internal characteristics of individuals (biology, motivation, and mental processes) (Hogan, 1976). Moreover, Durkheim and other sociologists build their view on the erroneous assumption that society precedes and is independent of people, even though a social structure does not or cannot exist without people. The sociocultural position does not account for individual differences or attend sufficiently to the human's capacity to think and act in a social context.

The possibility of new life and increased access to data for the sociocultural models comes from the field of *community mental health,* which bears such diverse and almost indistinguishable labels as community psychiatry, community psychology, social psychiatry, comprehensive mental health, and a host of others. Its major thrust in this country has been on certain socially oriented types of psychiatric and psychological practice. In addition, the techniques and theories of behavioral sciences are used to investigate sociocultural variables and to modify the existing body of literature in these areas (Sabshin, 1973, pp. 386–394).

On the basis of experimental programs developed within several comprehensive mental-health services that markedly reduced their caseload of chronic psychotics, Gruenberg constructed an interesting sociocultural model (Gruenberg, 1973, pp. 399–403). He used the term *social breakdown syndrome* (S.B.S.) to describe

. . . the deterioration in social functioning associated with mental disorders which can be prevented both by less harmful responses to those disorders and by changed community attitudes toward the mentally ill and their treatment (Gruenberg, 1973, p. 400).

There are seven steps in the development of S.B.S., beginning with the transient experiences everyone encounters, namely, the discrepancy between what one can do and what one is expected to do. Failure to meet these expectations, especially when they persist and the failure is recognized both by self and others, results in self-doubt and increased uncertainty. Actions initiated to meet the demands of the situation are usually unsatisfactory, and the person reacts with feelings of being misunderstood and of anger. These actions and reactions eventually lead to social exclusion or withdrawal, and then to some vague or specific labeling to the effect that the person is crazy, mentally ill, or psychotic. The labeling results in admission to the mental hospital where the environment fosters the further development of S.B.S. Institutionalization brings with it compliance to the hospital's rules and isolation from family and community. In the end, the patient identifies with other patients, and the patient's capacity to cope with ordinary social interactions and work tasks deteriorates (from disuse). Gruenberg claims that planned in-

tervention and prevention of S.B.S. can be instituted through knowledge of countermeasures specific to these developing steps.

Learning Models

In contrast to the medical-disease models, the learning approach optimistically views both normal and abnormal behaviors as primarily determined by learning, and, in turn, modifiable through the appropriate application of learning principles. Thus, abnormal behaviors are learned maladaptive responses that can be either eliminated or altered in favor of more adaptive ones, without having to make any additional assumption about an underlying disease process. In general, learning models reject the Freudian notion of the unconscious and its emphasis on symbolism in psychopathology, and the medical position of disease entities in preference to the parsimonious idea that aberrant behavior is either a failure to learn a response or the acquisition of a maladaptive response. Since we already have described (see Chapter 3) some of the basic principles, paradigms, and theoretical positions of learning, we shall in the following discussion illustrate how these same principles apply to the formation of abnormal behaviors.

In their effort to translate psychoanalytic theory into learning terms, Dollard and Miller (1950) described a neurosis as originating from an approach-avoidance conflict, that is, a conflict between two or more strong drives that create internal tension and produce responses that are incompatible. A conflict of this sort is illustrated by a person's strong need for sexual expression with a person of the opposite sex (approach), on the one hand, which is opposed by the person's fear of making overt sexual advances (avoidance), on the other hand. During development, children are required to learn socially acceptable outlets for their drives, especially those that are associated with eating, toilet training, and sexual and aggressive behaviors. As children seek expression of these drives, they are likely, at least on some occasions, to be punished for the responses (aggressive behavior toward parents likely will mean punishment by parents). Dollard and Miller have shown in animal studies that punishment leads to the emergence of fear as a learned drive. Moreover, fear can be conditioned as a response to a previously neutral stimulus, which then takes on the properties of a drive stimulus. In this way, it is possible for the same stimulus to elicit both the original drive and the learned fear drive.

In neurosis, the individual is unable to reduce the tension of the conflicting drives, but continually seeks responses that tend to reduce his or her suffering (subjective state of *misery*). Any response (symptom) that successfully reduces neurotic misery is reinforced, although it is not likely to solve the original conflict. Each successive reinforcement of the symptom increases the probability of its occurrence and strengthens it as a learned habit. For example, Dollard and Miller considered phobias (intense and persistent fears) as learned avoidance responses that are reinforced by the reduction in the strength of the fear drive. Although the original stimulus of the fear is frequently obscured in childhood conflicts over sexual and aggressive impulses (á la Freud), the intense fears transfer to new cues through stimulus generalization, higher order conditioning, and response-mediated generalization. Phobias persist because those affected usually manage to avoid the phobic situation with behaviors (withdrawal and avoidance) that reduce the fear but do not

resolve the basic and underlying conflict (intrapsychic conflict).

While Dollard and Miller's innovative effort brought new respectability for psychoanalytic theory within the camp of empirically minded psychologists, and admiration from clinically oriented ones for making learning theory relevant to "real" human problems, it also stimulated its share of criticisms. Objectors to the theory noted that it considered an extremely limited range of animal and human behaviors, and that it treated clinical phenomena with no more rigor than the way psychoanalysis used them. In addition, the theory's exclusive reliance on drive reduction as a reward mechanism for learning fails to deal effectively with the complexities of most clinical phenomena (Rapaport, 1953). Nevertheless, Dollard and Miller's theoretical model marked the first approximation in a series of subsequent learning formulations attempting to account for and understand human social behavior (including maladaptive behaviors).

According to the social-learning view of Julian Rotter, abnormal behaviors are "learned" and "thus maintained because the individual has a relatively high expectancy that such behavior will lead to a reinforcement of value (or avoid or reduce some potential punishment)" (Rotter, Chance, and Phares, 1972, p. 441). Moreover, most abnormal behaviors can be thought of as avoidance behaviors attributable to expectations of punishment or low expectancies of achieving important reinforcements. For example, if a youngster places a high value on athletic success but expects that he or she will not achieve this end, then the youngster is likely to employ avoidance behaviors or symptoms such as withdrawal from peer relations (especially those involving opportunities for athletics). The avoidant behavior eventually leads to the youngster's failure to develop competency which, in turn, tends to facilitate the development of other deviant behaviors. Withdrawal behavior precludes practice opportunities that could increase the youngster's athletic competence, and, instead, may lead to excessive and unrealistic fantasy activities about his or her extraordinary athletic prowess.

Another possible consequence of high need value may result in the person distorting reality or in his or her failure to make appropriate discriminations among social situations. If a need is excessive, every occasion becomes an opportunity for its attainment without regard for the propriety of the situation. Behavior, under these circumstances, is likely to be inappropriate and to elicit negative reactions from others, which, in the end, will lower the person's expectations about receiving the rewards.

With regard to other aspects of abnormal behavior, Rotter's theory "substitutes either low expectancy for success or high expectancy for failure" (Rotter et al., 1972, p. 447) for what is clinically considered anxiety. In addition, it rejects the dichotomy between neurosis and psychosis implied in the Kraepelinian classification system, and it attempts to deal specifically with certain forms of abnormal behavior, such as obsessions, compulsions, depressive reactions, and hypochondriacal behavior (frequent somatic complaints).

Bandura's social-learning view relies heavily on instrumental conditioning and imitation learning in arguing that abnormal response patterns are learned and maintained by a faulty conditioning history (Bandura, 1968, pp. 293–344). In some instances, the faulty prior learning involves a "behavioral deficit" in which there is a failure to acquire adequate responses that would enable the person to cope effectively with the demands of the environment. The failure to learn the requisite skills arises from inadequate modeling and reinforcements. The failure may lead to further adverse affects of impoverished performance, because insufficient rewards are given for the skills the individual has, while, at the same time, the behavioral deficit is negatively reinforced. Bandura suggests that the low levels of responsiveness of psychotic children and adults are manifestations resulting from behavioral deficits of this sort.

Deviant response patterns also may be attributable to the failure "to respond discriminately to important stimuli" (Bandura, 1968, p. 299) in people who possess "normal" responses in their repertoires. In the course of development, children learn to differentially respond to stimuli in terms of the consequences that are associated with particular stimuli. For example, they may consistently receive approval (reinforcement) for shedding their clothes at bath or bedtime and consistently receive disapproval (punishment) for undressing at other times. By introducing the discriminable stimuli and the different schedules of reinforcement, the behavior of undressing is brought under stimulus control. Through faulty training or a disruption of previously acquired discriminative responses, behaviors that are inappropriate to the situation may occur. Deviant (abnormal) responses of this sort are evident in psychotic individuals in the form of inappropriate or impoverished affect, delusions, and cognitive dysfunction.

In addition, deviant behaviors may arise when inappropriate stimuli acquire the capacity to produce intense emotional responses. "If a formerly ineffective conditioned stimulus occurs in conjunction with another stimulus which is capable of eliciting unpleasant autonomic responses, the former stimulus itself gradually acquires the power to evoke the same aversive emotional response pattern" (Bandura, 1968, p. 303). These deviant behaviors are manifested as somatic complaints and in psychophysiological disorders (see Chapter 11) such as asthma, ulcers, and hypertension. In addition, conditioned emotional reactions of phobias and other avoidance patterns are acquired in this way.

Bandura also described the faulty prior learning of either defective or inappropriate incentive systems as a condition that results in abnormal behaviors. In this instance, he referred to pleasurable but culturally unacceptable stimuli (sexual, alcohol, drugs), which in themselves function as strong positive reinforcers, that become associated with behaviors considered deviant in our culture, such as homosexuality, transvestism (a male dressing up as a female), or alcoholism. He cites the example of transvestism in a young boy who received the approval of mother, grandmother, and neighbors whenever he dressed up as a girl, or a mother's active positive conditioning of her son's exhibitionistic behaviors. In these illustrations, the previous positive reinforcement accounts for the acquisition and maintenance of sexually deviant response patterns.

In addition, Bandura discusses how aversive behaviors such as aggression are acquired, since these behaviors often are thought of as symptomatic of a personality aberration in our society. Experimental studies have shown that aggressive, punitive parents are likely to produce aggressive children, especially if the parents (models) are highly successful in controlling rewards (Bandura and Walters, 1963). Moreover, frustrated children, who under ordinary conditions respond with aggression, can be taught novel patterns in which they exhibit unaggressive and inhibited behavior after they observe the inhibited behavior of a model. Also, whether the aggressive behavior of the model is rewarded or punished differentially can affect the behavior of the children who are observers. Those who observe aggression rewarded are more aggressive than the children who observe aggression punished.

Research has also shown that positive reinforcement increases the child's aggressive behavior, and that the effects of this reinforcement transfer to new social situations. As expected, punishment tends to inhibit aggressive responses, although a great deal of punishment training may lead to aggression directed toward objects or persons who are not the punitive agent (displaced aggression). While less research evidence is available about the effect of reinforcement on dependency and sexual behavior, Bandura and Walters proposed that "reinforcement variables modify these classes of responses in much the same manner as they modify aggression" (Bandura and Walters, 1963, p. 160).

Humanistic Models

Falling somewhere between the global concepts of the sociocultural models and the more specific and mechanistic postulates of learning theories are a group of views known as *humanism* and *existentialism* in their orientation toward personality and abnormal behaviors. They are environmental positions because they stress experience and the individual's reaction both to self and the external world as essential determinants of behaviors. Instead of expressing concern with either the exploration of the person's unconscious (intrapsychic models) or the recounting and restructuring of past learning experiences (learning models), the humanistic approach tries to understand the whole person in terms of present functioning and capabilities for the future. Both humanism and existentialism are deeply rooted in philosophical ideas that regard human nature in a positive light, and that respect the worth of every person and their right to make choices about how they will live their lives.

According to Abraham Maslow, one of the pioneers of the humanistic movement in psychology,

Man demonstrates *in his own nature* a pressure toward fuller and fuller Being, more and more perfect actualization of his humanness in exactly the same naturalistic, scientific sense that an acorn may be said to be "pressing toward" being an oak tree, or that a tiger can be observed to "push forward" being tigerish, or a horse toward being equine. Man is ultimately *not* molded or shaped into humanness, or taught to be human. The role of the environment is ultimately to permit him or help him to actualize *his own* potentialities, not *its* potentialities. The environment does not give him potentialities and capacities; he *has* them in inchoate or embryonic form, just exactly as he has embryonic arms and legs. And creativeness, spontaneity, selfhood, authenticity, caring for others, being able to love, yearning for truth are embryonic potentialities belonging to his species-membership just as much as are his arms and legs and brain and eyes (Maslow, 1968, pp. 160–161).

For Maslow, every person has "an essential biological inner nature" that is, within limits, unchangeable, and which is partly unique and partly common to the species. The needs, emotions, and human capacities of this inner nature are either intrinsically neutral or "good," suggesting that people are not innately "evil" but manifest such behaviors as destructiveness, cruelty, and sadism as violent reactions to the frustration of their inner core. Maslow viewed the inner nature as weak and delicate, and

readily denied and overcome by habit and external forces, although it persists in striving for survival first and then actualization (self-fulfillment). Thus, Maslow emphasized the presence in all people of inherent tendencies for survival and for actualization, which if not thwarted or suppressed lead to both the maintenance and enhancement of life (Maddi, 1972). Needs associated with the survival tendency include physiological demands, safety, belongingness and love, and esteem, while the actualizing tendency incorporates the need for self-actualization and the need for cognitive understanding.

According to Maslow, when either of these tendencies are blocked, the person becomes "sick" or evidences maladaptive behaviors (Maslow, 1968). In the course of living, people continually face the conflict between the defensive forces of survival and the forces of growth, wherein they must choose between safety and growth, for example. People progress and move forward when the anxieties of safety are less than the "delights" of growth, and conversely, they regress or remain static when the anxieties of growth are greater than the "delights" of safety. Healthy people are those who are free to choose growth, while those who are "sick" are thwarted by the fears and anxieties of survival. Thus, the needs associated with the survival tendency (including safety needs) must be gratified before the growth needs can be met and before the person can feel safe enough to take the next step. For example, the young child can only venture forth to explore the surrounding environment when the mother-child relationship is secure, safe, and intact. However, if the mother-child relationship is impaired and uncertain, the child will cling to mother and be unable to take the growth step of freely interacting with the environment. Moreover, the maladaptive responses can be best treated when the therapist respects the fears of the "sick" person, and provides the security and safety needed for the person to be bold enough to choose a growth direction.

In a similar vein, Carl Rogers, one of the earliest and best known phenomenologists, conceptualized self-actualization as the core tendency of human personality (Maddi, 1972; Rogers, 1959, 1974). By this he meant that every person is born with inherent potentialities and that life experiences are perceived by the individual as either favorable or unfavorable in terms of self-actualization (the realization of these potentialities). The developing child gains a conscious sense of self by learning that it is highly desirable to be favorably regarded by parents, relatives, and others (the need for positive regard). The need for positive regard is internalized into the merging self through approval and disapproval received from others, while the child develops another important need, the need for positive self-regard. Under unusual circumstances, a person may receive unconditional approval from others, in which case, unconditional positive self-regard is developed, resulting in an ideal person who experiences no discrepancy between his or her self and potentialities. Less ideal, but more the rule, is the probability that the individual will receive conditional positive regard. This leads to a less favorable outcome in the sense that the person develops conditions of worth that give rise to anxiety about the occurrence of unworthy behaviors. Defenses (much like those noted by Freud) are constructed to deal with the anxiety and to ward off threats to the self. However, when defenses are inadequate, anxiety increases and abnormal behaviors appear.

So, for Rogers, the way of actualizing your potentialities in the fullest manner is to possess a self-concept that does not include conditions of worth, and therefore precipitates no defenses. It follows from this that you will (1) respect and value all manifestations of yourself, (2) be conscious of virtually all there is to know about yourself, and (3) be flexible and open to new experiences. In this way, the work of becoming what it is in your nature to be can go forward undisturbed. You will be what Rogers calls a *fully functioning* person (Maddi, 1972, p. 97).

Perhaps even more well known is Rogers' client-centered therapy, in which the therapist provides unconditional positive regard in a warm, reflective, and empathic manner to bolster the client's self-regard. This acceptance presumably decreases the client's need for defenses and facilitates acceptance of previously denied feelings and experiences. With increased freedom for clients to accept their feelings, they can perceive themselves and others more realistically, and they can form self-perceptions that are more congruent with their potentialities.

The existential view holds that human understanding cannot come from approaches that focus on the specific mechanisms of learning, the unconscious, or drive states (May, 1961; Maddi, 1972; Hogan, 1976). To do so is to talk about abstractions that lose sight of the existing human being, and to give precedence to mechanisms rather than people as beings. Existentialism is an attitude and an approach to humans instead of a theory or a special ideological school. It stresses the person's "unique pattern of potentialities" and his or her relationship to them as the person struggles to deal with "being" and "non-being." Accordingly, the major task that each person must deal with is to become self-aware or to seriously question who one is and what is the purpose of one's life. In this process, the person discovers that human existence is purposeless, which gives rise to *Angst,* a subjective state of dread or anxiety over the possibility of non-being that also serves as a basic source of motivation. A second motivational force, the *will to power,* permits the person to deal with Angst through knowledge of oneself. However, the anxiety that comes from the potential of non-being may, at times, be too high for some people to tolerate and too intense to prompt self-awareness. Therefore, many people choose self-deception because the more they seek self-knowledge the more they heighten the dread of non-being (Hogan, 1976).

To achieve self-awareness and an authentic (honest and true) being, people must accept the discomfort of non-being and find the courage to persist by recognizing that they have the power to create their own meaning and existence. This sense of human dignity not only recognizes and accepts the limits set by biological and social forces but also permits the individual to examine those remaining possibilities for freedom of action. People who see no options or alternatives (freedom) in their life circumstances (such as feeling trapped in a bad marriage) confuse the actual limits of the situation with the possible degrees of freedom that may be available. These reactions form the basis of psychopathology in which the individual blames others since he or she is unwilling to assume the responsibility for or take the necessary action that would further his or her authentic being. In this sense, psychopathology involves cowardice and self-deception, and a refusal to use one's wits (higher mental processes of symbolization, imagination, and judgment) to construct alternatives in situations where freedom of action was unnecessarily surrendered.

In general, humanistic models, while popular with clinical practitioners, have incurred their share of criticisms on the grounds of being vague and incomplete (for example, they provide few, if any, specifics with regard to the nature of inherent potentialities), of proposing formulations that are unsystematic and unintegrated, and of making naive and unverified assumptions. The idea "that man would be a constructive, rational, and socially conscious being, were he free of the malevolent distortions of society" (Millon, 1973, p. 267) is based on unsupported and perhaps romantic assumptions about the nature of man to which Millon makes the following cryptic comment: "There is something as banal as the proverbialism of a fortune cookie in the suggestion 'be thyself.' Conceiving man's emotional disorders as a failure to 'be thyself' seems equally naive and banal" (Millon, 1973, p. 267).

Critique of Environmental Models

Unlike the medical models that assume abnormal behaviors are disease entities caused by some sort of biological pathogen, the environmental models make no assumption about an underlying disease process. Instead, these models represent a diverse set of views that primarily emphasize environmental forces (factors external to the organism) as determinants of aberrant response patterns. To the extent that this is true, they can be criticized for not adequately considering the internal state of the organism and its influence on behavior, and for viewing people as passive, without any real impact on the environment. Both the sociological and humanistic models deal in variables that are vague and too broad to be either predictive or testable, and neither sufficiently attends to developmental principles or processes. The learning views tend to be mechanistic, molecular, and too often generalized from data generated from animal studies. Their attention to childhood usually takes the form of retrospective reinforcement histories that cannot be reconstructed with either the accuracy or precision needed to test their formulations. In their focus on behavior (both normal and abnormal), they, too, tend to disregard the internal processes of the organism and to discount (and possibly oversimplify) the psychopathological process itself. Indeed, as we shall see in our discussion of childhood psychosis (Chapter 8), symptoms can be modified or even eliminated without essentially altering the abnormal condition.

Although the environmental models can be additionally criticized for using correlational data for making cause and effect interpretations, these models (like the medical models) have not only significantly contributed to our understanding and treatment of childhood disorders, but they also have kept open alternative and promising avenues for investigating the etiological factors involved in psychopathology. Since it is doubtful that any single approach will provide the necessary data that will enable us to understand this very complex field, there is every reason to encourage the further development of these and other approaches, notwithstanding their methodological limitations.

Summary

Conceptual models are frames of reference that provide a broad but cohesive way of understanding and explaining abnormal behaviors. They make etiological assumptions that tend to persist in the absence of corroborative evidence. Adoption of a model increases the resistance to alternative views and sets into motion important consequences.

Selected positions within two broad categories of models, *medical-disease* and *environmental,* were discussed. The medical-disease models were described as a group of views which assumed that abnormal behaviors were disease entities, and that the pathological process occurred within the organism. Under this rubic, genetic, biochemical, neurophysiological, and intrapsychic models were considered.

Although all genetic views acknowledge the importance of heredity as a determinant of both the biological and psychological make-up of people, they vary in their emphasis on the relative contributions made by heredity versus environment. One extreme holds that genetic factors are the primary determinants of abnormal behaviors. A more moderate view proposes that heredity disposes the person to act in certain ways, but that these predispositions can be modified by learning and one's life experiences. A variant of this is the view of genetic vulnerability, which posits vulnerability as a predisposition that increases the risk of breakdown.

Stimulated by the various etiological trends in physical medicine, the biochemical model has focused on the search for a psychotoxic agent causing mental illness. Recent advances in research techniques have made it possible to map pathways in the brain mediated by specific neurotransmitters, and to formulate hypotheses concerning the possible alterations in the metabolism of the monoamines in the central nervous system.

The neurophysiological model assumes that the etiology of abnormal behaviors resides in brain pathology that is inherited, congenital, or acquired.

Psychoanalysis and other intrapsychic views were described as medical models, because they essentially regard abnormal behaviors as disease entities and the pathology as stemming from unresolved internal conflicts.

The intrapsychic views of Jung and Adler, who broke with Freud, were also discussed. An overall critique of the medical model was presented in which the disease concept was faulted as illogical, erroneous, and unsupported by empirical evidence.

The environmental models focus almost exclusively on external variables as primary determinants of abnormal behaviors. Sociocultural models deal with global variables of social systems and culture as they relate to abnormal behaviors, and they tend to oversimplify complicated relationships.

The discussion of learning models included Dollard and Miller's translation of psychoanalytic theory into a learning system based on classical conditioning and drive-reduction postulates. Rotter's and Bandura's approaches to social learning and the formation of abnormal behaviors were described. Abnormal behaviors are construed by Rotter as avoidance behaviors attributable to expectations of punishment or low expectancies of achieving important reinforcements. The avoidance behavior eventually leads to the failure to develop competency, which in turn often facilitates the development of other deviant behaviors. Bandura's social-learning theory emphasizes operant conditioning and imitation learning in the acquisition of both deviant and conforming behaviors. A number of conditions that give rise to the faulty conditioning history associated with aberrant behaviors were discussed. The theory also used data from both field and laboratory studies to show the influence of modeling and patterns of reinforcement in the learning of aggressive, dependent, and sexual behaviors.

The humanistic models (self-actualization and existential) were presented. These are environmental positions stressing experience and the individual's reaction both to self and to the external world as essential determinants of behavior. The humanistic approach focuses on the whole person in terms of present and future capabilities. Both humanism and existentialism are approaches to humans rather than theories or ideological schools.

A critique of the environmental models was also included.

Epilogue

The evaluation revealed that Eric's adjustment problems were rooted in early but long-standing faulty parent-child relationships, rather than possession, brain pathology, or genetic transmission. Mother's overprotectiveness and her strong inclination to treat Eric as a "baby" had been evident since birth, possibly because she experienced a mixture of inadequacy, anger, and guilt feelings over his premature birth, and/or because she viewed Eric as a substitute for her absent husband. Whatever her reasons, Eric became the beneficiary of her extra maternal care and attention. However, in order to obtain more gratification, she coerced him to behave in ways that would comply with her wishes. She helped to retard his social maturity by encouraging him to share in her household chores, and she literally reduced his chances of success in sports and in relating to his peers by overfeeding him. Eric, in turn, read the contingencies well and behaved accordingly.

He preferred being at home where he could be close to mother and be fed and nurtured by her. Going to school only deprived him of maternal relations and gratification, an event that neither Eric or mother really wanted. Father's dedication to his business, and his almost total abdication of parental responsibilities or involvement presented a distant, disinterested, and ineffective male model for Eric. Like father, Eric was passive and unassertive because he had learned that he would be indulged by mother (and perhaps others) if he permitted her to be dominant and overbearing.

Eric and his parents (his sister went off to college) became involved in weekly family therapy sessions that were intended to increase everyone's understanding of his or her role and contributions to Eric's problems, and to create a climate that would facilitate changes. Mother and father had to understand how Eric was both a victim and a participant in their marital conflicts. They needed to resolve their problems with each other and to deal with Eric in ways that would promote his personal growth. At the same time, Eric needed to find gratification in activities outside of the home and away from mother and to shift his identification toward father.

After four months of therapy, some improvements were noted. Father became more active in family matters and spent more time with his wife and Eric. He drew Eric into the business, which provided Eric with success experiences outside of the home, as well as a male model who he could emulate. Father's re-entry into the family eased mother's loneliness and decreased her need to hold onto Eric. Eric began to lose weight, feel better about himself, and to slowly establish relationships with peers. No essential change was evident in his academic performance.

REFERENCES

ARIETI, S. and E. B. BRODY. *American Handbook of Psychiatry* (Vol. III) (2nd ed.). New York: Basic Books, 1974.

BALINSKY, B. I. *An Introduction to Embryology* (2nd ed.). Philadelphia: Saunders, 1965.

BANDURA, A. and R. H. WALTERS. *Social Learning and Personality Development*. New York: Holt, Rinehart, and Winston, 1963.

BANDURA, A. "A Social Learning Interpretation of Psychological Dysfunctions." In P. London and D. Rosenhan (Eds.), *Foundations of Abnormal Psychology*. New York: Holt, Rinehart, and Winston, 1968, pp. 293–344.

BEATTY, J. *Introduction to Physiological Psychology*. Monterey, California: Brooks/Cole, 1975.

BOULTON, A. "Biochemical Research in Schizophrenia." *Nature*, 1971, *231*, 22–28.

BRILL, N. Q. "General Biological Studies." In L. Bellak and L. Loeb (Eds.), *The Schizophrenic Syndrome*. New York: Grune and Stratton, 1969, pp. 114–154.

CANTRIL, H. *The Invasion from Mars: A Study in the Psychology of Panic*. Princeton: Princeton University Press, 1940.

CHASSEN, J. B. *Research Design in Clinical Psychology and Psychiatry*. New York: Appleton-Century-Crofts, 1967.

COHEN, J., OFFNER, F., and C. W. PALMER. "Development of the Contingent Negative Variation in Children: *Electroencephalography and Clinical Neurophysiology*, 1967, *23*, 77–98.

COLEMAN, M. "Serotonin and Central Nervous System Syndromes of Childhood. A Review." *Journal of Autism and Childhood Schizophrenia,* 1973, *3,* 27–35.

DAVIS, J. M. "A Two Factor Theory of Schizophrenia." *Journal of Psychiatric Research,* 1974, *11,* 25–29.

DELGADO, J. M. R. *Physical Control of the Mind.* New York: Harper and Row, 1969.

DOLLARD, J. and N. E. MILLER. *Personality and Psychotherapy.* New York: McGraw Hill, 1950.

DOBZHANSKY, T. *Mankind Evolving.* New Haven: Yale University Press, 1962.

DRAGUNS, J. G. and L. PHILLIPS. *Psychiatric Classification and Diagnosis: An Overview and Critique.* Morristown, N.J.: General Learning Press, 1971.

DURHAM, H. W. "Social Structures and Mental Disorder: Competency Hypotheses of Explanation." *Milbank Memorial Fund Quarterly,* 1961, *39,* 259–311.

ERLENMEYER-KIMLING, L. "Discussion of Genetics and Mental Illness." *Behavior Genetics,* 1976, *6,* 285–290.

FREUD, S. "Neurosis and Psychosis" (Joan Riviere, trans.) (Vol. II). In E. Jones (Ed.), *The Collected Papers of Sigmund Freud.* New York: Basic Books, 1959, pp. 250–254.

GARMEZY, N. "The Experimental Study of Children Vulnerable to Psychopathology." In A. Davids (Ed.), *Child Personality and Psychopathology: Current Topics* (Vol. 2). New York: Wiley, 1975, pp. 171–216.

GODDARD, H. H. *The Kallikak Family.* New York: Macmillan, 1912.

GOLDFARB, J. and S. WILK. "Neuroanatomy, Neurophysiology, and Neurochemistry." In S. D. Glick and J. Goldfarb (Eds.), *Behavioral Pharmacology.* St. Louis: Mosby, 1976, pp. 14–57.

GOLDSTEIN, L. and A. A. SUGARMAN. "EEG Correlates of Psychopathology." *Proceedings of the American Psychopathological Association,* 1969, *58,* 281–309.

GROVES, P. M. and G. C. REBEC. "Biochemistry and Behavior: Some Central Actions of Amphetamine and Antipsychotic Drugs." *Annual Review of Psychology,* 1976, *27,* 91–127.

GRUENBERG, E. M. "From Practice to Theory—Community Mental-Health Services and the Nature of Psychoses." In T. Millon (Ed.), *Theories of Psychopathology and Personality: Essays and Critiques* (2nd ed.). Philadelphia: Saunders, 1973, pp. 399–403.

HANSON, D. R., GOTTESMAN, I. I., and L. L. HESTON. "Some Possible Childhood Indicators of Adult Schizophrenia Inferred from Children of Schizophrenics." *British Journal of Psychiatry,* 1976, *129,* 142–154.

HOGAN, R. *Personality Theory: The Personological Tradition.* Englewood Cliffs, New Jersey: Prentice-Hall, 1976.

JULIAN, R. M. *A Primer of Drug Action.* San Francisco: Freeman, 1975.

JUNG, C. G. *Man and His Symbols.* Garden City, New York: Doubleday, 1964.

KALLMAN, F. J. "The Genetics of Human Behavior." In T. Millon (Ed.), *Theories of Psychopathology and Personality: Essays and Critiques* (2nd ed.). Philadelphia: Saunders, 1973, pp. 24–28.

KLERMAN, G. "Clinical Research in Depression." *Archives of General Psychiatry,* 1971, *24,* 305–319.

KETY, S. S. "Biochemical Hypotheses and Studies." In L. Bellak and L. Loeb (Eds.), *The Schizophrenic Syndrome.* New York: Grune and Stratton, 1969, pp. 155–171.

KETY, S. S. "Biochemical Hypotheses of Schizophrenia." In T. Millon (Ed.), *Theories* of *Psychopathology and Personality: Essays and Critiques* (2nd ed.). Philadelphia: Saunders, 1973, pp. 92–103.

KETY, S. S. "Recent Biochemical Theories of Schizophrenia." In D. D. Jackson (Ed.), *The Etiology of Schizophrenia.* New York: Basic Books, 1960, pp. 120–145.

LEHMER, M. "Navajos Want Their Own Schools." *San Francisco Examiner and Chronicle,* December 14, 1969, p. D–4.

MADDI, S. R. *Personality Theories: A Comparative Analysis* (revised ed.). Homewood, Illinois: The Dorsey Press, 1972.

MASLOW, A. H. *Toward a Psychology of Being* (2nd ed.). Princeton, New Jersey: Van Nostrand Reinhold, 1968.

MAY, R. *Existential Psychology.* New York: Random House, 1961.

MEDNICK, S. A. "Breakdown in High-Risk Subjects: Familial and Early Environmental Factors. *Journal of Abnormal Psychology,* 1973, *82,* 469–475.

MEDNICK, S. A. and T. F. McNEILL. "Current Methodology in Research on the Etiology of Schizophrenia: Serious Difficulties Which Suggest the Use of the High-Risk Group Method." *Psychological Bulletin,* 1968, *70,* 681–693.

MEDNICK, S. A. and F. SCHULSINGER. "Some Premorbid Characteristics Related to Breakdown in Children with Schizophrenic Mothers." In D. Rosenthal and S. S. Kety (Eds.), *The Transmission of Schizophrenia.* New York: Pergamon Press, 1968, pp. 267–291.

MEDNICK, S. A., SCHULSINGER, H., and F. SCHULSINGER. "Schizophrenia in Children of Schizophrenic Mothers." In A. Davids (Ed.), *Child Personality and Psychopathology: Current Topics* (Vol. 2). New York: Wiley, 1975, pp. 217–252.

MENDELS, J. and A. FRAZER. "Brain Biogenic Amine Depletion and Mood." *Archives of General Psychiatry,* 1974, *30,* 447–451.

MERTON, R. "Anomie, Anomia and Social Interaction." In M. B. Clinard (Ed.), *Anomie and Deviant Behavior.* New York: Free Press of Glencoe, 1964, pp. 213–242.

MILLON, T. (Ed.). *Theories of Psychopathology and Personality: Essays and Critiques* (2nd ed.). Philadelphia: Saunders, 1973.

MITTLER, P. *The Study of Twins.* Middlesex, England: Penguin Books, 1971.

NAUTA, W. J. H. "The Problem of the Frontal Lobe: A Reinterpretation." In J. V. Brady and W. J. H. Nauta (Eds.), *Principles, Practices and Positions in Neuropsychiatric Research."* New York: Pergamon, 1972, pp. 167–187.

RAPAPORT, D. "A Critique of Dollard and Miller's *Personality and Psychotherapy."* *American Journal of Orthopsychiatry,* 1953, *23,* 204–208.

RITVO, E. R. "Biochemical Research with Hyperactive Children." In D. P. Cantwell (Ed.), *The Hyperactive Child: Diagnosis, Management and Current Research.* New York: Spectrum, 1975, pp. 83–91.

ROGERS, C. R. "A Theory of Therapy, Personality, and Interpersonal Relationships as Developed in the Client Centered Framework." In S. Koch (Ed.), *Psychology: A Study of a Science* (Vol. 3). New York: McGraw-Hill, 1959, pp. 184–256.

ROGERS, C. R. "In Retrospect: Forty-Six Years." *American Psychologist,* 1974, *29,* 115–123.

ROSENTHAL, D. *Genetics of Psychopathology.* New York: McGraw Hill, 1971, p. 3.

ROSENTHAL, D. *Genetic, Theory and Abnormal Behavior.* New York: McGraw-Hill, 1970, p. 2

Rotter, J. B., Chance, J. E., and E. J. Phares. *Applications of a Social Learning Theory of Personality.* New York: Holt, Rinehart, and Winston, 1972.

Sabshin, M. "Theoretical Models in Community and Social Psychiatry." In T. Millon (Ed.), *Theories of Psychopathology and Personality: Essays and Critiques* (2nd ed.). Philadelphia: Saunders, 1973, pp. 386–394.

Sager, C. J. "Alienation 'Can Be Said to Epitomize Our Times.'" *Roche Reports,* 1968, *5*:8, 1–2, 11.

Sarason, I. G. *Personality: An Objective Approach.* New York: Wiley, 1966.

Satterfield, J. H., Cantwell, D. P., and B. T. Satterfield. "Pathphysiology of the Hyperactive Child Syndrome." *Archives of General Psychiatry,* 1974, *31*, 839–844.

Selye, H. *Stress Without Distress.* Philadelphia: Lippincott, 1974.

Shagass, C. and J. J. Straumanis. "Evoked Potentials and Psychopathology." *Proceedings of the American Psychopathological Association,* 1969, *58*, 22–53.

Shapiro, J., Machattie, L., Eron, L., Ihler, G., Ippen, K., and J. Beckwith. "Isolation of Pur *Lac* Operon DNA." *Nature,* 1969, *224*, 768–774.

Small, J. G., DeMyer, M. K., and V. Milstein. "CNV Responses of Autistic and Normal Children." *Journal of Autism and Childhood Schizophrenia,* 1971, *1*, 215–231.

Snyder, S. H., Banerjee, S. P., Yamamura, H. I., and D. Greenberg. "Drugs, Neurotransmitters, and Schizophrenia." *Science,* 1974, *184*, 1243–1253.

Szasz, T. S. "The Myth of Mental Illness." *American Psychologist,* 1960, *15*, 113–118.

Thomas, W. I., and F. Znaniecki. *The Polish Peasant in Europe and America.* (Vols. I and II). New York: Dover Publications, 1958.

Vaughn, H. G. Jr. "Some Reflections of Stimulation of the Human Brain." In J. Zubin and C. Shagass (Eds.), *Neurobiological Aspects of Psychopathology.* New York: Grune and Stratton, 1969, pp. 66–77.

Venables, P. H. "The Electrodermal Psychophysiology of Schizophrenia and Children at Risk for Schizophrenia: Controversies and Developments." *Schizophrenia Bulletin,* 1977, *3*, 28–48.

Walter, W. G. "The Contingent Negative Variation as an Aid to Psychiatric Diagnosis." In M. L. Kietzman, S. Sutton, and J. Zubin (Eds.), *Experimental Approaches to Psychopathology.* New York: Academic Press, 1975, pp. 197–205.

Watson, J. D. and R. H. C. Crick. "Molecular Structure of Nucleic Acids: A Structure for Deoxyribose Nucleic Acid." *Nature,* 1953, *171*:4356, 737–738.

West, A. P. "Interaction of Low-Dose Amphetamine Use with Schizophrenia in Outpatients: Three Case Reports." *American Journal of Psychiatry,* 1974, *131*, 321–323.

Williams, R. J. "The Biological Approach to the Study of Personality." In T. Millon (Ed.), *Theories of Psychopathology and Personality: Essays and Critiques* (2nd ed). Philadelphia: Saunders, 1973, pp. 29–38.

Wittkower, E. D. and J. Fried. "Some Problems of Transcultural Psychiatry." *International Journal of Social Psychiatry,* 1958, *3*, 242–252.

Zubin, J. "The Biometric Approach to Psychopathology Revisited." In J. Zubin and C. Shagass (Eds.), *Neurobiological Aspects of Psychopathology.* New York: Grune and Stratton, 1969, pp. 281–309.

Zubin, J. "Scientific Models for Psychopathology in the 1970's." *Seminars in Psychiatry,* 1972, *4*:3, 283–296.

PART II   Methods of Evaluation and Intervention

Assessment Approaches:

clinical observation, the interview,

psychological tests and

behavioral assessment

5

PROLOGUE

After months of urging by the school principal, Mrs. B. telephoned the psychologist for an appointment for Freddy, her nine-year-old son. Although Freddy, a third grader, achieved at an academic level far below his intellectual potential, his social immaturity, isolation, and withdrawal worried the school officials even more. Mrs. B. balked at the psychologist's suggestion of seeing her and her husband first to obtain a more complete picture of Freddy's present problems and past history. She stated that she and Mr. B. both worked and couldn't get away, and that, after all, it was Freddy who needed professional attention. Several appointment times were offered, but Mrs. B. angrily rejected them saying she couldn't make any arrangements without checking with her husband. Days later, Mrs. B. telephoned again to set a definite time for their first visit. She reluctantly gave the psychologist permission to speak to the principal about Freddy, only after she repeatedly warned that he would be difficult to contact.

Mr. and Mrs. B. arrived separately, but on time for their appointment, seating themselves across from each other in an empty waiting room. The psychologist's greeting interrupted their silence and stark separateness. Mrs. B. quickly stood up and extended a firm hand, while Mr. B. slowly rose and timidly placed his limp hand into the clinician's. Mrs. B. was a tall woman whose big-boned frame and sturdy, matronly appearance made her look older than her stated age of forty-two. She was stylishly dressed with jet black hair that was obviously coiffed by a hairdresser. Although not a pretty woman, Mrs. B. created an air of attractiveness and poise in the way she put herself together. In sharp contrast, Mr. B. was several inches shorter, overweight, balding, and dressed in a worn and loosely fitting suit, suggesting that he had been even heavier at one time. He looked older than forty-one years, yet his appearance was discrepant with his boyish awkwardness in meeting people and his passive-dependent relationship with his wife.

Mrs. B. did all of the talking, even when questions were directed to her husband. She was organized, aggressive, firm, and unemotional in her presentation of Freddy's problems and history. She recognized her son's poor academic performance and acknowledged that he barely passed the first and second grades, and that it was doubtful Freddie would pass the third grade. Nevertheless, she regarded him as a "late bloomer" who would eventually catch fire and be an outstanding student. Bolstered by an agreeing nod from her husband, she expressed confusion and annoyance with the school principal for his insistence on the referral. At the same time, she praised the principal, and she indicated that she and her husband were here to make certain that they weren't neglectful of Freddy.

Mr. and Mrs. B. had married after they had both turned thirty. Neither had been married before, nor had they dated very much prior to their meeting. They wanted children immediately but had to wait several years, because they had difficulty conceiving. Mother had always worked as a bookkeeper, and father as a salesman. However, Mrs. B. quit her job when Freddy was born and did not return to full-time employment until he was three years old. At that time, Mr. B. became seriously ill with ulcerative colitis, which required several hospitalizations and eventually surgery. Mrs. B. went back to work to help support the family, leaving Freddy in a preschool and in the care of a housekeeper. When he entered the first grade, the housekeeper was discharged to cut expenses. However, their concern over Freddy's safety during the few hours between the close of school and the end of mother's work day prompted them to require that he stay close to home and not wander beyond their fenced yard. Freddy more than complied with their wishes in that he rarely, if ever, went out of doors after he returned from school. He chose to change into his pajamas and watch TV while holding on to his favorite baby blanket until mother arrived home at about 5:30 P.M. He made no friends, even though a number of boys his age lived in the neighborhood. Since Freddy was left alone so much, his parents never went out in the evenings or on weekends without taking him along.

Mother reported that Freddy was a fussy eater who often refused to eat the meals she prepared. On these occasions, father would interrupt his own dinner to go out and buy Freddy's favorite hamburger and french fries. The parents also had great difficulty in putting Freddy to bed at a regular and reasonable time, although after awhile Mr. B. usually resolved the problem by agreeing to Freddy's request that he sleep with him. Mr. B.'s frequent indulgence of his son met with Mrs. B.'s disapproval, opposition, and intense anger. However, the open battles between the parents over Freddy's management were short lived, because mother feared that the conflict would precipitate another hospitalization for her husband.

In this chapter, we shift emphasis from the discussion of the broad and substantive issues of the field to an in-depth look at the assessment process to see how the clinician functions in arriving at a diagnosis and a treatment plan for children like Freddy. Who and what does the clinician evaluate; what techniques are available for accumulating information; what information is needed; and how is it used are questions which we shall try to answer to remove the cloud of mystery that often surrounds the clinical process and to further our understanding of the significance of these data for the various clinical conditions that we will present in later chapters.

Referral

All clinical interactions begin with a referral that brings the child and the family to the attention of the clinician. Most clients [1] do not seek professional help on their own, and they usually experience some degree of resistance in admitting that "something is wrong." The nature of the referral often provides the clinician with early clues that aid in evaluating both the referrant's understanding and willingness to do something about the problem. For example, in her first telephone call, Mrs. B. communicated her reluctance to accept either the principal's initial referral or any involvement in her son's maladjustment. In addition, she readily constructed barriers to block a meeting with the psychologist, reflecting her resistance to becoming part of the evaluation and to admitting that problems exist.

[1] "Client" is used in this chapter to refer to the child and the parents, recognizing that in most instances diagnosing abnormal behavior in children minimally involves this trio.

In general, families who are aware of their problems and who willingly seek professional help are more cooperative and easier to work with than those who show resistance. The willing parents have taken that painful first step in identifying their undesirable behaviors and show the initial motivation to bring about needed changes. Those who are either unable or unwilling to face up to their problems not only require the direction of others to secure help, but also show poor motivation to alter their behavioral patterns. Mr. and Mrs. B. refused to acknowledge Freddy's deviant behaviors, although both his poor school performance and social adjustment were obvious to everyone else. It was the principal's unwillingness to tolerate Freddy's deteriorating behavior that pressed Mrs. B. into calling the psychologist. Their own wish to put an end to the principal's coercion and to avoid the socially unacceptable stigma of being neglectful parents motivated Mr. and Mrs. B. to reluctantly go through the motions of seeking professional assistance for problems they preferred to deny. Although recognition of one's problems and self-motivation are desirable, their absence does not preclude a favorable outcome. The important point is that the clinician has an early awareness of the referrant's motivation in order to construct a strategy that would increase cooperation and motivation. Frequently the behaviors of troubled children are a plea for help and a means of attracting the attention of some responsible adult. Acting-out children who disrupt class, fight with others, and refuse to obey rules attract more than their share of attention. Less noticeable to most adult observers are those aberrant behaviors of children that do not affect the lives of others. Excessive day dreaming, withdrawal from social interactions, disruptive sleep patterns, and unwillingness to try any new activity because of an intense fear of being physically hurt are some examples of adjustment problems that may be as serious as acting-out behaviors. However, these are more likely to go on for longer periods of time before professional services are sought.

Resistance to outside intervention is not uncommon in parents, who, like Mrs. B., wish to believe that this is a "passing phase" that the child will eventually "outgrow." Parental reluctance to seek clinical services is understandable, since the referral may imply that parents are responsible for the child's problems, that they have failed to be "good" parents, or that they conceived a damaged offspring. In addition, parental resistance may reflect a basic unwillingness to change their own behaviors or to give up using the child as a vehicle for expressing their conflicts.

Frequently, children also are reluctant to take professional help, because they feel put-down, unloved, and blamed for the problem. Consequently, they are likely to react with anger and anxiety for being singled out and brought to a specialist for help. Some youngsters may resist because they equate the need for psychological assistance with an open admission of a serious disability. In this instance, they may wish to deny or conceal their difficulties, because their integrity is threatened. Still others may show reluctance because they are fearful of the unknown and of what the "doctor" might do to them. Whatever the circumstances, the clinician must be aware as early as possible of the presence of fears and resistances and their potential effect on the relationship and the information gathered.

In addition, the referral should provide the clinician with an orientation to the referrant's major problems. A telephone conversation with the referrant can yield information about the primary symptoms, their duration, their onset (gradual or sudden), their effects on the functioning of the referrant and others, and the measures that have been tried to deal with them. It is also important to know the results of recent medical evaluations, and the kind and dosage of current medication, because of their possible confounding effects on the behavioral assessment of the client. Armed with this information, the assessment process begins to take shape, even before the referrant arrives for the initial visit. In those instances where a client is self-referred, some preliminary in-take procedure (either informally on the telephone or by some prepared written questionnaire) is often employed.

Clinical Methods

Typically, the diagnostic process is aimed at classifying the abnormal behaviors, arriving at working hypotheses about causal factors, and constructing a plan to remediate the condition. In later sections, we shall discuss the clinical methods by which these goals are met: clinical observations, the interview, psychological tests, and behavioral assessment. Keep in mind that while each of these methods offers advantages and disadvantages, the clinician does not typically rely on only one approach for gathering diagnostic information. Instead, the clinician recognizes that careful assessment involves a combination of methods to yield data that is reliable, complete, and accurate.

Clinical Observations

Observation is the chief method of study for every field of scientific inquiry, although its limitations are more pronounced when it is applied to the clinical setting. Human behavior is so complex and changeable that it overloads the sheer observational capacities of the observer. A child in a play situation may do many things (laugh, talk, run, throw, hit or catch a ball, and become involved in a fight with a playmate) within a short timespan of a few minutes. Obviously all of the behaviors evidenced cannot be accurately recorded. Laughing, for example, is sufficiently complex in itself to make the human observer's task of recording it extremely difficult. The observer must make decisions about what constitutes a laugh, what prompts it, as well as note all of the facial, bodily, and auditory components of the laugh. However, in the clinical setting not one but many behaviors are observed at the same time, increasing the difficulty of the task, and reducing the chances of obtaining high agreement between different observers.

Sources of Observational Error

Clinical observations are subject to the biases of the clinician (*observer bias*) in that a particular behavior might be interpreted to confirm a working clinical hypothesis. In addition, clinicians might overlook or underrate other behaviors that do not coincide with their a priori notions. Because the intrusion of observer bias is ever present, clinicians must not only be aware of this source of error, but also must guard against distorting what they see.

The client is another potential contributor to observational error (*subject bias*), especially early in the clinical interaction. Since most clients want to put their best foot forward, we can expect them to temporarily adopt behaviors that will create a favorable impression. Some may be

guarded and defensive because they fear being studied, or fear the prospect of being viewed as "crazy." Still others may attempt to behave in ways that they believe are expected of them. Any of these conditions will make client's behaviors difficult to note and even more hazardous to interpret.

Areas of Clinical Observation

In spite of these limitations, observation is an important and useful clinical method in generating diagnostic hypothesis that can be rejected or supported by further study. A sensitive and well trained clinical observer can gain valuable information from the following five categories of the client's behaviors: (1) general physical appearance and attire; (2) emotional gestures and facial expressions; (3) gross and fine motor acts; (4) the quality of the relationship between the client and others; and (5) the client's verbalizations.

General Appearance and Attire. Almost everyone is well practiced in forming initial impressions of strangers through their physical appearance and dress. Although clinicians use similar cues, their assessment is not intended to serve as an early basis of interpersonal attractiveness or as a guide for ensuing social interactions, but rather as sources of data on the physical, social, and personality characteristics of the client. In this light, clinicians look for extremes, incongruities, and peculiarities in both physical appearance and attire as early diagnostic clues that may require further evaluation. Is the child well proportioned and formed or does the child show physical deformities or abnormalities that should be noted for later study with respect to their organic and/or psychological implications for the child's adjustment? Similarly, observations about the client's general health, cleanliness, body surface signs (bruise marks, cuts, sores, scars, hair distribution and other secondary sexual characteristics, and so forth), and the condition and propriety of the client's clothes may provide gross indications of some diagnostic possibilities that can be either ruled in or out by additional data. For example, emaciation in a fifteen-year-old girl is one of the physical manifestations of a disorder known as anorexia nervosa (see Chapter 11) or an extremely large or small head disproportionate to the rest of the body in a five-year-old suggests macro- or microcephalus (congenital disorders that usually result in severe mental retardation). Black or blue bruise marks on the face and arms of a child may be the result of a convulsive disorder, accident proneness, or physical assault. Needle marks on the arm of an adolescent may indicate drug abuse, while extremely chafed and irritated hands may be the result of a handwashing compulsion.

Within limits acceptable to society, the child and the parents are expected to be dressed and be groomed in ways that are appropriate to their age, socioeconomic status, vocation, and to some extent educational level. Any gross disparity is worthy of note, although, on closer examination, some will not be of diagnostic significance. But the shabby, baggy, and worn condition of Mr. B's clothes gave the unmistaken impression of a down-trodden, dejected, and spiritless man who might be depressed. Moreover, Mr. B.'s attire was in sharp contrast to the way Mrs. B. was smartly dressed and groomed, and to Freddy's freshly cleaned and pressed shirt and trousers, suggesting gross neglect that was discrepant with his family, his middle-class socioeconomic level, and his job as a salesman.

Emotional Gestures and Facial Expressions. Most of us have learned to note and interpret body movements, gestures, and expressions as clues to the emotional state and reactions of those with whom we interact. The shrug of the shoulder that connotes either disapproval or apathy, the clenched fist and gritting of teeth that communicates anger, the hung head and the slumped bodily attitude that suggests dejection, and the wide open smile accompanied by hand clapping that expresses pleasure and approval illustrates some of these behaviors. We learn early to look for these signs to help us get along with those around us. The disapproving glance of a parent or teacher represents a nonverbal communication often sufficiently potent to control our behavior. For more than fifty years, psychologists have demonstrated that subjects can successfully identify emotions represented in either posed or candid photographs of faces (Munn, 1940; Schlosberg, 1952, 1954; Izard, 1971). Two additional studies support the notion that emotional gestures and facial expressions can provide valuable clues in the diagnostic interview (Ekman, 1964, 1965).

At the first meeting, the clinician looks for signs of tension, apprehension, fear, and other emotional states as well as for inappropriate emotional reactions that may be evidenced in the client's facial and body expressions. Additional observations should occur during subsequent meetings so that the clinician can confirm, reject, or elaborate initial impressions. Moreover, patterns of emotional responsivity should emerge over time and in different stimulus contexts. Thus, it is important not only for the clinician to observe signs of the initial emotional reaction but also to continue the observations to discern changes in emotionality, appropriateness, consistency of emotional reactions, and the range of the child's emotional repertoire.

Gross and Fine Motor Acts. Motor behavior interests the clinician because it is an area of responsivity that is affected by neurological, physiological, pharmacological, and psychological variables. Disturbances in motor behavior vary in degree or kind. The general activity level of the child should be noted, especially at either extreme. *Overactivity* represents heightened motor output in which there are quick and successive motor acts that are rarely completed or goal directed. An example of this is the hyperkinetic child (see Chapter 9) who is characterized by restlessness, fidgeting, flitting from one activity to another, and an inability to sit still for even a moment without getting into something (often destructively).

Underactivity, sometimes known as psychomotor retardation, represents reduced and slowed motor output that may be indicative of endocrine imbalance, drug effects, depression, mental retardation, or psychosis. The extreme of underactivity, paralysis or muscular weakness (asthenia), may reflect a neurological disorder, psychoneurosis (hysterical paralysis of the conversion reaction), or the effects of heavy sedation.

In addition to the general activity level, certain kinds of unusual motor behaviors are of diagnostic importance. A *tic* is an involuntary spasmodic twitching of the face or body parts that is repeated at frequent intervals. Its origin usually has an emotional component (anger, anxiety, grief, or shame), making it a valuable bit of diagnostic data. The child's unsolicited repeti-

tion and imitation of motor acts performed by the examiner or others is called *echopraxia.* This motor disturbance is most often associated with childhood psychosis. Another peculiar kind of motor behavior is known as *perseveration,* in which movements and actions just performed by the child are repeated. The initial action is usually appropriate for the stimulus, but its repetition is inappropriate. Perseveration should be noted because it is a behavior associated with brain pathology, mental retardation, and psychosis. *Ritualistic* or *compulsive* motor behaviors such as performing a prior sequential set of acts before performing another activity may be diagnostic clues of an obsessive-compulsive neurotic reaction (discussed in Chapter 11).

Quality of Relationships. Children almost never come to the evaluation sessions unattended, a circumstance that provides the clinician with opportunities to observe the nature of the relationship between both parents, and between the child and the parents. For example, the scene of silence, separateness, and emptiness enacted by Mr. and Mrs. B. in the waiting room along with Mrs. B.'s domination of her husband in the initial interview communicated so much about their relationship. Mrs. B.'s inclination to be aggressive and dominant was extended to her relationship with Freddy where it was noted that she criticized and directed his activities as they waited for the psychologist. A child and mother who totally ignore each other, sitting at different ends of an uncrowded waiting room and who show no visible sign of interest in each other, convey a picture of coldness and distance in their relationship. The kinds of interactions that may be observed are almost endless. The point to be made is that these should provide the clinician with sources of rich but tentative interpretative data, which the clinician can reject or later confirm.

Verbalizations of the Client. Verbal language is not only a unique characteristic of people, but it also represents the principal source of data used by the clinician in diagnosing abnormal behavior. As a trained observer, the clinician must listen carefully to both the *formal structure* of the client's verbalizations and the *content* of what the client says, because each of these areas can reveal important diagnostic information.

The formal structure of language is first learned in the home environment. It consists of such characteristics as grammar, sentence structure, choice of words, speed, flow, and length. It is then modified and developed in school, and constantly practiced within a cultural setting. It should tell us something of the client's educational level and the subculture that has been influential. The way language is structured should provide an estimate of the client's intellectual level and current functioning. For example, a middle-class Caucasian child of thirteen who speaks in short monosyllabic phrases with poor grammatical structure is probably intellectually limited. Table 5–1 summarizes some of the major deviations in the formal structure of verbal language indicative of disordered thought beyond the slips of the tongue, digressions from the main topic, or interruptions in the flow of ideas found in the speech of most people.

Observations of language content provide an important source of diagnostic data, since they permit a glimpse of human functioning in areas that tend to be impaired when abnormal conditions exist. In fact, careful listening to the content of

TABLE 5–1   Deviations in Language Structure Indicative of Psychotic Thinking

Deviation	*Description*
Neologisms	The coining of new words, i.e., "jampow" created to refer to the draining of one's strength by excreting feces.
Incoherence	Phrases connected without reason or logical sequence. "I am made of bones and blood much as the wind bends the trees and Napoleon feels his heart."
Verbigeration	Extreme of incoherence consisting of a flow of unrelated words.
Word Salad	Speech that includes neologisms, incoherent, and illogical phrases sequenced so that they lack meaning. "The world is jampow! What's the use (laughs) . . . no matter, the sky is purple. Let my face burn, cut the trees down, and we will shout thy commands."
Tangential, Circumstantial, Loss of Goal Ideas	Long winded, indirect, and round-about speech that includes irrelevant details to the extent that the original objective is forgotten.
Flight of Ideas	Continuous, rapid flow of speech in which the client jumps from one thought to another without any apparent connection.
Clang Associations	The sound of the word touches off a series of punnings and/or rhymings. "Goodbye! . . . sky and eye . . . don't fly, lie, die, die . . . "
Pressure of Speech	Markedly rapid speech that is almost impossible to interrupt.
Mutism	Absence of speech.
Blocking	Low verbal output in which there are numerous instances of sudden breaks (silence) in the stream of speech occurring to interval stimulation.

verbal language should reveal what people think, what they have learned and remembered, how they see themselves and their environment, and what they feel. Various signs of disordered thinking, especially in extreme forms, are readily apparent in the client's language content. For example, *bizarre ideas* such as "my limbs are made of jelly," or "the ear of corn can't hear if it is cooked too long" characterize the language content typically found in psychotic children. Similarly, the expression of fixed beliefs based on false premises, known as *delusions,* describes paranoid thinking. Delusions are not ordinarily shared by other members of the client's educational and socioeconomic group, which helps to distinguish them from common superstitions, as well as religious and political beliefs. The two most commonly observed types of delusions are of grandeur and persecution, although other types are known.

Content of speech may also reveal signs of memory impairment, in that partial or total inability to recall, a condition known as *amnesia,* may be evident in what the client says. *Anterograde amnesia* refers to loss of memory of those matters that occurred after the precipitant event and which tends to become progressively worse. This type of amnesia is characteristic of degenerative brain pathology, whereas, *retrograde amnesia,* the loss of memory for things that took place prior to the precipitant event (usually emotional trauma or head injury), may be indicative of either a neurotic reaction or brain damage. Sometimes brain damaged people fill in the gaps in their memory with imagined experiences they believe have really happened. This type of memory impairment, *confabulation,* is illustrated by the brain injured adolescent who recounts for the clinician the events of her day by saying she visited her parents in a neighboring city when in fact she never left the hospital. In contrast, *hyperamnesia* refers to the unusual ability to recall minute and sometimes insignificant details learned in the distant past. This exaggeration of memory may be evident in childhood psychosis, paranoid and manic states, and obsessive-compulsive neurotic reactions.

In addition, language content may indicate impairment of perceptual functioning. The ten-year-old child who sees snakes covering his bed is likely to be *hallucinating,* perceiving something that does not actually exist. Hallucinations of this sort may be suggestive of extremely high fever, toxic drug reactions, brain disorders, and psychotic reactions. Any of the senses may be involved in hallucinations, although visual and auditory experiences are most frequently observed.

Finally, the content of verbal language gives the clinician important diagnostic data about the client's range of emotions, the quality of feelings, the appropriateness of the emotional expression to the situation, and the degree of control exercised over impulses and feelings. Mrs. B.'s pervasive anger toward her husband, the school principal, and the examiner were reflected in what she said. Her words did not convey either elation or despondency, or inappropriateness of feelings (disparity between expressed feelings and the context in which the feelings occur), which may have suggested a psychotic reaction. Instead, Mrs. B.'s verbalizations revealed a cold, controlling, aggressive, domineering, and somewhat masculine woman who encouraged immaturity and dependency in both Freddy and her husband.

Let us now turn to consider the interview, the second method used by clinicians to evaluate the client. What has already been discussed about verbal language should be elaborated and better understood as we deal with the interview method in this next section.

The Interview

In today's world almost everyone has had some experience with the interview. We tend to think of it as a formal conversation between two or more people that has been prearranged for a specific purpose, be it admission to school, membership in a club, job placement, market research, or census taking. How the interview is conducted varies widely, depending on the orientation and training of the interviewer. For example, the psychoanalytically oriented clinician would want to know a great deal about the child's past history, especially early experiences, while the behaviorist would emphasize current unwanted behaviors and the conditions that maintain them. In addition, the nature of the interview may be influenced by the setting and the purpose of the interview, as well as by the special characteristics of the interviewee. A study of nine different interview schedules showed that only three kinds of information (identifying data, present problem, and family history) were included in all of them, while many other types of information were common to only a few schedules (Peterson, 1968).

The Initial Interview

This is the first of perhaps several interactions between the client and clinicians, and it is sometimes referred to as the intake interview. Although the intent may be to gather diagnostic data, it is difficult to separate diagnostic sessions from therapeutic ones. Consequently, a primary objective of the initial interview is to establish a positive relationship between clinician and client (known as *rapport*). The clinician must be sensitive to and aware of the client's attitudes and feelings about being evaluated. The clinician should remember that it is the client and not the clinician who feels scrutinized and who may enter into this first meeting with feelings of anxiety and mistrust. For various reasons, parents may not adequately prepare their youngsters for the interview, and this is likely to allow the child's imagination to run wild and arouse anxieties and fears. Clinicians can lessen these difficulties by helping parents to prepare the child prior to the visit with regard to what to expect and why the interview is necessary. In addition, the clinician's discussion of these matters early in the session will help to allay anxieties, so that the child can feel freer to cooperate and talk openly.

In dealing with young children, special problems of rapport may arise because of their limited verbal abilities, their fear of strangers, and their reluctance to separate from mother. The clinician can inspire trust and make the situation less formidable by introducing play materials and sitting on the floor and either playing or watching the child play. Moreover, giving the child freedom to move about the room realistically acknowledges the fact that the child can't sit still for a long period of time. Freedom of movement loosens the situation up to the extent that it will increase the child's spontaneity and verbalizations.

As a matter of practice, many clinicians (including the author) hold the initial interview with both parents, followed by several separate sessions with the child in which each parent is asked to bring the child to the practitioner at least one time. At the end of the evaluation process, a feedback session is held for the parents and, whenever possible, the child to discuss the findings and recommendations. The initial interview serves the multiple purposes of establishing rapport, eliciting information about the child's problems, seeing how parents relate to each other, and obtaining historical data on the family and child. In addition, it can give parents some help in learning how to prepare their child for subsequent visits. An account of the present problem is a natural starting point for most parents, since their chief complaints are likely to be uppermost in their minds, and thus the first area they would be willing to talk about. Following this discussion, the interview can turn to a detailed history in

TABLE 5–2

	Area of Inquiry	Information	Implication
I.	Prenatal, Birth, and Early Development	Pregnancy planned, legitimate, difficult?	Rejection
		Delivery: breach, section, induced?	Brain injury
		Mother's physical and emotional condition?	Infection, drugs, anxiety, depression.
		Infant's weight, height?	Premature birth
		Feeding: breast, bottle, problems, weaning?	Mother-child interaction and early signs of abnormal development and behavior, in eating, sleeping, toilet training, gross and fine motor coordination, and language acquisition.
		Sleep-patterns; restlessness, colic, problems associated with bedtime?	
		Toilet training: when, what problems, enuresis, how handled?	
		Motor patterns: crawl, walk, write, language patterns, talk?	
II.	Medical History	Patterns of illness and sequela, head injuries or signs of brain dysfunction, surgery.	Parental and client reaction to illness. Brain damage, emotional trauma, fears, anxieties.
III.	Educational History	Amount of education, grades, relations with school authorities and peers, and behavioral problems like truancy, dismissals. . . .	Intellectual and achievement pattern. Relations to both authority and peers. Acting out and delinquency.
IV.	Work History	Sequence of jobs held, how long, reasons for termination, special vocational skills.	Achievement motivation, reliability, sense of responsibility. . . .
V.	Social History	Nature of social adjustment, choice of interpersonal relations, social activities, interests, hobbies, and sexual adjustment and experiences such as masturbation, homosexuality, heterosexuality, sex fantasies, and particular difficulties. Handling of anger, and circumstances that give rise to hostile feelings. Drug or alcohol use.	Ability and kind of relationships, style of relating, range of interest, sex orientation, difficulties, and emotional reactions. Quality of feelings, acting out and delinquency. Drug or alcohol abuse.
VI.	Family History	Parents alive, other members of family . . . living together or when and how did separation occur. Indications of epilepsy, mental illness, or other diseases, and emotional stability.	Kinds of parental models, genetic influences, relations within family structure.

which a systematic study of the antecedent conditions that contributed to the child's personality and present difficulties are highlighted. This procedure is known as a *case history,* and much like the interview itself, it can vary considerably. Some clinicians routinely cover the same background areas in all cases, while others select only areas that seem especially relevant to the study of a given client. Still others vary in the extent of inquiry used in their review of pertinent historical material. In order to give the reader a look at what this procedure entails, a sample case history form is outlined and summarized in Table 5–2.

Sometime before the initial parent interview is over, the clinician describes what will be done with the child during the next two sessions and also tells the parents that the clinician will ask them to take some paper and pencil tests while the clinician and child interact. To reinforce the idea of parental involvement and to communicate it to the child, the clinician (as he or she initially interacts with the child and one parent) requires that the parent complete one or two tests at a desk in the outer office (Sentence Completion Test and The Minnesota Multiphasic Personality Inventory). They are both told that the parent will be working outside, while the child and the clinician are busy for approximately the same amount of time (one hour). The child is reassured by the knowledge that the parent is nearby and that both mother and father are actively involved in the evaluation process.

Critical Evaluation of the Interview

Although the interview is the most important and frequently used clinical method for diagnosing and understanding clients, it is a procedure that is subject to several sources of error that may significantly reduce its reliability. We know from earlier discussions that interviewers vary with respect to types of information they gather, their purpose for the interview, and, more subtly, in the way in which they establish rapport. Therefore, by keeping interview differences to a minimum, interview agreement for diagnosis or prognosis, could be increased. This could be accomplished by more routine use of a standardized interview format in which the clinician asks the same set of questions and accumulates the same set of data from every client seen. An example of a *standardized* or *structured interview,* as it is called, is the Psychiatric Evaluation Form: Diagnostic Version (Spitzer, Endicott, Mesnikoff, and Cohen, 1967–1968), which is partially shown in Table 5–3.

Sometimes the resolution of one problem leads to others. In adding more structure and uniformity to the interview, the clinician gives up the freedom to wander and shift about from area to area in ways that seem to best fit the client and to obtain maximum information. Moreover, the standardized interview imposes a style of inquiry that may be neither comfortable for the interviewer nor suitable for motivating the client to be productive.

Clinicians are responsible for charting and maintaining the direction of the interview as well as for its contents. Additionally, they are required to serve as recorders, observers, and skilled professionals who know how to pursue pertinent information while avoiding the blind alleys of unimportant material. Under these circumstances, it is not surprising that inaccuracies and errors are inadvertently introduced into the process by the interviewer. Untrained interviewers are likely to be so overly attentive to the mechanics of their multiple functions that they often lose sight of their major ob-

TABLE 5–3 *

PSYCHIATRIC EVALUATION FORM - DIAGNOSTIC VERSION

INTERVIEW GUIDE	SCALES

ORIGINAL COMPLAINT

If a psychiatric patient: Now I would like to hear about
your problems or difficulties and how they led to
your coming to the (hospital, clinic).

> **The time period for this
> section is the past month.**

GENERAL CONDITION

Tell me how you have been feeling recently.
    (Anything else been bothering you?)

PHYSICAL HEALTH

How is your physical condition?
Does any part of your body give you trouble?
Do you worry much about your health?

PHYSICAL HEALTH
214 SOMATIC CONCERNS

Excessive concern with bodily functions; preoccupation with one or more real or imagined physical
complaints or disabilities; bizarre or unrealistic
feelings or beliefs about his body or parts of body.
Do not include mere dissatisfaction with appearance.

?   1   2   3   4   5   6

**If necessary, inquire for doctor's opinion about
symptoms or illnesses.**

When you are upset do you react physically...like
    [stomach trouble, diarrhea, headaches, sick
    feelings, dizziness] ?

215 CONVERSION REACTION

Has a motor or sensory dysfunction which conforms
to the lay notion of neurological illness, for which
his doctors can find no organic basis (e.g., paralysis
or anesthesia).

?   1   2   3   4   5   6

216 PSYCHOPHYSIOLOGICAL REACTIONS

Is bothered by one or more psychophysiological
reactions to stress. Examples: backache,
headaches, hypertension, dizziness, asthma, spastic
bowel. **Note: the reaction may or may not involve
structural change.**

?   1   2   3   4   5   6

APPETITE-SLEEP-FATIGUE

**Disturbances in these areas are often associated
with Depression, Anxiety, or Somatic Concerns.**
What about your appetite for food?
Do you have any trouble sleeping or getting
    to sleep? (Why is that?)
How easily do you get tired?

MOOD

**This section covers several moods. The interviewer
must determine to what extent the symptoms are
associated with either one or the other or several
of the dimensions.**

What kinds of moods have you been in recently?

MOOD
217 ELATED MOOD

Exhibits or speaks of an elevated mood, exaggerated
sense of well being or optimism, or feelings of elation. Examples: Says "everything is great," jokes,
witticisms, silly remarks, singing, laughing, or trying
to get others to laugh or smile.

?   1   2   3   4   5   6

What kinds of things do you worry about?
    (How much do you worry?)

What kinds of fears do you have? (Any situation...
    activities...things?)

How often do you feel anxious or tense?
    (When you are this way, do you react phy-
    sically...like sweating, dizziness, cramps?)

218 ANXIETY

Remarks indicate feelings of apprehension, worry,
anxiety, nervousness, tension, fearfulness, or panic.
When clearly associated with any of these feelings,
consider insomnia, restlessness, physical symptoms
(e.g., palpitations, sweating, dizziness, cramps), or
difficulty concentrating, etc.

?   1   2   3   4   5   6

What about feeling restless?

219 PHOBIA
Has an irrational fear(s) of a particular object(s) or situation(s) which he tends to avoid. Consider number, interference in life and degree of irrationality.

?   1   2   3   4   5   6

How often do you feel sad, depressed, or blue?

When was the last time you felt like crying?

How do you feel about yourself?
(When you compare yourself with other people, how do you come out?)

Is it hard for you to concentrate on things?

Do you enjoy things now as much as usual?

220 DEPRESSION
Remarks indicate feelings of sadness, depression, worthlessness, failure, hopelessness, remorse, guilt, or loss. When clearly associated with any of these feelings, consider crying, insomnia, poor appetite, fatigue, loss of interest or enjoyment, difficulty concentrating, or brooding, etc.

?   1   2   3   4   5   6

221 GUILT
Feels he is either unworthy, sinful, evil, or has done something terrible, or feels he is being punished for his misdeeds.

?   1   2   3   4   5   6

OBSESSIONS-COMPULSIONS
Do you get thoughts that don't make sense that you can't get rid of or put out of your mind?

Is there any act which you have to repeat over and over or which you cannot resist repeating...like constantly washing your hands or constantly checking things or anything like that?

222 OBSESSIONS-COMPULSIONS
Has thoughts which occur repeatedly against his resistance, the content of which he regards as senseless, or performs some act or routine which he cannot resist repeating excessively (e.g., handwashing).

?   1   2   3   4   5   6

SUICIDE-SELF MUTILATION
When a person gets upset, depressed, or feels hopeless, he may think about dying. Do you?

Have you recently thought about killing yourself?
If yes: Determine degree of preoccupation, and presence of threats, gestures, or attempts.

(What about hurting yourself physically... other than suicide?)

223 SUICIDE-SELF MUTILATION
Suicidal thoughts, preoccupation, threats, gestures, or attempts, and thoughts or acts of self mutilation.

?   1   2   3   4   5   6

SOCIAL ISOLATION AND SUSPICION-PERSECUTION
This section covers both Social Isolation and Suspicion-Persecution. The interviewer must determine to what extent the symptoms are associated with either one or the other or both dimensions.

How are you getting along with people?

What kinds of trouble do you have with people?
(What about your family?)

Do you have much to do with [your neighbors, co-workers, students, the other people here]?

How do you usually feel when you are with people?

How do people generally seem to feel about you?

Whom do you feel you can trust the most?

Do you feel you have to be on guard with people?

SOCIAL ISOLATION AND SUSPICION-PERSECUTION
224 SOCIAL ISOLATION
Avoidance of contact or involvement with people; preference for being alone; feelings of isolation, rejection, or discomfort with people.

?   1   2   3   4   5   6

225 SUSPICION-PERSECUTION
From mild suspiciousness to belief that he is being persecuted. Examples: distrustfulness; feels mistreated, taken advantage of or tricked; feels that people are staring at him or talking about him when they aren't; believes he is being poisoned, his mind is being read, controlled, or influenced by others, or that there is a plot against him. **Do not include feelings or beliefs which are completely justified by the situation.**

?   1   2   3   4   5   6

* Spitzer, Endicott, Mesnikoff & Cohen, 1967–1968. Reprinted with permission from New York State State Psychiatric Institute.

jective—the client. Interview errors may also be introduced by transient personal events, such as fatigue from too much partying the night before or preoccupation about a sick child at home. Some interviewers bring with them certain biases, whether it be their inclination to overinterpret sexual data, or to overemphasize inadequacies and deficiencies in clients rather than strengths and resources. Daily (1960) identified a "pathology bias" in some clinicians who tend to see symptoms of abnormal behavior in everyone.

Another important source of interview error comes from the interviewee, whose predetermined attitudes, expectations, and feelings about the interview may influence what he or she says, what areas he or she will discuss truthfully, and how much cooperation will take place. In addition, clients are subject to the same sorts of transient effects from personal events as the interviewer. These may unduly color their usual behavior pattern on a given day. They may be erroneously interpreted if they are not confirmed by additional observations made over several separate occasions.

Apart from sources of errors that lower the reliability of the interview, questions concerning its predictive validity have been raised (Sarbin, 1943; Kelly and Fiske, 1951; Meehl, 1954; Matarazzo, 1965). Unequivocal answers are not forthcoming at present, because of the nature of inherent complexities and sources of error involved in the interview process itself, and of the poorly defined areas selected for prediction. To illustrate, we need only look at the problem of predicting school success. How well have we identified the characteristics that an individual must possess in order to succeed in school? Even if we could agree that both intelligence and motivation are im-

portant factors, we could not agree on the weight that should be assigned to each in arriving at a predictive formula. Obviously, if we were dealing with a graduate program in which candidates for admission were all intellectually bright, then we probably would give more attention to factors such as motivation and past demonstrated performance in a known setting. The problem of prediction is further complicated by the poorly defined criteria of school success. Should we use grade point average as our criterion, and, if so, is a "C" average adequate as a measure of success or should it be set higher, say "B" or "A"? Should the student's participation in extracurricular activities be included and how much weight should it be given? How about using eventual job placement as a criterion? But how do you grade or measure the quality of jobs, and how do you account for fluctuations in the job market at the time placement is made? Obviously, the problems involved in making predictions, be they from interviews, test results, grades, or other indicators of past performance, are numerous and complex.

The interview as a method, standing by itself, cannot be any more reasonably indicted for predictive inefficiency than most other methods. It is a procedure that is essential in establishing rapport between client and clinician. It is also useful in providing the clinician with first-hand observations and information for diagnosing and understanding the client, and in serving as a potential base for improving interpersonal relations between the client and others. Recent advances aimed at decreasing major sources of error, such as the standardized interview and computer interviewing, offer promise for more effective and systematic study of the interview process and its future clinical application.

Psychological Tests [2]

Of all the clinical methods available for diagnosing abnormal behavior, psychological tests are more closely identified with the activities of psychologists than with any other group of mental health specialists. Beginning with the study of individual differences at the close of the nineteenth century, psychology continues to make substantial contributions to the development of tests that measure a wide range of human behaviors. These efforts have produced a degree of precision and objectivity that is simply not attainable with other assessment approaches. Essentially, the test method provides for a standard procedure in which the same stimuli are presented to every client in a prescribed manner, and responses are then categorized in objective and quantitative terms. Many psychological tests have been devised to more reliably measure behaviors that are elicited in the course of clinical observations and the interview. However, there are other tests that measure behaviors that are not readily discernible in the clinical interaction, for example, fantasies, specific aspects of memory, perception, or academic achievement. Therefore, the use of psychological tests in the diagnostic process serves the dual function of increasing the accuracy and reliability of data already available through other clinical methods, and of providing additional data not accessible otherwise.

Intelligence Tests

No area of psychological testing has enjoyed greater success or public acceptance

[2] Only a sample of the available tests can be included here. For a more detailed and extensive coverage of tests, Buros' *Mental Measurement Yearbook* is recommended as a valuable reference.

than that of intelligence testing. It was the first to be widely recognized and the first of many to have been developed as a response to specific social needs. Today, the I.Q. as an index of intelligence is a household term that has implications for many aspects of a person's life, be it school success, vocational choice, employment opportunities, or economic and social potential. In the clinical setting, assessing intelligence is almost always important, because it establishes an overall baseline estimate of the child's intellectual capacities to cope with the environment. It also provides an evaluation of the child's functioning efficiency in a variety of cognitive areas where impairment may be of diagnostic significance. Intelligence tests are numerous and diverse in that they are designed for all ages, for either group or individual administration, and for people who may be otherwise excluded because of their verbal, motor, and/or educational disadvantages.

1. *The Binet Scales* that appeared at the turn of the twentieth century (as noted in Chapter 1) represented the first major breakthrough in intelligence testing. The scales were translated into English, revised several times, and improved as a psychometric instrument largely through the efforts of Lewis Terman and his associates at Stanford University (Terman, 1916; Terman and Merrill, 1937, 1960). Although the term Intelligence Quotient or I.Q. was first introduced by William Stern, it was Terman who was largely responsible for its current popularity, since he used it in his revision of the scales to express mental development and brightness. The I.Q. is computed by dividing mental age (MA), that is, the sum of the months of credit a respondent received for items passed, by chronological age (CA), that is the actual age of the respondent in months. The obtained

ratio is then multiplied by 100. Thus the I.Q. score of 100 is set as the average and reflects the child's mental ability to perform at a level equal to his or her actual age. In using the formula MA/CA × 100, the obtained I.Q. score yields a quantitative expression of the degree to which the child falls above or below the average. The latest revision of the Stanford-Binet (Form L-M) incorporates the best subtests from the 1937 L and M scales. As in previous editions, the scale consists of six subtests for age levels beginning with two years to the adult years. At the youngest level, the child is required to put each cut-out of a circle, square, and triangle into its appropriate hole in a form board, identify parts of a boy depicted on a large picture, build a tower with blocks, and point to the correct picture when a word is presented, such as airplane, telephone, hat and so forth. At age five, the child is asked to complete an incomplete drawing of a man, to imitate the examiner in folding a piece of paper into a triangle, to define words such as ball, hat, and stove, to copy a figure of a square, and so forth. Most children find the subtest interesting and pleasurable.

2. *The Wechsler Scales.* Because he was critical of the Stanford-Binet on the grounds that it only yielded one score which was heavily influenced by verbal skills, David Wechsler set out to construct a test of intelligence that would measure not only the aggregate of abilities involved in intelligence, but also provide separate scores for its important components (Wechsler, 1955). In addition, Wechsler devised a new method of calculating the I.Q. that was not dependent on the erroneous assumption that there is a linear relationship between MA and CA. He showed that intelligence does not proceed by equal amounts throughout its development, but instead tends to

increase until the very late teens and then levels off for a brief period before it gradually declines with age. Therefore, Wechsler did away with the MA score, and defined I.Q. in terms of deviation units from the average of scores obtained by people of a given age (which, incidentally, is the procedure for computing I.Q. that was adopted in the 1960 revision of the Stanford-Binet).

The first of Wechsler's tests appeared in 1939, but it was later substantially revised and called the Wechsler Adult Intelligence Scale (WAIS). The enormous popularity of the Wechsler tests with individuals ranging in age from sixteen to sixty-four years prompted the construction of two new tests that essentially followed the same format, but was for use with preschool and school-age children: the Wechsler Intelligence Scale for Children (WISC) and its recent revision, the WISC-R, and the Wechsler Preschool and Primary Scale of Intelligence (WPPSI) (Wechsler, 1974).

WISC-R consists of twelve subtests, six of which are considered verbal in nature and six nonverbal. Separate I.Q. scores are obtained for each grouping of subtests, that is, a Verbal Scale I.Q. and a Performance Scale I.Q. When the total weighted score of all of the subtests is computed, a third I.Q., known as the Full Scale I.Q., is established. The subtests of both the verbal and Performance Scales along with a sample item and a brief description of the tasks involved are summarized in Table 5–4. By and large, clinicians have found the Wechsler Scales very useful because they not only provide three separate I.Q. scores, but they also yield separate subtest scores that can be examined for potential diagnostic clues associated with areas of either impaired or enhanced intellectual functioning.

3. *Other Tests of Intelligence.* There are a number of other intelligence tests that

TABLE 5–4 Description of Subtests of the WISC-R and Sample Items

Verbal Scale Sub-Tests

Information	A simply stated set of questions that require memory of previously learned facts. (What must you do to make water boil?)
Similarities	A set of paired items that require verbal abstraction of similarity. (In what way are an apple and a banana alike?)
Arithmetic	A set of computation questions and problems. (At 8¢ each, how much will 3 candy bars cost?)
Vocabulary	A set of words to define. (What does "umbrella" mean?)
Comprehension	A set of questions dealing with judgment and common sense ways of coping with different situations. (What is the thing to do when you cut your finger?)
Digit Span	Immediate memory of a series of orally presented numbers. (I am going to say some numbers. When I am finished, say them right after me . . . 8–4–2–3–9.)

Performance Scale Sub-Tests

Picture Completion	Twenty simple line drawings, each with an important missing element. (Look at the picture and tell me what important part is missing?)
Picture Arrangement	A series of cards presented in a jumbled sequence. (Put the cards in the right order so they tell a story that makes sense.)
Block Design	Blocks are used to reproduce a series of designs. (Take these blocks and make a design with them that looks like the one on this card.)
Object Assembly	Scrambled pieces must be correctly assembled to make an object. (Put these pieces together correctly.)
Coding	Symbols attached to numbers must be correctly substituted in a series of numbered boxes. (Write in the open box the symbol that goes with the number above it.)
Mazes	A supplementary test requires finding one's way through a set of mazes, with a minimum of wrong turns and in the shortest period of time.

merit some attention because they are particularly suitable for either certain special circumstances or certain populations. The Binet and Wechsler scales are rather expensive and time consuming, in that they require prior training for the examiner, and they ordinarily take more than one hour to administer to an individual client. Group intelligence tests are paper-and-pencil devices that can be readily administered to large numbers of individuals by examiners who require only minimal training. Usually, these tests are used with a good deal of success in schools or other institutional settings for screening purposes.

The Peabody Picture Vocabulary (PPVT) and the Slosson Intelligence Test (SIT) are examples of two individually administered intelligence tests that are more economical than the Binet or WISC in that they take less time and can be given by relatively untrained examiners. The PPVT consists of a graded set of cards each containing four line drawn pictures (Dunn, 1959, 1965). The task is to identify the picture corresponding to the word presented by the examiner. The test applies to children ranging from two-and-one-half to eighteen years of age, and it can be administered in approximately fifteen minutes. The SIT can be used for children and adults, and it can be given in about twenty minutes. It consists of items taken from the Binet Scale and the Gesell Institute of Child Development Behavior Inventory (Slosson, 1963). Both the PPVT and the SIT are quick measures of intelligence and useful screening instruments but they should not be regarded as suitable substitutes for either the Binet or WISC (Sattler, 1974; Himmelstern, 1972).

An example of the oldest and one of the most widely used group intelligence tests is the Otis-Lennon Mental Ability Test, which includes six levels that are appropriate for school children from kindergarten through twelfth grade (Otis and Lennon, 1967). Like other group tests, the Otis is economical, but it has the disadvantages of precluding examiner observations and of penalizing children who are slow or poor readers and who are relatively unstimulated and unmotivated by an objective paper and pencil test.

If for some reason, perhaps for child adoption or early suspicion of mental retardation, an infant must be evaluated, the clinician may find an infant scale useful. For example, the Bayley Scales of Infant Development (BSID) is a well constructed and standardized measure of infant development from two to thirty months of age (Bayley, 1969). Bayley wisely cautions that the scales are not intended to predict a child's future abilities, but they are useful in identifying impairments in development that may suggest diagnostic inferences with respect to neurological defects, emotional disturbances, or sensory and environmental deficiencies. It should be emphasized that attempts to assess the intelligence of an infant have been uniformly unsuccessful. Infant intelligence tests are highly unreliable, and their validity with respect to future measure of intelligence have been quite low (McCall, Hogarty, and Hurlburt, 1972).

There are occasions when the clinician is confronted with a nonverbal client, or one who does not speak English. In such an event, the clinician may use a completely nonverbal test such as the Porteus Maze Test (Porteus, 1965). The test is easy to administer, fun to take, and it can be helpful in identifying both children and adults who fall in the borderline range of intelligence.

As useful as intelligence tests have been, they are not trouble free or without limitations. For some time, the I.Q. was assumed to have a constant meaning regardless of the age of the child, and regardless of what test was used to obtain it. We know that unless certain constant relationships are maintained between the dispersion of test scores at each age and the averages for successive ages, the I.Q. cannot remain constant either for individuals or for groups (Stodolsky and Lesser, 1967; Sattler, 1974). Moreover, tests of intelligence are different in their construction, norms, variability, and ways of calculating I.Q.'s, so that an I.Q. obtained from one is not the same as that derived from another (Anastasi, 1976). The popular idea of thinking of an I.Q. as an absolute number referring to the relative amount of brightness a person possesses is erroneous. Like all test scores, an I.Q. can vary as much as plus or minus fifteen points from one test administration to another. To avoid misinterpretations, clinicians rarely, if ever, report the obtained I.Q. score to the parents and child, but instead discuss the findings of terms of a descriptive range (retarded, borderline defective, dull normal, average, bright normal, superior, and very superior) of functioning. Also, many intelligence tests have limited applicability, since they excluded black and other minority groups from their normative population. Clinicians must exercise care in selecting the test that is most appropriate for each client and in interpreting the results in light of the available norms for that test.

Personality Tests

Most psychologists tend to divide personality tests into two types: self-report inventories and projective tests.

1. *Self-report inventories* are characterized by structured stimuli (test items) to which a client responds with a fixed number of specific choices. Frequently, they are paper and pencil tests that can be administered easily to many people at the same time and can be scored rapidly and objectively. While they are designed to measure discrete personality traits, most have been intended for use with literate adult and adolescent populations. *The Family Relations Test* represents one of the few inventories used clinically to assess the child's feelings toward various family members, as well as the members' regard for the child (Bene and Anthony, 1957). The child reads a series of statements (or they are read to young children) and is asked to assign a message to the most appropriate family member, or to oneself, or to "nobody." The messages are subdivided into a number of categories such as positive and negative feelings from the child to others, positive and negative feelings toward the child from others, dependence, maternal overprotection, paternal indulgence, and maternal overindulgence. Responses are tallied in each subcategory and patterns of scores are interpreted in terms of psychoanalytic theory. The tests boast good reliability, but validity studies and normative data are sorely needed.

The Minnesota Multiphasic Personality Inventory (MMPI) is unquestionably the best known and most widely used personality test of the self-report type (Hathaway and McKinley, 1943). Its success and popularity can be attributed largely to the care exercised by the authors in its original construction and to the voluminous research literature that has accumulated over the last thirty years. It was developed as an inexpensive diagnostic instrument that is easily administered to most people (usually adults) and as a psychometric device that eliminates many of the deficiencies of other inventories. It consists of nine clinical scales that describe the major psychiatric disorders. In addition, it has three validity scales that serve as internal checks of the respondent's tendency (1) to attribute socially desirable traits to himself; (2) to be careless or confused and thus give an invalid answer; and (3) to be either too open or too defensive. Early clinical application of the MMPI dampened the original idea that a deviant elevation on a single clinical scale would correspond to the psychiatric diagnosis of the client. However, MMPIers soon found that the instrument could be effectively used in making diagnostic decisions when combinations of scale scores (profile patterns) were interpreted (Dahlstrom, Welsh, and Dahlstrom, 1972). Within recent years, computer programs have become available for scoring and interpreting the MMPI. Imagine! The response can be scored, analyzed, and readied for a printout of the interpretation in narrative form in less time than it takes most people to say "Minnesota Multiphasic Personality Inventory" (Fowler, 1969).

In spite of its popularity and its demonstrated value in the diagnostic process, the MMPI is not without limitations. It is a test on which many normal persons achieve elevated scores on the clinical scales. In addition, disturbed persons with some superficial knowledge of abnormal behavior can minimize their psychopathology by not admitting to items that are characteristic of their disorder. The test may be too time consuming (taking about one and a half hours) and inappropriate for persons who are either illiterate or who have low reading competence. Although it is neither designed for or useful with young children, its demonstrated value in predicting juvenile delinquency has encouraged clinicians to include it in their test batteries for preadolescent and adolescent youngsters (Hathaway and Manachesi, 1953, 1963). In addition, it is sometimes a fruitful test to give to parents while the clinician works with the child, especially for those parents with suspected psychopathology.

2. *Projective tests* involve the presentation of unstructured and ambiguous stimuli to which people may respond freely. Test stimuli are standard in the sense that the same set is presented to each examinee in the same order and with the same instructions. However, the purpose for which the test is intended and the variables it is designed to assess are concealed from the respondent. In contrast to self-report inventories, the stimulus meaning of the projective test items are determined more by the responder than by the predetermined design of the test constructor. The open and free style of responding to projective devices allows wide variations in the number, length, and content of responses, as well as in interpretations that reflect the unique aspects of the respondent's personality.

Projective tests come in an extensive and diverse assortment of stimuli and task requirements that make categorization difficult (Lindzey, 1959). The stimulus material ranges from ink blots to pictures of various people, animals, scenes, as well as geometric designs, cartoons, words, and incomplete sentences. Most projectives assume that every response is psychologically determined and that the test stimuli provide ample opportunity for eliciting a sample of answers that reflect the person's basic personality. It is further assumed that the test's ambiguity and hidden intent will make the respondents less defensive and freer to reveal their personalities. Accordingly, a great deal may be inferred from these test responses, including the person's fantasies, defense mechanisms, unconscious motives, latent feelings, and sources of anxiety. Interpreters of projective tests typically adopt a holistic frame of reference, stressing the interaction among personality variables and the totality of personality.

The Rorschach (Ink Blots). Introduced in 1921 by the Swiss psychiatrist, Hermann Rorschach, the test consists of a standard series of ten ink blots, five of which are achromatic and five chromatic (Rorschach, 1921, 1942). Although a form is available for group administration, typically the test is given in a fixed sequential order to one person at a time. The test administration includes three separate phases known as *free association, inquiry,* and *testing the limits.* During free association the client is simply required to look at each card and to say aloud what it looks like. The examiner records the client's verbal and nonverbal responses as well as the time taken for the first association and for all associations to each card. The most crucial and difficult phase of administration is the inquiry, because it involves conducting a short nondirective interview to obtain answers concerning the location, the stimulus determinants, and the content of each response. This information enables the examiner to formally score the responses sometime later. When testing young children, some clinicians conduct the inquiry after the child has responded to each card rather than waiting until the free association is completed on all ten blots to avoid the possibility of the child forgetting. Testing the limits involves yet another presentation of the ten cards. It is useful in special circumstances, such as when few responses are given, or when the examiner wants to see if the client is capable of perceiving good form or popular responses.

The Rorschach test uses scores to describe the stimulus characteristics of the test responses and to reflect specific psychological processes. The most recent norms for children and adolescents have been published by Levitt and Trullmaa (1972). Interpretation of Rorschach protocols involves understanding of the conventional psychological meaning attached to the scoring categories and learning how and when to modify these interpretations, as scores are considered in the context of other scores. The interpretive process is quite complex because it is not only tied to the psychological meaning of a given scoring category and its relationship to other scores, but also to certain considerations such as the frequency of scores and their patterns and distribution. In addition, the formal structure and the content of the verbal response are analyzed and play an important part of the interpretation of Rorschach protocols.

We might properly ask, "Just how effective is the Rorschach as a psychodiagnostic instrument and as a measure of personality?" After more than fifty years of clinical use, and a voluminous literature that exceeds four thousand published papers and books, one would think that a definitive answer would be forthcoming. But the issue of the validity of the Rorschach is complicated by the controversy evidenced between research findings and the favorable experiences of clinicians who show continued confidence in its usage. As a psychometric instrument or a test, the Rorschach incorporates so many glaring weaknesses and inadequacies that it is clearly found wanting. The diversity of scoring systems and the idiosyncratic practices of clinicians introduce inconsistencies into interpretation that, in turn, lower predictive accuracy (Exner, 1969). Moreover, Rorschach scores do not occur with frequencies that even come close to approximating a normal distribution. Evidence based on 337 Rorschach protocols not only supports this finding but also notes that almost half of the scoring categories show average response frequencies of less than one (Knopf, 1956). In short, half of the scoring categories are rarely called into use, making them almost useless for differential diagnosis and as important indicators of psychological attributes.

Recent reviews of the Rorschach uniformly conclude that it is not a test but a rich and broad sample of an individual's personality (McArthur, 1972; Rabin, 1972; Reznikoff, 1972). There is a growing view that the Rorschach can be clinically useful if it is treated as a standard interview in which formal perceptual scoring is abandoned and only the content of the protocol is evaluated (Zubin, Eron, and Schumer, 1965). This position holds that it is the content of the Rorschach record and not the perceptual determinants that are the important ingredients for whatever success and clinical usefulness it has enjoyed. In this connection, Reznikoff aptly concludes:

Thus, while the Rorschach may be psychometrically moribund, there is convincing evidence that it is gaining new vigor as a very novel interview situation that has meaningful applications in exploring a broad spectrum of personality dimensions (Reznikoff, 1972, p. 176).

It is in this context that clinicians find it a fruitful device to use with children.

The Thematic Apperception Test (TAT). In 1935, Morgan and Murray introduced the TAT as a method of studying fantasy. They observed that literary works often reflect the authors' experiences even though these are distorted in fiction writings. Moreover, they contended that one could discern from the writings of a particular author certain common underlying patterns, attitudes, needs, and interests that reflect the author's personality.

As originally conceived, the TAT is a story-telling device that consists of thirty ambiguous black and white pictures plus one blank card. Some cards are intended for boys, girls, men, or women, but all thirty-one cards are seldom used with any given individual. Usually, the examiner administers ten cards that seem appropriate for the client. The examiner asks the respondent to make up a story that includes what is going on in the picture, what led up to the events depicted, how it turns out, and how people are feeling and thinking. The examiner may record the story along with aside comments and nonverbal behaviors, or the respondent may be asked to write it. Although there are formal scoring systems available, these are primarily used for research but seldom for clinical practice. Instead, clinicians usually analyze the stories as a sample of verbal behavior much like that obtained in an interview.

Occasionally the respondent's identification with the hero is so intense that it evokes obvious autobiographical data, as is the case illustrated in the following story given to Figure 5–1 by an adolescent client who was briefly hospitalized because of severe attacks of anxiety.

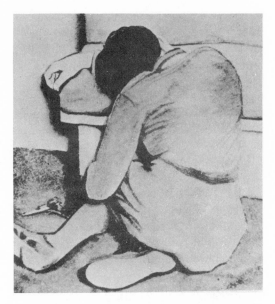

FIGURE 5–1   (Reprinted by permissions of the publishers from Henry A. Murray, *Thematic Apperception Test*, Cambridge, Mass.: Harvard University Press, Copyright © 1943 by the President and Fellows of Harvard College, © 1971 by Henry A. Murray.)

This, to me, is the scene of a boy who just learned about his father's death, and he went back to his room to cry where nobody could see him. Where should I go from here? . . . Again the boy is wondering why his father had to die at an early age, and nobody will tell him. Eventually he forgets about this, but he always had doubts in his mind about certain things that happened. Actually, this struck me as very personal. There is a question of religion involved, and the lack of any medical treatment. That's how my father died when he was forty-nine and I was about twelve years old. He probably died of a cerebral hemorrhage. It happened that this was a Christian Science family, and the boy wondered if medical treatment might have saved this tragedy, but he was never allowed to voice his opinion because of strict religious training. The boy's mother believed vigorously, and was very religious, and the boy had the impression that his father was going along with the mother rather than believing himself. It turned out that the boy finally leaves home, goes out on his own, raises his own family, and buries the feeling.

In an extensive review of validity studies with the TAT, it was found that deviant themes, deviant emotional tones, poorly organized stories, and incongruity among story elements are more apparent in the stories of schizophrenics and neurotics than in the responses of normal adults (Suinn and Oskamp, 1969). Moreover, overtly aggressive and delinquent adolescents are different from nonaggressive adolescents in that they respond with a greater number of aggressive stories and tell more aggressive stories to cards that infrequently elicit aggression. Other validity studies showing differential results with contrasting groups of subjects lend some additional justification for the inclusion of the TAT as part of a psychodiagnostic work-up (Fogel, 1967; Werner, Stabenau, and Pollin, 1970).

Story Telling Techniques for Children. Bellak (1954) designed a TAT-like test called the *Children's Apperception Test (CAT)* for children between the ages of three and ten. The CAT is based on the belief that it is easier for children to identify with animals than with the adult figures of the TAT. It consists of ten pictures of animals in situations that are intended to elicit responses focusing on the psychosexual development and conflicts initially formulated by Freud as occurring in young children. For example, Card 10 of the CAT was constructed to provide information about the child's toilet training, as shown in Figure 5-2 on page 148.

Research with the CAT has produced some normative data, but few studies have been directed toward validating the predictive accuracy of interpretations. As a matter of fact, there is evidence that casts doubt on the CAT's clinical usefulness and on Bellak's original assumption that children will more readily identify with animals than with human figures. Several studies have shown that children tell longer stories, manifest more feelings, and evidence greater identification when responding to human pictures than to the animal pictures of the CAT (Zubin, Eron, and Schumer, 1965).

Constructed as an alternative to the TAT for children of ages eight to fourteen, the *Michigan Picture Test (MPT)* consists of fifteen pictures plus one blank card of various people and scenes such as a classroom, a family in a variety of activities, and so forth (Andrew, Hartwell, Hutt, and Walton, 1953). Although the MPT normative data are quite adequate and some of the responses have been related to outside measures of maladjustment in children, the MPT has not enjoyed widespread clinical use.

Drawing Techniques. In 1926, Florence Goodenough introduced a technique for measuring intellectual levels of children from their drawings of a man (Goodenough, 1926). At the same time, she suggested that her test was also capable of reflecting personality factors. Since then, other writers have been even more impressed with this observation to the point where they contend that drawings yield more and richer data about personality than intelligence. Moreover, it is generally assumed that a human figure drawing is an unconscious projection of oneself, and that psychodiagnostic clues are qualitatively reflected in the drawing (Machover, 1949; Hammer, 1958). There are a number of variants of the draw-a-man test; the best known is described by Machover, who asks the client to first draw a picture of a person on a sheet of blank white paper, and then to draw a person of

FIGURE 5–2   (From Bellak and Bellak, 1961. Reprinted with permission
from Grune and Stratton Co.)

the opposite sex on a separate sheet. In addition, she proposed thirty-three questions to ask children to obtain more specific information about their performance (Machover, 1960, pp. 238–257).

Drawings of human figures are easy to administer and require little time and cost. As an added bonus, they have been known to offer fanciful but contradictory interpretations; for example, inadequacy feelings are either reflected in the drawing of very small figures or very large ones, or both intellectual strivings or feelings of intellectual inadequacy are given as interpretations of a drawing of a large head (Urban, 1963).

Drawing is a technique that has enjoyed a degree of clinical popularity exceeded only by the substantial body of negative findings concerning its validity.

Sentence Completion Techniques (SCT). Growing out of the word association technique where the client responds to a set of stimulus words with the first word that comes to mind, the SCT consists of a series of sentence stems that the client completes. For example, here are only a few items drawn from many that a client might be asked to complete:

I am afraid_____.
I got mad_____.
The people I like best_____.
My main trouble is_____.

The SCT is an extremely flexible device for measuring personality in that the stimuli (sentence stems) can readily be manipulated to assess specific areas of personality and to meet the requirements of different populations and situations. Thus, it is not surprising that there are many forms of the SCT that are applicable to children, adults, females, and males in such diverse settings as the classroom, mental-health clinic, and industry.

As with other projective techniques, the SCT assumes that the responses reveal information about the client's personality. Interpretation usually involves content analysis that ranges in clinical practice from formal scoring to intuitive inspection of the responses. Reliability and validity estimates are higher than those reported with most other projective techniques, making the SCT highly useful in clinical practice and research.

Tests of Brain Damage

The possibility that the abnormal behaviors of a child are the result or the by-product of some central nervous system dysfunction is one that is almost always under consideration in the psychodiagnostic process. Unfortunately, the area of brain dysfunction, which includes many vague but interchangeable terms such as brain damage, organic brain disorders, organicity, central nervous system damage, or dysfunction, is quite complex and imprecise. Reference to any one of these labels suggests the illogical struggle to fit under one broad rubric a set of very heterogeneous conditions that only belong together because "something" has happened to the brain. There is room in this category for such diverse causal agents as tumors and lesions, infections, toxic agents, brain injuries, and biochemical and hormonal imbalances. These circumstances are further complicated by the fact that there is no one-to-one relationship between brain damage and specific behavioral manifestations, although certain behavioral changes in memory, attention span, and perceptual-motor coordination, among others, have been associated with the performance of individuals with known brain damage. Moreover, since behavior is frequently determined by multiple factors, it is not easy to determine when a given behavior change is the product of psychological or organic influences, or both.

Therefore, it is not surprising that behavioral tests designed to determine the presence of brain damage, not to mention its location or extent, have encountered serious predictive difficulties. Often what is surprising is how well some actually do work in the clinical setting. We shall discuss several examples of tests intended specifically to assess brain damage, although we should also note that the clinician uses data obtained from many of the other tests (personality and intelligence) already presented in this chapter.

The Bender-Gestalt Test. First introduced in 1938 by Lauretta Bender (1938), the test consists of nine figures printed on separate white cards that were taken from designs Wertheimer initially used to demonstrate principles of perceptual organization. The designs are shown in Figure 5–3. They are given in a fixed order to both children and adults with the simple request to copy each design on one unlined sheet of white paper. Research has shown that sim-

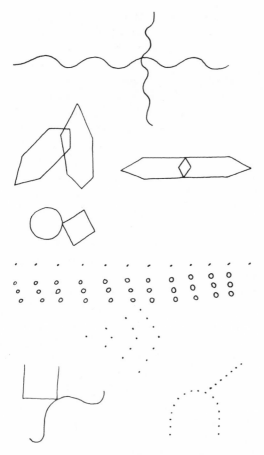

FIGURE 5–3   Bender-Gestalt Test (From Bender, L., 1946, p. 4. Reprinted with permission from the American Orthopsychiatric Association.)

of several scoring systems based on specific errors (distortions, rotations, integration failures, and others) found in the responses of young children ranging in age from five to ten years. Only its ease and economy and the occasional indication from the reproductions of the possible presence of brain damage seem to justify the popularity and widespread use of the Bender-Gestalt Test in clinical practice.

Graham - Kendall Memory - for - Designs Test. Inasmuch as memory is an area of functioning that often is affected by brain damage, tests that involve memory are important in the clinician's armamentarium. The Graham-Kendall Test requires an individual to draw from memory designs that are presented and exposed for five seconds. The test consists of fifteen figures, similar to the Bender except that they have been selected for their demonstrated discriminability between normal and brain damaged persons from ages nine to sixty. A highly reliable scoring system is available that is easy to use, especially by inexperienced examiners.

The Graham-Kendall offers the advantages of normative data, an easy scoring system, the added function of memory, and promising validity data to recommend its use in assessing brain damage.

Achievement and Ability Tests

In the course of a psychodiagnostic work-up, there are instances where special tests are used to answer specific questions or to provide data that would fill in existing gaps in the information already available. This is particularly true in evaluating children who are referred because they are experiencing some difficulties in school. It is often not enough to assess their intelligence,

ple changes in the instructions given to the respondent and whether or not the individual is permitted to move the stimulus cards affect differences in test performance (Hutt, 1972).

Bender provides no normative data nor a formal scoring system, preferring to inspect intuitively the child's performance and make interpretations about perceptual organization and maturation, perceptual motor coordination, and neurological impairment. Koppitz (1964) has developed one because these results do not shed much light on the child's actual performance or academic achievement.

A wide assortment of achievement tests are available for primary, middle, and high-school grades that measure achievement in a variety of academic subjects, such as reading, spelling, arithmetic, social studies, and science. Typically, these tests are of the paper-and-pencil variety that can be administered by the teacher to a group of youngsters. Most achievement tests are easily and quickly scored, and they provide the user with national and sometimes regional norms in order that the individuals' scores can be compared with the performance of others. The addition of data on the child's achievement allows the clinician an opportunity not only to make these comparisons, but also to relate the child's achievement scores to his or her overall intellectual abilities. Taken together, the clinician can more precisely determine whether or not the child's academic performance is discrepant with his or her overall capacity, in which subject areas the child is deficient and/or accelerated, and what performance patterns the child evidences that may serve as potential clues for differential diagnosis.

One test that is used to assist in diagnosing learning disability is the *Illinois Test of Psycholinguistic Abilities (ITPA)* (Kirk, McCarthy, and Kirk, 1968). The ITPA was constructed to serve as a diagnostic tool in assessing deficits in mental functions that are said to be manifest in mentally retarded youngsters and those who have learning disabilities. It can be given to children from age two to ten, and it includes the following subtests: auditory reception, visual reception, visual memory, auditory association, auditory memory, visual association, visual closure, verbal expression, grammatic closure, and manual expression.

The standardization population consisted of children of average intelligence who came from families with slightly above the national average income and educational levels. Thus, the norms underrepresent minority and lower income groups. Research aimed at evaluating the ITPA for diagnosing reading disorders has yielded both positive and negative findings, and it is apparent that more empirical evidence is needed to either support or refute its effectiveness in diagnosing learning disabilities (Carroll, 1972).

Behavioral Assessment

Behavioral assessment consists of procedures that grew out of behavior therapy (to be discussed in Chapter 6), in which the treatment strategies have been derived from learning principles and where abnormal behaviors are viewed as learned responses rather than as symptoms of some underlying disease process. The approach focuses on assessing unwanted behaviors and appraising the child's behavioral repetoire for the purpose of affecting behavior change in some desired direction. It is unlike psychological testing and diagnostic interviewing because it is not primarily aimed at understanding the client or in arriving at a proper classification of his/her abnormal condition. Moreover, it is not concerned with uncovering personality traits or dynamics nor with identifying the historical antecedents of a psychological disorder. Instead, behavioral assessment sets out to: (1) determine the frequency of unwanted behaviors in specific situations to obtain a reliable estimate of the magnitude of the problem, (2) identify the variables that are currently maintaining the client's abnormal thoughts, feelings, and behaviors, and (3) evaluate the responses the client is capable of making in order to plan the most effective treatment plan for the client.

Behavioral Observation

Direct observations of the child's actual behavior in a variety of settings and situations are the primary assessment data for the behaviorally oriented clinician. Accordingly, the clinician, aided by observations of the child's problem behaviors reported by parents, teachers, pediatrician, and other involved people, begins the assessment by delineating the target behaviors to be observed. This is usually followed by a *baseline* observational period in which either the frequency or the duration of the target behavior is systematically recorded on a daily basis or on the days when the child is in the situation where the behavior occurs. In this way, the frequency of temper tantrums or the duration of rocking behavior serves as a baseline from which to later measure the effect of behavior therapy.

Baseline observational data can be obtained in the actual setting in which the target behavior occurs, such as in the home and school, or in the clinic. Frequency measures are easy to do and can be recorded by the clinician and/or the person appropriate to the setting. This has the added benefit of making everyone concerned much more aware of the problem behavior. By dividing the number of times the target behavior occurs by the time of the specified observational period, the clinician can obtain a *response rate*. In instances where it is desirable to observe several behaviors at the same time, *interval recording* or *time-sampling* is ordinarily favored. This method divides each observation session into small time intervals (about twenty seconds) in which the clinician records the presence (+) or absence (0) of each behavior. Since only one occurrence of each behavior

is recorded for each interval, the method fails to yield an exact frequency tally of the behaviors under study. To obtain a measure of the duration of the behavior or *response duration,* the clinician notes the time interval between the beginning and the termination of the target behavior.

In order to identify the stimuli that maintain the target behavior, the clinician also records changes in environmental stimuli before and after the behavior occurs. Those stimuli that precede the target behavior, called *antecedent stimuli,* may be signals to the child that reinforcement will be given when the behavior is emitted, as illustrated in the attention and assistance a boy receives if he waits until father comes home before doing his homework. The stimuli events that occur after the behavior is emitted are known as *consequences* or *consequent stimuli,* and they may serve as reinforcers that increase the probability that the behavior will occur again. In this instance, the boy's refusal to do his homework until the evening is reinforced by his being permitted to play or watch TV. Information about the antecedent and consequent stimuli is necessary for the preparation of a behavioral intervention plan, since these stimuli play an important role in the maintenance of the unwanted behavior. Most often, the clinician gathers this information from the initial interview with the parents, from reports of teachers and others who have observed the child's problem behavior, and through direct observations of the child in a variety of settings.

Other Sources of Behavioral Assessment

1. *The behavioral interview* is an important tool in establishing a good working relationship with the parents and child, although it differs from the traditional inter-

view discussed earlier. Instead of focusing on historical information to understand the underlying psychopathology or to classify it, the behavioral interview takes a more contemporary perspective in seeking information about the child's present problem behaviors and the antecedent and consequent stimuli that may maintain them. The clinician may ask parents to aid in the assessment process by monitoring and recording the target behaviors, and by allowing the clinician to come into the home and/or school to make observations. The behavioral clinician emphasizes objective and specific descriptions of behavior that may require training parents to be more objective, accurate, specific, and reliable in their reporting (Mash and Terdal, 1976). In addition, the behavioral interview is more flexible, and less restricted to a particular place or time period, than the traditional interview in that it may take place in the home, classroom, or over the phone and involves several interviews of different people. Table 5–5 illustrates a sequential interview guide that one behavioral clinician has found useful in accumulating behavioral data and in training parents.

TABLE 5–5   Summary of an Interview Guide for Parents *

Sequential Points To Be Covered

1. Have the parents establish general goals and complaints.
2. Have the parents reduce the general goals and complaints to a list of discrete behaviors which require an increase or decrease in frequency.
3. Have the parents select from the ranked list a single problem behavior on which to concentrate their efforts.
4. Have the parents specify in behavioral terms the precise behavior that is presently occurring and which they desire to change.
5. Have the parents specify in behavioral terms the precise behavior which they desire.
6. Have the parents discuss how they may proceed to the terminal behavior in a step-by-step manner.
7. Have the parents list positive and negative reinforcers which they think will be effective in bringing about behavior changes.
8. Have the parents discuss what deprivations are possible.
9. Have the parents clearly establish what they want to do, either to increase or decrease a behavior or to do both.
10. Have the parents discuss the situation in which the desired behavior should occur.
11. Have the parents discuss the situation in which the undesired behavior should not occur.
12. Have the parents determine a situation which increases the likelihood that some form or portion of the desired behavior occurs.
13. Have the parents discuss how they may increase desired behavior by immediately giving a positive reinforcer following the behavior.
14. Have the parents discuss how they may increase desired behavior by immediately terminating a negative reinforcer following the behavior.
15. Have the parents discuss how they may decrease undesired behavior by withholding the reinforcers which follow it.
16. Have the parents discuss how they may decrease undesired behavior by removing a positive reinforcer.
17. Have the parents discuss how they may decrease undesired behavior by time-out.
18. Discuss with the parents how they may pattern the reinforcers they give to the child.
19. Have the parents discuss how they may vary the reinforcers they give to the child.
20. Have the parents discuss how they may apply two or more procedures simultaneously.
21. Have the parents rehearse verbally the entire program.

---

* From Holland, 1976. Reprinted with permission from the Springer Publishing Co.

2. *Structured self-report measures* have been used by behavioral clinicians in conjunction with direct observations as a way of providing initial data about problem behaviors, although this approach is subjective and runs the risk of poor reliability. Self-report measures vary considerably in terms of the number of items and the specifity and types of behaviors included, the way the items are rated and scored, as well as the age for which they are appropriate. In general, they are characterized by a series of items on which clients rate themselves with respect to the presence or absence or the degree of intensity of particular events or behaviors. For example, the Fear Survey Schedule–II (FSS–II) consists of fifty-one fears (empirically selected) that adolescents and college students can rate in terms of seven different intensities ranging from "none" to "terror" (Greer, 1976). Ratings on such items as sharp objects, dead bodies, failing a test, arguing with parents, and hypodermic needles enable the clinician to assess the various fear stimuli that the client tends to avoid. The FSS–II is often used as a research tool in selecting subjects who differ on specific fears.

3. *Situational observation* is another widely used assessment method in which the behavior sampling may occur in a clinical setting where the clinician can make observations in a systematic manner and under relatively controlled conditions. As an illustration, a youngster with a phobia for dogs might be asked to participate in a Behavioral Avoidance Test (BAT) in which he enters a room that houses a caged dog. He is asked to approach and if possible pet the dog, while his behavior is observed and monitored by the clinician (Bandura, Grusec, and Menlove, 1967). The BAT is used both as a way of assessing the severity of the youngster's phobia and as a means of

evaluating the effectiveness of the behavior therapy. Situational observations may also be used to assess mother-child interactions, let's say, with regard to understanding the antecedent and consequent stimuli reinforcing the child's passive and compliant behaviors. Under these circumstances, the clinician might observe and record mother's behavior toward the child whenever the child attempts to be assertive as well as what she does when the child is passive. In this way, the clinician can accumulate valuable data about the child's target behavior and some of the stimuli that maintain it for the construction of a behavioral intervention plan and for its assessment.

Evaluation of Behavioral Assessment

Behavioral assessment is a relatively new but exciting development that provides a detailed and systematic analysis of problem behaviors and the environmental stimuli that maintain them. It is an approach that is intimately tied to treatment and, therefore, it has the additional advantage of generating data that are used to evaluate the effectiveness of behavior therapy. If the treatment program fails, the clinician can then re-examine the data, gather more, and reformulate and test another remediation plan. While the traditional psychodynamic approach faults the behavioral orientation principally on the grounds that it deals only with symptoms and ignores the underlying basis of the disorder, there is essentially little evidence that the criticism is warranted. Technical advances in behavioral assessment have been abundant during recent years, and more extensive information may be found in the following recent publications: Gelfand and Hartmann, 1975; McReynolds, 1975; Mash and Terdal, 1976.

Summary

In this chapter the spotlight was on the clinical process in which the methods used by clinicians in diagnosing abnormal behavior—clinical observations, the interview, psychological tests, and behavioral assessment—were discussed and evaluated. In addition, a variety of specific behaviors that have potential value as diagnostic clues were identified and described.

The clinical process is initiated through a referral made either directly by the client, or through the intervention of others. Those who are self-referred are more likely to be more aware of their problems and to be more motivated to change their behavioral patterns than those who are directed to the clinician by others. Children are rarely, if ever, self-referred, although they may either directly or indirectly "cry out" for help.

The referral also serves to provide the clinician with an initial orientation to the client's major problems, and sometimes with additional information about the symptoms and what, if anything, has been done to deal with them. The diagnostic process is intended to gather sufficient data to classify the abnormal behavior, to identify the causes or arrive at a working hypothesis about causal factors, and to construct a remedial plan.

Observations of behaviors should be systematically made within each of the following areas: (1) general appearance and attire, and bodily surface signs; (2) emotional gestures and facial expressions; (3) gross and fine motor acts; (4) quality of relationship between client and others; and (5) verbalization of the client.

The interview is a formal conversation between two or more people that has been prearranged for a specific purpose. Interviews may be structured or unstructured. How they are conducted varies widely depending on the orientation and training of the interviewer, the setting and purpose of the interview, and the characteristics of the interviewee.

Rapport between the client and the clinician is the primary objective of the initial interview, along with the gathering of information about the client's current problems and symptoms, when and how they first appeared, the circumstances surrounding their development, and the stimulus events that seem to evoke them. The case history study which systematically reviews certain important past areas of the client's life is undertaken by some clinicians.

Problems of reliability and validity are associated with the interview process. These involve its complexity and variability, interviewer and interviewee biases, and its questionable efficiency in making predictions. Recent advances such as the standardized interview and computer interviewing provide opportunities for greater systematic study of the interview process.

Psychological tests are useful devices for obtaining important information about people. These instruments enable the collection of data in a standard, prescribed, and quantifiable manner.

A widely used class of measure are intelligence tests, illustrated by the Binet and Wechsler Scales. These instruments make possible the assessment of baseline cognitive capabilities, as well as the identification of specific intellectual impairments. Although I.Q. scores are often used in decision-making processes, they are not without their limitations.

There exist other types of intelligence measures used with special populations. Large numbers of people can be quickly assessed through the use of group intelligence tests. The Bayley Scales of Infant Development are employed in the identification of impairment of baby's functioning. For nonverbal individuals, the Porteus Maze Test is best in assessing intellectual level.

A second well-known type of psychological tests is personality measure. This group of tests is composed of self-report inventories and projective tests. Self-report inventories, such as the MMPI and Family Relations Test, represent structured devices that permit rapid and objective scoring. Projective tests, on the other hand, enable the free and open assessment of the needs, drives, and attitudes of people.

Several tests of brain damage that claim to identify central nervous system dysfunction were discussed. Generally, these tests require the copying of figures from cards such as the Bender-Gestalt or the reproduction of designs from memory as in the Graham-Kendall Memory-for-Design Test. Special tests of academic achievement and of assessing deficits in a wide array of mental functions were also presented.

Behavioral assessment sets out to: (1) determine the frequency of unwanted behaviors in specific situations to obtain a reliable estimate of the magnitude of the problem; (2) identify the variables that are currently maintaining the client's abnormal thoughts, feelings, and behaviors; and (3) evaluate the responses the client is capable of making in order to plan the most effective treatment plan. It includes direct observations of the child's actual behavior in a variety of settings and situations in which a baseline measure of the target behavior is obtained. Other sources of behavioral assessment such as the behavioral interview, structured self-report measures, and situational observation were also discussed.

Epilogue

Unfortunately there is little to say about what happened to Freddy and his family, because Mr. and Mrs. B. were unwilling to deal either with the problem or the results of the psychological evaluation. They acknowledged that they did not like some of Freddy's behavior at home, but quickly noted that these were minor and only transient (sleeping with father or refusing to eat what mother cooks). They completely rejected the possibility that Freddy's infantile patterns were in any way related to what they were doing. They excused Freddy's social withdrawal on the grounds of economic circumstances that required them to hold down full-time jobs. Being unable to accept much responsibility for Freddy's adjustment problems or to go along with treatment recommendations that would involve all of them, Mr. and Mrs. B. focused on the principal and the school as the scapegoat. Accordingly, they felt it was the school that failed in helping Freddy to adjust better, and probably it was to blame for providing a poor environment where these behaviors could develop. This became both the source of their anger and their justification for withdrawing Freddy from the school. Thus, they saw themselves as the injured parties, the family whose problems were the symptoms of Freddy's mistreatment at school, and the family who spent money it could not afford to have Freddy in a private school that did him in.

At the end of the term, Mr. and Mrs. B. transferred Freddy to a local public grade school, believing that they had taken a positive and major step in resolving his problems. They steadfastly refused additional sessions with the psychologist or any form of therapeutic assistance. They avoided in-depth conversations with the school principal about Freddy, by telling the school that they were removing him because of financial difficulties. No further follow-up was possible.

REFERENCES

ANASTASI, A. *Psychological Testing* (4th ed.). New York: Macmillan, 1976.

ANDREW, G., HARTWELL, S. W., HUTT, M. L., and R. E. WALTON. *The Michigan Picture Test.* Chicago: Science Research Associates, 1953.

BANDURA, A., GRUSEC, J. E., and R. L. MENLOVE. "Vicarious Extinction of Avoidance Behavior." *Journal of Personality and Social Psychology,* 1967, *5,* 16–23.

BAYLEY, N. *Bayley Scales of Infant Development. Manual.* New York: The Psychological Corporation, 1969.

BELLAK, L. *The Thematic Apperception Test and the Children's Apperception Test in Clinical Use.* New York: Grune and Stratton, 1954.

BELLAK, L., and S. S. BELLAK. *Children's Apperception Test (C.A.T.)* (4th ed.). P.O. Box 83, Larchmont, N.Y.: CP.S., Inc., 1961 (now published by Grune & Stratton, Inc., 381 Park Avenue, South, New York, N.Y.)

BENDER, L. "A Visual Motor Gestalt Test and Its Clinical Use." *The American Orthopsychiatric Association Research Monographs.* No. 3, 1938.

BENDER, L. *Instructions for the Use of Visual Motor Gestalt Test.* New York: The American Orthopsychiatric Association, 1946.

BENE, E. and J. ANTHONY. *Manual for the Family Relations Test.* London: National Foundation for Educational Research in England and Wales, 1957.

CARROLL, J. B. "Review of the ITPA." In O. K. Buros (Ed.), *The Seventh Mental Measurements Yearbook* (Vol. 1). Highland Park, New Jersey: Gryphon Press, 1972, pp. 819–823.

DAHLSTROM, W. G., WELSH, G. S. and L. E. DAHLSTROM. *An MMPI Handbook: Vol. 1: Clinical Interpretation. A Revised Edition.* Minneapolis: University of Minnesota Press, 1972.

DAILY, C. A. "The Life History as a Criterion of Assessment." *Journal of Counseling Psychology,* 1960, *7,* 20–23.

DUNN, L. M. *Expanded Manual for the Peabody Picture Vocabulary Test.* Minneapolis: American Guidance Service, 1965.

DUNN, L. M. *Peabody Picture Vocabulary Test Manual.* Nashville: American Guidance Service, 1959.

EKMAN, P. "Body Position, Facial Expression and Verbal Behavior During Interviews." *Journal of Personality and Social Psychology,* 1964, *68,* 295–301.

EKMAN, P. "Differential Communication of Affect by Head and Body Cues." *Journal of Personality and Social Psychology,* 1965, *2,* 726–735.

EXNER, J. E., Jr. *The Rorschach Systems.* New York: Grune and Stratton, 1969.

FOGEL, M. "Picture Description and Interpretation in Brain Damaged Patients." *Cortex,* 1967, *3,* 433–448.

FOWLER, R. D., Jr. "Automated Interpretation of Test Data." In J. N. Butcher (Ed.),

MMPI Research Developments and Clinical Applications. New York: McGraw-Hill, 1969.

GELFAND, D. M. and D. P. HARTMAN. *Child Behavior Analysis and Therapy.* Elmsford, New York: Pergamon Press, 1975.

GOODENOUGH, F. L. *Measurement of Intelligence by Drawings.* Yonkers, New York: World Press, 1926.

GREER, J. H. "The Development of a Scale to Measure Fear." In E. J. Mash, and L. F. Terdal (Eds.), *Behavior Therapy Assessment.* New York: Springer, 1976, 155–166.

HAMMER, E. F. (Ed.). *The Clinical Application of Projective Drawings.* Springfield, Illinois: Thomas, 1958.

HATHAWAY, S. R. and J. C. McKINLEY. *Manual for the Minnesota Multiphasic Personality Inventory.* Minneapolis: University of Minnesota Press, 1943.

HATHAWAY, S. R. and E. D. MONACHESI. *Adolescent Personality and Behavior:* MMPI *Patterns of Normal, Delinquent, and Other Outcomes.* Minneapolis: University of Minnesota Press, 1963.

HATHAWAY, S. R. and E. D. MONACHESI (Eds.). *Analyzing and Predicting Juvenile Delinquency with MMPI.* Minneapolis: University of Minnesota Press, 1953.

HIMMELSTEIN, P. "Review of the Slosson Intelligence Test." In O. K. Buros (Ed.), *The Seventh Mental Measurements Yearbook.* Highland Park, New Jersey: Gryphon Press, 1972, pp. 765–766.

HOLLAND, C. J. "An Interview Guide for Behavioral Counseling with Parents. In E. J. Mash and L. F. Terdal (Eds.), *Behavior Therapy Assessment.* New York: Springer, 1976, pp. 99–108.

HUTT, M. L. *Hutt Adaptation of the Gestalt Bender Test* (2nd ed.). New York: Grune and Stratton, 1969.

IZARD, C. E. *The Face of Emotion.* New York: Appleton-Century-Crofts, 1971.

KELLY, E. L. and D. W. FISKE. *The Prediction of Performance in Clinical Psychology.* Ann Arbor, Michigan; University of Michigan Press, 1951.

KIRK, S. A., McCARTHY, J. J., and W. D. KIRK. *Illinois Test of Psycholinguistic Abilities* (Rev. ed.). Urbana, Illinois: University of Illinois Press, 1968.

KNOPF, I. J. "Rorschach Summary Scores in Differential Diagnosis." *Journal of Consulting Psychology,* 1956, *20,* 99–104.

KOPPITZ, E. M. *The Bender Gestalt Test for Young Children.* New York: Grune and Stratton, 1964.

LEVITT, E. E. and A. TRUUMAA. *The Rorschach Technique with Children and Adolescents.* New York: Grune and Stratton, 1972.

LINDZEY, G. "On the Classification of Projective Techniques." *Psychological Bulletin,* 1959, *56,* 158–168.

MACHOVER, K. *Personality Projection in the Drawing of the Human Figure.* Springfield, Illinois: Thomas, 1949.

MACHOVER, K. "Sex Differences in the Developmental Pattern of Children as Seen in Human Figure Drawings." In A. I. Rabin and M. R. Haworth (Eds.), *Projective Techniques with Children.* New York: Grune and Stratton, 1960, pp. 238–257.

MASH, E. J. and L. F. TERDAL (Eds.). *Behavior Therapy Assessment.* New York: Springer, 1976.

MATARAZZO, J. D. "The Interview." In B. B. Wolman (Ed.), *Handbook of Clinical Psychology*. New York: McGraw-Hill, 1965, 403–450.

McARTHUR, C. C. "A Review of the Rorschach." In O. K. Buros (Ed.), *The Seventh Mental Measurements Yearbook* (Vol. 1). Highland Park, New Jersey: Gryphon Press, 1972, pp. 440–443.

McCALL, R. B., HOGARTY, P. S., and N. HURLBURT. "Transitions in Infant Sensori-motor Development and the Prediction of Childhood IQ." *American Psychologist*, 1972, *27*, 728–748.

McREYNOLDS, P. (Ed.). *Advances in Psychological Assessment* (Vol. 3). San Francisco: Jossey-Bass, 1975.

MEEHL, P. E. *Clinical versus Statistical Prediction: A Theoretical Analysis and a Review of the Evidence*. Minneapolis: University of Minnesota Press, 1954.

MUNN, J. L. "The Effect of Knowledge of the Situation upon Judgment of Emotion from Facial Expressions." *Journal of Abnormal and Social Psychology*, 1940, *35*, 324–338.

MURRAY, H. A. *Thematic Apperception Test*. Cambridge, Massachusetts: Harvard University Press, 1943.

OTIS, A. S. and R. T. LENNON. *Otis-Lennon Mental Ability Test*. New York: Harcourt, Brace, & World, 1967.

PETERSON, D. R. *The Clinical Study of Social Behavior*. New York: Appleton-Century-Crofts, 1968.

PORTEUS, S. D. *Porteus Maze Test. Fifty Years Application*. Palo Alto, California: Pacific Books, 1965.

RABIN, A. I. "A Review of the Rorschach." In O. K. Buros (Ed.), *The Seventh Mental Measurement Yearbook* (Vol. 1). Highland Park, New Jersey: Gryphon Press, 1972, pp. 443–446.

REZNIKOFF, M. "A Review of the Rorschach." In O. K. Buros (Ed.), *The Seventh Mental Measurement Yearbook* (Vol. 1). Highland Park, New Jersey: Gryphon Press, 1972, pp. 446–449.

RORSCHACH, H. *Psychodiagnostik*. Methodik und Ergebnisse eines Wahrnehmungsdiagnostischen Experiments (Deutenlassen Bon Zufallsformen). Bern and Leipzig: E. Bircher, 1921.

RORSCHACH, H. *Psychodiagnostics: A Diagnostic Test Based on Perception*. New York: Grune and Stratton, 1942.

SARBIN, T. R. A. "A Contribution to the Study of Actuarial and Individual Methods of Prediction." *American Journal of Sociology*, 1943, *48*, 593–602.

SATTLER, J. M. *Assessment of Children's Intelligence*. Philadelphia: Saunders, 1974.

SCHLOSBERG, H. "The Description of Facial Expressions in Terms of Two Dimensions." *Journal of Experimental Psychology*, 1952, *44*, 229–237.

SCHLOSBERG, H. "Three Dimensions of Emotion." *Psychological Review*, 1954, *61*, 81–88.

SLOSSON, R. L. *Slosson Intelligence Test for Children and Adults* (SIT). New York: Slosson Educational Publications, 1963.

SPITZER, R. L., ENDICOTT, J., MESNIKOFF, A., and G. COHEN. *Psychiatric Evaluation Form: Diagnostic Version*. Biometric Research, New York State Psychiatric Institute, 1967–1968.

STODOLSKY, S. S. and G. S. LESSER. "Learning Patterns in the Disadvantaged." *Harvard Educational Review*, 1967, *37*, 546–593.

SUINN, R. M. and S. OSKAMP. *The Predictive Validity of Projective Measures.* Springfield, Illinois: Thomas, 1969.

TERMAN, L. M. *The Measurement of Intelligence.* Boston: Houghton Mifflin, 1916.

TERMAN, L. M. and M. A. MERRILL. *Measuring Intelligence.* Boston: Houghton Mifflin, 1937.

TERMAN, L. M. and M. A. MERRILL. *Stanford-Binet Intelligence Scale: Manual for the 3rd Revision.* Form L.M. Boston: Houghton Mifflin, 1960.

URBAN, W. H. *The Draw-A-Person Manual.* Western Psychological Services, 1963.

WECHSLER, D. *Manual for the Wechsler Intelligence Scale for Children-Revised.* New York: The Psychological Corporation, 1974.

WECHSLER, D. *Manual for the Wechsler Adult Intelligence Scale.* New York: The Psychological Corp., 1955.

WERNER, M., STABENAU, J. R., and W. POLLIN. "Thematic Apperception Test Method for the Differentiation of Families of Schizophrenics, Delinquents and 'Normals.'" *Journal Abnormal Psychology,* 1970, *75,* 139–145.

ZUBIN, J., ERON, L. D., and F. SCHUMER. *An Experimental Approach to Projective Techniques.* New York: Wiley, 1965.

Treatment Approaches

6

INTRODUCTION

Knowing what's wrong with children like Freddy is of little practical value unless something can be done to correct their problems and promote their normal development. You will recall that Mr. and Mrs. B. sought professional help not because they recognized a need for it but because they felt pressured by the school principal. They reluctantly participated in the diagnostic process but promptly rejected the findings and the treatment recommendations, since they saw no real problem other than the school's failure to meet Freddy's needs. They angrily went through the motions of visiting the psychologist to placate the school and to show that they were not neglecting parents, but they had no expectation that the evaluation would have any meaning or impact. In the process, their belief hardened that Freddy was the victim of the school's incompetence and unwillingness to work with him, and their hostile feelings toward the school carried over to their relationship with the psychologist.

Although diagnosis and treatment may involve different techniques and goals, the two processes are not unrelated or independent of each other, in the sense that the success of each is greatly influenced by the nature of the relationship between client and clinician. The relationship (although colored by prior events and feelings) formally begins when the client and practitioner first meet, and ideally it grows until the child and parents experience positive feelings of confidence, trust, acceptance, and safety. Without this sort of rapport, clients such as Mr. and Mrs. B. tend to be defensive, unproductive, unreceptive, resistant, and difficult to work with. Perhaps Mr. and Mrs. B.'s strong negative feelings about the clinical sessions were unalterable, but hindsight suggests that greater effort by the psychologist to allay their anxieties and to deal with their anger may have brought about a more meaningful relationship and a different outcome. The important point is that rapport is a necessary initial step (whether the goal is diagnostic or therapeutic) that forms the basis for all subsequent clinical interactions, and that influences the extent to which the client will accept and carry out the clinical findings and treatment recommendations.

Freddy's case also may illustrate a number of other general issues meriting attention that are associated with treatment approaches. As so often happens, Mr. and Mrs. B. knew little about their psychologist other than that he was recommended by the school as a competent professional. They accepted the school's referral without fully realizing that practitioners differ widely in terms of their training, theoretical orientation, technical skills, experience, and personal style, and these differences introduce considerable variability into the quality and kinds of services they may receive. As we have already seen (Chapter 2), diversity among clinicians contributes to the problems of reliability in the classification of abnormal behaviors, and to differences in etiological formulations (Chapter 4) and treatment choices. The fact is that clinical practice still is more of an art than a science and an area with little uniformity in the way a given case is evaluated, conceptualized, and treated. The state of the art is such that each clinician has ample leeway to bring something of his or her own to a given clinical interaction, so that even those with similar training, experience, and theoretical bent are likely to vary with respect to the specifics of what they do. Consequently, it is important to recognize that this sort of heterogeneity in clinical practice does exist as unsystematic variations of the treatment approaches that will be described in this chapter. Moreover, and perhaps of greater significance, is the fact that heterogeneity represents a serious liability to the scientific study of treatment methods, since unsystematic variations in clinical practice make replication virtually impossible and restrict the possibility of either combining the data obtained from separate studies using the same treatment method or comparing the relative effectiveness of different methods.

Freddy's parents chose to reject the treatment recommendations of the psychologist, preferring instead to do nothing more than transfer him to another school. Unfortunately, we shall never know how Freddy fared in the new school environment since Mr. and Mrs. B. refused further contact with the clinician. But even under more favorable and cooperative circumstances, it would be extremely difficult to accumulate data that would adequately assess the effectiveness of their remedy. All too often treatment outcome and follow-up studies (when available) rely on parental reports that may be colored by their own needs and wishes. It would be foolhearty to accept Mr. and Mrs. B's observations as the sole measure of treatment outcome, since they chose the particular remedy, and inasmuch as they consistently demonstrated their inclination to lessen and deny their son's problems. Similarly, the therapist's progress reports may be subject to bias arising out of the need to see improvement in the child, and the need to validate the treatment. In either event, a more accurate appraisal of treatment outcome could be achieved through behavioral ratings made by independent observers (those who are not invested or involved in the treatment) who have ample opportunity to sample the child's behavior in different settings. In addition, the evaluation could be further enhanced if ratings were obtained on the specific target behaviors purported to change with treatment.

But even these precautionary measures are not sufficient to enable us to arrive at a definitive conclusion about the impact of the treatment. While Mr. and Mrs. B. might be inclined to attribute Freddy's improvement to the change of schools, his progress could have been the result of one or more less apparent factors for which there are no controls. In the absence of (1) data from a larger sample of youngsters who were given the same treatment as Freddy and who were similar to him in age, intelligence, sex, educational level, socioeconomic class, and apparent adjustment problems, (2) an untreated matched control group and a placebo control group, and (3) data indicating specific ways in which the two schools were similar and different, Mr. and Mrs. B.'s conclusion is no more warranted than one interpreting Freddy's progress as the result of chance, developmental factors, changes within the family, or the like.

The placebo effect refers to changes or benefits achieved from a treatment that has no known value other than the client's belief that it will help. The fact that something is being done or taken internally for the problem, even though the measure has no known curative effects, is frequently sufficient to produce significant changes (Shapiro, 1971). Indeed, some writers claim that the expectation for help (placebo) is as powerful as specific treatments if not more so in bringing about behavioral changes (Frank, 1961; Bergen, 1971). Consequently a placebo control is necessary to determine the effects of the specific treatment beyond that which may be produced by a placebo condition.

Even if these additional research data and controls were satisfied, we would still need long term follow-up data to rule out transient effects and to assess the extent to which the treatment approach brought about durable changes. In short, the intent of this analysis is to highlight the difficulties one encounters in doing research in this area, to specify some of the complex experimental demands that must be met, and to forewarn the reader that much of the available research literature fails in one or more ways to meet these methodological requirements.

Finally, Freddy's story raises the question of what is treatment, since we may tend to think of therapy as an intervention that actively involves the child and family, and one that is designed and carried out by a professional. In the strictest sense, Freddy was given a home remedy fashioned by his parents who believed that their son's academic failures and social immaturity were directly attributable to a damaging school situation. On the basis of their etiological formulation, Mr. and Mrs. B. took the logical action of changing Freddy's school environment. Environmental manipulation as a treatment approach has a long history dating back to Hippocrates, who prescribed removing some of his patients from the family setting (Zilboorg and Henry, 1941). Contemporary medical and psychological practice continues to employ such environmental changes as bed rest, a vacation, removal of a pet from the home, a change of residence to a drier or warmer climate, transfer to a different school, among others as viable treatments for a variety of diseases and abnormal behaviors.

Is the distinction between what is treatment and what is not to be made on the basis of whether the therapist is a qualified professional? Should it be restricted to procedures that are based on some theoretical or rational grounds? Does it require the active participation and involvement of the client? As Davison and Neale put it, "these are difficult questions, and, as in other areas of abnormal psychology, there is a lack of total agreement on the various points" (Davison and Neale, 1974, p. 459).

Since there are a number of treatment approaches for abnormal behaviors that have little or inadequate theoretical or rational basis (for example, electric convulsive therapy, psychosurgery, drug therapy), and some that vary considerably in the degree of participation by the client (hypnosis, behavior modification, psychotherapy), we cannot justifiably use either theoretical basis on client participation as criterion for defining treatment. To reflect the diversity of approaches in current practice, we favor the broad definition of treatment that includes any intervention or agent designed to alleviate or alter abnormal behaviors and facilitate normal personality development. The issue of who dispenses the intervention is essentially a social-ethical one in which society gives license to certain trained and qualified individuals as a means of protecting itself from charlatans. In this sense, conversations with friends, play, recreational activities, or taking hot baths may be therapeutic in their affect, but cannot be considered treatment *per se* by societal standards.

The primary intent of this chapter is to describe a representative sample of treatment approaches used to remove or alleviate abnormal behaviors in children in order to enhance our understanding of the diverse techniques that are available, and to provide the necessary background information for later discussions. While general in nature, these descriptions will emphasize the assumptions, rationale, and operational requirements of various treatment methods, and to a lesser extent will focus on a critical appraisal of their effectiveness, since subsequent clinical chapters will include more detailed evaluations of them as they are applied to specific clinical entities. Although there is no single acceptable way of classifying treatment methods, for pedagogical reasons we have arbitrarily organized them under the following categories—*psychological, somatic,* and *milieu*—to characterize and distinguish them by their rationale and by what is done with or to the client.

Psychological Approaches

Individual Psychotherapies

Psychotherapy as a treatment form began with the work of Sigmund Freud and Joseph Breuer who, toward the end of the nineteenth century, explored various procedures by which hysteria (a neurotic reaction now called *conversion reaction*) could be treated (Urban and Ford, 1971). In spite of the proliferation that has occurred since that time in the ways by which psychotherapy is conducted and in its numerous goals, it can be broadly defined as a psychologically planned and ongoing (at regular intervals) interaction between a trained person, the therapist, and a client who has adjustment problems. As it is practiced today, Freud's method of psychoanalysis involves frequent visits (as many as three to five each week) between the client and the therapist (known as the psychoanalyst) over a prolonged period that may range from one to ten years. Traditional psychoanalysts seat themselves out of view of their clients, who are asked to lie on a couch so that they can more comfortably and freely report whatever comes into their minds (free association), be it feelings, sensations, memories, or associations. Through the interpretation of free associations and dreams, conflicts that once were unconscious become conscious, and presumably this greater self-awareness enables the client to live a more conflict-free life (Fine, 1973).

Freud thought of his psychoanalytic method primarily as a treatment for adult neurotics, although in 1909 he published the now celebrated case history of a five-year-old phobic boy, Little Hans, who was analyzed by his father under Freud's supervision (Freud, 1955). Little Hans' case was important to Freud as a means of confirming his theoretical formulation of infant sexuality as the origin of adult neurotic symptomatology, and as a way of demonstrating that insight (understanding of the intrapsychic conflict) could dissolve phobic (neurotic) symptoms. However it was years later that the psychoanalytic treatment of children was developed and undertaken, primarily through the leadership of Melanie Klein and Freud's daughter, Anna Freud (Lesser, 1972). As practiced today, few children undergo classical psychoanalysis, although analytic concepts have been incorporated in a number of psychotherapies. In a recent review, Koocher and Pedulla (1977), who examined a variety of therapy approaches (including the psychoanalytic),

found that psychoanalytic theory still remains a potent force, although more frequently used by psychiatrists than psychologists. However, they concluded that regardless of theoretical orientation, different approaches in general may not vary significantly in child cases. For example, most psychologists and psychiatrists use art as a therapeutic medium and most employ parents as part of the treatment plan.

Play Therapy [1] Essentially, Anna Freud and Melanie Klein introduced play as a procedural modification of psychoanalysis. Their reason was that preadolescent children are unable to free associate because of their limited linguistic development and their less mature (than adults) ego organization. Accordingly, play and not free association was regarded as the natural communication media of children, enabling them to freely and safely express their rich fantasy life and reveal their unconscious processes and basic conflicts (Hammer and Kaplan, 1967). It has also been suggested that play facilitates the establishment of rapport by reducing the communication barrier between child and therapist and by making the therapeutic sessions more interesting to the child (Freud, 1946; Watson, 1951). But playing *per se* is not to be construed as therapy (although its effects may be therapeutic); rather it is an activity that enables the therapist to understand the child and which the therapist uses to promote the child's growth.

1. *Psychoanalytic Play Therapy*, as formulated by Anna Freud in 1926 and in

---

[1] For a more detailed description of play therapy the reader is referred to Hammer, M. and A. M. Kaplan. *The Practice of Psychotherapy with Children.* Homewood, Illinois: The Dorsey Press, 1967; and Axeline, V. M. *Dibs in Search of Self.* New York: Houghton Mifflin, 1964.

subsequent publications (Freud, 1936, 1946, 1965) emphasized the differences between child and adult analysis. She viewed children as relatively unmotivated for treatment since they usually don't seek help volitionally and they tend to see their problems as caused by the environment and not within themselves. In addition, she noted that children are unable to free associate and unlikely to develop a transference neurosis (the repetition of neurotic conflicts that are focused on the therapist in analysis) equal to that formed by an adult. Freud regarded play with toys and other materials such as drawing, painting, modeling, and dramatic role play as particularly useful in establishing early a positive working relationship between the child and the therapist, and for assessing the child's fantasies and unconscious conflicts. Free play was used not as a substitute for free association but as a technique that allowed the child to externalize internal (unconscious) material. By structuring the form and content of the play, the child has the opportunity to play out intrapsychic conflicts, while the therapist initially strengthens ego functioning by helping the child identify and verbalize what he or she is experiencing and feeling. Later, in the course of analysis, the analyst interprets these feelings and experiences to increase the child's conscious awareness of unconscious drives, past emotional traumatic experiences, and other sources of anxiety that impede functioning. Freud also emphasized the importance of working with the child's parents, since the course and outcome of the treatment is likely to be greatly influenced by their willingness to support the treatment and accept change in their child.

In contrast, Klein's approach, which is favored in Great Britain, equates the use of play with free association, and assumes that children are capable of developing transferences in the course of analysis that can be interpreted and understood in a way that is similar to adult analysis (Klein, 1949). Klein and her followers advocate the use of free play, especially with preschool children. Unlike Freudians, they interpret the play early in the analysis and in symbolic terms (the shape of an object represents male or female genitalia) that imply a direct relationship between the symbol and the unconscious conflict. They do not offer intermediate levels of interpretation or a progression of interrelated interpretations before they symbolically connect the child's play with its primitive libidinal impulse. Consequently, this approach has been criticized on the grounds that it reflects an overly simplistic view of the child's psychodynamics, as well as of the child's readiness to understand and deal with the original unconscious sources of anxiety (Lesser, 1972).

2. *Nondirective Play Therapy* with children grew out of Carl Rogers' client-centered therapy for adults and his view that all people possess the drive for self-realization and the capacity to solve their own difficulties (Rogers, 1951). Consequently, Rogers designed a treatment approach that encouraged self-realization by providing his clients with unconditional positive regard (unqualified acceptance), clarification of their thoughts and feelings through reflections, and opportunities for directing their own courses of action without interpretation or influence by the therapist. Virginia Axline fashioned her nondirective play therapy for children after Rogers' approach by assuming that play can serve as a substitute for words and can be just as therapeutic, provided that the children are given complete acceptance and freedom of expression

(Axline, 1969). Play takes place in a setting where the child's importance, integrity, and self-worth are emphasized and where he or she is free to express feelings without fear of censure or reprisals. The therapist reflects back to the child the feelings and attitudes expressed through play to help the child recognize and clarify his or her feelings and gain a better self-understanding. Throughout therapy, it is the child and not the therapist who is responsible for growth and self-realization.

Consistent with her positive view of human nature, Axline believes that children can be successfully treated in play therapy without treating the parents. While she notes that parental treatment may facilitate the therapeutic outcome for the child, she stresses the importance of the alliance between the therapist and the child, which must not be endangered by the therapist's involvement in the treatment of the parents.

3. *Filial Therapy* is a variant of play therapy in which parents are trained to conduct nondirective play with their emotionally troubled children (Guerney, 1964). Parents meet with the psychologist in groups on a weekly basis to learn the principles of nondirective play therapy and to air their children's problems for group discussion. Research data indicate that parents improved in ratings obtained on such behaviors as empathy, involvement, reflection of feelings, and permitting the child more self-direction, and they continued to improve after three post-training play sessions (Stover, Guerney, and O'Connell, 1971).

Indications and Contraindications for Play Therapy. In general, clinicians agree that play is a useful therapeutic technique for preadolescent children, especially for those who have limited verbal facility either because of developmental or psycho-

genic factors (Hammer and Kaplan, 1967). Children for whom this medium is appropriate would include: the preschooler, the mute or linguistically handicapped, the socially shy, the inhibited, the withdrawn, the emotionally constricted, the fearful, the obsessive ruminator, the daydreamer, and the fantasy-ridden youngster. For these children, play helps to establish rapport while it also provides a natural activity through which they can discharge pent up feelings, act out conflicts, and externalize psychic energies that were internalized as fantasies or obsessive thoughts. Play does not exclude or discourage verbal interactions between the child and therapist, although it is typically the major vehicle of expression and communication in therapy. Hammer and Kaplan (1967) note that play therapy, especially free play, is contraindicated for adolescents and children who evidence a high degree of emotional arousal or low cortical control of excitation, such as impulsive, acting out, or hyperkinetic (hyperactivity caused by brain damage) youngsters. These children need to learn to exercise more control over their feelings and impulses; a goal which can be better accomplished in situations with relatively low levels of stimulation and where structure and constraints are externally imposed on their acting-out tendencies.

But a note of caution must be added. These indications and contraindications are based on clinical experience and not on empirical findings. In fact, only a few studies have been done on play-therapy processes, and of those dealing with outcomes, most have been based on small numbers of cases and inadequate methodologies. After reviewing the available literature, Ginott (1961) and Lebo (1964) concluded that it is impossible to determine if changes that have occurred in children are attributable to play therapy *per se* or to a number of other possible factors, such as the placebo effect, spontaneous remission, increased attention or concern from significant others, and the like.

Experimental confirmation is needed of the effectiveness of play therapy in treating personality problems. Thus far, for example, there is no evidence to indicate the superiority of play therapy over dancing lessons in treatment of shyness or its superiority over boxing lessons in the treatment of aggressiveness. (Ginott, 1961, p. 154)

Psychotherapy. Verbal forms of one-to-one interactions between a therapist and a child are as numerous as there are therapists ranging widely in their theoretical underpinnings, goals, and techniques.

1. *Reality Therapy* is an interesting and relatively recent form of psychotherapy that differs markedly from the traditional psychoanalytic and client-centered approaches. The therapist focuses on the present while actively and deliberately encouraging the child to make a value judgment about his or her behavior, to make a plan that would achieve the desired goal, and to be committed to the plan (Glasser, 1965, 1969; Barr, 1974). Reality therapy assumes that people are accountable for their own actions and that responsible behaviors on their part will result in their happiness. In behaving responsibly, children satisfy their basic needs of involvement and self-worth without hurting others to the extent that they feel good about themselves and others. The therapist finds unacceptable such comments as "I can't help it," "I am unhappy," or "My father never showed me any affection" because the therapist emphasizes the positive or what the client can do. In addition, the therapist deals with the present, since nothing can be done to change the

past. Interpretations and attempts to provide insight are never part of the therapy in as much as these techniques serve to prompt excuses for irresponsible behaviors, and to delay efforts to formulate and commit oneself to a plan of action that will change unwanted behaviors. In adapting reality therapy principles to the classroom, Glasser (1969) suggested three different kinds of meetings between the teacher and groups of students to help them solve both behavioral and educational problems. In addition, he noted that his approach was very successful in treating institutionalized delinquent girls in that about eighty percent left the institution and failed to return (Glasser, 1965). However, there are sufficient ambiguities about these data to warrant a much more guarded conclusion (Glasser, 1965).

Recently a number of clinicians have attempted to adapt a form of psychotherapy known as *transactional analysis* for work with children. Essentially, transactional analysis focuses on intrapsychic learning, as well as interpersonal "games" (Berne, 1972). As applied to groups of children, Roth (1977) has found this technique effective in male adolescents in residential treatment programs, and Garber (1976) has employed this approach to alter self-perception in delinquent boys on probation. This therapy is quite new in terms of its application to children, and its potential value has yet to be empirically demonstrated.

While it is neither possible nor fruitful to attempt to describe other approaches here, some general comments concerning psychotherapy are in order. Reports based on reviews of the research literature on psychotherapy by Bergin (1966) and by Levitt (1971) are of special interest in providing us with a summary of the current status of psychotherapy, and in highlighting specific problems inherent in psychotherapy research with children.

Although Bergin's review focused on psychotherapy with adults, his conclusions, nevertheless, are relevant to the practice of psychotherapy with children. He noted the following:

1. The subsequent adjustment of people who receive psychotherapy may be better or worse as compared to those who were not afforded such treatment. The fact that the outcome may be positive or negative speaks more to our need to determine the characteristics of those who get better and those who do not and under what conditions, than to abandon the treatment form as ineffective.

2. Spontaneous remission (improvement over time) occurs in control subjects who did not receive psychotherapy. This finding underscores not only the importance of adequate control groups in studying the effectiveness of a given treatment form, but also the need to institute research that would tell us more about the variables producing spontaneous remission.

3. Progress in psychotherapy seems to be related to some characteristics of the therapist (such as personal adjustment, interpersonal warmth, empathy, and experience) that should be controlled for in research studies and that should be taken into account in the selection of a therapist.

4. The client-centered approach to psychotherapy is the only one that has shown consistently favorable results, while studies of classical psychoanalysis (over long periods of time) have produced the poorest outcomes. However, Levitt's findings based on outcome studies of child psychotherapy over a period of thirty-five years (up to 1960) are even more pessimistic, in that the data fail to demonstrate the effectiveness of psychotherapy with children beyond a spontaneous recovery rate of between sixty and seventy percent.

5. Not only are traditional psychotherapies

of questionable effectiveness, but also they are of limited pragmatic value in the sense that they are only applicable and available to a small number of those who need treatment for abnormal behaviors. We need to develop alternative treatment methods that are suitable and feasible for the many more people for whom treatment has not as yet been available.

6. The more recent behavior therapies should be studied more extensively since they have demonstrated considerable promise.

In discussing child psychotherapy research, Levitt (1971) identifies (but offers no solutions) several unique problems researchers face. The fact that children change as a function of developmental processes may account for the spontaneous remission in "normal children" of behaviors usually regarded as manifestations of emotional problems, such as enuresis, disruptions of sleep, persistent fears, and temper tantrums (MacFarlane, Allen, and Honzik, 1954; Lapouse and Monk, 1959). These behaviors tend to disappear without the assistance of some therapeutic intervention as the child grows older, but in all likelihood their remission is attributable to the child's development of new or more effective coping skills to handle stress. Levitt argues, with some support from the literature, that overly anxious mothers tend to seek professional help for symptomatic children such as these, and these children may then be counted as therapeutic success, although a developmental remission probably would have occurred without treatment. In addition, Levitt notes that symptoms that are indicative of an abnormal condition also may drop out because of developmental changes only to be replaced by other symptoms. He refers to this empirical finding as *developmental symptom substitution* and suggests that it reflects the probable occurrence of certain symptoms at certain ages, such as school phobia that most frequently occurs during the grade-school years and delinquency during adolescence. Without adequate experimental controls and follow-up data, one might erroneously attribute the disappearance of the first symptoms to the effectiveness of treatment, not knowing that a second set of symptoms has emerged later. Developmental factors may be responsible for the disappearance of the original set of symptoms and the reappearance of other ones, while in fact the child has made no significant improvement in adjustment with or without therapy. Finally, Levitt points out that the common practice of treating both the child and one or more members of the family makes the research prospects of separating treatment effects extremely difficult. If mother and child are treated separately and the child's outcome is favorable, we cannot draw any specific conclusions about the effectiveness of the child's therapy without knowing the relative contribution of the mother's therapy, or the accumulative benefit of both therapeutic interventions.

The dim view taken by Levitt, Bergin, and others about psychotherapy has by no means gone unchallenged, since it simply does not jibe with the experience of practicing clinicians who cite numerous instances from their caseloads attesting to its value as a treatment form. Perhaps the reaction of Lawrence Kubie, a well-known psychiatrist, analyst, and teacher, can be taken as a reflection of the opposition's stance.

We will soon be ashamed of the extent to which we may have been turned against the term by the recent flood of ignorant, naive and biased attacks on psychotherapy as a field. While pretending to be scientific, these studies have violated important principles of research design. Certainly a precise investigation of the psycho-therapeutic process . . . is urgently needed. But we do not yet have reliable techniques by which to make meaningful evaluation of results. Anyone who pretends today that he is making accurate evaluations or comparisons is merely exhibiting naivete, bias, and ignorance. (Kubie, 1971, p. 23)

Group and Family Therapy

In this section, we shall describe some of the widely used psychotherapies that involve multiple clients who are brought together at regular intervals to engage in psychologically planned verbal and nonverbal interactions with each other, and with one or more therapists. Group therapy may be distinguished from family therapy on the basis of the blood-tie relationships of the participants and on theoretical grounds, although in practice, the therapist is faced with the similar problem of working with several clients at the same time. In group therapy, several emotionally disturbed children (usually unknown to each other) meet together with a therapist to share and express their conflicts and feelings, to promote the development of social behaviors, and to support each other as they attempt to solve their problems. In contrast, in family therapy the family is the single interacting social system in which the behaviors of each member are the product of the pressures existing within that system. Abnormal behaviors of a child represent expressions of family transactions and pathology that can best be resolved through the participation and treatment of the family as a unit, and not through isolated attempts to bring about changes in the child (Bell, 1975).

Group Therapy. In current practice, group therapy may take a variety of forms, depending on such factors as the age of the child, the type of psychopathology, and the theoretical preference of the therapist. However, all types of group therapy provide a social and economic advantage over individual psychotherapy, since a group therapist can offer treatment services to a larger number of clients and at a reduced cost per client for each therapy session. In addition, group therapy recognizes that humans are social animals whose growth and development are greatly influenced by the attitudes and values held by the group. In the words of Slavson, a pioneer and chief proponent of group therapy,

The most important value to character formation of group experience is the modification or elimination of ego centricity and psychological insularity. It increases the ability to feel with other people, that is, to establish positive identification (Slavson, 1970).

1. *Activity Group Therapy* is a treatment method introduced by Slavson, designed for prepubetal youngsters of the same age and sex who have been rejected (directly through dislike or neglect or indirectly through overprotectiveness) by parents, siblings, school, and peers (Slavson, 1970; Slavson and Schiffer, 1975). These children are described as overtly hostile toward the world and they refuse to interact with it through either antisocial or nonsocial behaviors. Activity groups provide a sanctuary for these children wherein the stress of their disharmony with the environment is removed and replaced by a social setting characterized by acceptance and "unconditional love." Tendencies toward open expressions of aggression or withdrawal are tolerated and permitted to run their course (emotional release) without censure or interpretation from the therapist, although the other members of the group may exert control over these actions.

Although the emphasis is placed on activities that are functionally related to the clinical needs of the children either with age and sex appropriate play materials that are used separately or as a group project, verbal interactions can and do occur in the therapy sessions. The therapist assumes a neutral and impartial role but also serves as a model of restraint and of other socially desired behaviors, and as a reinforcer of desirable behaviors as they appear. Permissiveness and praise from both the therapist and other members of the group increase the child's self worth and gratifies his or her need for status and success.

Typically, Slavson works with children between the ages of seven and fourteen in groups containing from three to eight children. Hammer and Kaplan (1967) differ somewhat from Slavson in their opinions about the abnormal conditions that can be treated effectively by activity group therapy. They suggested that the treatment is most appropriate for youngsters with behavior disorders who are not extreme in their overt aggressive tendencies, and for mildly neurotic children without intense or pervasive anxiety. In addition, children who are overly inhibited, or emotionally constricted, or fearful of close interpersonal relations are said to be suitable for this treatment form. However, it must be emphasized again that which children are successfully treated by activity group therapy and which are not are very much empirical questions that have not, as yet, been adequately answered through research.

2. *Group Play Therapy,* like individual play therapy, may follow psychoanalytic or nondirective theoretical lines or some variant of both. It is usually intended for young children between the ages of five and nine years for whom play is a natural mode of expressing conflicts, feelings, and fantasies that have impeded personality development and social adjustment. A play group should

consist of no more than six children who are homogeneous with respect to age and sex (Schiffer, 1969). Psychoanalytically oriented therapists have suggested that the presence of several children makes the therapy less threatening and facilitates the early establishment of rapport (Ginott, 1961; Schiffer, 1969). They also have claimed that group play provides opportunities for catharsis (emotional release) and subsequent reduction of guilt and anxiety, enhancement of self-worth through support and reinforcement given by the therapist and the group members, and the development of social skills and activities in which sublimation (acceptable outlets for id impulses) can occur. Nondirective play groups closely follow the approach used by Axline in her individual play therapy, in which play is the primary vehicle through which children express and clarify their feelings, and where growth and self-realization are promoted by a therapeutic attitude of unconditional acceptance.

3. *Verbal Group Therapy* is viewed by its proponents as particularly suitable for adolescents who may regard play as too child-like, and for whom peer relations and group affiliation are important (Berkovitz and Sugar, 1975). As contrasted to individual psychotherapy, group therapy comforts adolescents with the reassurance that others are "in the same boat," as well as provides them with the safety of numbers to help diffuse the fear and distrust frequently associated with adult therapists. Although adolescents may enter group therapy as a result of parental or other external pressures, the group does not become viable unless and until its members experience a sense of belonging and accept their responsibility to participate in it (MacLennan and Felsenfield, 1968).

Group therapy has been described as appropriate for a variety of settings (out-patient, hospital, school, and residential), for different patient populations, and with divergent ideas concerning the group composition (in terms of such variables as age, sex, and types of psychopathology) (Hammer and Kaplan, 1967; Reckless, 1968; Franklin and Nottage, 1969; Yalom, 1970; Berkovitz, 1972; Sugar, 1975). For example, Sugar (1975) suggested that young adolescents between twelve and fourteen years of age should be placed in groups that are homogeneous in age (not greater than a three-year age span) and sex to increase peer harmony and interests, and to avoid the additional stress of relating to the opposite sex before a better self-understanding is achieved. Grouping for middle to late adolescents tends to become increasingly heterosexual, since these youngsters now are faced with the real problem of relating to the opposite sex. Sugar also acknowledged that clinicians have varying opinions about the composition of the group with respect to the homogeneity or diversity of psychopathology. Anderson (Anderson and Marrone, 1977) described a method of group therapy for emotionally disturbed children where regular sessions were held in the school and teachers acted as co-therapists. Anderson reported that their method was more effective than group or individual treatment given outside of the school, although the outcome variables and adequate controlled treatment comparisons were not provided. It is noteworthy that most of the variations and applications of group therapy described in the literature reflect clinical experience, preference, and bias, and not differences that are firmly rooted in empirical data.

Family Therapy. From a historical perspective, family therapy is a relatively recent innovation that began to take on significance for clinical practice in the mid-

1950s and early 1960s, with the appearance of a body of literature dealing with its description and theoretical basis (Brown, 1972). In the course of the intervening years, family therapy has been influenced primarily by two views: psychoanalysis and systems theory (Offer and VanderStoep, 1975). Psychoanalytically oriented family therapists find family interviews useful in diagnosing the psychopathology of the child and the family, and in forming a basis for planning a suitable treatment strategy. If, for example, the evaluation revealed that the child's problem was an intrapsychic one, then individual psychotherapy would be indicated, whereas family therapy would be the preferred treatment for children whose problems were primarily interpersonal (Kramer, 1970). In addition, analytically oriented therapists view the child as the outlet for the expression of unresolved parental conflicts, and through which parental anxieties are re-experienced in day-to-day family transactions. The child, then, becomes the victim and (to some extent) a participant in unresolved parental battles which are enacted in daily family interactions, such as that described between Mr. and Mrs. B. in their management of Freddy.

In contrast, system theorists (usually behaviorally oriented nonmedical practitioners) regard the diagnostic process and the concern over psychopathology as potential sources of interference to an open and flexible interaction between the therapist and the family. These therapists perceive the family as a unit, a biosocial system, in which there is reciprocal interaction among the members and where the child's disturbance fulfills a psychologically meaningful function for that system. Consequently, changes in the child's behavior without concommitant changes in the family system may result in the appearance of new symptoms in family members or the destruction of the family as a unit. Within this perspective, Mr. and Mrs. B.'s reluctance to seek professional help and their refusal to accept treatment might be interpreted as their resistance to change the family interactive patterns (albeit maladaptive) that have successfully kept their family system intact.

In practice, family therapy varies widely, as evidenced by a survey of 300 therapists who described differences in procedures that ranged from the use of family therapy as an extension or supplement to individual therapy, to discrepant views about which family members should be included in the treatment and about what kinds of emotional disturbances are effectively treated by this approach (Group for the Advancement of Psychiatry, 1970). For example, John Bell (1975), a pioneer in family therapy, begins with a joint interview of both parents (1) to obtain their version of the child's problems, (2) to gain historical data about the child's development, and (3) to inform them about his approach to family therapy. He tells the parents that he will act as a referee to assure that every member of the family has an opportunity to participate in the sessions, but that he will be especially supportive of the child (or children) to gain his or her confidence and to provide a safe setting for the open expression of feelings. Usually the parents and all of the children over eight years of age then convene, while Bell gives a similar orientation of his role to the children, adding that the parents are willing to change and that everyone can work together to decide on the plans for the family. Following these initial sessions, Bell describes his approach to family therapy in three sequential phases. In the *child-centered phase*, the child is encouraged to express his or her thoughts and feelings about what makes the family unhappy. According to Bell, children typically use this opportunity to voice their irritation over some aspect of the rules and routine of their family lives, such as bed time hours, keeping their room clean, or who gets to watch which T.V. show and when. Bell works with these complaints by asking the child for solutions that perhaps parents can accept tentatively with the proviso for a trial period and future discussions. The *parent-centered phase* starts when "everything is going good" for the child, although considerable hostility has accumulated for the parents during the first phase of therapy. Bell permits the expression of these feelings, but at the same time tries to safeguard the rapport he has with the child by telling the parents that the child must also have a say in the matter, by noting that the child's behavior corresponds to developmental norms (when this is so), and by helping the child to explicate the reasons for his or her actions. This phase of therapy usually involves the catharsis of negative feelings and the greater understanding of both the emotional ties between family members and the nature of parental problems. The final stage of therapy, the *family-centered phase,* occurs when many of the referral problems have disappeared, and the sessions during this stage are punctuated with laughter and reports of the family enjoying shared activities and working together to solve problems.

Unlike Bell, Haley (1963), approaches family therapy with the idea that family members engage in a power struggle with the therapist, and that the therapist must construct various strategies to maintain authoritative control. Family members consistently try to wrestle control in whatever way they can to render the therapist ineffective, since they perceive the therapist as a threat to the equilibrium of the family. Haley responds to these defensive ploys

by forcing the family to look at itself and by pressing for more open and direct communication with him and among family members. He downplays psychodynamics, interpretation, and insight as useful ingredients for therapy, and emphasizes the importance of relationships within the family system and the need to establish different interpersonal operations within the family for therapy to be effective.

Block (1976) advocates a procedure wherein all family members are initially included in a series of open-ended contracts concerning family problems. These contracts then are dealt with in separate sessions that include only those members of the family necessary for that phase of the work. Presumably, this method is intended to reduce the scapegoating of a particular child, to eliminate symptomatic behavior, and to establish the family system as the unit of the malfunction. Other variations of family therapy include multiple families meeting together in group therapy, a combination of family and group therapy, and social networks in which families and their support systems are brought together for regularly scheduled therapy sessions (Mendell, 1975; Attneave, 1976; Strelnick, 1977).

Family therapists also tend to have their own system of categorizing families as a way of describing different family structures and patterns, and as a diagnostic indication for therapy and therapy outcome. However, as Brown so aptly noted,

A satisfying classification seems not yet at hand. Descriptive characterizations of families are everyday language among family therapists. These include such terms as *sick* families, *chaotic* families, *multiple-problem* families, *psychosomatic* families, *obsessional-compulsive* families, *regressive* families, *hostile* families, *hypomanic* families, *sensitive* families, *violent* families, families with a sense of destiny, families with purpose, stable families, stable-unstable families, likeable families and difficult families (Brown, 1972, p. 986).

Outcome Research with Group and Family Therapy

Although the literature on group and family therapy is extensive, relatively few adequately controlled studies are available that shed light on the effectiveness of these treatment methods. A recent review of group psychotherapy included only studies that met the following criteria: (1) provided quantitative pre- and post-therapy measures of behavioral and psychosocial adjustment, and (2) did not combine group therapy with any other treatment intervention (Abramowitz, 1976). These studies tended to focus on immaturity, social isolation, poor self-concept, or academic achievement as the four major problem areas of the identified children. The survey showed that about one-third of the studies yielded positive outcome results, about one-third reported mixed outcomes (some positive, some negative, and some with no change), while the remaining one-third of the studies yielded findings of no improvement. There were no apparent differences among types of group therapy, although behavioral approaches were over-represented in both the positive and mixed results. These outcome data are far from impressive in demonstrating the effectiveness of group therapy.

Unfortunately, the empirical support for family therapy is no greater than it is for group therapy, in spite of the enthusiasm of its proponents. The results of a recent study are fairly typical in that they shed more light on the many methodological problems involved in outcome research than on the question of whether or not family therapy is effective. Sigal, Barrs, and Doubilet (1976) compared treated and untreated families with respect to the following criteria of effectiveness: (1) status of presenting symptoms at least a year after termination, (2) appearance of new symptoms, and (3) parental reports of satisfaction. They found that on follow-up the treated families were no better or worse than the untreated families. However, their measures of effectiveness were not objective, the assignments of families to either the experimental or control groups were not random, and the untreated group, in fact, saw a therapist for one or two sessions before terminating themselves. Indeed, it is difficult to do meaningful (well-controlled) outcome studies because, as Ross points out:

. . . relevant control groups are hard to find, therapies and therapists are difficult to equate, a sufficient number of subjects with the same problem behavior is rarely available, and objective criterion measures are often unacceptable or irrelevant to therapists of a different theoretical orientation (Ross, 1972, p. 307).

Behavior Therapy

Broadly speaking, behavior therapy or behavior modification refers to the treatment of abnormal behaviors by methods and techniques that have been derived from experimental psychology and the principles of learning. Although its beginnings can be traced to the 1920s, the meteoric rise of behavior therapy as a body of literature and as a promising treatment approach has occurred only within the brief span of the last twenty-five years (O'Leary and Wilson, 1975). Laboratory experiments in this country and in Russia demonstrated the acquisition of a phobic reaction through classical conditioning in a little boy, named Albert (Watson and Rayner, 1920), and the extinction of children's fears by the pairing of the feared object with food (something highly pleasant) (Jones, 1924), and the treatment of sexual perversions and alcoholism through conditioning procedures (Yates, 1970). Some years later, Dunlap (1932) described the acquisition of maladaptive habits and the methods he devised to weaken or eliminate them, while the Mowrers (Mowrer and Mowrer, 1938) showed that enuretic children can be treated successfully by conditioning procedures that involved the sounding of a loud buzzer as soon as the child wet an electrically wired pad placed on the bed.

Unlike other practitioners, behavior modifiers find it unnecessary to diagnose psychopathology or use traditional assessment techniques to uncover the origins of abnormal behavior in order to plan a corrective action. What they do need to assess is the current conditions that either influence the occurrence of the behavior in question or its failure to occur (Ross, 1972). In addition, the construction of a realistic behavioral plan requires that the therapist learn as much as possible about the child's capabilities, that is, his or her response repertoire and the range of stimuli that can be processed, as well as those stimuli that have reinforcement value for maintaining the behavior. Initially, the therapist, together with the parents and the child, identifies the specific behavior *(target behavior)* to be modified, which then makes the treatment goal clear to all parties concerned and establishes a clear-cut behavioral criterion for the evaluation of treatment outcome. Treatment strategy is then devised in terms of whether the desired effect involves: (1) a decrease in the emission of a target behavior, (2) an increase in the occurrence of a wanted response or class of responses, or (3) a combination of increasing the rate of

wanted behaviors and eliminating unwanted ones.

1. *Decrease of target behavior* can be achieved in various ways. Jones (1924a,b), was the first to introduce the idea that the pairing of an incompatible experience (the enjoyment of eating a favored food) with the gradual presentation of the fear evoking stimulus (the furry rabbit) would lead to the elimination of the learned fear response. Some years later, Wolpe (1958) referred to this principle as *reciprocal inhibition* and proposed a procedure called *systematic desensitization* (sometimes known as *counterconditioning*) for the treatment of a learned fear in adults. Desensitization pairs the incompatible response of relaxation (induced by suggestion, hypnosis, or drugs) with a graded series of anxiety stimuli in such a way as to prevent the occurrence of the fear response (avoidance), and allow the anxiety to extinguish. Wolpe's method involves the training of muscle relaxation, the preparation (by the therapist and the client) of a hierarchy of fear-evoking stimuli (arranged in order from the least to the most fearful), and finally the actual desensitization. In the last stage, the client relaxes and then is asked to imagine the least fearful stimulus, then the next in the hierarchy, and so on, until the client reports that relaxation has given way to anxiety. At this point, relaxation is re-established and the process is repeated until the client successfully goes through the entire hierarchy without anxiety. Wolpe's approach has been modified for children, since training in deep muscle relaxation is difficult to accomplish with youngsters (Lazarus and Abramovitz, 1962; Wolpe and Lazarus, 1966). The modification, known as *emotive imagery*, uses imagery of pleasurable scenes that are incompatible with anxiety, and that are, in effect,

substitutes for muscle relaxation. While the child enjoys the pleasurable fantasy, the anxiety arousing stimulus is gradually introduced (much like Jones gradually introduced a rabbit as the child ate his favored food) via the previously constructed hierarchy of the least to the most fearful stimulus.

Systematic desensitization has been used successfully with a wide range of phobias (Garvey and Hegrenes, 1966; Chapel, 1967; Lazarus and Rachway, 1967; Bandura, 1969; Obler and Teriwelliger, 1970), although the paucity of research leaves the claim for its effectiveness virtually unsubstantiated (Lazarus and Abramovitz, 1962).

In contrast to desensitization, where therapy is conducted in a way that minimizes anxiety arousal, *flooding* or *implosive therapy* is based on the principle of maximal anxiety arousal. This approach involves the induction of intense anxiety by exposing the client to highly threatening stimuli. The idea is to induce and sustain high levels of anxiety without relief, until the aversive reactions are extinguished (Stampfl and Levis, 1967; Watson and Marks, 1971). Flooding has been used successfully in treating phobic and obsessive-compulsive reactions, although thus far most of the studies have been done with adults (Boulougouris and Bassiakos, 1973; Mathews and Shaw, 1973; Morganstern, 1973; Watson, Mullett, and Pillay, 1973; Emmelkamp, 1974).

Modeling is another behavioral technique that has been effective in reducing avoidance behaviors in children, as evidenced by a carefully controlled study in which children fearful of a dog reduced their avoidance behavior after being exposed to a fearless peer model who comfortably approached the feared animal (Bandura, Grusec, and Menlove, 1967). *Extinction* of a target behavior also can be

brought about through the discontinuance of the reinforcement for some unwanted behavior usually given to the child by the parents, through the use of punishment, or through a technique known as *time out,* in which the child is isolated from positive reinforcing conditions for a period of time. Strong punishment (electric shock and slapping) has been shown to extinguish self-destructive and mutilating behaviors of psychotic children, while a combination of mild punishment and time out was effectively used in the treatment of a five-year-old acting-out and destructive child (Boardman, 1962; Lovaas, Freitag, Gold, and Kassorla, 1965; Lovaas, Koegel, Simmons, and Long, 1973).

Positive reinforcement can be used indirectly to decrease unwanted target behaviors by giving rewards when low-frequency prosocial behaviors occur. For example, hyperactivity, or the social unresponsiveness of schizophrenic children (the target behavior) can be effectively reduced by positively reinforcing attentive and more sedentary behaviors, such as listening to the teacher or sitting quietly (Patterson, Jones, Whittier, and Wright, 1965; Doubros, and Daniels, 1966; Lovaas, Koegel, Simmons, and Long, 1973).

2. *Increase of prosocial behaviors* can be accomplished most effectively by behavioral strategems that either use positive reinforcement or modeling. By making the reinforcement or the reward contingent on the performance of some wanted response, children can be taught a variety of social behaviors, to improve their academic habits and performance, and to emit new responses (Stolz, Wienckowski, and Brown, 1975). There have been numerous successful applications of positive reinforcement for the purpose of increasing prosocial behaviors. They have been evidenced in such

diverse behaviors as the smiling of an infant at an adult, toilet training, cooperation between schizophrenic children, social interaction between severely retarded youngsters, or increasing young children's creativity in block building (Brackbill, 1958; Madsen, Hoffman, Hingtgen, Saunders, and DeMyer, 1965; Thomas, Koropsak, and Madsen, 1969; Whitman, Mercurio, and Caponigri, 1970; Goetz and Baer, 1973). Moreover, the use of tokens as reinforcers (sometimes referred to as token-economy systems), which can be accumulated and cashed in at some later time for privileges or some tangible item, has tended to offset the problem of a child becoming satiated with a particular reinforcer and has enabled teachers and the personnel of institutions greater opportunities for the control and management of relatively large groups of children (Ayllon and Azrin, 1968; O'Leary and Drabman, 1971; Kazdin, 1977). Another application of positive reinforcement is known as *contingency contracting*, in which the therapist and the client agree together on the behavioral goals and the reinforcement to be received when the goals are reached. For example, a contract between a child and parents might deal with such matters as the child agreeing to do homework on a daily basis, or to go to bed at a specified hour, or to perform certain household chores in exchange for something he or she wants from the parents. Therefore, both parties involved in the contract agree to meet their commitments so that when one party changes behavior the other provides reinforcement for that behavioral change. Behavioral contracting has been effectively used within families of delinquents to reduce such behaviors as sexual promiscuity, drug abuse, and truancy (Stuart, 1971; Stuart, Jayaratne and Tripoldi, 1973).

New behaviors also can be acquired through modeling when the model (actual, depicted, or imagined) demonstrates the desired behavior for a child who is learning (Rachman, 1972). Recent work in assertiveness training illustrates the application of modeling for persons who have difficulty in asserting themselves. Successful results have been reported when the client is taught to imagine people who are engaged in assertive behavior that they would like to do or when they are exposed to a model who role plays and demonstrates assertiveness (Hersen, Eisler, Miller, Johnson, and Pinkston, 1973; Kazdin, 1974; Stolz, Wienckowski, and Brown, 1975).

3. *Combining procedures* that *decrease* maladaptive behaviors and *increase* adaptive ones is a favored strategy of behavior therapists, since it meets the dual purpose of dealing with the child's problem behavior and providing him or her with alternative and socially acceptable ways of responding. The approach has been applied to a wide range of problems, including school phobia, social behaviors of psychotic and mentally retarded children, and the antisocial behaviors of delinquents. For example, when a school-phobic child was given positive reinforcement for going to school coupled with the discontinuance of positive consequences of staying at home, and the mother experienced aversive consequences when the child failed to attend school, the technique proved to be effective in extinguishing the school refusal and in achieving the child's regular school attendance (Ayllon, Smith, and Rogers, 1970). By using a favored food as a positive reinforcer, a psychotic boy was taught to wear his eye glasses, while his disruptive table manners were modified by removing his plate, or removing him from the dining room when he ate with his fingers, ate from the plate

of others, or threw food (Wolf, Risley, and Meers, 1964). Similarly, a combination of punishment and positive reinforcement was used to reduce undesirable mealtime behavior of mental retardates, and to increase their desirable eating responses (Henriksen, and Doughty, 1967). Behavioral intervention that included token reinforcement, a contract system, and time-out from reinforcement significantly reduced aggressive and nonconforming responses and markedly improved family relations and functioning in a group of acting-out boys (Patterson and Reid, 1973).

Evaluation of Behavior Therapy

In the aggregate, behavior therapy has demonstrated considerable promise as a treatment approach for a wide range of abnormal behaviors and for a substantial age span in children and adolescents. Because assessment of target behaviors are typically an integral part of the treatment process, evaluation of outcome in behavioral terms is readily accomplished. However, much of the research data in this area are based on single cases or on very small samples in a research design in which the subject is his or her own control (*ABAB* design). Studying too few subjects makes the kind of interpretation and conclusions drawn from the results rather tentative, while the *ABAB* design makes it impossible to compare the effectiveness of behavior therapy with other treatment methods in a single study (Ross, 1972). In addition, follow-up data over long periods of time are not generally available to assess the durability of the behaviors modified with behavior therapy, and to unequivocally answer the nagging question of symptom-substitution raised by traditional therapists. While the research data support the overall effectiveness of behavior

therapy, the sobering thoughts of Ross (1972) place its evaluation in a more appropriate perspective.

It is unlikely that behavior therapy, as presently conceived and practiced, is the treatment of choice for every conceivable form of psychological disorder and it is to be hoped that, in addition to the conditioning and social learning paradigms now applied in treatment, other aspects of psychology, such as the study of cognitive processes, modeling procedures, developmental phenomena, physiological correlates, and group dynamics, will eventually be brought to bear on clinical problems. (Ross, 1972)

Somatic Approaches

The somatic therapies that include *shock therapy* (chemical or electrical), *psychosurgery,* and *psychoactive drugs* are radical forms of treatment that must be administered under medical supervision. With the exception of drug therapy, these therapies are used infrequently with children since they are poorly understood and have the potential for producing untoward neurophysiological effects (Shaw, 1966). Lauretta Bender (1953), a chief proponent of shock treatment, used both Metrazol (a convulsion producing drug) and electric shock with schizophrenic children (see Chapter 8) as a means of stimulating the maturation and patterning of what she regarded as an inadequately developed nervous system in these youngsters. She claimed that twenty-five percent of the shock-treated children on long term follow-up had higher adjustment ratings than members of the nonshock group (four percent) evidenced. However, Eisenberg (1957) argued convincingly against Bender's claim by showing that a very high percentage of the shock-treated group (eighty-nine percent) continued to be schizophrenic at the time of the follow-up and that approximately twenty-five percent of psychotic children could be expected to spontaneously recover without any treatment. Bender's use of shock treatment has been regarded by others as indiscriminant and distasteful (Wing, 1966), and in the end, even she abandoned it in favor of LSD and other psychotomimetic drugs (Bender, Goldschmidt, and Sankar, 1962).

Psychosurgery was introduced in 1936 by Moniz and again in 1942 by Freeman and Watts (1950) for chronic and difficult-to-manage adult mental patients and for individuals suffering from intractable pain. Crude surgical procedures were used in severing or removing portions of the prefrontal lobe of the brain to disconnect the nerve fibers that normally connect the frontal lobe and the dorsomedial nucleus of the thalamus (believed to be the center of emotions). In 1951, two Japanese neurosurgeons, Narabayashi and Uchimura introduced human stereotaxic surgery, in which the amygdala (part of the temporal lobe and the limbic system) was destroyed. This surgery was designed as a treatment for behavior problems in children and adults who evidenced hyperexcitability, destructiveness, and violent behaviors (Narabayashi, 1972). The procedure was extended to feebleminded epileptic patients who also were violent and uncontrollable. Narabayashi reported that there were no fatalities in well over 100 surgical cases, and that sixty-seven percent showed improvement consisting of calm, obedient, and cooperative behaviors. The calming effect was even stronger in children who showed better improvement than adults. Other investigators in different parts of the world (India, the United States, and Japan) have since reported similar findings in which hostile, aggressive, destructive, and uncontrollable children and adults have been made more

manageable and docile by the surgical destruction of the amygdala or the posterior hypothalamus (Heimburger, Whitlock, and Kalsbeck, 1966; Balasubramaniam, Kanaka, and Ramamurthi, 1970; Sano, Mayanagi, Sekino, Ogashiwa, and Ishijima, 1970).

Psychosurgery has been sharply criticized on both socioethical and methodological grounds. Some argue against using such a radical and potentially dangerous procedure with human subjects when the surgical effects (either good or bad) are inadequately documented, and where controls (when used) are subjected to "sham" operations in which a superficial incision is made in the cerebral cortex and a small portion of the skull is removed (Breggin, 1972). In addition, the vast majority of studies thus far reported have used unclear criteria for patient selection; few, if any, objective measures (other than the biased observations of the surgeon) to assess either short or long-term outcome; and are riddled with other serious methodological flaws (too few subjects, no control groups, and so forth) to yield definitive results (Mark and Ervin, 1970; Valenstein, 1973; Shevitz, 1976). Indeed, the justification for the continuance of psychosurgery with patient populations can come only after it has survived the most careful empirical scrutiny possible and unequivocal confirmation of its benefits are firmly established.

Psychoactive drug therapy, especially with children, is clearly the major somatic approach in clinical practice today, having gained its popularity from demonstrations of its effectiveness and in some cases its superiority over other treatment methods with adult mental patients (Group for the Advancement of Psychiatry, 1975). Unfortunately, the application of drug therapy to children and adolescents has not been supported by a vast body of research data, but it has occurred in spite of the fact that there is a dearth of adequately controlled studies demonstrating its benefits or comparing its effectiveness with other therapies for this age group (Christensen and Sprague, 1973; Gittelman-Klein, 1975). With the possible exception of hyperkinesis or minimal brain dysfunction (see Chapter 9), the effect of drug treatment in children with other disorders has been studied infrequently, unsystematically, and with a lack of concern for determining its long-term adverse consequences.

The paucity of studies may be attributable largely to the difficulties a researcher may encounter in trying to assess the efficacy of drugs in light of the many almost insurmountable methodological problems involved. There is no single diagnostic classification system for children and adolescents that is uniformly used by clinicians, nor is there evidence of high reliability among practitioners when they diagnose from the same classification schema. Outcome criteria are often difficult to specify and even more difficult to evaluate, since too few objective measuring devices (behavioral rating scales, psychological tests) of demonstrated reliability and validity are available. Moreover, drug effects may be confounded or obscured by developmental changes in the child, obvious and subtle changes in the child's environment (loss of a parent, change of school, change in parental attitudes and child rearing practices), or inadequate supervision of the child's drug intake (Lucas, 1970). Lucas also noted that physicians often are reluctant to prescribe high doses of drugs to children they see on an outpatient basis that otherwise they feel safe to give in the more controlled inpatient setting. Under these conditions, many drug treated outpatients are not likely to receive the therapeutic dose of the drug that is

necessary to produce a beneficial effect (Sprague and Sleaton, 1975). Finally, the problem of suggestion or the placebo effect discussed earlier in this chapter is especially important in drug therapy, not only because it requires an appropriate control group, but also because the ethical and service considerations involved in withholding treatment from some children may discourage clinical facilities from undertaking drug therapy research.

For our purposes, we will consider three major categories of psychoactive drugs and their effects: stimulants, tranquilizers, and antidepressants. Table 6–1 lists the generic and trade names for some of the more widely used drugs under each major category.

1. *Stimulant drugs* were first used for the treatment of acting-out behavior disorders in children in 1937 by Bradley, who reported children showing marked improvement in school performance especially in arithmetic, a decrease in mood swings, and a calmer more comfortable adjustment (Bradley, 1937). After more than ten years of experience with Benzedrine and Dexedrine, Bradley (1950) found improvement on such variables as academic performance, drive for achievement, attention span, school adjustment, and control of behavior in sixty to seventy-five percent of the treated children, while fifteen to twenty-five percent were unchanged, and ten to fifteen percent were worse.

Since the appearance of Bradley's early work, many other studies have been reported in which stimulant drugs were used to treat conditions (psychoneuroses, psychopathic personality, schizophrenia, delinquency, hyperkinesis) and an array of disruptive behaviors (temper outbursts, fighting, hyperactivity, restlessness, disobedience, lying, defiance) (Office of Child Development,

TABLE 6–1   Generic and Trade Names of Psychoactive Drugs within Each Major Category

	Generic Name	Trade Name
1. Stimulants		
	Amphetamine	Benzedrine
	Dextroamphetamine	Dexedrine
	Methylphenidate	Ritalin
	Magnesium Pemoline	Cyclert
2. Tranquilizers		
Phenothiazines	Chlorpromazine	Thorazine
	Triflupromazine	Vesprin
	Thioridazine	Mellaril
	Fluphenazine	Permitil
	Trifluoperazine	Stelazine
Thioxanthenes	* Thiothixene	Navane
	Chlorprothixene	Taractan
Butyrophenones	* Haloperidol	Haldol
Dihydroindolones	Molindone	Moban
3. Antidepressants		
	Imipramine	Tofranil, Presamine, Pramine, Imavate
	* Amitriptyline	Elavil
	* Nortriptyline	Aventyl
	* Phenelzine	Nardil
	* Nialamide	Niamid
	* Tranylcypromine	Parnate

* Not recommended for children under twelve years of age.

1971; Conners, 1972). However, the most systematic research with stimulant drugs has been cases with minimal brain dysfunction (MBD), where a paradoxical effect is noted in which the drug has a calming rather than a stimulating effect on these hyperactive children (Conners, 1972). The weight of the evidence thus far accumulated indicates that stimulant drugs (amphetamine, dextroamphetamine, methylphenidate, magnesium pemoline) have a positive effect on the disruptive, impulsive, and acting-out symptoms of children evidencing MBD (Werry, Sprague, Weiss, and Minde, 1970; Weiss, Minde, Douglas, Werry, and Sykes, 1971; Dykman, McGrew, and Ackerman, 1974; Page, Bernstein, Janicki, 1974; Lambert, Windmiller, Sandoval, and Moore, 1976).

In addition, a number of studies have examined more specific effects of stimulant drugs on various spheres of functioning in MBD children. With respect to activity level and motor performance, these drugs seem to lower aimless and nongoal directed activity, and to improve motor steadiness, accuracy, and reaction times, suggesting faster but more controlled and effective motor performance (Knights and Hinton, 1969; Sprague, Barnes, and Werry, 1970). This salutory effect on motor performance apparently extends to other areas, as reflected in studies that indicate higher intelligence test scores (I.Q.s) in children treated with stimulant drugs, especially since the elevation occurred primarily in performance I.Q.s (based on motor and nonverbal responses) or on tests involving perceptual motor coordination, spatial relations, human figure drawings, and tracing one's way through a maze with a pencil (Conners and Rothschild, 1968; Millichap, Aymat, Sturgis, Larsen, and Egan, 1968; Knights and Hinton, 1969). However, two recent studies showed that Ritalin does not enhance learning in underachieving children, and that it may, in fact, conceal learning problems from teachers who may erroneously equate behavioral changes in the classroom with positive changes in achievement (Rie, Rie, and Stewart, 1976; Rie, Rie, Stewart, and Ambuel, 1976).

The results of studies dealing with the effect of stimulants on mood and personality have been sketchy, inconsistent, and unsystematic. There are data that indicate that these drugs produce happier, more cooperative, energetic, task and achievement oriented youngsters, while a recent committee of experts were apparently unimpressed with the evidence since they concluded that stimulants do not produce mood improvement effects (Conners, 1972). In a recent review of research on stimulant drugs, Whalen and Henker (1976) have proposed that in evaluating the effectiveness of these medications, it is important to consider their potency in causing attributional change, that is, where the responsibility of the disorder lies (external conditions versus internal dysfunctions).

The known side effects of stimulant drugs include loss of appetite and weight, insomnia, headaches, abdominal pain, irritability, aggressiveness, and tearfulness (Aman and Werry, 1974; Campbell and Small, 1978). Moreover, recent data suggested that the long-term administration of

stimulants adversely affects growth in terms of height and weight (Safer, Allen, and Barr, 1972; Quinn and Rappoport, 1975; Safer and Allen, 1975).

2. *Tranquilizers* (see Table 6–1) have been credited with radically changing the practice of adult psychiatry, particularly in reducing the length of hospitalization for many seriously disturbed mental patients, and in keeping so many of them functioning within the community. However, their usefulness with emotionally troubled children is limited to the control of certain symptoms, such as severe hypermotility, excitability, insomnia, and stereotyped behaviors, and to effects that are usually quite small (Brummit, 1968; Fish, 1968; Campbell, 1976). In fact, the risks with major tranquilizers seem to be greater than the gains, in that tranquilizers are known to impair cognitive functioning and learning, as well as to produce serious extrapyramidal symptoms (tremors and excessive salivation), dyskinetic symptoms (abnormal movements of the face, neck, jaw, tongue, difficulties in swallowing), and convulsive seizures (Campbell and Small, 1978).

Many sedatives and minor tranquilizers are now employed with anxious and neurotic children, because their untoward effects are minimal (Yaffe and Danish, 1977). Those most commonly used in clinical practices include the minor tranquilizers (such as Valium and Librium) and the antihistamine sedatives (such as Benadryl).

However, Patterson and Pruitt (1977) conclude that "there is no absolute documentation of benefit for the use of sedatives and minor tranquilizers in children. . . . Drugs are not a substitute for the care and caring that should be given by the health professional to the affected child and the parents" (p. 176).

3. *Antidepressant drugs* have neither been studied nor used extensively with children, although tricyclic amines have shown promise in the treatment of enuresis and school phobias in children between the ages of six to fourteen years, and with adolescents who manifest moderate to severe depression (Gittelman-Klein and Klein, 1971; Bakwin and Bakwin, 1972; Gittelman-Klein and Klein, 1973; Campbell and Small, 1978). Conners (1972) also noted some interesting but tentative findings worthy of further exploration. These suggest that antidepressant drugs (imipramine) may have a similar positive action on behavior disorders and MBD as they do on depression.

Socioethical Issues of Drug Therapy with Children

Recently, public concern was aroused by newspaper accounts appearing in 1970 that claimed as many as twenty percent of our school-aged children showed learning and behavioral characteristics of MBD, and that large numbers of these youngsters (between 300,000 and 2,000,000) were being drugged to control and manage their classroom behavior (Brown and Bing, 1976). The fact that MBD is an ambiguous and little understood condition and that stimulants and tranquilizers were increasingly used without data on their long-term effects and for a disorder about which the experts cannot agree brought a storm of public protests (Ladd, 1973). Local physicians defended their practice, and they were supported by a panel of experts brought together by the Office of Child Development and the Department of Health, Education and Welfare, who were favorable about the effects of these drugs in treating MBD children

(Office of Child Development, 1971). Apparently, parents of the treated children and the school officials involved also were unperturbed by the situation, although one well known educator, Edward T. Ladd, sharply criticized the practice and raised some important issues (Ladd, 1973). Ladd noted five serious risks involved in the use of these drugs: (1) the possibility of the drugs producing undesirable physiological effects, even addiction; (2) the possibility of faulty diagnoses since the diagnostic judgment is frequently based on teachers' observations of the child's behavior; (3) the possibility that this practice will further encourage a positive attitude toward taking "pills" in a culture already inclined to think of chemical substances as a "cure-all" for anything or everything; (4) the likelihood that the use of drugs deprives children of opportunities for controlling and regulating their own behavior and for developing independence; and (5) the belief that drug use infringes on the legal rights and civil liberties of children, since it is doubtful that the schools have a legal right to attempt to control their students' hyperactive behaviors.

Eisenberg (1971) dealt with the issue of drug therapy from another perspective. He described the medical reluctance and the ethical concerns of experimental drug research with normal children as largely responsible for the paucity of laboratory data on the effectiveness and the safety of the various drugs used today. He also highlighted our need to know the long-term effects of chronic drug use on the growth and development of children, because adverse and permanent consequences are real possibilities. As a means of minimizing risks and abuses, Eisenberg discussed the principles of drug therapy that he believed should be carefully weighed and followed when administering drugs to children as part of a larger therapeutic program.

Milieu Approaches

These treatment methods refer to ongoing experiences in which the daily environment is ordered, arranged, and planned as either a partial or a complete therapeutic program. The possibilities of such programs are numerous, although the prototype is ordinarily thought of as a residential treatment facility where the treatment philosophy is expressed in almost every aspect of the environment, including the attitudes and activities of the staff, the design of living, the way the child is managed, and the specific therapeutic programs the child is offered (Shaw, 1966). Obviously, not all inpatient units meet these standards, since some only provide custodial care while others offer no more than hospital maintenance, regular visits with a therapist, and a structured and controlled setting. Residential treatment centers are typically quite expensive, but they are very valuable when either the child or the family is too disturbed to be managed and treated on an out-patient basis. Under these conditions, the residential program may be the best solution because it provides the child with a total therapeutic environment as well as the necessary external controls to prevent the child from becoming involved in conflicts with society. However, most therapists whenever possible prefer to keep the child in the home and functioning in the community by using alternative milieu approaches, such as special education programs and summer camps. In describing these approaches, it is important to recognize that at this time few if any controlled studies exist that evaluate the effectiveness of one treatment relative to other treatments, assess what aspects of the milieu approach contribute most significantly to improvement, or determine the specific ways in which children benefit, if at all.

Residential Treatment Centers

These vary widely in size, philosophy, goals, and methods, but as a milieu approach, they all provide children with greater tolerance and consistency, firmer control, and more frequent contacts with adults who are warmer and more understanding of their problems than those they otherwise would encounter on the outside. While not all aspects of a residential facility are of equal therapeutic value, Redl (1972) compiled a list of important ingredients that he believes would make a difference in the treatment of disturbed children when they are organized in accord with the therapeutic goals. He stresses that the social structure of a residential facility more closely resembles a harem society or a sleep-away camp than a family unit, and that the roles, responsibilities, pecking order, and communication network of the staff must be articulated clearly to avoid confusion and mixed messages. Routines, rituals, and regulations of daily living should be managed within the context of therapeutic goals, since they have a strong impact on the child's behavior, such as whether he or she is encouraged to control impulses or act them out. Since other youngsters and their personality characteristics (and psychopathology) have significant but possibly different stimulus values and effects on different children, it is important to order the interpersonal living arrangements in ways that best meet the psychological needs of each child. Redl also stresses the importance of staff attitudes and feelings, the daily assessment of each child's behaviors in terms of their implications, the planning of activities, and the use of space, equipment, and time as having a substantial therapeutic effect on the child.

Residential centers offer multifaceted programs with a multidiscipline professional staff to carry them out. Professionals include psychiatrists, clinical psychologists, psychiatric social workers, psychiatric nurses, special education teachers, language therapists, occupational and recreational therapists, and child-care workers. In performing their respective roles, each staff member should have an understanding of the individual child and his or her psychopathology, as well as maintain continuous communication with other staff members to coordinate their efforts within the total treatment plan. The child's therapist usually directs the therapeutic program, which involves decisions about living arrangements, visitors, the activities that the child will participate in, and the short- and long-term goals the staff and child should accomplish. When indicated, the therapist also meets with the child in regularly scheduled sessions of individual or group psychotherapy. Milieu residential centers rely heavily on their special school as an integral part of the treatment plan, not only to provide continuing education, but also to function as a prime force in promoting the child's social, physical, and emotional development. Language specialists to remediate reading and speech problems, occupational therapists to help the children learn to manipulate craft materials in an organized and constructive way, and recreational therapists to plan and supervise athletic and play activities are almost always available as supportive components of this milieu approach. In addition, a cadre of nurses usually function as ward or cottage supervisors, as administrators of

medications and arrangers of daily activities, and as supervisors of child-care workers who are responsible for managing the children in the morning, at mealtimes, during free activity periods, and at bedtime.

Project Re-Ed, launched by federal funds and consisting of residential schools under the state mental health department of Tennessee and South Carolina, is an example of a residential milieu that emphasizes an educational approach in helping emotionally disturbed children to adapt to living at home and within the community (Hobbs, 1966). Unlike residential treatment centers described above where psychotic and severely disturbed children are "treated" for their psychopathology, project Re-Ed is not intended to be a psychiatric institution but is designed to service children who are less disturbed and for whom institutionalization is not required. The children are six to twelve years of age, average or higher in intelligence, but often academically deficient. They are enrolled in the residential schools in groups of eight with teams of teacher-counselors, teacher-counselor trainees, teacher aides, and resource specialists (art, music, and physical education) assigned to work with each group. Volunteer workers and professional consultants from the fields of psychiatry, psychology, social work, and education are also available. Children live in the schools during the week and spend weekends with their families at home. The thrust of the program is two-fold: (1) re-educating the children to live effectively in the outside world by enhancing self-competence, and learning to cognitively control their behavior, and (2) training a new type of mental health worker, the teacher-counselor.

The evaluative results of one study suggest that Re-Ed has promise as a milieu approach (Weinstein, 1969). Ratings made by parents, teachers, and referring agencies showed that seventy-five percent of the children were regarded as moderately to greatly improved after six months with respect to their symptomatology, although no academic improvement was noted. Moreover, the project demonstrated a significant reduction in per child cost (about one-third less) over the expenditures necessary in the psychotherapeutically oriented residential centers.

Special Education Programs

Various estimates have been cited indicating the numbers of school-age children who are emotionally disturbed, or who require special help either for emotional difficulties or academic problems, or both. One investigator suggested that three children in the average classroom evidence a classifiable abnormal condition, while another reported a higher figure of nine when mild and moderate problems were included (Glidewel and Swallow, 1968; Bower, 1969). When the numbers of children in kindergarten through the third grade who have received special help from a professional worker or who had to repeat a grade are considered, the estimate reaches an even more staggering figure of forty-one percent (Rubin and Balow, 1971). The fact that the bulk of the mentally retarded and sensory handicapped children are not included in these estimates makes the sheer demand and need for special educational programs more apparent, especially in light of recent legislation that guarantees the right of every child to publically supported education.

Special education programs are now available for mentally retarded, sensory handicapped, emotionally disturbed, and learning disabled children either in full day schools, in self-contained classes, or in resource rooms. The social stigma, the isolation from normal peers, and the self-limiting availability of resources associated with full day school or self-contained programs are among the disadvantages noted by educators who argue against this form of special education. The concept of the resource room was developed to overcome some of the criticisms of the isolated special class by providing these students with a classroom and a special education teacher with whom they work during several periods of the day, while for the remainder of the school day they attend regular classes.

Summer Camps

Full day and sleep-away camps for emotionally disturbed and mentally retarded children provide recreational programs as well as opportunities for the development of social, personal, and physical skills, such as peer relations and group affiliation, a sense of independence and personal competence, and the acquisition of new skills in crafts and in outdoor athletic activities. Special academic instructional programs are sometimes available in reading and other areas in which the child needs help. Group therapy and activities planned to meet therapeutic goals for each child (similar to a residential treatment center) reflect the program emphasis of a few of the camps, usually ones that are quite expensive and limited in the numbers of children they can handle.

Summary

In this chapter, we initially discussed the issues associated with treatment approaches, such as rapport and the heterogeneity of clinical practice, as well as the methodological problems involved in doing research to evaluate treatment outcome, the relative merits of different therapies, and the durability of behavioral changes on follow-up. We also considered the question of what is treatment and arrived at a broad definition that would satisfy our purposes and reflect the diversity of approaches in current practice. Therefore, treatment is regarded as any intervention or agent designed to alleviate or alter abnormal be-

haviors and facilitate normal personality development. The remainder of the chapter was devoted to descriptions and to a lesser extent critical appraisals of various *psychological, somatic,* and *milieu* treatment approaches. Tables 6–2, 6–3, and 6–4 summarize the treatment methods described under each of these categories.

TABLE 6–2 Psychological Treatment Approaches

Method	
I. Individual Psychotherapies	Psychologically planned interaction between therapist and client.
A. Play Therapy	Suitable for prepubertal children where play rather than words is natural mode of expression.
1. Psychoanalytic	Procedural modification of psychoanalysis in which play is used as media of expressing and understanding unconscious processes and conflicts.
2. Nondirective	Adapted from client centered therapy in which the feelings and attitudes of child are reflected and clarified by therapists.
3. Filial Therapy	Variant of nondirective play in which parents are trained to conduct therapy.
II. Group and Family Therapy	Involve multiple clients and are distinguishable on the basis of blood-tie relations of participants and on theoretical grounds.
A. Group Therapy	Multiple clients meeting together in planned group experience intended to foster personal and social development.
1. Activity Group	Designed for prepubertal children where play activities for each child or the group are used to enhance self worth and imitation of socially desired behaviors.
2. Group Play a. Psychoanalytic	Offers children emotional release, reduction of guilt and anxiety, and more acceptable outlets for id impulses.
b. Nondirective	Offers opportunities for self-realization under conditions of unconditional acceptance.
3. Verbal Group	Suitable for adolescents who are reassured and comforted by presence of others and for whom peer relations and group affiliation are important.
B. Family Therapy 1. Psychoanalytic	Members of the family are brought together for treatment. Diagnose psychopathology of child and family, and view the child as the victim and participant of unresolved parental conflicts.
2. Systems Theory	View diagnosis as interference with open interaction between therapist and family, and perceive of the family as a biosocial system in which there is a reciprocal interaction among family members.

TABLE 6–2 Psychological Treatment Approaches (*cont.*)

III. Behavior Therapy	Treatment of abnormal behaviors by methods derived from experimental psychology and the principles of learning.
A. Decreasing Target Behaviors	
1. Reciprocal Inhibition: systematic desensitization and emotive imagery	Pairing of incompatible responses of relaxation or imaging pleasurable scenes with a graded series of anxiety stimuli to prevent fear response and extinguish anxiety.
2. Flooding or Implosive Therapy	Induces the arousal of maximal anxiety without relief until the aversive reactions are extinguished.
3. Modeling	Learning to reduce avoidance behaviors through vicarious imitation of a model.
4. Extinction	Target behavior eliminated through the discontinuance of reinforcement, by punishment or time-out.
B. Increasing Prosocial Behaviors	
1. Positive Reinforcement	Making reinforcement (reward) contingent on the performance of some wanted response.
a. Token Economy	Use of tokens as reinforcers which can be accumulated and later cashed in for desired privilege or tangible item.
b. Contingency Contract	Therapist and client agree on behavioral goals and the reinforcement to be received when goals are reached.
2. Modeling	New behaviors are acquired by means of a model (actual, depicted, or imagined) who demonstrates the desired behavior.
C. Combined Procedures	Strategies that involve the decrease of maladaptive behaviors and the increase of adaptive ones.
1. Positive Reinforcement, Discontinuance of Positive Consequences, and Aversive Consequences	Reward for wanted behavior, remove rewards from target behavior, and punish parents when child fails to emit wanted response.
2. Positive Reinforcement and Punishment	Use of reward for wanted behavior and aversive controls from unwanted ones.

TABLE 6–3 Somatic Treatment Approaches

Method	
I. Shock Treatment (Chemical or Electrical)	Electric current passed through two electrodes attached to the skull or chemical substances used to produce convulsions. Has been tried with psychotic children by Bender primarily, but with no demonstrated benefits.
II. Psychosurgery	Sterotaxic destruction of the amygdala or posterior hypothalamus in children who evidenced hyperexcitability, violent, and uncontrollable behaviors. No fatalaties reported with claims of positive calming effects. The approach has been criticized on both socioethical and scientific grounds.
III. Psychoactive Drug Therapy	The use of certain chemical substances to alter mood and behavior, although there is a dearth of adequately controlled studies.

TABLE 6–3 Somatic Treatment Approaches (*cont.*)

A. Stimulants	Used for acting-out behaviors, hyperactivity, and minimal brain dysfunction where a paradoxical effect is noted in which the drugs have a calming rather than a stimulating effect. The evidence suggests a positive effect on symptoms of MBD children, improvement in goal directed activity, motor steadiness, and reaction time. Treated MBD children also show higher performance I.Q.s, but no consistent changes in mood and personality
B. Tranquilizers	Usefulness limited to the control of certain symptoms, and to effects that are usually quite small. Risks of side effects seem to be greater than benefits.
C. Antidepressants	Neither studied or used extensively with children, although tricyclic amines show promise with enuretics, school phobics, and adolescent depressions.

TABLE 6–4 Milieu Treatment Approaches

Method	
I. Residential Treatment Centers	Multifaceted programs with multi-discipline staff providing live-in environment that is ordered, arranged, and planned as a total therapeutic program. Children receive greater tolerance, consistency, firmer control, and more frequent contacts with understanding adults than they would get on the outside. Centers are usually psychodynamically oriented and quite expensive, but useful for psychotic or very severely disturbed children and/or families.
A. Project Re-Ed	Residential milieu approach that emphasizes an educational approach to emotionally disturbed children. It also was designed to train a new type of mental health worker, the teacher-counselor. Results of one study thus far showed that the project has promise in decreasing symptoms and in reducing cost of residential treatment.
II. Special Education Programs	Specially designed instructional programs given by trained teachers for the retarded, sensory handicapped, emotionally disturbed, and learning disabled children either in full day schools, self contained classes, or in resource rooms.
A. Day schools or self-contained classes	Criticized because of their social stigma, isolation of children from normal peers, and their limited access to material resources.
B. Resource rooms	Developed to overcome some of the criticisms of day or self-contained classes. Provides students with special education teacher with whom to work for several periods of the day, but rest of the day students attend regular classes.
III. Summer Camps	Either full day or sleep-away summer camps are available for emotionally disturbed and retarded children. Recreational, social, and academic programs are offered.

REFERENCES

ABRAMOWITZ, C. V. "The Effectiveness of Group Psychotherapy with Children." *Archives of General Psychiatry,* 1976, *33,* 320–326.

AMAN, M. G. and J. S. WERRY. "Methylphenidate in Children: Effects on Cardiorespiratory Function in Exertion." In Conners, C. K. (Ed.), *Clinical Use of Stimulant Drugs in Children.* Amsterdam: Excerpta Medica, 1974, pp. 119–131.

ANDERSON, N., and R. T. MARRONE. "Group Therapy for Emotionally Disturbed Children: A Key to Affective Education." *American Journal of Orthopsychiatry,* 1977, *47,* 97–103.

ATTNEAVE, C. L. "Social Networks as a Unit of Intervention." In Guerin, P. J., Jr., (Ed.), *Family Therapy:* Theory and Practice. New York: Gardiner Press, 1976, 220–231.

AYLLON, T. and N. H. AZRIN. *The Token Economy: A Motivational System for Therapy and Rehabilitation.* New York: Appleton Century Crofts, 1968.

AYLLON, T., SMITH, D., and M. ROGERS. "Behavioral Management of School Phobia." *Journal of Behavior Therapy and Experimental Psychiatry,* 1970, *1,* 125–128.

AXLINE, V. M. *Dibs in Search of Self.* Boston: Houghton Mifflin, 1964.

AXLINE, V. M. *Play Therapy* (revised edition). New York: Ballantine Books, 1969.

BAKWIN, H. and R. M. M. BAKWIN. *Behavior Disorders in Children* (4th ed.). Philadelphia: W. B. Saunders Company, 1972.

BALASUBRAMANIAM, V., KANAKA, T. S., and B. RAMAMURTHI. "Surgical Treatment of Hyperkinetic and Behavior Disorders." *International Surgery,* 1970, *54,* 18–23.

BANDURA, A. *"Principles of Behavior Modification."* New York: Holt, Rinehart and Winston, 1969.

BANDURA, A., GRUSEC, J. E., and F. L. MENLOVE. "Vicarious Extinction of Avoidance Behavior." *Journal of Personality and Social Psychology,* 1967, *5,* 16–23.

BARR, N. "The Responsible World of Reality Therapy." *Psychology Today,* 1974, 7:9, 64–68.

BELL, J. E. *Family Therapy.* New York: Jason Aronson, 1975.

BENDER, L. "Childhood Schizophrenia." *Psychiatric Quarterly,* 1953, *27,* 633–681.

BENDER, L., GOLDSCHMIDT, L., and D. SANKAR. "Treatment of Autistic Schizophrenic Children with LSD-25 and UML 491." *Recent Advances in Biological Psychiatry,* 1962, *4,* 170–177.

BERGIN, A. E. "Some Implications of Psychotherapy Research for Therapeutic Practice." *Journal of Abnormal Psychology,* 1966, *71,* 235–246.

BERGIN, A. E. "The Evaluation of Therapeutic Outcomes." In Bergin, A. E. and S. L. Garfield (Eds.), *Handbook of Psychotherapy and Behavior Change: An Empirical Analysis.* New York: Wiley, 1971, 217–270.

BERKOVITZ, I. H. "On Growing a Group: Some Thoughts on Structure, Process and Settings." In I. H. Berkovitz (Ed.), *Adolescents Grow in Groups: Experiences in Adolescent Group Psychotherapy.* New York: Brunner/Mazel, 1972, 6–28.

BERKOVITZ, I. H. and M. SUGAR. "Indications and Contraindications for Adolescent Group Psychotherapy." In Sugar, M. (Ed.), *The Adolescent in Group and Family Therapy.* New York: Brunner/Mazel, 1975, 3–26.

BERNE, E. *What Do You Say after You Say Hello?* New York: Bantam Books, 1972.

BLOCK, D. A. "Including the Children in Family Therapy." In Guerin, P. J. (Ed.), *Family Therapy: Theory and Practice*. New York: Gardner Press, 1976, 168–181.

BOARDMAN, W. K. "Rusty: A Brief Behavior Disorder." *Journal of Consulting Psychology*, 1962, *26*, 293–297.

BOULOUGOURIS, J. C. and L. BASSIAKOS. "Prolonged Flooding in Cases with Obsessive-Compulsive Neurosis." *Behavior Research and Therapy*, 1973, *11*, 227–231.

BOWER, E. M. "Mental Health." In Ebel, R. (Ed.), *Encyclopedia of Educational Research*, (Fourth Edition). New York: Macmillan, 1969, 811–828.

BRACKBILL, Y. "Extinction of the Smiling Response in Infants as a Function of Reinforcement Schedule." *Child Development*, 1958, *29*, 115–124.

BRADLEY, C. "The Behavior of Children Receiving Benzedrine." *American Journal of Psychiatry*, 1937, *94*, 577–585.

BRADLEY, C. "Benzedrine and Dexedrine in the Treatment of Children's Behavior Disorders." *Pediatrics*, 1950, *5*, 24–36.

BREGGIN, P. R. "The Return of Lobotomy and Psychosurgery." *Congressional Record*, February, 1972, *118*:26, E1602–E1612.

BROWN, J. L. and S. R. BING. "Drugging Children: Child Abuse by Professionals." In Roocher, G. P. (Ed.), *Children's Rights and the Mental Health Profession*. New York: Wiley, 1976, 219–228.

BROWN, S. L. "Family Group Therapy." In Wolman, B. B. (Ed.), *Manual of Child Psychopathology*. New York: McGraw-Hill, 1972, 969–1009.

BRUMMIT, H. "The Use of Long Acting Tranquilizers with Hyperactive Children." *Psychosomatics*, 1968, *9*, 157–159.

CAMPBELL, M. "Biological Interventions in Psychoses of Childhood." In Schopler, E. and R. J. Reichler (Eds.), *Psychopathology and Child Development: Research and Treatment*. New York: Plenum, 1976, 243–270.

CAMPBELL, M. and A. M. SMALL. "Chemotherapy." In Wolman, B. B., Ross, A. O., and J. Egan (Eds.), *Handbook of Treatment of Mental Disorders in Childhood and Adolescence*. Englewood Cliffs, New Jersey: Prentice-Hall, 1978.

CHAPEL, J. L. "Treatment of a Case of School Phobia by Reciprocal Inhibition." *Canadian Psychiatric Association Journal*, 1967, *12*, 25–28.

CHRISTENSEN, D. E. and R. L. SPRAGUE. "Reduction of Hyperactive Behavior by Conditioning Procedures Alone and Combined with Methylphenidate (Ritalin)." *Behavior Research and Therapy*, 1973, *11*, 331–334.

CONNERS, C. K. "Psychological Effects of Stimulant Drugs in Children with Minimal Brain Dysfunction." *Pediatrics*, 1972, *49*, 702–715.

CONNERS, C. K. "Pharmacotherapy of Psychopathology in Children." In Quay, H. C. and J. S. Werry (Eds.), *Psychopathological Disorders of Childhood*. New York: Wiley Interscience, 1972, 316–347.

CONNERS, C. K. and G. H. ROTHSCHILD. "Drugs and Learning in Children." In Hellmuth, J. (Ed.), *Learning Disorders, Volume III*. Seattle, Washington: Special Child Publications, 1968, 191–224.

DOUBROS, S. G. and G. J. DANIELS. "An Experimental Approach to the Reduction of Overactive Behavior." *Behavior Research and Therapy*, 1966, *4*, 251–258.

DUNLAP, K. *Habits: Their Making and Unmaking*. New York: Liveright, 1932.

DAVISON, G. C. and J. M. NEALE. *Abnormal Psychology: An Experimental Clinical Approach*. New York: Wiley, 1974, 459.

DYKMAN, R. A., McGREW, J., and P. T. ACKERMAN. "A Double Blind Clinical Study of Pemoline in MBD Children: Comments on the Psychological Test Results."

In Conners, C. K. (Ed.), *Clinical Use of Stimulant Drugs in Children.* Amsterdam: Excerpta Medica, 1974, 125–129.

EISENBERG, L. "The Course of Childhood Schizophrenia." *Archives of Neurology and Psychiatry,* 1957, *78,* 69–83.

EISENBERG, L. "Principles of Drug Therapy in Child Psychiatry with Special Reference to Stimulant Drugs." *American Journal of Orthopsychiatry,* 1971, *41,* 371–379.

EMMELKAMP, P. M. G. "Self-observation versus Flooding in the Treatment of Agoraphobia." *Behavior Research and Therapy,* 1974, *12,* 229–237.

FINE, R. "Psychoanalysis." In Corsini, R. (Ed.), *Current Psychotherapies.* Ithaca, Illinois: Peacock, 1973, 1–33.

FISH, B. "Drug Use in Psychiatric Disorders of Children." *American Journal of Psychiatry,* 1968, *124,* 31–36.

FRANK, J. D. *Persuasion and Healing:* A Comparative Study of Psychotherapy. New York: Schocken Books, 1961.

FRANKLIN, G. and W. NOTTAGE. "Psychoanalytic Treatment of Severely Disturbed Juvenile Delinquents in a Therapy Group." *International Journal of Psychotherapy,* 1969, *19,* 165–175.

FREEMAN, A. M. and J. W. WATTS. *Psychosurgery in the Treatment of Mental Disorders and Intractable Pain* (Second Edition). Springfield, Illinois: Charles C Thomas, 1950.

FREUD, A. *The Ego and the Mechanisms of Defense* (1936). New York: International Universities Press, 1946.

FREUD, A. *The Psychoanalytical Treatment of Children: Lectures and Essays.* London: Imago, 1946.

FREUD, A. *Normality and Pathology in Childhood.* New York: International Universities Press, 1965.

FREUD, S. *Analysis of a Phobia in a Five-Year-Old Boy* (1909). Vol. 10 (Standard Edition). London: Hogarth, 1955.

GARBER, J. "A Psychoeducational Therapy Program for Delinquent Boys: An Evaluation Report." *Journal of Drug Education,* 1976, *6,* 331–342.

GARVEY, W. P. and J. R. HEGRENES. "Desensitization Techniques in the Treatment of School Phobia." *American Journal of Orthopsychiatry,* 1966, *36,* 147–152.

GITTELMAN-KLEIN, R. (Ed.). *Recent Advances in Child Psychopharmacology.* New York: International Arts and Science Press, 1975.

GITTELMAN-KLEIN, R. and D. F. KLEIN. "Controlled Imipramine Treatment of School Phobia." *Archives of General Psychiatry,* 1971, *25,* 204–222.

GITTELMAN-KLEIN, R. and D. F. KLEIN. "School Phobia: Diagnostic Considerations in the Light of Imipramine Effects." *Journal of Nervous and Mental Disease,* 1973, *156,* 199–215.

GINOTT, H. G. *Group Psychotherapy with Children: The Theory and Practice of Play-Therapy.* New York: McGraw-Hill, 1961.

GLASSER, W. *Reality Therapy: A New Approach to Psychiatry.* New York: Harper and Row, 1965.

GLASSER, W. *Schools Without Failure.* New York: Harper & Row, 1969.

GLIDEWELL, J. and C. SWALLOW. *The Prevalence of Maladjustment in Elementary Schools.* Chicago, Illinois: University of Chicago Press, 1968.

GOETZ, E. M. and D. M. BAER. "Social Control of Form Diversity and the Emergence of New Forms in Children's Blockbuilding." *Journal of Applied Behavior Analysis,* 1973, *6:2,* 209–217.

GROUP FOR THE ADVANCEMENT OF PSYCHIATRY (GAP). *Pharmacotherapy and Psychotherapy: Paradoxes, Problems and Progress.* 1975, Vol. IX, Report No. 93.

GUERNEY, B., Jr. "Filial Therapy: Description and Rationale." *Journal of Consulting Psychology*, 1964, *28*, 304–310.

HALEY, J. Strategies of Psychotherapy. New York: Grune and Stratton, 1963.

HAMMER, M. and A. M. KAPLAN. *The Practice of Psychotherapy with Children.* Homewood, Illinois: Dorsey Press, 1967.

HEIMBURGER, R. F., WHITLOCK, C. C., and J. E. KALSBECK. "Stereotaxic Amygdalectomy for Epilepsy with Aggressive Behavior." *Journal of the American Medical Association*, 1966, *198*, 741–745.

HENRIKSEN, K. and R. DOUGHTY. "Decelerating Undesirable Mealtime Behavior in a Group of Profoundly Retarded Boys." *American Journal of Mental Deficiency*, 1967, *72*, 40–44.

HERSEN, M., EISLER, R. M., MILLER, P. M., JOHNSON, M. B., and S. G. PINKSTON. "Effects of Practice, Instructions and Modeling on Components of Assertive Behavior." *Behaviour Research and Therapy*, 1973, *11*, 443–451.

HINGTGEN, J. N., SAUNDERS, B. J., and M. K. DeMYER. "Shaping Cooperative Responses in Early Childhood Schizophrenics." In Ullmann, L. P. and L. Krasner (Eds.), *Case Studies in Behavior Modification.* New York: Holt, Rinehart and Winston, 1965, 130–138.

HOBBS, N. "Helping Disturbed Children: Psychological and Ecological Strategies." *American Psychologist*, 1966, *21*, 1105–1115.

JONES, M. C. "The Elimination of Children's Fears." *Journal of Experimental Psychology*, 1924(a), *7*, 382–390.

JONES, M. C. "A Laboratory Study of Fear: The Case of Peter." *Journal of Genetic Psychology*, 1924(b), *31*, 308–315.

KAZDIN, A. E. "Effects of Covert Modeling and Model Reinforcement on Assertive Behavior." *Journal of Abnormal Psychology*, 1974, *83*, 240–252.

KAZDIN, A. E. *The Token Economy.* New York: Plenum Press, 1977.

KLEIN, M. *The Psycho-analysis of Children* (1932). London: Hogarth Press, Ltd., 1949.

KNIGHTS, R. M. and G. G. HINTON. "The Effects of Methylphenidate (Ritalin) on the Motor Skills and Behavior of Children with Learning Problems." *The Journal of Nervous and Mental Disease*, 1969, *148*, 643–653.

KOOCHER, G. P. and B. M. PEDULLA. "Current Practices in Child Psychotherapy." *Professional Psychology*, 1977, *8*, 275–287.

KRAMER, C. H. "Psychoanalytically Oriented Family Therapy: Ten Year Evolution of a Private Child Psychiatry Practice." *Family Institute of Chicago Publications*, 1970, No. 1., 1–42.

KUBIE, L. S. "A Doctorate in Psychotherapy: The Reasons for a New Profession." In Holt, R. R. (Ed.), *New Horizon for Psychotherapy: Autonomy as a Profession.* New York: International Universities Press, 1971, pp. 11–36.

LADD, E. T. "Pills for Classroom Peace?" In Davis, A. (Ed.), *Issues in Abnormal Child Psychology.* Monterey, California: Brooks, Cole, 1973, 289–296.

LAMBERT, N. M., WINDMILLER, M., SANDOVAL, J., and B. MOORE. "Hyperactive Children and the Efficacy of Psychoactive Drugs as a Treatment Intervention." *American Journal of Orthopsychiatry*, 1976, *46*, 335–352.

LAPOUSE, R. and M. A. MONK. "Fears and Worries in a Representative Sample of Children." *American Journal of Orthopsychiatry*, 1959, *29*, 803–818.

LAZARUS, A. A. and A. ABRAMOVITZ. "The Use of 'Emotive Imagery' in the Treatment of Children's Phobias." *Journal of Mental Science,* 1962, *108,* 191–195.

LAZARUS, A. A. and S. RACHMAN. "The Use of Systematic Desensitization in Psychotherapy." *South African Medical Journal,* 1967, *31,* 934–937.

LEBO, D. "The Present Status of Research on Nondirective Play Therapy." In Haworth, M. R. (Ed.), *Child Psychotherapy: Practice and Theory.* New York: Basic, 1964, 421–430.

LESSER, S. R. "Psychoanalysis with Children." In Wolman, B. B. (Ed.), *Manual of Child Psychopathology.* New York: McGraw-Hill, 1972, 847–864.

LEVITT, E. E. "Research on Psychotherapy with Children." In Bergin, A. E. and S. L. Garfield (Eds.), *Handbook of Psychotherapy and Behavior Change: An Empirical Analysis.*" New York: Wiley, 1971, 474–494.

LOVAAS, O. I., FREITAG, G., GOLD, V. J., and I. C. KASSORLA. "Experimental Studies in Childhood Schizophrenia: Analysis of Self-Destructive Behavior." *Journal of Experimental Child Psychology,* 1965, *2,* 67–84.

LOVAAS, O. I., KOEGEL, R., SIMMONS, J. Q., and J. S. LONG. "Some Generalizations and Follow-Up Measures on Autistic Children in Behavior Therapy." *Journal of Applied Behavioral Analysis,* 1973, *6,* 131–166.

LUCAS, A. R. "Psychopharmacologic Treatment." In Shaw, C. R. (Ed.), *The Psychiatric Disorders of Childhood* (2nd ed.). New York: Appleton Century Crofts, 1970, pp. 436–456.

MACFARLANE, J. W., ALLEN, L., and M. HONZIK. *A Developmental Study of the Behavior Problems of Normal Children Between 21 Months and 14 Years.* Berkeley, California: University of California Press, 1954.

MACLENNAN, B. W. and N. FELSENFIELD. *Group Counseling and Psychotherapy with Adolescents.* New York: Columbia University Press, 1968.

MADSEN, C. H., HOFFMAN, M., THOMAS, D. R., KOROPSAK, E., and C. K. MADSEN. "Comparisons of Toilet Training Techniques." In Gelfand, D. M. (Ed.), *Social Learning in Childhood.* Belmont, California: Brooks, Cole, 1969, 124–132.

MARK, V. H. and F. R. ERVIN. *Violence and the Brain.* New York: Harper and Row, 1970.

MATHEWS, A. and P. SHAW. "Emotional Arousal and Persuasion Effects in Flooding." *Behavior Research and Therapy,* 1973, *11,* 587–598.

MENDELL, D. "Combined Family and Group Therapy for Problems of Adolescents: A Synergistic Approach." In Sugar, M. (Ed.), *The Adolescent in Group and Family Therapy.* New York: Brunner/Mazel, 1975, 231–247.

MILLICHAP, J. G., AYMAT, F., STURGIS, L. H., LARSEN, K. W. and R. A. EGAN. "Hyperkinetic Behavior and Learning Disorders III: Battery of Neuropsychological Tests in Controlled Trial of Methylphenidate." *American Journal of Diseases of Children,* 1968, *116,* 235–244.

MORGANSTERN, K. P. "Implosive Therapy and Flooding Procedures: A Critical Review." *Psychological Bulletin,* 1973, *79,* 318–334.

MOWRER, O. H. and W. M. MOWRER. "Enuresis: A Method for Its Study and Treatment." *American Journal of Orthopsychiatry,* 1938, *8,* 436–459.

NARABAYASHI, H. "Stereotaxic Amagdelectomy." In Eleftheriou, B. E. (Ed.), *The Neurobiology of the Amygdala.* New York: Plenum Press, 1972, 459–483.

OBLER, M. and R. F. TERWILLIGER. "Pilot Study on the Effectiveness of Systematic Desensitization with Neurologically Impaired Children with Phobic Disorders." *Journal of Consulting and Clinical Psychology,* 1970, *34,* 314–318.

OFFER, D. and E. VANDERSTOEP. "Indications and Contraindications for Family Therapy." In Sugar, M. (Ed.), *The Adolescent in Group and Family Therapy.* New York: Brunner/Mazel, 1975, 144–160.

OFFICE OF CHILD DEVELOPMENT, DEPARTMENT OF HEALTH, EDUCATION AND WELFARE. *Report of the Conference on the Use of Stimulant Drugs in the Treatment of Behaviorally Disturbed Young School Children.* Washington, D.C. 1971.

O'LEARY, K. D. and R. DRABMAN. "Token Reinforcement Programs in the Classroom: A Review." *Psychological Bulletin,* 1971, *75,* 379–398.

O'LEARY, K. D. and G. T. WILSON. *Behavior Therapy: Application and Outcome.* Englewood Cliffs, New Jersey: Prentice-Hall, 1975.

PAGE, J. G., BERNSTEIN, J. E., JANICKI, R. S., and F. A. MICHELLI. "A Multiclinic Trial of Pemoline in Childhood Hyperkinesis." In Conners, C. K. (Ed.), *Clinical Use of Stimulant Drugs in Children.* Amsterdam: Excerpta Medica, 1974, 98–124.

PATTERSON, G. R. and J. B. REID. "Intervention for Families of Aggressive Boys: A Replication Study." *Behavior Research and Therapy,* 1973, *11,* 383–394.

PATTERSON, G. R., JONES, R., WHITTIER, J., and M. A. WRIGHT. "A Behavior Modification Technique for the Hyperactive Child." *Behavior Research and Therapy,* 1965, *2,* 217–226.

PATTERSON, J. H. and A. W. PRUITT. "Treatment of Mild Symptomatic Anxiety States." In Weiner, J. M. (Ed.), *Psychopharmacology in Childhood and Adolescence.* New York: Basic Books, 1977, pp. 169–178.

QUINN, P. O. and J. L. RAPPOPORT. "One Year Follow-Up of Hyperactive Boys Treated with Imipramine or Methylphenidate." *American Journal of Psychiatry,* 1975, *132*:3, 241–245.

RACHMAN, S. "Clinical Applications of Observational Learning, Imitation, and Modeling." *Behavior Therapy,* 1972, *2,* 379–397.

RECKLESS, J. B. "Pseudosociopathic Neurotic Behavioral Disturbances in Adolescent Girls." *North Carolina Medical Journal,* 1968, *29,* 1–12.

REDL, F. "The Concept of 'Therapeutic Milieu'." In Whittaker, J. K. and A. E. Trieschman (Eds.), *Children Away from Home: A Sourcebook of Residential Treatment.* Chicago, Illinois: Aldine, Atherton, 1972, 55–70.

RIE, H. E., RIE, E. D., and S. STEWART. "Effects of Methylphenidate on Underachieving Children." *Journal of Consulting and Clinical Psychology,* 1976, *44,* 250–260.

RIE, H. E., RIE, E. D., STEWART, S., and J. P. AMBUEL. "Effects of Ritalin on Underachieving Children: A Replication." *American Journal of Orthopsychiatry,* 1976, *46,* 313–322.

ROGERS, C. R. *Client-Centered Therapy: Its Current Practice, Implications, and Theory.* Boston: Houghton-Mifflin, 1951.

ROSS, A. O. "Behavior Therapy." In Quay, H. C. and J. S. Werry (Eds.), *Psychopathological Disorders of Childhood.* New York: Wiley, 1972, 237–315.

ROTH, R. "A Transactional Analysis Group in Residential Treatment of Adolescents." *Child Welfare,* 1977, *56,* 776–786.

RUBIN, R. and B. BALOW. "Learning and Behavior Disorders: A Longitudinal Study." *Exceptional Children,* 1971, *38,* 293–299.

SAFER, D. J. and R. P. ALLEN. "Side Effects from Long-Term Use of Stimulants in Children." In Gittelman-Klein, R. (Ed.), *Recent Advances in Child Psychopharmacology.* New York: International Arts and Science Press, 1975, 109–122.

SAFER, D. J., ALLEN, R., and E. BARR. "Depression of Growth in Hyperactive Children on Stimulant Drugs." *New England Journal of Medicine,* 1972, *287*:5, 217–232.

SANO, K., MAYANAGI, Y., SEKINO, H., OGASHIWA, M., and B. ISHIJIMA. "Results of Stimulation and Destruction of the Posterior Hypothalamus in Man." *Journal of Neurosurgery,* 1970, *33,* 689–707.

SCHIFFER, M. *The Therapeutic Play Group.* New York: Grune and Stratton, 1969.

SHAPIRO, A. K. "Placebo Effects in Medicine, Psychotherapy, and Psychoanalysis." In Bergin, A. E. and S. L. Garfield (Eds.), *Handbook of Psychotherapy and Behavior Change: An Empirical Analysis.* New York: Wiley, 1971, 439–473.

SHAW, C. R. *The Psychiatric Disorders of Childhood.* New York: Appleton Century Crofts, 1966.

SHEVITZ, S. A. "Psychosurgery: Some Current Observations." *American Journal of Psychiatry,* 1976, *133*:3, 266–270.

SIGAL, J. J., BARRS, C. B., and A. L. DOUBILET. "Problems in Measuring the Success of Family Therapy in a Common Clinical Setting: Impasse and Solutions." *Family Process,* 1976, *15*:2, 225–232.

SLAVSON, S. R. *An Introduction to Group Therapy.* New York: International Universities Press, 1970, 1.

SLAVSON, S. R. and M. SCHIFFER. *Group Psychotherapies for Children: A Textbook.* New York: International Universities Press, 1975.

SPRAGUE, R., BARNES, K., and J. WERRY. "Methylphenidate and Thioridazine: Learning Activity and Behavior in Emotionally Disturbed Boys." *American Journal of Orthopsychiatry,* 1970, *40,* 615–628.

SPRAGUE, R. L. and E. K. SLEATON. "What Is the Proper Dose of Stimulant Drugs in Children?" In Gittelman-Klein, R. (Ed.), *Recent Advances in Child Psychopharmacology.* New York: International Arts and Sciences Press, 1975, 79–108.

STAMPFL, T. G. and D. J. LEVIS. "Essentials of Implosive Therapy: A Learning-Theory-Based Psychodynamic Behavioral Therapy." *Journal of Abnormal Psychology,* 1967, *72,* 496–503.

STOLZ, S. B., WIENCKOWSKI, L. A., and B. S. BROWN. "Behavior Modification: A Perspective on Critical Issues." *American Psychologist,* 1975, *30,* 1027–1048.

STOVER, L., GUERNEY, B. G., Jr., and M. O'CONNELL. "Measurements of Acceptance allowing Self-Direction, Involvement and Empathy in Adult-Child Interaction." *Journal of Psychology,* 1971, *77,* 261–269.

STRELNICK, A. H. "Multiple Family Group Therapy: A Review of the Literature." *Family Process,* 1977, *16*:3, 307–325.

STUART, R. B. "Behavioral Contracting within Families of Delinquents." *Journal of Behavior Therapy and Experimental Psychiatry,* 1971, 2, 1–11.

STUART, R. B., JAYARATNE, S. and T. TRIPOLDI. "Changing adolescent deviant behavior through reprogramming the behavior of parents and teachers: an experimental evaluation." *Canadian Journal of Behavioural Science,* 1976, *8,* 132–44.

SUGAR, M. "The Structure and Setting of Adolescent Therapy Groups." In Sugar, M. (Ed.), *The Adolescent in Group and Family Therapy.* New York: Brunner, Mazel, 42–48.

URGAN, H. B. and D. H. FORD. "Some Historical and Conceptual Perspectives on Psychotherapy and Behavior Change." In Bergin, A. E. and S. L. Garfield (Eds.), *Handbook of Psychotherapy and Behavior Change: An Empirical Analysis.* New York: Wiley, 1971, 3–35.

VALENSTEIN, E. S. *Brain Control: A Critical Examination of Stimulation and Psycho-surgery.* New York: Wiley, 1973.

WATSON, J. P., MULLETT, G. E., and H. PILLAY. "The Effects of Prolonged Exposure to Phobic Situations upon Agoraphobic Patients Treated in Groups." *Behavior Research and Therapy,* 1973, *11,* 531–545.

WATSON, J. P. and I. M. MARKS. "Relevant and Irrelevant Fear of Flooding: A Cross-over Study of Phobic Patients." *Behavior Therapy,* 1971, *2,* 275–293.

WATSON, J. B. and R. RAYNER. "Conditioned Emotional Reactions." *Journal of Experimental Psychology,* 1920, *3,* 1–14.

WATSON, R. I. *The Clinical Method in Psychology.* New York: Harper and Row, 1951.

WEINSTEIN, L. "The Project Re-ED Schools for Emotionally Disturbed Children: Effectiveness as Viewed by Referring Agencies, Parents and Teachers." *Exceptional Children,* 1969, *35,* 703–711.

WEISS, G., MINDE, K., DOUGLAS, V., WERRY, J., and D. SYKES. "Comparison of the Effects of Chlorpromazine, Dextroamphetamine and Methylphenidate on the Behavior and Intellectual Function of Hyperactive Children." *Canadian Medical Association Journal,* 1971, *104,* 20–25.

WERRY, J. S., SPRAGUE, R. L., WEISS, G., and K. MINDE. "Some Clinical and Laboratory Studies of Psychotropic Drugs in Children: An Overview." In Smith, W. L. (Ed.), *Drugs and Cerebral Function.* Springfield, Illinois: Charles C Thomas, 1970, 134–144.

WHALEN, C. K. and B. HENKER. "Psychostimulants and Children: A Review and Analysis." *Psychological Bulletin,* 1976, *83,* 1113–1130.

WHITMAN, T. L., MERCURIO, J. R., and V. CAPONIGRI. "Development of Social Responses in Two Severely Retarded Children." *Journal of Applied Behavior Analysis,* 1970, *3,* 133–138.

WING, J. "Diagnosis, Epidemiology and Etiology." In Wing, J. (Ed.), *Early Childhood Autism: Clinical, Educational, and Social Aspects.* Oxford: Pergamon, 1966, 3–50.

WOLF, M. M., RISLEY, T. R., and H. L. MEERS. "Application of Operant Conditioning Procedures to the Behavior Problems of an Autistic Child." *Behavior Research and Therapy,* 1964, *1,* 305–312.

WOLPE, J. *Psychotherapy by Reciprocal Inhibition.* Stanford, California: Stanford University Press, 1958.

WOLPE, J. and A. A. LAZARUS. *Behavior Therapy Techniques: A Guide to the Treatment of Neuroses.* Oxford: Pergamon Press, 1966.

YALOM, I. D. *The Theory and Practice of Group Psychotherapy.* New York: Basic Books, 1970.

YAFFE, S. J. and M. DANISH. "The Classification and Pharmacology of Psychoactive Drugs in Childhood and Adolescence." In Weiner, J. M. (Ed.), *Psychopharmacology in Childhood and Adolescence.* New York: Basic Books, 1977, 41–47.

YATES, A. J. *Behavior Therapy.* New York: Wiley, 1970.

ZILBOORG, G. and G. W. HENRY. *A History of Medical Psychology.* New York: Norton, 1941.

PART III   Clinical Syndromes

Abnormalities of Early Childhood

eating, sleeping, and elimination

7

PROLOGUE

Sandy was a four-year-old girl who was referred by her pediatrician because she refused to feed herself and to eat table food. Instead she ate only strained foods, and, at that, restricted her diet to oatmeal, cottage cheese, and occasionally some types of fruit. Several months before the referral, Sandy underwent successful surgery for a congenital heart defect, and she now was in fine health. Actually, her feeding problem was long-standing, having begun when she almost choked on a piece of string bean at nine months of age. Frightened by this event, mother cautiously refrained from giving Sandy any table foods for several weeks. Later when she tried to introduce solid foods, Sandy balked and this was the beginning of many battles over food. Sandy managed to win most of the battles, because she was fragile and her parents did not want to risk aggravating her already weakened health.

Sandy was feeding herself by the age of twenty months, although her refusal began around this time following another battle over food. The pediatrician advised that Sandy would learn to eat solid foods if she were forced to do so by not having other foods available as alternatives. Mother instituted this strategy and Sandy responded by crying for thirty-six hours as she persisted in her refusal to eat table foods. It was when she began to have dry heaves that mother became afraid to continue the struggle. Not only did Sandy receive strained foods again, but she also capped her victory when mother shortly thereafter succumbed to her demands to be fed (Excerpts from Bernal, 1972).

Sandy's story illustrates the importance of a basic function, such as eating, as a potential seedbed for the development and maintenance of abnormal behaviors. Infants do little else but eat, sleep, and eliminate waste; and, in turn, parental energies are almost totally consumed by these functions. These are the basic rhythmic patterns of infancy that come in for early habit training and regulation, and that greatly influence the nature of later relationships between mother and child. Before Sandy was a year old, she already had exercised control over her mother's (parent's) behavior, especially when the battleground was eating, because this battleground heightened mother's anxiety about Sandy's health.

Mothering parents quickly become powerful reinforcers as they satisfy the child's essential needs of hunger, thirst, comfort (avoidance of pain), and sleep, while the child serves to gratify mother's need to love and be needed. As both mother and child strive to bring these basic functions under increased control, the interplay provides frequent opportunities for irritability, impatience, conflict, and tension to arise between them. For example, the inconsistent mother who is unpredictably both stringent and lax about the child's bedtimes reinforces irregular sleep patterns that are likely to be a source of continued conflict in their future relationships. Similarly, the failure of the young child to respond positively to toilet training efforts, before he or she is physiologically ready, may evoke feelings of disappointment and anger in mother who interprets the child's behavior as obstinate and uncooperative.

In this chapter, we shall consider abnormal behaviors associated with eating, sleeping, and elimination, because these functions predominate early mother-child interactions in ways that establish patterns that may persist and lead to later adjustment problems. In addition, these functions are so paramount during infancy that any one or all of them are likely to evidence impairment when the young child's physical, social, or personal equilibrium is seriously disturbed.

Problems of Eating

Undoubtedly, eating is the foremost activity of awakened babies, especially during their first year of life. The infant's biological need and total dependence on adults for food and emotional security become linked with the patterns of eating and hunger in ways that have profound implications for later physical and personality development. The weight of this responsibility falls on the mothering parent who eagerly but anxiously follows the pediatrician's feeding instructions. Minor deviations from the expected eating pattern produce sufficient concern in the inexperienced mother to prompt her to call the doctor for advice and reassurance. Pediatricians usually attempt to deal with the more serious eating problems, but they seldom refer the baby for psychiatric or psychological assistance unless other abnormal behaviors also are manifested. There are some disturbances of eating that are serious only because they are potential sources of stress between the mother and child, and others that additionally may result in physiological damage to the child.

Colic

Because of its early onset and symptom picture, strictly speaking, colic is not a disturbance of eating, although it is often associated with hunger and feeding. It is a condition characterized by loud and per-

Because Americans live in relative abundance and are well fed, we may find it difficult to believe that as many as one-half of the world's children suffer some degree of malnutrition. Severe malnutrition may be either a protein deficiency *(kwashiorkor)* or an overall deficit of food or calories *(marasmus)*. Kwashiorkor often occurs at or after weaning when the infant who was fed on milk, known to be high in protein, is given as a replacement starchy foods that are low in protein. The condition produces stunted growth, swelling, skin sores, and dislocation of dark hair color to red or blond. Infantile marasmus frequently results from early cessation of breast feeding, overdilution of the bottle-fed formula, or gastrointestinal infection that occurs early in infancy. There is extreme retardation of development and wasting away of tissues in babies affected by marasmus.

Severe malnutrition of this sort is extremely rare in the United States, and only evident in one to two percent of children in the world. Moderate malnutrition or chronic undernutrition is much more common, affecting about half of the world's children, and between twenty to thirty percent of children under six years of age in this country, especially those from low-income families. Few preschool children have insufficient protein intake, whereas the preponderance of malnutrition comes from insufficient intake of calories. A surprising finding is that there is an iron deficiency in more than fifty percent of American children between one and five years of age, and that this inadequacy is not restricted to lower socioeconomic levels.

Animal research has shown that malnutrition between the third trimester of pregnancy and through the first year of life can produce irreversible brain deficits both in reduction in the size of the brain and in the number of brain cells. In addition, severe malnutrition that occurs prenatally or during infancy leads to permanent abnormal behaviors in animals, including apathy, reduced exploratory behavior and problem-solving ability. More direct evidence of the effect of malnutrition in humans indicates that malnourished babies have short attention spans, poor concentration, poor fine motor coordination, and impaired ability to learn. It is also known that undernourished children are more susceptible to infection than well-fed youngsters, because their body defenses against disease are impaired. Irreversible effects on human behavior are probably rare since they occur only when severe malnutrition has been of long duration during infancy and continued through childhood with undernutrition. Iron deficiency (the most frequent form of undernutrition) may lead to anemia, decrease in attentiveness and persistence, and an increase in irritability (Sidelight based on Read and Felson, 1976).

sistent crying that occurs within the first few weeks of the infant's life, and lasts for about three to five months. The infant appears to be suffering from intestinal cramps or pain that is inferred from the sound and character of the cry, as well as from the physical signs of abdominal distention and flexion of the legs. Initially, worried parents look for its cause in factors relating to eating, such as the type or temperature of the baby's formula, or the possibility that the baby swallowed too much air as he or she ingested food.

Colic is found more frequently among first born infants, and there are those who report that it is rarely observed while the baby is in the hospital (Kessler, 1966). For these reasons, it has been conjectured that psychological factors, principally anxiety, tension, and ambivalence in mother, play a significant causal role in producing colic. However, Illingworth (1954) found that sixty-six percent of the babies studied showed symptoms of colic before leaving the hospital, and eighty-five percent manifested symptoms within their first fifteen days of life. Furthermore, overfeeding or underfeeding, diet of nursing mothers, techniques of feeding, swallowing air, spoiling the baby, or allergy were not implicated as causative factors. Supporting a psychogenic view is the study by Lakin (1957), who reported that mothers of colicky infants were more tense and anxious during pregnancy, less sure of themselves and adjusted to their maternal role, and less satisfied with their marriage than mothers of noncolicky babies. In contrast, the well known pediatrician, Benjamin Spock, suggested that many colicky infants are easily startled and unusually tense, active, and restless, which he was inclined to view as innate characteristics (Spock, 1963).

Although the etiology of colic has not been established, almost all observers agree that the condition is temporary and presents no substantial physical danger to the infant. The major consideration and deleterious effect lies in the potential damage colic can produce in the mother-child relationship. Consider, if you will, the prolonged distress of the infant who is in pain that cannot be readily alleviated, and the anxiety, guilt, fatigue, and frustration of the parent who day after day is faced with the almost futile task of trying to bring some relief to the suffering baby. Surely, this situation is charged with emotion and increased tension for both mother and child, which can seriously mar their future relationship.

There is no known specific treatment for colic, although the distressed baby seems to gain temporary relief from being picked up, held, and walked. Parents are best advised about the temporary nature of the condition and about the fact that their baby is not in any physical danger. At the same time, they need to know that they are not responsible for the discomfort so that their guilt and/or feelings of inadequacy are allayed. With patience, tender care and concern, and sharing between parents of the baby's needs, both parents and child can weather this stormy period without ill effects.

Obesity

Obesity is a condition that is all too well known in our society, affecting more than fifty million overweight Americans and some ten to fifteen percent of our adolescent population. Gross obesity occurring either during childhood or at puberty is both a physical and psychological disability that may have serious consequences for later life. There is some evidence to indicate that excessive weight gains in infancy are associated with a high incidence of obesity at age six, seven, and eight (Eid, 1970). It is also likely that fat children will become obese adults, because overfed babies have a permanent increase in the total number of fat cells in the body (Brook, Lloyd, and Wolf, 1972). In addition, the degree of obesity in childhood is related to excesses in weight in the adult years. Abraham and Nordsieck (1960) found that eighty percent of those children who were considered extremely obese were fat as adults, as contrasted to forty-two percent of the boys and eighteen percent of the girls judged to be average in weight who later were obese as adults. Thus, the long range outlook for obese youngsters is pessimistic, notwithstanding temporary losses in weight during adolescence or other periods during their lifetime.

Obesity is clinically diagnosed either by a body weight that is greater than twenty percent of the norm for height and weight, or by skin fold measurements (pinching the skin in the triceps area) to obtain an estimate of subcutaneous fat. The obvious symptom of obesity is a marked excess of body fat. While it has been found that obese youngsters do not differ from non-obese children in food habits, food choices, or the proportion of calories obtained from various foods, they do evidence a higher frequency of *abnormal inactivity* (expend far less energy). This finding is particularly important in light of the fact that the reduction of activity is not accompanied by a corresponding decrease in food intake (Bullen, Monello, Cohen, and Mayer, 1963; Mayer, 1966). The clinical behavior of these youngsters has been described as immature, excessively dependent on mother, shy, fearful, timid, clumsy, slow, and apathetic (Bruch, 1941, 1957). In addition, most obese people are tall as children but are below average in height as adults (Lloyd, Wolff, and Whelen, 1961; Illingworth, 1971). This growth pattern is attributable to an early but temporary spurt in skeletal maturation. In addition, the characteristic of tallness rules out rare endocrine disorders as the cause of obesity, because hormonally pro-

duced obesity is typically found in children who are short in stature.

It is quite clear that there is no single cause of obesity, but instead the condition can arise from multiple factors. Hereditary tendencies toward obesity are strongly inferred from studies that have consistently reported a significant relationship between obesity in the child and in one or both parents. Estimates of family occurrence have ranged from sixty-nine percent to eighty percent in which fat children have one or both parents who also are obese (Carrera, 1973, pp. 113–124). While suggestive, the evidence is not persuasive or conclusive inasmuch as obesity can be explained equally as well on environmental grounds. However, the significance of environmental factors is undermined by the observations of Bakwin and Bakwin (1972), who noted that no significant relationship exists between the weights of adopted children and their foster parents as is found customarily between obese children and their natural parents. Most observers now agree that even if genetic factors are involved in obesity, heredity does not set, in any precise way, the body weight of the child; it merely establishes the boundaries within which the child's weight will vary depending on caloric intake and psychological factors.

Contrary to the widespread belief that obesity in childhood is the result of endocrine disorders, it is now recognized that most fat children do not have any demonstrable hormonal disturbance.

Far more attention has been given to psychogenic considerations where mother-child relationships have been viewed as critical. For example, after extensive work on obesity, Bruch (1961) suggested that the frequent feeding of the child by mother on occasions when the child is not hungry produces a deficit in the ability to correctly identify the bodily sensations of hunger and satiation. Accordingly, the child fails to learn the appropriate labels for these bodily sensations and therefore does not learn the specific behaviors relevant to these sensations. Children reared under these circumstances do not know when they are hungry and when they are satiated. Another learning interpretation emphasizes the family occurrence data by suggesting that obese children imitate the eating behaviors of their obese parents who serve as their models. A more Freudian view of obesity regards eating and excessive oral gratification as a manifestation of deep seated, but thwarted, needs for love and affection from a mother who is rejecting, but who attempts to conceal her feelings by overzealous demonstrations of nurturance. The child seeks comfort and escape from anxiety and stress by self-indulgence through eating, which reinforces ties to and dependency on mother.

While there is no overwhelming evidence favoring one psychogenic view over another, there is ample data indicating that psychological factors are significantly related to obesity. The research literature reports that there are emotional disorders and psychological disturbances in anywhere from forty to eighty-one percent of obese children and adolescents studied (Tolstrup, 1953; Ostergaard, 1954; Bruch, 1955; Monello and Mayer, 1963). There is also evidence indicating that chronically obese children who have been brought for medical treatment have more undifferentiated and immature body images than their nonobese peers (Nathan, 1973).

Whether obesity is caused by psychological variables or vice-versa is as yet uncertain, although it may be more important to underscore the damaging effects of obesity on the personal and social adjustment of so many of these children. Fat youngsters are often embarrassed, ridiculed, and rejected by their peers, and they are unable to successfully compete in athletic and other play activities. They often become social isolates with strong inclinations toward withdrawing from potential sources of failure and conflict, and toward reducing their anxiety by eating (Mobbs, 1970). In addition to the psychological dangers of obesity, there are physical problems associated with this condition. Many of these youngsters walk late and have orthopedic problems of the legs and feet. Obese infants have a higher incidence of lower respiratory infections than nonobese babies, and these ailments are especially dangerous and serious in very obese children (Hutchinson-Smith, 1971). Furthermore, individuals who have been obese since childhood are likely to have a shortened lifespan, because they are prone to such potentially fatal conditions as hypertension and cardiovascular disease.

Obesity in children is particularly difficult to treat in that most youngsters neither manifest the sustained motivation for long-term self-control of food intake or activity level, nor the independence from parents who hold the major responsibility for providing them with a proper diet. Bruch (1957) found that individual psychotherapy was ineffective when obesity was the only complaint because these children failed to cooperate. Group psychotherapy appears to be a more promising treatment procedure because peer approval is quite important to most of these youngsters (Craddock, 1973). Several studies undertaken recently in the United States and Great Britain have shown significant weight loss in group treatment of obese youngsters who ranged in age from ten to sixteen years. However, the group programs varied considerably from biweekly sessions on diet, nutrition, and exercises during a three-week summer camp program to sessions over a period of eighteen months. Follow-up data in which the long term effects are assessed are not as yet available.

Diet restrictions along with increased physical exercises are the most obvious and effective means of reducing excess weight, although this approach is dependent on the cooperation of both parents and child. The specifics of the program must be carefully designed and monitored by a physician who would evaluate the child's health, growth patterns, and caloric needs. Typically, a favorable initial response is obtained with this approach, but often the enthusiasm of mother and child wanes and the child regains weight. In order to increase the incentive to participate, and to reinforce the desired changes in the child's eating behavior, behavior modification techniques could be employed to maximize the likelihood of obtaining long term positive effects. The use of behavior modification in the management of obesity in adults is well established (see reviews by Abramson, 1973; Hall and Hall, 1974; Stunkard and Mahoney, 1976). Social reinforcement from the therapist, group members, and important figures in the environment; tangible reinforcers such as tokens, personal valuables, and money; and techniques such as self-monitoring and behavioral contracting are among the many approaches that have been employed successfully (Jeffrey, 1976). However, to date, behavior modification has not been applied to the management of obesity in children, although on rational and empirical grounds it should prove useful. Studies of this sort will undoubtedly be forthcoming within the next several years (Personal communication with D. B. Jeffrey).

Pica

Occurring in children over the age of one and disappearing in the fourth and fifth year of life, pica involves the consumption of substances not ordinarily considered edible, such as dirt, clay, plaster, paint, hair, paper, and coal. Children with pica prefer these unnatural substances and purposefully seek them out as distinguished from normal youngsters of this age who indiscriminately mouth almost everything they touch. In general, this depraved appetite is not troublesome, although in some special instances it may lead to serious health hazards. The ingestion of lead-based paint from peeling walls or baby furniture, so often characteristic of the economically impoverished, may result in lead poisoning, which can produce brain damage, mental retardation, behavior disorders, and possible death. Frequent and repeated eating of hair may result in hairball tumors that can cause intestinal obstruction (Bakwin and Bakwin, 1972). While pica is not restricted to any specific intelligence level, it is more commonly found in mentally retarded children who not only persist in mouthing objects longer than normal children, but also who are unable to discriminate between food and nonfood substances.

Millican and Lourie (1970, pp. 333–348) found that pica was more frequent among low socioeconomic southeastern black families whose subculture sanctions the custom of eating laundry starch and earth containing clay. Furthermore, mothers of children with pica showed a significantly higher incidence of having had pica than mothers of nonpica children. For these families, learning, either through direct instruction or by way of parental modeling, is substantially implicated as the primary determinant of pica. The authors also noted that children with pica manifested an excessive amount of oral activity, such as thumb sucking, nail biting, and mouthing of inedible objects, as well as oral disturbances such as feeding problems and retarded or no speech. In addition, these children showed a variety of other symptoms including rocking, head-banging, hair pulling, enuresis, nightmares, temper tantrums, firesetting, stuttering, phobias, and compulsive masturbation. Interestingly enough, mothers who had pica also exhibited signs of oral disturbances in the form of obesity, alcoholism, and drug addiction.

It has often been suggested that pica is caused by a nutritional deficiency, especially of iron, but clinical and laboratory tests as well as double-blind studies in which iron was intramuscularly given failed to support this hypothesis (Millican and Lourie, 1970). Aside from constitutional factors that result in brain damage and mental retardation with which pica may be associated, there is more evidence supporting an environmental basis for this condition than there is for substantiating a biological view. Family disorganization, broken homes, parental neglect, poor physical environment, and poverty conditions all seem to play a causative role (Gutelius, Millican, Layman, Cohen, and Dublin, 1962; Millican and Lourie, 1970). Most observers consider persistent pica beyond the age of six rare but serious in that it is frequently a sign of severe psychopathology requiring professional attention and intervention.

There is little known or written about the treatment of pica principally because it tends to disappear in most children of normal intelligence by age five with proper diet and careful supervision as to what the child is permitted to eat. Since persistent pica is considered a symptom of some serious abnormal disorder, the choice of treatment is usually tied to the eventual diagnosis and not to the specific eating problem. Millican and Lourie (1970) proposed a combined program of educational sessions with mothers to inform them of the potential health hazards of pica and to persuade them to spend more time with their children and to discourage excesses in oral gratification. In addition, these authors suggested psychotherapy for those older children who manifested persistent pica and other abnormal behaviors.

Refusal to Eat (Anorexia)

This is a condition that varies in severity from ordinary fussy appetites to rare life-endangering self-starvation. Mild and moderate forms of refusal to eat appear most frequently in youngsters between the ages of one and five. Generally, these are children with poor appetites who are finicky about foods and resist trying new ones. They chew poorly and insist on the repetition of special rituals associated with eating, such as drinking from a particular cup or being fed by the same person who is expected to make a game of eating. Although these youngsters usually enjoy good health, they successfully manipulate their parents by the threat of failing health and the prospect of impaired growth and development.

During this age period, the child's physical growth is relatively slow as compared to infancy, and weight gains are slight and irregular from month to month. Under these circumstances the child's need for food is less, although many uninformed parents have difficulty accepting this as a normal pattern. Instead, they tend to be so anxious about their child's poor appetite and slow growth rate that they may place undue emphasis on eating and continually battle with the child to alter the feeding pattern. In the course of these events, refusal to eat is reinforced by the additional attention mother gives to her problem child (something like what Sandy's mother did), and through the satisfaction the child derives from resisting mother and in annoying her. The problem is likely to continue and perhaps worsen as long as parents persist in encouraging it.

Treating the younger child who refuses to eat is not a formidable problem. Simple and direct information about normal physical development and appetite changes as a function of growth patterns can be extremely helpful in reducing parental anxiety, and in avoiding parent-child battles over food. Parents need to know that children differ in terms of food preferences, and that it is all right for a child to have likes and dislikes. Feeding should be at regular times and intervals with a minimum of distractions and with regard for the child's needs. Portions should be small to avoid the inevitable problem of forcing the child to finish everything on the plate. Self-feeding should be initiated as early as possible, although parents must understand that the child's table manners will be far from impeccable.

Problems of Sleep

Another essential need of the human organism is sleep, which is periodic and rhythmic in nature. Disruptions or difficulties in sleep can arise in early childhood. While no thoroughly adequate explanation is available to account for this need, it appears that sleep permits the body to regulate itself and to preserve its energy for later activity. Children vary considerably with respect to their sleep requirements,

although most parents have some preconceived notion of how much sleep their children need for normal and healthy development. When the child's sleep pattern fails to correspond to this expectation, parents are likely to enter into an early and prolonged battle with the child over the regulation of sleep, a state of affairs that is frought with the real possibility of damaging personality development. Sleep disturbances may have their origin in this sort of struggle over training and regulation, or they may be important manifestations of other difficulties the child is experiencing. In either event, sleep problems may be considered as falling into two broad categories: those involving failure to go to sleep and those disrupting the continuity of sleep.

Difficulties in Falling Asleep

In infancy, babies are unable to sleep because of some bodily discomfort arising from hunger, thirst, irritation and pain of wet or soiled diapers, intestinal cramps, indigestion and gas, or extreme temperature conditions. Infants quickly and loudly communicate their distress by crying until they are restored to a more comfortable state or they are overcome by their stronger need to sleep. All children have occasional insomnia brought on by physical illnesses, such as head colds, earaches, sore throats, itchy skin rashes, and stomach upsets. Emotional or environmental conditions that produce intense feelings or overstimulation at or near bedtime may also interfere with falling asleep. Most parents are understanding and accepting of the infrequent bouts of insomnia, but they are frustrated, angered, and concerned by the child's persistent failure to go to sleep.

By and large, children are not eager to go to bed, but they prefer to postpone bedtime as long as they can with whatever device, excuse, or scheme that might work. The American household is quite familiar with bedtime rituals that run the gamut from the child demanding a story read by a parent, a drink of water, a trip to the bathroom, a round of good night kisses for everyone, a bedtime prayer, and finally being tucked into bed. The parent tiptoes away in eager anticipation of a well-earned period of relaxation only to hear the child call out for another drink of water or for something else. The ritual surely continues and becomes even more embellished if parents participate and encourage it. Through this device, the child gains additional parental attention that may be needed to allay the fears of being left alone, or to win a favored position over siblings, or (in Freudian terms) to reduce the child's unconscious fears of losing control over aggressive and sexual impulses while asleep. Some children dread going to sleep because they fear that they will not awaken again, or that someone close to them will die. There are others who are reluctant to retire because they simply have been put to bed earlier than their sleep needs require.

The possible causes of insomnia or the child's unwillingness to fall asleep are too numerous to exhaust here. If, however, the problem persists and becomes troublesome, treatment can be appropriately and effectively designed in light of the special sets of conditions causing and maintaining the sleep problem. In order to arrive at an appropriate remedial strategy, it is necessary to assess both the child and the family. The clinician can best determine the factors involved in the child's unwillingness to fall asleep by identifying conflicts between parents, attitudes toward the child, sibling rivalries, child-rearing practices, and the specific aspects surrounding the sleep pattern. The problem may stem from improper training as evidenced by parental inconsistency, failure to set limits, and reinforcement of behaviors that tend to postpone going to sleep. Under these circumstances, treatment can be directed toward the modification of parental practices and the unwanted behaviors associated with sleep. However, if the insomnia originates in the child's intrapsychic conflicts about self-adequacy, guilt feelings about behaviors that are unacceptable, or fears of separation, then more extensive therapeutic intervention may be necessary for both the child and parents. Perhaps the simplest form of insomnia to remedy occurs when the child's sleep requirements are less than the preconceived expectations of parents. Given the evidence that the child is happy and active and is in good health, parents can be reassured that the problem will dissipate as they adjust the bedtime hour to conform more closely to the child's needs.

Disruptions in the Continuity of Sleep

1. Nightmares and Night Terrors. Most normal children occasionally experience fright reactions during sleep. Only when these reactions are frequent do they require professional consideration and attention. Although both nightmares and night terrors are fear responses that disrupt sleep, they are sufficiently different to be regarded as distinct phenomena. Sleep research has shown that nightmares are relatively common, and they occur during the last third of the night in a stage of sleep known as stage 1—REM (rapid eye movement) where most dreams take place. In contrast, night terrors are rare, and they occur within the first two hours of the night in stage 4—NREM (non-REM) dreamless sleep, which is also recognized as the period of deepest sleep. Night terrors are also accompanied by severe autonomic discharges marked by steep increases in respiratory rate and amplitude, and a profound acceleration in heart rate (Broughton, 1968; Fisher, Kahn, Edwards, and Davis, 1973). They are found more often in boys than girls, and they occur most frequently between the ages of five and seven, decreasing through early adolescence (Jacobson, Kales, and Kales, 1969, pp. 109–118).

In addition to the differences found in the physiological monitoring of sleep, a number of important differences have been observed in the clinical manifestations of these fright reactions. Table 7–1 summarizes the distinctive clinical features of both nightmares and night terrors.

The causes of nightmares and night terrors are, as yet, little understood. The literature in sleep research consistently indicates that nightmares occur during REM sleep and are properly regarded as a dream phenomena. In contrast, evidence suggests that

TABLE 7–1 *   Differences in the Clinical Picture Between Nightmares and Night Terrors

Nightmares	*Night Terrors*
1. Fearful sleep experience after which the child wakes. The fear may persist for a while, giving way to good orientation and clear realization.	1. Fearful experience taking place in sleep or in a somnolent twilight state, not followed by waking.
2. Slight defense movements or moaning immediately before waking are the only noticeable activities.	2. Facial features are distorted and express terror. The eyes stare, wide open. The child sits up in bed or even jumps to the floor in great agitation, runs helplessly about, clutches at persons or objects, cries out that someone is after him or her, implores an imaginary dog or burglar to leave him or her alone, shouts for help, or screams inarticulately.
3. The child is already awake when the parents notice his or her distress and, after he or she has been calmed, is able to give a coherent account of what has happened.	3. The child, sleeping through the episode, is unable to give any account of his or her distress, which the child is living out in all details while the parents look on and infer from his or her shouts and actions what might go on within the child. The attack cannot be cut short by any amount of calming and reassurance.
4. The child, after waking knows all the persons and objects of his or her surroundings.	4. The persons and objects of the environment are often not recognized and may be mistaken for others and woven into the dream content.
5. No hallucinations ever occur.	5. The child hallucinates the frightening dream objects into the room.
6. There is usually no perspiration.	6. The attack is usually accompanied by perspiration.
7. A long period of waking and conscious going over of the dream situation may follow.	7. Peaceful sleep instantly follows the termination of the reaction.
8. The entire episode rarely lasts longer than one or two minutes.	8. The terror may last for some time, up to fifteen or twenty minutes.
9. The contents are remembered more or less clearly. The incident itself is always recalled.	9. There is complete amnesia for the contents as well as for the occurrence of the episode.

* Reproduced from Kanner, 1972, pp. 478–479 with permission from the Charles C Thomas Publishing Co.

night terrors are not associated with dream states. Instead, they are more closely akin to an arousal response much like that observed in "sleep drunkenness," where the child is awakened out of stage 4 sleep by a parent, spontaneously walks to the toilet, urinates, and returns to bed without any recollection of what has transpired (Gastaut and Broughton, 1965, pp. 197–221). On the basis of their extensive physiological study of nightmares and night terrors, Fisher et al. (1973, p. 96) noted:

That the night terror is not a dream at all in the ordinary sense, but a symptom, a pathological formation emerging from NREM sleep, brought about by a rift in the ego's capacity to control anxiety. Although the REM nightmare shows evidence of attempts at mastery of the traumatic experience, the night terror seems to be a manifestation of the failure of mastery, which may explain why it may endure unchanged and unabated for periods of a quarter of a century. It is evident that some night terrors have a posttraumatic origin. However, severity of trauma and degree of pre-existing psychopathology do not appear to be sufficiently differentiating factors.

Although it has been demonstrated that night terrors can be produced by the sounding of a buzzer during stages 3 and 4 of NREM sleep, the question raised by the work of several investigators concerning the trigger mechanism of night terrors is, as yet, unanswered (Broughton, 1968; Fisher et al, 1973). It is conjectured by these authors that night terrors may be set off by recurrent ongoing mental activity or previous psychological factors, or both.

Most writers view the basis of nightmares along the lines suggested by Freud, who believed that dreams were the product of unconscious impulses and conflicts, particularly those that are aggressive and sexual in nature. It is also possible that previously frightening experiences, and upsetting events of the day, such as peer rejection or

failing an important test in school, can precipitate nightmares (Ellis and Mitchell, 1973).

Other than a few reports in the psychoanalytic literature, little has been written on the remedial approaches to nightmares and night terrors. This is probably attributable to the fact that only a relatively small number of children with these fright reactions are brought for professional attention, and to the fact that these conditions ordinarily subside without intervention. Either extensive individual psychotherapy or family therapy is likely to be used in instances in which these sleep disruptions persist and become management problems. Several studies have found that the drug Valium has reduced the incidence of night terrors by eighty to ninety percent (Kahn, Fisher, Byrne, Edwards, and Frosch, 1970; Fisher, Kahn, Edwards, and Davis, 1972).

Sleepwalking (Somnambulism)

Sleepwalking is a disruption of sleep that is manifest in approximately six percent of children (Bakwin and Bakwin, 1972) and is often triggered by an upsetting emotional experience or event. Night terrors and somnambulism frequently co-exist, and they share other common features such as occurring during the first two hours of the night in NREM sleep. In either case, there is a clouding of consciousness, amnesia for the period, and in both victims, are difficult to awaken (Jacobson, Kales, and Kales, 1969, pp. 109–118). In contrast to night terrors, sleepwalkers bear no observable sign of fright, but instead they locomote without any emotional display. Walking is carried out with eyes open, rigid movements that are somewhat unsteady, and the appearance of a definite goal in mind. In most instances, obstacles are avoided, although occasionally the child will trip over some object in his or her path. Except for locomotion, the somnambulists' senses are blunted, and there is potential danger in their activities. They may fall down stairs, climb out of a window, walk out of the house, or run into an object that may inflict injury, but these occasions are rare. However, necessary precautions need to be taken by parents to prevent possible injuries to sleepwalking children.

Sleepwalking may have a genetic basis in that the condition is found in two or more members of the immediate family in approximately forty percent of the cases (Bakwin and Bakwin, 1972). In addition, the concordance rate for monozygotic twins is significantly higher than it is for dizygotic twins. Like night terrors, the sleep-research literature links sleep-walking to disorders of arousal, but the precise nature of the trigger mechanism is unknown. Anxiety, prior fearful experiences, emotional conflict, loud noises, and stomach distress are illustrative of psychogenic factors that may precipitate somnambulism. It also is possible to induce sleepwalking by standing the sleeping child up, an action that does not have the same effect on the nonsomnambulistic child. Virtually nothing is known about the treatment for this condition, other than that most observers agree that drug therapy is usually ineffective. Somnambulism that is frequent and associated with night terrors and other problems is ordinarily approached by psychotherapeutic intervention involving the child, the parents, or both.

Problems of Elimination

In this section, we shall consider *enuresis* and *encopresis*, the two major problems of the rhythmic biological functions of elim-

ination that are associated with or have their origin in early childhood. Even more than the problems of eating and sleep, the failures in toilet training are likely to be troublesome to parents and to prompt them to seek professional attention and intervention. Our culture places a high premium on cleanliness and personal hygiene, reflected in the aversion and even in the repugnance for the "dirty" job of handling soiled or wet diapers. Under these circumstances, it is reasonable to expect that the early achievement of bladder and bowel control is desirable, if not enviable. At the same time, disturbances in toilet training greatly increase the probability of parent-child conflicts, damage to the child's self-esteem, and problems of social adjustment in school and at home.

Enuresis

Enuresis, like so many other abnormal conditions, is difficult to define because of (1) the variability in age at which it is maturationally possible to establish bladder control (age criteria), (2) the differences in time and training procedures by which bladder control is attempted (training criteria), and (3) the problems of how often it must occur to be considered as properly falling within this category (frequency criteria). Nevertheless, most observers tend to apply the term arbitrarily to the involuntary passage of urine primarily during night-time sleep (nocturnal) in children past the age of three or four in which the cause is not linked to any demonstrable organic pathology. Most children develop the necessary physiological and social maturity by the age of fifteen to eighteen months for controlling the bladder, although parental practices differ widely as to when training is initiated and how the control is taught. The question of how often wetting must occur to be regarded as abnormal is not easily answered and is an area of some controversy. Some writers accept the frequency of once a month, while others consider weekly or more frequent wetting as satisfying the criteria for enuresis. While daytime wetting (diurnal) is known to occur and to properly fit the definition of enuresis, nocturnal wetting during sleep is by far more frequent and common. Diurnal wetting rarely occurs in the absence of nocturnal enuresis. It happens at times when the child is so engrossed in play that time out is not taken to go to the toilet, or when the child is under nervous tension that tends to exaggerate the urgency to urinate.

Because of the problems involved in the definition of enuresis, incidence estimates are quite variable and difficult to compare from study to study. Kanner (1972) reported an incidence of enuresis in twenty-six percent of the children referred to his clinic for psychiatric consultation. The enuretic children ranged in age from three to fourteen years, with the highest frequency occurring between eight and eleven years of age and in more boys than girls (sixty-two percent boys, thirty-eight percent girls). Somewhat lower estimates were obtained when enuresis was the primary referral problem. Gilbert (1957) reported an incidence of twelve percent referred to a Child Guidance Center for enuresis, but only an incidence of one percent referred to clinics located in schools. A study of school children revealed that eight percent were once a month or more frequent nocturnal bedwetters (Lapouse and Monk, 1959). Bakwin and Bakwin (1972) estimate from the available literature that approximately fifteen percent of children are enuretic.

Enuresis usually persists from early childhood until the time of referral as almost a lifelong pattern in some seventy-eight to ninety percent of the cases (Kessler, 1966; Kanner, 1972). It is more prevalent among children of manual workers and least frequent in children of professional and high salaried families (Blomfield and Douglas, 1956). The relationship between enuresis and socioeconomic status of the family suggested by this study was even more marked as the age of the children increased. This may be attributable to such factors as differences in attitudes toward cleanliness, accessibility to toilet facilities, consistency in training practices, and possible differences in the temperature of the home, since being cold will increase the tendency to urinate. Enuresis is found in all levels of intelligence, but it rarely occurs as an isolated symptom. Instead, clinical observations indicate that it is highly associated with general immaturity (manifest in such behaviors as whining, moodiness, irritability, restlessness, overactivity, excitability, stubbornness, disobedience, and oversensitivity), and a wide array of acting-out behaviors (that include temper tantrums, nail biting, fear reactions, encopresis, masturbation, tics, health concerns, thumb sucking, stuttering, stealing, and truancy) (Kanner, 1972).

Like night terrors and sleep-walking, enuresis occurs in the first few hours of sleep (NREM), and it is not temporally associated with dream sleep (REM) (Pierce, 1963). This finding was substantiated by Broughton (1968), who also showed more frequent and intense bladder contractions prior to micturition in enuretic children as compared to nonenuretics, and significantly higher heart rates in enuretics before sleep, in stage 4 sleep, during arousal, and after micturition. Broughton hypothesized that it is these autonomic changes that occur throughout the night (independent of bedwetting) which predispose the child to micturition.

Since 1550 B.C. when enuresis was first reported, it has been attributed to a variety of unverified causes such as intestinal parasites, laziness, dreams, deep sleep, weak bladder, acid urine, excessive secretion of urine, weakened musculature, and even allergy (Glicklich, 1951; "Causes of Enuresis," 1969). However, most contemporary writers now regard the condition as determined by several factors. Although relatively rare (five to ten percent), there are cases in which organic factors produce urinary incontinence. For this reason, diseases of the genito-urinary tract and the kidneys, congenital malformations of the bladder, lesions of the spinal cord, diabetes, or nocturnal epileptic seizures initially must be explored and ruled out (Ellis and Mitchell, 1973).

The theory that hereditary factors are involved is largely based on the long established observation that parents and siblings of enuretic children have histories of wetting, and that the concordance rate for enuretic monozygotic twins is significantly higher than that found for dizygotic enuretic twins (Frary, 1935; Hallgren, 1957; Bakwin, 1971). However, the fact that enuresis seems to run in families cannot be taken as evidence to support a genetic view, because, as we have noted before, this relationship has been obtained without proper control for environmental factors. Might it not be just as reasonable to suppose that those parents who suffered the problems of enuresis during their childhood would be more accepting of it and more likely to provide faulty toilet training for their youngsters? The confounding of genetic and environmental variables in studies of this sort makes it difficult to evaluate either set of conditions in identifying the etiology of enuresis. Nevertheless, it is entirely possible that some cases of enuresis are determined by a genetic predisposition that is modifiable by environmental factors.

Most instances of enuresis are thought to be the product of psychological and environmental conditions, primarily of faulty habit training in which the regulation is started too early, too late, or with training practices that are inconsistent and emotionally charged. Training that begins before the child is maturationally ready sets the stage for parental disappointment, anger, and possibly rejection of the child. At the same time, the child not only senses these parental attitudes and feelings, but also reacts to them with anxiety, insecurity, lowered self-esteem, and hostility. Disharmony and strain between parent and child originating from these early failures will make later attempts at training tense and difficult. Training that is initiated too early may reflect parental aversion for the dirty job of handling eliminative wastes, or the premature encouragement of self-sufficiency in the child. In contrast, lack of training or regulation that begins late may suggest maternal overprotectiveness and mother's wish to continue the child's dependency as long as possible. Under these circumstances, the child may be reinforced for the infantile behavior of wetting. These parents may put the child to sleep with diapers, forget to awaken the child to void during the early portion of the night, or make it difficult for the child to go to the toilet by keeping the household dark and cold.

In this connection, MacKeith (1968) proposed a "critical period" between one-and-a-half to four-and-a-half years of age for learning bladder control. Training beyond the upper limit of this age period would be difficult to successfully institute, and wetting is likely to continue for years before it is finally brought under control.

In addition, MacKeith emphasized anxiety from situational events such as the birth of a sibling, hospitalization, illness, injury, or moving as important sources of intrusion in the achievement and maintenance of bladder control. In order to bolster the argument supporting the role of anxiety, he cites the available data in the literature that indicated the following: (1) more than eighty percent of 320 enuretic children had experienced anxiety-provoking conditions in their first three years of life; (2) illness was most common in the third year of life for enuretic children; (3) the prevalence of enuresis is significantly higher at age five among children from severely disturbed families; (4) the incidence of enuresis is much lower than found in the general population when an anxiety-free training procedure is used; and (5) the physical and mental stress occurring in enuretic children between the ages of two and three is related to the persistence of bedwetting beyond the age of four. More recent data support the implication of anxiety and disturbances in the family as etiologic factors of enuresis, and suggest that the anxiety of the mother is significantly related to the rate of progress the child makes in treatment (Young and Morgan, 1973a).

Even within the psychogenic view of enuresis, there are those who have recognized that it is erroneous to consider one etiology common to all cases. The early work of Gerard highlights this point and illustrates that enuresis can arise from a variety of emotional conflict situations (Gerard, 1939). For example, she notes instances of enuresis that appeared to be regressive, arising out of situational stressors such as the arrival of a new sibling. In addition, she cites cases of revenge in which the wetting represented retaliation toward a punitive mother, and cases that seemed neurotic in nature because the bedwetting was based on unresolved psychosexual conflicts and unconscious fears of castration.

Whatever the primary cause or causes, it is generally agreed that enuresis is a problem that is not only burdensome to all concerned, but also one that may contribute to serious adjustment difficulties in the affected child. The spectacle of parental behaviors that begin with patience and persuasion need only be reviewed to sense what the enuretic child experiences at home. Parents try rewards for successive nights of dryness, then shaming, and then even more punitive tactics of scolding without success. They may then adopt a "get-tough" policy by refusing to change pajamas or bed linens, and then resort to spankings. And sometime before parents turn to professional help, they may try a more rational approach that includes special remedial activities such as reducing fluid intake in the evening and waking the child several times during the night to take him or her to the toilet. The child becomes the focus of negative attention with the clear message that he or she has failed to achieve what others have, and that there is something wrong with him or her. Shame, guilt, feelings of inadequacy, rejection, despondency, and hostility both for self and others simply must arise out of this situation for most enuretic children. Problems of alienation and withdrawal from peer relationships must also occur for these children. Therefore, it is advisable to institute remedial measures as early as possible to maximize the chances of resolving the problem and to minimize the psychological damage associated with it.

In days of old, the remedies suggested for enuresis included such exotic and repugnant preparations as powdered goat claws or cock trachea, hare's brain in wine, hare's testicles, roast mouse, gastric mucose of a hen, or the roasted bladder of a pig sprinkled on the bed, as well as such painful techniques as pouring collodian on the prepuce, placing an inflated rubber bag in the vagina, clamping the penis, applying irritants to the glans or silver nitrate to the urethral passage to make micturition painful ("Causes of Enuresis," 1969). Fortunately, we can report that treatment advances have progressed considerably since that time, and there are several approaches that seem to work quite well.

The most effective and promising drug therapy is a single dose of imipramine given daily at bedtime. Dinello and Champelli (1968) reviewed some forty papers in which imipramine was used for the treatment of enuresis. These authors found that only seventeen studies used adequate controls, and of these eleven reported positive results with the drug. In all six studies in which negative findings were obtained, the reviewers noted that the drug dosages were too small. They concluded that imipramine works best with enuretic children (as contrasted to adults) who are frequent bedwetters and when treatment is on an outpatient basis and the drug is given in single doses of 50 mg or higher. Bakwin and Bakwin (1972) suggested that the drug should be given for an eight-week period at high dosage and then gradually diminished. Imipramine may produce the untoward effects of irritability and awakening during the night, but these side effects are transient and temporary. In a more recent study, the efficacy of placebo, imipramine, and classical conditioning treatment approaches were compared in groups of enuretic school children between eight and ten years of age. Those treated with either imipramine or conditioning showed more improvement than the placebo group after

two months (when treatment ended) and after a four month follow-up. Imipramine-treated youngsters showed an almost immediate improvement after treatment was begun, but the improvement declined considerably after treatment was terminated. In contrast, the conditioning group was slower to show improvement although the gains were better maintained after the treatment was stopped (Kolvin, Taunch, Currah, Garside, Nolan, and Shaw, 1972). These findings suggest that relapses are likely to occur when imipramine is used as the only treatment for enuresis.

Psychological approaches to the treatment of enuresis, primarily those that incorporate the essential paradigm of classical conditioning, are well known, since the Mowrers first introduced the method in 1938 (Mowrer and Mowrer, 1938). The basic procedure consists of the temporal pairing of the interoceptive cues of bladder distension present during bedwetting with the sound of a buzzer or bell that is activated when urine falls on an electrically sensitive pad. The bell serves to awaken the child and is a signal for the child to cease micturition. At the same time, it summons the parent to take the child to the toilet to void, and to reset the pad and return the child to bed. The object of this conditioning procedure is to replace the buzzer with interoceptive cues in consistently waking the child and in establishing the sphincter responses necessary for continence. Obviously, the effectiveness of the method is dependent largely on the child's ability to hear the sounding of the buzzer, and on the cooperation of the parents. Treatment continued in the Mowrers' study until the child achieved seven consecutive dry nights, and then, under conditions of increased fluid intake prior to bedtime, the experimenters administered another series until the child achieved another seven consecutive dry nights. Early objections to this and similar studies centered around three major issues: (1) the absence of control groups, (2) the belief that other symptoms of the presumed underlying emotional disturbance would surface as a substitute for wetting, and (3) the lack of evidence indicating that successes achieved through this method would indeed be maintained over a long period of time.

Studies that have used control groups have appeared in the literature since the 1960s, and they have shown that conditioning was more effective than either no treatment or psychotherapy in producing bladder control (DeLeon and Mandell, 1966; Baker, 1969). Moreover, the Baker study found no evidence of symptom substitution but rather that parents rated their children as happier and more independent than before treatment, as the children themselves scored higher on a measure of self-image and less neurotic on a neurotic inventory. At this point in time, there is little doubt that an initial arrest of wetting can be brought about by conditioning in about ninety percent of unselected enuretic cases (Lovibond and Cotte, 1970).

The early concern about relapse under a conditioning procedure is still legitimate and very real. When relapse was defined as renewed wetting occurring more than once a week, the relapse rate reached as high as thirty to forty percent over a two-year period following treatment (Lovibond, 1964). Lovibond also found that age, sex, adjustment, personality factors, or wetting patterns were unrelated to failure to maintain continence. After examining the relationship of some forty factors to relapse, Young and Morgan (1973b) concluded that relapse is not a function of patient and background variables but a product of de-

ficiencies in the treatment. Two additional studies by these authors provide evidence that a procedure of overlearning in which the child is required to regain bladder control through conditioning trials until achieving fourteen consecutive dry nights (under conditions of increased fluid intake) significantly decreases the relapse rate (Young and Morgan, 1972a,b).

The popularity of psychotherapy as a treatment approach for enuresis was particularly evident during the first half of the twentieth century, when psychoanalytic theory was most influential, and before the usefulness of drug and conditioning therapy was demonstrated. There was strong support for the view that held that enuresis was a symptom of some underlying emotional conflict and disturbance. In accordance with this assumption, treatment (usually psychodynamically oriented psychotherapy) was aimed at resolving the basic emotional problems rather than at eliminating the symptom. Unless the cause could be treated, symptom removal would not only be temporary, but also it would result in symptom substitution (the appearance of other symptoms). At present, conditioning and drug therapy have proved more effective than psychotherapy, although psychotherapy is still used and recommended for those cases of enuresis in which deep-seated psychological problems are evident.

Encopresis

Involuntary defecation not directly caused by physical disease that occurs in children beyond the age of about two or three years is known as encopresis or fecal soiling. In addition to soiling, encopresis is almost always associated with constipation in which alternating periods of loss of bowel control and withholding of feces are characteristic. As objectionable and aversive as the soiling may be to parents, it is far less hazardous physiologically to the child than constipation. Persistent withholding results in impacted feces, enlarged colon (megacolon), and loss of tone and sensitivity of the colon that eventually leads to its improper functioning (Ellis and Mitchell, 1973). Unlike enuresis, encopresis is primarily a diurnal phenomenon that more often occurs after bowel control has been established. Incidence estimates are infrequently cited in the literature, and those that are available vary considerably depending on such factors as the size of the sample, the age of the children, the frequency of soiling, and the criterion used with regard to withholding. Shirley (1938), in one of the earliest studies, found an incidence of almost three percent with a male to female ratio of 5:1, while Anthony showed a sex ratio of 6:1 favoring boys (Anthony, 1958). The incidence of encopresis decreases sharply to one and a half percent when children over seven years of age are sampled (Bellman, 1966).

As difficult as it may be to interpret these incidence data, it is apparent that encopresis is rare, extremely infrequent beyond age seven, and it is a condition that is predominantly found in boys. In Shirley's sample of cases, approximately thirty-seven percent obtained I.Q. scores below seventy (mental retardation), suggesting that limited intelligence may account for these failures in bowel training and control. Nevertheless, a sizable number of encopretic children remains in whom psychogenic factors appear primary. Encopresis was noted as a problem in children who were evacuated from London during the period of heavy German air-raid bombings in World War II (Burns, 1941). Further

support for its psychogenic origin comes from the finding that encopretic children who have experienced the emotional stress of separation, arrival of a new sibling, or the illness of mother also evidence regressive behavior, feeding problems, and temper tantrums (Kanner, 1972). Conflicts between parent and child over bowel control are both more probable and more severe than those that arise from bladder regulation, because of our greater aversion to one over the other. In addition, defecation becomes the battleground for the child's struggle for assertion and independence, because it is an event that often meets with parental resistance (Anthony, 1957; Erikson, 1963). When the child's efforts are blocked or thwarted, the child may become defiant by soiling or withholding. Reactions of disgust to incontinence may encourage the child to withhold or to conceal the evidence of soiled clothes in order to avoid parental punishment and rejection. The encopretic child also faces social alienation and ridicule from others, which impairs the child's peer relationships, self-concept, and social adjustment. As we shall see in our discussion of childhood psychoses (Chapter 8), encopresis may be an accompanying symptom of this severe form of abnormal behavior.

Before treatment is instituted, incontinence resulting from some organic pathology such as Hirschsprung's disease (neurogenic megacolon that results from an absence of anglionic cells of the rectum or large intestine), or megacolon caused by obstructive lesions should be ruled out medically. Beyond this, encopretic mental retardates, psychotic children, and encopretic children with less serious associated abnormal behavior have been successfully treated by operant conditioning procedures that used positive reinforcement when appropriate bowel movements were achieved (Neal, 1963; Gelber and Meyer, 1965; Hundziak, Mauer, and Watson, 1965; Balson, 1973). The work of Neal with four hospitalized encopretic children illustrates, in a general way, the procedures used in operant conditioning. The children were accompanied to the toilet four times daily (after each meal and at bedtime) by a nurse who was known to the child and who tried to reduce the anxiety associated with defecation by permitting the child to close the toilet door if the child wished, or to eat candy and read a comic book. Each child sat on the toilet until either a bowel movement occurred or five minutes had elapsed. Bowel movements were lavishly praised, and the child was given candy or some other appropriate reward. No punishment or critical comments were made when bowel movements were not obtained; and clean pants were given to the child to replace soiled ones whenever soiling occurred. Once the child was free from soiling and was accustomed to sitting on the toilet, the four times a day routine was abandoned and replaced with voluntary trips to the toilet whenever the child felt the sensation of rectal fullness. The child was rewarded for each successful bowel movement. Rapid success, that is, within three months, was achieved in two cases, and in one child after a full year; the fourth case represented a therapeutic failure.

Wright (1973) reported dramatic success (one failure in approximately thirty-six cases) in eliminating encopresis by using a conditioning procedure that involved two positive and one negative reinforcer, morning trips to the toilet, and the use of cathartics. Children unable to defecate were given suppositories and then permitted to have breakfast. In the event that the suppository did not work, the child was given

an enema, a set of conditions that were designed to result in defecation at a specific and regular time (early in the morning). Positive reinforcers were given when defecation occurred, while negative reinforcers were used whenever soiling was noted. Once daily bowel movements were established and soiling extinguished for two weeks, the use of cathartics was gradually reduced. Their use was completely discontinued when the child had no soiling for eight consecutive weeks.

Encopresis is a messy problem that frequently comes to the attention of the professional because parents and others find it so objectionable. The prognostic outlook is related to the age of the child, the duration of the condition, and the severity of the underlying or associated psychopathology.

Summary

During early childhood, the bodily functions of eating, sleeping, and elimination are of primary interest as they undergo dramatic modification through maturation and habit training. Behavioral problems may either become evident or originate in the regulation of these functions. Failures in training may reflect early or continued difficulties in the mother-child relationship, the presence of some serious organic or psychological disorder, and secondary effects that make for subsequent personal and social maladjustment. The major problems associated with each of these rhythmic patterns are presented in tabular form which summarizes the symptoms, variables related to the condition, possible causal factors, and the most promising treatment approaches.

A. Problems of Eating

Colic

Symptoms	Related Factors	Causal Factors	Treatment
Intestinal pain, abdominal distention, flexion of legs. Incessant and persistent crying.	Begins in first few weeks of life, and lasts three–five months. Found frequently in first born. Stressful and disruptive of mother-child relationship.	No known cause. First inclination to look at diet or factors related to eating. Tension and anxiety of mother. Innate tendency.	No known effective treatment. Temporary relief of symptoms by holding, rocking, and walking with baby.

Obesity

Symptoms	Related Factors	Causal Factors	Treatment
Body weight greater than twenty percent of norm. Excessive body fat. Abnormal inactivity. Immature, dependent on mother, shy, fearful, timid, clumsy, slow, and apathetic. Most obese children are tall for their age—a factor that distinguishes it from endocrine disease.	Fat infants tend to be obese later in childhood, and as adults. Pessimistic outlook. Secondary effects of obesity are in damaging self-esteem, in peer relations, and social adjustment, as well as in health hazards. Tall for age rules out hormonal basis of obesity. Below average in height as adults.	No single cause. Hereditary tendencies that may set weight boundaries. Small percentage caused by endocrine disorders. Psychogenic. Rejecting mother tends to overfeed which leads to child's failure to distinguish correct bodily sensations of hunger and satiation. Modeling of obese parents.	Difficult to treat. Diet restrictions, increased physical exercise, and behavior modification (although no modification program available as yet for children). Individual psychotherapy not effective. Group therapy and special group programs show promise but no follow-up data available yet.

Pica

Symptoms	Related Factors	Causal Factors	Treatment
Purposeful eating of inedible substances beyond age one. Usually disappears during fourth or fifth year of life. Excessive oral activities and feeding and speech problems. Also head banging, rocking,	Ingestion of toxic materials such as lead can result in brain damage, mental retardation, and death. Not limited to any specific level of intelligence, although often found in mental retardates.	Not caused by nutritional deficiency. Family disorganization. Modeling of parents.	Little known about treatment. Education of parents. Psychotherapy for older and more persistent cases.

A. Problems of Eating (con't.)

Pica (con't.)

Symptoms	Related Factors	Causal Factors	Treatment
hair pulling, enuresis, nightmares, temper tantrums, etc.	More frequent in low socioeconomic black families of the southeast.		
	Mothers often show pica, obesity, alcoholism, and drug addiction.		
	Pica beyond age of six is rare and considered sign of serious abnormal condition.		

Refusal to Eat

Symptoms	Related Factors	Causal Factors	Treatment
Refusal to eat.		Parental anxiety. Maternal attention reinforces the refusal to eat.	Education and reassurance of parent.
Weight loss.			Acceptance of child's food preference and regularity of feeding. Small portions and self-feeding.
Fussy and variable appetite.			
			Behavior modification.

B. Problems of Sleep

Falling Asleep

Symptoms	Related Factors	Causal Factors	Treatment
Wakefulness, restlessness, and insomnia.	Children differ in their sleep needs.	Physical discomfort and distress.	Modification of parental training practices.
Refusal or reluctance to go to bed.	Parents often have their own expectations.	Emotional and environmental conditions that produce intense feelings and overstimulation.	Adjust sleep schedule to fit child's needs.
Crying and distress.			Psychotherapy for those cases arising out of intrapsychic conflicts and fears.
		Reinforcement of bedtime rituals.	
		Inconsistent and faulty training.	

B. Problems of Sleep (con't.)

Disruptions of Sleep

Symptoms	Related Factors	Causal Factors	Treatment
Nightmares, night terrors, sleep walking. See Table 6–1 for differences in clinical picture between nightmares and night terrors.	Nightmares are frequent and occur during REM sleep when most dreaming occurs. Night terrors are rare, occur in NREM sleep, and are accompanied by severe autonomic discharges. Night terrors are more frequent in boys. Sleep walking is found in about six percent of children, and it occurs in NREM sleep. There is a potential danger of child hurting self while walking. Terrors and sleep walking frequently coexist.	REM nightmares may be attempts at mastery of traumatic experiences, while terrors may represent failure to master. Terrors are independent of mental activity. Nightmares may be products of unconscious impulses and conflicts. Sleep walking is often triggered off by upsetting emotional experiences. Sleep walking is found to run in families and has a higher concordance rate for monozygotic twins than dizygotic twins.	Nightmares are not often brought to attention of professional. Little is known about their treatment. Severe fright reactions that are frequent and persistent are treated with individual psychotherapy, but no hard data is available to evaluate its effectiveness. Valium also has been recommended. Special care needs to be taken so that accidents are prevented for sleep walkers. Psychotherapy is used for those cases that show sleep walking, night terrors, and other problems.

C. Problems of Elimination

Enuresis

Symptoms	Related Factors	Causal Factors	Treatment
Involuntary passage of urine mostly during the night but diurnal wetting may also occur. Wetting must be in children beyond age of three or four, occur at least once a month, and not be linked to organic pathology. General immaturity with such behaviors as: whining, moodiness,	Occurs most often between eight and eleven years of age, and in more boys than girls. It usually persists from early childhood. More prevalent in children of manual workers and less frequent in children of professional and high salaried families.	Only five to ten percent of cases caused by organic pathology. Runs in families with higher concordance rate for monozygotic twins. Studies, however, confound genetic and environmental factors. Primarily thought of as psychogenic in nature . . . faulty training,	Most effective drug is imipramine in daily dose of 50 mg or more for eight weeks and then gradually diminished. High relapse rate after four months. Classical conditioning is best psychological approach. Relapse rate can be significantly reduced with over-learning.

C. Problems of Elimination (con't.)

Enuresis (con't.)

Symptoms	Related Factors	Causal Factors	Treatment
irritability, restless-ness, overactivity, excitability, stubbornness, disobedience, over-sensitivity, as well as problems of eating, temper, nail biting, fear reactions, encopresis, tics, health concerns, masturbation, and stealing.	Found in all levels of intelligence.

Rarely occurs as an isolated symptom.

Occurs in NREM sleep.

Leads to serious difficulties in personal and social adjustment. | maternal overprotec-tiveness, situational anxiety, disturbances in the family.

No single cause (even psychogenic) that can account for all instances of enuresis. | Psychotherapy has been shown to be less effective than conditioning. However it is still used when enuresis is regarded as symptom of more serious underlying problem.

Conditioning removes symptom without evidence of symptom substitution. |

Encopresis

Symptoms	Related Factors	Causal Factors	Treatment
Involuntary fecal soiling in child beyond age of two or three, not directly related to organic disease.

Soiling alternates with periods of constipation that may be serious health hazard. It may lead to psychogenic megacolon, and improper functioning of the colon. | Primarily a diurnal condition.

It is rare with an incidence of about three percent with a male to female ratio of about 5:1 or 6:1.

Incidence sharply decreases to one and a half percent beyond age of 7.

Highly associated with mental retardation, although it occurs in all levels of intelligence.

Outlook is related to age of child, duration of the condition, and severity of underlying or associated psycho-pathology. | Primarily viewed as psychogenic in origin.

Situational anxiety.

Regressive behavior.

Conflict between mother and child. Child seeks independence and self-asser-tion. He reacts to con-trolling parent with defiance, hostility, and withholding of feces.

In rare instances, organic diseases produce incontinence and these must be ruled out medically. | Traditional individual psychotherapy has been used for chronic and persistent cases or for those where deep seated psycho-logical problems are apparent. No hard data to evaluate its effectiveness, however.

Operant conditioning has been used more recently with promising results. |

Epilogue

Interested readers will be happy to learn that Sandy's problems of refusal to self-feed and to eat solid foods were successfully treated (Bernal, 1972). Her parents were trained to gradually exert increasing control over her eating habits through the restriction of normal food intake and through providing her with the opportunity to earn social and food rewards for eating solid foods. Similarly, her parents rewarded Sandy for feeding herself. At the end of thirty-two weeks, Sandy's diet successfully included all table foods, and new foods were introduced. Sandy now fed herself, and her eating behavior improved so noticeably that her parents were no longer concerned.

While this behavioral approach eliminated Sandy's unwanted behaviors, we must not allow this positive outcome to blur our ability to view this treatment method critically. Essentially, we have evidence of symptom (or behavior) removal, but we would need long-term follow-up data to tell us that the symptoms have not reappeared or that new ones have not replaced them. Perhaps more important is the absence of data dealing with the nature of the mother-child battle that gave rise to the symptoms in the first place. In what ways have the relationships between mother and daughter changed, what brought about the change, and is the change the result of the treatment used? What is Sandy's adjustment like with respect to mother, other members of the family, nursery school, and so forth? Since there was no untreated child like Sandy to serve as a control subject, we have no way of knowing whether Sandy's eating behaviors would have changed over time without treatment. In fact, we could conjecture that Sandy's successful heart surgery and her clean bill of health were sufficient to allay her parents' fear of doing battle with her. Under these conditions, they may be less inclined to cater to Sandy's wishes, and more apt to hold the line in combating her eating problems.

REFERENCES

ABRAHAM, S. and M. NORDSIECK. "Relationship of Excess Weight in Children and Adults." *Public Health Reports*, 1960, *75*, 263–273.

ABRAMSON, E. E. "A Review of Behavioral Approaches to Weight Control." *Behaviour Research and Therapy*, 1973, *11*, 547–556.

ANTHONY, E. J. "An Experimental Approach to the Psychopathology of Childhood Encopresis." *British Journal of Medical Psychology*, 1957, *30*, 146–175.

BAKER, B. L. "Symptom Treatment and Symptom Substitution in Enuresis." *Journal of Abnormal Psychology*, 1969, *74*, 42–49.

BAKWIN, H. "Enuresis in Twins." *American Journal of Diseases of Children*, 1971, *121*, 222–225.

BAKWIN, H. and R. M. BAKWIN. *Behavior Disorders in Children* (4th ed.). Philadelphia: Saunders, 1972.

BALSON, P. M. "Case Study: Encopresis: A Case with Symptom Substitution?" *Behavior Therapy*, 1973, *4*, 134–136.

BELLMAN, M. "Studies on Encopresis." *Acta Paediatrica Scandinavia*, 1966, Supplement 170.

BERNAL, M. E. "Behavioral Treatment of a Child's Eating Problem." *Journal of Behavior Therapy and Experimental Psychiatry*, 1972, *3*, 43–50.

BLOMFIELD, J. M. and J. W. B. DOUGLAS. "Bedwetting, Prevalence among Children Aged 4–7 Years." *The Lancet*, 1956, *1*, 850–852.

BROOK, C. G. D., LLOYD, J. K., and O. H. WOLF. "Relation Between Age of Onset of

Obesity and Size and Number of Adipose Cells." *British Medical Journal*, 1972, *2*, 25–27.

BROUGHTON, R. J. "Sleep Disorders: Disorders of Arousal?" *Science*, 1968, *159*, 1070–1078.

BRUCH, H. "Obesity in Childhood and Personality Development." *American Journal of Orthopsychiatry*, 1941, *11*, 467–474.

BRUCH, H. "Fat Children Grown Up." *American Journal of Diseases of Children*, 1955, *90*, 501.

BRUCH, H. *The Importance of Overweight*. New York: Norton, 1957.

BRUCH, H. "Transformation of Oral Impulses in Eating Disorders: A Conceptual Approach." *Psychiatric Quarterly*, 1961, *35*, 458–481.

BULLEN, B. A., MONELLO, L. F., COHEN, H., and J. MAYER. "Attitudes Towards Physical Activity, Food and Family in Obese and Nonobese Adolescent Girls." *American Journal of Clinical Nutrition*, 1963, *12*, No. 1:1–11.

BURNS, C. "Encopresis (Incontinence of Faeces) in Children." *British Medical Journal*, 1941, *2*, 767–769.

CARRERA, F. III. "Obesity in Adolescence." In Kiell, N. (Ed.), *The Psychology of Obesity, Dynamics and Treatment*. Springfield, Illinois: Charles C Thomas, 1973, 113–124.

"Causes of Enuresis" (Editorial). *British Medical Journal*, 1969, *2*, 63–64.

CRADDOCK, D. *Obesity and Its Management* (2nd ed.). Edinburgh: Churchill Livingston, 1973.

DeLEON, G. and W. MANDELL. "A Comparison of Conditioning and Psychotherapy in the Treatment of Functional Enuresis." *Journal of Clinical Psychology*, 1966, *22*, 326–330.

DINELLO, F. A. and J. CHAMPELLI. "The Use of Imipramine in the Treatment of Enuresis" (Review). *Canadian Psychiatric Association Journal*, 1968, *13*, 237–241.

EID, E. E. "Follow-up Study of Physical Growth of Children Who Had Excessive Weight Gain in First Six Months of Life." *British Medical Journal*, 1970, *2*, 74–76.

ELLIS, R. W. B. and R. G. MITCHELL. *Disease in Infancy and Childhood* (7th ed.). Baltimore: William and Wilkins, 1973.

ERIKSON, E. *Childhood and Society* (2nd ed.). New York: Norton, 1963.

FISHER, C., KAHN, E., EDWARDS, A., and D. DAVIS. "Effects of Valium on NREM Night Terrors." *Psychophysiology*, 1972, *9*, 91.

FISHER, C., KAHN, E., EDWARDS, A., and D. M. DAVIS. "A Psychophysiological Study of Nightmares and Night Terrors." *Journal of Nervous and Mental Disease*, 1973, *157*, 75–98.

FRARY, L. G. "Enuresis: A Genetic Study." *American Journal of Diseases of Children*, 1935, *49*, 557–578.

GASTAUT, H. and R. BROUGHTON. "A Clinical and Polygraphic Study of Episodic Phenomena During Sleep." In J. Wortis (Ed.), *Recent Advances in Biological Psychiatry* (Vol. VII). New York: Plenum Press, 1965, pp. 197–221.

GELBER, H. and V. MEYER. "Behavior Therapy and Encopresis: The Complexities Involved in Treatment." *Behaviour Research and Therapy*, 1965, *2*, 227–231.

GERARD, M. W. "Enuresis: A Study in Etiology." *American Journal of Orthopsychiatry*, 1939, *9*, 48–58.

GILBERT, G. M. "A Survey of 'Referral Problems' in Metropolitan Child Guidance Centers." *Journal of Clinical Psychology*, 1957, *13*, 37–42.

GLICKLICH, L. B. "An Historical Account of Enuresis." *Pediatrics*, 1951, *8*, 859–876.

GUTELIUS, M. F., MILLICAN, F. K., LAYMAN, E. M., COHEN, G. J., and C. C. DUBLIN. "Nutritional Studies of Children with Pica." *Pediatrics*, 1962, *29*, 1012–1023.

HALL, S. M. and R. G. HALL. "Outcome and Methodological Considerations in Behavioral Treatment of Obesity." *Behavior Therapy*, 1974, *5*, 352–364.

HALLGREN, B. *Enuresis: A Clinical and Genetic Study.* Copenhagen: Munksgaard, 1957.

HUNDZIAK, M., MAUER, R. A., and L. S. WATSON, JR. "Operant Conditioning in Toilet Training of Severely Mentally Retarded Boys." *American Journal of Mental Deficiency*, 1965, *70*, 120–124.

HUTCHINSON-SMITH, B. H. "Obesity and Respiratory Infection of Children." *British Medical Journal*, 1971, *1*, 460–461.

ILLINGWORTH, R. S. "Three Months' Colic." *Archives of Disease in Childhood*, 1954, *29*, 165–74.

ILLINGWORTH, R. S. *Common Symptoms of Disease in Children* (3rd ed.). Oxford: Blackwell Scientific Publications, 1971.

JACOBSON, A., KALES, J. D., and A. KALES. "Clinical and Electrophysiological Correlates of Sleep Disorders in Children." In Kales, A. (Ed.), *Sleep: Physiology and Pathology, A Symposium*. Philadelphia: Lippincott, 1969.

JEFFREY, D. B. "Behavioral Management of Obesity." In Craighead, W. E., Kazdin, A. E., and M. J. Mahoney (Eds.), *Behavior Modification: Principles, Issues, and Applications*. Boston: Houghton Mifflin, 1976.

KAHN, E., FISHER, C., BYRNE, J., EDWARDS, A., and A. FROSCH. "The Influence of Valium, Thorazine, and Dilantin on Stage 4 Nightmares." *Psychophysiology*, 1970, *7*, 350.

KANNER, L. *Child Psychiatry* (4th ed.). Springfield, Illinois: Charles C Thomas, 1972.

KESSLER, J. W. *Psychopathology of Childhood*. Englewood Cliffs, New Jersey: Prentice-Hall, 1966.

KOLVIN, I., TAUNCH, J., CURRAH, J., GARSIDE, R. F., NOLAN, J., and W. B. SHAW. "Enuresis: A Descriptive Analysis and a Controlled Trial." *Developmental Medicine and Child Neurology*, 1972, *14*, 715–726.

LAKIN, M. "Personality Factors in Mothers of Excessively Crying (Colicky) Infants." *Monographs of the Society for Research in Child Development*, 1957, *22*, Serial No. 64, No. 1.

LAPOUSE, R. and M. A. MONK. "Fears and Worries in a Representative Sample of Children." *American Journal of Orthopsychiatry*, 1959, *29*, 803–818.

LLOYD, J. K., WOLFE, O. H. and W. S. WHELEN. "Childhood Obesity: A Long-Term Study of Height and Weight." *British Medical Journal*, 1961, *5245*, 145–148.

LOVIBOND, S. H. *Conditioning and Enuresis*. Oxford: Pergammon Press, 1964.

LOVIBOND, S. H. and M. A. COOTE. "Enuresis." In Costello, C. G. (Ed.), *Symptoms of Psychopathology: A Handbook*. New York: Wiley, 1970, 373–396.

MACKEITH, R. "A Frequent Factor in the Origins of Primary Nocturnal Enuresis: Anxiety in the Third Year of Life." *Developmental Medicine and Child Neurology*, 1968, *10*, 465–470.

MAYER, J. "Some Aspects of the Problem of Regulation of Food Intake and Obesity." *New England Journal of Medicine, 274*: 610–616, 17 March, 1966: contd, 662–673, 24 March, 1966; 722–731, concl. 31 March, 1966.

MILLICAN, F. K. and R. S. LOURIE. The Child with Pica and His Family." In Anthony, E. J. and C. Koupernik (Eds.), *The Child in His Family* (Vol. 1). The

International Yearbook for Child Psychiatry and Allied Disciplines. New York: Wiley, 1970, 333–348.

MOBBS, J. "Childhood Obesity." *International Journal of Nursing Studies,* 1970, *7,* 3–18.

MONELLO, L. F. and J. MAYER. "Obese Adolescent Girls: Unrecognized 'Minority' Group?" *American Journal of Clinical Nutrition,* 1963, *13,* 35–39.

MOWRER, O. H., and W. A. MOWRER. "Enuresis: A Method for Its Study and Treatment." *American Journal of Orthopsychiatry,* 1938, *8,* 436–459.

NATHAN, S. "Body Image in Chronically Obese Children as Reflected in Figure Drawings." *Journal of Personality Assessment,* 1973, *37,* 456–463.

NEAL, D. H. "Behavior Therapy and Encopresis in Children." *Behaviour Research and Therapy,* 1963, *1,* 139–150.

OSTERGAARD, L. "On Psychogenic Obesity in Childhood." V. *Acta Paediatrica,* 1954, *43,* 507–521.

PIERCE, C. M. "Dream Studies in Enuresis Research." *Canadian Psychiatric Association Journal,* 1963, *8,* 415–419.

READ, M. S. and D. FELSON. *Malnutrition, Learning, and Behavior.* National Institute of Child Health and Human Development Center for Research for Mothers and Children, DHEW Publication No. (NIH) 76–1036, April 1976.

SHIRLEY, H. F. "Encopresis in Children." *Journal of Pediatrics,* 1938, *12,* 367–380.

SPOCK, B. *Baby and Child Care* (Revised Cardinal Giant Edition). New York: Pocket Books, 1963.

STUNKARD, A. J., and M. J. MAHONEY. "Behavioral Treatment of the Eating Disorders." In Leitenberg, H. (Ed.), *Handbook of Behavior Modification.* Englewood Cliffs, New Jersey: Prentice-Hall, 1976, 45–73.

TOLSTRUP, K. "On Psychogenic Obesity in Children." IV. *Acta Paediatrica,* 1953, *42,* 289–304.

WRIGHT, L. "Handling the Encopretic Child." *Professional Psychology,* 1973, Vol. IV, 137–144.

YOUNG, G. C. and R. T. T. MORGAN. "Overlearning in the Conditioning Treatment of Enuresis." *Behavior Research and Therapy,* 1972 (a), *10,* 147–151.

YOUNG, G. C. and R. T. T. MORGAN. "Overlearning in the Conditioning Treatment of Enuresis: A Long-Term Follow-up Study." *Behavior Research and Therapy,* 1972 (b), *10,* 419–420.

YOUNG, G. C. and R. T. T. MORGAN. "Analysis of Factors Associated with the Extinction of a Conditioned Response." *Behavior Research and Therapy,* 1973 (a), *11,* 219–22.

YOUNG, G. C. and R. T. T. MORGAN. "Rapidity of Response to the Treatment of Enuresis." *Developmental Medicine and Child Neurology,* 1973 (b), *15,* 488–496.

Childhood Psychosis

8

PROLOGUE

I don't know where to begin, doctor, except that our pediatrician sent us to you because we are very worried about Henry, our oldest child. Oh, he's a healthy and fine-looking boy . . . and he was such a good baby. He rarely cried or demanded much attention. He seemed content and so self-sufficient that I was able to leave him alone and get other things done around the house. I remember feeling pleased with how easily I managed everything, and also a little resentful that Henry did not appear to need me more. After a while I couldn't help recognize that he was not interested in anyone, not even toys.

There were times when his eyes were bright and he looked alert. But he would often stare off into space and be so far away. Really, I tried everything to get his attention, but I just couldn't get through to him. We thought that he might be . . . deaf, but his hearing was checked and it was normal. We worried because he didn't walk by himself until months after his second birthday, but we were relieved that he repeated a few words before he was a year old. However, he never really put words together on his own, and he never has really entered into anything resembling a conversation. We struggled for several years to toilet train him but without success. He's five years old now, and he still wets and soils himself.

Henry won't feed himself and he's an absolute disaster at the dinner table. He throws food, bangs on the table, and shoves dishes within his reach until something spills or breaks. He likes to rock back and forth for hours on end, and sometimes he bangs his head as part of his rocking pattern. He doesn't play with other children, and at unexpected times he becomes angry and unmanageable for no apparent reason. My husband and I thought Henry would outgrow whatever stage he was going through, and that things would get better.

Believe me doctor, we have tried so hard to be patient with him. It's almost time for him to start school, but we're afraid that he won't be ready . . . (mother breaks into tears), maybe he'll never be ready! Oh, doctor, . . . help us . . . help us find out what's wrong with Henry.

Henry's mother settled down temporarily after the psychologist reassured her that everything possible would be done to uncover her son's difficulties. However, her basic anxiety came from the nagging fear that Henry was an abnormal child who was suffering from an irreparable disorder. Unfortunately, the psychologist could not dispel her fear, because he viewed Henry's long standing symptoms of social isolation and inaccessibility, of severe impairment of motor and language development, and of eating and toilet habits as falling within the broad category of childhood psychosis. But determining exactly what's wrong with Henry is an illusive and complex task that is much like one's first encounter with a mirage—now you see it . . . now you don't.

On the surface, the childhood psychoses of *schizophrenia, early infantile autism,* and *symbiotic infantile psychosis* have been described as separate, distinguishable conditions. However, on closer examination, their boundaries are actually quite fuzzy. In clinical practice, these diagnostic labels are all too often used interchangeably and inconsistently. There is disparity in the description of the symptom picture within each category, and even greater disagreement over the diagnostic signs used to discriminate among them. In addition, the difficulty encountered in differentiating childhood psychoses from mental retardation and organic brain syndromes only serves to increase diagnostic confusion. For these reasons, data on the incidence, family characteristics, etiological factors, and treatment effects for the separate diagnostic categories are inaccurate and difficult to interpret.

Nevertheless, in this chapter we shall try to bring some measure of clarity and orderliness to this fascinating area of study. We shall examine the symptom picture of the three major childhood psychoses, discuss the various criteria used to differentiate among them and other abnormal conditions, consider etiological views, and describe those treatment methods that seem to be most promising.

Childhood Schizophrenia

A sustained interest in childhood psychosis is relatively recent. It began with a paper published by Potter (1933), who outlined a set of diagnostic criteria for childhood schizophrenia drawn from a sample of six children. Through the years, childhood schizophrenia has remained the central focus of study, and the primary classification category of psychosis of children. However, the diversity of symptoms included within this category has tended to make it a "catch-all" classification that has resulted in even greater diagnostic imprecision. Indeed, it is difficult to understand how children who behave so differently can be considered to have the same disorder.

This apparent inconsistency interested several investigators who sought further diagnostic specificity by identifying distinctive conditions within or apart from the poorly defined boundaries of childhood schizophrenia. For example, Lauretta Bender described three discrete forms of this disorder; Leo Kanner proposed the syndrome of early infantile autism; and Margaret Mahler differentiated symbiotic infantile psychosis from childhood schizophrenia. Yet even to the present controversy continues about the validity and diagnostic usefulness of these separate entities.

In addition, it is still uncertain whether schizophrenia is the same condition in children and adults, even though the one label implies a congruence of the disorder over time. Schizophrenic youngsters display symptoms dissimilar to those displayed by schizophrenic adults, but this has been attributed to the more restricted behavioral repertoire and life experiences of children rather than taken as evidence of two different disorders (Potter, 1933; Kanner, 1972). Indirect evidence that schizophrenia is the same condition for children and adults comes from follow-up studies showing that children who were earlier diagnosed as schizophrenia were given the same diagnosis years later when they were adolescents or adults (Bender, Freedman, Grugett, and Helme, 1952; Bennett and Klein, 1966; Bender and Faretra, 1972). However, these data must be interpreted cautiously, since the second diagnosis was not independent of the first.

Clinical Description

For reasons already apparent, there is no simple, single description of this disorder, but instead a diversity of definitions that have been proposed by various clinicians. Nevertheless, as noted by Goldfarb and his colleagues:

Whatever the descriptive label, the criteria for the diagnosis of childhood schizophrenia refer to extreme impairments in human relationships, to inadequate perceptual and conceptual responses, to abnormalities of psychomotor behavior and communication, and to unusual preoccupations. These criteria are broad in scope, and the children classified as schizophrenic are highly diversified in the kind and quantity of their defects.

Varied as they may be, however, all schizophrenic children show massive gaps in the framework of their personalities and constitute an enormous burden to themselves, their families, and the community at large (Goldfarb, Mintz, and Strook, 1969, p. 1).

Childhood schizophrenia usually occurs gradually between the second and eleventh year of life. Most clinicians characterize the disorder as an impairment in *interpersonal relations* and in *motor behavior*. Moreover, they specify that it includes disturbances in *intellectual* and *cognitive functioning, affective responses,* and *language*. Table 8–1 summarizes the diagnostic criteria proposed by various investigators that are most widely used in clinical practice today.

The symptom picture varies with the child's developmental level, age of onset, nature of early experiences, and type of defense mechanisms used. Yet, in almost all instances, there is a profound decrease of interest in the external world of people, events, and activities, together with an absorption in oneself and loss of contact with reality. Schizophrenic children, like Henry, don't play with toys and refuse to look directly at familiar people. In the presence of people, some of these children may only glance upwards or sideways, while others may go as far as covering their ears in response to speech (Norman, 1954, 1955). Paradoxically, their usual avoidance of human contact suddenly can be interrupted by physical clinging, as if extreme fearfulness prompted their behavior (Creak, 1961; Goldfarb, 1963; Despert, 1968).

TABLE 8–1 Diagnostic Criteria of Childhood Schizophrenia

	Potter (1933)	Bradley and Bowen (1941)	Kaufman, Rosenblum, Heims, and Willer (1957)	Bender (1947)	Creak (1961)
I. Social and Interpersonal	Retraction of interest from environment.	Seclusiveness, irritability if disturbed. Decrease in number of personal interest; regressed nature of personal interests. Daydreaming.	Special interest and information (object or area) related to child's pathology; denial of human quality of people.	Inability to relate to people or play materials. Withdrawal (only for early onset).	Gross and sustained impaired emotional relations with others; unawareness of own identity. Pathological preoccupation with objects.
II. Intellectual and Cognitive	Autistic thinking, and acting show poor ties with reality.	Daydreaming.	Distorted time and space orientation.	Perceptual problems	Abnormal perceptual experiences.
III. Language	Decrease of speech—sometimes mutism.		Disturbances in speech structure and content; mutism; asynchrony of verbal content and tone.	Language disturbances.	Language disturbances.

TABLE 8–1 (Continued)

IV. Affect	Defect in emotional rapport; decrease, rigidity and distortion of affect.	Sensitivity to comment and criticism.	Inappropriate affect.	Lack of concern about body secretions.	Acute anxiety.
V. Motor	Hyperactivity, immobility, or bizarre, stereotyped and perseverative behavior.	Bizarre behavior. Physical inactivity.	Bizarre body movements. Repetitive and stereotypy motions; distorted use of body.	Motor awkwardness; continuation of early reflex patterns; postural reflex responses; bodily dependence.	Distortion in mobility.
VI. Physical Development				Disturbances of normal rhythmic patterns. Unevenness in somatic growth. Dysrythemia in EEG. Disturbance in vasovegetative functioning.	

Schizophrenic children have the blank and unexpressive facial stare suggestive of remoteness and inaccessibility. Parents often comment that they cannot "get close" or "make contact." They may show flatness and inappropriateness of affect along with unpredictable mood changes. At times, the child may be extremely withdrawn, while at other times the child may show sudden uncontrolled anger and assaultiveness toward self or those around him or her.

Intellectual and cognitive deficits also have been reported as part of the symptom picture of schizophrenic children. The literature between 1937 and 1965 indicates that at least one third of these youngsters scored an I.Q. of below 80 (Pollack, 1967). A more recent study involving 120 schizophrenic boys indicated that as many as half had I.Q.s below 80 (Walker and Birch, 1974). When compared with nonschizophrenic controls, all of the studies surveyed reported that the schizophrenic children were significantly inferior in their intellectual performance. Most observers emphasize disturbances in the thought processes of these youngsters as evidenced by autistic (highly personalized) thinking, incoherence, neologisms, perplexity, perseveration, and somatic delusions. In addition, obsessions, compulsions, and preoccupation with matters of an abstract character and with sexual material are commonly found in schizophrenic children.

Another prominent characteristic of the disorder is a language disturbance, which is sometimes symptomatic of their impaired thought processes. Some schizophrenic children are mute, only rarely uttering single words. Those who do possess speech do not use it to communicate. Instead, they repeat words in parrot-like fashion, use words in bizarre sequences, and give them new and highly personalized meanings. The resultant verbalizations have a wooden quality that fails to convey either the child's feelings or thoughts (Goldfarb, Goldfarb, and Scholl, 1966).

Usually schizophrenic children show some disturbances in bladder and/or bowel control, as well as in bodily movements and activity level. They may have alternate periods of *hypoactivity* and *hyperactivity* which are ordinarily purposeless, repetitious, stereotyped, and rhythmic. Bizarre body movements, such as whirling, body rocking, head banging, rigid posturing, choreiform (spasmodic twitching) hand movements, facial grimacing, and excessive masturbation may be present. An interesting example of this is cited by Despert, who described a four-year-old boy having an acute schizophrenic episode.

. . . (he) stated it very clearly when he complained: "I can't be myself, I'm scared I'm not myself." Identified at intervals with a rhinoceros, a dog, a woodpecker, etc., he exhibited neuromuscular patterns of considerable interest, in that they demonstrated the profound personality disorganization. On many occasions this boy, as a rhinoceros, spontaneously performed movements of the mouth muscles (a sort of a snarl) which, anatomically, are impossible in man, and were so unlike the human faces that each time they threw the mother into a panic. Everything happened as if, at such times, even the neuromuscular and vegetative systems had regressed to a lower phylogenetic level of functioning. The same was true when, as a dog, he uncovered his upper teeth in a pattern that no human feat of mimic would make possible. Two years later, when his contact with reality was considerably more normal, he recalled the identifications and, at the physician's suggestion, attempted to reproduce the facial expression, but never succeeded (Despert, 1968, pp. 133–134.)

Several investigators believe that the general clinical picture of childhood schizophrenia is too broad to fit into one diagnostic category, and they have tried instead to identify several specific subgroups. The best known of these are the three subtypes proposed by Bender (1955).

1. The *pseudodefective syndrome* is characteristic of schizophrenic youngsters who appear retarded from birth, or who, during the first three years of life, regress after reaching a higher level of functioning. These children tend to show high susceptibility to somatic illnesses, inadequate muscle tone (either hyper- or hyposensitive to stimulation), and immature areas of motor behaviors (clinging, whirling, and rocking).

2. The *pseudoneurotic syndrome* occurs during early or middle childhood and is marked by neurotic-like symptoms, such as severe anxiety, phobias, obsessions, stereotyped movements, and compulsive activities. Psychosomatic complaints or concerns about body boundary, body image, and orientation in time and space are often present. These children may be highly verbal and intellectually bright.

3. The *pseudopsychopathic syndrome* is seen in children of ten years or older who tend to act out antisocially, and who show paranoid ideation, compulsions, aggressive and potentially dangerous behavior, and little evidence of insight, guilt, and anxiety.

Etiological Views

The etiology or etiologies of childhood schizophrenia and the other childhood psychoses are, at present, little understood and highly speculative. In discussing the genetic, biological, and psychogenic positions, it is important to recognize that they are neither mutually exclusive nor as contradictory as some of their ardent supporters would have us believe.

1. Genetic Considerations. The bulk of human genetic research has focused on schizophrenia in adults. The extent to which these data are applicable to schizo-phrenia in children hinges on the unanswered question of whether schizophrenia is the same condition for both age groups. The major study with preadolescent schizophrenics found concordance rates of seventy-one percent for monozygotic twins, and seventeen percent for dizygotic twins (Kallman and Roth, 1956). These data compare favorably to those obtained with adult schizophrenics and suggest that genetic factors (as with adults) are implicated in the development of childhood schizophrenia.

Lauretta Bender, an important contributor to the literature on childhood schizophrenia, stresses the interrelatedness of genetic and biological factors. She believes that the disorder is caused by an inherited vulnerability that is activated by physiological crises, such as damage or trauma occurring prenatally, at birth, or in infancy. She considers childhood schizophrenia a neurological disorder with diffuse pathology involving a maturational lag that begins sometime during the embryonic period. The condition is revealed at all levels and areas of integration within the central nervous systems (Bender, 1961).

In a series of studies spanning almost twenty years, Fish (1971) noted irregularities in the rates of development in various areas in infants who later in childhood were diagnosed as schizophrenic. She claims that the neurological impairment is not fixed, but that it is evident in the variability of the child's development leading to the contradictory impression of retardation and precocity. These infants have arousal and attention problems and often are abnormally quiet and lethargic when compared to normals who are quite active. They tend to show gastrointestinal disturbances that include spastic constipation, absence of hunger, difficulty in swallowing solid foods, and an inability to suck. The more severe the lag and disruption in development, the greater the impairment of intellectual and social functioning, and the greater the resistance to modification. Fish sees the poorly integrated biological and psychological functions that are under the control of the central nervous system as the underlying disturbance responsible for the disparate behaviors of childhood schizophrenia.

The problem with this sort of genetic hypothesis is that its specific nature is unelaborated. It is a vague and untestable formulation that posits some predisposing inherited factor that is present in a wide variety of children. Moreover, it presumes that vulnerable youngsters would manifest the disorder only if they were exposed to certain damaging experiences. Until the inherited susceptibility is identified by some physical and/or behavioral evidence, this etiologic explanation must remain in the realm of supposition. In this connection, it is interesting to note that attempts to identify genetic vulnerability in adult schizophrenia by studying biochemical substances excreted in the urine have been promising, but inconclusive (Pollin, 1971; Wyatt, Murphy, Bellmaker, Cohen, Donnelly, and Pollin, 1973).

2. Biological Considerations. Like a number of others holding a biological view of the disorder, Ornitz and Ritvo (1968) share the observation that a perceptual disturbance is fundamental to schizophrenia and other psychotic disorders in children. They believe that the basis for perceptual inconstancy in psychotic children involves central nervous pathology of a specific but unknown type. Perceptual difficulties are evident in the failure of these children to distinguish between themselves and their environment, and in their inability to imitate and to modulate sensory input. The problems they have in maintaining body image can be illustrated in the following clinical observations:

> When asked to locate on a picture the finger that had been touched by the examiner, this child, whom I shall call Ann, had to grasp the involved finger with the other hand while looking for its equivalent in the picture. In a similar fashion, many of the schizophrenic children literally had to hold on to and to keep their eyes on the touched finger in order to identify it on the picture: Or . . . After teasing by another child with the taunt "your mother's ass!" she ran to the counselor, pushed her buttocks toward the latter, and cried "take away ass. I don't like ass!" She seemed confused about whether the buttocks belonged to her or her mother. (Goldfarb, 1963, p. 49).

While schizophrenic children do not differ from normal children in sensory acuities on tests of either visual, auditory, or touch thresholds, they do show receptor aberrations in all modalities. For example, "Cathy was observed today cutting paper with scissors. At one point she continued to cut directly into her skin so as to cause bleeding, without expression of pain." (Goldfarb, 1963, p. 50). It is inferred from these findings that the problem is not caused by impairment of peripheral sensory receptors, but is reflective of some deficit in the integration of sensory stimuli within the central nervous system. Ornitz and Ritvo (1968) stress that no specific central nervous system cause has been found as yet and perhaps never will be, because the etiology may be heterogeneous with one common central nervous system pathway.

The work of Goldfarb and his associates at the Henry Ittleson Center in New York suggests that childhood schizophrenia is caused by multiple factors. These factors range in a continuum from organic defects in the child to psychosocial inadequacies within the family. Either variable or some combination of the two leads to weakened ego boundaries that leave the child without predictable expectancies and environmental referents. Primary anxiety and panic are clinically evident as the child makes a variety of compensatory attempts (often in vain) to find sameness and constancy in the environment (Goldfarb, 1961).

Fairly extensive research over a decade has shown the following:

1. Schizophrenic children fall into two major groups, that is, organic and nonorganic.
2. Families of organic children are more "normal" than are the families of nonorganics.
3. The symptoms of the organic child arise from family-child interactions in which the parents stimulate the child too much, too little, or in a confusing way.
4. The symptoms of the nonorganic child are attributable to environment-parent indecisiveness, insensitivity to the child's needs, or bewilderment with the child's behavior; and
5. The nonorganics are more capable than the organics of proceeding through school almost without difficulty.
6. Schizophrenic boys have a significantly greater amount of reproductive complications than either their siblings or normal boys. This finding is related to the fact that many more boys than girls are organic, become schizophrenic, and are affected by disorders involving brain damage (Goldfarb, 1961; Meyers and Goldfarb, 1961; Goldfarb, 1971).

Unfortunately, Goldfarb, like others, used diagnostic criteria that have been too inconclusive to allow drawing definitive conclusions. As a matter of fact, he recently noted that some of the cases studied could very well fit the symptoms of early infantile autism (Goldfarb, 1970). The problem of heterogeneity of samples with respect to diagnostic criteria is characteristic of the clinical and research literature in general, a state of affairs that makes inferences about etiology uncertain and inconclusive.

3. Psychogenic Considerations. Beginning with Potter and continuing through the 1950s, many writers considered faulty mothering (usually from a psychoanalytic point of view) to be the fundamental cause of childhood schizophrenia. For example, Potter noted maternal overprotectiveness as a primary contributor to the disorder in four of his six cases, while Despert was impressed with the aggressive, overanxious, oversolicitous, and marked ambivalence these mothers displayed toward their children (Potter, 1933; Despert, 1938). Although constitutional vulnerability and biological factors were recognized as possible causes, the spotlight illuminated primarily the etiological contributions of the mother who is referred to as *schizophrenogenic.*

A maternal attitude inventory was administered to mothers of psychotic, mongoloid, and normal children who were matched for age, socioeconomic level, and family size. Mothers were told to answer the inventory in terms of children in general, and not with reference to their own offspring. It was found that mothers of mongoloid children were stricter and more regimented than mothers of psychotic or normal children. However, mothers of psychotic youngsters were more indulgent and more uncertain about their behavior than mothers of the other two groups (Pitfield and Oppenheim, 1964). More recent data showed that parents of psychotic children are neither emotionally disturbed nor impaired in their thinking (Schopler and Loftin, 1969). Furthermore, a study by Florsheim and Peterfreund (1974) found that parents of psychotic children fell within the normal range of intelligence.

In an effort to obtain specific information about parental practices, parents of neurotic, schizophrenic, asthmatic, and chronically ill children were given the Rorschach, TAT, and the MMPI. The groups were similar to each other with respect to age of the child, age of parents, size of family, socioeconomic status, and educational level. The results were equivocal in that mothers of schizophrenic children, although more isolated, were quite similar to the mothers of neurotic youngsters. Further analysis of the data showed that there was no difference among the groups of mothers in terms of previously identified characteristics often ascribed to mothers of asthmatic and schizophrenic children (Block, 1969).

One of the earliest studies in this area found that the child-rearing attitudes of mothers of brain damaged, retarded youngsters were more pathological than either the attitudes of mothers of schizophrenic or of normal children. While mothers of schizophrenics were more pathological than mothers of normals, the data were interpreted as indicative of maternal attitudes that were the *result* of dealing with impaired children, instead of the *cause* of their disturbance (Klebanoff, 1959).

More recent research dealing with family communication and behavioral patterns suggests that parents of schizophrenic children communicate with their children as clearly as those of normal youngsters, and that differences in family discussion are more likely to be a response to the severity of the child's symptoms and not the basis for the schizophrenic reaction itself (Haley, 1968; Zevin, 1973; Bender, 1974).

At present, it seems reasonable to conclude that there is no overwhelming evidence showing that parents of schizophrenic children display distinctive child-rearing attitudes, personality traits, or behavioral patterns that would substantially support faulty mothering as a fundamental causal condition.

Early Infantile Autism (EIA)

Clinical Description

Normal babies want to be picked up, held, and played with on almost any occasion. They react with animation and enthusiasm to the mere appearance of a familiar person, and they show displeasure when left alone. They enjoy human contact and place unquestioning trust in others. In dramatic contrast, Leo Kanner described psychotic children who as early as four months of age fail to show the normal anticipatory postural movements before being picked up (Kanner, 1943). They remain somewhat stiff and rigid, and do not conform to the body of the person holding them. These are the earliest indications of what he referred to as "extreme autistic aloneness," a primary symptom of early infantile autism (EIA), in which the child is unable to relate to people and insists on being left alone. Autistic babies show no interest in people or their conversation. An adult who reaches out to such a child is likely to receive an angry or irritated response. These children rarely, if ever, make direct eye contact with others. They may sit motionless, staring into space for hours, as if mentally preoccupied. They may smile to themselves momentarily, but other people are usually unable to attract their attention.

On the basis of case histories and clinical observations, Kanner concluded that many youngsters who had been labeled as either deaf or mentally retarded were, instead, experiencing symptoms that were associated with EIA (Kanner, 1943, 1949). He maintained that these children were of good intellectual potential and showed no evidence of auditory impairment. Kanner gave the new syndrome its name to convey its early onset, and to reflect the autistic personality characteristics of inaccessibility, aloofness, and isolation. Although much has been written about EIA since, the descriptive standard most widely accepted for the syndrome comes from data compiled by Kanner on the first 100 cases seen at John Hopkins Hospital Clinic (Kanner, 1954; Kanner and Lesser, 1958).

Pregnancies of mothers of autistic children were described as normal and uncomplicated, although the rate of premature births in Kanner's sample was higher than normal (twelve out of the first 100 cases were born prematurely). During the first few months of life, the infant manifests few, if any, apparent abnormal behaviors. Some youngsters may be apathetic and unresponsive, while others are inclined to cry excessively. Feeding may be a problem during the second half of the first year or later. The infant may either eat very little and show disinterest in food, or eat a great deal and have an enormous appetite. Parents may notice peculiar eating habits and food preferences. For example, several studies describe autistic children who would refuse all foods and would drink only milk, or would only drink liquids from a transparent container, or who would eat chocolate if it were cut in squares, but would refuse it if it were offered in round pieces (Rimland, 1964).

While autistic children reject human interactions, they have a very active interest in and fondness for inanimate objects in which they can be absorbed for prolonged periods. Mechanical objects such as light switches, plumbing faucets, and household appliances seem to be especially attractive to these children. They usually have good motor coordination together with a high level of spatial ability. Numerous reports cite these children accomplishing remarkable feats of agility and dexterity at an early age, such as balancing a dime on its edge at age three, or catching and throwing a ball with either hand at age fourteen months (Rimland, 1964).

Insistence on the maintenance of sameness in the environment along with autistic aloneness represent the two principal diagnostic signs of EIA. Unless the child introduces the changes, any alteration of furniture, toys, or clothes, or interruptions of routines (as bedtime rituals) results in the child's violent temper tantrums and eventual despair. In this regard, autistic children demonstrate remarkable memory, since they can notice small changes in their immediate environments even in those that they have not seen in several days.

Approximately fifty percent of autistic youngsters acquire speech. Even when speech is present, there is virtually no conversational interaction, because language is not used as a means of communication. Generally, it is parrot-like, repetitious, monotonous, and noncommunicative. Since these children invest their emotional and intellectual energies in things rather than people, they tend to ignore verbal suggestions and signs of praise or punishment. Often, they will repeat TV commercials verbatim, or statements made to them by a parent. They may reverse pronouns so that "you" may be used in place of "I." Both the words "I" and "yes" are frequently absent until the sixth year of life. The language of autistic children is very literal so that the meaning of words does not generalize from one situation to another. For example, "yes" may be used in the specific context, let's say, of wanting a certain toy, but it may not be used as an affirmative response to other things. Part-whole confusion may also be present so that the expression "hurt my head" may mean "I want comforting," regardless of what part the child may or may not have hurt (Rimland, 1964).

The prognosis for EIA is likely to be better in youngsters who have acquired speech as compared to those who are mute. Follow-up studies of sixty-three autistic children in adolescence showed that thirty-two had by age five developed communicative speech, while thirty-one had not. Moreover, one-half of the speaking youngsters achieved a rating of "fair" or "good" on social adjustment as compared to only one such success in the nonspeaking group of children (Eisenberg, 1956; Kanner and Lesser, 1958). Similarly, Lotter (1974) found that "the ability to use speech communicatively was the best predictor of outcome in late adolescence" (p. 271). This evidence was from an eight-year follow-up of thirty-two autistic children. I.Q. was also found to be a good predictor of outcome. DeMyer, Barton, DeMyer, Norton, Allen, and Steele (1973) report some pessimistic figures from both the literature and their own study: one to two percent recover to be normal, five to fifteen percent attain "borderline" functioning, sixteen to twenty-five percent have "fair" adjustment, and sixty to seventy-five percent remain in the "poor" category.

The following case resume illustrates a child who presents the clinical picture and diagnosis of EIA:

The patient, a five-year-old boy, was brought for professional attention because of a history of withdrawn and socially isolated behavior. He was uncommunicative and showed intense insistence on the sameness of the environment, hyperactivity, and repetitive and destructive activity. Both the pregnancy and delivery were normal. He smiled in the early weeks of life, but not necessarily in response to anyone. By the end of the first year his smiling decreased considerably, and it was difficult to get him to smile. He showed little anticipation at being picked up, and he appeared to draw back when held. He did not follow mother with his eyes, and he was neither alert to nor interested in the environment. Rocking, especially to music, appeared toward the end of the first year. His sleep was poor, and he was selective of and insistent on certain special foods before age one. In spite of this, he showed a rapid weight gain. He sat at six months, stood at seven months, walked at ten and a half months. His brother was born when he was approximately one year old.

During the second year of life, he was hyperactive and destructive. Severe tantrums and unresponsiveness to others were evident in that he neither permitted nor sought physical contact. He became adept at spinning objects and tearing paper, but showed no interest in toys. He spoke a few words at age two, but only for a brief period, and even then, words or vocalized sounds were not used for communication. Instead, he made his demands known by pushing and pulling. Intelligence testing at age three and a half showed a pattern of atypical retardation with successes on a few tasks at his age level.

The patient's mother, age thirty-eight, had been a successful business woman and an active, aggressive person who openly rejected the patient whom she could not control. She reported that since childhood she has been repelled by "little boys," but thought it would be "good for her" to have a boy. The patient's father is a passive and good-natured man who has suffered business reverses in the last several years. Both parents had difficulty in accepting the child's abnormal condition. Neither the patient's sister or brother show signs of abnormal behavior similar to the patient.

Clinical examination revealed a hyperactive boy who was out of contact with reality. He spun objects in a highly organized ritualistic manner. Speech was absent as was affective contact (Adapted from Despert, 1968, pp. 181–182).

TABLE 8–2 * Kanner's 100 Cases— Educational Level

	High School Graduate	Entered College	Graduated College	Post Graduate Work
Fathers	96	87	74	38
Mothers	92	70	49	11

* Kanner, 1954, pp. 378–385.

Kanner emphasized one common denominator in the backgrounds of autistic children. All of his patients were born to parents who were highly intelligent. This is demonstrated both by their scholastic accomplishments, which are summarized in Table 8–2, and by the many highly skilled and professional positions held by these fathers and mothers. He also described the parents as obsessive, preoccupied with abstractions, and emotionally cold, with little or no interest in people. They are polite, formal, bookish, humorless, and serious individuals who prefer solitary activities. They are undemonstrative but respectful and loyal to their spouses. Divorce or separation is extremely rare.

It has been argued that we cannot infer that parents of autistic children have unusually high intellectual levels, since Kanner's sample was biased because it represents only people who sought Kanner's services (Bender, 1959). However, later studies have corroborated the finding that parents of autistic children are significantly higher in educational level than parents of other severely disturbed youngsters, although not to the extent originally reported by Kanner (Lotter, 1966; Rimland, 1968; Treffert, 1970).

Kanner's observation concerning the personality of the parents of autistic children has stirred yet another controversy in the literature. As we shall elaborate in our discussion of etiology, there are those who view the highly intellectual, obsessive, aloof, and ice-box personality of these parents as the principal causative agent of EIA. Those who favor a biological interpretation of the disorder, however, dispute the importance and reliability of these parental personality characteristics.

SIDELIGHT 8–1

Discussions about psychotic children typically focus on a description of their symptoms, etiologies, and treatments with little attention drawn to the impact these children may have on their families. In 1972, a book appeared in which Josh Greenfeld gives us a poignant and sometimes painful account of his thoughts, feelings, and reactions to the problems he, his wife (Foumi), and oldest son (Karl) faced in recognizing and coping with his psychotic son, Noah. We hope the following excerpts from this highly recommended book will give us some insight into the family reactions.

4-16-67

"We've decided to stop worrying about Noah. He isn't retarded, he's just pushing the clock hands about at his own slow speed. Yet . . ."

8-16-67

"We took Noah to a pediatrician in the next town, who specializes in neurology. He said that since Noah is talking now there was little cause to worry; that

Noah seemed "hypertonic," a floppy baby, a slow developer, but that time would be the maturing agent. We came away relieved. But I also have to admit that lately I haven't worried that much."

9-16-67

"I've been reading child-care books. It seems I've been doing everything wrong."

3-11-68

"Noah kept us up half the night, giggling to himself and bouncing in his crib. I became annoyed with him and finally slapped him. He laughed back at me."

7-1-68

"Noah is two. He still doesn't talk, but I do think he's trying to teach himself how to stand up. We're still concerned. And I guess we'll remain concerned until he stands up and walks like a boy."

6-6-69

"Our fears about Noah continue to undergo dramatic ups and downs. Because of his increased opacity, the fact that he doesn't respond when we call his name and fails to relate completely to his immediate environment—a pattern of retardation or autism—we took him to a nearby hospital. . . I guess we both fear that what we dread is so, that Noah is not a normal child, that he is a freak, and his condition is getting worse."

7-14-69

"Somehow the rhythm of our lives, the good fortune of our marriage, seems to have dissipated."

8-1-69

"Meanwhile, last night, as I tried to fall asleep I heard Foumi crying. Why? She was crying for Karl, for the difficulties he would have with other children because he had an abnormal brother. I tried to comfort her, but I know she's right."

9-13-69

"I'm a lousy father. I anger too easily. I get hot with Karl and take on a four-year-old kid. I shout at Noah and further upset an already disturbed one. Perhaps I'm responsible for Noah's problems."

2-19-70

"Foumi keeps complaining about how it's impossible to keep Noah from being destructive about the house. Anything on a table, in a cabinet, on a floor is fodder for him to break. Poor Foumi, she can't afford to take her eyes off him for a second. Poor Noah."

8-70

"I also must note how very few people can actually understand our situation as a family, how they assume we are aloof when we tend not to accept or extend the usual social invitations. Nor have I mentioned the extra expenses a child like Noah entails—those entries I keep in another book."

8-70

"Even more heartbreaking has been the three-year period it has taken us to pierce the organized-medicine, institutionalized-mental-health gauze curtain. Most doctors, if they were unable to prescribe any form of curative aid, did their best to deter us from seeking it. Freudian-oriented psychiatrists and psychologists, if ill-equipped to deal with the problems of those not verbal, tried to inflict great feelings of guilt upon us as all-too-vulnerable parents. Neurologists and pediatricians, if not having the foggiest notions about the effects of diet and nutrition, vitamins and enzymes and their biochemical workings would always suggest such forms of therapy as practiced only by quacks. And county mental-health boards, we discovered, who have charge of the moneys that might be spent helping children like Noah, usually tossed their skimpy fundings away through existing channels that do not offer proper treatment for children like Noah."

8-71

"I still don't know exactly what's wrong with Noah. I only know something is profoundly wrong with him. I still don't know what to do—I only know I must do whatever I possibly can. Although Noah is too young for an institution now, I know I must still accept the very real possibility of his eventual institutionalization. I also know I must try not to feel more sorry for myself than Noah, but some days I forget . . ." (Greenfeld, 1972, pp. 22, 26, 29, 35, 38, 51–52, 56, 63, 71, 81, 90, 91, 92, and 97).

Etiological Views

1. Genetic Considerations. In his initial paper on autism, Kanner assumed:

That these children have come into the world with innate inability to form the usual biologically-provided contact with people, just as other children come into the world with innate physical or intellectual handicaps. If this assumption is correct, a further study of our children may help furnish concrete criteria regarding the still diffuse notions about the constitutional components of emotional reactivity. For here we seem to have pure-culture examples of *inborn autistic disturbances of affective contact* (Kanner, 1943, p. 250).

Albeit vague, Kanner made reference to an inherited and biological etiology for EIA, a view that parallels the thesis of genetic vulnerability. More than twenty years later, Rimland (1964) proposed a more specific view of genetic predisposition. He suggested that autistic children (because they come from parents who are intellectually bright) inherit a high capacity for blood circulation in the brain. He further conjectured that this makes them highly susceptible to "oxygen-produced" vascular destruction and damage, especially to the part of the brainstem known as the *reticular formation.* An excess of oxygen damages the connection between incoming sensory information and previously learned material normally stored in the brain. The result is a cognitive dysfunction.

Little data are, as yet, available with regard to chromosomal or twin studies, primarily because autism is so rare, and the incidence of psychiatric abnormalities is so low in the families of these children. Nevertheless, there are some indications of a high but not perfect concordance for autism in monozygotic twins, and an absence of chromosomal abnormalities in a small sample of autistic children (Judd and Mandell, 1968).

2. Biological Considerations. In the past ten years, there have been a number of investigations aimed at discovering a biochemical "marker" of early infantile autism. Along these lines, since attention has been focused on the role of the monoamines in the development of adult schizophrenia (see Chapter 4), researchers have been measuring monoamine levels in whole blood (Coleman, 1973), in platelets (Bouillin, Coleman, O'Brien, and Rimland, 1971), and in urine (Landgrebe and Landgrebe, 1976) in children diagnosed as autistic. Although differences in monoamine levels are often found when compared to normal children, they do not appear to be specific for autism in that these differences are observed in other pathological conditions as well. Other efforts are being aimed at finding biochemical indices for distinguishing childhood schizophrenia and infantile autism, which would support diagnoses made on the basis of clinical criteria (Bouillin, Bhagaven, O'Brien, and Youdim 1976). Many of these studies are hampered by issues of diagnosis and classification.

Physiological arousal has been an important variable in the biological views of a number of investigators who have been concerned with EIA. It has been postulated that autistic children have high thresholds against stimuli impinging on them from both within and outside (*interoceptive* and *exteroceptive stimulation*). At the same time, *they experience low maternal stimulation* (Schopler, 1965). Therefore, they are abnormally *under*aroused (hypoaroused). Yet, evidence suggests that autistic children are abnormally *over*aroused (hyperaroused) (Hutt and Hutt, 1970). Telemetered EEG recordings and behavioral observations were used to study autistic children in a variety of familiar and unfamiliar situations. EEG patterns of high arousal and even a chronic state of hyperarousal were found, as was an increase in stereotyped behavior patterns to more complex environmental settings.

DesLavriers and Carlson (1969) have brought these opposing views on arousal together in formulating their theory that autistic children are either chronically hyperaroused or chronically hypoaroused. Their hypothesis is based on Routtenberg's (1968) carefully considered proposal that the ascending reticular activating system (ARAS) and the limbic system are involved in a reciprocal relationship. The ARAS is thought to control general energy and motivation, while the limbic system (long thought to be involved in emotions) controls pleasure, and reinforcement or reward. Normally, these two systems are in balance, with each suppressing the activity of the other.

EIA is understood by assuming a disequilibrium between the two systems. In the hypoactive autistic child, that is, the child who is described as being a good, quiet, and undemanding baby, the ARAS is dominant and the limbic system is suppressed. Both systems function at a *hyponormal* level. In contrast, the hyperactive autistic child is described as an irritable baby who manifests irregularities of sleep and/or eating from birth on. This sort of child is hypersensitive to new and complex environmental stimuli, but he or she is unable to organize them because the limbic system is impaired. For this child, the inbalance is more severe as both systems operate at a *hypernormal* level. In effect, the hypoactive child receives only a minimum of stimulus input (both systems abnormally low), whereas the hyperactive child receives hypernormal stimulus input (both systems abnormally high). In either case, both types of autistic children may be thought of as sensory deprived in that few meaningful stimuli reach either of them.

Although unspecific with regard to the nature and location of the damage, some investigators have suggested a neurologically determined deficit. Abnormal behaviors of autistic children are the result of a central disorder of cognition involving deficits in the use and comprehension of language and in conceptual abilities (Rutter, 1968). Similarly, Ricks and Wing (1975) believe that the difficulty in handling symbols is the central problem in EIA, and that this deficit disrupts verbal and nonverbal communication and other aspects of the child's cognitive and social functioning. In this connection, experiments have shown that the memory of autistic children is good, but that they obtain low scores on tests involving concepts, abstractions, or symbolization (Hermelin and O'Connor, 1970).

These findings have led some to favor a neurological view of EIA, which claims that the deficit is in the encoding and expressive function of the nervous system rather than in the reception of sensory stimuli from the environment. The behavior of autistic children has been likened to that of brain damaged youngsters who are unable to process incoming sensory patterns (auditory and visual) into meaningful experiences because of some neurological deficit (Kugelmass, 1970).

Questionnaire data obtained from parents of autistic, retarded, aphasic, and sensory handicapped children revealed behavior characteristics in autistic children that were similar to those evident in other multiple handicapped youngsters. Autistic children have speech and body orientation problems also found in aphasics. In addition, they have visual abnormalities, abnormal body movements, and a preference for proximal senses similar to the characteristics of partially deaf and blind children (Wing, 1969). These similarities between autistic children and youngsters with perceptual and communication disorders were interpreted as evidence for a neurological cause of EIA. In support of the biological view, several investigators have found that about one third of the children with EIA strongly evidence neurological damage. Furthermore, seizures have been noted in adolescence in a small but significant number of these children (Rutter and Lockyer, 1967; Lotter, 1974).

While the specific nature and location of the impairment remains speculative, there is mounting evidence that strongly implicates neurological factors as the underlying etiology of EIA. Nevertheless, psychogenic considerations cannot be ignored because the quality of the continued interaction of child and family will have important consequences for the child's subsequent adjustment.

3. Psychogenic Considerations. Kanner's description of parents of autistic children as bright and well educated, relatively free of mental illness, stable in marriage, but emotionally cold and aloof personalities has led some writers to emphasize faulty parental patterns as the primary basis for the disorder. However, present research findings fail to corroborate this position. In the area of child rearing practices, four semistructured interviews were conducted with parents of autistic, brain damaged, and normal youngsters between four and five years of age (DeMyer, Pontius, Norton, Baron, Allen and Steele, 1972). The children were matched for age, sex, ordinal position in the family, number and sex of siblings, race, socioeconomic level, and religion of parents. The autistic group consisted of thirty-three youngsters, seven of whom were diagnosed as schizophrenic. The alleged cold, over-intellectualized, and nonstimulating characterization of parents of autistic children was not confirmed. In fact, it was found that parents of brain damaged children were the least stimulating, least warm, and the most restrictive in the physical freedom they permitted their children.

Projective techniques (Rorschach and TAT) have been used to compare personality characteristics of the parents of psychotic (schizophrenic and autistic) and neurotic children, and adult schizophrenics (Singer and Wynne, 1963). Parents of psychotic children were described as cynical, dissatisfied, and superficial. Their interpersonal relationships were characterized as passive, distant, intellectual, and obsessive. Although these findings can be taken as support of Kanner's observations, they do not provide evidence that warrant a cause and effect conclusion. It is not possible to determine whether these parental traits were present prior to the birth of the autistic child, or if they developed later in response to a disturbed child. Moreover, we are again faced with data that make no distinction between childhood schizophrenia and EIA, even though the personality features are supposed to be descriptive of one group of parents and not the other.

Although many etiological factors have been implicated as the basis of EIA, the recent literature strongly favors the view that attributes the disorder to some as yet unspecified neurological defect or multiple deficits. In this connection, the National Society for Autistic Children has initiated efforts to facilitate autopsy studies of the few autistic and schizophrenic children who die annually (Schopler, 1976).

Differentiating Childhood Schizophrenia from EIA

The process of systematically distinguishing one condition from others is complex and difficult, primarily because diagnostic categories (especially those of childhood psychoses) overlap considerably. However, the importance of differential diagnosis is rooted in etiological, therapeutic, and prognostic considerations. How can etiologic factors be studied and isolated without differentiating among diagnostic groups? How can the uses and limitations of a therapeutic drug such as penicillin be determined without the clinician being able to differentiate among colds, pneumonia, and lung cancer? Without differential diagnosis, the early identification of problems and the specific planning for future treatment and management cannot take place.

The task of differentiating autism from childhood schizophrenia is not made easier by the current literature. Some view schizophrenia broadly and see no meaningful distinction between the two conditions. Others, like Kanner himself, now regard EIA as a distinguishable subtype of schizophrenia. Rimland is perhaps the strongest American advocate for considering EIA as a separate disorder. He claims "that there is sufficient information at hand to demonstrate clearly that early infantile autism is not the same disease or cluster of diseases which has come to be called childhood schizophrenia, and that autism can and should be distinguished from it at all levels of discourse." (Rimland, 1964, p. 68).

A summary of the various points of differentiation noted by Rimland is shown in Table 8–3. Rimland also constructed two checklists to be completed by the child's parents in an effort to increase the accuracy of differentiating between the two conditions. Recent results involving more than 2,000 psychotic children showed that the diagnosis given by other professionals varied extensively with as many as ten different diagnoses given per child (Rimland, 1971). In addition, five diagnostic systems used to differentiate EIA from schizophrenia (including Rimland's checklist) were compared (DeMyer, Churchill, Pontius, and Gilkey, 1971). Even though the diagnostic criteria used for EIA differed from both Kanner's and Rimland's, the results showed that the Rimland checklist correlated highest. Continued support of the checklist comes from Davids (1975), who found that Rimland's checklist was the most effective in discriminating EIA from other disorders.

Based on an extensive review of the literature, Ward (1970) described two distinguishable types of autism: (1) those who lack object relations, insist on sameness, have been disturbed from birth, but who are physically healthy; and (2) those with a history of pre- and perinatal difficulties, developmental and perceptual problems, normal families, and regression after a period of normality. Ward suggested that the lack of object relations from birth, useful speech, and neurologic and developmental dysfunction along with maintenance of sameness differentiates autism from other disorders.

In contrast, Rutter (1972) argues that the term "childhood schizophrenia" should be abandoned and used only for those who evidence the classical symptoms of adult schizophrenia (regardless of age). He believes that EIA is a separate entity in that it occurs earliest and is clearly distinguishable from other psychotic disorders on seven points (which are similar to those noted in Table 8–3).

At this point, there should be little doubt that the differentiation between EIA and childhood schizophrenia is dependent on (1) the clinician's position concerning the distinctiveness of the two conditions; (2) the criteria employed for diagnostic decisions; (3) the extent to which symptomatology overlaps; and (4) the reliability of the diagnosis even when the same criteria are applied. To date, there is little agreement and uniformity with respect to any of these variables. Until agreement is reached, significant advances in our knowledge cannot occur.

Symbiotic Infantile Psychosis

Clinical Description

Rachel, a four-year-old, clung desperately to her mother in a manner that forced mother to attend to her needs exclusively. There seemed to be no pleasure that either Rachel or her mother achieved from this closeness because Rachel was rigid and panic-stricken. She reacted to the slightest frustration with piercing screams that kept mother from leading any independent existence. For example, she could not tolerate mother talking to anyone, either in person or on the telephone (adapted from Bergman, 1971, pp. 328–331).

Children like Rachel were first described by Margaret Mahler as distinct from EIA, and as suffering from symbiotic infantile

TABLE 8–3 Summary of Characteristics that Differentiate EIA from Childhood Schizophrenia (Adapted from Rimland, 1964)*

Characteristic	Early Infantile Autism	Childhood Schizophrenia
Onset	Almost from beginning of life.	Between the second and eleventh year of life.
Course	Continue to show early retardation and detachment as adults.	Gradually develop the delusions and hallucinations typical of adult form of schizophrenia.
Physical Appearance and Health	Handsome, well formed, usually of dark complexion, and almost always in good health.	Light complexion with pale and translucent skin. Poor health from birth and neurologically immature.
EEG	Normal.	Abnormal.
Anticipatory Postural Movements	Absent, and when picked up they are stiff and unresponsive.	Present, and inclined to mold and conform to the body or the holder.
Autistic Aloneness	Considered a principal sign.	Not usually evident.
Perseveration of Sameness	Considered a principal sign.	Uncommon.
Hallucinations	Virtually absent.	Both visual and auditory hallucinations are present.
Motor Performance	Both gross movements and finger dexterity are excellent. Twirling and spinning of small objects is evident.	Poor coordination, motor awkwardness, and clumsiness are typical. Twirling and spinning of small objects is evident.
Language Patterns	Indicating affirmation by repetition, absence of words "yes" and "I," delayed echolalia, part-whole confusion, and metaphoric language are typical.	None of these specific language patterns are ordinarily noted.
Special and Unusual Abilities	Extraordinary feats of memory and/or of music or mechanical performance are typically reported.	No reports of special or unusual abilities.
Personal Orientation	Unoriented, detached, aloof, and oblivious to the environment.	Disoriented, confused, and anxious about their relationship and the environment. More accessible than autistic children.
Conditionability	Classical conditioning is difficult to establish.	Classical conditioning occurs easily and rapidly.
Twins	Unusually high number of twins (especially monozygotic) are found.	No high frequency of occurrence in twins has been observed.
Family Backgrounds	Parents are highly educated, significantly above average in intelligence, and have a low divorce rate. There is also a very low incidence of mental illness found in parents and grandparents.	Unstable home backgrounds are frequently noted with a high incidence of mental illness found in these families.

* Rimland, 1964, pp. 67–76.

psychosis (Mahler, 1952). This very rare syndrome is chiefly characterized by symptoms of intense anxiety and panic over mother-child separation. It occurs between two-and-one-half to five years of age and is usually preceded by a history of normal development in the first two years of life. In sharp contrast to the autistic child who insists on aloneness, the symbiotic child is virtually unable to tolerate even the briefest separation from mother. At a time when the normal child becomes increasingly aware of his or her own capacities and individuality, the symbiotic child literally clings to the mother with a strong physical attachment to avoid any prospect of separation. The panic reaction of symbiosis may be triggered off by potential threats of separation, such as the birth of a sibling, enrollment in nursery school, or developmental periods that require increasing independence.

Symbiotic children are incapable of delineating self-boundaries and of seeing themselves as separate and adequate entities. Therefore, they cannot establish relationships with others apart from their marked interdependent ties to mother. Their frustration tolerance is so low that minor deviations in routine or mild thwartings throw them into a state of panic. They may have extreme reactions to small failures, as illustrated by the symbiotic child who gave up walking for months because he had tripped and fallen while moving about in his room. When threatened, symbiotic children exhibit panic-stricken agitation and severe temper tantrums that often are followed by bizarre ideas and behavior. These children rarely display curiosity, exploratory behavior, initiative, or normal aggressiveness. In contrast, they tend to present a rather bland and colorless picture of selflessness. Mahler and Furer (1972) have iden-

tified a "symbiotic phase" as part of normal development. They point out that the psychotic child has attained a grossly distorted fashion of this stage, and has not reacted to "inherent maturational pressures toward separation from the mother" (Mahler and Furer, 1972, p. 216).

As the psychosis persists, other symptoms emerge. The children become withdrawn, seclusive, and disinterested in their surroundings. Their contact with reality gradually weakens. They stay close to mother and live a very restricted life, mostly confined to the home. Disturbances in their thinking such as neologisms, incoherence, and bizarre ideas become evident, and previously acquired toilet, sleep, and eating habits become disrupted. Eventually, these secondary symptoms together with the tendency to insist on the sameness in the immediate environment overlap with the clinical picture of EIA. In fact, the two disorders become almost indistinguishable except for the history of an early intimate relationship between mother and infant (Mahler, 1968).

Rachel's history illustrates the typical picture of symbiotic infantile psychosis:

Mother maintained that Rachel was an easy baby to care for. She sat up at eight months, crawled by ten, and walked at fifteen months. She toilet trained herself by the age of two-and-a-half years. Her difficulties started in the second year of life when she became intensely negativistic and fearful. It was during this time that mother had to be hospitalized and out of the home for several days. When mother returned, Rachel was even more unresponsive than she had been earlier. In addition, Rachel's parents (who had not been getting along) decided to separate for good when she was two-and-a-half years of age.

At the time of the evaluation, mother and daughter lived together apart from father. Mother had given up all normal social relationships, partly because of Rachel's clinging and partly because of mother's tendency to be overly critical of herself and others. By this time Rachel showed a mixture of symbiotic and autistic behaviors. She did not use language for direct communication or put together words in a spontaneous way. Instead, Rachel quoted from books, records, songs, and television commercials. Although she spoke clearly, her voice was lifeless and unmodulated as were her facial expressions and body movements. Even her frequent shrieks seemed to lack emotional participation.

Motor activities were severely restricted in that she walked cautiously with small steps. She didn't run and was unable to climb, swing, throw a ball, or use her hands in any kind of manipulative activity. Most of her movements were confined to either bouncing from foot to foot or jumping and waving her arms.

Rachel showed no interest in toys, except as objects to chew on and hold in her mouth. She spent hours during the day listening to records or looking at some particular book that caught her fancy. She worked strenuously at shutting out the outside world. When unsuccessful, she reacted with anger and fear. For example, if anyone tried to interest her in a new toy, she would ignore it. However, if she were not permitted to ignore the toy, she would knock it down, drop it, or break into loud shrieks. A trip to the shoe store was an ordeal for mother, who could not quiet Rachel's screams. Rachel was afraid of strangers, especially children, of going in cars, and of all sorts of ordinary household appliances (adapted from Bergman, 1971, pp. 328–331).

Etiological Views

1. Genetic Considerations. Virtually no data exist that bear directly on the influence of genetic factors. In all probability, this is because the disorder is so rare, and frequently it is not differentiated from EIA or from childhood schizophrenia.

2. Biological Considerations. From the beginning, Mahler regarded symbiotic psychosis as a psychogenic disorder rooted in the psychopathology of the mother. Later,

she shifted her view to a position of constitutional vulnerability, a view influenced by Freud's idea of the protective barrier of ego functioning. The barrier is thought to be a mechanism that provides the organism with protection against incoming stimuli. When the barrier is impaired, the ego is unable to inhibit and select incoming stimuli, and differentiation of self becomes extremely difficult.

Evidence of this vulnerability comes from a study that reported certain unusual behaviors in five infants who later became psychotic (Bergman and Escalona, 1951). These infants exhibited extreme reactions to auditory and tactile stimulation, unusually sensitive discriminations, extreme likes and dislikes, and profound aversion and unresponsiveness to being picked up and cuddled by mother. However, these observations do not tell us whether the vulnerability is constitutionally determined or psychologically induced by poor mothering.

Apart from this view, there are no specific references to a biological formulation of this disorder. However, since symbiosis and autism are often undifferentiated, the biological considerations described under EIA may be applicable here.

3. Psychogenic Considerations. In the course of normal development, the child at first is totally dependent on mother for survival. Soon, this phase is followed by a growing realization by the child that he or she is separate from mother, and that he or she has a body of his or her own, and a separate self. In symbiotic psychosis, this normal process is disrupted either by constitutional vulnerability or by a mother who fosters the totally dependent relationship and discourages any development of independence on the part of the child. The mother may be overprotective and too attentive to the child, or she may be anxiously possessive and intensely jealous of normal contacts between the child and the outer world, or she may unconsciously view the infant as a representation of her "self" (Mahler, 1968).

The key to the psychogenic view of symbiotic psychosis is a pathological mother, who, for a variety of conjectured reasons, prevents the child from breaking previously established mother-infant ties. Other than clinical reports, no research data directly test this thesis. Even if this position was confirmed, it neither could exclude the genetic and/or biological view nor provide evidence to clarify the question of which came first, the neurologically damaged child or the pathological mother.

Differentiating Symbiotic Psychosis from EIA and Childhood Schizophrenia

The clinging and panic-stricken reaction to the threat of separation from mother in a child between the ages of two-and-one-half and five following a period of normal development are the principal identifying characteristics of symbiotic psychosis. Unfortunately, symbiotic children are rarely seen clinically during this early phase of the disorder. More likely, referrals come at a later time when the secondary symptoms (which Mahler herself finds almost indistinguishable from EIA) have developed. Under these circumstances, the clinician is dependent on the accuracy of historical data from parents in order to make the differential diagnosis. As a matter of fact, it has been suggested that the two conditions are, in practice, lumped together as either autistic or symbiotic because the secondary symptoms of symbiosis are so similar to autistic symptoms (Lowe, 1966). The sym-

biotic attachment and physical clinging, the severe anxiety about mother-infant separation, and the onset of the disorder following a period of normal development are key aspects of the psychosis that set it apart from childhood schizophrenia.

Although Mahler's description of symbiotic psychosis is well accepted, there is, to date, little systematic research on the syndrome. Moreover, several writers have noted that the condition is extremely rare, perhaps occurring too infrequently to be established as a "real clinical entity" (Eisenberg, 1967; McDermott, Harrison, Schrager, Lindy, and Kellens, 1967).

Childhood Psychosis versus Mental Retardation and Organic Brain Syndrome

In considering the diagnostic possibilities for any of the childhood psychoses, the suspicion of mental retardation is almost always evident. Remember, Kanner's initial cases of autism were thought to be either feebleminded or deaf. However, he ruled out mental retardation because autistic children usually demonstrated normal to excellent motor development, alertness, a remarkable memory for details in their environment, and special or unusual musical and mechanical talents. Information from case histories and clinical observations are necessary in this regard.

The most obvious source of information for differentiating psychosis from retardation are tests of intelligence, even though children affected by either condition may obtain equally low I.Q.s. In this event, the clinician examines the child's intratest performance as well as the qualitative aspects of the child's responses for clues that would aid differential diagnosis. For example, most individually administered intelligence scales have their items arranged in ascending order of difficulty. Usually, mental retardates correctly complete successive items until they reach their upper limit. Thereafter, they fail to answer correctly additional items. Thus, they show little variability in performance until such time as repeated failures occur. In contrast, psychotic children are generally more variable in their performance. They may show a pattern of failing some "easy" items along with succeeding on some "very difficult" ones. While the total number of correct items may be the same for both groups, the important difference is in the variability of successes and failures. To the clinician, this unevenness in performance is reflective of higher intellectual potential than the total score would indicate. It suggests impairment of current intellectual functioning by factors other than mental retardation.

In addition, the clinician may examine the responses given to each test item in search of qualitative clues that reveal poor contact with reality and disturbances in thinking. These are characteristics ordinarily associated with psychosis, but not with mental retardation. In this regard, some clinicians prefer to use projective techniques to further explore the presence or absence of a thought disorder.

Another condition that may closely resemble psychosis in children is neurological impairment. This is especially true in those instances where language is disturbed, and where gross and fine motor coordination difficulties are evident. In addition, stereotyped ritualistic behavior and severe anxiety reaction to changes in the environment are symptoms that are likely to occur in both psychotic and brain damaged children. Complicating the diagnostic picture is the fact that psychotic children with

I.Q.s of less than 80 have patterns resembling brain-damaged children (Walker and Birch, 1974).

In order to make this difficult differential diagnosis, the clinician may use data from psychological tests purporting to measure behaviors that may be impaired as a function of brain damage. However, many of these sensitive areas of functioning, such as perceptual-motor coordination, visual memory, abstract thinking, organizing part-whole relationships, and attention span, are also affected by the restricted abilities of the mental retardate. Since the overall performance may be equally poor for both abnormal conditions, the clinician may look for additional distinguishing clues in the type of errors committed and in the qualitative aspects of the child's responses. (See Figure 8–1 below and Figure 5–3 on p. 150.)

Additional clues concerning neurological impairment can be obtained from case history materials that may reflect prenatal and birth complications, and brain damage from childhood illnesses or accidental injuries. Medical and neurological examinations including an EEG can provide further corroborative data. Finally, clinical observations concerning the child's ability and willingness to relate socially is most important in arriving at a differential diagnosis. In most instances, psychotic children will show a marked disturbance in their relationship to people, while brain damaged youngsters ordinarily show normal emotional warmth and social capacity.

Incidence of Childhood Psychoses

Considering the general problems of gathering incidence data and the diagnostic confusion associated with childhood psy-

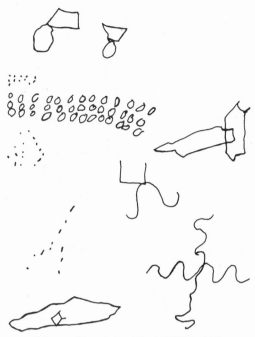

Eight-year-old boy who has a full-scale WISC I.Q. of 112.

FIGURE 8–1   Bender-Gestalt performance of an eight-year-old brain-damaged boy who obtained a full scale WISC IQ of 112

ner's two cardinal signs, the incidence rate declined to 2.1 per 10,000 children. Based on cases seen over a nineteen-year period, Kanner estimated the incidence of EIA as 0.7 per 10,000; a figure that has since been corroborated (Kanner, 1958, Treffert, 1970). After eliminating duplicated cases, these data showed a combined incidence of 3.1 per 10,000 for childhood schizophrenia and EIA.

It seems clear from the available estimates that childhood psychoses occur infrequently, and that the specific psychotic disorders are even rarer. Interestingly enough, there is consistent evidence of a high frequency of occurrence of childhood psychosis in boys as compared to girls. Estimates of boy-girl ratios have ranged from approximately 2:1 to slightly higher than 9:1 (Werry, 1972). Although this disproportionate sex distribution is sometimes used to bolster a genetic or biological view of childhood psychosis, there is no substantiated explanation at present for this empirical finding. As a matter of fact, as we shall see repeatedly, for unknown reasons boys typically exceed girls in the frequency of occurrence of most other forms of abnormal behavior.

choses, it should not be surprising that accurate estimates of the frequency of psychosis in children are difficult to come by. A recent report suggests that the incidence of childhood psychoses does not exceed the rate of six per 10,000 children (Werry, 1972). However, an accurate breakdown of incidence data for the specific psychotic disorders cannot be reliably obtained at present. Two studies in England found a 4.5 per 10,000 rate of EIA in children between the ages of eight and ten years (Lotter, 1966; Wing, O'Connor, and Lotter, 1967). However, when the diagnosis was restricted to those children who exhibited only Kan-

Treatment Approaches

Treatment approaches with psychotic children have been numerous and greatly dependent on the etiological position of the therapist. While it is not possible to review all of these variations, we shall consider and evaluate a sample of the most widely used or promising procedures under the following broad headings: psychological, milieu, and somatic therapies.

Psychological Therapies

1. Individual Psychotherapy. Individual psychotherapy is a general term used to refer to an ongoing interaction between therapist and the client. However, the nature of the interaction, the techniques used, the goals, the frequency of sessions, and the duration of therapy varies tremendously. Because of this diversity and the difficulty in establishing uniform criteria for improvement, psychotherapy is a formidable treatment method to assess.

Almost all variations of individual psychotherapy have been tried with psychotic children, although the early literature reflected a preference for a psychoanalytic approach. In this context, the psychotic child is said to have a severely impaired ego that is either the result of or further fragmented by a pathological mother-child relationship. For example, one psychoanalytically oriented therapist suggested that the psychotic child is the victim of gross emotional deprivation from a mother who is very immature, narcissistic, and incapable of emotional relationships (Rank, 1949). This psychodynamic formulation influences both the goal of therapy and the strategy necessary to achieve it. The therapist acts as a mother substitute who, in a totally accepting and loving manner, tries to provide the child with the ego support and emotional gratification that the real mother was unable to give. When the therapist establishes a relationship with the child (a condition that may take several years to accomplish), the therapist turns to the uncovering of traumatic experiences and unconscious conflicts and their resolution. In addition, many clinicians maintain that individual therapy is also necessary for mother in order to deal with her problems and to help her to eventually take over and meet the needs of her child.

Except for anecdotal accounts and clinical case reports, there have been few empirical efforts to evaluate the effectiveness of this approach. In two separate studies, no differences were found on any treatment variable between psychotic children who were considered to have either the best or the worst outcome in therapy. Moreover, no differences were found in outcome between psychotic children who were treated with individual psychotherapy for six months and psychotic youngsters who were untreated (Brown, 1960, 1963). In light of these negative results and the great expense involved (both in money and time), one cannot but wonder whether the gains are sufficient to merit continued clinical confidence in this approach.

2. Behavior Modification Approaches. At a time when clinicians were discouraged by the failure of individual psychotherapy to dramatically change the behavior of psychotic children, a relatively new and promising approach was introduced. Rooted in basic behavioral research, this approach includes many variations and is known by such diverse labels as behavior modification, behavior therapy, operant conditioning, aversive conditioning, desensitization, or token economy systems.

Although behavior modification had been successfully employed earlier with psychotic adults, Ferster and DeMyer (1962) were among the first to systematically shape the behavior of psychotic children by an operant conditioning procedure in which food was used as reinforcement. Since then, reinforcement procedures have been used with psychotic children to increase social responsiveness, eye contact, speech, and imitation in order to facilitate their learning of play, writing, and self-help skills (Hingtgen and Trost, 1966; Blake and Moss, 1967; Lovaas, 1967; Lovaas, Freitas, Nelson, and Whalen, 1967).

Punishment in the form of electric shock, isolation, and slapping have been used to eliminate unwanted behaviors. Mild electric shock was introduced to decrease a schizophrenic girl's bizarre inattentiveness that was interfering with her academic training (Lovaas, Freitag, Gold, and Kassorla, 1965). It has also been found to be very effective in controlling self-mutilative behavior of severely disturbed psychotic children (Lovaas, Schaeffer, and Simmons, 1965). An alternative to the use of punishment for self-mutilators has been reported recently in which air splints have been applied to the child's limbs. By controlling the air pressure in the splint, the limbs can be either partially or totally restrained, thus permitting the use of positive reinforcement in shaping new adaptive behaviors (Paul and Romanczyk, 1973).

Tokens acquire reinforcing value through pairings with food. They have been used to train autistic children in school behaviors such as sitting quietly at a desk, identifying objects, answering questions. and matching pictures. More impressive is the finding (contrary to what others found) that children trained this way later were able to transfer these behaviors to a group classroom situation (Martin, England, Kaprowy, Kilgour, and Pilek, 1968; Koegel and Rincover, 1974). The success with which parents, teachers, and other caretakers have been trained to carry out operant conditioning procedures has offered hope of providing the child with continued treatment at home or in school (Zimmerman and Zim-

merman, 1962; Wolf, Risley, and Mees, 1964; Merbaum, 1973). Using significant lay people in the therapy of psychotic children provides a continuity and consistency of treatment that increase the likelihood that desirable behaviors learned in therapy will be maintained outside of the treatment setting.

This sample of the literature illustrates some of the favorable results obtained with behavior modification and the clinical popularity it currently enjoys. Improvements in the behavior of psychotic children with this approach have been impressive, especially in light of the extreme inaccessibility of these children. Without a doubt, it has achieved its measure of acclaim, because it has brought about dramatic behavioral changes that have made these children more manageable in the home and school environment. It has modified such severely disruptive behaviors as self-mutilation, extreme inattention, lack of eye contact, or refusal to eat with utensils, and it has produced spoken words in children who appeared to be permanently mute.

However, we must inject a critical note. Behavior modification is not the treatment panacea for psychotic children. With all of its successes, behavior modification has been unable to significantly transform the psychotic child into a normal one, or even to change some of the child's impaired functioning to normal levels. For example, the enormous and painstaking efforts involved in increasing the number of words a psychotic child can say, unfortunately, offers no assurance that the gains will lead to the child's using language for communication purposes. In fact, the evidence indicates that with or without operant procedures, improvement in language development rarely brings with it a change in language from the mechanical and concrete mode to the spontaneous and communicative one (Rutter, 1968). Within recent years, promising reports have described nonverbal language training as a means of improving expressive language in speech deficient psychotic children (Miller and Miller, 1973; Devilliers and Naughton, 1974; McLean and McLean, 1974).

In 1969, Margaret Creedon began teaching sign language to autistic children with surprising success. The idea has caught on, and now there are scores of programs that use sign language to teach communicative skills to autistic and even retarded children (Offir, 1976).

Even though the results have been promising, there is no agreement as to why the approach works. Many theorists and researchers of EIA have pointed out that a language deficit is at the heart of the disorder. Also, language has been shown repeatedly to be the best predictor of prognosis. There are basically two views: One states that autistic children need all the language cues they can get, and the opposite view claims that these children can only attend to one mode of communication at a time—preferably the visual.

Sign language provides autistic children with a means to interact with the world. They can request things, ask questions, and even express their feelings. Fulwiler and Fouts (1976) reported on their work with a five-year-old autistic boy. After twenty sessions, not only was he using several signs appropriately, but he also increased his vocal language. These results were observed outside of the training sessions, and he became more attentive and manageable as well.

Although this is only one case (among several), it is an area that is quickly expanding. It is hoped that increased use will prove the effectiveness of sign language in bringing autistic children into contact with the human world.

Enthusiasm for behavior modification is further dampened when we recognize that its therapeutic benefits are lost if they are not constantly reinforced, and that the child rarely, if ever, initiates additional changes of his or her own (Pawlicki, 1970). The approach is also limited in that in most cases psychotic children seem to have great difficulties in generalizing what they learned in one situation to new situations. Finally, we must temper the enthusiasm for the use of parents and paraprofessionals as behavior therapists until such time as their potential and limitations are fully studied.

Milieu Therapy

Perhaps the best known milieu treatment program for severely disturbed children is the one developed by Bruno Bettelheim at the Orthogenic School in Chicago. Essentially, Bettelheim holds to a psychogenic view of childhood psychosis, in which the hostile rage of the mother severely threatens the child to the point where he or she is afraid to enter into human interactions. Therefore, the child withdraws from the surrounding world. Bettelheim argues that it is necessary to remove the child from the destructive mother-child relationship into a residential environment that is designed to satisfy the child's emotional needs. His milieu program includes psychoanalytic therapy (other residential settings may provide somatic and/or behavior therapy), physical and occupational therapy, and a daily life situation that is structured but permissive. Formal school is provided, although the initial emphasis is on nonacademic activities such as caring for animals, drawing, painting, and other simple crafts. In addition to a therapist, the child has a counselor who is responsible for a small number of children. The counselor, who usually eats with the children, is expected to give support and understanding, to interpret the child's words and actions, and to encourage the child's advances toward ego integration (Bettelheim, 1950).

Bettelheim reported unusually high success with autistic children, that is, of thirty-nine children he considered, fifteen (forty-eight percent) "rehabilitated," eleven (thirty-five percent) "much improved," and three "somewhat improved," and two "no lasting improvement" (Bettelheim, 1966, p. 15). However, his claims are difficult to interpret inasmuch as they were based on "impressions" at the time the children left the Orthogenic School, and inasmuch as the clinical symptoms of these youngsters did not fit Kanner's diagnostic criteria or even those of researchers who use more inclusive criteria for the diagnosis of EIA.

In evaluating the effectiveness of the Ittleson Center's residential program, Goldfarb, Goldfarb, and Pollak (1966), compared thirteen matched pairs of schizophrenic youngsters who were either treated in a daycare or a residential program. Neither treatment program was found to be more effective for the organic schizophrenic children, while the residential program yielded greater improvement than the daycare program for the nonorganics. Milieu therapy provides a full, varied, and extensive treatment plan for these children and a program that holds, at present, the most promise for improving the chances for psychotic children to make future satisfactory adjustments in society. Its greatest limitation is its unavailability in many states as either a public or private facility and its prohibitive cost when available.

Somatic Therapies

1. Electroconvulsive Shock Treatment (ECT). In 1947, Bender recommended the use of ECT to stimulate the maturation of psychotic children and to reduce their anxiety in order to make them more amenable to psychotherapeutic intervention (Bender, 1947). Later, she suggested that ECT promoted some type of reorganization, which resulted in a more integrated body image (Bender and Keeler, 1952). Followup studies of a large number of psychotic children treated with shock claimed that shock produces no intellectual impairment or other adverse effects, and that more than half of these youngsters improved socially, especially if they were treated before age seven (Bender, 1960).

A survey of hospital ECT practices found that four of nineteen institutions employed ECT with schizophrenic children (Szurek, Berlin, and Boatman, 1971). Those institutions with the longest and most extensive experience with this treatment used a series of twenty grand mal convulsions, one treatment per day for six days a week.

ECT is a radical treatment that is difficult to evaluate, particularly with regard to its long-term effects. In spite of the favorable results reported by a few clinicians, there is, to date, insufficient evidence from well-controlled studies to warrant its unconditional use.

2. Drug Therapies. Drugs are used rather extensively to treat psychotic children, or as some have suggested, to improve the psychotic child's accessibility to stimulation and influence (Eisenberg, 1964). It has been stressed recently that drugs in themselves do not eliminate previously learned maladaptive responses, and they do not create new social or personal patterns

(Goldfarb, 1970). The use of drugs is rarely sufficient to induce normal behavior, although they may help to reduce symptoms that interfere with the psychotic child's interaction with his environment.

Nevertheless, some researchers persist in reporting drug effects in terms of improvement ratings as if the source of the psychotic disturbance has been ameliorated.

Moreover, many studies are inadequately designed or have failed to employ sufficient experimental controls, rendering their results difficult to interpret in any conclusive way.

Tranquilizers, antidepressants, and hallucinogenic drugs (LSD) have been used. Bender (1966) began giving LSD and UML-491 (a derivative of LSD) to autistic children in 1961 and reported that these children did not show the expected psychotomimetic effects, but they did show heightened mood and responsivity, increased awareness, and a lessening of stereotypic behavior. After six weeks of treatment with either LSD or UML, all of the autistic children improved in I.Q., school work, motivation, and affect, and they manifested fewer signs of a thought disorder. A review and comparison of seven studies in which psychedelic agents had been used with autistic children noted that the studies had not been controlled for the psychedelic agent used, dosage level, frequency, demographic variables, specific disorder, duration, and severity of symptoms (Mogar and Aldrich, 1969). However, in all of these studies, some similar results were obtained that showed improvement in speech, elevation in mood, more interaction with people, and less ritualistic behavior. Mogar and Aldrich concluded that the effects of LSD seem only transient, and that psychotherapy must accompany the use of LSD to effect long term changes. They also emphasized the fact that

follow-up studies must be done to further evaluate the effectiveness of the drug.

3. Body Manipulation. DesLauriers and Carlson (1969) fashioned a promising treatment program based on their belief that there is a neurophysiological imbalance in EIA that produces a lag or an arrest in all areas of human development. Autistics evidence a high threshold of affective arousal, impaired responsivity to sensory stimulation, and a severely restricted capacity to derive pleasure or displeasure from human contacts. In order to overcome these difficulties, DesLauriers and Carlson proposed persistent stimulation of the child through a variety of tactile contacts and motor activities until the child showed that he or she actually experienced the sensory stimulation. This should be done in a setting where there are few distractions and where the continuous but pleasurable presence of the therapist vis-à-vis the child is paramount. Interactions between the therapist and the child focus on increasing the child's capacity to experience pleasure and displeasure, as well as on the child's emotional responsivity to human stimulation. In addition, the variety of sensory messages given to the child facilitates his or her ability to respond adaptively with intelligent and goal directed behaviors. The treatment approach varies depending on whether the child is considered hyperactive or hypoactive. For example, a two-and-a-half-year-old hyperactive autistic boy was approached with caution.

. . . we had to make our presence felt, not by moving forcefully on him and aggressively drawing his attention to us, but by allowing him to "bump" into us, so to say. This we did by placing ourselves on the floor in such a way that he had to move around us; and, secondly, by slowly making the area of restless roaming smaller and smaller, until the only thing he could move around and explore were our own bodies. It was like approaching an eight-month-old baby who does not know you; the most successful way is to back up on the baby and allow him to touch you first. By contrast, our approach to Kathy, whose typical early behavior consisted of standing quietly facing and scratching a wall, called for a more directly intrusive maneuver. As Kathy stood there, isolated in this quietly stereotyped, repetitive activity, the therapist placed herself beside her at the wall, and just as quietly began to scratch at the wall. After quite awhile, Kathy heard the scratching noise made by the therapist and looked at her fingers. The therapist then moved her fingers toward Kathy's fingers and touched them, as if by accident. The fifth or sixth time that this happened, Kathy seemed to become aware of this and pulled her own fingers away. Insistently, the therapist repeated the maneuver until it was Kathy herself who moved her fingers toward the therapist's hand, and a small game of finger touching began. The initiative of the child, in both instances, has to be counted on and respected; but this initiative has to be exploited in the direction of alerting the attention of the child to the physical presence of the therapist (DesLauriers and Carlson, 1969, pp. 136–137).

To ensure the continuity of treatment and to reduce parental guilt and anxiety from dealing with their autistic children, DesLauriers and Carlson included parents as co-therapists. Each parent initially spent twenty to thirty minutes in the therapy session with the child while observations and movies of the interactions were made. Parents then viewed themselves working with their child to see which responses were effective and which were not, and to overcome their fears and inhibitions over their child's prospect for improvement. Moreover, parents were given the opportunity to discuss with the therapist what they were doing and their feelings about it as a way of helping them discover that they could be real parents with meaningful functions. Finally, the therapist involved the schools in the re-educational process by sending the autistic child to school as soon as possible to widen his or her world of experiences.

To the extent possible, DesLauriers and Carlson assessed autistic children (between two and five years of age) before, during, and after treatment, and they demonstrated dramatic improvement in motoric, adaptive, communicative, and social development. Even more impressive is the finding that the developmental gains made by the five treated youngsters were maintained after almost a one-year follow-up.

4. Sensory Deprivation. Interesting but scant findings are available at present concerning the use of isolation or sensory deprivation in the treatment of autistic children. Three male autistic children were isolated in a room containing only a mattress and sheet and illuminated by a 25-watt bulb (Schechter, Shurley, Tousseing, and Maier, 1969). The room temperature was controlled and constant, and meals were brought in. The therapist visited the child two times a day for ten to fifteen minutes, and observations were made every two hours through a window. The authors found that all of the boys became increasingly alert to noise, although they were earlier thought to be deaf, engaged in eye contact with the therapist, ate well, seemed happy, and did not try to leave the room when the door was open. At the end of the isolation period (forty, sixty-eight and seventy-four days) all of the boys ran to their parents, sat in their laps, and held them. Follow-up of these children (twelve to twenty-four months later) found them to be attending nursery school and living at home as tolerable members of the family.

Isolation therapy is based on the rationale that the autistic child requires sensory reduction because he or she is impaired neurologically in such a way that the child is overwhelmed by incoming stimuli. Considerably more careful research is necessary before the effectiveness and the usefulness of this approach can be determined.

Summary

The area of childhood psychoses that subsumes childhood schizophrenia, early infantile autism, and symbiotic infantile psychosis is characterized by confusion and controversy. There is disparity about whether these are separable conditions and about the symptomatology included within each category, and even greater disagreement among clinicians with respect to the diagnostic criteria used to differentiate one disorder from another. In practice, these categories are used interchangeably and inconsistently, so that data with regard to incidence, family characteristics, etiological factors, and treatment effects are imprecise and difficult to interpret.

Through the years, childhood schizophrenia has been the central focus of study and the primary classification category of psychosis in children. Although longitudinal studies of children diagnosed as schizophrenics indicate that a significant number are later diagnosed as organic, there is still controversy as to whether schizophrenia is the same disorder in both children and adults. In general, childhood psychoses occur infrequently (from three to six per 10,000 children under twelve years of age), and the specific psychotic disorders in children are even more rare (approximately one per 10,000 for early infantile autism using Kanner's primary criteria). There is consistent evidence of a higher incidence of childhood psychoses in boys as compared to girls (ranging from 2:1 to 9:1).

Table 8–4 summarizes the primary characteristics of the clinical picture for childhood schizophrenia, early infantile autism, and symbiotic infantile psychosis.

Differential diagnosis among the psychotic disorders and mental retardation and organic brain syndrome was discussed.

Early infantile autism is differentiated from childhood schizophrenia on the basis of age of onset and Kanner's two primary signs of autistic aloneness and the insistence on sameness in the environment. In addition, a differentiating characteristic is that autistic children manifest special and unusual abilities, good memory, good motor coordination, and normal EEG patterns, whereas schizophrenic children do not. Symbiotic psychosis is differentiated from the other two psychotic conditions by an early and primary panic reaction to the threat of separation from mother. Secondary symptoms of symbiosis appear as the psychosis progresses, and these are almost indistinguishable from autism. Mentally retarded youngsters typically show no intratest variability on tests of intelligence but they are apt to be warm and responsive to human interactions, in contrast to psychotic children. Performance on tests purporting to measure behaviors that are often impaired as a function of brain damage, along with medical and neurological data, may be helpful in differentiating brain damaged children from psychotic and mentally retarded ones.

Genetic, biological, and psychogenic views concerning the etiology of childhood psychoses were discussed. While the data for any particular etiological position are incomplete and inconclusive, mounting evidence and support implicates neurological (perhaps genetically determined in

TABLE 8–4 Summary of the Clinical Picture for the Three Childhood Psychoses

Clinical Picture	Childhood Schizophrenia	Early Infantile Autism	Symbiotic Infantile Psychoses
Onset	Gradual between age two to eleven after period of normal development.	Gradual from birth.	Between two and one-half to five years after normal development.
Social and Interpersonal	Decreased interest in external world, withdrawal, loss of contact, impaired relations with others.	Failure to show anticipatory postural movements; extreme aloneness; insistence on sameness.	Unable to tolerate briefest separation from mother; clinging and incapable of delineating self.
Intellectual and Cognitive	Thought disturbance; perceptual problems; distorted time and space orientation; below average I.Q.	High spatial ability; good memory; low I.Q. but good intellectual potential.	Bizarre ideation; loss of contact; thought disturbance.
Language	Disturbances in speech; mutism, and if speech is present, it is not used for communication.	Disturbances in speech; mutism, and if speech is present it is not used for communication. Very literal; delayed echolalia; pronoun reversal, I and Yes are absent till age six.	
Affect	Defect in emotional responsiveness and rapport; decreased, distorted, and/or inappropriate affect.	Inaccessible and emotionally unresponsive to humans.	Severe anxiety and panic over separation from mother; low frustration tolerance; withdrawn and seclusive as psychosis persists.
Motor	Bizarre body movements; repetitive and stereotyped motions; motor awkwardness; distortion in mobility.	Head banging and body rocking; remarkable agility and dexterity; preoccupied with mechanical objects.	
Physical and Developmental Patterns	Unevenness of somatic growth; disturbances of normal rhythmic patterns; abnormal EEG.	Peculiar eating habits and food preferences; normal EEG.	Disturbed normal rhythmic patterns.
Family	High incidence of mental illness.	Aloof, obsessive, and emotionally cold; high intelligence and educational and occupational levels; low divorce rate and incidence of mental illness.	Pathological mother who fosters the symbiosis.

the form of an inherited vulnerability) factors in the development of psychosis in children.

Almost every form of treatment has been tried with psychotic children, including individual psychotherapy, behavior therapy, milieu therapy, electro-convulsive shock treatment, drug therapy, and sensory deprivation, but no treatment approach has been successful in bringing about major improvements in any significant number of psychotic children. Behavior modification approaches have been extremely promising and useful in altering or controlling behaviors that make psychotic youngsters much more manageable at home and in school. However, they have not, in the main, been successful in transforming the psychotic child into a normal one. In general, the prognosis for psychotic youngsters is poor, although the evidence suggests that those who have language and show some improvement before age five have a more favorable outlook than those who are mute and who show no signs of early improvement.

Epilogue

The diagnosis of childhood schizophrenia, confirmed by separate additional evaluations by a psychiatrist and a neurologist, was poorly received by the family, especially by the father. Primarily because of the father's reluctance and the fact that he had ample financial resources, Henry was taken for a lengthy series of examinations to centers out of the state. The results were usually the same, but father persisted for more than eighteen months in the hope that he would hear better news and that he would locate someone who would miraculously restore his son to normality. Finally, the father more agreeably turned to the recommendations made by the local professionals.

Behavior modification helped in toilet training and in increasing Henry's vocabulary, although it did not improve significantly his use of language for communication. He was enrolled in a special day-school program that not only gave his family a much needed respite during the day, but also provided him with continued language, motor, and social training. Socialization gradually occurred in the sense that he was more readily managed, that he began to acknowledge the presence of others, and that he learned more acceptable eating and personal hygiene habits. While Henry changed in the course of two years, his parents steadfastly refused therapy for themselves to help them deal with their feelings. At this point, Henry is easier to manage in school and at home, and more pleasant to be around. He likes painting, cutting out and pasting pictures in an album, and he is beginning to learn how to write his name.

REFERENCES

BENDER, L. *Instructions for the Use of Visual Motor Gestalt Test.* New York: The American Orthopsychiatric Association, 1946.

BENDER, L. "One Hundred Cases of Childhood Schizophrenia Treated with Electric Shock." *Transaction of the American Neurological Association,* 1947, *72,* 165–169.

BENDER, L. "Twenty Years of Clinical Research on Schizophrenic Children with Special Reference to Those Under Six Years of Age." In Caplan, G. (Ed.), *Emotional*

Problems of Early Childhood. New York: Basic Books, 1955.

BENDER, L. "Autism in Children with Mental Deficiency." *American Journal of Mental Deficiency,* 1959, *64,* 81–86.

BENDER, L. "Treatment in Early Schizophrenia." *Progress in Psychotherapy,* 1960, *5,* 177–184.

BENDER, L. "The Brain and Child Behavior." *Archives of General Psychiatry,* 1961, *4,* 531–547.

BENDER, L. "D-Lysergic Acid in the Treatment of the Biological Features of Childhood Schizophrenia." *Diseases of the Nervous System,* 1966 (Suppl. 7), *27,* 43–46.

BENDER, L. "The Family Patterns of 100 Schizophrenic Children Observed at Bellevue, 1935–1952." *Journal of Autism and Childhood Schizophrenia,* 1974, *4,* 279–292.

BENDER, L. and G. FARETRA. "The Relationship Between Childhood Schizophrenia and Adult Schizophrenia." In Kaplan, A. R. (Ed.), *Genetic Factors in "Schizophrenia."* Springfield, Illinois: Charles C Thomas, 1972.

BENDER, L., FREEDMAN, A. M., GRUGETT, A. E., Jr., and W. M. HELME. "Schizophrenia in Childhood: A Confirmation of the Diagnosis." *Transaction of the American Neurological Association,* 1952, *77,* 67–73.

BENDER, L. and W. R. KEELER. "The Body Image of Schizophrenia Children Following Electroshock Therapy." *American Journal of Orthopsychiatry,* 1952, *22,* 335–355.

BENNETT, S. and H. R. KLEIN. "Childhood Schizophrenia: Thirty Years Later." *American Journal of Psychiatry,* 1966, *122,* 1121–1124.

BERGMAN, A. "I and You: The Separation-Individuation Process in the Treatment of a Symbiotic-Psychotic Child." In McDevitt, J. B. and C. F. Settlage (Eds.), *Separation-Individuation: Essays in Honor of Margaret S. Mahler.* New York: International Universities Press, 1971, pp. 328–331.

BERGMAN, P. and S. K. ESCALONA. "Unusual Sensitivities in Very Young Children." In *Psychoanalytic Study of the Child* (Vols. III–IV). New York: International Universities Press, 1949.

BETTELHEIM, B. *Love Is Not Enough.* New York: Free Press, 1950.

BETTELHEIM, B. *The Empty Fortress.* New York: Macmillan, 1966.

BLAKE, P., and T. MOSS. "The Development of Socialization Skills in an Electively Mute Child." *Behavior Research and Therapy,* 1967, *5,* 349–356.

BLOCK, J. "Parents of Schizophrenic, Neurotic, Asthmatic, and Congenitally Ill Children." *Archives of General Psychiatry,* 1969, *20,* 659–674.

BOUILLIN, D. J., BHAGAVAN, H. N., O'BRIEN, R. A., and M. B. H. YOUDIM. "Platelet Monoamine Oxidase in Children with Infantile Autism." In Coleman, M. (Ed.), *The Autistic Syndromes.* Amsterdam, Holland: North-Holland Publishing Company, 1976, pp. 51–63.

BOUILLIN, D. J., COLEMAN, M., O'BRIEN, R. A., and B. RIMLAND. "Laboratory Predictions of Infantile Autism Based on 5-Hydroxytryptamine Efflux from Blood Platelets and Their Correlations with the Rimland E-2 Score." *Journal of Autism and Childhood Schizophrenia,* 1971, *1,* 63–71.

BRADLEY, C. and M. BOWEN. "Behavior Characteristics of Schizophrenic Children. *Psychiatric Quarterly,* 1941, *15,* 296–315.

BROWN, J. L. "Prognosis from Presenting Symptoms of Preschool Children with Atypical Development." *American Journal of Orthopsychiatry,* 1960, *30,* 382–390.

BROWN, J. L. "Follow-up of Children with Atypical Development (Infantile Psychosis)." *American Journal of Orthopsychiatry,* 1963, *33,* 855–861.

COLEMAN, M. "Serotonin and Central Nervous Syndromes of Childhood: A Review." *Journal of Autism and Childhood Schizophrenia,* 1973, *3,* 27–35.

CREAK, M. "Schizophrenia Syndrome in Childhood. Progress Report of a Working Party." *British Medical Journal,* 1961, *2,* 889–890.

DAVIDS, A. "Childhood Psychosis: The Problem of Differential Diagnosis." *Journal of Autism and Childhood Schizophrenia,* 1975, *5,* 129–138.

DEMYER, M. K., BARTON, S., DEMYER, W. E., NORTON, J. A., ALLEN, J., and R. STEELE. "Prognosis in Autism: A Follow-up Study." *Journal of Autism and Childhood Schizophrenia,* 1973, *3,* 199–246.

DEMYER, M. K., CHURCHILL, D. W., PONTIUS, W., and K. M. GILKEY. "A Comparison of Five Diagnostic Systems for Childhood Schizophrenia and Infantile Autism." *Journal of Autism and Childhood Schizophrenia,* 1971, *1,* 175–189.

DEMYER, M. K., PONTIUS, W., NORTON, J., BARON, S., ALLEN, J., and R. STEELE. "Parental Practices and Innate Activity in Normal, Autistic, and Brain Damaged Infants." *Journal of Autism and Childhood Schizophrenia,* 1972, *2,* 49–66.

DESLAURIERS, A. N. and C. F. CARLSON. *Your Child Is Asleep.* Homewood, Illinois: Dorsey, 1969.

DESPERT, J. L. "Schizophrenia in Children." *Psychiatric Quarterly,* 1938, *12,* 365–371.

DESPERT, J. L. *Schizophrenia in Children:* Collected Papers (1st ed.). New York: Brunner/Mazel, 1968.

DEVILLIERS, J. G. and J. M. NAUGHTON. "Teaching a Symbol Language to Autistic Children." *Journal of Consulting and Clinical Psychology,* 1974, *42,* 111–117.

EISENBERG, L. "The Autistic Child in Adolescence." *American Journal of Psychiatry,* 1956, *112,* 607–612.

EISENBERG, L. "Role of Drugs in Treating Disturbed Children." *Children,* 1964, *11,* 167–173.

EISENBERG, L. "Psychiatric Disorders of Childhood, 42.1. Psychotic Disorder. I: Clinical Features." In Freedman, A. M. and H. I. Kaplan (Eds.), *Comprehensive Textbook of Psychiatry.* Baltimore: Williams and Wilkins, 1967, 1433–1438.

FERSTER, C. B. and M. K. DEMYER. "A Method for the Experimental Analysis of the Behavior of Autistic Children." *American Journal of Orthopsychiatry,* 1962, *32,* 89–98.

FISH, B. "Contributions of Developmental Research to a Theory of Schizophrenia." In J. Hellmuth, (Ed.), *Exceptional Infants: Studies in Abnormalities* (Vol. 2). New York: Brunner/Mazel, 1971, pp. 473–482.

FLORSHEIM, J. and O. PETERFREUND. "The Intelligence of Parents of Psychotic Children." *Journal of Autism and Childhood Schizophrenia,* 1974, *4,* 61–70.

FULWILER, R. L. and R. S. FOUTS. "Acquisition of American Sign Language by a Noncommunicating Autistic Child." *Journal of Autism and Childhood Schizophrenia,* 1976, *6,* 43–51.

GOLDFARB, W. *Childhood Schizophrenia.* Cambridge, Massachusetts: Harvard University Press, 1961.

GOLDFARB, W. "Self-awareness in Schizophrenia Children." *Archives of General Psychiatry,* 1963, *8,* 47–60.

GOLDFARB, W. "Childhood Psychoses." In Mussen, P. M. (Ed.), *Carmichael's Manual of Child Psychology* (Vol. 2). New York: Wiley, 1970.

GOLDFARB, W., GOLDFARB, N., and H. SCHOLL. "The Speech of Mothers of Schizophrenic Children." *American Journal of Psychiatry*, 1966, *122*, 1220–1227.

GOLDFARB, W., GOLDFARB, N., and R. A. POLLAK. "Treatment of Childhood Schizophrenia: A Three Year Comparison of Day and Residential Treatment." *Archives of General Psychiatry*, 1966, *14*, 119–128.

GOLDFARB, W. "The Causes and Treatment of Childhood Schizophrenia." From *Program Reports of NIMH: The Mental Health of the Child*, 1971, 293–301.

GOLDFARB, W., MINTZ, I., and K. STROOK. *A Time to Heal*. New York: International Universities Press, 1969.

GREENFELD, J. *A Child Called Noah*. New York: Holt, Rinehart and Winston, 1972.

HALEY, J. "Testing Parental Instructions to Schizophrenic and Normal Children: A Pilot Study. *Journal of Abnormal Psychology*, 1968, *73*, 559–565.

HERMELIN, B. and N. O'CONNOR. *Psychological Experiments with Autistic Children*. New York: Pergammon Press, 1970.

HINGTGEN, J. N., and F. C. TROST, Jr. "Shaping Cooperative Responses in Early Childhood Schizophrenics: II. Reinforcement of Mutual Contact and Vocal Responses." In Ulrich, R., Statchnick, T. and J. Mabry (Eds.), *Control of Human Behavior*. Glenview, Illinois: Scott, Foresman, 1966.

HUTT, S. J. and C. HUTT (Eds.). *Behavior Studies in Psychiatry*. New York: Pergammon Press, 1970.

JUDD, L., and A. MANDELL. "Chromosome Studies in Early Infantile Autism." *Archives of General Psychiatry*, 1968, *18*, 450–457.

KALLMAN, F. J. and B. ROTH. "Genetic Aspects of Preadolescent Schizophrenia." *American Journal of Psychiatry*, 1956, *112*, 599–606.

KANNER, L. "Autistic Disturbances of Affective Contact." *Nervous Child*, 1943, *2*, 217–250.

KANNER, L. *Child Psychiatry* (4th ed.) Springfield, Illinois: Charles C Thomas, 1972.

KANNER, L. "Problems of Nosology and Psychodynamics of Early Infantile Autism." *American Journal of Orthopsychiatry*, 1949, *19*, 416–426.

KANNER, L. "The Specificity of Early Infantile Autism." *Zeitschrift fur Kinderpsychiatrie*, 1958, *25*, 108–113.

KANNER, L. "To What Extent Is Early Infantile Autism Determined by Constitutional Inadequacies?" *Association for Research on Nervous and Mental Diseases* Proceedings, 1954, *33*, 378–385.

KANNER, L. and L. I. LESSER. "Early Infantile Autism." *Pediatric Clinics of North America*, 1958, *5*, 711–730.

KAUFMAN, I., ROSENBLUM, E., HEIMS, L., and L. WILLER. "Childhood Psychosis: I Childhood Schizophrenia: Treatment of Children and Parents." *American Journal of Orthopsychiatry*, 1957, *27*, 683–690.

KLEBANOFF, L. B. "Parental Attitudes of Mothers of Schizophrenic, Brain Injured and Retarded and Normal Children." *American Journal of Orthopsychiatry*, 1959, *29*, 445–454.

KOEGEL, R. L. and A. RINCOVER. "Treatment of Psychotic Children in a Classroom Environment: I. Learning in a Large Group." *Journal of Applied Behavior Analysis*, 1974, *7*, 45–59.

KUGELMASS, I. N. *The Autistic Child*. Springfield, Illinois: Charles C Thomas, 1970.

LANDGREBE, A. R., and M. A. LANDGREBE. "Urinary Catecholamine Screening in Autistic Children." In M. Coleman (Ed.), *The Autistic Syndromes*. Amsterdam, Holland: North-Holland Publishing Company, 1976, pp. 65–72.

LOTTER, V. "Epidemiology of Autistic Conditions in Young Children." *Social Psychiatry*, 1966, *1*, 124–137.

LOTTER, V. "Factors Related to Outcome in Autistic Children." *Journal of Autism and Childhood Schizophrenia*, 1974, *4*, 263–277.

LOVAAS, O. I. "A Behavior Therapy Approach to the Treatment of Childhood Schizophrenia." In J. P. Hill, (Ed.), *Minnesota Symposium on Child Psychology* (Vol. I). Minneapolis: University of Minnesota Free Press, 1967, 108–159.

LOVAAS, O. I., FREITAG, G., GOLD, V. I., and I. C. KASSORLA. "Experimental Studies in Childhood Schizophrenia: Analysis of Self-Destructive Behavior." *Journal of Experimental Child Psychology*, 1965, *2*, 67–84.

LOVAAS, O. I., FREITAS, L., NELSON, K., and C. WHALEN. "The Establishment of Imitation and Its Use for the Development of Complex Behavior in Schizophrenic Children." *Behavior Research and Therapy*, 1967, *5*, 171–181.

LOVAAS, O. I., SCHAEFFER, B., and J. Q. SIMMONS. "Building Social Behavior in Autistic Children by Use of Electric Shock." *Journal of Experimental Research in Personality*, 1965, *1*, 99–109.

LOWE, L. H. "Families of Children with Early Childhood Schizophrenia." *Archives of General Psychiatry*, 1966, *14*, 26–30.

MAHLER, M. S. "On Child Psychosis and Schizophrenia: Autistic and Symbiotic Infantile Psychosis." *Psychoanalytic Study of the Child*, 1952, *7*, 286–305.

MAHLER, M. S. *On Human Symbiosis and the Vicissitudes of Individuation*. Vol. I. *Infantile Psychosis*. New York: International Universities Press, 1968.

MAHLER, M., and M. FURER. "Child Psychosis: A Theoretical Statement and Its Implications." *Journal of Autism and Childhood Schizophrenia*, 1972, *2*, 213–218.

MARTIN, G. L., ENGLAND, G., KAPROWY, E., KILGOUR, K., and V. PILEK. "Operant Conditioning of Kindergarten Class Behavior in Autistic Children." *Behavior Research and Therapy*, 1968, *6*, 281–294.

McDERMOTT, J. F., HARRISON, S. I., SCHRAGER, J., LINDY, J., and E. K. KILLENS. "Social Class and Mental Illness in Children: The Question of Childhood Psychosis." *American Journal of Orthopsychiatry*, 1967, *37*, 548–557.

McLEAN, L. P., and J. E. McLEAN. "A Language Training Program for Nonverbal Autistic Children." *Journal of Speech and Hearing Disorders*, 1974, *39*, 186–193.

MERBAUM, M. "The Modification of Self-destructive Behavior by a Mother-therapist Using Aversive Stimulation." *Behavior Therapy*, 1973, *4*, 442–447.

MEYERS, D. I. and W. GOLDFARB. "Studies of Perplexity in Mothers of Schizophrenic Children." *American Journal of Orthopsychiatry*, 1961, *31*, 551–564.

MILLER, A. and E. E. MILLER. "Cognitive Developmental Training with Elevated Boards and Sign Language." *Journal of Autism and Childhood Schizophrenia*, 1973, *3*, 65–85.

MOGAR, R. E. and R. W. ALDRICH. "The Use of Psychedelic Agents with Autistic-Schizophrenic Children." *Behavioral Neuropsychiatry*, 1969, *1*, 44–50.

NORMAN, E. "Reality Relationships of Schizophrenic Children." *British Journal of Medical Psychology*, 1954, *27*, 126–141.

NORMAN, E. "Affect and Withdrawal of Schizophrenic Children." *British Journal of Medical Psychology*, 1955, *28*, 1–18.

OFFIR, C. W. "Visual Speech—Their Fingers Do the Talking." *Psychology Today*, June, 1976, pp. 72–78.

ORNITZ, E. M., and RITVO, E. R. "Perceptual Inconstancy in Early Infantile Autism: The Syndrome of Early Infantile Autism and Its Variants, Including Certain

Cases of Childhood Schizophrenia." *Archives of General Psychiatry*, 1968, *18*, 76–98.

PAUL, H. A., and R. G. ROMANCZYK. "Use of Air Splints in the Treatment of Self-Injurious Behavior." *Behavior Therapy*, 1973, *4*, 320–321.

PAWLICKI, R. "Behaviour-Therapy Research with Children: A Critical Review." *Canadian Journal of Behavioural Science*, 1970, *2*, 163–173.

PITFIELD, M. and A. N. OPPENHEIM. "Child-Rearing Attitudes of Mothers of Psychotic Children." *Journal of Child Psychology and Psychiatry*, 1964, *5*, 51–57.

POLLACK, M. "Mental Subnormality and 'Childhood Schizophrenia'." In Zubin, J. and G. A. Jervis (Eds.), *Psychopathology of Mental Development*. New York: Grune and Stratten, 1967, 460–471.

POLLIN, W. "A Possible Genetic Factor Related to Psychosis." *American Journal of Psychiatry*, 1971, *128*, 311–317.

POTTER, H. W. "Schizophrenia in Children." *American Journal of Psychiatry*, 1933, *12*, 1253–1270.

RANK, B. "Adaptation of the Psychoanalytic Technique in the Treatment of Young Children with Atypical Development." *American Journal of Orthopsychiatry*, 1949, *19*, 130–139.

RICKS, D. M. and L. WING. "Language, Communication, and the Use of Symbols in Normal and Autistic Children." *Journal of Autism and Childhood Schizophrenia*, 1975, *5*, 191–221.

RIMLAND, B. "On the Objective Diagnosis of Infantile Autism." *Acta Paedopsychiatrica*, 1968, *35*, 146–161.

RIMLAND, B. *Infantile Autism*. New York: Appleton Century Crofts, 1964.

RIMLAND, B. "The Differentiation of Childhood Psychoses: An Analysis of Checklists for 2218 Psychotic Children." *Journal of Autism and Childhood Schizophrenia*, 1971, *1*, 161–174.

ROUTTENBERG, A. "The Two Arousal Hypothesis: Reticular Formation and Limbic System." *Psychological Review*, 1968, *75*, 51–80.

RUTTER, M. "Concepts of Autism: A Review of Research." *Journal of Child Psychology and Psychiatry*, 1968, *9*, 1–25.

RUTTER, M. "Childhood Schizophrenia Reconsidered." *Journal of Autism and Childhood Schizophrenia*, 1972, *2*, 315–337.

RUTTER, M. and L. LOCKYER. "A Five to Fifteen Year Follow-up Study of Infantile Psychosis—I. Description of Sample." *British Journal of Psychiatry*, 1967, *113*, 1169–1182.

SCHECHTER, M. D., SHURLEY, J T., TOUSSIENG, P. W., and W. J. MAIER. "Sensory Isolation Therapy of Autistic Children: A Preliminary Report." *Journal of Pediatrics*, 1969, *74*, 564–569.

SCHOPLER, E. "Early Infantile Autism and Receptor Processes." *Archives of General Psychiatry*, 1965, *13*, 327–335.

SCHOPLER, E. "Childhood Psychosis—Etiology and Autopsy." *Schizophrenia Bulletin*, 1976, *2*, 194–195.

SCHOPLER, E., and J. LOFTIN. "Thought Disorders in Parents of Psychotic Children: A Function of Test Anxiety." *Archives of General Psychiatry*, 1969, *20*, 174–181.

SINGER, M. and L. C. WYNNE. "Differentiating Characteristics of Parents of Childhood Schizophrenics, Childhood Neurotics, and Young Adult Schizophrenics." *American Journal of Psychiatry*, 1963, *120*, 234–243.

SZUREK, S. A., BERLIN, I. N., and M. J. BOATMAN. *Inpatient Care of the Psychotic Child.* Palo Alto, California: Science and Behavior Books, 1971.

TREFFERT, D. A. "Epidemiology of Infantile Autism." *Archives of General Psychiatry,* 1970, *22*, 431–438.

WALKER, H., and H. G. BIRCH. "Intellectual Patterning in Schizophrenic Children." *Journal of Autism and Childhood Schizophrenia,* 1974, *4*, 143–161.

WARD, A. "Early Infantile Autism: Diagnosis, Etiology, and Treatment." *Psychological Bulletin,* 1970, *73*, 350–362.

WERRY, J. S. "Childhood Psychosis." In Quay, H. D. and J. S. Werry (Eds.), *Psychopathological Disorders of Childhood.* New York: Wiley, 1972, pp. 83–121.

WING, J. K., O'CONNOR, N., and V. LOTTER. "Autistic Conditions in Childhood: A Survey in Middlesex." *British Medical Journal,* 1967, *3*, 389–392.

WING, L. "The Handicaps of Autistic Children: A Comparative Study." *Journal of Child Psychology and Psychiatry,* 1969, *10*, 1–40.

WOLF, M. M., RISLEY, T. R., and H. L. MEES. "Application of Operant Conditioning Procedures to the Behavior Problems of an Autistic Child." *Behavior Research and Therapy,* 1964, *1*, 305–312.

WYATT, R. J., MURPHY, D. L., BELLMAKER, R., COHEN, S., DONNELLY, C. H., and W. POLLIN. "Reduced Monoamine Oxidase Activity in Platelets: A Possible Genetic Marker for Vulnerability to Schizophrenia." *Science,* 1973, *170*, 916–918.

ZEVIN, B. "Family Communication with Schizophrenic and Nonschizophrenic Siblings." *Proceedings of the 81st Annual Convention of the American Psychology Association, Montreal, Canada,* 1973, *8*, 471–772.

ZIMMERMAN, E. and J. ZIMMERMAN. "The Alteration of Behavior in a Special Classroom Situation." *Journal of Experimental Analysis of Behavior,* 1962, *5*, 59–60.

Abnormalities of Middle Childhood:

language disorders, learning disabilities, and hyperkinesis

9

The period of childhood that broadly ranges from five through preadolescence is truly a time of remarkable growth, especially in the child's emotional, cognitive, and social functioning. It is also a time of transition for both parents and child in which the child's world is extended from the secure and familiar walls of the home to new situations and relationships. Parents transfer some of their child-rearing responsibilities primarily to the school, and to a lesser extent, to other community agencies. At the same time, children are called upon to acquire new skills and behaviors in order to cope with the demands of a more complex environment. The role of the school in the child's cognitive and social development cannot be overemphasized. However, the school is by no means an exclusive influence in shaping the child. Obviously the attitudes, values, and stimulation within the home, along with neighborhood peer relationships and participation in a variety of other outside activities also affect the development of the child.

The extent to which children successfully

adapt during the school years is not only dependent on the impact of new experiences, but to a greater degree, on the influence of many prior biological and environmental conditions. Antecedent events that are likely to lead to serious adjustment difficulties during the school years are numerous. To illustrate, let us consider a symbiotic mother-child relationship that produces intense anxiety in the child who is threatened by the prospect of separation from mother, or the shattered self-concept of the enuretic who has failed to achieve parental approval, or the slow and limited language development of the retardate. Without adequate physical and mental endowment, proper habit training, emotional gratification, encouragement for independence, and values that prompt academic and social achievement, the child cannot be expected to fly smoothly from the nest and soar to great heights. However, not all of the problems of the school years have their beginnings in early childhood. The enthusiasm of the normal child who eagerly looks forward to school may be quickly dampened and transformed to aversion by a hostile and rejecting teacher or by a humiliating event that results in prolonged peer criticism and alienation. It also may be dampened for those youngsters who are unaccustomed to sedentary and highly structured demands of the usual classroom setting. Without a sensitive teacher and a flexible school program, these children are likely to receive a disproportionate share of both negative attention and academic failures that almost always leads to self-doubt and feelings of inadequacy. The school's emphasis on academic achievement and competition is communicated early to students who, in turn, easily decipher the all too familiar code names given to groups of fast, intermediate, and slow learners (redbirds, bluebirds, and yellowbirds). At best, these conditions can serve to increase motivation and reward for those who are capable of succeeding, while they can heighten anxiety and failure for those who are not. Repeated failures to achieve often result in poor motivation, avoidance of academics, withdrawal and day dreaming, or acting-out behaviors that are designed to replace the ego gratification and positive support that are denied these youngsters. In addition, events that occur outside of the school, such as illness or death of a parent, marital discord, disruptions in family and/or peer relations, and social disappointments, may be sufficiently stressful to impede academic progress and personal adjustment.

It is during this period that previously tolerated or unnoticed behaviors, as well as newly acquired ones, surface as trouble signs that indicate some impairment of academic success and social adjustment. The behavioral possibilities are too numerous and varied to be organized along a single common feature other than the dimension of time. For this reason, we shall consider a sample of abnormal behaviors that are most frequently brought to the attention of professionals during the school years. More specifically, we shall discuss *language disorders, learning disabilities,* and the *hyperkinetic syndrome.*

Language Disorders

Language acquisition and the ability to speak in words and sentences distinguish human beings from all other living creatures. Normal speech emerges during the second year of life, following a period of spontaneous vocalizations of sounds known as babbling. Once the child begins to talk, language dramatically multiplies from a few spoken words at eighteen months to more than two thousand words at age five (Smith, 1926). At this point, the child is verbally fluent and capable of combining words into sentences in ways that reflect a mastery of the complex structure of language. Yet, ". . . language development is far from complete when the child reaches his fifth birthday" (Palermo and Molfese, 1972, p. 425).

In light of this rapid progress and because speech is so necessary for the multiple demands of daily living, it is not surprising to find that children with speech problems come to the attention of professionals at an earlier age (between four and five) than the referral age for most other forms of abnormal behavior (between eight and nine) (Chess and Rosenberg, 1974). There is also a higher frequency of speech disorders in boys (sex ratio of 3:1) as compared to non-language problems where boys exceed girls by a 2:1 ratio. Incidence estimates of speech problems in school populations and referrals to child guidance centers have been reported in the neighborhood of five to six percent, while the estimate jumped to twenty-four percent when referrals to a private practitioner from an upper-middle-class sample were tallied (Gilbert, 1957; Mysak, 1972; Chess and Rosenberg, 1974).

Speech is a complex function that is dependent on the integrity of the brain, auditory apparatus, and the anatomy of the many structures involved in the formation and production of speech, such as lips, tongue, palate, vocal chords, and so forth. Hearing is intimately related to speech in that a child who cannot hear either will be unable to speak or will show profound voice and articulation problems depending on the severity of the hearing loss and the age at which it occurs. For example, partial or complete deafness before age five will result in severe speech problems, even when the child is given extensive training. However, deafness that occurs after nine years of age will have less severe effects, although abnormalities of the voice are likely to be present (Bakwin and Bakwin, 1972). Anatomic defects such as *harelip* and *cleft palate* illustrate structural causes of speech disorders, because they prevent proper closure of the mouth in the formation of consonants and vowels.

Injuries and diseases of the brain also may result in speech disorders, although we should bear in mind that the term "brain damage" is too broad and heterogeneous to imply specific behavioral effects. Even in those instances where brain damage leads to speech problems, the consequences will differ as to what aspect of language is disabled. The mentally retarded may show delayed and slow speech development because of cognitive damage, while the cerebral palsied child may have articulation problems because of damage to the mus-

culature structure involved in the formation of words.

Aphasia (from the Greek, meaning "without speech") is one of the many possible outcomes of brain damage, although the neurological deficit often is unsubstantiated in children. It is a term used to designate an impairment of symbolic language, not only of speech, but also of the other language modalities (gestures and writing), and of comprehension of language. Aphasic children frequently manifest multiple problems that include perceptual, learning, behavioral, and emotional difficulties (Wood, 1964). But the child's ability to recover from aphasia resulting from injury to the speech area of the brain is amazing, especially as compared to the adult. The younger the child, the better the prognosis and recovery continues to be favorable until the early teen years. Permanent impairment is likely to occur after this age (Lenneberg, 1964, 1969). Childhood aphasia is the subject of considerable disagreement and confusion centering around the need to corroborate its neurological premise, and the imprecise terminology used to describe the specific impairments of the central language process (Perkins, 1977).

The literature dealing with the relationship between speech disorders and intelligence consistently indicates "that the lower the intelligence level, the greater incidence of defective speech" (Eisenson, 1965, p. 769). School children with speech problems are characteristically lower in intelligence than controls, and speech defects are more frequently found among mental retardates than among youngsters of normal intelligence. While the relationship between low intelligence and speech disorders is well established, it should not be taken to mean that speech problems are found only in retarded children. To the contrary, they can and do occur in children of all levels of intelligence.

If speech acquisition involves imitation and modeling, then problems of articulation and delayed speech surely can arise from faulty parental reinforcement patterns. Perhaps as a way of prolonging the period of infancy and maintaining dependency, some mothers reward their babies' use of nonverbal communication. Under these conditions, the children are rewarded for not speaking, since their needs are met promptly without the necessity for verbal language. It is also true that some mothers reinforce baby-talk, which increases the probability that the child will repeat lisps and other articulation errors. The fact that Irwin (1960) showed that vocabulary of one-year-old children can be significantly increased by reading to them suggests that some instances of delayed speech may arise in households in which there is insufficient verbal stimulation. In addition, emotional trauma, illness and hospitalization, birth of a sibling, parental rejection, and negativism are among the psychogenic factors implicated in speech disorders (Mysak, 1972).

Of the many possible types of speech disorders, only three will be singled out for discussion, primarily because *delayed speech, articulation problems,* and *stuttering* collectively represent more than eighty percent of all of the serious speech difficulties found in school age children ("Need for Speech Pathologists," 1959).

Delayed Speech

For most parents, the emergence of developmental milestones—the first smile, the first step, the first tooth, or the first spoken word—are eagerly greeted as reassuring

signs that their babies are healthy and progressing normally. We tend to regard acceleration in these growth patterns as reflecting superiority, and slowness as some measure of mental or biological inferiority. Inasmuch as there is considerable variability within the normal developmental limits of speech acquisition, simple two-word utterances may not appear before the child is thirty months old. However, failure to talk beyond this age or by the time the child is three is sufficient indication of an abnormal delay in speech (Worster-Drought, 1968). Delayed speech may also refer to speech that appears within the normal age range, but in which there is very slow progress in new word acquisition and in the formation of sentences. Either delayed onset or retarded progress requires prompt and careful evaluation to determine the basis of the problem and what can be done about it.

Etiological Considerations

Intellectual evaluation of children with delayed speech is of primary importance, inasmuch as over half of the cases are caused by or associated with mental retardation (Bakwin and Bakwin, 1972). Hearing also should be tested early in the evaluation process, because we know that children who suffer a significant hearing loss will have either or both delayed onset of speech and slow language development. It is evident that a severe hearing loss following the normal onset of speech results in the gradual deterioration of the child's speech not only in acquisition, but also in articulation, quality of tone, and loudness (Davis and Silverman, 1970).

The suggestion that auditory memory is related to or accounts for some instances of delayed speech has been seriously entertained by some writers, although the results of controlled investigations have been equivocal (Eisenson, 1965). Operationally, auditory memory is studied by the oral presentation of a series (of varying length) of numbers, words, sentences, or nonsense syllables that the subject is asked to recall immediately or at some later time. Eisenson (1965) posited that many children with delayed speech, particularly those who are brain damaged, are impaired in their ability to handle the complex process of analyzing auditory sequences and reproducing them from memory to the listener in an intelligible form. Other neurological deficits (as noted earlier) can result in delayed speech and language retardation such as brain damage that seriously affect hearing or impair intellectual functioning.

If environmental factors play an influential role in speech disorders, they are probably most significant in delayed speech and articulation problems. According to Emerick and Hatton (1974), "the quantity and quality of language stimulation, motivation to speak, number of siblings, and order of birth, have long been cited as critical to the development of language in the child. . . . A child apparently is capable of learning the basic systems of his language under, or perhaps, in spite of, the most adverse learning conditions. However, he will probably show the effects of his experience in his vocabulary, grammar, and articulation" (p. 107). Perhaps this view will permit us to interpret in another light the well-established findings that ghetto and socioeconomically deprived children have impoverished speech, poor language comprehension, limited vocabularies, and use immature and incorrect grammar (Gerber and Hertel, 1969; Perkins, 1977). These language deficiencies are real if we apply middle-class caucasian standards as the basic yardstick. However, as Baratz (1968, 1969) noted, the speech of lower-class black children is not deficient but, instead, reflective of their subculture. These children are not impaired or impoverished in their ability to acquire language; to the contrary, they demonstrate that they can and do learn a complicated language and structure that permits them to communicate effectively within their own subculture. In this connection, ghetto children are taught a new linguistic system, that of middle-class society, when they begin their formal schooling, which, in effect, requires them to be bilingual. Lahey (1973) discusses in greater detail these issues and surveys some recent studies that use positive reinforcement and modeling to alter various aspects of the speaking behavior of minority children.

Therapeutic Approaches

Behavior modification procedures have been employed with severely and moderately retarded children, some of whom were brain damaged, to teach them grammatical rules (Guess, Sailor, Rutherford, and Baer, 1968; Baer and Guess, 1971). By means of imitation and differential reinforcement, it was demonstrated that retardates learned the correct grammatical usage of the training examples, and they generalized appropriately from this limited experience to new instances that were not part of the original practice material. Although only moderately successful, behavior modification has been used to increase the retarded language development of severely psychotic children (see Chapter 8). In addition, verbal stimulation, instructions to parents in encouraging verbalizations from the child, and family and child psychotherapy have been suggested as remedial approaches to children with delayed speech.

Problems of Articulation

Imprecise production of speech sounds frequently are a major characteristic of many types of speech disorders. For this reason alone, articulatory problems are the most prevalent of all speech aberrations, representing more than eighty percent of the cases treated by speech therapists in the public schools (Bingham, VanHuttam, Paulk, and Taussig, 1961). Defective articulation and the degree of imprecision in producing speech sounds is determined by listening to phonetic behavior. The smallest unit of distinguishable speech sounds is a *phoneme,* which serves as a standard against which articulatory errors can be compared and corrected. According to Perkins (1977), there are four types of faulty articulation in which phonemes are either omitted, substituted, distorted, or added.

With the exception of the high incidence of faulty articulation found in mental retardates, intelligence at other levels bears no significant relationship to articulatory proficiency (Winitz, 1969). However, based on a careful review of the literature, Winitz noted a positive relationship between defective articulation and academic achievement, grades, as well as reading and spelling performance. Additionally, evidence suggests that children with articulatory difficulties show slower development of vocabulary and verbal output, and they tend to be restricted and underdeveloped in the way they arrange words to form phrases or sentences ("Human Communication and Its Disorders: An Overview," 1969; Shriner, Holloway, and Daniloff, 1969; Templin, 1973). The evidence is such that at this time

it is not possible to determine whether inadequate articulation impairs the development of vocabulary, syntax, and educational performance, or if these are simply part of a more pervasive symptom picture associated with some language or learning disorder. The fact that studies consistently report a higher incidence of articulatory deficits in low socioeconomic level children is not surprising in that subculture speech sounds are likely to differ from the standard phonemes used to determine misarticulations (Adler, 1973). Winitz (1969) suggested that this finding is explicable on the basis of the differences in language stimulation and reinforcement between socioeconomic levels.

Etiological Considerations

Problems of articulation are attributable to a number of possible causal factors, the most obvious of which are those physiological, neurological, and sensory conditions that hamper proficiency in the formation of speech sounds. Children who have physiological abnormalities, such as hare lip, cleft palate, dental obstructions, and tongue malformations, are structurally impaired in ways that make normal movement of the speech apparatus difficult. Central nervous system injury or damage that affects hearing, neuromuscular control of the speech mechanism, or respiratory regulation (resulting in either insufficient air supply for speaking or inefficient control of speech sounds) are well-established determinants of articulatory errors (Hardy, 1968; Darley, Aronson, and Brown, 1969). Anyone who has received an injection of Novocaine to reduce the discomfort of dental drilling or extraction can recall the loss of sensation in the tongue, the lips, and part of the face that temporarily reduced their proficiency in articulation. Moreover, auditory acuity and discrimination among pitches of tones, vowels, and consonants, and complex patterns at some level are necessary for accurate articulation. Unfortunately, at present the research evidence is too inconclusive and incomplete to provide specific data as to the precise level of acuity and discrimination needed to enable proper articulation.

At the same time, there are many articulatory problems for which no organic cause can be found. These instances are considered to result from faulty learning in which poor speech models, low levels of stimulation and motivation, or some underlying personality disorders are viewed as prime contributors (Goodstein, 1962).

Therapeutic Approaches

Most articulatory problems are appropriately treated by a trained speech therapist, since these speech difficulties do not ordinarily give rise to serious emotional or personality consequences. A review of the literature revealed no consistent evidence that either parents of children with cleft palates or the children themselves manifest emotional disturbances to any substantial degree (Goodstein, 1969). Whenever social and personal adjustment problems are associated with misarticulations, speech therapy and psychological intervention may be an effective remedial combination. While it is beyond the scope of our discussion to consider the specific treatment approaches used by speech therapists, it is important to note that learning principles have been increasingly applied to the construction of techniques employed to modify articulatory problems. Essentially, the procedure involves the same set of steps (or some variant) that are applicable to the modifica-

tion of a wide variety of unwanted behaviors.

In order to change behavior, it is necessary to select an unwanted behavior (the *target*) that can be reliably observed and manipulated (increased or decreased). Then instructional or other cues should be provided to elicit the desired response, and consequences should be found that will strengthen it and weaken the target behavior. Records of response frequencies prior to, during, and following the intervention must be kept in order to assess the effectiveness of the modification. Those readers interested in more detailed information are referred to two recent books that review and describe behavior modification approaches to articulatory and other language disorders (Lahey, 1973; Wolfe and Goulding, 1973).

Stuttering

Although stuttering, or stammering, is easily recognized by most laypeople, it is a condition that specialists in speech pathology find difficult to define because the boundary between stuttering and dysfluence in normal speech (irregularities in the flow of speech) is ambiguous. In fact, the task of making auditory judgments about stuttering is highly unreliable since listeners (judges) disagree among themselves more than half of the time (Perkins, 1977). Nevertheless, we shall, for our purposes, use the term "stuttering" to refer to a particular breakdown in speech fluency characterized by *blocking* (inability to articulate), *repetition,* and *prolongation of speech sounds.*

Blocking is said to be stressful to the stutterer (Jones, 1970, pp. 336–358), as well as a possible consequence of strong anxiety for even normal speakers (Herbert, 1974).

It occurs most often in the first words, phrases, or sentences of speech as is the case with repetitions. The fact that repetitions typically are found in normal speech of young children makes it all the more understandable that the early diagnosis of stuttering on this basis is difficult. In contrast, the infrequent occurrence of prolongation of vowels in normal speakers of any age may, if present in young children, be of diagnostic significance.

Stuttering begins between the ages of two and five, and almost always before eight. It occurs more frequently in boys, with estimated sex ratios ranging from 3:1 to as high as 8:1 (Jones, 1970; Bakwin and Bakwin, 1972), and it is extremely rare in adult females. Socioeconomic factors and intelligence are unrelated to stuttering, although vast differences among cultures seem to be evident (Stewart, 1971). Yet, stuttering is not universal, since it is unknown in undeveloped areas of the world and among the American Indians. Persistent stuttering is found in only one to two percent of the population, while transient stuttering appears in four or five percent (Jones, 1970; Bakwin and Bakwin, 1972). Fortunately, most cases of stuttering are temporary in that more than fifty percent recover by puberty without treatment and eighty percent have normal speech by the time they reach their late teens (Glasner and Rosenthal, 1957; Sheehan and Martyn, 1966, 1967). No satisfactory explanation exists for these findings, although the gradual nature of recovery tends to support a maturational view so popularly expressed about many other forms of abnormal behavior in children with the pronouncement, "he will outgrow it." Happily this seems to be the case for four out of every five stutterers.

Etiological Considerations

While the literature on stuttering is neither sparse nor wanting for causal hypotheses, as yet it has provided no single explanation that is acceptable. The search for biological or constitutional (including genetic) factors has focused on the exploration of difference between stutterers and nonstutterers in cerebral dominance (neither of the two cortical hemispheres are alleged to be dominant in stutterers, resulting in poor synchrony and control of the central mechanisms of speech), in metabolic organization, in sensory feedback, in EEG recordings, and in air and bone conduction of the auditory mechanism, among others ("Human Communication and Its Disorders: An Overview," 1969; Travis, 1971; Perkins, 1977). The data thus far accumulated, although inconsistent, have failed in any substantial way to provide confirmation for a biological view of stuttering.

Psychogenic interpretations of stuttering also have been plentiful in the literature. One large segment of these studies has its origin in the premise that stuttering is a symptom of a basic neurotic disorder. This view assumed a psychodynamic orientation in which stuttering was a primary expression of anxiety that resulted from unconscious conflicts. In addition, it was conjectured that feelings of embarrassment, failure, and lowered self-esteem associated with stuttering would further enhance the development of neurotic reactions and defenses (Barbara, 1959). However, neither aspect of this position is supported by the research evidence. Although considerable effort has been expended toward this end, there are neither special personality patterns that can reliably identify stuttering children, nor indications that neurosis occurs more frequently among stutterers than nonstutterers (Goodstein, 1962; Sheehan, 1962).

This is apparently true, in spite of the fact that Johnson (1961), one of the most distinguished researchers in this area, believed that parents of stutterers were more anxious about the speech and other aspects of their children's behavior and tended to be more unrealistic in their demands. The inclination of these parents to be overprotective, critical, perfectionistic, and covertly rejecting has been reported by others, but there is no support for the view that parents of stutterers are grossly maladjusted or emotionally disturbed (Perkins, 1977).

At present, the most viable viewpoint seems to be that stuttering is learned, although different theorists have not always emphasized similar environmental conditions and learning paradigms. Johnson and his colleagues (Johnson, 1956; Johnson, Brown, Curtis, Edney, and Keaster, 1956) posited that dysfluencies occur in the normal speech of children, which are reacted to by parents of stutterers with negativism and an unrealistic expectation of fluency. Through this type of interaction, stuttering becomes a learned avoidance reaction in which the child struggles to avoid all instances of dysfluencies and subsequent negative reactions from parents. Failure to achieve fluent speech is inevitable, and this in turn heightens anxiety and the likelihood of more interruptions in the flow of speech. Cast in a somewhat different light, Sheehan (1953, 1968) argues that stuttering represents an approach-avoidance conflict in which the child vacillates between the opposing needs to speak and to avoid speaking. The avoidance stems from the embarrassment and other unpleasant feelings that the child associates with previous failures in speech fluency. Probably the most sophisticated learning view of stuttering is the *two-process theory* of Brutten and Shoemaker (1967, 1969, p. 51). Their view holds that the primary speech disorganization is acquired through classically conditioned anxiety, while the secondary aspects of stuttering (eye-blinks, wrinkling of the nose) are instrumentally conditioned. Therefore, in order to modify stuttering, both classes of responses must be extinguished.

Therapeutic Approaches

Treatment plans and procedures for stutterers are numerous and diverse, so much so that an extensive review is beyond our scope. Consequently, we shall consider only a sample of the major approaches. Van Riper (1963) proposed a program that combines psychotherapy and speech practice under conditions of progressive stress (similar to desensitization), which effectively reduced or eliminated stuttering in fifty percent of the cases that were followed up five years after therapy. A wide variety of delayed auditory feedback techniques in which very brief delays in hearing one's own voice to improve or eliminate (during practice) speech dysfluencies have been employed both to study organic components of the disorder and to treat the condition (Jones, 1970). In general, the results using this approach have been disappointing, although a few stutterers have shown dramatic improvement.

Beginning with the work of Flanagan and his associates (Flanagan, Goldiamond, and Azrin, 1958), principles derived from operant conditioning have been shown to modify stuttering behavior. Early studies demonstrated that the frequency of stuttering can be operantly manipulated. However, as Martin and Ingham (1973) conclude following their critical review of the literature:

The reports of response contingent stuttering therapy programs of techniques reviewed above are far from satisfactory. There is evidence that the procedures may affect changes within some therapy programs, but the data are difficult to evaluate. Most reports are premature and do not include carefully obtained carryover or follow-up data (p. 126).

For the long-term chronic stutterer whom Jones (1970) regards as primarily neurotic, psychotherapy along with some technique to interrupt the persistence of stuttering are recommended. Essentially, these individuals need to deal with the anxiety and fear of failure associated with their long history of stuttering, and to have the opportunity of resolving conflicts that have diminished self-confidence and impaired their social adjustment.

Learning Disabilities

Herman is a nine-year-old boy of average intelligence who is of great concern to his third-grade teacher. He is unable to read beyond the first-grade level, and his writing is poor and rather uncoordinated. Although his reading difficulties had been noted earlier, he now shows a reluctance to read aloud in class or work on improving his proficiency in this area. Instead, he is a disruptive influence by talking incessantly, poking his classmates, and refusing to remain in his seat for any prolonged period of time. Herman is easily distracted by the sights and sounds around him, and seems to have attentional and concentrational difficulties. Except for arithmetic where he clearly achieves at a level better than most of his peers, his teacher finds little in his performance that she can reward. Because Herman is clumsy and awkward, he is often excluded from playground athletic games that require good motor coordination. Numerous school conferences with Herman's parents and the likelihood of his having to repeat the third grade finally resulted in a referral to a psychologist.

Every elementary classroom teacher and practicing clinician recognizes Herman's story as representative of a sizeable number of school-age youngsters with learning difficulties. Learning disability is only one of many labels used interchangeably as a large umbrella that refers to a discrepancy between anticipated and actual academic achievement in children who otherwise are not handicapped in intelligence, sensory processes, emotional stability, or opportunities to learn. Yet, there is a good deal of confusion and disagreement about which label to use and which criteria to set for judging children as falling within the category. This is evident by the fact that there are more than forty terms used in the literature to refer to essentially the same condition, although one is hard pressed to comprehend how such diverse labels as learning disorders, learning dysfunction, minimal brain damage, minimal cerebral dysfunction, or perceptual problem can have the same connotation for classification, etiology, or remediation (McDonald, 1968).

Most writers and school systems exclude the mentally retarded in defining learning disabilities, although this may be based more on practical considerations than on ideological grounds. If the definition of learning disabilities implies a discrepancy between expected (based on the child's assets) and actual achievement in one or more specific areas of learning, then it follows logically that the retarded child can also have a learning disability in which such disparities may be present. Admittedly, it is much more difficult to establish evidence for specific discrepancies in retarded children because of the pervasive and generalized effect of mental retardation on so many areas of functioning, and because the discrepancy is likely to be smaller (perhaps imperceptible) as the expected capacity decreases in measurable units.

It is also customary to exclude children who are primarily emotionally disturbed from the rubric of learning disability, although the distinction between primary and secondary emotional problems is sometimes difficult to make, and most observers believe that learning disabilities are almost always accompanied by some emotional difficulties (Giffin, 1968; Harris, 1970). Efforts to set learning disabilities apart from psychotic and severely neurotic conditions are based on both practical and substantive considerations. There is marked dissimilarity between these groups in that children with severe emotional disorders are impaired and disturbed in many areas of functioning, whereas those with learning disorders are essentially intact except for a deficit in one or more of the basic learning processes (McCarthy, 1971).

Before the 1960s, relatively little interest was noted in the area of learning disabilities, except for some research on childhood aphasia and other language disturbances, and some remedial reading programs spotted in strong public school systems around the country. Since that time, specialists in speech, education, medicine, and psychology have made major contributions to the area, which were to some extent prompted by the interest of an aroused and supportive citizenry. Today we have public funds supporting the training of specialists and enabling public schools to establish special educational programs for children with learning disabilities. Accurate incidence

figures are difficult to obtain because of the controversy that continues over which term to use and which children appropriately fit the category. Nevertheless, estimates are available that range from five to twenty percent of grade-school children who show multiple or single signs of learning disability (Wender, 1971), and most observers agree that learning disability represents a large, if not the largest, referral problem in school-aged youngsters (Clarizio and McCoy, 1970; Wender, 1971).

Reading Difficulties

Achievement in reading below the child's level of accomplishment in other academic areas or below the potential for learning in general is undoubtedly the most frequent of the specific learning disabilities. This reason alone would justify its consideration here. But, at a different level of discourse, reading disabilities also illustrate the similarity of issues and areas of controversy that are so characteristic of the entire field of learning disabilities. Disparities in incidence estimates, definition of terms, etiological views, and remedial approaches are found in both learning disorders in general and reading difficulties in specific.

Authoritative sources estimate that more than ten percent of the school population in the United States experience reading problems, and at least one source believes that it may be as high as twenty to forty percent ("Reading Disorders in the United States," 1969; Goldberg and Schiffman, 1972). Like so many other disorders of childhood, reading problems are found more frequently in boys than in girls with estimates ranging from 3:1 to 5:1 (Goldenson, 1957; Myklebust and Johnson, 1962). Interesting, but somewhat puzzling, is the finding that reading problems are ten times more prevalent in Western countries than in Japan (Makita, 1968).

While these incidence figures tell us too little about the criteria used to establish the disability or the differential effectiveness of school reading programs across the country, they do impress us with the enormity and seriousness of the problem. Early acquisition of reading proficiency is a necessary skill for satisfactory progress in most other areas of study, and an important determinant of later vocational, economic, and social prospects. Poor readers make poor students who face limited vocational choices and restricted income potential. While cause and effect is not clear, the fact remains that juvenile delinquency and other forms of antisocial behaviors are highly associated with reading difficulties (Margolin, Roman, and Harari, 1955). The repeated experiences of failure in reading generalizes to other academic areas and contributes to increasing feelings of inadequacy, alienation, and frustration. Acting-out behaviors and conduct problems in the classroom may provide emotional outlets and gratification of attentional needs. Should this behavioral pattern be reinforced in the absence of other successes, then it is possible for it to become dominant. In this connection, there is evidence that reading failures become chronic and difficult to modify (fifteen percent success) if the disability is not identified and treated before the fifth grade. In contrast, more than eighty percent of children diagnosed and remediated as reading problems in the second grade were able within two years to read at their normal grade level (Schiffman and Clemmens, 1966).

Since Kussmaul (1877) used the term "word blindness" to refer to an inability to read in the absence of any demonstrable impairment of vision, speech, or intelligence, a wide array of labels have appeared in the literature to designate the same or a similar phenomenon. In 1937, Orton (1937) introduced *dyslexia* to describe significant underachieving specific to reading (much below the level of accomplishments in other academic areas) in which there is a persistent tendency to reverse letters and words, and a general confusion among words. Other terms such as primary reading disability, specific developmental dyslexia, congenital word blindness, developmental lag, and specific reading disability have been used interchangeably and synonomously with dyslexia. Generally speaking, dyslexia now is employed to designate those children of average or slightly below average intelligence with specific retardation in reading who have not been deprived of educational opportunities, or who do not show any gross evidence of either sensory or neurological impairment.

Typically, dyslexic children have difficulty comprehending written language and competently managing other language functions of spelling, writing, and speech. They may be left-handed or ambidextrous, and they are inclined to be poorly coordinated, awkward, and clumsy. Before beginning school, many are considered intellectually bright, an observation that is periodically supported by their good verbal responses to classroom discussions. Their initial grades in arithmetic are high, but they are likely to decline as reading proficiency becomes more essential in working written problems and in taking examinations. They frequently show emotional disturbances as a reaction to repeated failures and a lowering of self-esteem.

Two primary types of difficulties have been suggested, each involving impairment in either the auditory or visual modality (Johnson and Myklebust, 1967; Clark,

1973). Dyslexic children with auditory defects have trouble learning to read, because they are unable to develop phonetic skills. Auditory perceptions are made, but some defect in the neurological pathway prevents the information from being integrated in the language area of the brain. Thus, these children are said to have poor auditory association with what they see. As a group they are more difficult to remediate than those youngsters with visual defects, especially when auditory spatial perceptions are disturbed. In contrast, youngsters with visual defects typically have phonetic skills, but they are apt to have problems in spelling; in reading maps, graphs, floor plans; or in dealing with spatial symbols necessary for proficiency in mathematics. They often omit letters in reading a word that may change its meaning, such as "mit for might." Recent research has demonstrated significant differences between dyslexic and normal children in visual information processing, in memory for visual information, and in the perception and organization of broken-up words embedded in ambiguous stimuli (Stanley and Hall, 1973; Feild and Feild, 1974).

Etiological Considerations

It is apparent that reading problems much like the broader category of learning disabilities represent heterogeneous conditions for which there is no single cause. Proponents of a genetic view find support in data from twin and family studies that indicate a high prevalence of reading problems in monozygotic twins and in close relatives (parents and siblings) of dyslexic children (Hallgren, 1950; Tenhunen, Widholm, and Hortling, 1967; Symmes and Rapoport, 1972; Matheny and Dolan, 1974). But as we have noted in previous discussions of genetics, data of this sort can be interpreted as equally supportive of either a genetic or social transmission view.

Although evidence of gross neurological involvement or impairment is not usually discernible, there is a persistent assumption by a large segment of contemporary writers that implicates brain dysfunction as the etiological basis of reading and other learning disabilities. This view excludes easily detectable brain damage, which may be responsible for such conditions as cerebral palsy, epilepsy, mental retardation, or sensory disorders. Instead, it refers to instances where no obvious signs of brain pathology are evident, and where inferences are made from certain behaviors that presumably reflect minimal neurological impairment or brain dysfunction. Gross motor functioning such as sitting, crawling, and walking develop normally, while problems in fine motor coordination are likely to be evident. Handedness is often established late, riding a bicycle is extremely difficult, as is fastening buttons, cutting with scissors, or tying shoelaces. In forming fine motor acts, these children are awkward and clumsy to the extent that they require and usually receive parental assistance. Sharp and sudden mood swings ranging from timidity to violent emotional outbursts, along with hyperactivity, distractability, and short attention span are additional characteristics of these youngsters. They have few, if any, friends, either because they have run them off through their display of emotional instability and hyperactivity, or because other children are forbidden to play with them (Goldberg and Schiffman, 1972).

Evidence supportive of this view is indirect and inconclusive. Prematurity and complications of birth and birth weight are among the early and potential signs of neurological impairment that have been

shown to be related to later academic problems in more of these children than normal
controls (Wender, 1971). However, it is not
at all clear why the vast majority of these
high-risk infants never become learning disabled. As noted by Grossman (1966):

Actually, there is no syndrome, no aggregate of
neurological signs, that can be correlated with
any specific learning and/or behavior disorder.
Indeed, many youngsters with profound aberrations of motor functioning do well in school, in
their studies and in their interpersonal relationships (p. 63).

There are those who regard minimal brain
dysfunction as an unproven and strictly inferred diagnosis that has little meaning and
application for educational remediation.
In this connection, the extensive study of
Paine and his associates (Paine, Werry, and
Quay, 1971) showed that minimal cerebral
dysfunction is not a homogeneous diagnostic condition, but essentially a descriptive
label for a diverse set of neurological, behavioral, and cognitive dysfunctions.

Satz (Satz, Radin, and Ross, 1971; Satz
and Ross, 1973) and his associates favor
the view that dyslexia is a maturational lag
in brain development that differentially
impedes progress in those skills that are in
primary ascendancy at different times in
the child's life. For example, the skills that
normally develop early will be delayed in
young children with maturational lags,
while the skills that show a slower rate of
development will be delayed in older
youngsters who have this maturational immaturity. Since reading proficiency is dependent on the prior development of perceptual discrimination and analysis, according to this view, a lag in the maturation of
the brain should be evident early in poor
perceptual functioning. Moreover, measures
of these behaviors should be predictive of

subsequent reading disabilities. In a recent
report of a two-year follow-up study of almost 500 kindergarten boys who were initially given an extensive developmental and
neuropsychological test battery, Satz and
Friel (1974) obtained data that supported
their theory.

Another view implicates the long-term
effects of nutritional and environmental
deprivation as sufficiently potent to produce
neurological dysfunction (Hallahan and
Cruickshank, 1973). Inasmuch as nutrition
is a basic determinant of growth and development, it should also affect the maturation of higher brain functions. For the human infant, the first six months of life is
probably the most critical as a nutritional
period, because it is during this time that
maximal postnatal brain-cell division occurs. Of equal significance is the maternal,
sensory, and environmental deprivation
that some writers suggest can produce
neurologic deficits or a nondeveloping
nervous system capable of producing learning disabilities (Grotberg, 1970).

The psychodynamic influence of Freud
highlighted intrapsychic conflicts and motivational variables as important determinants of reading and other learning disabilities. Clinical reports in which inhibition
of curiosity, repression of scoptophilic
impulses (wishes to forbidden and anxiety-
laden events), fantasies of aggression, and
family tendencies to deny and distort the external reality, among other fanciful notions,
have been generated as untested causes of
learning problems (Kessler, 1966; Heineke,
1972). More empirically oriented work has
shown that academic underachievers as compared to controls have poor self-concepts
and are more hostile toward their environment (Shaw, 1968). It has also been found
that boys with learning difficulties experi-

enced more specific emotional traumas, but these findings were so general that they would be difficult to replicate (Brodie and Winterbottom, 1967). Families of under-achievers tend not to place a high value on formal learning for their children, and they tend to show less mutual acceptance among family members, less sharing and communication, less awareness of each other, and less satisfaction in their family relationships (Morrow, 1970).

In general, the evidence for a psychogenic view of learning disabilities is inconclusive, imprecise, and not any more convincing than that which favors a biological position. While clinicians believe that emotional factors play an important role in many instances of disturbed learning, the ultimate question of demonstrating their role as etiological variables is still very much an empirical matter.

Therapeutic Approaches

The heterogeneity of terminology and of etiological possibilities in the area of learning disabilities is only exceeded by the diversity of remedial approaches suggested in the literature. As a matter of fact, clinical reports and testimonials can be found lauding the effectiveness of almost every treatment method from psychodynamically oriented psychotherapy, to special training in the development of perceptual and perceptual motor skills, to behavior modification, to educational remedies, and to chemotherapy. Heinicke (1972) cited a number of his own studies using psycho-analytic psychotherapy, along with a review of other investigations that employed remedial education with children who had reading disabilities. He found that both types of treatment tended to improve read-ing, although the gains were not sustained after treatment was terminated.

A variety of special training programs designed to facilitate perceptual skills and the neurological organization necessary for learning in general, and reading in particular, have received widespread popularity and recognition. The notable contributions of Kephart, Getman, Barsch, and Frostig, along with the controversial work of Doman and Delacato, share (with slight variations) the assumption that early motor development is necessary for normal perceptual development and for later emergence of conceptual abilities in children (Hallahan and Cruickshank, 1973). Doman and Delacato asserted that brain damage or "poor neurological organization" was responsible for most learning disabilities (Doman, Spitz, Zucman, Delacato, and Doman, 1960). Their view and training procedures, which have been negatively evaluated, relied heavily on outdated concepts of localization of function within the brain and hemispheric dominance (Robins and Glass, 1969). Training consisted of practice in specific motor patterns to (1) stimulate various areas of the brain; (2) impose hemispheric dominance; and (3) give carbon dioxide to increase blood circulation in the brain.

The use of drugs in the treatment of learning disabilities is complex and perplexing because of the heterogeneity inherent in the disorder, and the variable and sometimes unknown effects that drugs have on children. According to Goldberg and Schiffman (1972), a drug such as Dilantin is best used with children who have minimal neurological signs and abnormal EEG tracings, while ritalin is recommended for those who are both learning disabled and hyperactive. For emotionally disturbed

children, thorazine may help to reduce anxiety and increase learning. Stimulant drugs
such as the amphetamines may be useful
with children who have both behavioral
and learning difficulties, but these should
not be prescribed beyond the age of twelve.
Barbiturates and phenothiazines should not
be used because they are likely to depress
learning and contribute to a decline in intellectual functioning. Moreover, the following caution should be sounded whenever
drugs are used:

Laymen and professional people alike will do
well, in their involvement in the learning problems of children, to be more aware of the potential dangers in administering drugs to children.
The indiscriminate and unsupervised administration of tranquilizers in the home or classroom
to children who manifest behavioral and/or learning problems is a form of Russian roulette (Goldberg and Schiffman, 1972, p. 154).

Although behavior modification has
been widely employed as a technique in the
teaching and management of children in
the classroom, there are relatively few studies available that have involved either a
substantial number of subjects with specific learning disabilities or follow-up data.
The evidence of the effectiveness of either
a token economy procedure or positive reinforcers has not been impressive in demonstrating reading improvement in children
with reading problems (Staats, Minke,
Goodwin, and Landeen, 1967; Hewett, Taylor, and Artuso, 1969).

The Hyperkinetic Child

Beth was five-and-a-half years old at the time her
parents arranged for her evaluation at a guidance
clinic. The parents noted that they had considerable difficulty in disciplining her and that
similar problems were reported by her kindergarten teacher. The teacher also observed that

Beth was easily distracted, inattentive, hyperactive, and impaired in visual-motor coordination, raising the possibility of a perceptual
problem.

Beth was the oldest of three, and she came from
a lower-middle-class background. Mother's pregnancy with Beth went quite well, but the labor
and delivery were difficult in that labor lasted
about twenty hours and forceps were necessary
to deliver the child. She was born with the umbilical cord wrapped around her neck and she
was slightly blue at birth (indicating anoxia).
She was in intensive care for the first 48 hours
of her life. Her development proceeded at a
slower than average rate; she was unable to sit
unaided until she was nine months. She crawled
at thirteen months and walked at nineteen
months. While she spoke (single words) by twenty
months, she did not speak in sentences until
she was thirty-three months. Toilet training was
difficult and completed at three years. However,
mother reported that she (Beth) continues to wet
the bed on infrequent occasions. When she was
two years old, there were four separate times
that she fell on her head, but she never lost consciousness or evidenced any symptoms following
the accidents.

Mother reported that Beth would not follow her
instructions, and that she was frequently given
to temper tantrums primarily when Beth was required to do something that she did not want
to do. Threats, shouting, and spankings apparently did nothing to change Beth's behavior.
The child was extremely active and never played
in one place for any length of time. She tired
quickly of whatever activity she was involved
in, and as she moved from one thing to another
she left a litter of toys and objects which she
refused to pick up. Beth's constant penchant
for getting into trouble through overactivity, short
attention span, frequent temper tantrums, and re-
fusals to respond to parental directions tended
to place a heavy strain on her interactions with
members of her family.

In school, Beth was overactive, highly distractible,
and unable to persist in an activity for any length
of time. Her teacher noted that she tended to
run into or over objects that were in her way,
and that her performance on perceptual motor
tasks was well below the average (cutting and

pasting, drawing, building objects with blocks, and copying letters or numbers).

A neurological examination revealed a normal EEG, and no evidence of either generalized or localized abnormalities in brain functioning. Reflex development and motor coordination were below age level, but not considered grossly abnormal. On the basis of her difficulty in fine motor coordination and in perceptual tasks, the neurologist concurred with the diagnosis of minimal brain damage (Excerpts from Leon, 1974, pp. 35–42).

Children like Beth stand out in a crowd because their activity level and their disruptive behaviors demand attention and usually elicit negative responses from others. They are management problems wherever they are, be it at home or in school, and they require constant supervision because they never seem to respond favorably to corrective measures. Although Beth is clearly hyperactive, the nature of her problem and what to do about it are complex issues that have been the subject of considerable clinical and research interest and controversy.

The term *hyperactivity* has been used for a *symptom* describing heightened activity level, or more often for a *syndrome* that collectively reflects a specific disease (Ross and Ross, 1976). It falls short as a purely quantitative measure of behavior, since norms for children's activity level are virtually nonexistent, and because children vary considerably in activity output within themselves across different situations and among themselves in specific situations (Rapoport and Benoit, 1975; Schleifer, Weiss, Cohen, Elman, Cvejic, and Kruger, 1975). To date, there are only a few studies that report data on activity level and restlessness in hyperkinetic children who are otherwise physically and intellectually normal (Pope, 1970; Sykes, 1971). Pope meas-

ured activity level by means of a device (accelerometer) worn on the wrist and ankle that reliably recorded leg and arm movement. She found that greater locomotor and total motor activity along with shorter attention span characterized hyperkinetic children. Moreover, her results suggested that excessive activity in the hyperactive child is specific to a situation (found only on difficult tasks) rather than general to all situations. The other study used a stabilimetric cushion (a device to measure motor activity while the subject is stationary) to measure restlessness, and to show that hyperkinetic children were significantly more restless than the controls. These studies not only indicated differences in motor activity between hyperactive and normal children, but also empirically suggested for the first time that the type and amount of activity is influenced greatly by the specific situation.

Even more unsatisfactory is the use of hyperactivity for a clinical syndrome, since whether the symptoms form a unitary dimension or reflect a common etiology is questionable (Werry, 1968). At one time, children who are persistently overactive, distractable, impulsive, and emotionally excitable were thought to be neurologically impaired or brain damaged (Strauss and Lehtinen, 1947). However, more recent research has shown that this hyperkinetic behavior pattern is neither an inevitable or even a likely consequence of brain pathology, and that the syndrome is often seen in children who show no history or clinical evidence of brain injury (Chess, 1960; Ernhart, Graham, Eichman, Marshall, and Thurston, 1963; Schulman, Kaspar, and Thorne, 1965; Stewart, Pitts, Craig, and Dieruf, 1966; Paine, Werry and Quay, 1968; Sroufe, 1975). Moreover, Ross and Ross (1976) make the excellent observation that

. . . there are many statements in the literature accompanied by extensive research evidence that support the view that hyperactivity is a non-specific symptom occurring in a variety of medical and behavioral disorders and associated with a heterogeneous group of etiological factors. Yet, *for the most part,* research on pharmocologic, behavioral, and educational intervention has treated hyperactive children as a homogeneous group of subjects. As the label *hyperactive child syndrome* is commonly used it implies that there is *one* kind of hyperactive child, a belief that has been detrimental to progress in research on and treatment of hyperactivity (p. 11).

As a syndrome, hyperactivity has been known by various interchangeable labels such as hyperkinetic child, hyperkinesis, hyperactive child syndrome, minimal brain dysfunction, minimal brain damage, and even learning disability. None of these should be taken to imply a specific etiology. Instead, the behavioral pattern should be viewed as arising from a variety of causative factors. Because hyperactivity, short attention span, and restlessness often accompany learning problems, some writers have tended to include the syndrome under the general rubric of learning disabilities (Keogh, 1971; Wender, 1972). Unfortunately, as we have already seen, the category of learning disabilities is ambiguous and heterogeneous, and it may include a number of specific learning difficulties either with or without any behavioral evidence of an hyperactive pattern. In order to minimize the confounding of these conditions and to identify a more homogeneous syndrome, in this section we shall focus on those children who manifest the behavioral patterns of hyperactivity but who are otherwise physiologically and intellectually normal.

Hyperactivity in children is harrassing, frustrating, exasperating, and extremely troublesome to others, especially to parents and teachers who must deal with it on a daily basis. It is one of the most frequent reasons for referral in child guidance clinics and it represents about ten percent of referrals to a private practitioner (Chess, 1960; Patterson, Jones, Whittier, and Wright, 1965; Safter, 1971). Other data estimate its occurrence in from three to ten percent of children (Burks, 1960; Pitts, Craig, and Dieruf, 1966; Comly, 1971; Miller, and Palkes, 1973). Hyperkinesis is found more frequently in boys than girls with sex ratios ranging anywhere from 5:1 to 9:1 (Eisenberg, 1966; Stevens, Sachden, and Milstein, 1968; "Report of the Conference on the Use of Stimulant Drugs in the Treatment of Behaviorally Disturbed Young School Children," 1971; Silver, 1971).

A review of the research literature indicates a fairly consistent behavioral picture associated with the hyperkinetic syndrome (Kleemeier, 1974). One study surveyed five professional groups (pediatricians, teachers, psychologists, psychiatrists, and social workers) with respect to the criteria each used in diagnosing hyperkinesis (Schrager, Lindy, Harrison, McDermott, and Killens, 1966). The professionals were given a fifty-five-item behavioral checklist and instructed to choose those six behaviors that they regarded as most significant in the determination of the hyperkinetic syndrome. The six behaviors rated by each group as frequently as seventy-five percent or more were fidgeting, inattentiveness, hard-to-manage, easily distracted, can't sit still, and low frustration tolerance. In another study, data obtained from an extensive standardized interview of mothers of hyperactive and normal elementary-school children were compared (Stewart, Pitts, Craig, and Dieruf, 1966). Marked differences were found between the groups in such behaviors as overactiveness, can't sit still, can't accept correction, temper tantrums, irritable, destructiveness, unresponsiveness to disci-

TABLE 9–1 * Profile of the Hyperactive Child

I. At home
1. Cannot remain still
2. Cannot conform to limits or prohibitions
3. Makes excessive demands
4. Has sleeping problems
5. Shows unwarranted aggression
6. Is general "pest"
II. At school
1. Is talkative
2. Fidgets continuously
3. Cannot concentrate
4. Has short attention span
5. Cannot conform to limits or prohibitions
6. Shows poor school achievement
III. Relationships with other children
1. Cannot make friends
2. Fights without provocation
3. Has poor manners
4. Is extremely bossy
5. Disregards rights of others
6. Is constantly rejected

* Ross and Ross, 1976, p. 276. Reprinted with permission from John Wiley & Sons, Inc.

pline, defiance, doesn't complete project, doesn't listen to whole story, doesn't follow directions, recklessness, and unpopularity with peers. Table 9–1 shows the behavioral profile of the hyperactive child.

In addition, some clinicians agree on the typical descriptive patterns of these children, without implicating a specific or single etiology (Stewart and Olds, 1973; Laufer, 1967, pp. 1442–1452). Onset is ordinarily noted early in life (usually before six years of age), and the disorder is especially common in first-born males. The newborn may be extremely sensitive to external stimuli, tending to respond to them in a massive and undifferentiated manner. The child is very active in the crib and playpen, often wearing mother out with repeated escapes whenever she turns her back. Successful escapes may lead to a path of destruction as the child touches everything in sight, or spills, breaks, empties, and disturbs almost all of the contents of the room as he or she

moves purposelessly about. The child sleeps little and is reluctant to go to bed, but is often up before someone in the household can prevent the child from either disturbing the family or getting into some sort of trouble. The child is restless and fidgety at mealtimes and actively disruptive in school, where he or she is apt to be up and out of his or her seat much of the time. Short attention span is to be expected, although occasionally the child may be able to sit for lengthy periods of time watching television or reading a book. Any pressure to complete a task triggers activity and increases the likelihood of failure and interpersonal squabbles. Blurting out an answer in class before being called on, hitting a friend, playing hookey, losing things, or in some other way getting into trouble is characteristic of the hyperkinetic child, probably because the child is impulsive and disinclined to think before acting. The child is also excitable, emotionally labile, and easily frustrated; at one moment the child can be happy, and in the next irritable, hostile, or tearful. Although it had long been clinically accepted that hyperactivity dissipates with age, the results of recent follow-up studies indicate that children of this sort continue to be academic failures, emotionally immature, impaired in attention and concentration, and even behavior (antisocial) problems. Apparently, restlessness and activity level tend to decrease with age, although many of the other major symptoms persist through the teen-age years (Minde, Lewin, Weiss, Lairgueur, Douglas, and Sykes, 1971; Weiss, Minde, Werry, Douglas, and Nemeth, 1971).

Etiological Considerations

While hyperactivity following some type of brain damage is possible, most hyperkinetic children show no evidence or history that would suggest injury to the central nervous system. Yet, many writers in the field still cling to a biological view, by including the disorder under the general category of minimal brain dysfunction. This term, like the label of learning disabilities, is used to refer to a number of disparate conditions. Consequently, it is imprecise, and perhaps more important, it is misleading. Surely if brain dysfunction is involved, the damage must be more than minimal to produce such serious and disruptive behavioral patterns. In addition, the vague etiological assumption of this diagnosis tends to confuse and frighten parents who take it to mean that their child's brain is damaged in some unknown but irreparable way.

SIDELIGHT 9–1

The following is a transcript of a doctor's inadequate discussion of the diagnosis and treatment of minimal brain dysfunction with a young mother. This interaction occurred in a university clinic where pediatricians from the community regularly gave volunteer hours; all interactions with the patients were routinely recorded for teaching purposes, and a red indicator light informed the doctor that his conversation was being taped:

Doctor: It seems as though this young man (taps chart) has brain damage, well, uh, not brain *damage*, MBD, that is, minimal brain *dysfunction*.

Mother: (clearly shocked) You mean it's his *brain*? All the school said was that he was hyperkinetic and very distractible.

Doctor: Oh, sure, well, MBD and hyperkinetic are really the same thing. MBD just means that his brain isn't working properly right now so things get a bit out of control especially in school. But he'll probably grow out of it, a lot of these MBD kids are fine by the time they get to adolescence. It's not his intelligence, there isn't anything wrong with *that*, he's a bright boy.

Mother: (sounds very troubled) I never thought of him having anything wrong with his *brain*. How does this brain dysfunction happen, like what caused it? It is something we did?

Doctor: Well, now, we don't really know what caused it. A lot of this kind of thing happens before birth or at birth. It's pretty difficult to pinpoint the cause. We aren't really sure most of the time how it happened.

Mother: You mean he might have had it all his life?

Doctor: That's right.

Mother: How could he have had it all this time and never had any trouble until he's seven years old and in the second grade?

Doctor: Oh, well, that's when MBD shows up. In school. These MBD children often don't have any trouble until they get in school. But don't worry, we can fix him up with some medication. He'll be fine in school once he's on medication.

Mother: What will the medication do? It's not drugs, is it? What kind of medication is it?

Doctor: It'll quiet him down and he'll get on a lot better in school . . . the teacher'll love him now. The medication we're going to try first is a stimulant called

Mother: (interrupting) *A stimulant!* That's the last thing he needs. Is that some kind of drug?

Doctor: (coldly) Mrs. A., with these brain-damaged children stimulants have a quieting effect. You'll be *amazed* at the difference. We'll try one kind for a week or two and see how it goes; you just have to play it by ear at the beginning because we never know which kind will work best for a child, and if it doesn't

The interview was obviously flawed by the doctor's confusion and his failure to deal with the mother's anxiety about her son's problem and her role in it. Nevertheless, it reflects the potential danger involved in the etiological assumption about the diagnosis and in the indiscriminate use of drugs in the treatment of the disorder.

A recent review of the research on the genetics of the hyperactive child syndrome indicates that there is evidence supporting family transmission (1) in the higher prevalance rates of the syndrome in first and second degree relatives of probands than normal controls, (2) in a higher incidence of the syndrome in biologic relatives when nonbiologic parents of adopted hyperactive children were compared with biologic parents of nonadopted hyperactives, and (3) in twin studies that find a higher concordance for monozygotic pairs (Cantwell, 1975). However, the evidence is based on relatively few studies that were frequently marred by methodological inadequacies.

A neurochemical hypothesis of minimal brain dysfunction that involves the catecholamines (dopamine and norepinephrine) has been proposed by a number of investigators (Brase and Loh, 1975). One study generates an interesting model for the minimal brain dysfunction syndrome from data obtained from selective depletion of brain dopamine in developing rats (Shaywitz, Yager, and Klopper, 1976). Neo-natal rats depleted of brain dopamine showed increased levels of activity between twelve to twenty-two days as compared to controls, but their hyperactivity declined as they reached maturity. At the same time, the treated rats continued to evidence learning deficits in adulthood. The study suggests that early dopamine depletion produces hyperactivity that declines around the time of puberty, while the cognitive, perceptual, and emotional problems persist. In this connection, and in support of a biological view, Rapoport, Quinn, and Lamprecht (1974) delineated a group of severely hyperkinetic boys who had a high frequency of minor physical anomalies (large head circumference, low-set ears, curved fingers, large gap between first and second toe, and so forth). These children evidenced a high frequency of either hyperactivity in the father or obstetrical difficulties at birth. In addition, the plasma levels of dopamine-beta-hydroxylase (an enzyme involved in the synthesis of norepinephrine) were correlated positively with the physical anomalies in their sample of youngsters. Those who favor a biological view also tend to cite studies that have found a higher incidence of abnormal EEGs in hyperkinetic children as compared to controls. However, many would argue that the abnormality in EEG tracings alone is insufficient as evidence of any specific etiological factor (Stevens et al., 1968).

Both cortical overarousal and underarousal have been posited as the basic cause of the hyperkinetic syndrome. In 1957, Laufer and Denhoff suggested that hyperactivity is the result of an oversensitivity of the central nervous system to external and internal stimuli. These authors implicated the posterior portion of the forebrain, known as the *diencephalon,* as the site of the dysfunction which, according to the theory, rendered the cortex susceptible to an unusually large amount of stimulation. Burks (1960) similarly concluded that hyperkinesis was the result of overstimulation of the cortex, although he suggested that the dysfunction was located in the reticular formation (a system of nerve paths and connections within the brainstem) through its failure to inhibit incoming impulses. Similar theoretical viewpoints emphasizing cortical overarousal have been proposed by Eisenberg (1966), Keogh (1971), and Solomons (1971). However, empirical tests of these theories are essentially unavailable except for supportive inferences that come from the experimental work of Laufer and his associates (Laufer and Denhoff, 1957; Laufer, Denhoff, and Solomons, 1957).

Quite unexpectedly, Satterfield and Dawson (1971), who had initially set out to test the excessive physiological arousal view of hyperkinesis, found results that were contradictory to this hypothesis but congruent with an underarousal interpretation. They had predicted that hyperkinetic children would have significantly higher basal skin conductance (SCL) than normals, that the frequency of magnitude of the nonspecific skin response (GSR) would be significantly greater, that specific GSRs for the onset of a tone would also be greater, and that the stimulant drugs dextroamphetamine sulfate and methylphenidate would reduce these SCL and GSR levels in hyperkinetic children (making them more like normals). In contrast to their expectations, hyperkinetic children showed lower SCL values, smaller frequencies of nonspecific GSRs, and smaller specific CSRs. All measures changed in the direction of normals when the hyperkinetic children received stimulant drugs.

On the basis of these results, it was posited that hyperkinetic children had lower reticular excitation and that their motor hyperactivity was actually an attempt to facilitate and increase sensory input to a more optimal level. Moreover, the apparent paradoxical effect of amphetamines (stimulants acting as depressants) was not paradoxical at all, but, in fact, the amphetamines acted as a stimulant to bring these youngsters up to an appropriate level of arousal. A second study was undertaken in order to replicate these findings (Satterfield, Cantwell, Lesser, and Podosin, 1972). The results indicated that the best responders to drug treatment were those who showed the lowest initial physiological arousal level, and the worst drug responders were those who were considered overaroused. In support of this view, Kleemeier (1974) re-examined the studies that found higher incidence of abnormal EEGs in hyperkinetic children, and she showed that there is a significant relationship between hyperactivity and slow wave activity (or slow cortical activity). The possibility that hyperkinetic children are underaroused continues to gain experimental support (Grunewald-Zuberbier, Grunewald and Rasche, 1975;

Zahn, Agate, Little, and Wender, 1975). It promises a rational explanation for the effectiveness of stimulant drugs, and it could open up new vistas in the treatment and educational management of these youngsters.

While few would argue against the view that experiential factors are associated with hyperkinesis, the question of whether environmental conditions play a primary causal role in producing the disorder is still very controversial. We know that high degrees of anxiety can be manifested behaviorally in restlessness, impaired learning, distractibility, and emotional excitability (symptoms that at least resemble hyperkinesis). In fact, Chess (1960) found that hyperactivity occurred in a variety of disturbed behaviors such as psychotic, neurotic, brain damaged, mentally retarded, and in a group of youngsters she called "physiologic" (not associated with any other pathology). At present, we do not have the evidence to resolve this controversy one way or the other, although we need to be mindful of the emotional components in both parents and child that are often part and parcel of the disorder. It is the rare parent who is not eventually harrassed, fatigued, worried, guilt ridden, and angered by the hyperactive child. This child is difficult to manage, frustrating to be with, and quite disappointing to those who hold expectations for the child's academic and social achievement. It is little wonder that the child is rejected, avoided, and disliked by almost everyone with whom he or she comes in contact. The child's self-esteem is typically quite low, and the child is aware that he or she is alienated from others and that there is something radically wrong with him or her.

Conflicts are inevitable between the child and the parents, siblings, teachers, and peers. Tension in the home often increases and, unfortunately, the situation deteriorates before it gets better. The child's behavior worsens, and the child is apt to be blamed for any sort of trouble whether or not he or she actually has been involved. Environments that are characterized by disorganization, conflicts, destruction, impulsiveness, emotional lability, and restlessness provide modeling opportunities for hyperactivity. Under these living conditions, a child either with or without minimal brain dysfunction should evidence a clear symptom picture of hyperkinesis. Regardless of the primary etiology, by the time the family brings the child to a professional, the problem will most likely involve many serious emotional facets that must be dealt with.

Therapeutic Approaches

Our society's penchant for taking medicines is perhaps most clearly reflected in the preferred treatment approach for hyperactive children. Chemotherapy using two types of drugs, amphetamines and methylphendiate (*stimulants*), and phenothiazines (*tranquilizers*) is so commonplace that teachers and other nonmedically trained professionals as well as physicians rely heavily on medication as a first line of defense. The widespread use of drugs, unfortunately, is not supported by a substantial number of carefully controlled research studies, or by investigations designed to answer important questions such as what is the long-term effect of drugs on intellectual abilities, academic achievement, or other cognitive functions. The literature is characterized primarily by clinical reports, although a sparse number of controlled studies have focused on activity level as the chief measure of therapeutic effectiveness. Millichap and Fowler (1967) reviewed drug

TABLE 9–2 *   Index of Optimum Therapies

Stimulants	Dose, Mg per Day	Percent Improved	Percent Side Effects
Ritalin	5–60	83	14
Dexedrine	5–30	69	12
Tranquilizers			
Thorazine	10–20	55	25
Deaner	50–150	47	7
Serpasil	0.25–0.5	34	>19

* Adapted from Millichap and Fowler, 1967, p. 775.

studies with hyperactive children who had learning disabilities, and they compiled the following index of optimum therapies (see Table 9–2).

On the basis of this review and Table 9–2, it appears that stimulants effect greater numbers of improvement and less frequent side effects than tranquilizers. Moreover, Ritalin seems to be the most effective stimulant drug.

A more recent review of the literature noted that the findings with respect to the use of tranquilizers with hyperactive children were conflicting and inconclusive (Werry and Sprague, 1970).

Imipramine, a long-acting antidepressant, has been tried because it is regarded as a drug that produces less undesirable side effects than control nervous-system stimulants such as amphetamines and methylphenidate. One study reported improvement in hyperactive children treated with imipramine during an eight-week period, as compared to deterioration in behavior in those youngsters when they were given a placebo over a period of four weeks (Waizer, Hoffman, Polizos, and Engelhardt, 1964). However, Rapoport et al. (Rapoport, Quinn, Bradford, Riddle, and Brooks, 1974) demonstrated that the stimulant was more effective than imipramine on all measures of improvement.

Those few studies that have attempted to determine the effect of stimulants and tranquilizers on school achievement generally showed no substantial change when either drug was given in normal clinical doses. If anything, stimulants facilitated performance slightly, while tranquilizers tended to minimally depress some areas (Werry and Sprague, 1970). But too little is known about the effect of these drugs on learning and memory in hyperactive children who have been medicated over a period of several years. Perhaps the greatest problem in evaluating the specific efficacy of this treatment approach is the confounding but popular practice of using drug therapy in some combination with other remedial techniques, such as psychotherapy, special educational programs, and environmental manipulations.

A recent study offers promise that a token reinforcement program can be used as an effective alternative to drug control (Ayllon, Layman, and Kandel, 1975). Ritalin was discontinued in three hyperactive school-aged children after baseline rates of their activity levels and mathematics and reading performance were obtained. Without medication their activity level increased markedly, while the introduction of the reinforcement program (tokens for correct responses in math and reading) controlled their hyperactivity at a level comparable to the baseline data (while subjects were on ritalin). In addition, their math and reading performance increased from a baseline rate of about twelve percent correct to over eighty-five percent correct on the no drug reinforcement program. Interesting as these findings are, we need to accumulate data on many more subjects and over much longer periods of time before we can be confident of this type of treatment program.

Psychotherapy as an approach for changing the hyperactive child's behavior through the resolution of conflicts and the strengthening of self-esteem has been favored by many clinicians, although little proof of its usefulness is empirically available. Differences in orientation, techniques, goals, and amount of psychotherapy among therapists and for each child treated are so vast that systematic research is difficult to undertake. When some of these variables are controlled for research purposes, there is the risk that the ensuing evaluation of the effectiveness of psychotherapy will be highly specific to the experimental conditions and not to the usefulness of psychotherapy in general (as clinically practiced or as defined in other empirical studies). For example, the results of the study by Eisenberg and his associates (Eisenberg, Gilbert, Cytryn, and Molling, 1961), which indicated that short-term psychotherapy is not effective in changing the behavior of hyperactive children, cannot be taken as a broad indictment of psychotherapy. The findings must be interpreted within the special conditions of the study, and in light of the criteria used to measure its effects. It seems unreasonable to expect that any form of brief treatment, including psychotherapy, would significantly alter the well established behavioral patterns of hyperactive children.

Based on the assumption that overactivity in brain damaged children is attributable to an inability to inhibit and delay incoming and background stimuli, Strauss and Lehtinen (1947) were the first to advocate a maximal reduction of distracting stimuli in the immediate environment as an important aspect of a treatment program for these youngsters. Some years later, Cruickshank et al. (Cruickshank, Bentzen, Ratzeburg, and Tannhauser, 1961) in a demonstration-pilot project used the principles of reduced environmental stimulation and a structured educational program with brain damaged and hyperactive children in a public school setting.

Their results, although difficult to interpret because of methodological limitations, provided some evidence supportive of the restricted environment view of Strauss and Lehtinen. More recently data were reported that indicated better performance under conditions of reduced environmental stimulation, although familial and brain damaged mental retardates were used as subjects (Gorton, 1972). Considerably more evidence is needed, but the idea of restricting environmental stimulation, if confirmed by research, would have useful implications for both the classroom and home management of hyperactivity.

Summary

The period of childhood between the ages of five and twelve is one of dramatic growth and transition for both parents and children. While many diverse forms of abnormal behaviors can occur during this period, special detailed attention was given to the three most frequently noted problems, those of language disorders, learning disabilities, and the hyperkinetic syndrome.

Disorders of speech are among the earliest referral problems most often occurring between the ages of four and five, wth a sex ratio of approximately 3:1 in favor of boys. More than eighty percent of all the serious speech difficulties found in school-aged children involve problems of delayed speech, articulation, and stuttering.

The term *learning disability* is one of many labels used interchangeably and imprecisely as a broad category referring to a discrepancy between anticipated and perceived academic achievement in children who otherwise are not handicapped in intelligence, sensory processes, emotional stability, or opportunities to learn. Learning problems are estimated to occur in between five and twenty percent of school-aged youngsters. The specific learning disability of reading was considered because it is found in more than ten percent of the school population, and because it is illustrative of the issues and areas of controversy characteristic of the entire field of learning disabilities.

Hyperkinesis in children has become a syndrome of increasing interest to clinicians and researchers. The term does not imply a specific etiology, and it is often included under the general rubric of learning disabilities. We considered the hyperkinetic syndrome as a separate condition in order to lessen the confounding of these categories that exists in the literature.

The clinical picture, etiological considerations, and therapeutic approaches of the disorders covered in this chapter are summarized in the following tables.

A. Disorders of Speech

1. Delayed Speech

Clinical Picture	Etiology	Treatment
Failure to speak in at least two-word utterances by the time child is three years of age	More than half of the cases are caused by or are associated with mental retardation.	Behavior modification in which imitation and differential reinforcement are used to improve correct grammatical structure.
or		
Slow progress in new word acquisition, and in the formation of sentences.	Partial or complete hearing loss.	Verbal stimulation and instructions to parents to encourage verbalizations from the child.
	Brain injury that affects hearing or intelligence.	Psychotherapy.
	Language stimulation, motivation to speak, number of sibs, order of birth, and socioeconomic deprivation.	

2. Articulation Problems

Clinical Picture	Etiology	Treatment
Imprecise production of speech sounds are the most prevalent of all speech problems.	Physiological abnormalities that make normal movement of speech apparatus difficult.	Speech therapy.
It is determined by listening to smallest unit of distinguishable speech sounds, phoneme.	CNS damage that affects hearing, neuromuscular or respiratory control.	Speech therapy and psychotherapy.
There are four types of faulty articulation: phonemes are either omitted, substituted, distorted, or added.	Loss of sensation in tongue, lips, or face.	Behavior modification to strengthen the desired response and weaken the unwanted behavior.
Higher incidence in low socioeconomic children.	Auditory acuity and discrimination impairment.	
Positive relationship between it and academic achievement, and grades.	Faulty learning such as poor speech models, low stimulation and motivation, and an underlying personality disorder.	

A. Disorders of Speech (con't.)

3. Stuttering

Clinical Picture

Although easily recognized by laypeople, it is difficult to define because the boundary between it and dysfluence in normal speech is ambiguous.

It is characterized by blocking, repetition, and prolongation of speech sounds.

Persistent stuttering is found in one to two percent and transient stuttering is found in four to five percent of the population.

More than fifty percent of cases recover by puberty without treatment, and eighty percent have normal speech by late teens.

No relationship found with intelligence or socioeconomic factors.

Begins between two and five and almost always before eight. More frequent in boys (estimates range from 3:1 to 8:1).

Etiology

No single causal explanation is as yet acceptable.

Data have failed to confirm a biological view.

No research evidence supporting a neurotic basis.

Most viable view is that it is a learned avoidance reaction in which the child struggles to avoid all instances of dysfluencies. Failure heightens anxiety and the likelihood of more dysfluencies.

Alternative is the two-process theory in which the primary speech disorganization is acquired through classically conditioned anxiety while secondary aspects are instrumentally conditioned.

Treatment

Psychotherapy and speech practice under conditions of progressive stress reduced stuttering in fifty percent of the cases.

Delayed auditory feedback techniques have been disappointing in general.

Operant conditioning has been used but results are far from satisfactory, difficult to evaluate, and most reports do not include follow-up data.

For chronic stutterers who are primarily neurotic, psychotherapy is recommended.

B. Learning Disabilities

1. Reading Failures

Clinical Picture

Found in more boys than girls (ranging from 3:1 to 5:1).

Poor readers make poor students who face limited vocational choices and restricted income potential. There is a high association with antisocial behaviors.

Reading failure becomes chronic and difficult to modify if not identified before fifth grade.

Etiology

It represents heterogeneous conditions for which there is no single cause.

High prevalence of reading problems in close relatives of dyslexic children is often used to support a genetic view, but these data can be used equally well to support a social transmission view.

While evidence of CNS involvement is not usually apparent, many hold some sort of brain

Treatment

Heterogeneity of terms and etiological views is only exceeded by diversity of remedial approaches.

Dynamically oriented psychotherapy has been used and reported but improvements were not sustained after treatment was terminated.

Various special education programs to improve perceptual skills and neurological organization have been popular but

B. Learning Disabilities (con't.)

1. Reading Failures (con't.)

Clinical Picture

Dyslexia is used to designate children of average or slightly below average intelligence with specific retardation in reading who have not been deprived of educational opportunities or show any gross evidence of either sensory or neurological impairment.

They have difficulty in comprehending written language, and managing other language functions of writing and speech. They may be lefthanded or ambidextrous, poorly coordinated and awkward. Considered bright intellectually before school and get good grades in arithmetic at first. Emotional disturbances and low self-esteem are noted.

Two primary types: impaired in either auditory or visual modality. Auditory defects are more difficult to remediate than visual ones.

Significant differences noted in visual information processing, in memory for visual information, and in the perception and organization of broken-up words embedded in ambiguous stimuli.

Etiology

dysfunction as the primary cause. Hence the term "minimal brain dysfunction" is used.

Some regard minimal brain dysfunction as an unproven and inferred diagnosis that has little meaning and application for educational remediation, while others believe that it will enable further understanding of the neurophysiological basis of learning.

Maturational lag in brain development is another view which has some empirical support through a study which permitted correct classification of both high and low risk children in better than ninety percent of the cases.

Psychogenic view involving poor self-image or more fanciful psychoanalytically derived interpretations tend to be imprecise and difficult to substantiate. However, most clinicians are convinced that emotional factors play an important role in many cases of disturbed learning.

Nutritional and environmental deprivation have been recently implicated as potential determinants of neurological dysfunction.

Treatment

evidence to date is inconclusive.

Chemotherapy has been used —with Dilantin best for those with minimal neurological signs, Ritalin for those who are both hyperactive and disabled in learning, and Thorazine for emotionally disturbed children with learning problems. Barbiturates and phenothiazines should not be used.

Behavior modification in the teaching management of children in classroom has been used, but data are too sparse to evaluate.

C. Hyperkinetic Syndrome

Clinical Picture

Persistent overactivity, distractibility, impulsivity, emotional excitability, low frustration tolerance, short attention span, and in some cases antisocial behavior.

Onset is usually early in life,

Etiology

Biological view is prevalent although there is usually no evidence or history of brain injury.

Both cortical overarousal and underarousal have been suggested as the basic cause. Underarousal is a more viable and

Treatment

Chemotherapy is the most favored approach. Two types of drugs are used: stimulants and tranquilizers. Evaluation of drug effectiveness is difficult because there are few controlled studies. However, stimulants seem to be more effective than tranquilizers.

C. Hyperkinetic Syndrome (con't.)

1.Reading Failures (*cont.*)

Clinical Picture	*Etiology*	*Treatment*
and the behaviors become troublesome to parents and teachers especially when child enters school.	promising position, but more data are necessary.	Studies assessing the long term effects of drugs on learning and memory are not available.
It is more frequent in boys (estimates range from 5:1 to 9:1) and it is found in between three and nine percent of elementary school children.	Psychogenic factors such as conflicts and environments that are disorganized, destructive, impulsive, emotional, and restless provide modeling opportunities for hyperactivity.	Psychotherapy to resolve unconscious conflicts and strengthen self-esteem has been used but evaluation is difficult at present.
Specific learning disabilities may be present.	Whether emotional factors are primary or secondary can not be determined from data available.	Restriction of environmental stimulation has been tried with promising but inconclusive findings.
These children are otherwise physiologically and intellectually normal.		
While it had been thought that the syndrome dissipates with age, recent data indicate persistence of behaviors through the teenage years.		

REFERENCES

ADLER, S. "Articulatory Deviances and Social Class Membership." *Journal of Learning Disabilities,* 1973, *6,* 650–654.

AYLLON, T., LAYMAN, D., and H. J. KANDEL. A Behavioral Educational Alternative to Drug Control of Hyperactive Children. *Journal of Applied Behavioral Analysis,* 1975, *8,* 137–146.

BAER, D. M. and D. GUESS. "Receptive Training of Adjectival Inflections in Mental Retardates." *Journal of Applied Behavior Analysis,* 1971, *4,* 129–139.

BAKWIN, H. and R. M. BAKWIN. *Behavior Disorders in Children* (4th ed.). Philadelphia: Saunders, 1972.

BARATZ, J. "Language in the Economically Disadvantaged Child: A Perspective." *American Speech and Hearing Association,* 1968, *10,* 143–145.

BARATZ, J. "Language and Cognitive Assessment of Negro Children: Assumptions and Research Needs." *American Speech and Hearing Association,* 1969, *11,* 87–91.

BARBARA, D. A. "Stuttering." In Arieti, S. (Ed.). *American Handbook of Psychiatry,* Vol 1. New York: Basic Books, 1959, pp. 950–963.

BINGHAM, D. S., VAN HATTUM, R., FAULK, M. E., and E. TAUSSING. Program Organization and Management. *Journal of Speech and Hearing Disorders.* Monograph Supplement, 1961, *8,* 33–49.

BRASE, D. A. and H. H. LOH. "Possible Role of 5-hydroxytryptamine in Minimal Brain Dysfunction." *Life Sciences,* 1975, *16,* 1005–1015.

BRODIE, R. D. and M. R. WINTERBOTTOM. "Failure in Elementary School Boys as a Function of Traumata, Secrecy, and Derogation." *Child Development,* 1967, *38,* 701–711.

BRUTTEN, E. J. and D. J. SHOEMAKER. *The Modification of Stuttering.* Englewood Cliffs, New Jersey: Prentice-Hall, 1967.

BRUTTEN, E. J. and D. J. SHOEMAKER. "Stuttering: The Disintegration of Speech Due to Conditioned Negative Emotion." In Gray, B., and G. England (Eds.). *Stuttering and the Conditioning Therapies.* Monterey, California: Monterey Institute for Speech and Hearing, 1969, p. 51.

BURKS, H. "The Hyperkinetic Child." *Exceptional Children.* 1960, *27,* 18–26.

CANTWELL, D. P. "Genetics of Hyperactivity." *Journal of Child Psychology and Psychiatry, and Allied Disciplines,* 1975, *16,* 261–264.

CHESS, S. "Diagnosis and Treatment of the Hyperactive Child. *New York State Journal of Medicine,* 1960, *60* (July-December), pp. 2379–2385.

CHESS, S. and M. ROSENBERG. "Clinical Differentiation among Children with Initial Language Complaints." *Journal of Autism and Childhood Schizophrenia,* 1974, *4,* 99–109.

CLARIZIO, H. F. and G. F. McCOY. *Behavior Disorders in School-Aged Children.* Scranton, Pennsylvania: Chandler Publishing Co., 1970.

CLARKE, J. L. "Verbal and Nonverbal Learning Disabilities." In Burkowsky, M. R. (Ed.) *Orientation to Language and Learning Disorders.* St. Louis, Missouri: Warren H. Green, 1973, pp. 54–100.

COMLY, H. "Cerebral Stimulants for Children with Learning Disorders." *Journal of Learning Disabilities,* 1971, *4,* 484–490.

CRUICKSHANK, W. M., BENTZEN, F. A., RATZEBURG, F. H., and M. T. TANNJAUSSER. *A Teaching Method for Brain Injured and Hyperactive Children;* A Demonstration-Pilot Study. Syracuse, New York: Syracuse University Press, 1961.

DARLEY, F. L., ARONSON, A. E., and J. R. BROWN. "Clusters of Deviant Speech Dimensions in the Dysarthrias." *Journal of Speech and Hearing Research,* 1969, *12,* 462–496.

DAVIS, H. and S. R. SILVERMAN. *Hearing and Deafness* (3rd ed.). New York: Holt, Rinehart, and Winston, 1970.

DOMAN, R. J., SPITZ, E. B., ZUCMAN, E., DELACATO, C. H., and G. DOMAN. "Children with Severe Brain Injuries: Neurological Organization in Terms of Mobility." *Journal of the American Medical Association,* 1960, *174,* 257–262.

EISENBERG, L. "The Management of the Hyperkinetic Child." *Developmental Medicine and Child Neurology,* 1966, *8,* 593–598.

EISENBERG, L., GILBERT, A., CYTRYN, L., and P. A. MOLLING. "The Effectiveness of Psychotherapy Alone and in Conjunction with Perphenazine or Placebo in the Treatment of Neurotic and Hyperkinetic Children." *American Journal of Psychiatry,* 1961, *117,* 1088–1093.

EISENSON, J. "Speech Disorders." In Wolman, B. B. (Ed.). *Handbook of Clinical Psychology.* New York: McGraw Hill, 1965, pp. 765–784.

EMERICK, L. L. and J. T. HATTEN. *Diagnosis and Evaluation in Speech Pathology.* Englewood Cliffs, New Jersey: Prentice-Hall, 1974.

ERNHART, C. B., GRAHAM, F. K., EICHMAN, P. L., MARSHALL, J. M., and D. THURSTON. "Brain Injury in the Preschool Child: Some Developmental Considerations. II. Comparison of Brain Injured and Normal Children." *Psychological Monographs: General and Applied,* 1963, *77* (No. 574), 17–33.

FEILD, C. T. and H. S. FEILD. "Performance of Subjects with Reading Disabilities on a Series of Perceptual Closure Tasks." *Perceptual and Motor Skills,* 1974, *38,* 812–814.

FLANAGAN, B., GOLDIAMOND, I., and N. H. AZRIN. "Operant Stuttering: The Control of Stuttering Behavior Through Response Contingent Consequences." *Journal of the Experimental Analysis of Behavior,* 1958, *1,* 173–177.

FRISK, M., WEGELIUS, E. B., TENHUNEN, T., WIDHOLM, O., and H. HORTLING. "The Problem of Dyslexia in Teenage." *Acta Paediatrica Scandinavia,* 1967, *56,* 333–343.

GERBER, S. E. and C. G. HERTEL. "Language Deficiency of Disadvantaged Children." *Journal of Speech and Hearing Research,* 1969, *12,* 270–280.

GIFFIN, M. "The Role of Child Psychiatry in Learning Disabilities." In Myklebust, H. R. (Ed.). *Progress in Learning Disabilities.* Vol. 1. New York: Grune and Stratton, 1968, pp. 75–97.

GILBERT, G. M. "A Survey of 'referral problems' in Metropolitan Child Guidance Centers." *Journal of Clinical Psychology,* 1957, *13,* 37–42.

GLASNER, P. J. and D. ROSENTHAL. "Parental Diagnosis of Stuttering in Young Children." *Journal of Speech and Hearing Disorders,* 1957, *22,* 288–295.

GOLDBERG, H. K. and G. R. SCHIFFMAN. *Dyslexia: Problems of Reading Disabilities.* New York: Grune and Stratton, 1972.

GOLDENSON, R. M. *Helping Your Child to Read Better.* New York: Crowell, 1957.

GOODSTEIN, L. D. "Functional Speech Disorders and Personality: A Survey of the Literature." In Trapp, P. and P. Himelstein, (Eds.). *Readings on the Exceptional Child.* New York: Appleton-Century-Crofts, 1962, pp. 399–419.

GOODSTEIN, L. D. "Psychosocial Aspects of Cleft Palate." In Spriesterbach, D.C., and D. Sherman (Eds.). *Cleft Palate and Communication.* New York: Academic Press, Inc. 1969, pp. 201–224.

GORTON, C. E. "The Effects of Various Classroom Environments on Performance of a Mental Task by Mentally Retarded and Normal Children." *Education and Training of the Mentally Retarded,* 1972, *7,* 28–38.

GROSSMAN, H. J. The child, the teachers, and the physician. In W. M. Cruickshank. (Ed.). *The Teacher of Brain Injured Children: A Discussion of the Bases for Competency.* Syracuse, N.Y.: Syracuse University Press, 1966, pp. 57–67.

GROTEBERG, E. G. Neurological Aspects of Learning Disabilities: A Case for the Disadvantaged. *Journal of Learning Disabilities,* 1970, *3,* 25–31.

GRUNEWALD-ZÜBERBIER, E., GRUNEWALD, G., and A. RASCHE. Hyperactive Behavior and EEG Arousal Reactions in Children's Electroencephalograms. *Clinical Neurophysiology,* 1975, *38,* 149–159.

GUESS, D., SAILOR, W., RUTHERFORD, G., and D. M. BAER. "An Experimental Analysis of Linguistic Development: The Productive Use of the Plural Morpheme." *Journal of Applied Behavior Analysis,* 1968, *1,* 297–306.

HALLAHAN, D. P. and W. M. CRUICKSHANK. *Psychoeducational Foundations of Learning Disabilities.* Englewood Cliffs, New Jersey: Prentice Hall, 1973.

HALLGREN, B. "Specific Dyslexia (Congenital and Word Blindness)." *Acta Psychiatrica et Neurologica,* Supplementum 65, 1950.

HARDY, J. "Respiratory Physiology: Implications of Current Research." *American Speech and Hearing Association.* 1968, *10,* 204–205.

HARRIS, A. J. *How to Increase Reading Ability: A Guide to Development and Remedial Methods.* 5th ed. New York: McKay, 1970.

HEINICKE, C. M. "Learning Disturbance in Childhood." In Wolman, B. B. (Ed.). *Manual of Child Psychopathology.* New York: McGraw-Hill, 1972.

HERBERT, M. *Emotional Problems of Development in Children.* New York: Academic Press, 1974.

HEWETT, F. M., TAYLOR, F. D., and A. A. ARTUSO. "The Santa Monica Project: Evaluation of an Engineered Classroom Design with Emotionally Disturbed Children." *Exceptional Children,* 1969, *35,* 523–529.

"Human Communication and Its Disorders: An Overview. A Report of the Subcommittee on Human Communication and Its Disorders." *National Advisory Neurological Diseases and Stroke Council,* Monograph No. 10. U.S. Department of Health, Education and Welfare, National Institute of Neurological Diseases and Stroke, 1969.

IRWIN, O. C. "Infant Speech: Effect of Systematic Reading of Stories." *Journal of Speech and Hearing Research.* 1969, *3,* 187–190.

JOHNSON, D. J. and H. R. MYKLEBUST. *Learning Disabilities, Educational Principles and Practices.* New York: Grune and Stratton, 1967.

JOHNSON, W. (Ed.). *Stuttering in Children and Adults; Thirty Years of Research at the University of Iowa.* Minneapolis: University of Minnesota Press, 1956.

JOHNSON, W. *Stuttering and What You Can Do about It.* Minneapolis: University of Minnesota Press, 1961.

JOHNSON, W., BROWN, S., CURTIS, J., EDNEY, C., and J. KEASTER. *Speech Handicapped School Children.* New York: Harper and Row, 1956.

JONES, H. G. "Stuttering." In C. G. Costello, (Ed.). *Symptoms of Psychopatholgy: A Handbook.* New York: Wiley, 1970.

KEOGH, B. "Hyperactivity and Learning Disorders: Review and Speculation." *Exceptional Children,* 1971, *38,* 101–109.

KESSLER, J. *Psychopathology of Childhood.* Englewood Cliffs, New Jersey: Prentice-Hall, 1966.

KLEEMEIER, C. P. "A Comparative Evaluation of the Theoretical Relationship Between Arousal and Learning as Demonstrated by the Hyperkinetic Syndrome." Unpublished Comprehensive Examination Paper, Department of Psychology, Emory University, April, 1974.

KUSSMAUL, A. Disturbances of Speech. In *Encyclopedia of Practical Medicine,* 1877, *14,* 581–875.

LAHEY, B. B. "Minority Group Languages." In Lahey, B. B. (Ed.). *The Modification of Language Behavior.* Springfield, Illinois: Thomas, 1973, pp. 270–315.

LAUFER, M. W. "Brain Disorders." In Freedman, A. M., and H. I. Kaplan (Eds.). *Comprehensive Textbook of Psychiatry.* Baltimore: Williams and Wilkins, 1967, pp. 1442–1452.

LAUFER, M. W. and E. DENHOFF. "Hyperkinetic Behavior Syndrome in Children." *Journal of Pediatrics,* 1957, *50,* 463–474.

LAUFER, M. W., DENHOFF, E., and G. SOLOMONS. "Hyperkinetic Impulse Disorder in Children's Behavior Problems." *Psychosomatic Medicine,* 1957, *19,* 38–49.

LENNEBERG, E. H. (Ed.). "Language Disorders in Childhood." *Harvard Educational Review,* 1964, *34,* 152–177.

LENNEBERG, E. H. "On Explaining Language." *Science,* 1969, *164,* 635–643.

LEON, G. R. *Case Histories of Deviant Behavior: A Social Learning Analysis.* Boston: Holbrook Press, 1974, 35–42.

McCARTHY, J. M. "Learning Disabilities: Where Have We Been? Where Are We

Going?" In Hammill, D. D. and N. R. Bartel (Eds.). *Educational Perspectives in Learning Disabilities.* New York: Wiley, 1971.

McDonald, C. W. "Problems Concerning the Classification and Education of Children with Learning Disabilities." In Hellmuth, J. (Ed.). *Learning Disorders.* Vol. 3. Seattle, Washington: Special Child Publications, 1968, pp. 371–389.

Margolin, J. B., Roman, M., and C. Harari. "Reading Disability in the Delinquent Child: A Microcosm of Psychosocial Pathology." *American Journal of Orthopsychiatry.* 1955, *25*, 25–35.

Martin, R. and R. Ingham. "Stuttering." In B. B. Lahey, (Ed.). *The Modification of Language Behavior.* Springfield, Illinois: Thomas, 1973, pp. 91–129.

Matheny, A. P., Jr., and A. B. Dolan. "A Twin Study of Genetic Influences in Reading Achievement." *Journal of Learning Disabilities,* 1974, *7*, 99–102.

Miller, R. G., Jr., Palkes, H. S., and M. A. Stewart. "Hyperactive Children in Suburban Elementary Schools." *Child Psychiatry and Human Development,* 1973, *4*, 121–127.

Millichap, J. G. and G. W. Fowler. "Treatment of 'Minimal Brain Dysfunction' Syndromes." *The Pediatric Clinics of North America,* November 1967, Vol. 14, No. 4, 767–777.

Minde, K., Lewin, D., Weiss, G., Lairgueur, H., Douglas, V., and R. Sykes. "The Hyperactive Child in Elementary School: A Five Year Old Controlled Follow Up." *Exceptional Children,* 1971, *38,* 215–221.

Morrow, W. R. "Academic Underachievement." In Costello, C. G. (Ed.). *Symptoms of Psychopathology: A Handbook.* New York: Wiley, 1970, pp. 535–559.

Myklebust, H. R. and D. Johnson. "Dyslexia in Children." *Exceptional Children.* 1962, *29,* 14–25.

Mysak, E. D. and G. M. Gilbert. "Child Speech Pathology." In Wolman, B. B. (Ed.). *Manual of Child Psychopathology.* New York: McGraw-Hill, 1972, pp. 624–652.

"Need for Speech Pathologists." American Speech and Hearing Association, Committee on Legislation. *Journal of the American Speech and Hearing Association,* 1959, *1,* 138–139.

Orton, S. T. *Reading, Writing and Speech Problems in Children.* New York: Norton, 1937.

Paine, R. S., Werry, J. S., and H. C. Quay. "A Study of Minimal Cerebral Dysfunction." *Developmental Medicine and Child Neurology,* 1968, *10,* 505–520.

Paine, R. S., Werry, J. S., and H. C. Quay. "A Study of Minimal Cerebral Dysfunction." In Hammill, D. D. and N. R. Bartel (Eds.). *Educational Perspectives in Learning Disabilities.* New York: Wiley, 1971, pp. 59–79.

Palermo, D. S. and D. L. Molfese. "Language Aquisition from Age Five Onward." *Psychological Bulletin,* 1972, *78,* 409–428.

Patterson, G. R., Jones, R., Whittier, J., and M. A. Wright. "A Behavior Modification Technique for the Hyperactive Child." *Behavior Research and Therapy,* 1965, *2,* 217–226.

Perkins, W. H. *Speech Pathology: An Applied Behavioral Science* (2nd ed.). St. Louis: Mosby, 1977.

Pope, L. "Motor Activity in Brain-Injured Children." *American Journal of Orthopsychiatry.* 1970, *40,* 783–794.

Rapoport, J. L. and M. Benoit. "The Relation of Direct Home Observations to the Clinic Evaluation of Hyperactive School Age Boys." *Journal of Child Psychology and Psychiatry and Allied Disciplines.* 1975, *16,* 141–147.

Rapoport, J. L., Quinn, P. O., Bradbard, G., Riddle, K. D., and E. Brooks. "Imipramine and Methylphenidate Treatments of Hyperactive Boys." *Archives of General Psychiatry*, 1974, *30*, 789–793.

RAPOPORT, J. L., QUINN, P. O., and F. LAMPRECHT. "Minor Physical Anomalies and Plasma Dopamine-Beta-Hydroxylase Activity in Hyperactive Boys." *American Journal of Psychiatry*, 1974, *131*, 386–390.

Reading Disorders in the United States. National Advisory Committee on the Dyslexia and Related Reading Disorders. Washington, D.C.: U.S. Department of Health, Education and Welfare, August, 1969.

"Report of the Conference on the Use of Stimulant Drugs in the Treatment of Behaviorally Disturbed Young School Children." *Journal of Learning Disabilities*, 1971, *4*, 523–530.

ROBBINS, M., and G. V. GLASS. "The Doman-Delacato Rationale: A Critical Analysis." In Hellmuth, J. (Ed.). *Educational Therapy*. Vol. II. Seattle, Washington: Special Child Publications, 1969, pp. 321–377.

ROSS, D. M. and S. A. Ross. *Hyperactivity: Research, Theory and Action*. New York: Wiley, 1976.

SAFER, D. J. "Drugs for Problem School Children." *Journal of School Health*, 1971, *41*, 491–495.

SATTERFIELD, J. H., CANTWELL, D. P., LESSER, L. I., and R. L. PODOSIN. "Physiological Studies of the Hyperkinetic Child: I." *American Journal of Psychiatry*, 1972, *128*, 1418–1424.

SATTERFIELD, J. H. and M. E. DAWSON. Electrodermal Correlates of Hyperactivity in Children. *Psychophysiology*, 1971, *8*, 191–197.

SATZ, P., RARDIN, D., and J. Ross. "An Evaluation of a Theory of Specific Developmental Dyslexia. *Child Development*, 1971, *42*, 2009–2021.

SCHIFFMAN, G. and R. L. CLEMMENS. "Observations on children with severe reading problems." In J. Hellmuth. *Learning Disorders*, Vol. 2. Seattle, Washington: Special Child Publications, 1966, pp. 297–310.

SCHLEIFER, M., WEISS, G., COHEN, N., ELMAN, M., CVEJIC, H., and E. KRUGER. "Hyperactivity in Preschoolers and the Effect of Methlphenidate." *American Journal of Orthopsychiatry*, 1975, *45*, 38–50.

SCHRAGER, J., LINDY, J., HARRISON, S., McDERMOTT, J., and E. KILLINS. "The Hyperkinetic Child: Some Consensually Validated Behavior Correlates." *Exceptional Children*, 1966, *32*, 635–637.

SCHULMAN, J. L. KASPER, J. C., and F. M. THRONE. *Brain Damage and Behavior*. Springfield, Illinois: Thomas, 1965.

SHAW, M. C. "Underachievement. Useful Construct or Misleading Illusion." *Psychology in the Schools*. 1968, *5*, 41–46.

SHAYWITZ, B. A., YAGER, R. D., and J. H. KLOPPER. "Selective Brain Dopamine Depletion in Developing Rats: An Experimental Model of Minimal Brain Dysfunction." *Science*, 1976, *191*, 305–308.

SHEEHAN, J. G. "Theory and Treatment of Stuttering as an Approach Avoidance Conflict." *Journal of Psychology*, 1953, *36*, 27–49.

SHEEHAN, J. G. "Stuttering as a Self-Role Conflict." In Gregory, H. H. (Ed.). *Learning Theory and Stuttering Therapy*. Evanston, Illinois: Northwestern University Press, 1968, pp. 72–83.

SHEEHAN, J. G. and M. M. MARTYN. "Spontaneous Recovery from Stuttering." *Journal of Speech and Hearing Research*, 1966, *9*, 121–135.

SHEEHAN, J. G. and M. M. MARTYN. "Methodology in Studies of Recovery from Stuttering." *Journal of Speech and Hearing Research*, 1967, *10*, 396–400.

SHEEHAN, J. G. "Projective Studies of Stuttering." In Trapp, E. P. and P. Himmelstein. *Readings on the Exceptional Child.* New York: Appleton-Century-Crofts, 1962, pp. 419–429.

SHRINER, T. H., HOLLOWAY, M. S., and R. G. DANILOFF. "The Relationship Between Articulatory Deficits and Syntax in Speech Defective Children." *Journal of Speech and Hearing Research,* 1969, *12,* 319–325.

SILVER, L. A. "A Proposed View on the Etiology of the Neurological Learning Disability Syndrome." *Journal of Learning Disabilities.* 1971, *4,* 123–133.

SMITH, M. E. "An Investigation of the Development of the Sentence and the Extent of Vocabulary in Young Children." *University of Iowa Studies in Child Welfare,* 1926, *3,* Np. 5.

SOLOMONS, G. "Guidelines on the Use and Medical Effects of Psychostimulant Drugs in Therapy." *Journal of Learning Disabilities,* 1971, *4,* 470–475

SROUFE, L. A. "Drug Treatment of Children with Behavior Problems." In Horowitz, F. (Ed.). *Review of Child Development Research,* Vol. 4. Chicago: University of Chicago Press, 1975, pp. 347–407.

STANLEY, G. and R. HALL. "Short-term Visual Information Processing in Dyslexics." *Child Development,* 1973, *44,* 841–844.

STEVENS, J. R., SACHDEV, K., and V. MILSTEIN. "Behavior Disorders of Childhood and the Electroencephalogram." *Archives of Neurology,* 1968, *18,* 160–177.

STEWART, J. L. "Cross-cultural Studies and Linguistic Aspects of Stuttering." *Journal of the All India Institute of Speech and Hearing,* 1971, 2, 1–6.

STEWART, M. A. and S. W. OLDS. *Raising a Hyperactive Child.* New York: Harper and Row, 1973.

STEWART, M. A., PITTS, F. N., CRAIG, A. G., and W. DIERUF. "The Hperactive Child Syndrome." *American Journal of Orthopsychiatry,* 1966, *36,* 861–867.

STRAUSS, A. A. and L. E. LEHTINEN. *Psychopathology and Education of the Brain Injured Child.* New York: Grune and Stratton, 1947.

SYKES, D. H., DOUGLAS, V. I., WEISS, G., and K. K. MINDE. "Attention in Hyperactive Children and the Effect of Methylphenidate (Ritalin)." *Journal of Child Psychology and Psychiatry and Allied Disciplines,* 1971, *12,* 129–139.

SYMMES, J. S. and J. L. RAPOPORT. "Unexpected Reading Failure." *American Journal of Orthopsychiatry,* 1972, *42,* 82–91.

TEMPLIN, M. C. "Developmental Aspects of Articulation." In Wolfe, W. D. and D. J. Goulding, (Eds.). *Articulation and Learning: New Dimensions in Research, Diagnostics, and Therapy.* Springfield, Illinois: Thomas, 1973, pp. 51–83.

TRAVIS, L. *The Handbook of Speech Pathology and Audiology.* New York: Appleton-Century-Crofts, 1971.

VANRIPER, C. G. *Speech Correction: Principles and Methods* (4th ed.) Englewood Cliffs, New Jersey: Prentice-Hall, 1963.

WAIZER, J., HOFFMAN, S. P., POLIZOS, P., and D. M. ENGELHARDT. "Outpatient Treatment of Hyperactive School Children with Imipramine." *American Journal of Psychiatry,* 1974, *131,* 587–591.

WEISS, G., MINDE, K., WERRY, J. S., DOUGLAS, V., and E. NEMETH. "Studies on the Hyperactive Child: VIII. Five Year Follow-up." *Archives of General Psychiatry,* 1971, *24,* 409–414.

WENDER, P. H. *Minimal Brain Dysfunction in Children.* New York: Wiley-Interscience, 1971.

WERRY, J. S. "Studies on the Hyperactive Child. IV. An Empirical Analysis of the

Minimal Brain Dysfunction Syndrome." *Archives of General Psychiatry.* 1968, *19,* 9–16.

WERRY, J. S. and R. L. SPRAGUE. "Hyperactivity." In Costello, C. G. (Ed.). *Symptoms of Psychopathology: A Handbook.* New York: Wiley, 1970.

WINITZ, H. *Articulatory Acquisition and Behavior.* New York: Appleton-Century-Crofts, 1969.

WOLFE, W. D., and D. J. GOULDING (Eds.). *Articulation and Learning: New Dimensions in Research, Diagnostics, and Therapy.* Springfield, Illinois: Thomas, 1973.

WOOD, N. E. *Delayed Speech and Language Development.* Englewood Cliffs, New Jersey: Prentice-Hall, 1964.

WORSTER-DROUGHT, C. "Speech Disorders in Children." *Developmental Medicine and Child Neurology,* 1968, *10,* 427–440.

ZAHN, T. P., ABATE, F., LITTLE, B. C., and P. H. WENDER. Minimal Brain Dysfunction, Stimulant Drugs, and Autonomic Nervous System Activity. *Archives of General Psychiatry,* 1975, *32,* 318–387.

10

Mental Retardation

PROLOGUE

Regina was a seven-year-old first grader who was a source of great concern to her parents, although they did not openly discuss their fear of what might be wrong with her. References to Regina's apparent "slowness" were met with defensiveness, denial, or attempts to conceal the obvious facts. It was only after several parent-teacher conferences, and the school's insistence that she be placed in a special class for slow children, that her parents agreed to have her evaluated by a clinical psychologist. In the process, it was established that Regina was unable to read, write, recognize alphabet letters or numbers, or in any way meet the minimal learning requirements of the first grade. Her history revealed consistent evidence of delay in motor, speech, self-help, and social development, although she was physically normal and emotionally stable. On the basis of all the findings, including her I.Q. score of 61, she was given the diagnosis of mental retardation—mild.

Regina's story is all too familiar, because it describes youngsters we have known, and it reflects our pessimistic attitudes about the future prospects of those who fall into the category of the mentally retarded. Yet, we must not subscribe to the popular notion that Regina is representative of a homogeneous entity who share similar behavioral characteristics, comparable educational handicaps, and predictable social and voca-tional outcomes. In fact, the term *mental retardation,* or synonymous labels such as mental deficiency, feeblemindedness, amentia, or mental handicap, refers to a heterogeneous condition involving many different patterns of assets and limitations, and a diversity of etiologies. Moreover, mental retardation (as we have noted previously) may be associated with or actually mimic the symptoms of a variety of abnormal behaviors to the extent that discrimination between the two conditions is difficult. The coexistence of mental retardation and personality disorder is not uncommon, although the underlying nature of the relationship may differ in one of the following ways:

1. The relationship may be coincidental in that the two conditions may be present in the same individual.
2. Both forms of abnormal behavior may be the expression of a single pathological process of the brain.
3. The personality disorder may be the result of a primary deficit in intelligence, reflecting the retardate's limited capacity to cope with stressful situations.
4. The subnormal intelligence may be the product of a primary personality disorder, reflecting behaviors that are characteristically impaired in the particular aberrant personality. (Benton, 1964; Benton, 1970; Bialer, 1970).

In this chapter, we shall consider the major clinical and research issues about mental retardation, including the definition, the incidence, the descriptive levels of retardation, the divergent etiological factors, and the institutional and remedial provisions.

Definition

The most current and accepted definition of mental retardation is the one offered by the American Association on Mental Deficiency (AAMD), which states:

Mental retardation refers to significantly subaverage general intellectual functioning existing concurrently with deficits in adaptive behavior, and manifested during the developmental period. (Grossman, 1973, p. 11).

While this definition emphasizes intelligence, it also acknowledges that intelligence is neither a sufficient nor an exclusive criterion of mental retardation. The additional criterion of deficits in adaptive behavior restricts reliance on measured intelligence and requires evidence of a broader and more consistent nature. For example, it guards against the possibility of misdiagnosing youngsters who for reasons of educational deprivation or sensory handicap (the blind and deaf) cannot be assessed accurately by traditional tests of intelligence. Some writers question the test constructors' assumption that intelligence is normally distributed on a bell-shaped Gaussian curve, on the grounds that the experiential components of intelligence (social and educational) are not equally available to everyone (Wortis, 1970). Wortis points out that based on current I.Q. scores there is a higher incidence of mental retardation found in the lower socioeconomic level, a finding that unduly penalizes this population because they have been deprived of social and educational opportunities afforded others.

The inclusion in the AAMD manual of an adaptive behavior scale by which various aspects of development, social behavior, and independent functioning can be rated is an important step in assessing adaptive behaviors. Unless this scale is refined empirically or new ones are devised, the undue emphasis given to intelligence scores is likely to continue (Robinson and Robinson, 1970). But adaptive capacity is difficult to measure because it rests with social change and is dependent on the individual's life situation. In a society such as ours, in which technological advances and urbanization are commonplace, and where human existence is complex and difficult, we would expect to find many individuals who are unable in some way to adapt to these demands. What sort of adaptive failures are indicative of mental retardation? Does the increase in impaired adaptive behavior associated with social change mean that mental retardation is on the rise? The problem encountered here can be illustrated in the relationship found between age and the incidence of mental retardation; that is, during infancy and preschool years, the incidence is relatively low but it rises sharply in the school years until fourteen or fifteen, while the number of people first diagnosed as mentally retarded declines in adult life (Lemkau and Imre, 1969). It is reasonable to conjecture that changes in the level of adaptive behavior account for this relationship, in that children who are intellectually subaverage (at least those moderately impaired) can cope successfully with the minimal social demands made during infancy and preschool, while at a later age the demands become more complex, making adaptation more difficult. The fact that there is a decline in the incidence of detection of mental retardation during adulthood suggests that these cases have already been identified, and it is in accord with the finding that many forms of mental retardation are associated with a short life expectancy. If adulthood has been reached without prior evidence of mental retardation, clinicians are inclined to look upon impaired adaptive behaviors as manifestations of an abnormal condition other than mental deficiency.

Because the AAMD definition is purely behavioral in nature and makes no attempt to account for etiological factors, it may be less than satisfactory to those who are primarily concerned with the issues of causation and prevention. Zigler (1967) has argued that a greater degree of order could be brought to the field if distinctions were made between physiological and cultural-familial etiologies. He maintains that the difference between the cultural-familial retardate and the nonretardate is attributable to differing motivational systems and not to mental retardation per se.

It is significant that no implication concerning outcome is included in the current definition. The popular expectation that the mentally retarded are doomed to a life behind institutional walls because they are unable to work or engage in any social relations is intentionally avoided, because it simply isn't true. As we shall see, there are many retardates (especially those falling into the borderline level and even some in the mild category) who are capable of holding employment, of getting married, and of having and raising children.

Incidence

As with so many of the other abnormal conditions we have considered, the incidence of mental retardation is virtually impossible to estimate accurately because it varies with the definition, the diagnostic criteria (especially the I.Q. cut-off point), and the age and socioeconomic level on which prevalence figures are based. In the absence of a national survey of all instances of mental retardation, incidence estimates tend to come from small sample surveys, extrapolated guesses, and the experience of workers in the field.

Within these limitations, mental retardation is recognized as a major problem with an incidence rate exceeded only by mental illness, cardiac disease, arthritis, and cancer (*The First Report to the President on the Nation's Progress and Remaining Great Needs to the Campaign to Combat Mental Retardation*, 1962). Based on the I.Q. score of 70 or below, there is a consensus that more than six million Americans, or three percent of the population, are retarded. As substantial as this figure is, there are those who regard it as low because it fails to include those borderline retarded (I.Q. scores that fall one standard deviation from the mean) in whom we find evidence of slow rate of learning, difficulty in comprehending complex ideas, limited ability to generalize from one experience to another, and poor academic achievement. If this group were included, as suggested by the American Psychiatric Association (*Diagnostic and Statistical Manual of Mental Disorders,* 1968), the incidence of mental retardation would be in excess of thirty-two million, or sixteen percent of the population. However, the 1973 AAMD definition specifically deleted the borderline category because it was impractical and potentially damaging to label so many as mentally retarded, and because a large number of persons falling in this group are able to make adequate adjustments within the community. It is for this reason that we shall restrict our discussion to the consideration of those persons who meet the intellectual and adaptive criteria of the AAMD definition (I.Q. scores that are two standard deviations or below the mean I.Q. score).

Most studies show that mental retardation is higher in males than females, in black children than white, in lower socioeconomic levels as contrasted with middle and upper classes, and in different geographical areas of the country where there are striking variations in the availability of facilities and services for the retarded (Robinson and Robinson, 1965; Smith, 1971). In addition, approximately ten percent of the mentally retarded population have I.Q.s below 50, while about ninety percent have I.Q.s between 50 and 70 (Dingman and Tarjan, 1960; *The Decisive Decade,* 1970).

Levels of Retardation

It is customary to subdivide mental retardation in terms of degree of intellectual and adaptive impairment, although the primary importance of the I.Q. is reflected in most, if not all, classification systems. The AAMD manual (Grossman, 1973) describes four categories: *Mild, Moderate, Severe, and Profound,* and it carefully specifies that intelligence is to be measured by standardized intelligence tests that are administered individually by trained professionals. Each level of mental retardation is expressed by a range of I.Q. scores corresponding to a standard deviation unit that describes the distribution of I.Q. scores in the general population on the most widely used tests of intelligence. Because an I.Q. score is subject to errors of measurement, it can be expected to vary from one time to another. Therefore, it is arbitrary and misleading to regard an I.Q. near the top of one range as fixed within this level, since actually it may reflect the individual's capacity to function in the lower portion of the next higher category.

Another problem associated with the classification of mental retardation by levels stems from the inclination to use the scores to draw inferences about the child's future behavior, in spite of the fact that test scores (and I.Q.s) only reflect present performance. The danger in inferring future potential lies in the possibility that planning for the child will be limited by his presumed capacity, which may preclude opportunities for education and training beyond this predicted level. In the absence of any preconceived notion about a child's limited potential, achievement can reach heights that exceed prior expectation (Birnbrauer, Wolf, Kidder, and Tague, 1965). Consequently, scores and levels of retardation must be interpreted as indicative of present functioning, rather than as a stereotyped and fixed prediction of the child's future limitations.

1. Mild Mental Retardation (I.Q. range of 52 to 67) is the largest category, accounting for almost ninety percent of all retardates. Although as adults their intellectual level is much like that of children aged eight to eleven, with proper training and special education many of the mildly retarded are able to make an adequate social and vocational adjustment. When employed, they typically hold unskilled jobs that yield no more than a low socioeconomic income. They frequently need supervision in the management of their social and financial affairs, and because of their limited work skills, they are particularly vulnerable to unemployment as the economy fluctuates. Some find employment in sheltered workshops where supervision is provided and where working conditions are uncomplicated and nonstressful. The vast majority show no signs of brain pathology or physical aberrations that would readily distinguish them from normals. In fact, it has been estimated that only about one percent of this group are institutionalized (Hobbs, 1964). Many mildly retarded children are unidentified until the academic demands of school make their deficiencies apparent. Once they are diagnosed, the school regards them as educable (a descriptive label that corresponds to this I.Q. range) and as eligible for special education classes (if available). Unfortunately, only one out of three is placed in a program where the teacher is a specialist, where the classes are small, and where students learn at their own pace without the social stigma of failure (Mackie, 1965).

2. Moderate Mental Retardation (I.Q. range of 36 to 51) is a category that accounts for approximately six percent of retardates. Persons who function at this level are very slow to learn, and their conceptualization skills are extremely limited. While they have some command of the spoken language, typically they cannot read or write. With proper training, they are capable of acquiring self-care behaviors and of performing routine chores in the home or in a sheltered workshop. In school, they are considered *trainable,* and are eligible for special education classes that emphasize the development of practical and basic self-help skills in lieu of academic matters. Most moderately retarded individuals stand out as different from others in that they have poor motor coordination, as well as physical deformities and anomalies. They require close supervision in almost everything they do, and they have few, if any, friends. Institutionalization is dependent on their level of social competence and the extent to which their families are willing and able to care for them in the home.

3. Severe Mental Retardation (I.Q. range of 20 to 35) represents approximately three and a half percent of the retarded population, most of whom are institutionalized or under constant supervision in the home. Only the upper range are eligible for trainable classes, while the others are not accepted by most school systems. The vast majority of the severely retarded exhibit genetic disorders, brain pathologies, sensory defects, or, in some instances, severe emotional disturbances. Their learning capacity is very limited, to the extent that

SIDELIGHT 10–1: IDIOT SAVANT [1]

Yoshihiki Yamamoto is a famous and gifted Japanese artist, although he has never obtained an I.Q. score above 47. When he was six months old, it was learned that he had hydrocephalus (a condition that involves an abnormal accumulation of fluid on the brain) and that in all likelihood he would be mentally retarded. His retardation was more apparent when he was old enough to start school, in that he had a moderate hearing loss, could not talk, and was not toilet trained. Because special education was not available, his parents were forced to place him in the regular elementary school from which he graduated at age twelve at the very bottom of the class. On an evaluation before entering junior high, he obtained an I.Q. of 23 (or a mental age of three), indicating that he was unable to continue in the regular school program. It was Yamamoto's good fortune to be placed in a special class with a teacher, Takashi Kawasaki, who patiently developed a special curriculum around Yamamoto's artistic talent, promoted and sold his art work in order to purchase additional art supplies, and helped his student maintain a rigid and intensive daily work schedule.

Two illustrations of Yamamoto's work are included here to reflect the unbelievable quality and beauty of his artistic talent. Yet Yamamoto may be referred to as an *idiot savant,* a retardate with some highly developed skill that is grossly discrepant with his level of functioning in other areas. Stories similar

FIGURES 10–1 and 10–2 (From Morishima, 1975, p. 72 and 73 and reprinted with permission of the Ziff-Davis Publishing Co.).

[1] Adapted from Morishima, 1975, pp. 72–73.

to Yamamoto's (but probably less gifted) have appeared in the literature, albeit infrequently. There is no satisfactory explanation for the rare appearance of specific superior skills in these mentally retarded individuals, although Yamamoto's story provides the optimistic suggestion that with special care, interest, program construction, and supervision some retardates may achieve unexpected levels of performance.

they require prolonged training in order to acquire minimal self-help skills. Their motor, speech, and social development are severely retarded.

4. Profound Mental Retardation (I.Q. under 20) is the rarest and most extreme category, accounting for about one and a half percent of all retardates. Ordinarily individuals in this group are institutionalized and require constant supervision and frequent medical care. Many are confined to a bed or are unable to move about unaided because of central nervous system disorders, sensory and motor disturbances, metabolic aberrations, and other physical disabilities. As a group, their life expectancy is short, with death often occurring during the childhood years. They show little evidence of learning, although some manage to learn to walk, to speak one or two simple phrases, or to acquire partial self-care in feeding and in going to the toilet.

Etiological Considerations and Related Clinical Disorders

It should be apparent from what has been said that mental retardation is not a unitary entity that appears in the same form, to the same degree, at the same time. It is not always produced by the same causal factors and can result from one circumstance or from the interaction among a number of circumstances that may occur before, during, or after birth. Moreover, the condition varies in severity and in the behavioral characteristics of those affected. It has been estimated that there are more than 300 known or suspected causes of mental retardation, yet these account for not more than twenty-five percent of all the cases (Love, 1973). In approximately seventy-five percent of retarded individuals, there is no evidence of brain pathology. These cases are usually referred to as the cultural-familial defectives, in whom incompletely understood sociocultural, psychological, and hereditary factors are implicated as etiological variables.

We turn now to the consideration of the major biological and environmental factors leading to mental retardation, and to the description of some of the distinguishable clinical types of retardation especially associated with known biological causes. At the same time, we note that our efforts to separate biological and environmental forces are intended for convenience and ease of exposition, and not to deny or ignore the important interplay that exists among them. The baby who is born with the rare hereditary milk sugar disease known as *galactosemia* will suffer permanent brain damage and will eventually die if fed with milk that contains lactose. However, with early identification and proper environmental changes in diet, the baby may develop normally. Thus, the interaction of both biological and environmental factors contributes significantly to the critical questions of whether and how the infant survives.

Heredity and Chromosomal Abnormalities

There is a long-standing popular view that heredity plays a primary causative role in mental retardation. Stimulated by Darwin's theory of natural selection, Galton studied the family trees of certain distinguished British families and arrived at the conclusion that genius was inherited (Hunt, 1961). In this country, Goddard in 1912 published the results of his well-known study of the Kallikak family, in which he argued that feeble-mindedness and certain other undesirable traits were genetically transmitted. The pioneer constructors of intelligence tests (Simon, Binet, Stern, and Goddard) were influenced by this view, and to varying degrees regarded intelligence as fixed and genetically predetermined (Sattler, 1974). Subsequent research evidence indicating that (1) the I.Q. was constant from one age level to another, (2) Binet-type intelligence tests were highly intercorrelated, and (3) the tests results were good predictors of general academic achievement led many to believe that intellect was a fixed and genetically determined characteristic. Further support came from animal studies in which Coghill demonstrated that development proceeded on an orderly basis and was rarely affected by exigencies of the external environment (Coghill, 1929), and from infant studies showing that the emergence of a fundamental skill such as walking was unaffected by the deprivation of practice opportunities (Dennis and Dennis, 1940). Thus, there seemed to be strong evidence to support the view that development was genetically regulated and relatively uninfluenced by experiential factors.

But soon the weight of research support shifted to the importance of prior experiences in determining whether or not certain patterns of behavior would be exhibited. The effects of early stimulation on both the rate and quality of development, and the influence of many environmental factors on such primary areas as learning, memory, thinking, perception, and personality formation were considered increasingly important. The battle between hereditarians and environmentalists over the nature-nurture problem continues to the present without resolution. Most contemporary students of behavior regard it as an insoluble problem, principally because it begins with an erroneous assumption and asks the wrong questions. Heredity and experiential factors interact, and both contribute to human development and behavior. Instead of pitting one set of variables against another, it is more appropriate to attempt to study the effects of one factor while the other is held constant, and to determine the specific conditions under which both heredity and environment may influence behavior (Hebb, 1965).

While it is true that many forms of mental retardation tend to run in families, known hereditary diseases or chromosomal abnormalities are evident in only a small number of these cases. The most prevalent are the cultural-familial type who fall within the mildly retarded category, and who best exemplify the interactive effects of both genetic and environmental factors. We shall consider this group when we discuss environmental factors, since little is known about the specific genetic defect or mode of transmission for this population. In the meantime, let us direct our attention to those already identified genetic conditions that lead to mental retardation. Obviously, only a selected sample of these disorders can be included here to provide the reader with some better understanding of the variety of genetic effects and the resulting types of clinical symptoms.

Recessive Genetic Disorders. Within recent years, technical advances in laboratory methods in the field of genetics have made possible significant contributions to our understanding of the etiology of mental retardation. At present, most of the genetically determined syndromes involve recessive genes that alter in some way the development of an enzyme essential for normal metabolism, or that impair metabolic processes.

1. *Abnormalities of Amino Acid Metabolism.* Although recessive disorders affect the metabolic processes in different ways, the largest number of known syndromes is associated with faulty metabolism of amino acids (Robinson and Robinson, 1970). Donohue (1967) noted that there are at least eighteen different types of amino acid metabolic disturbances associated with mental retardation and neurological dysfunction. While these account for approximately three percent of the institutionalized retardates, about one third of this group are affected by a disorder known as *Phenylketonuria* or *PKU* (Holmes, Moser, Halldorsson, Mack, Pant, and Matzilevich, 1972).

Phenylketonuria is an autosomal recessive metabolic disorder in which the affected infant lacks a liver enzyme needed to oxidize phenylalanine (an amino acid found in protein food) to tyrosine. As a result, phenylalanine is improperly utilized by the body, and its accumulation in the blood stream causes brain damage and mental retardation. Large amounts of phenylpyruvic acid are excreted in the urine, which gives the urine a characteristic musty odor. As a matter of fact, this odor led to the identification of PKU by Folling in 1934 after mothers of retarded children called it to his attention. Although it is a rare disorder occurring in one in 10,000 to one in 20,000 Caucasian births, PKU has received a good deal of public attention because it illustrates a form of mental retardation that can be prevented by early detection and low phenylalanine diets (Bakwin and Bakwin, 1972).

Evidence of mental retardation may appear within the first few months of life, and almost certainly between six and twelve months after birth. Behaviorally, PKU is characterized by hyperactivity, bizarre body movements, severe temper outbursts, and retardation that is most often severe (although moderate cases can occur). There are reports of rare instances in which intelligence is normal or even superior in persons whose phenylpyruvic acid is high (Perry, 1970). Some cases exhibit eczema, vomiting, and convulsions. Hair, skin, and eye color is usually lighter than that of the unaffected members of the family (Gellis and Feingold, 1968).

The diagnosis may be made by adding a few drops of ferric chloride to an infant's urine and observing the subsequent color stain. A green or greenish-blue color indicates the presence of PKU. However, the absence of a green color obtained within six weeks of birth may not be a true indication of normality because an excess of phenylalanine may be absorbed in the mother's blood during fetal life. A blood test measuring the level of phenylalanine and tyrosine is a more reliable method of identifying PKU early, and this is now required in most states as a means of prevention (Berman, Cunningham, Day, Ford, and Hsia,

1969). Treatment by controlled intake of phenylalanine is ordinarily effective if initiated prior to the age of three months; otherwise, the resultant brain damage is irreversible and mental retardation cannot be arrested. Some infants are damaged by the elevated level of phenylalanine of their mothers, a condition that can be prevented if mother's phenylalanine intake is controlled during pregnancy (Holmes et al., 1972).

Other amino acid metabolic disorders leading to mental retardation include: Menkes' syndrome or Maple-Syrup disease, Hartnup's disease, Citrillinuria, and Homocystinuria, all of which are extremely rare and are best treated early by special diets.

2. *Amaurotic Family Idiocy: Abnormalities of Lipid Metabolism.* In general, these disorders are transmitted genetically as autosomal recessive traits and result in the faulty metabolism of fatty compounds needed for the development of the central nervous system. They are characterized by progressive mental and physical deterioration that almost always results in early death.

Tay-Sachs disease is probably the best known of this group of disorders. It is found most frequently among children of eastern European Jewish ancestry, who represent some fifty to sixty percent of these cases (Carter, 1970). Affected infants appear normal at birth and only begin to show gradual signs between four and eight months of age, when they display sensitivity to noise, tremors of the extremities, listlessness, and retarded motor development. The disorder is progressive, and the child exhibits signs of muscular spasticity, muscular degeneration, blindness, convulsions, and accentuation of hearing, and of the startle reflex. The child's head and abdomen enlarge, and typically a cherry red

spot on the eyegrounds is present. Death occurs usually before the age of four years. There is no known treatment for this disorder.

Prospective parents of eastern European Jewish ancestry can be tested for the presence of the recessive gene (blood is analyzed for the level of the enzyme produced by normal genes). If both the father and mother carry the gene, amniocentesis can determine whether the fetus has inherited the fatal double dose. If only one member of the couple carries the recessive gene, then the child may also be a carrier, but he or she will not have the disease. In other words, this disease could really be eliminated from the population through genetic testing and abortion of fetuses found to have the disease.

Niemann-Picks' disease is rarer but quite similar to Tay-Sachs disease in that it also affects more Jewish children, has an early and gradual onset of common symptoms, and results in early fatality (Carter, 1970). Distinction between the two conditions is made by the absence of the eyeground sign characteristic of Tay-Sachs disease. If there is a family history of the disease a skin biopsy of prospective parents will reveal the presence or absence of the recessive gene.

In two other types of Amaurotic Idiocy, the clinical picture is somewhat the same as already described, but the onset occurs either in young children between six and eight years old *(Early Juvenile Cerebral Lipoidosis)* or later in life between twenty and thirty years of age *(Early Adult Amaurotic Idiocy or Kuf's disease).*

3. *Abnormalities of Carbohydrate Metabolism.* The best known form of these disorders is *Galactosemia* (referred to earlier), another autosomal recessive metabolic condition, which, in this case, impairs the

infant's ability to metabolize galactose. The disorder appears immediately after birth or as soon as the child begins to ingest milk. Symptoms include vomiting, diarrhea, colic, weight loss (or failure to gain weight), and cataracts, which may later be followed by jaundice and cirrhosis of the liver (Carter, 1970). Although the disorder usually produces mental retardation, it can be prevented by early detection (through a test of the urine) and treated by the elimination of lactose in the diet, probably for the duration of the child's life.

4. *Abnormalities of Endocrine Function.* The labels *hypothyroidism* or *cretinism* are used to designate several aberrant conditions of the thyroid that may be associated with mental retardation. Hypothyroidism could result from thyroid or iodine deficiency in the mother during pregnancy, from an absence of the thyroid gland, or less frequently from a genetically determined enzyme defect that interferes with the proper synthesis of thyroxine (Heber, 1970). According to Holmes et al. (1972), instances of congenital hypothyroidism resulting from different causes are clinically indistinguishable except for the presence of a goiter early in life in nongenetic cases, in contrast to a later appearance of this symptom (between the ages of five and ten) in genetically caused cases. Children who are cretins have a characteristic appearance that includes puffy eyelids, flat nasal bridge, open mouth with a thick protruding tongue, short and thick neck, enlarged abdomen, dry and mottled skin, short stature, stubby fingers, and, if untreated, delayed or no sexual maturation. In addition, their motor and mental development is retarded; the degree of retardation is proportional to the severity and early occurrence of the thyroid deficiency. Thyroid extract is often successfully used to reverse the symptoms of congenital hypothyroidism, although evidence suggests that only fifty percent of infants treated before six months of age had average or better I.Q. scores (Wilkins, 1965).

Chromosomal Abnormalities. It is estimated that the prevalence of chromosomal abnormalities in live-born infants is about one in 20,000. This estimate is even higher if fetuses are considered, since ninety percent of fetuses carrying such an abnormality are spontaneously aborted (Holmes et al., 1972). In general, infants born with chromosomal abnormalities are equally divided between those with autosomal abnormalities and those with sex chromosomal abnormalities. We shall consider an example of each type of chromosomal abnormality.

1. *Down's syndrome* or *Mongolism* is a disorder that was described clinically well over 100 years ago, although its identification as an autosomal syndrome associated with an extra Group-G chromosome (trisomy 21) was discovered in 1959 by Lejeune, Gautier, and Turpin (1963). Mongolism occurs more frequently in boys than girls, and it is seen in all racial, ethnic, and socioeconomic groups. It has been estimated that approximately one out of every 600 live births and about ten to fifteen percent of all institutionalized retardates are mongoloid (Heber, 1970). These children typically fall within the moderate to severe categories of mental retardation, and they are characterized by distinctive physical features, deficient muscle tone (hypotonia), congenital heart defects, and feeblemindedness.

The mongoloid has almond-shaped, slanting eyes, with the skin of the eyelids very thick. The lips are thin and appear fissured and dry, with the tongue also showing deep fissures. The teeth are usually small and misshapen; the nose is flat; hair is generally sparse, fine and straight. Hands and feet are broad and clumsy, and the mongoloid is awkward in both gross and fine motor coordination. He has fingerprints with L-shaped loops rather than the usual whorls. One other outstanding characteristic of the mongoloid is his deep voice, which is often helpful in making a diagnosis (Love, 1973, p. 59).

Mongolism is a chromosomal aberration that does not follow simple Mendelian genetic transmission. Research investigating the factors that cause the chromosomal aberration has failed to yield definitive results. Reported correlations with viral hepatitis and with fluoride in the drinking water have been soundly criticized, and seem unpromising at present. However, it is well established that older mothers run a high risk of bearing mongoloid children, in that more than half of these youngsters are produced by mothers who are in their late thirties and forties. Moreover, the approximate risk per pregnancy in mothers under twenty-nine years of age is one in 3,000, contrasted to a risk of one in fifty-five for mothers in their forties (Koch, Fishler, and Melnyk, 1971). Faulty intrauterine conditions that are more likely to occur in older pregnant women have been thought to produce the chromosomal abnormality, although the specific factors have not as yet been identified.

Down's syndrome is irreversible and not amenable to treatment, although chromosomal analysis of mother after conception helps provide an estimate of risk and helps prevent the disorder in most instances.

2. *Klinefelter's syndrome* (47/XXY) illustrates a group of disorders associated with chromosomal abnormalities of the sex chromosome. In this condition which affects only males, there is an extra X chromosome. The disorder is characterized by a tall and effeminate body build, sterility, small testes, breast enlargement (in adolescents and adults), and diminished facial and body hair. Although the frequency of mental deficiency among those with Klinefelter's syndrome is higher than in the general population (about twenty-five percent), in a large number of the cases intelligence is either unaffected or slightly lower than average.

The most common anomaly of the sex chromosome in females is *Turner's syndrome* (XO), in which approximately twenty percent of those affected are mentally retarded. Sexual infantilism, short stature, webbing of the neck, flat nasal bridge, epicanthal folds, and protruding and/or low set ears are common features associated with this disorder. Hormonal treatment given at the proper time for both Klinefelter's and Turner's syndromes helps increase the maturation of secondary sexual characteristics (Gellis and Feingold, 1968).

Other Biological Factors. In this section we shall consider a number of other biological determinants of mental retardation that may occur before, during, or after birth.

1. *Infections and Toxins.* Obviously not all infections give rise to brain damage and mental deficiency, although some that are contracted by the mother during pregnancy and others that occur in the child postnatally are known to produce neurological and intellectual deficits. For example, mothers who have rubella (German measles) during the first trimester of pregnancy give birth to offsprings who show an array of congenital anomalies, including sensory defects (deafness and cataracts),

heart lesions, and mental retardation. However, the discovery of a vaccine to protect youngsters against rubella has radically reduced the serious consequences of this infectious disorder. During the twenty-year period between 1935 and 1955, the danger of fetal infection from mothers infected with syphilis decreased as this venereal disease declined. Within recent years, the frequency of syphilis has increased, making this form of transplacental infection more likely (Heber, 1970). Congenital syphilis is associated with premature births, copper-colored or red spots on the buttocks, saddle-nose deformity, seizures, brain damage, and mental deficiency. The greatest risk of fetal infection occurs after the first four months of pregnancy in mothers who have recently contracted syphilis (Holmes et al., 1972). Postnatally, encephalitis (viral infections of the brain) and infections of the meninges (membrane cover of the brain) result in brain damage and mental retardation in about ten to twenty percent of the children affected (Koch, 1971). Early symptoms of fever, stiff neck and back, and headache are usually exhibited. Fortunately, these infections are rare in this country.

Toxic substances such as lead and carbon monoxide also can produce brain damage and mental retardation. Lead ingestion (from old paint) interferes with brain-cell metabolism and may result not only in severe retardation, but possibly in death. Jaundice occurring after twenty-four hours in the newborn is a sign of possible incompatibility of blood types between the mother and the fetus. If untreated by proper blood-exchange transfusions, it usually leads to kernicterus (a yellow bilirubin staining of brain areas) and mental retardation. The two most common types of blood incompatibility are Rh-factor and ABO.

SIDELIGHT 10-2: FETAL ALCOHOL SYNDROME

At a recent conference on birth defects Dr. Sterling Clarren reported that he could smell alcohol on the breath of a baby he had delivered. The child's mother was a heavy drinker who had continued to imbibe during the course of the pregnancy. At birth, "the child's eyes were small. His nose and cheekbones were flat. The child's growth was stunted—he weighed in at under five pounds—and the joints got stuck. He couldn't move his fingers."

First identified as *fetal alcohol syndrome* by Dr. David Smith, the problem is said to occur in one of every 4,000 births and possibly more frequently. Clarren estimates that the disorder ranks as the third leading cause of mental retardation.

Apparently, alcohol is particularly damaging to the early development of the fetus during the first eighty-five days of pregnancy, although the specific manner by which the damage occurs is not now known. The extent of the impairment is said to be dependent on the amount of alcohol used by the pregnant mother. Unfortunately, the defect cannot be detected before birth and in time for a therapeutic abortion. Of course, the disorder would be prevented entirely if pregnant mothers would abstain from drinking (from "Baby Born Deformed with Alcohol on Breath UPI," January 5, 1977, p. 9B).

2. *Trauma, Injury, or Physical Agent.* The potentially harmful effects of irradiation and nuclear fall-out have been well known since the atomic bombing of Hiroshima and Nagasaki at the close of World War II. Pregnant women who have been exposed to large amounts of irradiation of the uterus run the risk of giving birth to offsprings who are microcephalic (small head), mentally retarded, and structurally deformed in the eyes and the limbs. Birth is a physically demanding and traumatic event for the newborn, and either precipitous or prolonged labor, the fetal position, the baby's head size, uterine and pelvic anomalies, and hazards associated with the umbilical cord can lead to either intracranial hemorrhage or anoxia. Either condition may produce brain damage and mental retardation, although medical advances have substantially reduced the probability of mental deficiency occurring from birth trauma (*Infant Care,* 1968). Unconsciousness, persistent vomiting, and possible mental confusion are common symptoms of trauma to the brain. Head injuries caused by household or automobile accidents also may result in brain damage and impaired cognitive functioning. Nylander and Nylander (1964) made the interesting observation that head injuries are more likely to occur in retarded than in normal youngsters, and that most head injuries are too mild to be regarded as a cause of mental retardation.

3. *Premature Birth.* Follow-up studies of premature infants with birth weights less than three pounds and five ounces indicate a high incidence of physical and mental disorders, including mental deficiency. However, many of these studies have been criticized for their failure to account for the relationship between social class and birth weight, and for their tendency to ignore the

fact that the expected distribution of intelligence for prematures is below the normal mean. Nevertheless, the results of the more carefully controlled studies consistently show that prematurity is associated with a higher rate of mental retardation in both white and non-white populations (Pasamanick and Lilienfeld, 1955; Masland, 1960; McDonald, 1964).

4. *Nutritional Deprivation.* Malnutrition, especially deficiencies of certain vitamins during early development, can cause physical and intellectual deterioration (Cravioto, Delicardie, and Birch, 1966). Moreover, vitamin deficiency, particularly of Vitamins A and E, in the mother during pregnancy has been associated with prematurity, congenital malformations of the central nervous system, and mental retardation (Carter, 1970). Several experimental studies involving both humans and animals have demonstrated that protein deprivation reduces appetite and adversely affects brain growth and mental performance (Barnes, Moore, Reid, and Pond, 1967; Winick, 1968; Zamenhof, van Marthens, and Margolis, 1968). Although comparable evidence for humans is not available, it is interesting to note that animals deprived of proper nutrition over successive generations are less efficient in reproduction and in mothering, and tend to have smaller litters with lower birth weights and higher mortality (Stein and Kassab, 1970). At present, the social and preventative implications of these animal studies for those people who live under poverty conditions from one generation to another are striking, although tentative.

Environmental Factors and Cultural-Familial Retardation. In the absence of demonstrable evidence of genetic and/or biological factors causing more than seventy-five percent of all cases of mental retardation, there is a strong inclination to turn to environmental influences as a viable alternative. In this light, the importance of the environment in shaping behavior is secondary to biological considerations, and instances of unknown (organic) etiology become attributed to psychosocial determinants. The issue is not over which of the two classes of variables is of primary significance, but over the implication that the absence of one set of conditions can be taken as supportive evidence for the other. Obviously, in order to consider a variable as a causal agent, its influential effects must be demonstrated empirically. Therefore, we shall examine the sociocultural forces that appear to play a significant role in determining mental retardation.

Cultural-Familial Mental Retardation. Although the current AAMD definition of mental retardation avoids etiological considerations, it is generally accepted that the cultural-familial type of mental deficiency refers to those mildly retarded individuals in whom no biological or genetic abnormality can be found, and who have a retarded parent or sibling. This implies that both heredity and environment play a causal role, and yet, almost without exception, discussions take the form of heredity versus environment where the two are in opposition to each other. Girardeau (1971), after an extensive and critical review of the literature, concludes that there appears to be no scientific evidence at present to confirm either heredity or environment as a major causative factor in cultural-familial retardation. The question of how these factors interact "could be approached more appropriately in terms of specific experimental questions rather than as a gross generalization" (p. 341).

It is well established that mental retardation is essentially a lower-class phenomenon for those cases (primarily falling between I.Q.s of 50 to 75) in which there is no evidence of neurological and/or genetic abnormalities (Hardy, 1965; Kushlick, 1966). Persons of low socioeconomic level often have incomes that do not permit adequate nutrition, medical care, housing and living conditions, or social and intellectual enrichment. Children in this group tend to be less supervised during the day, having working parents or one parent who had been abandoned by the other and left with the full responsibility of managing the household. Their schools are apt to have poor facilities and educational programs, while the availability of academic, verbal, or intellectual materials is likely to be extremely limited in both the schools and the home. Therefore, poverty may indirectly or directly lead to some of the biological determinants of mental deficiency already discussed such as prematurity, infections and toxins, birth injuries, or malnutrition.

Support for the influence of social and economic deprivation on brain weight, learning, and intellectual development is derived from a variety of sources. Tests show that animals reared in enriched environments with bright lights and with conditions that facilitate play and exploration have heavier cerebral cortices and greater cortical activity than those reared in a sensory deprived environment (Bennett, Diamond, Krech, and Rosenzweig, 1964). Restricted environments impair the learning performance of preadult rodents. However, as Meier points out, "primate studies indicate that any laboratory rearing procedure leads to defective behavior, especially of connotative rather than cognitive behavior, when these animals are compared with feral or socially reared controls" (Meier, 1970, p. 291). Thus, there is a disparity in results between the two animal species which Meier believes is attributable to a failure to understand differences among species and among the variables that affect their behavior. More importantly, he criticizes the categorical generalization of findings based on animal data to rearing practices in humans. Nevertheless, longitudinal studies with humans have shown that lower-class children, as compared to those of the middle class, receive from their mothers significantly fewer vocalizations, smiles, rewards for developmental progress, or prolonged periods of play (Kagan, 1969). Kagan argues that deprivation of these early experiences has a deleterious effect on mental development, which is reflected in lower I.Q. scores.

We know that the usual outcome of socioeconomic deprivation is academic failure and restricted employment potential after school. The academic progress of many lower-class children may be impaired because of their bilingualism and the negative attitude that disadvantaged communities hold toward education and their prospect of social and economic upward mobility. Data on the effects of early sensory and maternal deprivation largely derived from animal studies are provocative, but too tenuous to extend to humans without considerably more research. It is entirely possible that the atypical social histories associated with low social and economic class membership have a greater deleterious influence on emotional and motivational factors than on cognition.

As a matter of fact, there is ample evidence that the mentally retarded (stemming from a history of repeated experiences of failure) expect little success, set low goals for themselves, accept levels of success that are much below their cognitive abilities, and tend to exhibit avoidance behavior under conditions of heightened expectations of failure (MacMillan, 1969; Zigler, 1971). Zigler (1971) also notes that social deprivation largely contributes to an array of overdependent behaviors often observed in retardates (especially the institutionalized familial retardate), such as seeking attention and affection. He suggests that their perseverative behavior can be more properly attributed to their heightened motivation for adult support than to an inherent cognitive rigidity. Moreover, Zigler convincingly argues that observed change in I.Q. scores following some environmental intervention is a reflection of motivational changes and is not attributable to the influence of intellectual stimulation.

One of the most impressive and convincing demonstrations of the potent influence of environmental factors on later intellectual and social functioning is Skeels' follow-up study of infants evaluated some thirty years earlier (Skeels, 1966). Skeels studied two groups of children mostly from poor family backgrounds, many of whom had mentally retarded mothers and were illegitimate. After evaluation, the two groups received different treatments. One group was transferred before age three from an overcrowded and unstimulating orphanage to an institution for the mentally retarded, where the environment was regarded as more enriched in interpersonal relationships, and where there were mother-surrogates and a greater amount of developmental stimulation. The second group, known as the contrast group, was confined for a prolonged period of time to the nonstimulating orphanage environment. Children in the experimental group remained in the institution for the retarded until they had received maximum benefit, and then they were either placed in adoptive homes or returned to the orphanage for transfer to an adoptive home. The length of stay in the institution for the retarded ranged from 5.7 to 52.1 months. Children in the contrast group remained in the orphanage until placement, for periods of time ranging from 21.4 to 43.1 months.

Over the first two years of the study, the experimental group showed a dramatic average gain of 28.5 I.Q. points, while the contrast group, which was initially higher in intelligence, showed an average decline of 26.2 I.Q. points. After twenty-one years, all subjects were located and further studied. Essentially, the divergent patterns noted earlier for the two groups persisted into adulthood. All of the experimental subjects were self-supporting, and all had completed an average of twelve grades in school. Eleven were married, and nine had children whose I.Q.s ranged from 86 to 125. In the contrast group, one member had died in adolescence, and four were still institutionalized. The contrast group completed, on the average, less than three grades of school; only sixty-four percent were employed and those who were employed held menial and unskilled jobs. Only two members of this group were married, and one was subsequently divorced.

Skeels' findings suggest that nurturance and cognitive stimulation early in childhood are important determinants of intellectual, personality, and social development through adulthood.

Remedial Approaches

In the early 1960s, the President's panel on mental retardation sent missions to several European countries in order to learn more about their progress in the care, education, and rehabilitation of the mentally retarded. The initial task of identifying those promising aspects of facilities and programs for later replication in this country was relatively easy. But, as is the case with most transplants, the ultimate success largely depends on the extent to which the donor and the recipient are compatible. Compatibility here refers to the attitudes and values held by different societies toward mental retardation, which greatly influence the basic policies and programs selected and how they are implemented. Lippman (1972) contends that the advances he observed in Scandinavia as compared to the United States primarily are attributable to attitudinal differences between the countries. He identified the following three fundamental attitudes in Scandinavia that seemed to be responsible for their successful programs and services:

1. Mentally retarded people are human beings. They should therefore be treated with respect for their individual dignity.
2. We do not always know what capabilities a retarded person may have, but we must do all we can to help each one achieve his (or her) fullest potential.
3. It is society's responsibility to help the retarded, as it must help others who are handicapped or dependent; and society works most effectively through the state (Lippman, 1972, p. 7).

In Scandinavia, comprehensive health services, special education, sheltered workshops, hostels for community living, and residential facilities are provided when needed for all citizens, whereas in the United States a full range of these services is not uniformly available. Scandinavian residential programs are state operated or sponsored, and they are designed to provide for a smaller number of clients than most state institutions for the retarded in this country. Living conditions are rarely crowded and overpopulated, as we know them here, because privacy and individuality are highly regarded, and because the Scandinavians hold different attitudes toward the retarded than Americans do. Consequently, the Scandinavian countries typically design their facilities to provide clean, colorful, and well furnished surroundings with space for personal belongings, attractive pictures hanging on the walls, an absence of locks, and strict adherence to the simple amenity of knocking on closed doors before entering a room. In contrast, many of our institutions are drab, sterile, and impersonal, and they are operated on the premise that the retarded are just as personally insensitive and unaware of the environment as they are intellectually limited. Inactivity is uncommon in Scandinavian residences, even for those who are severely retarded. All are encouraged to participate in some productive activity and to utilize their resources to the fullest. Most Scandinavian retardates live in the community, where a large proportion find employment without resistance or prejudice. Apparently, they are judged by the same criterion of productivity that other employees are expected to meet.

While little, if any, data are available to assess public attitudes toward mental retardation in this country, inferences can be drawn from an examination of the institutional environment in which some retardates are required to live. The deplorable living conditions in institutions for the retarded, together with an analysis of the political and social forces that interfere with improvement, have been candidly described elsewhere (Blatt and Kaplan, 1966; Blatt, 1970).

A severe indictment of institutions for the mentally retarded is voiced by Braginsky and Braginsky (1971), who argue that many children have been institutionalized because they were rejected and unwanted by their families and not because of mental retardation *per se*. They claim that residential facilities and labels such as "mental retardation" are used primarily by society and parents as ways to justify their acts of abandonment and to alleviate the guilt that accompanies these actions. It is not unusual for the retardate to be rejected by his or her family, shunned by employers, ostracized by peers, denied heterosexual relationships, and ignored by the community (Love, 1973).

As unpleasant as these revelations may be, it is necessary to understand our attitudes toward the retarded as we consider the kinds of programs and services offered in this country.

Overcoming Parental Resistance

All prospective parents hope for a "normal and healthy child." While any abnormality is disappointing, emotionally disturbing, and difficult to accept, the diagnosis of mental retardation is particularly shocking and troublesome for most affected parents. Perhaps this is attributable to the pessimistic assumptions commonly held in our society that imply that the retarded child's potential and future outlook are dismal and hopeless. It may be that such a diagnosis is threatening and guilt provoking to parents, because it reflects uncomfortably on the family "line" in terms of either inheritance or some biological defect. The fear that the child will have to be banished permanently to an institution, or, if kept at home, will become the object of ridicule and embarrassment to members of the family are real possibilities and problems. Moreover, the sudden prospect of having to cope with and manage a poorly understood condition is sufficient in itself to arouse a great deal of anxiety in most parents.

There is general agreement that parental attitudes and reactions to their mentally retarded child are important influences in shaping the life of both the family and the handicapped child. It has been found that parents of retarded children are quite anxious about the future, and are especially concerned about what will happen to the child when they are no longer able to care for him or her (Condell, 1966). Other research data are interpreted as indicating that parents of retarded children are more rejecting than those of average youngsters, and that fathers have more difficulty in accepting retarded sons than daughters (Worchel and Worchel, 1961; Paymer, 1965; Levine, 1966). Parental guilt, ambivalence, anger, shame, and grief are some of the other parental reactions that are likely to disturb the relationship between parents, affect child-rearing practices, and have a significant impact on the adjustment of normal children in the family.

In dealing with the problem of mental retardation, the clinician cannot function merely as a thorough diagnostician, since parents are neither unaffected by the clinical findings, nor knowledgeable and omnipotent enough to manage the situation without any further professional assistance. Counseling over a period of time is necessary in order to provide information to parents with regard to their specific questions about the diagnosis, etiology, prognosis, and immediate and long-range therapeutic plans for their child (Kanner, 1961, pp. 453–461). In addition, the clinician must be prepared to deal with the emotional reactions of parents and to help them work through their feelings to the point where they can be comfortable with themselves and the limitations of the child. Toward these ends, participation in group sessions with other parents who are experiencing similar difficulties, and availability of counseling services at various stages of the child's life, may be very beneficial.

Programs for the Institutionalized Retarded

No type of retardation in itself indicates the need for residential care, although most institutionalized retardates are classed as severe or profound and require almost constant and specialized management. There is general agreement that the retarded child should remain in the home and function in the community for as long as possible. However, the extent to which this can be accomplished will depend on the adequacy and stability of the family, its economic resources, and its capacity to cope with the special needs and problems of the child. In addition, the child's placement is influenced by the availability and strength of the educational programs, the vocational training and placement opportunities, and other resources in the community. Thus, a mildly or moderately retarded child from a broken home may require institutionalization or foster-home placement, because the remaining working parent is unable to provide proper supervision and care. In circumstances where the community fails to provide the necessary program or service, residential care may be the most desirable placement for the child.

Privately supported residential facilities are available throughout the country, but the cost is usually prohibitive for most middle and lower socioeconomic families. Publicly supported state institutions typically are overcrowded, with waiting periods that may be longer than a year before admission is possible. With increasing frequency, state institutions are occupied by the more severely and profoundly retarded, where there is a higher incidence of multiple problems that cannot be readily managed on the outside. Medical advances have significantly increased the life expectancy for some of these children, which, in effect, has unexpectedly decreased the turnover rate in most state institutions.

Residential facilities offer such varied services as nursing, medical and dental care, special education, vocational training, and recreational activities. However, institutions have been criticized on the grounds that they tend to process patients in a depersonalized way, shifting them from service to service rather than using existing resources flexibly (Kirman, 1972; Gunzburg, 1973). Moreover, many severely retarded, institutionalized individuals spend between one third to one half of their waking day doing absolutely nothing, and up to one fifth additional time engaging in autistic behaviors (Klaber, 1969).

However, in recent years dramatic changes have been taking place in the institutional programs, in the attitudes of the staff, and in the behavior of the residents. These changes can be attributable largely to the systematic application of learning principles known as *behavior modification*. This approach is essentially positive in nature, in that it assumes that retardates can learn, can do things for themselves, can function more effectively, and can profit from and enjoy a wider range of experiences. As Bigelow (1977) so aptly stated:

The focus is always upon improvement. No limit is set on what an individual can learn, other than the limits of his own rate of progress. Some individuals may progress quickly, others more slowly, but all are capable of learning. This positive approach of focusing upon teaching specific skills can drastically alter one's view of retardation. Frustration and pessimism is minimized once we see the residents learning (p. 18).

Illustrations of behavior modification with the mentally retarded are numerous, demonstrating that new behaviors can be acquired and maintained, and that old unwanted behaviors can be eliminated. Beginning with Fuller's (1949) interest in showing that through operant conditioning an eighteen-year-old vegetative idiot (who was thought hopelessly unable to learn) could learn the simple response of moving his arm in order to receive a food reinforcer, behavior modification has been used with increasing frequency and effectiveness to alter the behavior of retardates. Since that time, a variety of self-help behaviors have been taught successfully to the severely retarded, such as bowel and bladder control, tying shoes, fastening buttons, and washing. In addition, language acquisition, speech correction, and increased social competence in the acquisition of table manners or in the elimination of fighting and other disruptive behaviors have been accomplished with behavior modification (Weisberg, 1971; Thompson and Grabowski, 1972). The ease with which behavior modification can be taught to the nonprofessional staff makes possible and economically feasible the involvement of a larger number of caretakers in teaching new behaviors to the retarded. Those using this approach must first select target behaviors for improvement that are both useful to the resident in normal living and in keeping with his or her limitations. Errors that ordinarily slow the learning process are lessened by breaking the target behavior into a series of small steps. Thus, learning to name colors may be approached by learning to name one color at a time and even by dividing this task into specific simple components, such as looking at the stimulus, saying the name, and then saying the correct name when the stimulus is presented. Of course, the learning of each step is accomplished primarily through the careful arrangement of the consequences of the behavior, that is, giving a reward immediately following the correct response while incorrect responses are unrewarded. At present, the use of behavior modification extends beyond institutional programs to community-based special education and vocational activities.

Programs for the Community-Based Retarded

In this section, we mainly shall direct our attention to the mildly retarded and to the two major programs, special education and vocational training and placement, that seem to play the most significant role in their future adjustment.

Special Education. Programs in special education are neither uniform from state to state nor necessarily uniform among cities and counties of a given state. Some communities are entirely without special education programs for the educable retarded, while others differ with regard either to the maintenance of a separate facility apart from the regular public schools, or to the segregation by classes within the regular school of programs that service the mentally retarded. The community special school is designed to meet the needs of those children who are unable to cope with and

profit from a normal school situation and who presumably require a specialized environment that is too costly for decentralization (Cruickshank, 1967). Youngsters who are isolated in such an environment may or may not have their special educational needs met there, but all are deprived of opportunities to learn to socially interact with normal children, with whom they must successfully relate if they are to make an adequate adjustment as adults. This concern is also raised by some educators who prefer not to have separate self-contained classes for the retarded as part of the regular school program, but rather would handle retarded students through *mainstreaming,* where the retarded could participate at some time during the school day in normal classes and activities. The effectiveness of mainstreaming has not yet been evaluated systematically, although some studies are in progress with regard to preschool and school-aged children (Ingram, 1976; Cooke, Appolloni, and Cooke, 1977; Levitt, 1977). Another variant of special education is the resource teacher who provides special assistance to students only in specific areas where they require additional help, such as reading, braille for blind students, speech correction, or arithmetic.

Unfortunately, special classes for the mentally retarded service only about twenty percent of those who need it (*The Decisive Decade,* 1970). When they are available, there may not be enough classes to accommodate all those who should be placed there. In addition, some schools attempt to move disruptive but otherwise normal children from the regular program into special classes, but in most instances, the special teacher can resist such efforts by adhering to the standards of eligibility established by the school system (I.Q. scores below a certain cut-off point).

At the elementary age level, special education curricula for the mentally retarded generally include information that will help the retardate function in the normal environment, and skills that will enable social, personal, and vocational self-sufficiency. These programs seek to maintain adequate levels of performance for appropriate interaction with the environment (Smith, 1971). Class size should be small enough to enable the teacher to provide each student with individual attention to his or her needs and to facilitate maximum growth. Ample opportunities for successful experiences are needed to build self-confidence and to motivate students to make additional progress. At the secondary level, the curriculum is ordinarily structured to continue the efforts of the elementary school program and to teach social and vocational skills that will maximize the retardate's personal adjustment and employment potential.

Vocational Training and Placement

Among the mildly retarded, training and personality rather than intellectual ability appear to be the most influential determinants of employment success. Inadequate performance and difficulties in interpersonal relationships are the chief reasons for their adjustment failures (Shawn, 1964; Gorelick, 1966). Schools and sheltered workshops have been the primary vocational training grounds for the mentally retarded. On the basis of observations of school programs across the country, Gold (1973) draws the following conclusions:

1. Little connection exists between classroom activities and work activities.

2. Where work experience is part of the program, training is left to the student's job supervisors.

3. Criteria for success are poorly defined.

4. Subjective evaluation of student performance by the job supervisor is often the only measure by which the student is judged.

5. There is a reliance on the creativity and enthusiasm of staff in the absence of a technology of systematic training (pp. 101–102).

Workshops may be either transitional or permanent, and students may prepare for later placement or work for indefinite periods of time, because they are incapable of competitive work assignments. Work contracts are obtained from the business world to provide vocational training and actual paid work experience for the trainees. Research has shown that work performance can be increased by means of a token reinforcement system, by giving a bonus, or by isolating the student from other trainees if the work production fails to meet a certain level (Campbell, 1971). The relatively recent development and success of autoinstructional techniques to teach new work skills to the retarded is extremely promising in increasing the employability of the retarded and the willingness of industry to contract with sheltered workshops.

Prevention

Although some progress has been made in preventing mental retardation, it is curious and deplorable that in a society such as ours, preventive measures and programs have not kept pace with our knowledge of the etiological factors involved in this disorder. Not all states require either the various laboratory tests of newborns that would provide the early detection of known metabolic disorders, such as phenylketonuria or galoctosemia, or the routine tests for red-cell ABO antibodies in the cord blood of babies whose mothers are group O. Genetic counseling based on laboratory evaluation of chromosomal numbers and types occasionally is available to assist parents about future pregnancies which, in turn, could affect the future frequency of mental retardation. However, most states and communities throughout the country do not have a premature infant program that experts believe would significantly reduce the incidence of multiple handicaps, mental retardation, and fatalities. Rh-blood testing of pregnant mothers prior to delivery should be routinely performed, and standard nursery provisions should be established in all hospitals handling newborns in order to reduce the problem of infection and crowding. We need to make available to more expectant mothers adequate nutritional and medical care throughout the entire period of pregnancy, not just near the time of delivery, because it is now apparent that many of the etiological factors are related to intrauterine conditions.

More and more attention needs to be given to postnatal environmental forces, primarily those associated with poverty and low socioeconomic status. Variables known to affect intellectual and social development, such as nutritional deficiencies, deprivation of sensory, intellectual, and social stimulation, infections and poisonings, and family disorganization, are frequently found in slum environments.

Programs of sex education and family planning, such as measures to reduce venereal disease and prevent unwanted pregnancies, are of particular importance to the cultural-familial group of retardates. In this connection, there is a segment of society who advocates sterilization and eugenics in order to significantly reduce mental retardation; but a discussion of the moral, ethical, and social implications of this view is beyond the scope of this presentation.

Increased support for research in the areas of etiology and prevention is of course necessary, even though we lag behind in the development of preventive programs that are commensurate with our current knowledge.

Summary

Mental retardation is an heterogenous condition involving many different patterns of assets and liabilities, and a diversity of etiologies. It may be associated with or mimic the symptoms of a variety of abnormal behaviors that often make the discrimination between the two conditions difficult. The current definition of mental retardation specifies two concurrent criteria, subaverage intellectual functioning as measured by standardized individual intelligence tests (I.Q. scores), and deficits in adaptive behavior for which assessment is less refined and available. Based on an I.Q. score of 70 or below, more than six million Americans, or three percent of the population, are retarded.

Approximately ninety percent of the mentally retarded population have I.Q.s between 50 and 70, while about ten percent have I.Q.s that fall below 50. The following four levels of mental retardation have been used to describe the degree of intellectual and adaptive impairment:

Mild .... I.Q.s between 52 and 67
Moderate .... I.Q.s between 36 and 51
Severe .... I.Q.s between 20 and 35
Profound .... I.Q.s below 20

These categories are arbitrary inasmuch as an I.Q. score is subject to errors of measurement and can be expected to vary from one time to another.

More than 300 known or suspected biological causes account for approximately twenty-five percent of all cases of retardation, whereas there is no evidence of brain pathology for the vast majority of the cases (seventy-five percent). These cases are usually called *cultural-familial retardates,* in whom incompletely understood sociocultural, psychological, and hereditary factors are implicated as etiological variables. Recessive genetic disorders affecting amino acid, lipid, and carbohydrate metabolism and endocrine functioning were discussed and illustrated with such specific conditions as PKU, Tay-Sachs disease, galactosemia, and cretinism.[1]

Approximately one in 20,000 live-born infants have chromosomal abnormalities either of the autosomal or sex chromosome type. Down's syndrome or mongolism is the best known and most frequent of the autosomal abnormalities (trisomy 21) that occurs more in boys than girls, and in babies of older pregnant women. Although specific causal factors have not as yet been identified, it is thought that faulty intra-uterine conditions produce the chromosomal anomaly. Klinefelter's and Turner's syndromes were described as disorders associated with chromosomal abnormalities of the sex chromosome. Other biological factors such as infections and toxins, trauma, injury, irradiation, prematurity, and nutritional deprivation were also considered.

There is evidence that sociocultural forces play a significant role in mental retardation, especially the cultural-familial type which, essentially, is a lower-class phenomenon. Poverty environments are characterized by poor nutrition, poor medical care, and deprivation of the sociocultural stimulation needed for normal growth and development. These early and continued deprivations not only have a deleterious effect on cognitive development but perhaps an even greater influence on the individual's emotional and motivational structure.

Management and remedial programs for the retarded in the Scandinavian countries were contrasted to the programs offered in the United States.

In general, most authorities agree that retarded youngsters should live at home and function in the community for as long as possible. Residential facilities are occupied by the more severely and profoundly retarded, although some mild and moderate retardates are also institutionalized. The use of behavior modification has dramatically changed the institutional programs, staff attitudes, and the behavior of the residents.

Special education classes for the retarded serve only about twenty percent of those who need it. At the elementary school level, the program strives to provide the retardate with information that will help him function in the normal environment, and with skills that will facilitate social, personal, and vocational self sufficiency. Sheltered workshops are either transitional or per-

[1] These disorders, with the exception of Tay-Sachs disease, can be successfully treated if started early by special diets or hormones.

manent in providing retardates preparation for later placement or opportunities to work for indefinite periods of time. Token reinforcement systems, work for pay, financial bonus, or social punishment are among the various behavior modification techniques used successfully in vocational training and placement.

Preventative programs have failed to keep pace with our current knowledge of the etiological factors involved in mental retardation. Laboratory tests for the early detection of known metabolic disorders, for red cell ABO antibodies, and Rh-blood testing of pregnant mothers should be routinely required. Genetic counseling to assist parents in making decisions about future pregnancies along with maintaining adequate prenatal medical and nutritional care, and premature infant programs should be available in or near all communities. Postnatal environmental factors, particularly those associated with low socioeconomic status, need more attention in order to reduce their adverse affect on intellectual and social development.

Epilogue

Regina's parents found it difficult to accept the diagnosis of mental retardation, even though (or perhaps because) it confirmed their worst fear. It took several sessions with the psychologist to explore their feelings and concerns about Regina and her condition. As they became more open and willing to discuss the situation, they agreed to participate in group sessions with other parents of retarded children, and to begin to make short- and long-term plans for Regina. Discussions between the school authorities, the parents, and the psychologist were initiated and continued until Regina was properly placed in a special class. At home, the parents were more accepting of Regina in terms of both her assets and limitations. They all worked hard at increasing Regina's social competence, and in giving her support and positive reinforcement for her accomplishments and for her gradual independent functioning in certain areas. Regina's small successes delighted her parents, who in turn spontaneously showed their pleasure with appropriate rewards. Two years later, Regina shows definite but slow signs of learning in school, along with better social skills in greeting people, in her eating behavior, and in her personal hygiene and appearance. She is a happy child at school and at home with parents and teachers, who are working together to provide her with understanding and the assistance she needs to make most use of her resources.

REFERENCES

"Baby Born Deformed with Alcohol on Breath." *Atlanta Journal,* January 5, 1977, p. 9B.

BAKWIN, H. and R. M. BAKWIN. *Behavior Disorders in Children* (4th ed.). Philadelphia: Saunders, 1972.

BARNES, R. H., MOORE, A. U., REID, I. M., and W. G. POND. "Learning Behavior Following Nutritional Deprivations in Early Life." *Journal of the American Dieticians Association,* 1967, *51,* 34–39.

BENNETT, E. L., DIAMOND, M. C., KRECH, D., and M. R. ROSENZWEIG. "Chemical and Anatomical Plasticity of the Brain." *Science,* 1964, *146,* 610–619.

BENTON, A. L. "Psychological Assessment and Differential Diagnosis." In Stevens, H. A. and R. F. Heber (Eds.), *Mental Retardation: A Review of Research* (1st ed.). Chicago: University of Chicago Press, 1964, pp. 16–56.

BENTON, A. L. "Interactive Determinants of Mental Deficiency." In Stevens, H. A. and R. F. Heber (Eds.). *Mental Retardation: A Review of Research* (1st ed.). Chicago: University of Chicago Press, 1970, pp. 661–671.

BIALER, I. "Relationship of Mental Retardation to Emotional Disturbance and Physical Disability." In Haywood, H. C. (Ed.), *Social-Cultural Aspects of Mental Retardation.* New York: Appleton-Century-Crofts, 1970, pp. 607–660.

BERMAN, J. L., CUNNINGHAM, G. C., DAY, R. W., FORD, R., and D. Y. Y. HSIA. "Causes of High Phenylalanine with Normal Tyrosine in Newborn Screening Programs." *American Journal of Diseases of Children,* 1969, *117,* 54–65.

BIGELOW, G. "The Behavioral Approach to Retardation." In Thompson, T. I. and J. Grabowski (Eds.), *Behavior Modification of the Mentally Retarded* (2nd ed.). New York: Oxford University Press, 1977, pp. 17–45.

BIRNBRAUER, J. S., WOLF, M. M., KIDDER, J. D., and C. E. TAGUE. "Classroom Behavior of Retarded Pupils with Token Reinforcement." *Journal of Experimental Child Psychology,* 1965, *2,* 219–235.

BLATT, B. *Exodus from Pandemonium: Human Abuse and a Reformation of Public Policy.* Boston: Allyn and Bacon, 1970.

BLATT, B. and F. KAPLAN. *Christmas in Purgatory: A Photographic Essay on Mental Retardation.* Boston: Allyn and Bacon, 1966.

BRAGINSKY, D. D. and R. M. BRAGINSKY. *Hansels and Gretels: Studies of Children in Institutions for the Mentally Retarded.* New York: Holt, Rinehart and Winston, 1971.

CAMPBELL, N. "Techniques of Behavior Modification." *Journal of Rehabilitation,* 1971, *37,* 28–31.

CARTER, C. H. *Handbook of Mental Retardation Syndromes* (2nd ed.). Springfield, Illinois: Thomas, 1970.

COGHILL, G. E. *Anatomy and the Problem of Behavior.* New York: Macmillan, 1929.

CONDELL, J. F. "Parental Attitudes Toward Mental Retardation." *American Journal of Mental Deficiency,* 1966, *71,* 85–92.

COOKE, T. P., APPOLLONI, T., and S. A. COOKE. "Normal Preschool Children as Behavioral Models for Retarded Peers." *Exceptional Children,* 1977, *43,* 531–532.

CRAVIOTO, J., DELICARDIE, E. R., and H. G. BIRCH. "Nutrition, Growth and Neurointegrative Development: An Experimental and Ecologic Study." *Pediatrics,* 1966, *38,* 319–372.

CRUICKSHANK, W. M. "Current Educational Practices with Exceptional Children." In Cruickshank, W. M. and G. O. Johnson (Eds.), *Education of Exceptional Children and Youth* (2nd ed.). Englewood Cliffs, New Jersey: Prentice-Hall, 1967, pp. 43–93.

The Decisive Decade. President's Committee on Mental Retardation. Washington, D.C.: Government Printing Office, 1970.

DENNIS, W. and M. G. DENNIS. "The Effect of Cradling Practice upon the Onset of Walking in Hopi Children." *Journal of Genetic Psychology,* 1940, *56,* 77–86.

Diagnostic and Statistical Manual of Mental Disorders (2nd ed.). Washington, D.C.: American Psychiatric Association, 1968.

DINGMAN, H. F. and G. TARJAN. "Mental Retardation and the Normal Distribution Curve." *American Journal of Mental Deficiency,* 1960, *64,* 991–994.

DONOHUE, W. L. "Lesions in the Central Nervous System Associated with Inborn Errors of Amino Acid Metabolism." *Acta Paediatrica,* 1967, *56,* 116–117.

The First Report to the President on the Nation's Progress and Remaining Great Needs to the Campaign to Combat Mental Retardation. President's Committee on Mental Retardation. MR 67. Washington, D.C.: U.S. Government Printing Office, 1962.

FULLER, P. R. "Operant Conditioning of a Vegetative Human Organism." *American Journal of Psychology,* 1949, *62,* 587–590.

GELLIS, S. S., and M. FEINGOLD. *Atlas of Mental Retardation Syndromes.* U.S. Department of Health, Education and Welfare. Washington, D.C.: U.S. Government Printing Office, 1968.

GIRARDEAU, F. L. "Cultural–Familial Retardation." In Ellis, N. R. (Ed.), *International Review of Research in Mental Retardation* (Vol. 5). New York: Academic Press, 1971, pp. 303–348.

GOLD, M. W. "Research on the Vocational Habilitation of the Retarded: The Present, the Future." In Ellis, N. R. (Ed.), *International Review of Research in Mental Retardation* (Vol. 6). New York: Academic Press, 1973, pp. 97–147.

GORELICK, M. C. *An Assessment of Vocational Realism of High School and Post–High School Educable Mentally Retarded Adolescents.* Los Angeles: Exceptional Children's Foundation, 1966.

GROSSMAN, H. J. (Ed.). *Manual on Terminology and Classification in Mental Retardation: 1973 Revision.* Special publication of the American Association on Mental Deficiency, 1973.

GUNZBURG, H. C. "The Role of the Psychologist in Manipulating the Institutional Environment." In Clarke, A. D. B. and A. M. Clarke (Eds.), *Mental Retardation and Behavioral Research. Study Group # 4.* Baltimore: Williams and Wilkins, 1973, pp. 57–67.

HARDY, J. B. "Perinatal Factors and Intelligence." In Osler, S. F. and R. E. Cooke (Eds.), *The Biosocial Basis of Mental Retardation.* Baltimore: Johns Hopkins Press, 1965, pp. 35–60.

HEBB, D. O. "Heredity and Environment in Mammalian Behavior." In Anastasi, A. (Ed.), *Individual Differences.* New York: Wiley, 1965, pp. 160–170.

HEBER, R. *Epidemiology of Mental Retardation.* Springfield, Illinois: Thomas, 1970.

HOBBS, M. T. "A Comparison of Institutionalized and Noninstitutionalized Mentally Retarded." *American Journal of Mental Deficiency,* 1964, *69,* 206–210.

HOLMES, L. B., MOSER, H. W., HALLDORSSON, S., MACK, C., PANT, S. S., and B. MATZILEVICH. *Mental Retardation: An Atlas of Diseases with Associated Physical Abnormalities.* New York: Macmillan, 1972.

HUNT, J. McV. *Intelligence and Experience.* New York: Ronald Press, 1961.

Infant Care. U.S. Government. Washington, D.C.: Universal Publishing and Distributing Corporation, 1968.

INGRAM, S. H. "An Assessment of Regular Classroom Teachers' Attitude Toward Exceptional Children Subsequent to Training on Mainstreaming." *Dissertation Abstracts International,* 1976, *37* (3–A), 1307.

KAGAN, J. "Inadequate Evidence and Illogical Conclusions." *Harvard Educational Review,* 1969, *39,* 126–129.

KANNER, L. "Parent Counseling." In Rothstein, H. (Ed.), *Mental Retardation.* New York: Holt, Rinehart, and Winston, 1961, pp. 453–461.

KIRMAN, B. H. *The Mentally Handicapped Child.* London: Thomas Nelson, Ltd., 1972.

KLABER, M. M. "The Retarded and Institutions for the Retarded—A Preliminary Research Report." In Sarason, S. B. and J. Doris (Eds.), *Psychological Problems in Mental Deficiency.* New York: Harper and Row, 1969, pp. 148–185.

KOCH, R. "Postnatal Factors in Causation." In Koch, R. and J. C. Dobson (Eds.), *The Mentally Retarded Child and His Family: A Multi-disciplinary Handbook.* New York: Brunner/Mazel, 1971, pp. 87–94.

KOCH, R., FISHLER, K. and J. MELNYK. "Chromosomal Anomalies in Causation: Down's Syndrome." In Koch, R. and J. C. Dobson (Eds.), *The Mentally Retarded Child and His Family: A Multi-disciplinary Handbook.* New York: Brunner/Mazel, 1971, pp. 111–137.

KUSHLICK, A. "Assessing the Size of the Problem of Subnormality." In Meade, J. E. and A. S. Parkes (Eds.), *Genetic and Environmental Factors in Human Ability.* A symposium held by the Eugenics Society in September–October, 1965. New York: Plenum Press, 1966, pp. 121–147.

LEJEUNE, J., GAUTIER, M., and R. TURPIN. "Study of the Somatic Chromosomes of Nine Mongoloid Idiot Children." In Boyer, S. H. (Ed.), *Papers on Human Genetics.* Englewood Cliffs, New Jersey: Prentice-Hall, 1963, pp. 238–240.

LEMKAU, P. V. and P. D. IMRE. "Results of a Field Epidemiologic Study." *American Journal of Mental Deficiency,* 1969, *74,* 858–863.

LEVINE, S. "Sex-Role Identification and Parental Perceptions of Social Competence." *American Journal of Mental Deficiency,* 1966, *70,* 822–824.

LEVITT, M. L. "Former Special Education Pupils in the Mainstream: A Descriptive Follow-up Study." *Dissertation Abstracts International,* 1977, *37* (8–A), 5039.

LIPPMAN, L. D. *Attitudes toward the Handicapped: A Comparison Between Europe and the United States.* Springfield, Illinois: Thomas, 1972.

LOVE, H. D. *The Mentally Retarded Child and His Family.* Springfield, Illinois: Thomas, 1973.

MACMILLAN, D. L. "Motivational Differences: Cultural-Familial Retardates vs. Normal Subjects on Expectancy for Failure." *American Journal of Mental Deficiency,* 1969, *74,* 254–258.

McDONALD, A. D. "Intelligence in Children of Very Low Birth Weight." *British Journal of Preventative Social Medicine,* 1964, *18,* 59–74.

MACKIE, R. P. "Spotlighting Advances in Special Education." *Exceptional Children,* 1965, *32,* 77–81.

MASLAND, R. L. "Current Knowledge Regarding the Prenatal and Environmental Factors in Mental Deficiency." *Proceedings of the London Conference on the Scientific Study of Mental Deficiency,* 1960, *Part 1,* 55–76.

MEIER, G. W. "Mental Retardation in Animals." In Ellis, N. R. (Ed.), *International Review of Research in Mental Retardation* (Vol. 4). New York: Academic Press, 1970, pp. 263–309.

MORISHIMA, A. "His Spirit Raises the Ante for Retardates." *Psychology Today,* June 1975, pp. 72–73.

NYLANDER, B. H. and I. NYLANDER. "Acute Head Injuries in Children: Traumatology, Therapy and Prognosis." *Acta Paediatrica,* 1964, *152–157* (Suppl.), 1–34.

PASAMANICK, B. and A. M. LILIENFELD. "Association of Maternal and Fetal Factors with Development of Mental Deficiency." *Journal of American Medical Association,* 1955, *159,* 155–160.

PAYMER, S. S. "Reciprocal Role Expectations and Role Relationships: The Adjustment of the Mentally Retarded." *American Journal of Mental Deficiency,* 1965, *70,* 382–388.

PERRY, T. "The Enigma of PKU." *The Sciences,* 1970, *10,* 12–16.

ROBINSON, H. B. and N. M. ROBINSON. *The Mentally Retarded Child: A Psychological Approach.* New York: McGraw-Hill, 1965.

ROBINSON, H. B. and N. M. ROBINSON. "Mental Retardation." In Mussen, P. H. (Ed.), *Carmichael's Manual of Child Psychology* (Vol. 2) (3rd Ed.). New York: Wiley, 1970, pp. 615–666.

SATTLER, J. M. *Assessment of Children's Intelligence.* Philadelphia: Saunders, 1974.

SHAWN, B. "Review of a Work Experience Program." *Mental Retardation,* 1964, *2,* 360–364.

SKEELS, H. M. "Adult Status of Children with Contrasting Early Life Experiences: A Follow-up Study." *Monographs of the Society for Research in Child Development,* 1966, *31,* Serial No. 105.

SMITH, R. M. *An Introduction to Mental Retardation.* New York: McGraw-Hill, 1971.

STEIN, Z. A. and H. H. KASSAB. "Nutrition." In Wortis, J. (Ed.), *Mental Retardation: An Annual Review II.* New York: Grune and Stratton, 1970.

THOMPSON, T. I. and J. GRABOWSKI (Eds.). *Behavior Modification of the Mentally Retarded.* New York: Oxford University Press, 1972.

WEISBERG, P. "Operant Procedures with the Retardate: An Overview of Laboratory Research." In Ellis, N. R. (Ed.), *International Review of Research in Mental Retardation* (Vol. 5). New York: Academic Press, 1971, pp. 113–145.

WILKINS, L. *The Diagnosis and Treatment of Endocrine Disorders in Childhood and Adolescence* (3rd ed.). Springfield, Illinois: Thomas, 1965.

WINICK, M. "Changes in Nucleic Acid and Protein Content of Human Brain During Growth." *Pediatric Research,* 1968, *2,* 352–355.

WORCHEL, T. and P. WORCHEL. "The Parental Concept of the Mentally Retarded Child." *American Journal of Mental Deficiency,* 1961, *65,* 782–788.

WORTIS, J. "Introduction: What is Mental Retardation?" In Wortis, J. (Ed.), *Mental Retardation. An Annual Review II.* New York: Grune and Stratton, 1970, pp. 1–6.

ZAMENOF, S., vanMARTHENS, E., and F. L. MARGOLIS. "DNA (Cell Number) and Protein in Neonatal Brain: Alterations by Maternal Dietary Protein Restriction." *Science,* 1968, *160,* 322–323.

ZIGLER, E. "Familial Mental Retardation: A Continuing Dilemma." *Science,* 1967, *155,* 292–298.

ZIGLER, E. "Motivational Aspects of Mental Retardation." In Koch, R. and J. C. Dobson (Eds.), *The Mentally Retarded Child and His Family: A Multi-disciplinary Handbook.* New York: Brunner/Mazel, 1971, 369–385.

Psychoneuroses and Psychophysiological Disorders

11

PROLOGUE

Billy was an eight-year-old who was referred to a psychiatrist for symptoms of increasing anxiety, extreme fearfulness, night terrors, and phobias that had prevented him from attending school for a period of about eight months. He spent most of the time at home either playing or reading alone in his room, although on occasion he went out into the yard to play with a friend in the clubhouse they had made. For the most part, he was an active boy who liked to make things with his hands and who seldom was bored because of his capacity to be inventive and imaginative. However, daily (at least once) attacks of panic and apprehension disrupted his state of tranquility. These attacks occurred especially in the evening when father came home or at bedtime. At times, Billy would lie awake in crippling terror as he imagined the presence of strange creatures in the closet, or the movement of shadows in his darkened room. He would hold his breath out of fear of being heard, and sometimes, after a long period of silence and rigid immobility, he would jump out of his bed and run into his parents' bedroom. In addition, Billy had phobias about dirt, germs, and bugs that interfered with his daily living. He meticulously washed his hands before each meal or whenever he touched anything he considered dirty. He had numerous somatic complaints that took the form of a headache, stomachache, fatigue, or merely "I feel bad all over."

Billy's birth and early development were normal, except that during the first year of life he had severe colic that continued far beyond the usual three-month period. He screamed almost constantly during this first year and was unable to sleep longer than two or three hours at a time. His language developed precociously as did his sense of humor, sensitivity, empathy, and personal charm. He was well liked by adults, but he never seemed comfortable with peers. He was quite content and felt safe being alone in his room with a book, and when he was seven he confessed that people had hurt him or disappointed him so often that he felt better off staying away from them. He did well in school but seldom performed at a level commensurate with his ability. His teachers noted that he was often preoccupied, unwilling or incapable of applying himself, and incomplete with assignments. He tended to be late to school and late getting home, and his inclination to be slow in almost everything exasperated both his teachers and parents.

Billy was an only child, although his mother was previously married and had a son sixteen years older than Billy. Mother was an outgoing person but tense, emotional, and given to occasional episodes of "nervous exhaustion," and to periods of incapacitation (each winter) from severe bronchial asthma. Father was a stoic, apathetic, but quick-tempered man who worked as a laborer, had few interests, limited ambition, and who led a routine life that consisted of working, eating, reading the evening paper, and sleeping. He was virtually a stranger to Billy as he sat silently in his chair for hours while at home, only to break the silence with an occasional unpredictable outburst of anger. Billy lived in fear of his father and could only relax when father was absent from the home. When it came time for father to return from work each day, Billy became tense.

There was a very close bond between Billy and his mother. She recognized that she was overprotective and that their relationship was abnormally close. The overinvolvement between them was further enhanced by the mother's asthmatic condition. During her severe attacks both she and Billy feared that she would die, and he would sit by her bedside for hours on end in a kind of deathwatch. The onset of his severe symptoms and his refusal to attend school occurred at the time of her worst asthma attack eight months prior to his psychiatric evaluation (Excerpts of a clinical case from Shaw. *The Psychiatric Disorders of Childhood*, 1966. Courtesy of Appleton-Century-Crofts, Publishing Division of Prentice-Hall, Inc.)

The diagnosis of psychoneurosis used to classify Billy's condition illustrates one set of disorders we shall discuss in this chapter. In addition, we shall consider the psychoneuroses and the psychophysiologic disorders of childhood by describing the clinical picture, the frequency of occurrence, etiological considerations, and therapeutic approaches that are popular or promising for both forms of abnormal behavior.

Psychoneuroses

Although psychoneurotic disorders can take many forms, according to psychoanalytic theory, all of them display the common ingredients of intense feelings of anxiety, personal suffering and discomfort, and self-directed or internalized reactions to the stress of intrapsychic conflicts (Kessler, 1972). There can be little doubt that Billy's anxiety was severe and progressive. He suffered painfully from the fear of imagined creatures and moving shadows as he lay awake in his darkened room, from his phobias of germs and dirt, and from his many somatic ailments. His behavioral symptoms were self-directed or internalized (washing hands or having a headache) rather than externalized (expressing anger toward father or acting out his ambivalent feelings toward mother). Similarly a learning-oriented view of psychoneuroses emphasizes the presence of an uncomfortable level of anxiety as a chief component of these disorders. The anxiety is accompanied by personal discomfort and the persistence of coping responses that are inappropriate and ineffective for the situation.

The differences between these theoretical positions center largely on the nature of the conflicts or the anxiety producing stimuli, the manner by which the coping responses are established, and the purpose these responses serve. Psychoanalytic thinking regards psychoneuroses as a fundamental outgrowth of unconscious conflicts over the handling of sexual and aggressive impulses. In its mediating role, the ego struggles to maintain equilibrium between the expression of id impulses and the censorship of these responses by the superego. The ego expends a great deal of energy in dealing with the intrapsychic conflict and in attempting to maintain some semblance of harmony between these warring personality factions. In the process, ego functioning is often impaired, and the resulting behavioral patterns (symptoms) symbolize the unconscious conflict as well as the ego's efforts to reduce the anxiety level. When the conflict is unresolved, two forms of neurotic disturbance tend to occur. One type is restricted to the stage of psychosexual development of the current conflict and is indicative of a favorable prognosis. Children with this type usually have an uneventful premorbid history with no significant parental problems or contributing constitutional factors. The second type occurs more frequently and is usually evident as a multisymptom blend of two or more neurotic reactions, as illustrated in Billy's clinical picture. In these instances, there is evidence of family pathology, constitutional predisposing factors, prior history of neurotic behaviors, and primitive defense mechanisms.

In contrast, a learning view neither restricts the anxiety producing stimuli to specific kinds of impulses nor postulates separate and combating components of the personality. It more parsimoniously states that the child, in the face of high anxiety, will seek ways to reduce it to more tolerable levels. Any response of the child that promptly decreases the anxiety (even responses not appropriate for the demands of the situation) will be reinforced and will be more likely to occur again in response to the same or similar anxiety arousing stimuli. Thus, through learning paradigms such as classical conditioning and phenomena such as generalization and reinforcement, the child establishes complex associations between the anxiety producing stimuli (that is, any stimulus that arouses anxiety) and the responses he or she uses to cope with that anxiety.

As a point of departure, it matters little which of these views seems to be more persuasive because there are several important areas of agreement that could further our understanding of psychoneurotic disorders. Clearly, these abnormal behaviors involve severe anxiety that prompts responses, albeit inappropriate or inefficient, aimed at allaying the tension. These responses form a persistent behavioral pattern as the child's energies increasingly become tied up in trying to deal with high-anxiety levels. The resultant neurotic child is painfully uncomfortable, grossly unhappy, and noticeably impaired in functioning since he or she is occupied in playing out the repetitious cycle of high anxiety and attempts to reduce it.

Therefore, anxiety plays a key role in the development of psychoneuroses, and it is responsible for the emergence of a variety of counterreactions. In some instances, the child may experience diffuse (free-floating) but intense anxiety that is not attached to an object or event, while in others the anxiety is displaced onto some symbolic object or even converted into somatic symptoms. In still other instances, anxiety may be counteracted by ritualistic and repetitious behaviors, or it may be dissipated by self-deprecation. These various ways of dealing with the central problem of high anxiety represent the diverse forms of neurotic reactions seen clinically. Some Freudians also have given the affective state of depression a similar place of conceptual importance as an arousing state in which the child defends himself or herself against it by various neurotic reactions (Anthony, 1972). The question of why the child chooses a particular technique (set of symptoms) and not another is one that has been especially troublesome for both psychoanalytic and learning theories to answer.

With this as a background for understanding psychoneuroses in general, we now turn to a more specific discussion of the major types of neurotic reactions.

also present. Physical symptoms become prominent especially during an acute anxiety attack, where the child often manifests shortness of breath, palpitations, profuse sweating, faintness, dizziness, nausea, abdominal pain, and diarrhea. Many of these youngsters have anxiety attacks at bedtime, possibly because their sleep pattern is frequently interrupted by nightmares and night terrors, or because their fantasies involve fear of potential threats. In almost all instances, their symptoms bring secondary gain from the special concern and attention that parents usually show. For some of these youngsters, the anxiety level may be chronically high and persistent to the point that their self-preoccupation results in indecisiveness, excessive worrying, and impaired attention. The uneasiness and distress that come with chronic anxiety also encourage timidity and withdrawal from people and outside activities.

Anxiety Reaction

Children who are given this diagnosis experience intense anxiety as vague, undifferentiated, and free-floating (not anchored to a particular object or event) feelings that carry the dreadful expectation of impending doom or catastrophe. Their anxiety is the central symptom, and it goes beyond the apprehensions and fears experienced by almost all children. It is more severe and usually unrelated to external reality, although it may be triggered by a variety of events ranging from the inocuous experience of being called in for dinner to the more serious happenings of failing in school, falling ill, or losing a pet. Irritability, bodily and health concerns, and sudden and severe attacks of anxiety are

Phobic Reaction

This form of neurosis consists of persistent, severe, and irrational fear of which the child is aware but from which he or she cannot free himself or herself. Some observers regard the irrational nature of the fear as the important element in distinguishing phobias from ordinary fears, while others contend that the experience of fear is the same regardless of whether its origin is real or imagined (Jersild, 1968; Kessler, 1972). The ingredient of severity is probably more important since a phobia is usually so debilitating that it interferes with the child's daily functioning. In addition, a phobia has an obsessional quality in that the child ruminates about it and cannot completely free his or her thoughts from it.

In young children, fears and phobias are particularly difficult to distinguish, because fears occur with regularity during the course of normal development. All infants show a startle response (freeze reaction) to loss of support or to any sudden and loud noise. Later, during the first year of life (between five and ten months), babies evidence a fear of strangers in which they react with fear-like panic to unfamiliar people, objects, or situations (see Chapter 4). Between the ages of two and three, fear of animals tends to appear, while beginning with the third year of life, children become fearful of the dark, perhaps because they feel alone and vulnerable to outside forces they can't control. Animal fears increase during the preschool years as animals become part of frightening dreams, and as children become more aware of the powerful and dangerous aspects of animals. Frequently, animal fears are learned and heightened by contagion, that is, through parents, siblings, and others in the environment transferring their own anxiety and fear of animals. "Don't get too close to the dog, he may bite," or "Be careful, the cat may scratch," or "My God! There's a mouse in the room . . . somebody quick do something and catch it!" are only a few of many illustrations of people communicating fear and arousing it in others who may not have been previously affected.

A full-blown *animal phobia* occurs when the fear of the animal becomes unwarranted, intense, and persistent. Freudians maintain that children invest human characteristics in animals, and that animals appear to give free and open expression to children's sexual and aggressive impulses, because animals are not bound by social controls. Therefore, animals provide safer and more primitive objects on which children can project their unacceptable libidinal feelings (Anthony, 1972).

School phobia is of special significance because it represents a frequent problem of school-aged children, especially during the middle years. School phobia is a disruptive condition characterized by acute anxiety, reluctance to go to school, or refusal to leave the home, and numerous somatic complaints. Its onset may be quite sudden and unexpected, although it can ordinarily be traced to some significant precipitating event, such as the change of school or classes, the prospect of returning to school following an illness, hospitalization, or serious illness of a parent (especially mother) an embarrassing incident at school, academic or social failure, and death or fear of death (one's own or that of another) (Leventhal and Sills, 1964; Tietz, 1970). The reaction is one of extreme anxiety, in which many possible somatic symptoms are evident, such as trembling, hyperventilation, headaches, nausea, diarrhea, dysmennorrhea, and sleep and stomach disturbances.

In this country, school phobia occurs at an approximate rate of three per 1,000, while the incidence is slightly higher, 3.8 per 1,000, in England (Clarizio and McCoy, 1970; Smith, 1970). The disorder occurs most often in the first four or five grades of school, and the incidence is about the same for boys and girls in this age group, but higher in girls during the secondary school years (Leton, 1962; Chapman, 1974). There seems to be a positive relationship between age and severity of the underlying disturbance, and between age and prognosis. Children with school phobia are good academic performers, and they are no different in intelligence from children in the general population (Nichols and Berg, 1970;

Hampe, Miller, Barret, and Noble, 1973). They are distinguished from truants by their acute anxiety, somatic symptoms, overattachment to home and family, refusal to leave the home, good academic performance, and absence of antisocial behaviors.

Although generally considered to be a neurotic reaction, there are those who regard school phobia as a complicated entity that may reflect different disorders, causes, and, in turn, require different treatment (Shapiro and Jegede, 1973). For example, in a seven-year-old, refusal to go to school may reflect separation anxiety and the thwarting of dependency needs, whereas in an older adolescent, this behavior may represent a more serious withdrawal pattern that is part of a schizophrenic reaction. Nevertheless, the most frequent cause of school phobia is thought to be a specific form of separation anxiety in which fear of separation is mutually shared by mother and child (Johnson, Falstein, Szurek, and Svendsen, 1941; Kelly, 1973). For the child, a school phobia occurs when this anxiety is repressed and is displaced onto the school environment. Mothers of school-phobic children are viewed as overprotective, ambivalent, fearful of aggression, and inconsistent in their child-rearing practices, while these children evidence immaturity and excessive dependency on their mothers (Davidson, 1961; Nichols and Berg, 1970; Berg and McGuire, 1974).

Evidence of separation anxiety, dependency, and depression was found more frequently in school-phobic children than in controls (Waldron, Shrier, Stone, and Tobin, 1975). Moreover, other data indicated that mothers of school-phobic children tend to be older, since these youngsters appeared late in the birth order of the family, and that these mothers preferred excessively dependent children (Berg and McGuire, 1974; Veltkamp, 1975). Taken collectively, the studies suggest that separation anxiety exists for both mother and child, and that these relatively older mothers are more apt to encourage and nurture dependency in their young offspring as a way of prolonging motherhood and of holding on to their youth. In these cases, the mutual dependency tie is so strong that the school phobia may serve to maintain this attachment for both the mother and child.

Leventhal and Sills (1964) present a somewhat different viewpoint that holds that phobic children tend to overvalue themselves and their achievements. As they try to maintain their unrealistic self-image, they invariably suffer anxiety when their overestimated self-perception is threatened in the school situation. They avoid the threatening situation by withdrawing from it and by the use of helplessness, which, in turn, stimulates the mother to act as the child's protector, enabling the child to seek refuge in the home where mother can repair the damaged self-image. These children vigorously resist attempts to return them to school, since they are oriented toward maintaining their unrealistic self-image or power beliefs.

Another way of explaining school phobia has been through learning principles, especially classical conditioning. According to this view, the school environment acquires the capacity to elicit anxiety or fear through repeated pairings of the neutral stimulus (school) with the fear arousing one (separation from mother). In the presence of situations in which the loss of mother is either real or imagined, fear is intensified and the phobia is formed. In a similar manner, a fear reaction to some specific aspect of school (a punitive teacher or a bully) can generalize to the total school situation, making it a highly anxious place that must be avoided.

Obsessive-Compulsive Reaction

In this particular type of neurotic reaction, the anxiety is isolated from its origin (the unacceptable impulse) through recurrent thoughts (obsessions) or acts (compulsions) or both that the child must perform in spite of the fact that the ideas or the behaviors seem silly or unreasonable. Although the child is unaware of the original source of the anxiety, it is very much tied to the maintenance of obsessions and compulsions in that the child experiences marked apprehension when something or someone interferes with their completion. Minor obsessions and compulsions occur in all children and in many different forms, such as bedtime or feeding rituals that must be played out in proper sequence, walking on the sidewalks without stepping on the cracks, the reverberation of a tune or a jingle in one's thoughts, or the ritualistic behaviors performed by the young baseball batter or the basketball player at the foul line. These reactions are distinguishable from the neurotic in severity and in the degree to which they affect functioning.

Obsessive-compulsive reactions occur with equal frequency in boys and girls and in children of above average intelligence (Judd, 1965; Templer, 1972). The onset may be either sudden or gradual, but in either case, the symptoms often put the child in conflict with the environment and produce guilt feelings. One recent study showed no differences between parents of obsessive children and their middle-class, white, Anglo-Saxon, Protestant counterparts, although it has been long maintained that these youngsters come from obsessional parents (Adams, 1972; Anthony, 1972).

Conversion Reaction

In this neurotic reaction, the original anxiety is transformed into a dysfunction of body parts that are under the voluntary control of the central nervous system. The symptoms symbolically express the underlying conflict and decrease the anxiety generated from it to the extent that the child appears to be relatively indifferent to the physical dysfunction. This has been referred to as *la belle indifference,* reflecting the absence of marked anxiety that one would ordinarily expect to be associated with impaired bodily functioning. The physical symptomatology in conversion reactions can mimic almost any organic disease, although it can be influenced by suggestion, and it ordinarily does not follow anatomical lines. Frequent symptoms involving motor disturbances include paralysis, tics, and tremors, while those involving sensory difficulties include loss of sensation (anesthesia), a peculiar skin sensation without objective cause (paresthesia), and extreme sensitivity (hyperesthesia).

Conversion reactions are as common among boys as girls, although more frequent in female adolescents and adults and in black children (Proctor, 1967). Proctor indicates that these youngsters tend to be older than others who come to clinics for abnormal behaviors, but that this may reflect his observation that many conversion reactions are seen more frequently and given symptom relief by pediatricians and other physicians. Thus, he contends that earlier instances are both unrecognized and unrecorded as conversion reactions. A number of observers (Proctor, 1967; Anthony, 1972; Kessler, 1972) note that conversion reactions have declined, especially in the middle and upper social classes, and now they are largely confined to working-class and educationally unsophisticated people. The facts that there have been cultural changes from strict to permissive in child-rearing practices and sexual attitudes, and that people are more knowledgeable than ever before about their biological functioning, suggest a decrease in the superego's need to use repression, and a decline in the influence of suggestion in the formation of neurotic reactions.

Depressive Reaction

Children with depressive reactions internalize their original conflict through self-deprecation and despondency. These youngsters experience guilt, loss of self-esteem, ambivalent feelings toward significant people in their environment, helplessness, and loneliness. But because we don't expect children to be depressed and because they are frequently unable to verbalize or describe their feelings, these reactions often go undetected by parents and professionals alike. In fact, some clinicians say that depressive reactions make up about twenty-five percent of their caseload, and that almost all of them are associated with real-life events affecting the child and involving the parents (Clark, 1977). Depressive symptoms in children may be masked by apathy, social withdrawal, somatic complaints (headache or abdominal pain), and even by a display of aggressive behaviors such as vandalism, sexual acting-out, or truancy, especially in older children. Poor appetite, weight loss, and disturbed sleep patterns so characteristic of severe depressions in adults may be present, although some youngsters have been known to increase their intake of food and gain weight during bouts of depression.

In addition to the difficulties already noted in recognizing depressive reactions in children, the diagnosis is further complicated by the fact that depression may be present as a symptom associated with some other disorder, as an acute grief reaction to a loss of a loved one, as a temporary state of a developmental crisis, or as a separate psychotic condition.

Mixed Reaction

This form of neurosis is probably one of the most frequently seen in children, because it provides for the occurrence of a combination of symptoms that are characteristic of the other reaction types. It is particularly common in children since they are immature and ever-changing organisms whose personality traits and neurotic character structure are much less defined than that of adults. Consequently, the neurotic symptoms of children typically do not follow the classical form noted in adults; but, instead, their symptoms may occur in isolation or in combination with other symptoms that may be unrelated in origin (Freud, 1965). Changes in parental behaviors, the family circumstances, or even fortuitous events in school or outside of the home may be sufficient to reduce unconscious conflicts and the necessity for neurotic behaviors. In addition, the mixed reaction is a catch-all category that tends to be abused by clinicians who are uncertain of what specific neurotic reaction to use as a diagnostic entity. Nevertheless, the category serves a useful function for cases such as Billy, where the symptom picture is truly a blend of several neurotic behaviors such as anxiety attacks, phobias, compulsions, and possibly conversion reactions.

Incidence

Estimates of the incidence of psychoneuroses have been plagued by the paucity of data based on large samples and adequately controlled studies. To make matters worse, these estimates seem to vary with the theoretical orientation of the clinician, the willingness of the clinician to use a psychiatric label that may stigmatize the child and influence how others react to him or her, and the type of clinical setting to which the child is referred. Hospitalized cases should be fewer since the rather drastic measure of removal from the home often implies a serious disturbance such as a psychosis. In contrast, outpatient cases should be greater in number, although these services may be more inclined to focus on situational factors and not on intrapsychic conflict as a source of the child's difficulties. Moreover, neurotic reactions in children frequently are masked by the presence of somatic complaints that are likely to be evaluated and symptomatically treated by pediatricians. If pediatricians find no organic basis for the complaint, the reassured parents may very well be less inclined to attend to the child's symptoms. It is also true that neurotic behaviors in young children are difficult to distinguish from behaviors that occur with normal development. Therefore, it is almost impossible to determine how many of these instances go undetected and unrecorded as neurotic reactions.

In light of these limitations, it is not surprising to find that incidence estimates of neurotic reactions vary considerably. One report noted that children under eighteen years of age comprised slightly more than one-half of the patients serviced at community mental-health clinics throughout the country for the year 1961, and that ten percent of these children were diagnosed as psychoneurotic (Rosen, Barn, and Cramer, 1964). As might be expected, these authors found a slightly lower incidence of psychoneuroses (eight percent) when hospitalized youngsters under the age of fifteen were tallied. Their data also suggested a significant interaction between the variables of sex and age, indicating that boys between the ages of nine and fourteen years had a higher incidence of neurotic reactions than girls of the same age, while there was a reversal of this sex trend between the ages of fourteen and sixteen years. At age ten, there were twice the number of boys classified as neurotic as there were girls; but, by the age of 20, girls outnumbered boys by the same ratio. Perhaps the highest incidence estimate comes from data involving children referred to a child guidance clinic, where between twenty-five and fifty percent of them were diagnosed as psychoneurotic (Kurlander and Colodny, 1965). Later findings based on the GAP classification but consisting of different populations of outpatient children showed the incidence of neurotic reactions to be approximately six to eleven percent, a figure that is more in line with earlier estimates (Sabot, Peck, and Raskin, 1969; Bemporad, Pfeiffer, and Bloom, 1970).

Etiological Considerations

Biological Views

In the course of contemporary history, two major views, psychoanalytic and learning theory, have received unparalleled acceptance in the formulation of psychoneurotic reactions to the extent that biological causative factors have been virtually ignored. In fact, the weight of the meager evidence that could implicate central nervous system dysfunction thus far has been negative, adding further credence to the psychogenic position. Indeed, studies based on the comparison of EEG tracings and neurological signs have shown less frequent abnormalities in neurotic children than in either psychotic or hyperkinetic children (Ellingson, 1954; Kennard, 1960; White, DeMyer, and DeMyer, 1964). Moreover, it has been argued that even when autonomic and central nervous system differences are present, they cannot be considered as causal factors since they are more likely the result of psychoneurosis (Cohen, 1974).

As early as 1951, Hans Eysenck, one of the leading proponents of genetic involvement in neurosis, statistically isolated a dimension related to emotional instability and a poorly integrated personality that successfully predicted scores on several objective personality tests. He labeled this factor *neuroticism* and demonstrated a higher concordance for neuroticism with monozygotic (identical) twins than with dizygotic (fraternal) twins (Eysenck and Prell, 1951). However, the conclusion that neurotic behavior is largely determined by genetic factors must be tempered by the fact that only normal subjects were used in the study. In later studies, concordance rates of neuroses for monozygotic twins were found to range from one and a half to almost two times greater than that for dizygotic pairs (Shields and Slater, 1961; Pollin, Allen, Hoffer, Stabenau, and Hrubec, 1969; Schepank, 1971). But in considering their data, Pollin and his colleagues reached the conclusion that heredity is implicated only minimally as a cause of psychoneuroses. Despite the resurgence of interest in the relationship between heredity

and a variety of abnormal behaviors, there is a dearth of unequivocal evidence that would warrant any other conclusion at this time.

Psychogenic Views

Psychoanalytic Theory. By all scientific yardsticks, the enormous popularity enjoyed by psychoanalytic theory as an explanation of neurotic reactions is truly remarkable. The voluminous psychoanalytic literature is replete with pronouncements and untested hypotheses that were drawn from either the clinical experiences of various writers or their analyses of the psychodynamics of small samples (sometimes a single case) of illustrative clinical cases. Restatements of Freud's position and neo-Freudian interpretations of the development of one or several neurotic reactions have been plentiful. The obvious limitations of these reports and the absence of empirical studies designed to test the theory have made it virtually impossible to evaluate it as a valid explanation of psychoneuroses. Yet, the theory's widespread acceptance has given it an aura of validity that is a tribute to Freud's personal persuasiveness, the innovativeness and completeness of his system, and his clinical genius in carefully analyzing a small number of neurotic cases.

According to this view, the distinguishing cornerstone of psychoneuroses is intrapsychic conflict arising from the battle over the expression of unconscious impulses (sex and aggression) on the one hand, and the repression of these libidinal forces on the other. The conflict between the id and superego produces anxiety that is allayed by the ego's attempts to mediate between these two rather unyielding components of the personality. While the measures taken by the ego to counteract the anxiety do not effectively resolve the intrapsychic conflict, they do reduce the tension if they are to persist. Consequently, neurotic behaviors are maintained because they allay anxiety, and they can be eliminated only when the basic intrapsychic conflict is resolved.

How do intrapsychic conflicts arise? Freud believed that they stem from environmental stimuli and events that take on particular significance during a given stage of psychosexual development. For example, the horse phobia manifested by Hans, a five-year-old boy whose analysis Freud supervised, occurred during the oedipal stage when boys allegedly have incestuous wishes for mother, death wishes for father (or at least a wish for his absence), and the fear of castration as retaliation by father should he find out about these wishes. Hans was terrified of being harmed or bitten by horses, or of their falling, and of things associated with horses such as carts and vans (Freud, 1955). Apparently Hans' fear of horses followed a specific frightening event in which he saw a horse fall and he thought it was dead. At about this time, Hans was very sexually aroused by sleeping with his mother whenever his father was away from home. He masturbated nightly, but he was apprehensive that his sexual actions would lead to the disappearance of his penis since he noted that his mother did not have one. The fact that his sexual fantasies were gratified when father was absent and that he was not the primary object of mother's affection when father was home fostered rivalry, resentment, and the inevitable conclusion that he was better off without father. But how could Hans get rid of a father he also loved, whom he had enjoyed as a playmate, and who had cared for him

throughout his lifetime? Thus, according to Freud, Hans' sexual impulses resulted in death wishes for father, which were banished from consciousness through repression. Hans handled the fear that was generated from his aggressive impulses (death wishes) by projection, that is, by turning them into fears that he will be harmed by external forces. Horses became the specific object of the fear because of his one frightening experience (trauma) and because they served as a symbolic substitute for father, with whom he had played "horsey" on many prior occasions.

As for the other forms of psychoneuroses, Freud suggested that each is distinguishable by the primary defense mechanisms the child uses to reduce the anxiety generated by intrapsychic conflicts. As we have already seen, Hans displaced his projected fear of being harmed by father onto horses, whereas hysterical youngsters allay their anxiety by converting it into some somatic disturbance. Obsessive-compulsive children set standards for themselves that are impossible to reach, and they often are guilt-ridden because their superegos tend to be strict and stern (Kessler, 1972). They behaviorally express their banished impulses through excessive virtue (reaction formation), and defend themselves against intrapsychic anxiety primarily through the mechanism of undoing. The defense of undoing serves the superego in that it provides for repetitive acts that appease or alleviate guilt, such as seen in the symbolic cleansing of the compulsive handwasher who is extremely guilty about forbidden sexual thoughts or acts. Similarly, depressive reactions reflect rigid and strict superego development in which the intrapsychic anxiety (often over hostile impulses) is internalized in the form of self-depreciation, condemnation, and guilt feelings.

Learning Theory. Actually, there is no single theory *per se* that serves as a systematic explanation of psychoneuroses, although various learning theorists and data from learning studies have contributed to our understanding of it. The first direct attempt to relate learning to neurotic-like behavior came in the early 1900s in an experiment in which classical conditioning was used to demonstrate that an eleven-month-old child, Albert, could learn to be afraid of a white rat and subsequently of other small furry animals (Watson and Rayner, 1920). Watson and Rayner paired the previously neutral white rat with a noxious sound that was frightening to Albert in order to establish the conditioned fear. Unfortunately, Albert and his family moved away before the experimenters could use learning principles to eliminate the specific and generalized fear. However, several years later, Mary Carver Jones (1924) successfully treated a boy by the name of Peter (age two years and ten months) who was afraid of a white rabbit and other small, furry animals by pairing pleasurable experiences with the feared stimulus and using social imitation. Jones paired the pleasurable activity of eating with the incompatible fear-evoking presentation of the rabbit which initially was introduced in a cage at a distance far enough away from Peter so as not to interfere with his eating. Gradually, the rabbit was brought closer to Peter, and eventually the animal was released from the cage. In addition, Jones periodically brought children who were unafraid of the rabbit into the experimental session as social models for Peter.

In 1938, a conditioning technique was introduced as a treatment for enuresis (Mowrer and Mowrer, 1938). The technique consisted of placing an electric pad in the child's bed that activated a bell when the child wet the pad to both waken the child and inhibit urination. Successive pairings of the bell with the sphincter contraction that results in the cessation of urination proved to be successful in eliminating nocturnal enuresis in all of the children studied, although some relapses occurred later.

As noted in Chapter 3, the first theoretical attempt came with Dollard and Miller's (1950) ingenious effort to translate psychoanalytic postulates into a more systematic and testable drive-reduction model of learning. Their reinterpretation of Freudian concepts into learning terms corresponded closely with psychoanalytic assumptions about unconscious conflicts and the conditions under which specific symptoms developed. Although their work brought more scientific respectability to psychoanalytic theory and underscored the importance of learning in the etiology of abnormal behaviors, especially neurotic reactions, it did little to stimulate innovations or to discourage clinicians from using their own experience rather than empirical tests to validate psychoanalytic theory (Bandura and Walters, 1963).

Since it was first reported in Pavlov's laboratory, there have been ample demonstrations showing that conflict situations can produce experimental neuroses or a behavioral breakdown that simulates neurotic symptoms (Pavlov, 1928; Masserman, 1950; Wolpe, 1958, 1973). These studies have shown that anxiety can be induced by certain (external) environmental conditions that, in turn, give rise to abnormal behaviors. We now know that when two valued goals conflict, the choice of either alternative leads to the frustration of the other. The choice may be between two positive goals (approach-approach), two negative ones (avoidance-avoidance), or the positive and negative aspects of the same goal (approach-avoidance). Approach-approach conflicts are readily resolved without creating any significant disruption in most individuals by choosing one of the desirable alternatives. Blocking and failing to respond is ordinarily the reaction to avoidance-avoidance conflicts, while approach-avoidance conflicts tend to produce vascillation and are usually the most difficult conflicts to resolve.

On the basis of research on experimental neuroses, Wolpe (1958, 1973) used learning principles to formulate a view of the disorder in which anxiety plays a primary role in the acquisition and maintenance of these maladaptive habits. He proposed that anxiety responses can be conditioned by either specific noxious stimuli that evoke anxiety or ambivalent ones that heighten anxiety levels. Noxious stimuli include those producing pain or discomfort such as loud sounds, and those thwarting pleasure, while ambivalent stimuli involve situations in which the organism is required to make a fine choice between opposing responses, such as the situation in which Pavlov's dog had to make a discrimination (between a circle and ellipse) that exceeded its sensory capacity. However, Wolpe's major contribution was in the development of a treatment strategy, called *reciprocal inhibition* (discussed in Chapter 6), designed to eliminate neurotic symptoms by inhibiting anxiety responses through the conditioning of new and more adaptive responses to the same conditions that gave rise to the original anxiety. More specifically, anxiety is reduced by introducing responses that are either incompatible or antagonistic to those produced by the original situation. Typically, Wolpe teaches his patients deep relaxation because he believes that it is antagonistic to anxiety responses, and because

it provides a method for its *systematic desensitization*.

The work of Skinner and his followers in operant conditioning (instrumental learning) and Bandura and others in modeling (imitation learning) was discussed more fully in Chapter 4. These studies have shown that these learning paradigms also can account for the acquisition of abnormal behaviors much like those evident in neurotic reactions. Accordingly, neurotic behaviors increase in their probability of occurrence as a function of either reinforcement or imitation of a model. Unlike psychoanalysis, learning approaches typically are less concerned with diagnosis and traditional classification, preferring to focus on the symptom or deviant behavior in order to construct a treatment strategy for its elimination or modification. In addition, learning-oriented clinicians differ from their psychoanalytic counterparts with respect to the goal of treatment, with the latter seeking to discover or resolve underlying unconscious conflicts, and the former directing their efforts toward modifying or alleviating neurotic behaviors in situations where they were previously manifested. There will be more about treatment in the next section.

Therapeutic Approaches

Somatic Therapies

In light of the minimal role played by biological factors in the etiology of psychoneuroses, it is not surprising that somatic therapies similarly are unimportant in the treatment of these reactions. Although tranquilizing drugs such as Benadryl and Thorazine sometimes are used by pediatricians for children experiencing anxiety attacks to make the children feel more comfortable and less anxious, chemotherapy is rarely, if ever, effective as a long-term remedy by itself (Bakwin and Bakwin, 1972). Antidepressant drugs sometimes are used for severe depressive reactions with "marked and persistent lowering of vitality, with associated sleep and appetite disturbance, reduced mobility and verbal retardation" (Graham, 1976, p. 104). Drugs in combination with other treatment procedures reportedly have been used, for example, with school-phobic children (Gittelman-Klein and Klein, 1973). Interestingly enough, imipramine was more effective than a placebo in returning these youngsters to school. However, since the drug was used in conjunction with parent and child counseling and a desensitization program, it was impossible to identify which of the several treatment approaches was responsible for the improvement. Confounding of treatment effects has been noted in many of the therapy studies reported in the literature. In addition, the frequency with which single cases are used as a measure of therapeutic effectiveness prohibits an adequate appraisal of the various treatment approaches to psychoneuroses. Yet, it seems safe to say that at present there is a consensus suggesting that psychological therapies and not somatic ones are the primary remedial measures to be used if neurotic reactions are to be successfully ameliorated.

Psychological Therapies

In one form or another, psychoanalytically oriented therapy has been the primary treatment approach for psychoneuroses for years, probably because of the theory's widespread popularity among clinicians with regard to normal and abnormal personality development. The object of this treatment is to uncover the underlying intrapsychic conflict that gives rise to the neurosis and to provide the child with an opportunity to resolve it. Although overt symptoms give much needed information about the conflict, the defenses, and the character structure, they are not the chief targets of treatment. In fact, Freudians contend that symptom removal without resolving the basic conflict leads to symptom substitution, that is, other and different symptoms soon appear. This assumption has been the subject of much controversy, since learning-oriented therapists argue that neurotic behaviors and not their conjectured cause should be the object of treatment, and that symptom substitution will not occur if the child learns new behaviors in the place of unwanted ones (Spiegel, 1967; Cahoon, 1968).

Dynamic therapy with children involves the establishment of a relationship between therapist and child, therapy with one parent—usually the mother, play activities along with conversation, ventilation and acceptance of feelings, and interpretations by the therapist (Kessler, 1972). Traditionally, the child is seen weekly or biweekly by a therapist, while the mother is seen by another collaborating therapist to deal with her feelings and reactions to the child, with any changes that occur, and with day-to-day reality events. Play is used, especially for young children, as a natural medium for understanding the child's conflicts and feelings, for the expression of unacceptable feelings without disapproval, and for interpretations of unconscious conflicts. Within recent years, therapy involving the entire family (parents, child, and siblings) or the parents and the child has received increased attention as a promising technique for the treatment of psychoneuroses and other forms of abnormal behavior. Family therapy is thought to be useful when the child's symptoms are viewed as expressions of a disturbed family, when the child is old enough to comprehend the verbalizations of the therapy sessions, when no improvement has been noted in individual psychotherapy, and when individual therapy results in stress for other family members (Glick and Kessler, 1974). In contrast, it is not considered useful when the family is in the actual throes of a break-up, and when the child's problems are either intrapsychic or stem from specific stressors outside of the family, such as school.

Behavior therapies are now the chief rival of psychodynamic ones in the treatment of neurotic behaviors, especially phobic reactions. We already have described the basic characteristics of Wolpe's theory of reciprocal inhibition and his technique of systematic desensitization. On the basis of a review of studies using desensitization for phobias, we can conclude that the treatment was effective in the majority of the cases, and that the successes were achieved without recurrence of the symptoms and without symptom substitution (Rachman, 1967). Because deep relaxation is difficult to teach children, Lazarus (1971) has used emotive imagery. He presents children with increasingly fearful stimuli that are "woven into progressively more enjoyable fantasies" (Lazarus, 1971, p. 211). Several studies have demonstrated that desensitization in combination with operant-conditioning techniques has been quite successful in treating school-phobic youngsters (Lazarus, Davison, and Polefka, 1965; Garvey and Hegrenes, 1966). For example, Garvey and Hegrenes (1966) constructed an anxiety hierarchy that consisted of a graded series of twelve steps ranging from proximity to the school to actually attending classes. The therapist met with the child,

Jimmy, each school morning to take him through each step until the point when Jimmy reported anxiety or fear. The therapist then terminated the session and positively reinforced Jimmy's behavior with both praise and candy. After twenty sessions, Jimmy was able to resume normal school attendance and after a two-year follow-up he remained free of any adjustment difficulties.

Modeling also has been effective in eliminating phobic reactions. This was illustrated in a study that treated youngsters having a dog phobia by exposing them to a fearless peer model who comfortably approached a dog (Bandura, Grusec, and Menlove, 1967). The mere viewing of the unafraid peer model with the dog resulted in the reduction of the avoidance responses noted in the previously phobic children. Another behavior therapy, known as *implosive therapy*, stems from the proposition that anxiety or fear responses will be extinguished when high anxiety-evoking stimuli are presented in the absence of the primary aversive stimulus. This technique was used to successfully treat a school phobia by constructing vivid descriptions of intense anxiety arousing scenes related to school, and then presenting them to the boy to extinguish his fear of attending school (Smith and Sharpe, 1970). The improvement in the boy's adjustment to school remained unchanged after a thirteen-week follow-up.

In general, the literature on psychological therapies abounds with testimonials, descriptions of successfully treated single cases, or otherwise uncontrolled reports about their effectiveness. Frequently, it is difficult to assess any given therapy, since in practice therapists employ a mixture of methods and introduce, in some unknown way, their own special orientation and skills. Fortunately, most neurotic children have a favorable prognosis with the expectation that one-third of the cases will be completely "cured," one-third improved, and one-third unimproved regardless of the treatment method used (Clarizio and McCoy, 1976). Indirect support for this conclusion comes from a review of studies designed to assess the effectiveness of group therapy in children (Abramowitz, 1976). One-third of the studies yielded positive treatment results, one third mixed results, and another third negative results. Moreover, there were no apparent differences between types of therapy, although there seemed to be more behavior modification techniques than other therapies represented in the positive and mixed-outcome results.

Some data, although meager, are now available that bear on the question of long-term prognosis. One study showed that the symptoms of indecision, fear of thunder, headaches, and insomnia could be predicted in adult women by their presence in childhood, while another found that neurotic adults had significantly more school phobias during childhood than a matched group of orthopedic and dental patients (Abe, 1972; Tyrer and Tyrer, 1974). Finally, recent data suggest that the prognosis for child neurotics may not be as favorable as we had once thought. Waldron (1976) compared forty-two young adults who had neurosis in childhood with twenty controls on various aspect of their functioning. The results indicated that seventy-five percent of the former patients were at least "mildly ill" at follow-up, in contrast to only fifteen percent of the controls. While these data point to a more pessimistic outlook for neurotic children, at this point they can only be regarded as tentative until the findings are replicated with larger and more completely defined samples.

Psychophysiologic Disorders

Unlike most of the previously discussed clinical conditions where behavioral maladjustment is the chief problem, *psychophysiologic disorders* are characterized by physical symptoms arising from dysfunctioning and structural damage to a single organ system usually innervated by the autonomic nervous system. Typically, these disorders involve a significant interplay between physiological and psychological forces, since the physical changes are to a great extent caused by prolonged psychological and social stress. They have also been referred to as *psychosomatic* and *somatization reactions,* although the specific label *psychophysiologic disorders* is preferred to avoid confusion with the more general term *psychosomatic* that refers to an orientation and approach common to medical practice today. In addition, this label circumvents the implication of somatization reactions wherein psychophysiologic disorders would be classified as merely another form of psychoneurosis (GAP Report No. 62, 1966). While somatic complaints are evident in neurotic reactions, the physical symptoms of psychophysiologic disorders differ in a number of important ways. They neither serve to allay anxiety as the various neurotic counterreactions do, nor do they characteristically affect those bodily parts that are under the voluntary control of the central nervous system, as illustrated by the paralysis of the conversion reaction. Instead, psychophysiologic disorders are those in which emotional factors primarily cause actual changes and even damage to a single organ system (respiratory, digestive, genitourinary, cardiovascular) that is regulated by the involuntary portion of the nervous system. The idea that psychological and social stress may trigger off or contribute to physical symptoms should not be taken to imply that these disorders are imagined, contrived, or trivial. In fact, they are very real and important since they involve irreversible damage to bodily tissues that may prove fatal, or at the least may require a good deal of medical attention.

Stress and Psychophysiologic Disorders

The pioneer work of Hans Selye in constructing a theory that involves the endocrine system in relation to bodily or psychological stress is particularly pertinent to the study of psychophysiologic disorders (Selye, 1956, 1969). Selye identified the pattern of reactions to prolonged stress as the general adaptation syndrome (GAS), which consists of three temporal phases repeated in sequence: the *alarm reaction,* the *stage of resistance,* and the *stage of exhaustion.* When a stressor exists for a prolonged period of time, it serves initially (alarm reaction) to stimulate the production of corticosteroids throughout the body. In the second stage of resistance, the body's defensive response becomes more localized and confined to the specific body area of stress. As the stress continues, these localized defensive reactions become exhausted (stage of exhaustion), while at the same time the body is stimulated to produce certain corticosteroids that inhibit these localized reactions. Under conditions of severe stress and prolonged exhaustion, death is likely to occur.

We have known for a long time from both human and animal studies that a variety of psychological stressors such as war, maternal separation and inadequate stimulation, and conflict can bring about physiological changes in the function and structure of bodily organs. The effect on English civilians of the prolonged stress of almost constant enemy bombings during World War II was associated with a precipitous rise in the incidence of perforated peptic ulcers (Stewart and Winser, 1942). Other and more recent reports indicate that increases in the number of psychiatric casualties are associated with either the prolonged stress of military operations, the prolonged stress of work requirements without rest or sleep, or the accumulated effect of a number of life stressors (Selye, 1969; Myers, Lindenthal, and Pepper, 1971; Birley, 1972). Pediatricians are quite aware of a condition known as *marasmus* in which infants evidence progressive emaciation and possible death as a result of malnutrition. A similar condition was identified by Spitz (Spitz, 1945; Spitz and Wolf, 1946) who described the wasting away of marasmus, along with the sadness, immobility, apathy, and poor appetite and sleep patterns of what he called *anaclitic depression* in infants who were subjected to the stress of prolonged maternal separation and inadequate stimulation.

Studies with human subjects have indicated that conflict tends to produce physiological changes, especially in the autonomic nervous system, such as increases in vasoconstriction levels under conditions of competing instructions, and increases in heart rate and galvanic skin responses (GSR) when discrimination between two stimuli is difficult (Johnson, 1963; Moss and Edwards, 1964). Even more dramatic physiological changes have been brought about in animals under conflict situations. When hungry and thirsty rats were placed in a chronic approach-avoidance conflict requiring them to live for about two weeks in a chamber in which strong electric shock was given whenever they approached food or water, many of the experimental animals developed gastric ulcers and some died from intestinal bleeding, while the controls showed none of these effects (Sawrey and Weisz, 1956; Sawrey, Conger, and Turrell, 1956). In addition, ulcers were experimentally produced in monkeys who were restrained in chairs and for whom it was possible to avoid electric shock by being vigilant to a signal and then pressing a lever that deactivated the shock (Brady, Porter, Conrad, and Mason, 1958). These so called "executive monkeys" were paired with controls who were unable to do anything about the electric shock or stress conditions, and in whom ulcers did not develop. Brady and his colleagues argued that the stress of the constant vigil required for the decision of avoiding the shock was the ingredient that produced the tissue damage in the executive monkeys, in contrast to the effect of electric shock which the controls received but could do nothing about.

Theoretical Models
of Psychophysiologic Disorders

Most theories dealing with these disorders begin with the premise that psychological stress can bring about physiological malfunctioning and actual tissue change. This proposition gives rise to several important questions for which theorists with different orientations have sought answers. The first question asks who are the people likely to develop a psychophysiologic disorder and why are they affected by stress in this way while others are not? The second question focuses on the problem of uncovering the factors that determine why a particular organ system is affected and another is not. And finally, an acceptable theory must grapple with the issue of how or by what mechanisms psychological stres-

sors become translated into physical symptoms (Purcell, Weiss, and Hahn, 1972). Let us consider some of the major theoretical models, although, as we shall see, they tend to be general and not sufficiently specific or comprehensive to adequately explain or predict psychophysiologic disorders.

1. Two biological views have aroused considerable interest and popularity in the literature. They are the ideas of *genetic vulnerability* or *somatic weakness,* and of *innate specific autonomic response patterns.* The premise of genetic vulnerability or somatic weakness attributable to constitutional factors, prior illness, toxic substances, and the like is neither new nor specific to psychophysiologic disorders, since we have seen a similar model proposed for other disorders, especially childhood psychoses. In this instance, these factors are believed to predispose or weaken a particular bodily system, leaving it more susceptible to damage from stress. The vulnerable or weakened somatic area is selected as the affected organ system when noxious psychological stress conditions occur and persist. It is a view analogous to a rubber band flawed by a pinhole that eventually breaks at that vulnerable point under the stress of stretching.

The specific response theory holds that people differ in their physiological reactions to stress, and that these specific patterns are probably of genetic origin. Autonomic reactivity to stress is regarded as idiosyncratic (Lacey and Lacey, 1958), although the individual pattern tends to be quite consistent and similar from one stressor to another. Thus, on the basis of their specific autonomic response patterns to stress, people may be considered as primarily "stomach reactors," or "heart reactors," or "skin reactors," and so forth (Wolff, 1950; Coleman, 1972). In this way, "stomach reactors" are persons who are likely to respond to stress with increased secretion of stomach acid that would, in turn, make them more vulnerable to stomach ulcers.

2. One of the earliest *psychological views* suggested a relationship between certain personality traits and intrapsychic conflicts on the one hand, and psychosomatic disorders and organ choice on the other (Dunbar, 1943; Alexander, 1950). As an example of this psychoanalytically oriented position, Alexander suggested that unresolved dependency conflicts were involved intimately in the production of ulcers. He believed that the stomach and food were symbolically equated with parental love, and that the thwarting of long-standing childhood dependency wishes results in autonomic overactivity of the stomach and eventually ulcers. However, the weight of subsequent research failed to support the claim that there are specific personality types for each psychophysiologic disorder (Hamilton, 1955). More recent work along similar lines argued for a relationship between people's characteristic attitudes toward stress and the particular psychophysiologic disorder they are likely to evidence (Graham, 1962). To illustrate, Graham found, along with other relationships, that hypertension patients feel endangered and are on constant guard to ward off the threat of danger, while ulcer patients seek to get even with people or situations that have injured or deprived them of something promised.

From the time that Pavlov demonstrated that autonomic changes in heart and respiration rate could be conditioned, there has been ample evidence not only to support this finding, but also to foster the belief that physiological symptoms mediated by the autonomic nervous system can be learned only through classical conditioning. However, Miller and his colleagues (DiCara and Miller, 1968; Miller and Banuazizi,

1968; Miller, 1969) have opened up the real possibility that physical changes in visceral and glandular responses (heart rate and rate of intestinal contraction) can be produced by operant conditioning procedures, and that these learned alterations can be maintained for several months in the absence of additional practice. Miller (1969) argues that children may learn certain psychophysiological patterns as a function of parental concern and parental reinforcement of specific behaviors. Thus, when a child evidences several physiological responses to a stressful situation, the parent may inadvertently reinforce one, such as gastric distress, by permitting the child to avoid the stress as a result of the intestinal symptoms. Although this work has been impressive and has led others to a behavioral interpretation of all psychophysiologic disorders, replication of these findings along with new data are needed before the theory can be confirmed (Lachman, 1972).

Psychophysiological disorders are subcategorized by types according to the particular organ system affected. The GAP classification system lists eleven different types that include all of the major bodily systems and reflect the enormous variety of diseases thought to be influenced by psychogenic factors (GAP, 1966). For our purposes, it is neither possible nor necessary to cover all of these disorders, since we can obtain a reasonable grasp of them by limiting our discussion to the presentation of the most common psychophysiologic disorder in children, bronchial asthma, and an intriguing adolescent condition known as anorexia nervosa.

Bronchial Asthma

This is a disorder of the respiratory system more commonly found in children than in adults and in boys than in girls by a ratio of about 2:1 (Apley and McKeith, 1962; Graham, Rutter, Yule, and Pless, 1967; Purcell, Weiss, and Hahn, 1972). While the incidence of asthma falls somewhere between 2.5 and 5 percent for the general population, the vast majority of the cases (approximately sixty percent) consists of children under the age of seventeen who are sufficiently debilitated that they are responsible for nearly twenty-five percent of the total school days missed by all children (Purcell, Weiss, and Hahn, 1972). The seriousness of the disorder is further reflected in the fact that there are approximately 1.5 deaths per 1000 each year directly attributable to asthma (Mustacchi, Lucia, and Jassy, 1962). Yet, the long-term prognosis for many children in whom asthma began before the age of thirteen seems favorable, since data from a twenty-year follow-up study indicates that over seventy percent improved during or shortly after adolescence and continued to do well through the early adult years (Rackeman and Edwards, 1952).

Bronchial asthma involves an episodic contraction of the muscles of the bronchial tubes restricting air exchange, especially in expiration, and producing the frightening physical symptoms of convulsive coughing, wheezing, labored respiration (dyspnea), difficulty in drawing deep breaths, and tightness in the chest. Asthmatic attacks may range from mild to severe in which the child has a great deal of difficulty getting air in and out of the lungs and experiences the fear of suffocation. Repeated serious attacks can result in progressive deterioration of the bronchial system, where air exchange becomes even more difficult because the bronchial muscles lose their elasticity, the bronchial tissues swell, and mucous accumulates. Asthmatic attacks also vary in duration from a few minutes to several hours, and they are accompanied by

feelings of anxiety, irritability, and depression. Obviously things go better for these youngsters between attacks, although the children understandably experience apprehension about future episodes and the stimuli that trigger them off. The physical symptoms can be a painful source of embarrassment to youngsters who face a sudden eruption at almost any time and under a variety of circumstances. These children often feel "different," frustrated, and inadequate, because the disorder impairs their social ability for normal peer interactions especially in physical activities. Asthmatic children also affect others who become frightened when they witness an attack and feel helpless to alleviate it. Many parents feel guilty because they believe that they are in some way responsible for producing a damaged child and because they periodically resent the additional expenditure of time and money that these children frequently require. Purcell and Weiss suggest, "this guilt appears to be one of the antecedents of the commonly observed overprotective maternal attitude toward the asthmatic child, with reciprocal overdependence of the child on the mother" (Purcell and Weiss, 1970, pp. 601–602).

Etiological Views

The etiology of asthma may be caused by the primary influence of a single factor, or; more frequently, by the complex interaction of a number of contributing variables. The widespread belief that heredity plays a role in the disorder is supported by data indicating a much higher incidence of asthma in the families of these patients than in nonasthmatic families (Criep, 1962). However, the specifics of just how and where the genetic factor is implicated remains uncertain, although it is likely that it causes the respiratory apparatus to be

Knapp writes of a patient whose asthma began at age nine while he and his father were walking in the woods. Although his condition worsened over the next several years, he was symptom-free from the age of thirteen to twenty-three. From that time on his asthma became progressively more severe and chronic until his death at age fifty-two.

Abundant data from this patient's life suggest the importance of emotional factors in precipitating exacerbations of his asthma. He gives a graphic description of developing wheezing and shortness of breath upon separation from his mother. Once, while away on a trip with either her or his grandmother (it is not clear which), in a strange hotel, separated from his companion by a wall, he suffered through the night, having the feeling that his wheezes might be loud enough to be heard and bring her in to rescue him.

He described clearly the relationship of his symptoms to odors. His response to the scent of flowers may have had an allergic basis. That seems less likely in the case of the scent of "lovely ladies," which he stated also gave him asthma. So did certain "bad" smells, of asparagus and cigar smoke. . . . He had many conflicts around weeping, frequently described being dissolved in tears, but always with the implication that he never really was exhausting the reservoir of "sobbing." Less conspicuous was the role of excitement, which at times appeared to provoke his attacks. Some of his written associations lead from sexualized recollections directly to descriptions of asthma. Underneath the excitement were not only forbidden sexual impulses but also deep hostile ones. At the time of his brother's marriage, the patient was jealous; he managed to forget to mail the 150 invitations to the ceremony that had been entrusted to him. In the church he was almost more prominent than the bride, walking down the aisle just before the ceremony, gasping for breath, and wearing a fur coat, although the month was July. (P. H. Knapp, "The asthmatic and his environment," Journal of Nervous and Mental Diseases, © 1969 The Williams and Wilkins Co., Baltimore.)

more responsive to a variety of stimuli (genetic vulnerability) which in turn can excite an attack (Purcell, Weiss, and Hahn, 1972). At present, three classes of stimuli (*infections* such as whooping cough, pneumonia, or tonsillitis; *allergens* such as pollen, foods, and dust; and *emotional factors*) have been identified as causative agents that either act alone in relatively few cases or in most instances in combination with each other (Rees, 1964). Our discussion focuses on emotional factors, since the diagnosis of psychophysiologic disorders applies to those conditions that are caused primarily by psychological variables. This focus should be interpreted in the context that the dis-

order is most often determined by the interaction of a number of etiological agents.

Through the years, studies have shown that various emotional stressors can either induce an asthmatic attack or produce some of the physiological changes associated with the disorder. Experimenters have brought these alterations about by using, among other tactics, stressful interviews, emotional stimuli selected from the patient's history, the arousal of resentment and anxiety, and even the radical measure of confining a patient in a locked but allergen-free chamber (Treuting and Ripley, 1948; Dekker and Groen, 1956; Stein, 1962; Dudley, Martin, and Holmes, 1964). In addition, there have been many reports suggesting that asthmatic attacks in humans or symptoms resembling the labored breathing of asthmatics in animals can be conditioned classically. While much of these data implicate learning as an important contributor to asthma in some people, the findings are by no means convincing that asthma is acquired through conditioning because the subjects either failed to show all of the important physiological signs of the disorder or the findings were not replicated. After critically reviewing the literature, Purcell and his colleagues concluded, "it appears accurate to state that with either animals or human beings, the successful conditioning of asthma remains to be demonstrated, even in the opinion of those investigators whose original positive reports on conditioning are cited frequently" (Purcell, Weiss, and Hahn, 1972, p. 715).

Without much success, researchers also have pursued the psychoanalytically influenced notion that asthmatics have a common personality profile with a particular type of unresolved intrapsychic conflict (heightened dependency on mother), that some regard as the causative agent of the disorder, while others view the conflict as developing from the disorder. Working from a different premise, namely that asthmatics are heterogeneous, Purcell and his associates identified two subgroups of asthmatic children: (1) those who showed rapid remission of their symptoms when they were separated from their families and admitted to a hospital setting shortly after (RR), and (2) those who required continued steroid medication after they were separated and institutionalized (SD). The RR youngsters reported the more frequent occurrence of emotions, such as anger, anxiety, and depression, as precipitating their

asthma attacks while at home than the SD children (Purcell, 1963). More recently, differential predictions were made successfully for two groups of carefully evaluated asthmatic children who were separated from their families while their physical surroundings were kept relatively constant (Purcell, Brady, Chai, Maser, Molk, Gordon, and Means, 1969). The family of each asthmatic child lived in a motel for two weeks and had no contact with the child who was cared for in the home by a surrogate parental figure. All of the measures of asthma used in the study significantly improved during the separation period and declined when the family and the child were once again united for the group of children who were predicted to be affected by family interactions. The predicted nonresponders showed no difference during or after separation except for one measure.

In addition, parents of RR children hold stronger authoritarian and punitive attitudes than their SD counterparts, raising the possibility that neurotic conflict and emotional states are primary causes of asthma in the RR group, while allergens and infections are more important etiological factors in the SD youngsters (Purcell, Bernstein, and Burkantz, 1961; Purcell, 1975). Subgroupings of this sort seem to be a promising line of inquiry, since they tend to reduce the variability of an otherwise heterogenous and multiply determined disorder and enable more specific assessment of the relative contributions each class of stimuli makes in triggering asthmatic attacks in certain children.

Therapeutic Considerations

With some optimistic report of success, almost every form of treatment has been tried with asthmatics including drugs, suggestion and hypnosis, relaxation, behavior therapies, individual, group, and family therapy, long-term psychoanalysis, and institutionalization (separation from family) (Knapp, Mathé, and Vachon, 1976). Rapid or immediate symptomatic relief or recovery usually can be brought about by the administration of a number of drugs, primarily corticosteroids and sympathomimetic amines, depending on the severity of the attack and the status of the child. Preventive measures typically are suggested for those asthmatics in which allergens are involved. They may either take the form of environmental manipulation, as in the removal of rugs that tend to collect dust, or of prescribing medicines that tend to bolster the body's tolerance to the allergen.

The array of psychological treatments used for asthmatic children is particularly difficult to assess since too few studies are available, and, more often than not, these studies are flawed by methodological errors. However, the literature does suggest that individual, group, and family therapy may be instrumental in aiding asthmatic children to deal more effectively with the emotional stimuli that may trigger their attacks and to cope more effectively with their symptoms. For example, one study showed that systematic relaxation was successful in reducing the severity of symptoms for those asthmatic children in whom emotional factors played a prominent role in precipitating asthma attacks (Alexander, 1972). Another possible benefit of these therapies may be that some parents learn to modify those attitudes and behaviors that seem to contribute to the child's illness. Weekly family therapy sessions aimed at discovering and then changing those family and emotional situations that excite and maintain asthmatic symptoms did prove helpful in several cases in which acute attacks leading

to hospitalization were almost totally eliminated (Liebman, Minuchin, and Baker, 1974).

A relatively new therapeutic approach called *biofeedback* seems to hold particular promise for psychophysiologic disorders. Biofeedback monitors the physiological responses of the patient and provides information to the patient about the performance of various physiological functions that he or she could then learn to control sometimes with the aid of positive reinforcement. Ordinarily, the subject is provided with an electronic signal that varies with some aspect of a physiological response and is told to try to control the electronic signal. For example, one recent study showed that muscle relaxation associated with pulmonary function could be learned through biofeedback with and without the use of reinforcement (Kotses, Glaus, Crawford, Edwards, and Scherr, 1976). Using operantly manipulated levels of muscle tension, this group of investigators are actively studying the relationship between muscular and respiratory events that seem applicable to the control of asthma in children (Glaus, 1976: Kotses, Glaus, Crawford, Edwards, and Scherr, 1976; Kotses, Glaus, Bricel, Crawford, and Edwards, 1977). They have found that tension levels in or around the frontalis muscle (forehead) significantly influence measures of lung airway resistance, that frontalis tension is inversely related to peak expiratory flow rate, that this relationship holds for both asthmatic and nonasthmatic subjects, and that the effects of frontalis tension changes on airway resistance are immediate in that they are observable after a single training session. Experiments are now underway to evaluate a self-management program in which the child learns behaviors through biofeedback that will decrease the symptoms of bronchial asthma (Glaus, Private communication). In evaluating biofeedback techniques, it is important to be sure what component of airflow is being measured and to decrease the effects of suggestion and possible hidden reinforcers (Feldman, 1976).

Anorexia Nervosa

Anorexia nervosa refers to the most extreme form of refusal to eat where persistent aversion to food continues for long periods of time resulting in marked weight loss and emaciation (Bruch, 1973). It is a physiological disorder that affects mostly females (9 or 10 to 1) during early adolescence and through the teenage years, and it is fatal in about ten percent of all cases. Most often anorexic youngsters come from middle-class and upper-class families, where both family closeness and ambition are valued. Characterized by average or better intelligence, perfectionistic tendencies, and high achievement needs, these children are morbidly preoccupied with dieting and concerned about being overweight. Their pursuit of thinness results in self-starvation and a loss of as much as twenty-five to fifty percent of their body weight. Dieting also reflects their disturbed self-perception in that they continue to see themselves as too fat even when they are quite emaciated. Their energy is rigidly and almost totally tied up in a self-imposed regimen of restricted caloric intake to the extent that they are likely to induce vomiting if and when any increase in eating takes place. In fact, their refusal to eat inevitably brings them into a severe battle with their families since they will do anything to resist eating. They will gag and vomit, empty their plates into the trash when not watched, and pad themselves with a pillow or extra clothing before stepping onto a scale to prove that they haven't lost weight. Many of these youngsters eventually require hospitalization in order to bring their food intake under careful regulation and to begin psychotherapy.

Observations of anorexic youngsters have led to the widely accepted view that the disorder represents an attempt to cope with the frightening demands and responsibilities of approaching maturity (Thoma, 1967; Dally, 1969). Anorexic girls fear their own sexuality and the prospect of functioning as a woman. The disorder appears at a time when they begin to show signs of sexual maturation, and when interest in boys and dating occur. By reducing their body weight, they restore themselves to childlike physical characteristics, make themselves unattractive to boys, become amenorrheic and safe from the anxiety and threat of mature heterosexual relationships. Disturbed mother-daughter relationships in which the youngster has been both overly dependent on and rebellious against maternal domination, or the fear of oral impregnation (the association of growing fat with being pregnant) also have been proposed as etiological factors (Warren, 1968). As interesting as these hypotheses are, the psychological and physiological aspects of anorexia nervosa as yet are poorly understood. In fact, there is considerable uncertainty and disagreement among clinicians as to what diagnostic category anorexia nervosa properly belongs.

The treatment of anorexics is often difficult, and it requires a combination of medical and psychotherapeutic procedures. Many of these youngsters are best treated in a hospital where special feedings (liquid diet, intravenous or tube feeding) and close nursing supervision can be readily obtained. Feedings must be observed until everything is eaten in order to guard against the possibility of food being concealed, disposed of, or vomited by the youngster. Sometimes medical management includes the administration of drugs to reduce anxiety and to stimulate the appetite. While most clinicians tend to focus on the prompt stabilization of the anorexic's physical state by whatever measures necessary, at least one group makes no attempt to coerce or control food intake beyond the wishes of the client (Reinhart, Kenna, and Succop, 1972). Because these workers believe that the disorder is a psychological one, they emphasize psychological and not physiological factors. Consequently, they maintain that outpatient treatment is preferable to hospitalization, and that psychotherapy should begin promptly. They give the responsibility for eating to the child to foster her independence and bolster her attempts to separate from highly anxious parents. Frequent goals of psychotherapy include understanding and resolving fears of becoming fat and of growing up, and ambivalent (dependent and angry) feelings toward mother. Treatment aimed at restoring food intake without relapse can be achieved in a variety of ways in about one-half to two-thirds of the cases, whereas treatment intended to remove the underlying psychopathology is only successful with a few of these youngsters (Tolstrup, 1975).

Summary

In this chapter, two sets of disorders, the psychoneuroses and the psychophysiologic, were discussed. All types of psychoneurotic reactions display the common ingredients of intense anxiety, personal discomfort, persistence of coping responses that are inappropriate or ineffective for the situation, and self-directed or internalized reactions to anxiety-producing stimuli. Although similarities and differences between a psychoanalytic and a learning view of psychoneuroses were described, there is agreement that anxiety plays a key role in the development of these reactions and is responsible for the emergence of the variety of counterreactions seen clinically. A summary of the primary descriptive characteristics of each type of neurotic reaction follows.

Anxiety Reaction:	Intense free-floating anxiety with feelings of impending doom usually unrelated to external reality that may be triggered off by a variety of events. Sudden and severe attacks (either acute or chronic) are often accompanied by physical symptoms of shortness of breath, palpitations, sweating, faintness, dizziness, nausea, abdominal pain, and diarrhea.
Phobic Reaction:	Persistent, severe, and irrational fear that usually interferes with the child's daily functioning. *Animal phobia* is an unwarranted, intense, and persistent fear especially common in children. Freudians suggest that animals provide safer and more primitive objects on whom children can project their unacceptable libidinal feelings. *School phobia* represents a frequent problem of school aged children characterized by acute anxiety, refusal to go to school, and numerous somatic complaints. It is distinguished from truancy by the presence of acute anxiety, somatic symptoms, overattachment to home and family, good academic performance, and the absence of anti-social behaviors. Separation anxiety mutually shared by mother and child is often viewed as its cause.

Obsessive-Compulsive Reaction:	Characterized by recurrent thoughts, acts, or both which the child must perform although the ideas or the behaviors seem silly and unreasonable. Although the child is unaware of the original source of the anxiety, anxiety is responsible for the maintenance of these behaviors since the child experiences marked apprehension when its completion is interfered with.
Conversion Reaction:	Dysfunction of body parts that are under the voluntary control of the central nervous system. Anxiety is converted into symptoms that symbolically express the basic conflict and reduce the anxiety generated from it. The symptomatology can mimic almost any organic disease, but it ordinarily does not follow anatomical lines. These reactions have declined and are now seen in older children of working class and educationally unsophisticated families.
Depressive Reaction:	Internalization of the original conflict through self-depreciation and despondency manifested in guilt, loss of self-esteem, helplessness, and loneliness that may be masked by apathy, withdrawal, somatic complaints, and acting-out behaviors. The diagnosis is difficult to make, because children are not expected to be depressed, are unable to verbalize their feelings, and because depression is often a symptom associated with other disorders.
Mixed Reaction:	Characterized by a combination of symptoms manifested in other reaction types. The category is often a catch-all for clinicians who are uncertain about what specific diagnostic entity to use.

Etiological considerations of psychogenic variables primarily derived from psychoanalytic and learning theories were presented and critically evaluated as the most likely origin of these reactions, since there is both a lack of interest and evidence reflected in the literature supporting biological causes. Data from experimental studies using both humans and animals indicate that various learning models (classical and instrumental conditioning, modeling, and reciprocal inhibition) play a major role in the formation of psychoneuroses, but also have contributed to the development of specific treatment strategies.

Except for the use of drugs to reduce the symptoms associated with anxiety, or to alleviate the discomforting aspects of depression, somatic therapies have been relatively unimportant as a remedial approach for neurotic reactions. Psychological therapies comprised the major thrust of the discussion, which focused on the description and evaluation of psychodynamic individual therapy, group and family therapy, systematic desensitization, conditioning, modeling, and implosive therapy.

Psychophysiologic disorders are characterized by physical symptoms that arise from dysfunctioning and structural damage to a single organ system innervated by the autonomic nervous system. They involve a significant interaction between physiological and psychological forces since the physical changes are primarily caused by psychological and social stress. These disorders differ from neuroses in that the physical symptoms neither serve to allay anxiety nor do they characteristically affect those bodily parts that are under the voluntary control of the central nervous system. The importance of stress to psychophysiologic disorders was noted in Selye's general adaptation syndrome, and experimental studies involving a variety of psychological stressors such as war, maternal separation and inadequate stimulation, and conflict. Theoretical models of genetic vulnerability, somatic weakness, specific autonomic response patterns, specific personality types and conflicts, and learning views were discussed, although none were considered sufficiently specific or comprehensive to adequately explain or predict psychophysiologic disorders.

Finally, bronchial asthma, the most common of these disorders in children, and anorexia nervosa, an adolescent condition, were selected for discussion with regard to their clinical picture, incidence, etiological considerations (especially emotional factors), and therapeutic approaches.

Epilogue

As is so often the case, decisions about a treatment plan for youngsters like Billy are influenced by a variety of interacting factors that usually differ in importance from one situation to another. While the nature of the child's difficulties and needs must be the overriding consideration, the treatment choice also depends on the extent to which a full range of treatment options are available and the child's support systems (family and community) are both capable and willing to help. In Billy's case, the treatment program was dictated primarily by his mother's poor health (her asthmatic condition had worsened) and her inability to manage him any longer at home and his persistent school refusal. Moreover, the positive decision to admit Billy to a hospital (residential treatment center) was possible only because the family was both able, and willing, to pay for the costly services, and such a treatment center was available nearby. While most neurotic children are treated as outpatients, Billy's story provides us with an opportunity to see how the controlled environment and multitherapeutic approaches of a hospital setting were used to bring about significant changes in his personal, academic, and social adjustment.

On admission, Billy was homesick and despondent, although he slept comfortably and without interruption that night. His night terrors promptly disappeared, and he slept better throughout his nine months of hospitalization than he ever did at home. From the first day, he attended the in-patient school, where he participated readily and performed at a superior level. These early signs of improvement can be attributed to environmental changes, in which he moved from a home situation that was charged with anxiety to one that was orderly, controlled, comforting, attentive, and less threatening and conflictual. In addition to the day-school program, the hospital setting also provided Billy with recreational activities and opportunities to socialize with peers. He had his own therapist who saw him on a regular basis and on occasions when he needed more help. Hospital personnel and his cottage parent were also available for daily interactions, as sources of support, and as sensitive people who could observe and deal with his progress and setbacks.

Billy's academic gains were outstanding to the point where he had easily caught up with his grade level in all areas and was very well prepared to resume his regular class by the end of his hospitalization. Although not as substantial, his social gains were impressive as well. He participated in many of the games and peer activities and was more comfortable relating to others than before, although he never became close friends with any of the other children. He tended to avoid the overt expression of aggression but enjoyed it vicariously as he watched other youngsters fight, and he listened to their verbal outbursts of profanity with a grin of pleasure on his face. However, if Billy could not allow his language to become "dirty," the same could not be said of his person. His prior metic- ulousness and compulsive attention to cleanliness gave way to the other extreme in which he seemed to take delight in wal- lowing in "dirt" and in becoming the filthi- est kid at the hospital. Finally, and ap- parently after his messiness was sufficiently gratified, his personal cleanliness shifted to a middle position between these two ex- tremes.

During the first four-and-one-half months of psychotherapy, Billy was friendly but distant, preferring to talk about his symp- toms rather than play games or draw (as many youngsters of his age seem to prefer). He thought that play was a waste of time when he could be talking about his problems and trying to understand them. He wanted to go straight to the heart of the matter so that he would learn how to make his symp- toms "disappear" without any digression, not even to take time to talk about his friends back home, his family, his daily ac- tivities in the hospital, or his roommate in the cottage. In fact, Billy was dissatisfied with therapy when he was not talking about his symptoms; all else made him feel cheated and put off by his therapist.

After six months of hospitalization, Billy's treatment took a dramatic turn one morning. He had been in bed for three days with a severe cold and was supposed to return to school that morning. However, after breakfast he was found sitting alone on his bed crying. His therapist went to see him; and, when asked what was wrong, Billy burst into tears and said, "Everything has gone wrong." They talked for awhile, and Billy began to cheer up. When the therapist suggested that he might go to school rather than sit around in the cottage, he again burst into tears saying, "That's what the trouble was before I came here. When my nerves were like this, I didn't

feel like going to school, but they made me go and then I would feel worse." Sensing that Billy wanted desperately to relate, the therapist suggested that Billy might like to come to his office and talk. He readily ac- cepted the invitation, and in a period longer than two hours he poured out all of the feelings and thoughts that he had kept to himself for so long. He told of the fears that he had felt, especially toward father, fears that his father might kidnap him and do terrible things to him. He had fantasies while driving in a car with his father, that his father was a member of a bandit gang who intended to deliver him to the gang for some sort of harm. He felt that his mother wanted to protect him, but that she had to give in to the father's will. He resented her for this weakness and felt that she had failed him. He also talked about fears that went back to memories of early childhood.

Billy also talked of his great need to tell somebody about his fear and of his awful feeling that he could never be close enough to anyone to confide in them, that nobody could really understand or accept his feel- ings, and that if he told somebody they would laugh at him or reject him. He used the word "trust" often, prompting the therapist to ask, "Do you trust me?" to which Billy replied, "Not completely." When the therapist reflected, "But you are telling me about many things," he said, "Yes, and you're the only person I could tell these things to. I couldn't tell them to my mother or dad, or any other doctor or any other counselors, or anybody." The therapist acknowledged that being able to tell him these things was a very good sign. Billy looked thoughtful, then smiled and said, "Maybe I can get to trust you, then it will spread to other people and then I will get better."

Indeed, Billy did get better. He returned

home and to school managing both very well. There were a few occasions when his old fears returned, but he mastered them. He continued in therapy as an outpatient for about a year until his family moved away, primarily because of mother's health.

Annual letters from mother revealed that Billy continued to do well in school, was maturing normally, and is well liked by his peers (adapted from Shaw, 1966, pp. 123–126).

REFERENCES

ABE, K. "Phobias and Nervous Symptoms in Childhood and Maturity: Persistence and Associations." *British Journal of Psychiatry*, 1972, *120*, 275–283.

ABRAMOWITZ, C. V. "The Effectiveness of Group Psychotherapy with Children." *Archives of General Psychiatry*, 1976, *33*, 320–326.

ADAMS, P. "Family Characteristics of Obsessive Children." *American Journal of Psychiatry*, 1972, *128*, 1414–1417.

ALEXANDER, B. A. "Systematic Relaxation and Flow Rates in Asthmatic Children: Relationship to Emotional Precipitants and Anxiety." *Journal of Psychosomatic Research*, 1972, *16*, 405–410.

ALEXANDER, F. *Psychosomatic Medicine. Its Principles and Application.* New York: Norton, 1950.

ANTHONY, E. J. "Neurosis of Children." In Freedman, A. M. and H. I. Kaplan (Eds.), *The Child: His Psychological and Cultural Development* (Vol. 2). New York: Atheneum Press, 1972, pp. 105–143.

APLEY, J. and R. C. McKEITH. *The Child and His Symptoms: A Psychosomatic Approach.* Philadelphia: Davis, 1962.

BAKWIN, H. and R. M. BAKWIN. *Behavior Disorders in Children* (4th ed.). Philadelphia: Saunders, 1972.

BANDURA, A., GRUSEC, J. E., and F. L. MENLOVE. "Vicarious Extinction of Avoidance Behavior." *Journal of Personality and Social Psychology*, 1967, *5*, 16–23.

BANDURA, A. and R. H. WALTERS. *Social Learning and Personality Development.* New York: Holt, Rinehart, and Winston, 1963.

BEMPORAD, J., PFEIFFER, C., and W. BLOOM. "Twelve Months' Experience with the GAP Classification of Childhood Disorders." *American Journal of Psychiatry*, 1970, *127*, 658–664.

BERG, I. and R. McGUIRE. "Are Mothers of School Phobic Adolescents Overprotective?" *British Journal of Psychiatry,* 1974, *124*, 10–13.

BIRLEY, J. L. "Stress and Disease." *Journal of Psychosomatic Research*, 1972, *16*, 235–240.

BRADY, J. V., PORTER, R. W., CONRAD, D. G., and J. W. MASON. "Avoidance Behavior and the Development of Gastroduodenal Ulcers." *Journal of Experimental Analysis of Behavior*, 1958, *1*, 69–72.

BRUCH, H. *Eating Disorders: Obesity, Anorexia Nervosa, and the Person Within.* New York: Basic Books, 1973.

CAHOON, D. D. "Symptom Substitution and the Behavior Therapies: A Reappraisal." *Psychological Bulletin*, 1968, *69*, 149–156.

CHAPMAN, A. H. *Management of Emotional Problems of Children and Adolescents* (2nd ed.). Philadelphia: Lippincott, 1974.

CLARIZIO, H. F. and G. F. McCOY. *Behavior Disorders in School-Aged Children*. Scranton: Chandler, 1970.

CLARK, M. "Troubled Children: The Quest for Help." In Annual Editions, *Reading in Human Development 77/78*. Guilford, Connecticut: Dushkin Publishing Group, 1977, pp. 167–171.

COHEN, D. B. "On the Etiology of Neurosis." *Journal of Abnormal Psychology*, 1974, *83*, 473–479.

COLEMAN, J. C. *Abnormal Psychology and Modern Life* (4th ed.). Glenview, Illinois: Scott, Foresman, 1972.

CRIEP, L. H. *Clinical Immunology and Allergy*. New York: Grune and Stratton, 1962.

DALLY, P. *Anorexia Nervosa*. New York: Grune and Stratton, 1969.

DAVIDSON, S. "School Phobia as a Manifestation of Family Disturbance: Its Structure and Treatment." *Journal of Child Psychology and Psychiatry*, 1961, *1*, 270–287.

DEKKER, E. and J. GROEN. "Reproducible Psychogenic Attacks of Asthma." *Journal of Psychosomatic Research*, 1956, *1*, 58–67.

DiCARA, L. V. and N. E. MILLER. "Changes in Heart Rate Instrumentally Learned by Curarized Rats as Avoidance Responses." *Journal of Comparative and Physiological Psychology*, 1968, *65*, 8–12.

DOLLARD, J. and N. E. MILLER. *Personality and Psychotherapy*. New York: McGraw-Hill, 1950.

DUDLEY, D. L., MARTIN, C. J., and T. H. HOLMES. "Psychophysiologic Studies of Pulmonary Ventilation." *Psychosomatic Medicine*, 1964, *26*, 645–660.

DUNBAR, H. F. *Psychosomatic Diagnosis*. New York: Hoeber, 1943.

ELLINGSON, R. "The Incidence of EEG Abnormality Among Patients with Mental Disorders of Apparently Nonorganic Origin: A Critical Review." *American Journal of Psychiatry*, 1954, *111*, 263–275.

EYSENCK, H. J. and D. B. PRELL. "The Inheritance of Neuroticism: An Experimental Study." *Journal of Mental Science*, 1951, *97*, 441–465.

FELDMAN, G. M. "The Effect of Biofeedback Training on Respiratory Resistance of Asthmatic Children." *Psychosomatic Medicine*, 1976, *38*, 27–34.

FREUD, A. *Normality and Pathology in Childhood*. New York: International Universities Press, 1965.

FREUD, S. *Analysis of a Phobia in a Five-Year-Old Boy (1909)* (Standard ed.) (Vol. X). London: Hogarth Press, 1955.

GAP Report No. 62. Group for the Advancement of Psychiatry, Committee on Child Psychiatry. *Psychopathological Disorders in Childhood: Theoretical Consideration and a Proposed Classification*. New York, June 1966.

GARVEY, W. P. and J. R. HEGRENES. "Desensitization Techniques in the Treatment of School Phobia." *American Journal of Orthopsychiatry*, 1966, *36*, 147–152.

GITTELMAN-KLEIN, R. and D. F. KLEIN. "School Phobia: Diagnostic Considerations in the Light of Imipramine Effects." *Journal of Nervous and Mental Diseases*, 1973, *156*, 199–215.

GLAUS, K. D. "The Effects of Conditioned Muscle Tension Changes on Respiration." Unpublished doctoral dissertation, Ohio University, 1976.

GLICK, I. D. and D. R. KESSLER. *Marital and Family Therapy*. New York: Grune and Stratton, 1974.

GRAHAM, D. T. "Some Research on Psychophysiologic Specificity and Its Relation to Psychosomatic Disease." In Roessler, R. and N. S. Greenfield (Eds.), *Physiological*

Correlates of Psychological Disorder. Madison, Wisconsin: University of Wisconsin Press, 1962, pp. 232–238.

GRAHAM, P. "Management in Child Psychiatry: Recent Trends." *British Journal of Psychiatry,* 1976, *129,* 97–108.

GRAHAM, P., RUTTER, M., YULE, W., and I. PLESS. "Childhood Asthma: A Psychosomatic Disorder? Some Epidemiological Considerations." *British Journal of Preventive and Social Medicine,* 1967, *21,* 78–85.

HAMILTON, M. *Psychosomatics.* New York: Wiley, 1955.

HAMPE, E., MILLER, L., BARRET, C., and H. NOBLE. "Intelligence and School Phobia." *Journal of School Psychology,* 1973, *11,* 66–70.

JERSILD, A. T. *Child Psychology.* Englewood Cliffs, New Jersey: Prentice-Hall, 1968.

JOHNSON, A. M., FALSTEIN, E. I., SZUREK, S. A., and M. SVENDSEN. "School Phobia." *American Journal of Orthopsychiatry,* 1941, *11,* 702–711.

JOHNSON, H. J. "Decision Making, Conflict, and Physiological Arousal." *Journal of Abnormal and Social Psychology,* 1963, *67,* 114–124.

JONES, M. C. "The Elimination of Children's Fears." *Journal of Experimental Psychology,* 1924, *7,* 383–390.

JUDD, L. L. "Obsessive Compulsive Neurosis in Children." *Archives of General Psychiatry,* 1965, *12,* 136–143.

KELLY, E. "School Phobia: A Review of Theory and Treatment." *Psychology in the Schools,* 1973, *10,* 33–42.

KENNARD, M. A. "Value of Equivocal Signs in Neurologic Diagnosis." *Neurology,* 1960, *10,* 753–764.

KESSLER, J. W. "Neurosis in Childhood." In Wolman, B. B. (Ed.), *Manual of Child Psychopathology.* New York: McGraw-Hill, 1972, pp. 387–435.

KNAPP, P. H. "The Asthmatic and His Environment." *Journal of Nervous and Mental Diseases,* 1969, *149,* 133–151.

KNAPP, P., MATHÉ, S. A., and L. VACHON. "Psychosomatic Aspects of Bronchial Asthma." In Weiss, E. and M. Segal (Eds.), *Bronchial Asthma: Mechanisms and Therapeutics.* Boston: Little Brown, 1976, pp. 1055–1080.

KOSTES, H., GLAUCK, K. D., BRICEL, S. K., CRAWFORD, P. L., and J. E. EDWARDS. *Muscle Relaxation Effects on Peak Expiratory Flow Rate in Asthmatic Children.* Paper presented at annual meetings of the Biofeedback Society, Orlando, March, 1977.

KOSTES, H., GLAUS, K. D., CRAWFORD, P. L., EDWARDS, J. E., and M. S. SCHERR. "Operant Reduction of Frontalis EMG Activity in the Treatment of Asthma in Children." *Journal of Psychosomatic Research,* 1976, *20,* 453–459.

KURLANDER, L. F. and D. COLODNY. "Pseudoneurosis in the Neurologically Handicapped Child." *American Journal of Orthopsychiatry,* 1965, *35,* 733–738.

LACEY, J. F. and B. C. LACEY. "Verification and Extension of the Principle of Autonomic Response-Stereotypy." *American Journal of Psychology,* 1958, *71,* 50–73.

LACHMAN, S. J. *Psychosomatic Disorders: A Behavioristic Interpretation.* New York: Wiley, 1972.

LAZARUS, A. A. *Behavior Therapy and Beyond.* New York: McGraw-Hill, 1971.

LAZARUS, A. A., DAVISON, G. C., and D. A. POLEFKA. "Classical and Operant Factors in the Treatment of a School Phobia." *Journal of Abnormal Psychology,* 1965, *70,* 225–229.

LETON, D. A. "Assessment of School Phobia." *Mental Hygiene,* 1962, *46,* 256–264.

LEVENTHAL, T. and M. SILLS. "Self-image in School Phobia." *American Journal of Orthopsychiatry,* 1964, *34,* 685–695.

LIEBMAN, R., MINUCHIN, S., and L. BAKER. "The Use of Structural Family Therapy in the Treatment of Intractable Asthma." *American Journal of Psychiatry*, 1974, *131*, 535–540.

MASSERMAN, J. H. "Experimental Neuroses." *Scientific American*, 1950, *182*, 38–43.

MILLER, N. E. "Learning of Visceral and Glandular Responses." *Science*, 1969, *163*, 434–445.

MILLER, N. E. and A. BANUAZIZI. "Instrumental Learning by Curarized Rats of a Specific Visceral Response, Intestinal or Cardiac." *Journal of Comparative and Physiological Psychology*, 1968, *65*, 1–7.

MOSS, T. and A. E. EDWARDS. "Conflict vs. Conditioning: Effects upon Peripheral Vascular Activity." *Psychosomatic Medicine*, 1964, *26*, 267–273.

MOWRER, O. H. and W. M. MOWRER. "Enuresis: A Method for Its Study and Treatment." *American Journal of Orthopsychiatry*, 1938, *8*, 436–459.

MUSTACCHI, P., LUCIA, S. P., and L. JASSY. "Bronchial Asthma: Patterns of Morbidity and Mortality in the United States; 1951–1959" *California Medicine*, 1962, *96*, 196–200.

MYERS, J. K., LINDENTHAL, J. J., and M. P. PEPPER. "Life Events and Psychiatric Impairment." *Journal of Nervous and Mental Diseases*, 1971, *152*, 149–157.

NICHOLS, K. A. and I. BERG. "School Phobia and Self-evaluation." *Journal of Child Psychology and Psychiatry and Allied Disciplines*, 1970, *11*, 133–141.

PAVLOV, I. P. *Lectures on Conditioned Reflexes*, Vol. 1 (translated by W. H. Gantt). London: Lawrence and Wishart, 1928.

POLLIN, W., ALLEN, M. G., HOFFER, A., STABENAU, J. R., and Z. HRUBEC. "Psychopathology in 15,909 Pairs of Veteran Twins. Evidence for a Genetic Factor in the Pathogenesis of Schizophrenia and Its Relative Absence in Psychoneurosis." *American Journal of Psychiatry*, 1969, *126*, 597–609.

PROCTOR, J. T. "The Treatment of Hysteria in Childhood." In Hammer, M. and A. M. Kaplan (Eds.), *The Practice of Psychotherapy with Children*. Homewood, Illinois: Dorsey Press, 1967, pp. 121–150.

PURCELL, K. "Distinctions Between Subgroups of Asthmatic Children: Children's Perceptions of Events Associated with Asthma." *Pediatrics*, 1963, *31*, 486–495.

PURCELL, K. "Childhood Asthma: The Role of Family Relationships, Personality, and Emotions." In Davids, A. (Ed.), *Child Personality and Psychopathology: Current Topics* (Vol. 2). New York: Wiley, 1975, pp. 1010–1035.

PURCELL, K., BERNSTEIN, L., and S. C. BURKANTZ. "A Preliminary Comparison of Rapidly Remitting and Persistently 'Steroid Dependent' Asthmatic Children." *Psychosomatic Medicine*, 1961, *23*, 305–310.

PURCELL, K., BRADY, K., CHAI, H., MASER, J., MOLK, K., GORDON, N., and J. MEANS. "The Effect on Asthma in Children of Experimental Separation from the Family." *Psychosomatic Medicine*, 1969, *31*, 144–164.

PURCELL, K. and J. H. WEISS. "Asthma." In C. G. Costello (Ed.), *Symptoms of Psychopathology*. New York: Wiley, 1970, pp. 601–602.

PURCELL, K., WEISS, J., and W. HAHN. "Certain Psychosomatic Disorders" in Wolman, B. B. (Ed.), *Manual of Child Psychopathology*. New York: McGraw-Hill, 1972, pp. 706–740.

RACHMAN, S. "Systematic Desensitization." *Psychological Bulletin*, 1967, *67*, 93–104.

RACKEMAN, F. H. and M. D. EDWARDS. "Medical Progress: Asthma in Children: Follow-up Study of 688 Patients After 20 Years." *New England Journal of Medicine*, 1952, *246*, 815–858.

REES, L. "The Importance of Psychological, Allergic, and Infective Factors in Childhood Asthma." *Journal of Psychosomatic Research,* 1964, *7,* 253–262.

REINHART, J. B., KENNA, M. D., and R. A. SUCCOP. "Anorexia Nervosa in Children." *Journal of the American Academy of Child Psychiatry,* 1972, *11,* 114–131.

ROSEN, B. M., BARN, A. K., and M. CRAMER. "Demographic and Diagnostic Characteristics of Psychiatric Clinic Outpatients in the U.S.A., 1961." *American Journal of Orthopsychiatry,* 1964, *34,* 455–468.

SABOT, L. M., PECK, R., and J. RASKIN. "The Waiting Room Society: A Study of Families and Children Applying to a Child Psychiatric Clinic." *Archives of General Psychiatry,* 1969, *21,* 25–32.

SAWREY, W. L., CONGER, J. J., and E. S. TURRELL. "An Experimental Investigation of the Role of Psychological Factors in the Production of Gastric Ulcers in Rats." *Journal of Comparative and Physiological Psychology,* 1956, *49,* 457–461.

SAWREY, W. L. and J. D. WEISZ. "An Experimental Method of Producing Gastric Ulcers." *Journal of Comparative and Physiological Psychology,* 1956, *49,* 269–270.

SCHEPANK, H. "Hereditary and Environmental Influences in 50 Neurotic Pairs of Twins (English summary)." *Zeitschrift fur Psychotherapie und Medizinische Psychologie,* 1971, *21,* 41–50.

SELYE, H. "Stress: It's a G.A.S." *Psychology Today,* 1969, *3:4,* 24–26.

SELYE, H. *The Stress of Life.* New York: McGraw-Hill, 1956.

SHAPIRO, T. and R. O. JEGEDE. "School Phobia: A Babel of Tongues." *Journal of Autism and Childhood Schizophrenia,* 1973, *3,* 168–186.

SHAW, C. R. *The Psychiatric Disorders of Childhood.* New York: Appleton-Century-Crofts, 1966, pp. 121–126.

SHIELDS, J. and E. SLATER. "Heredity and Psychological Abnormality." In Eysenck, H. J. (Ed.), *Handbook of Abnormal Psychology.* New York: Basic Books, 1961, pp. 298–343.

SMITH, R. E. and T. M. SHARPE. "Treatment of a School Phobia with Implosive Therapy." *Journal of Consulting and Clinical Psychology,* 1970, *35,* 239–243.

SMITH, S. L. "School Refusal with Anxiety: A Review of 63 Cases." *Canadian Psychiatric Association Journal,* 1970, *15,* 257–264.

SPIEGEL, H. "Is Symptom Removal Dangerous?" *American Journal of Psychiatry,* 1967, *123,* 1279–1282.

SPITZ, R. A. "Hospitalism: An Inquiry into the Genesis of Psychiatric Conditions in Early Childhood." *Psychoanalytic Study of the Child,* 1945, *1,* 53–74.

SPITZ, R. A. and K. M. WOLF. "Anaclitic Depression: An Inquiry into the Genesis of Psychiatric Conditions in Early Childhood." *Psychoanalytic Study of the Child,* 1946, *2,* 113–117.

STEIN, M. "Etiology and Mechanisms in the Development of Asthma." In the First Hahnemann Symposium on Psychosomatic Medicine, Philadelphia: Lea and Febiger, 1962.

STEWART, D. N. and D. M. WINSER. "Incidence of Perforated Peptic Ulcer: Effect of Heavy Air-raids." *Lancet,* 1942, *1,* 259–261.

TEMPLER, D. "The Obsessive-Compulsive Neurosis: Review of Research Findings." *Comprehensive Psychiatry,* 1972, *13,* 375–398.

THOMA, H. *Anorexia Nervosa.* New York: International Universities Press, 1967.

TIETZ, W. "School Phobia and the Fear of Death." *Mental Hygiene,* 1970, *54,* 565–568.

TOLSTRUP, K. "Treatment of Anorexia Nervosa in Childhood and Adolescence." *Journal of Child Psychology, Psychiatry, and Allied Disciplines*, 1975, *16*, 75–78.

TREUTING, T. F. and H. S. RIPLEY. "Life Situations, Emotions and Bronchial Asthma." *Journal of Nervous and Mental Diseases*, 1948, *108*, 380–389.

TYRER, P. and S. TYRER. "School Refusal, Truancy, and Adult Neurotic Illness." *Psychological Medicine*, 1974, *4*, 416–421.

VELTKAMP, L. "School Phobia." *Journal of Family Counseling*, 1975, *3*, 47–51.

WALDRON, S. "The Significance of Childhood Neurosis for Adult Mental Health: A Follow-up Study." *American Journal of Psychiatry*, 1976, *133*, 532–538.

WALDRON, S., SHRIER, D. K., STONE, B., and F. TOBIN. "School Phobia and Other Childhood Neuroses: A Systematic Study of the Children and Their Families." *American Journal of Psychiatry*, 1975, *132*, 802–808.

WARREN, W. "A Study of Anorexia Nervosa in Young Girls." *Journal of Child Psychology and Psychiatry*, 1968, *9*, 27–40.

WATSON, J. B. and R. RAYNER. "Conditioned Emotional Reactions." *Journal of Experimental Psychology*, 1920, *3*, 1–14.

WHITE, R. T., DeMYER, W., and M. DeMYER. "EEG Abnormalities in Early Childhood Schizophrenia: A Double-Blind Study of Psychiatrically Disturbed and Normal Children During Promazine Sedation." *American Journal of Psychiatry*, 1964, *120*, 950–958.

WOLFF, H. G. "Life Stress and Cardiovascular Disorders." *Circulation*, 1950, *1*, 187–203.

WOLPE, J. *The Practice of Behavior Therapy* (2nd ed.). New York: Pergamon Press, 1973.

WOLPE, J. *Psychotherapy by Reciprocal Inhibition*. Stanford: Stanford University Press, 1958.

PROLOGUE

Gather ye rosebuds while ye may,
   Old time is still a-flying;
And this same flower that smiles today
   Tomorrow will be dying.

The glorious lamp of heaven, the sun,
   The higher he's a-getting,
The sooner will his race be run,
   And nearer he's to setting.

That age is best which is the first,
   When youth and blood are warmer;
But being spent, the worse, and worst
   Times still succeed the former.

Then be not coy, but use your time,
   And, while ye may, go marry;
For, having lost but once your prime,
   You may forever tarry.

ROBERT HERRICK

The poet's admonition to fully spend one's youth while it lasts is echoed by our culture in its hopes that this developmental period will be used fruitfully to produce adults who will be responsible and productive citizens. But adolescence is a period when young people also are placed in limbo, inasmuch as they are neither regarded as children nor quite ready to assume the responsibilities of adulthood. It is a stage of life that is not the same in all cultures, although we tend to think of it in terms with which we are most familiar. In some societies, adolescence is characterized by an uneventful and untroubled transition from childhood to adulthood, while in our society, it is a very stressful and tumultuous period. The timespan can be very brief or even omitted in societies that are well organized around the family and tightly controlled by their elders. Under these circumstances, the role of the adolescent in the family and in the community is relatively fixed, leaving little room for experimentation or mobility (Cavan and Cavan, 1968). The rite of passage into adulthood usually occurs at the time of physical maturity, and, in some instances, after a ritualistic period of formal initiation. In fact, before the twentieth century, adolescence was almost nonexistent in our culture as a separate stage of development. However, later advances in technology and industrialization have lengthened the period of adolescence considerably to meet the necessary demands of training and formal education for vocational specialization.

Prolongation of adolescence has kept many young people dependent on their families (at least financially) not only during high school but through most of the college years as well. Our society provides no well structured role for its adolescents, and none that recognizes them either as useful or as contributors to the community. Instead, a nagging public uneasiness exists about the activities of young people that periodically heightens around a particular issue. Some years ago, this was reflected in the results of a June, 1970, Gallup Poll in which "campus unrest"

aroused such intense reactions that it was considered our country's major problem (Keniston, 1975). Although this no longer is an issue, young people of each generation express dissatisfaction and disenchantment with some aspects of the adult world, and many are quite hesitant to join the adult world. "Far from seeking adult prerogatives of their parents, they vehemently demand a virtually indefinite prolongation of their nonadult state" (Keniston, 1975, p. 8).

With its rapid and dramatic physical changes especially in the development of adult sexual characteristics, puberty marks the beginning of adolescence. However, before this period is over profound social and psychological changes will occur that can affect the young person's self-perception, relationships with peers and others, self-control, autonomy and independence, academic and vocational competence, and sexual adjustment. Conflicts between parents and the adolescent are common, particularly conflicts involving the relinquishing of parental authority as the youngster wishes to assume more freedom and adult privileges. The specific battle may be over the choice of friends, or clothes and appearance, or such restrictions as dating, curfew, and the use of the family car. Inevitably, the power struggle generates resentment, resistance, and sometimes rebellion. In addition, there are internal conflicts that are concerned with impulse control, shifting moral standards, self-acceptance and inadequacy, and the uncertainty of goals and directions. From all indications, more than enough turmoil and volatility exist during this transitional period to produce a variety of serious behavior problems.

In this chapter, we shall focus on *delinquency, runaways,* and *drug abuse* as problems of adolescence that appear to have reached growing proportions in both frequency and severity.

Delinquency

Tom, a sixteen-year-old high schooler, was sent to a state hospital by the juvenile court after being charged with illegal possession of a pistol that was used in the fatal shooting of a child. Tom told several versions of what happened, although it was clear that he had found an old German Luger and a box of bullets while rummaging through closets of a neighbor's home. Pleased with his find and eager to show them off, Tom took them to the school playground where he met a little girl who lived in the neighborhood. The child did not believe that the gun was real, so Tom loaded it. At this point the story becomes confused, although there is no doubt that the gun went off, hitting her in the temple and killing her instantaneously. When she fell to the ground, Tom became frightened and fled the scene on his bicycle. He threw the pistol and bullets away in a deserted lot, and then returned to the playground to see if he could help the wounded child. By this time the police had arrived after being summoned by people who had heard the shot and saw Tom riding away. Apparently no one had witnessed the shooting. Initially Tom accused another boy of the crime and calmly maintained that he had just arrived for the first time. He later admitted that he did the shooting, although he insisted that it was accidental. He took the police to the abandoned gun and said that he was too frightened to tell the truth earlier.

Tom had a checkered history of attending many schools and of being a behavior problem in each. He was disrespectful to teachers, restless, very active, and involved in frequent fights and truancy. Outside of school he was also given to fighting and destructiveness. He lied and blamed others for any of his misbehaviors, even when he stole things and was apprehended with the objects in his possession. He was born out of wedlock and abandoned by his mother at birth. For the first seven years of his life, he was brought up in a large orphanage that provided minimal care. Prior to his legal adoption, he was placed twice but returned on each occasion because he had difficulties adjusting to siblings and other children in the neighborhood or because the foster parents did not like him. His adoptive parents worked and moved frequently, so that he was left at the homes of either relatives or neighbors and was enrolled in numerous new schools. For a long time Tom did not feel that he really belonged to them (Excerpts from case study pp. 238–39. Copyright © 1963 by Macmillan Publishing Co., Inc. Zax and George Stricker, reprinted with permission of Macmillan Publishing Co., Inc., from *Patterns of Psychopathology* by Melvin).

Tom's present difficulties along with his chronic history of acting-out behaviors represent a familiar pattern to most juvenile jurists, although the details of the story may differ from one youngster to another. As an abandoned and unloved child, Tom only gained attention when he responded in aggressive and antisocial ways. He did not have the benefit of parental models who could show him socially acceptable behaviors or who could provide him with a sense of belonging and security. He was a delinquent, but, strictly speaking, delinquency, much like the word "insanity," is a legal and not a psychological term that refers to the commission of an act by a minor that otherwise would be regarded as criminal if committed by an adult. Delinquent behavior also may include acts that are illegal specifically for minors (running away). In popular usage, "delinquency" is an ambiguous and catch-all label that may very well suggest different meanings to different people. For some, it may refer to young men with long hair and beards, or describe a wide range of mischievous acts (such as egging a car on Halloween), while to others, it may have a restricted use to teenagers who rob, steal, or murder. Even a legal definition lacks precision in light of the fact that statutory provisions differ widely among the states, and enforcement procedures and practices are noticeably heterogeneous. The tendency of different agencies and disciplines to formulate their own views of delinquent conduct further complicates the definitional problem (Eldefonso, 1972). For example, law enforcers may classify delinquents into two groups: those impulsive and/or immature youngsters who commit a delinquent act for the first time and respond to corrective measures, and those incorrigible recidivists who have failed to respond to many previous remedial efforts. Educators may view delinquency as academic underachievement, and disruptive and unmanageable behavior in the classroom, while many psychologists may be inclined to think of delinquency as a manifestation of some abnormal condition.

Problems with Incidence Data

It is apparent from the above discussion that the incidence of delinquency should vary with its definition; that is, estimates should be different depending on whether we view delinquents as minors committing illegal acts or as academic underachievers, or as youngsters repeatedly convicted for antisocial behaviors. Almost all youngsters at one time or another are guilty of some unlawful behavior, whether it be shoplifting, engaging in sex with a minor, vandalism, or smoking pot. However, there are fewer who are underachievers in a school population, and probably even a small number who are incorrigible recidivists. Incidence data also will be affected by differences in state laws with respect to the type of offenses and the age criterion used to define a minor over whom the juvenile court has jurisdiction. In addition, communities differ in the availability of child-related service agencies as alternatives to the court that are equipped to deal with cases of delinquency. Unfortunately, juvenile offenders who are handled by agencies other than the police or the courts are not included in the primary data that describe the problem. Thus, it is important to note that we have no precise measure of either crime or delinquency, although we do have estimates that are based on records maintained by law enforcement agencies and the juvenile courts.

The Magnitude and Seriousness of Delinquency[1]

In 1970 alone more than one million cases of juvenile delinquency, excluding traffic offenses, were handled by our nation's juvenile courts. Because some youngsters were referred more than once during the year, the actual number of children involved is somewhat lower and estimated at 907,000. This figure represents two and eight-tenths percent of the population between the ages of ten and seventeen. A substantially higher estimate of approximately five percent of children falling within this age group is given when cases of delinquency that are handled by the police or the family are included. Even more alarming is the fact that the rate of delinquency continues to increase with each passing year. More specifically, juvenile delinquency increased 106 percent between 1960 and 1970, as compared to a twenty-eight percent growth in the number of children falling into this age group during the same

[1] Information reported in this section is based primarily on two publications. *Juvenile Court Statistical Series*, U.S. Department of Health, Education and Welfare, Washington, D.C.: U.S. Government Printing Office, 1970; and *Uniform Crime Reports*, Federal Bureau of Investigation. Washington, D.C.: U.S. Government Printing Office, 1973.

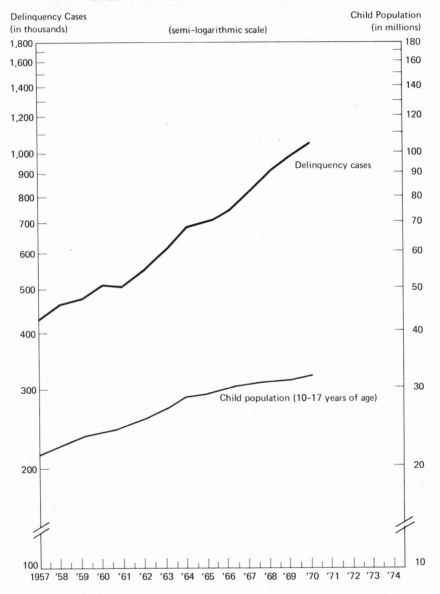

TREND IN JUVENILE COURT DELINQUENCY CASES AND
CHILD POPULATION 10-17 YEARS OF AGE, 1957–1970

FIGURE 12–1   Trend in juvenile court delinquency cases and child population 10–17 years of age, 1957–1970. (From *Juvenile Court Statistics,* 1970, p. 10.)

period of time. This upward trend is graphically illustrated in Figure 12–1, which plots the growth in both delinquency and child population over thirteen years (1957–1970).

Does the increase in delinquency over a decade merely reflect a surge in minor offenses? If we could answer yes to this question then we would be consoled and comforted that things are not as bad as they might seem. Unfortunately, the data lead to a negative interpretation and provide ample justification for the heightened public concern about delinquency and crime in this country. While all types of offenses (combined) more than doubled between 1960 and 1970, serious acts, including criminal homicide, forcible rape, burglary, robbery, aggravated assault, larceny, and auto theft together increased some ninety-five percent, and the most serious group of offenses (homicide, rape, aggravated assault, and robbery) dramatically increased by 167 percent during this ten-year period. The findings are incontrovertible that serious delinquent acts against person and property increased in greater proportion than did less serious offenses, although both minor and serious offenses occurred with increasing frequency in the decade of the 1960s.

When we think of crime and delinquency, we tend to regard it as almost the exclusive property of urban centers and especially of the inner cities. To some extent, this view is supported by the data showing that delinquency is between two and three times greater in cities than in other areas. However, rural areas are no longer as safe and secure as they once were. In 1969, there was a sixteen percent increase in delinquency in rural areas, and rural juvenile courts were busier than ever as they showed a higher percent increase in cases than either urban or semiurban

courts. If there once was a haven from this problem, there is now no area of the country that is unaffected. The rise in delinquency continues everywhere, and it seems to be spreading to our rural areas rapidly.

In the thirteen-year period between 1960 and 1973, crime increased for all ages some thirty-five percent, whereas the increase for youngsters under eighteen years of age was an astronomical 144 percent. A breakdown of arrests by type of offense and age for this period is provided in Tables 12–1 and 12–2, which shows that almost all offenses increased more rapidly for youngsters under eighteen than for adults.

Over the years, delinquency has been predominantly a male problem by a ratio of about 4:1, although the incidence of girls' delinquency has sharply increased to the extent that by 1970 the ratio was reduced to approximately 3:1. Between 1969 and 1970, arrests for girls under eighteen years of age increased more than twice as much as did arrests for boys (ten percent as compared to five percent), and this increase was equally evident in urban, semi-urban, and rural courts. The fact remains that since 1965 delinquency cases involving girls have increased by seventy-eight percent, as compared to a forty-four percent increase for boys. Moreover, the rise in arrests of girls under eighteen was considerably higher than for boys in both *violent* and *property* crimes. Perhaps this is a reflection of society's changing attitude toward females, who no longer are expected to assume passive, dependent, and compliant roles and functions.

Types of Delinquency

Through the years, investigators have recognized delinquency as a diverse and broad category that could be better studied,

TABLE 12–1 * Total Arrest Trends, 1960–1973 [2,378 agencies; 1973 population 94,251,000 [1]]

Offense charged	Number of persons arrested								
	Total all ages			Under 18 years of age			18 years of age and over		
	1960	1973	Percent Change	1960	1973	Percent Change	1960	1973	Percent Change
TOTAL	3,242,574	4,381,968	+ 35.1	466,174	1,138,046	+ 144.1	2,776,400	3,243,922	+ 16.0
Criminal homicide:									
Murder and nonnegligent manslaughter	4,541	10,629	+134.1	337	1,197	+ 255.2	4,204	9,432	+124.4
Manslaughter by negligence	1,766	1,660	− 6.0	132	216	+ 63.6	1,634	1,444	− 11.6
Forcible rape	6,857	13,823	+101.6	1,185	2,753	+ 132.3	5,672	11,070	+ 95.2
Robbery	31,197	83,012	+166.1	7,352	29,336	+ 299.0	23,845	53,676	+125.1
Aggravated assault	50,402	108,076	+114.4	6,306	19,306	+ 206.2	44,096	88,770	+101.3
Burglary—breaking or entering	117,084	211,029	+ 80.2	55,149	112,606	+ 104.2	61,935	98,423	+ 58.9
Larceny—theft	190,443	431,506	+126.6	91,375	204,913	+ 124.3	99,068	226,593	+128.7
Auto theft	54,202	87,975	+ 62.3	32,939	49,747	+ 51.0	21,263	38,228	+ 79.8
Violent crime [2]	92,997	215,540	+131.8	15,180	52,592	+ 246.5	77,817	162,948	+109.4
Property crime [3]	361,729	730,510	+101.9	179,463	367,266	+ 104.6	182,266	363,244	+ 99.3
Subtotal for above offenses	456,492	947,710	+107.6	194,775	420,074	+ 115.7	261,717	527,636	+101.6

Other assaults	115,156	182,985	+ 58.9	11,938	36,287	+ 204.0	103,218	146,698	+ 42.1
Forgery and counterfeiting	21,329	28,175	+ 32.1	1,502	3,081	+ 105.1	19,827	25,094	+ 26.6
Fraud and embezzlement	30,551	56,208	+ 84.0	779	2,376	+ 205.0	29,772	53,832	+ 80.8
Stolen property; buying, receiving, possessing	9,147	48,141	+426.3	2,531	15,925	+ 529.2	6,616	32,216	+386.9
Weapons; carrying, possessing, etc.	30,865	85,749	+177.8	6,353	13,950	+ 119.6	24,512	71,799	+192.9
Prostitution and commercialized vice	24,331	40,354	+ 65.9	413	1,595	+ 286.2	23,918	38,759	+ 62.0
Sex offenses (except forcible rape and prostitution)	39,582	35,693	− 9.8	8,738	7,078	− 19.0	30,844	28,615	− 7.2
Narcotic drug laws	29,889	328,670	+999.6	1,725	82,340	+4673.3	28,164	246,330	+774.6
Gambling	105,607	43,983	− 58.4	1,230	1,239	+ .7	104,377	42,744	− 59.0
Offenses against family and children	35,906	24,063	− 33.0	697	523	− 25.0	35,209	23,540	− 33.1
Driving under the influence	142,698	413,837	+190.0	1,125	5,640	+ 401.3	141,573	408,197	+188.3
Liquor laws	81,735	109,392	+ 33.8	17,207	43,329	+ 151.8	64,528	66,063	+ 2.4
Drunkenness	1,215,555	837,551	− 31.1	12,209	22,959	+ 88.0	1,203,346	814,592	− 32.3
Disorderly conduct	364,289	317,531	− 12.8	46,271	69,864	+ 51.0	318,018	247,667	− 22.1
Vagrancy	127,643	40,508	− 68.3	7,151	4,089	− 42.8	120,492	36,419	− 69.8
All other offenses (except traffic)	411,799	841,418	+104.3	151,530	407,697	+ 169.1	260,269	433,721	+ 66.6
Suspicion (not included in totals)	123,196	30,876	− 74.9	22,651	9,430	− 58.4	100,545	21,446	− 78.7

1 Based on comparable reports from 1854 cities representing 79,540,000 population and 524 counties representing 14,711,000 population.

2 Violent crime is offenses of murder, forcible rape, robbery, and aggravated assault.

3 Property crime is offenses of burglary, larceny, and auto theft.

* Uniform Crime Reports, 1973, p. 124–125.

373

TABLE 12–2 * Total Arrest Trends, 1968–1973 [3,256 agencies; 1973 estimated population 107,593,000]

Offense charged	Number of persons arrested								
	Total all ages			Under 18 years of age			18 years of age and over		
	1968	1973	Percent Change	1968	1973	Percent Change	1968	1973	Percent Change
TOTAL	4,257,707	4,826,192	+ 13.4	1,103,340	1,265,959	+ 14.7	3,154,367	3,560,233	+ 12.9
Criminal homicide:									
Murder and nonnegligent manslaughter	8,064	11,364	+ 40.9	785	1,249	+ 59.1	7,279	10,115	+ 39.0
Manslaughter by negligence	2,074	1,877	− 9.5	150	210	+ 40.0	1,924	1,667	− 13.4
Forcible rape	9,636	14,777	+ 53.4	1,959	2,972	+ 51.7	7,677	11,805	+ 53.8
Robbery	56,156	85,770	+ 52.7	18,482	29,718	+ 60.8	37,674	56,052	+ 48.8
Aggravated assault	84,563	115,244	+ 36.3	14,338	20,343	+ 41.9	70,225	94,901	+ 35.1
Burglary—breaking or entering	195,107	231,679	+ 18.7	106,466	125,560	+ 17.9	88,641	106,119	+ 19.7
Larceny—theft	367,227	474,905	+ 29.3	202,730	227,795	+ 12.4	164,497	247,110	+ 50.2
Auto theft	99,841	92,849	− 7.0	61,051	52,438	− 14.1	38,790	40,411	+ 4.2
Violent crime [1]	158,419	227,155	+ 43.4	35,564	54,282	+ 52.6	122,855	172,873	+ 40.7
Property crime [2]	662,175	799,433	+ 20.7	370,247	405,793	+ 9.6	291,928	393,640	+ 34.8
Subtotal for above offenses	822,668	1,028,465	+ 25.0	405,961	460,285	+ 13.4	416,707	568,180	+ 36.4

Other assaults	183,785	207,080	+ 12.7	32,471	40,486	+ 24.7	151,314	166,594	+ 10.1
Arson	6,685	7,837	+ 17.2	4,116	4,548	+ 10.5	2,569	3,289	+ 28.0
Forgery and counterfeiting	27,019	30,115	+ 11.5	3,321	3,362	+ 1.2	23,698	26,753	+ 12.9
Fraud	40,824	57,836	+ 41.7	1,902	2,272	+ 19.5	38,922	55,564	+ 42.8
Embezzlement	4,358	4,138	− 5.0	188	345	+ 83.5	4,170	3,793	− 9.0
Stolen property; buying, receiving, possessing	30,250	51,880	+ 71.5	10,304	17,603	+ 70.8	19,946	34,277	+ 71.8
Vandalism	79,750	84,811	+ 6.3	60,265	57,916	− 3.9	19,485	26,895	+ 38.0
Weapons; carrying, possessing, etc.	64,722	92,229	+ 42.5	11,583	14,870	+ 28.4	53,139	77,359	+ 45.6
Prostitution and commercialized vice	36,190	40,249	+ 11.2	754	1,540	+ 104.2	35,436	38,709	+ 9.2
Sex offenses (except forcible rape and prostitution)	35,721	37,702	+ 5.5	8,303	7,241	− 12.8	27,418	30,461	+ 11.1
Narcotic drug laws	130,228	356,460	+173.7	33,046	92,109	+ 178.7	97,182	264,351	+172.0
Gambling	58,359	47,054	− 19.4	1,282	1,258	− 1.9	57,077	45,796	− 19.8
Offenses against family and children	37,444	27,012	− 27.9	425	542	+ 27.5	37,019	26,470	− 28.5
Driving under the influence	232,222	461,620	+ 98.8	2,259	6,289	+ 178.4	229,963	455,331	+ 98.0
Liquor laws	155,131	127,773	− 17.6	49,495	50,662	+ 2.4	105,636	77,111	− 27.0
Drunkenness	1,161,516	913,625	− 21.3	29,678	26,538	− 10.6	1,131,838	887,087	− 21.6
Disorderly conduct	400,660	357,454	− 10.8	99,533	79,346	− 20.3	301,127	278,108	− 7.6
Vagrancy	88,140	43,633	− 50.5	9,598	4,809	− 49.9	78,542	38,824	− 50.6
All other offenses (except traffic)	479,526	631,247	+ 31.6	156,347	175,966	+ 12.5	323,179	455,281	+ 40.9
Suspicion (not included in totals)	81,415	31,436	− 61.4	18,927	9,034	− 52.3	62,488	22,402	− 64.1
Curfew and loitering law violations	77,207	96,372	+ 24.8	77,207	96,372	+ 24.8			
Runaways	105,302	121,600	+ 15.5	105,302	121,600	+ 15.5			

[1] Violent crime is offenses of murder, forcible rape, robbery and aggravated assault.

[2] Property crime is offenses of burglary, larceny and auto theft.

* *Uniform Crime Reports, 1973*, p. 125.

understood, and controlled if more specific and homogeneous subgroups could be identified. Attempts to grapple with the problem have failed to yield uniform results because of the differences in research purposes, procedures, and kinds of data gathered. For example, the classification of delinquent behavior in terms of statutory violations necessarily must result in typologies that are different from those designed to classify delinquency on the basis of the social factors, or those that search for its hereditary and physical characteristics (Reed and Baali, 1972). While it is not possible to consider all of the typologies formulated, we shall summarize the major psychological approaches to the typing of delinquency that have been regarded as both important and useful by workers in the field.

For more than thirty years, Jenkins and his collaborators have studied the clinical case records of large samples of delinquents who were either seen as outpatients of child-guidance clinics or as residents of a training school (Jenkins and Hewitt, 1944; Jenkins and Boyer, 1968; Jenkins, 1973). Influenced by a Freudian view of personality development, Jenkins hypothesized three types of delinquency that he considered to be the products of different early family-child relationships. He clinically judged data from the case records and later intercorrelated them for clusters of associated personality traits and family backgrounds. This procedure led to the identification of the following three major clusters for both boys and girls.

Type I. *The Socialized Delinquent* (or known as the cooperative delinquent, pseudosocial delinquent, or the gang delinquent) refers to children of normal personality structure and function who are not different in this regard from matched nondelinquent youngsters. Their inclination toward antisocial behavior is part of their socialization within a delinquent group to which they are extremely loyal, while they hold no sense of obligation toward members of any other group. These youngsters are the product of inadequate parental supervision, discipline, and control, and of families in which there is little cohesion, involvement, or loyalty.

Type II. *The Unsocialized Delinquent* (or known as the psychopathic personality, or the unsocialized-aggressive type) refers to those who have inadequate internal controls over their impulses and who are likely to display open hostility toward others. They are selfish, boastful, defiant, self-indulgent, and inclined to act out without feelings of guilt or remorse. Their hostilities and bitterness are attributable to early and continued parental rejection (especially by mother), and to an atmosphere of disharmony and instability in the home in which parents are unaffectionate, hot-tempered, and abusive. In a few cases, there is evidence of brain damage or neurological impairment.

Type III. *The Overinhibited Delinquent* (also referred to as the neurotic delinquent) are children characterized by internal conflict and anxiety stemming from an overly developed tendency to inhibit the expression of feelings and impulses. Their antisocial behaviors are considered to be manifestations of severe internal conflicts, although it is not at all clear why delinquent behavior appears in some and neurosis is evident in others. These youngsters come from cold, rigid, socially disciplined, and excessively repressed home environments in which they can gain approval only by being very good and inhibited. Neurotic symptoms such as sleep disturbances, fears, shyness and seclusiveness are likely to be evident in early childhood, while later on these youngsters are apt to have night terrors, anxiety attacks, or, in some instances, conversion symptoms.

Quay, both in collaboration with Peterson and Tiffany and independently, employed a different methodology (factor analysis) to identify distinguishing personality characteristics among delinquents (Peterson, Quay, and Tiffany, 1961; Quay, 1964, 1966). The results of this work revealed three broad personality types of delinquent behavior that are quite similar to those reported by Jenkins, although the labels attached to the types are different.

However, there is general agreement among these researchers as to the personality descriptions that are associated with each type of delinquent behavior. Table 12–3 summarizes the major personality traits and family characteristics for each of the three types of delinquency.

Factors Related to Delinquent Behaviors

Attempts to investigate the relationship between delinquent behavior and a host of sociological, psychological, biological, and legal variables have been voluminous. Yet,

TABLE 12–3 * Personality and Family Characteristics of Delinquency Types

Gang Delinquent	Psychopathic	Neurotic
Stable lower-class homes in communities that sanction delinquent conduct.	Lack of guilt or remorse for acts.	Behavior is prompted by prolonged internal conflicts and anxieties.
Basically of normal personality other than anti-social acts.	Defective moral development. Impulsivity and acting out without internal controls. Often in trouble in school, and with police.	Parents are often middle class, but cold, rigid, disciplined, and repressive.
Select undesirable models with whom to identify.		Homes are hostile and unloving, and sometimes delinquency is unconsciously encouraged by parents.
Steadfast loyalty to their group with no sense of loyalty to others.	Rebellious and defiant of authority.	
Most crimes committed in groups.	Make favorable impression as outgoing, gregarious, and manipulative.	Delinquent acts are ordinarily committed alone.
Values are high for duping others, physical prowess, defiance, excitement and thrills, and taking chances.	Self-centered, selfish, and self-serving.	
Their patterns reflect those of the lowerclass culture in which they were reared.	Unable to postpone or delay pleasure or gratification.	
	Disharmony and instability in the home. Parents are unaffectionate, and apt to be hot-tempered and abusive. Parental rejection is frequent and long standing.	

* Table based on findings in Jenkins, 1973. Courtesy of Charles C Thomas, Publisher, Springfield, Illinois.

the literature is not without its share of methodological limitations that have produced contradictory results and erroneous or overstated conclusions. In considering the summary of the major findings, we should bear in mind that these data reflect associational and not causal evidence.

1. Socioeconomic Level. While delinquency appears to be highly related to a background of socioeconomic deprivation, there are noteworthy qualifications that tend to reduce both the potency and clarity of this factor (*The Challenge of Crime in a Free Society*, 1967). To begin with, the relationship may be restricted to populations of delinquent youngsters drawn from large cities, inasmuch as studies conducted in small cities and communities failed to support the notion that delinquency is largely a lower socioeconomic phenomenon (Clark and Wenninger, 1962; Erickson and Empey, 1965). In addition, the urban relationship may simply reflect differing law enforcement practices and the availability of nonjudicial community agencies in dealing with lower-middle and lower-class offenders. Middle and upper-class youngsters are more likely to be the beneficiaries of more liberal enforcement policies, and they have greater access to alternative forms of intervention than inner-city impoverished children. Several studies have, in fact, shown that there is no difference in socioeconomic levels when unrecorded instances of delinquent behavior are obtained through an anonymous questionnaire procedure (Empey and Erickson, 1966; Haney and Gold, 1973).

2. Family and Home Environment. Substantially more delinquent than nondelinquent children come from broken homes in which one parent is absent through death, separation, divorce, or desertion (Anderson, 1968; Glueck and Glueck, 1968; Cortes and Gatti, 1972). It is interesting to note that many of the delinquent youngsters were between the ages of four to seven when the break occurred, suggesting that family instability may be more damaging to personality development in early childhood than in the later years. Obviously not every broken home is the same or necessarily one in which disorganization, tension, discord, or unhappiness exists. However, the fact remains that children reared in homes that are stable, cohesive, warm, loving, and happy are not likely to become involved in delinquent behavior (*The Challenge of Crime in a Free Society,* 1967).

Several forms of parental discipline have been found to be related to delinquency (McCord, McCord, and Zola, 1959; Glueck and Glueck, 1968; Trojanowicz, 1973). Permissiveness provides the child with an early opportunity to establish independent patterns of action without parental interference or restrictions. When the child's freedom is challenged or threatened by the demands of authority figures outside of the home, the child, being accustomed to behaving in terms of his or her own rules, tends to react with resentment, hostility, and open defiance. Extreme strictness in which physical punishment is used more than verbal discussion may produce negative attitudes toward parents, which, in turn, will reduce the child's desire to conform to parental wishes and to behave in ways that will please parents. However, parental control that lacks consistency appears to be the most damaging factor in that it is the most frequent parental pattern found in delinquent children. When parents vacillate, the child may lose respect for parental authority and control, lack consistent guidelines for behaving in a socially acceptable manner, and assume that he or she can avoid the consequences of his or her acts because it is unlikely that parents will respond in any consistent way (Aichhorn, 1969).

But more important than discipline as a correlate of delinquency is the affective quality of the parent-child relationship. As succinctly stated by Gibbons, "scientific candor compels us to conclude that the link between parental rejection and aggressive conduct is one of the more firmly established generalizations concerning delinquency" (Gibbons, 1970, p. 202). The failure of the delinquent boy to gain the favor and affection of his father appears to be a particularly significant background factor. Fathers of delinquent boys are rejecting and prone to be physically punitive to the extent that they arouse in their sons feelings of bitterness and hostility and aggressive antisocial behaviors as a means of retaliation. Jenkins (1957) noted that parental rejection adversely affected the child's development of an adequate conscience structure, which, when combined with feelings of hostility, opens the way for the unsocialized expression of aggression. Moreover, rejecting and abusive fathers are difficult to model or identify with, not only because of their poor relationships with their sons but also because they are often unemployed, alcoholic, or otherwise ineffective "heads" of their families. Glueck and Glueck (1968) observed that fewer than two out of ten of their delinquents regarded their fathers as the sort of men that they would like to emulate, as contrasted to more than half of the nondelinquents who viewed their fathers as positive models.

A relationship between delinquency and emotional instability of parents has also been reported (Glueck and Glueck, 1968; Aichhorn, 1969; Freeman and Savastona,

1970). Parental personality problems are likely to interfere with family relationships and with child-rearing practices in diverse ways. Especially in times of stress, the probability is high that psychotic, neurotic, alcoholic, retarded, or other seriously disturbed parents will be inconsistent, neglectful, and rejecting in both attitude and behavior toward their children. They may unconsciously encourage acting-out behaviors, or they may fail to provide the necessary sanctions and prohibitions that help to distinguish acceptable from unacceptable actions, or that serve as models for antisocial responses. Emotional instability in one or both parents is not only a frequent background finding of delinquent youngsters, but also a characteristic that can be traced to the previous generation of parents (Aichhorn, 1969).

3. School Performance. Delinquent youngsters are generally recognized as poor academic performers in school, although as a group they do not differ from nondelinquents in intelligence or achievement test scores (Hathaway and Monachesi, 1963; Elliott, 1966; Elliott, Voss, and Wendling, 1966). There is a consistently reported relationship between school dropout rate and delinquency; the delinquency rate for dropouts is estimated as ten times higher than the rate obtained for the total youth population (Schreiber, 1963; Jeffrey and Jeffrey, 1970). Lack of interest, carelessness, restlessness, tardiness, truancy, misconduct in school, and avoidance of anticipated failure are some of the reasons offered to explain delinquents' academic retardation. It is interesting to note that in a large-scale study of urban school children, early adolescents (between twelve and thirteen years old) exhibited more self-consciousness, increased instability of their self-image, lower self-esteem, and less favorable reactions by others than did younger children (Simmons, Rosenberg, and Rosenberg, 1973). In addition, these findings were more pronounced for those early adolescents who entered junior high school as compared to those who continued on in K–8 schools. It appears that the move from elementary school to junior high is a significant stressor for these youngsters in that the new school environment is more impersonal, less structured, and one in which teachers and students are more mobile and independent.

4. Biological Factors. As early as 1949, Sheldon, Hartl, and McDermott (1949) found a significant relationship between the mesomorphic (muscular) bodytype and delinquency. While Sheldon's findings were soundly criticized on methodological grounds, the Gluecks (1956) and others (Gibbens, 1963; Cortes and Gatti, 1972) have consistently obtained the same results, in spite of the fact that these studies used different criteria and methods to measure body type. Moreover, mesomorphs describe themselves as aggressive, active, adventurous, and impulsive, which are temperamental traits that have been found to be associated with delinquency (Cortes and Gatti, 1972).

Recent studies have shown that the presence of an extra Y chromosome is related to the increased probability of some psychological disorder in males, although little agreement exists as to the specific type of personality aberration (Hook, 1973). In spite of the fact that criminal behavior was found in many of these males, more research is needed to clarify the relationship. The current evidence is not sufficient to support the view that chromosomal abnormality plays a significant role in delinquent behavior. Abnormal brain waves (EEG), es-pecially positive spike patterns that occur at fourteen and six waves per second, have been observed in youngsters who manifest aggressive antisocial behaviors. However, inasmuch as this pattern occurs in approximately fifty percent of normal adolescents, its meaning and significance are greatly obscured (Solomon, 1967).

Etiological Considerations

From what has been said thus far, it should be apparent that there is no simple and single causal explanation of delinquency. Behaviors that are so inclusive, diverse, and intricately related to so many other variables must, in all likelihood, have multiple origins. At present, there are three prominent approaches to the etiology of delinquent behavior that reflect a sociological, a psychological, or multidiscipline view. As we summarize the major positions within each approach, it is important to note that these explanations should be considered not as oppositional but rather as alternative and supplementary ways of looking at the same problem.

Sociological Views

While only several of these formulations can be reviewed here, they all emphasize (although different in details) the contributions of the external environment as the primary cause of delinquency. This approach deals more effectively with the questions of how and why crime occurs in a society, but offers little explanation about how a particular individual becomes delinquent.

Thrasher (1936) suggested that delinquent gangs arise from play groups during adolescence as a result of conflict with other groups and as an organized means of banding individuals together to protect their rights and to satisfy needs that are not being met by their environments. Gangs fester in permissive and poorly controlled settings and in environments where adult crime is sanctioned. Thrasher also noted that members of the gang were involved in nondelinquent and normal teenage activities much of the time.

Other theorists have focused on lower-class youngsters and their difficulties in successfully achieving highly valued middle-class goals as the basis of gang delinquency. Cohen (1955), for example, believed that lower working-class boys are poorly prepared to cope with such demands of middle-class institutions as delay of gratification and pressures for achievement and success. Failure brings frustration, loss of status, and deep resentment over rejection by middle-class society. Affiliation with a gang subculture provides an important sense of belonging as well as performance and status criteria that these youngsters can meet. "The hallmark of the delinquent subculture is the explicit and wholesale repudiation of middle-class standards and the adoption of their very antithesis" (Cohen, 1955, p. 130). Delinquent activity within the confines and sanctions of the gang makes aggression against middle-class institutions legitimate while it bolsters and enhances self-esteem by group membership.

Taking a somewhat different tack, Ohlin and Cloward (1960) emphasized the very limited opportunity provided in the social order for lower-class youngsters to satisfy their needs. Under these conditions the stress of failure results in alienation and the use of illegitimate alternatives as possible routes to the successful fulfillment of goals. Ohlin and Cloward identified three differ-ent types of delinquent subcultures with which lower-class urban males affiliate in an attempt to adapt to the pressure created by the limited accessibility of middle-class channels to satisfy their aspirations. One is called the *criminal subculture,* in which there is a strong tie to adult criminal circles and where the youngsters learn patterns of criminal behavior through a sort of apprenticeship program. A second group is referred to as the *conflict subculture,* in which there is no direct connection with adult criminals but where the gang aggresses against others and uses physical violence to acquire status for itself and for its members. The third group is the *retreatist subculture,* in which members have reservations about committing criminal acts against persons or property, and instead engage in the use of drugs, sexual promiscuity, or other self-indulgent pleasurable experiences.

While most theorists have attended to delinquency in lower-class boys, Vaz (1967) is among the few who have made a major effort to deal with middle-class delinquency. He suggested that middle-class delinquency represents a gradual outgrowth of normal group activities in which deviant explorations for fun and excitement such as shoplifting or vandalism become, in time, the expected standard for the group. In a similar view, England (1972) proposed that hedonistic pursuits are fast becoming the articulated role of middle-class adolecents, because in the prolongation of this age period there are few opportunities to perform productive functions. Play and the seeking of fun and excitement are gratifying especially if they are supported and condoned by the group norms. Hedonistic behavior is readily maintained by the strong motivation of teenagers to share with and gain approval from their peers, even though the standards of behavior are discrepant with adult norms.

In the main, sociological views of delinquency are difficult to test empirically because they are so broad and general, and because they make assumptions about the responses of youngsters to the stress of the environment's social structure. In addition, these formulations fail to account for the large number of youngsters who do not become delinquent. Nevertheless, the sociological approach has been useful in identifying the social conditions "under which the psychological factors conducive to the development of antisocial behavior may more readily operate" (Bandura and Walters, 1959, p. 4).

Psychological Views

The psychological approach to delinquent or antisocial behavior can be characterized by attempts to account for its occurrence either through the psychodynamic development of basic personality structure in early childhood or through the acquisition of related behavioral traits by different learning paradigms.

Influenced by Freudian theory, a number of writers has assumed that delinquent youngsters are emotionally troubled (an erroneous assumption since there is a large number of delinquents who manifest no psychological disorder), and that the roots of their psychological disturbance can be found in unresolved and unconscious conflicts arising in early family relationships and in the management of sexual and aggressive impulses. Much of this work appeared in the literature during the 1940s and 1950s, and much was couched in Freudian language and concepts, particularly those studies dealing with the three components of personality—the *id, ego,* and

superego. Personality problems of delinquents are most likely to be in ego and superego functions inasmuch as delinquent behavior often involves the uncontrolled and outwardly directed expression of aggression without guilt, remorse, or pangs of conscience.

On the basis of their study of severely disturbed, unsocialized, aggressive delinquents, Redl and Wineman (1951) attempted to delineate some twenty-two functions of the ego in which their subjects were either deficient or impaired. Among the functions included as specific instances of faulty ego functions for these delinquent youngsters were low tolerance for frustration; inability to cope with inner feelings of anxiety and fear; poor control and disorganization when guilt is aroused; low responsivity to normal challenges of life such as games, school, and athletics; high responsivity to inner impulses; and inability to perceive external reality as manifested by blaming others and not themselves for their actions; expecting not to be caught; or engaging in infantile fantasies of aggrandizement.

The best known explanation of faulty superego function was formulated by Adelaide Johnson (1949) who referred to the deficiency as *superego lacunae* to connote an absence of the superego, rather than its weakness or ineffectiveness. Specific lacunae in certain areas of behavior in the child are similarly found in the parent's superego. Although unconscious and subtle, parental lacunae serve to sanction the child's behavior, since the parents experience vicarious pleasure when the behavior occurs. For example, excessive warnings and admonitions not to misbehave are interpreted as a parental invitation for misconduct. In this instance, either the wish or the fear that the child will get into trouble is likely to be realized. Superego lacunae are also apparent in the father who is told by his teenage son that the son has impregnated the girl next door. While the father expresses strong disapproval and concern, he also flashes a quick and faint smile as a reflection of pride and admiration for his son's sexual prowess. This illustration can be further extended to the girl's parents who may have encouraged her to act out sexually by displaying anxiety and excessive attention to what they suspect is going on when she is out with a boy. Under these conditions, both sets of parents derive vicarious pleasure from their children's sexual activities which were either unconsciously condoned or even encouraged by them. The acting-out behavior serves the dual purpose of gratifying forbidden parental wishes and of expressing hostility to the child for doing what he or she should not have done.

While these psychoanalytically inspired formulations have been interesting to and popular with clinicians, they remain difficult to test and verify. Another approach that has a more empirical basis has involved the systematic study of aggression and imitation, behaviors that are directly related to antisocial and delinquent conduct.

Contemporary research focusing on the determinants of aggressive behavior began with the formulation by Dollard and associates, who postulated that aggression is always elicited by frustration (Dollard, Doob, Miller, Mowrer, and Sears, 1939). They defined "aggression" as behavior that is intended to injure the person toward whom it is directed, and frustration as the blocking or thwarting of ongoing goal-directed activity. In addition, their frustration-aggression hypothesis consisted of a number of specific propositions beyond the major formulation that aggression is always

a response to frustration. These theorists suggested that social factors, such as low socioeconomic and educational level and marital instability, that are known to be related to antisocial behavior could be explained within the framework of the frustration-aggression hypothesis. More specifically, they regard the poor social conditions as sources of frustration provoking aggressive behavior that is likely to occur inasmuch as the fear of punishment (prison) is relatively weak.

However, subsequent research has uncovered some flaws in this theoretical formulation. Block and Martin (1955) demonstrated that frustration does not always lead to aggression, and it is now apparent that the instigator of aggression need not always be frustration. Moreover, the proposition that an act of aggression reduces the strength of other aggressive impulses has not been supported by the research data. Mallick and McCandless (1966) showed that children given the opportunity to engage in aggressive play after they were experimentally frustrated were no less aggressive than controls who were not permitted to play aggressively. Similar results were obtained by Kahn (1966), who found that college students, when compared to controls, expressed more aggression toward their frustrators if aggression was permitted following frustration. Thus, it seems clear that aggressive acts do not reduce the strength of subsequent aggressive behavior.

Buss (1966) took a different view of aggression in that he regarded it as an operant response that is maintained if it is instrumental in fulfilling the person's wants or if it removes a noxious stimulus. In a nicely designed study, he demonstrated that aggression increased when it had instrumental value but did not increase as a result of frustration. With respect to delinquent and antisocial aggressive behaviors, this view of aggression seems fruitful. It suggests that the aggressive behaviors of delinquents are maintained by reinforcements that are readily available in their environment. In fact, Patterson and Cobb (1971) observed and identified a number of such reinforcements for aggression in their studies involving institutionalized delinquents and families of aggressive children. These children obtain peer approval and recognition for delinquent acts, and their aggression often is reinforced as a response that is instrumental in limiting or terminating aggression from others (peers, family members, and authority figures).

Although first proposed more than thirty years ago (Miller and Dollard, 1941), the more recent work of Bandura (Bandura and Walters, 1959; Bandura, Ross, and Ross, 1963; Bandura, 1969a, b) emphasizes *imitation* as an instrumental response in the acquisition of aggressive and other behaviors. Preferring the term *modeling* to *imitation*, he showed that young children in an experimentally controlled situation model the aggressive behavior of both live and filmed adults (models) who act aggressively. Furthermore, parents of aggressive boys encouraged more aggression and more often served as aggressive models for their youngsters than parents of nonaggressive children.

Modeling of aggressive behavior by young children who are exposed to a heavy fare of television programs showing violence and crime has been a source of public concern and controversy. There is some evidence that measured aggression in nineteen-year-old males was positively correlated with their earlier viewing of TV shows containing violence when they were in the third grade (Eron, Husemann, Lefkowitz, and Walder, 1972). In addition, it

has been shown that experimental exposure to TV violence increases aggressive behavior in children (Murray, 1973). However, it is difficult to conclude from these data that television viewing of violence is a direct and major source of later aggression and crime.

Multifactor Views

Although this approach has been criticized as "a grab bag of superficial generalizations" (Trojanowicz, 1973, p. 54), it nevertheless attends to the many and diverse variables that seem to be implicated in this complicated problem of delinquency. The best known example of this approach stems from the long and extensive work of Sheldon and Eleanor Glueck (Glueck, 1950; Glueck and Glueck, 1968), who studied 500 delinquent and nondelinquent boys over a period of years in terms of a number of sociological, psychological, and constitutional (physique) variables. Based on their initial sample of boys who ranged in age from nine to seventeen years, they found an excess of mesomorphic (muscular) body builds in delinquents with corresponding personality traits of aggressiveness, adventurousness, and acquisitiveness. They also characterized delinquent youngsters by scholastic retardation (although no difference in intelligence was found between the two groups of boys), dislike for school, pugnaciousness toward schoolmates, truancy, and misconduct that occurred at an earlier age than in those few nondelinquents who also misbehaved. Delinquents tended to keep late hours, smoked and drank earlier, and ran away from home more frequently than nondelinquents. Delinquent youngsters gravitated toward gangs and were inclined to make friends with other delinquents. They lived in overcrowded homes and came from families who had a higher incidence of intellectual and emotional abnormalities, including alcoholism and criminality, and that were more often physically and/or psychologically broken. Delinquent boys, as compared to the controls, had fewer positive and warm relationships with their fathers and were inclined to reject fathers as desirable models to emulate.

In what they refer to as a "biopsychosocial" approach, Cortes and Gatti (1972) studied 100 delinquent and 100 nondelinquent boys who ranged in age from 16.5 to 18.5 years. Their findings were similar to those obtained by the Gluecks with respect to physique and personality traits. In addition, they found that delinquents had a high need for achievement, which was interpreted as a potential for successful entrepreneurship if their energies were more constructively channeled. Delinquents also were less religious and less supervised, but more rejected by parents. As found in the Gluecks' sample, more delinquents came from broken homes and had disrupted father-son relationships than the controls.

Therapeutic Considerations

The values, attitudes, and practices of our society toward antisocial acts are predicated on the Judaic-Christian ethic that dictates "an eye for an eye" or punishment to fit the crime. Our society's position with respect to the misbehavior of minors is somewhat more lenient, flexible, and influenced by a desire to remediate and rehabilitate. For example, if a young offender is called to the attention of the juvenile court, the judge, after studying the circumstances and information provided by the police, case workers, psychologists, and other professionals, may exercise one of several options. The judge may sentence the child to a training or detention facility for a designated period of time, or may place the child on probation where he or she will be supervised or guided by a case worker or probation officer, or may refer the child to his or her family or to some community agency for remedial measures. The fact is that many more delinquents are dealt with by the courts along the lines of the last two options than the more stringent one of incarceration.

Even when institutionalization occurs, most facilities are open in the sense that they are not designed to prevent escape (an event that happens frequently). Minimally funded and poorly conceived and implemented programs of educational and vocational training are often provided and sometimes psychological help is offered in the form of counseling, group therapy (especially oriented around the misuse of alcohol and drugs), and individual psychotherapy. In the main, young inmates removed from undesirable environments are placed in a setting that is possibly more corrupt and conducive to further criminal behavior than the conditions under which they previously lived. Most juvenile judges are reluctant to use incarceration as a remedial approach, because they are aware of the evidence that no more than twenty or thirty percent of delinquent boys improve after institutionalization to the extent that they have no subsequent arrest record (Gibbons, 1970; Cohen and Filipczak, 1971). Nevertheless, one study showed significant improvement in institutionalized delinquents in reading level, I.Q., and in social behaviors, such as trust, relations to others, especially authority figures, and control of aggression (Kahn and McFarland, 1973).

Unfortunately, it appears that a community-based remedial program involving individual and group psychotherapy, vocational counseling, and supervision by probation officer was no more effective in reducing recidivism than incarceration (Gibbons, 1970). Yet the results are not all negative. Nir and Cutler (1973) suggest that community-based psychotherapy can work and be effective in treating delinquent youngsters if the court authorizes treatment as a condition of probation for as long as it is necessary. Most delinquent youngsters are resistant and reluctant to enter into psychotherapy, and it is generally agreed that most will terminate treatment as early as possible unless some authority or dire consequence requires them to continue. In addition, the therapist is likely to find that parents resist treatment for their youngsters and subtly attempt to encourage their youngsters to terminate treatment. Unless there is a lever and control for the delinquent's continuance in psychotherapy, this treatment form is difficult to implement and often doomed to failure (Kaplan, Ryan, Nathan, and Bairos, 1969).

Special community-based residential facilities that have used a variety of so-called therapeutic milieu programs have been reported in the literature. Most of these programs emphasize group interaction to improve socialization, but they differ in the manner in which they are operated, ranging from staff control to inmate self-government. Counseling, individual and group psychotherapy, recreation, vocational training, and supervised work experiences are frequently offered. While programs of this sort usually arouse a good deal of public and professional interest, few can claim unequivocal success, and even fewer can muster sufficient evidence to justify their higher cost as compared to existing training schools.

A recent study demonstrated the effectiveness of training in role-taking skills with chronically delinquent boys (Chandler, 1973). Training consisted of writing, acting, and videotaping brief, life-like skits about people their own age. These three-hour session enabled the subjects to see themselves as others do and to learn to overcome their deficient role-taking skills. As compared to controls, delinquents who received the experimental training improved significantly in assuming roles that facilitated their social competence and cooperation. Moreover, follow-up data after eighteen months indicated that these improvements were associated with decreases in delinquent behavior. Another program involving a twenty-seven-day course in survival training claimed to be effective in reducing recidivism for as long as one year after parole of delinquent males (Kelly, 1971). The rationale for the program stemmed from the observation that delinquent boys prefer motoric over verbal expression. In addition, the idea of giving boys a severe physical test in which they could achieve beyond their expectations would increase the likelihood of their tackling heretofore unachieved goals (like going "straight").

One of the most promising treatment approaches is behavior modification, in which positive reinforcement, punishment (especially withholding rewards), and token systems are employed to alter antisocial behavior and to improve educational levels of delinquent youngsters. Schwitzgebel (1964) paid delinquent youngsters to talk to him about delinquency on the assumption that they would talk about their own delinquent acts and thus gain insight into themselves. In the process, he found that either they were tardy for appointments, or they did not arrive at all. He then used the payment to effect behavioral changes that could be carried over to daily living, such as being on time and performing well in a talk session.

The National Training School Project, which was implemented for one year as a pilot and demonstration program to alter delinquent behavior, is illustrative of the application of a token economy system. Points (each equal to one cent) that the student could use to purchase comfort and luxury items, such as snacks and clothing, were used to reinforce successful academic performance. Students were not required to study or work for points, although at the end of the year most of them had increased their achievement scores by several grades.

Parsons and Alexander (1973) significantly altered the destructive communication patterns of delinquent families in a short-term family therapy study. They formulated a token economy system on the basis of how each family member wanted to be rewarded by the others. They employed social reinforcement and modeling in the training of each family member in solution-oriented communication patterns, and they used a behavior modification primer to familiarize family members with the concepts and language of the treatment program. Families were trained over a three-week period of time and then they began the four-week therapy program. At the end of therapy, family interaction patterns were significantly modified in the direction of communicative patterns characteristic of normal families.

In spite of the promising findings, it is too early to render a final verdict regarding the effectiveness of behavior modification with delinquent children. To date, most studies have failed to include either no-treatment controls or reversal designs, leaving open the possibility of spontaneous improvement, especially since adolescents are at a point in their lives where

maturation often produces change. More research, especially studies to determine the long-term effects of this treatment approach, is needed (Davidson and Seidman, 1974).

The Runaway

At some time or another, almost every child entertains the idea of running away from home as an expression of dissatisfaction with parental controls or practices, or as a way of dealing with some of the tensions and pressures of growing up. Some may stay out late and then return home, some may leave for a few days, and others may disappear for long periods of time. In 1971, more than 200,000 youngsters between the ages of ten and seventeen were arrested as runaways, a figure that represents an increase of more than forty percent over the incidence reported in 1968 (*Uniform Crime Reports: 1968–1971*, 1972). Obviously this estimate reflects only a small portion of runaways (probably one-third to one-half of all runaways) in this country, although a more accurate accounting is not available or possible (Ambrosino, 1971). During the decade of the 1960s, almost every urban center had its special crowded area in which runaways could join other youngsters who were experimenting with drugs, sexual relations, and various patterns of group and communal living. Contrary to popular belief, ample evidence indicates that the number of children who run away from home each year continues to rise (Libertoff, 1976). In fact, it has been estimated that in 1972 alone the total number of runaways was more than two million children.

Jenkins (1973) regards the chronic runaway as a subgroup of the unsocialized aggressive-type delinquent. The degree of family pathology for this subgroup is greater than for any other type. His analysis of the case records of delinquent boys showed that runaways were involved in stealing from the home, in passive homosexuality, and in delinquent acts other than running away. These boys were especially immature, apathetic, and seclusive. They were often truant from school, rebellious toward authority, and inclined to be only a peripheral member of a delinquent group.

Most observers agree that runaways are frightened, angry, and desperate youngsters for whom home is much more of a threat than a refuge. Runaways are displeased with their environment and their lot in life, and they deal with the unhappy situation by fleeing from it. Running away may serve as an attention-getting device, a cry for help, an attempt to coerce the family to make changes that accommodate the youngster's wishes, a means of avoiding an intolerable home or school situation, or an act of liberation for pleasure-seeking purposes. Whether these or other reasons prompt their behavior, runaways sooner or later find themselves without the basic necessities (food, shelter, and medical care) previously provided by their environments. They are often vulnerable to and the victims of the attacks, thefts, abuse, and exploitation of others on the streets who deal in illicit drugs, heterosexual and homosexual favors, and the gamut of criminal activities.

While most of the available literature is in accord with Jenkin's characterization of runaways as disturbed, delinquent, or both, there is growing evidence that indicates that runaways represent a more diverse population ranging from severe personality difficulties to minor ones (Homer, 1973; Howell, Emmons, and Frank, 1973; Libertoff, 1976). Libertoff found that the majority of runaway children in Massachusetts came from unstable homes where parental discord, separation, divorce, and death of one parent were frequent. In addition to family disruption, many of these children had been subjected to physical restraint, beatings, sexual abuse, and highly combative home situations. They had long histories of psychological deprivation and physical abuse with little evidence of either parental or environmental support that would foster normal personality development. In contrast, Howell and his associates found that their sample of runaways came from stable two-parent homes, and that before running away the vast majority of these youngsters were troubled by ordinary problems of growing up rather than by any major or serious difficulties. In retrospect, two thirds of their sample considered running away as a positive and growing experience, although this view may have been largely colored by an attempt to rationalize their behavior and to resolve cognitive dissonance. Homer found that less than half of the runaway girls in her sample were responding to conflicts in the home, while the majority ran away to seek "a subculture which affords them specific pleasures and freedom from controls" (Homer, 1973, p. 479). She divided her runaway girls into two categories: *the running-from group*, who had both intrapsychic and family conflicts that exceeded their tolerance level; and *the running-to group*, who were pleasure seekers engaged in a variety of forbidden experiences, such as sex, drugs, drinking, truancy, and more serious crimes.

Both groups of runaways were given three types of therapeutic intervention: once a week individual psychotherapy, twice a week group therapy, and family therapy every other week. In addition, consultations with the schools and other community agencies were provided by professionals when needed. The results indicated that girls in the running-from group were effectively treated (six out of seven) with insight-oriented therapy and family therapy, while these therapies were ineffective in producing behavior changes in the nine girls of the running-to group. According to Homer, pleasure seekers are less open to modification and behavior change than conflict-troubled runaways, because pleasure seekers are determined to do their own thing and because they find external controls and limits on their behavior quite intolerable. Perhaps the major implication of these findings is the demonstration that runaways comprise a divergent population that requires careful case-by-case evaluation in order to select and construct effective treatment strategies.

Drug Abuse

We would be remiss if we didn't follow up the discussion of delinquency with the consideration of drug abuse in adolescence, inasmuch as the toll of deaths, addiction, and crime related to drugs has reached alarming proportions. Just in the thirteen years between 1960 and 1973 (see Table 12–1) arrests for drug offenses increased by a staggering 4,673.3 percent for youngsters under eighteen as compared to an increase of 774.6 percent for persons over eighteen. It is estimated that about one-ninth of our total population or some twenty-four million Americans over eleven years of age have experimented with marijuana (*Marijuana: A Signal of Misunderstanding,* 1972). Among college students sampled in 1971, fifty-one percent admitted having tried marijuana at least once, eighteen percent experimented with amphetamines, fifteen percent tried barbituates, seven percent had experience with cocaine, and two percent

admitted to using heroin (*Current View of College Students on Politics and Drugs,* 1972). Except for the reported use of heroin (which was about the same), somewhat lower incidence figures were obtained from high-school youngsters in that twenty percent had experience with marijuana, ten percent with amphetamines, and about six percent with barbiturates (Johnston, 1973). Self-report data obtained from about 5,000 high-school seniors from a county near San Francisco indicated that between 1968 and 1974, marijuana use rose (smoked at least one time each year) from thirty-eight percent to sixty percent and from twenty-two percent to forty-three percent (smoked ten times or more each year) (Blackford, 1974). The results also showed that the use of hallucinogens (LSD) has not declined but has remained stable at about seventeen percent over this six-year period.

Males typically have had a higher incidence of drug abuse than females by a ratio of about 2:1, although the ratio declined during the early 1970s as greater numbers of girls became involved with drugs. Adolescent drug users are inclined to use more than one drug, with the most likely combination being amphetamines, barbiturates, and hallucinogens (Johnston, 1973). In a sample of 100 adolescent marijuana users, Halikas and Rimmer (1974) found that all used one other drug and fifty-two percent used more than two other drugs. In addition, the factors of use of illicit drugs at an early age, poor high-school socialization, poor adolescent adjustment, antisocial behavior, homosexual experiences, and numerous parental conflicts were found to predict multiple drug abuse. It is also true that experiences with marijuana were found in more than ninety-six percent of heroin and cocaine users, and in eighty-five percent of the users of stimulants and depressants

(Gergen, Gergen, and Morse, 1972). However, these data cannot be interpreted to support the popular belief that marijuana leads to the use of more serious drugs, because correlational evidence cannot be taken to reflect a causal relationship. As a matter of fact, Johnston's data indicate that more than fifty percent of marijuana users failed to become involved with any of the more serious drugs after one year had elapsed.

It is entirely possible that estimates of the scope of the problem reflect only the tip of an iceberg that is very difficult to accurately and completely measure. Arrest data do not include the incidence with which prescription and over-the-counter drugs are used, such as alcohol, glue, lighter fluid, aerosols, caffein, and diet pills. In addition, they do not reflect the differences in law enforcement practices or availability of alternative community services, or the many instances of illegal drug abuse that are undetected and unreported. Self-report questionnaire data are influenced greatly by the willingness of the respondent to admit to illegal drug abuse, and by the nature and extent of the questions that deal with legal and over-the-counter substances. The patterns of drug use change over time, making it almost impossible for researchers to keep pace with current trends. Nevertheless, most observers would agree that drug abuse is a sizeable and serious problem occurring at all levels of the social scale, in all environments, and at all ages (some neonates are born addicted).

Types of Mood Altering Drugs

Drug abuse refers to an excessive use of one or more chemical substances that are illegal and/or considered harmful to the person's health, social and personal adjustment, or to society. These agents are taken ordinarily to achieve an unusual mood or state, or to obliterate unpleasurable and uncomfortable feelings. The list of substances that may be categorized as *mood* or *mind altering drugs* is quite extensive and diverse.

Heroin is the most frequently used narcotic or "hard" drug, claiming approximately 250,000 active addicts who live primarily in the economically impoverished areas of our country's urban centers. Users are predominantly male (about eighty-five percent) and about two-thirds of them are either black, Puerto Rican, or Mexican-American (Wald and Hutt, 1972). Because they are members of minority groups and come from broken and/or disrupted homes and poverty conditions, they are apt to have low self-esteem, low frustration and anxiety tolerance, and inadequate defenses to cope with the stress and strain of daily living. Baer and Corrado (1974) confirmed the importance of parent-child relationships as predisposing factors in heroin addiction. They found that addicts were more likely to have experienced an unhappy childhood, harsh physical punishment, and little parental concern for their schoolwork, sexual conduct, careers, or choice of friends. Heroin users have low self-esteem, are only capable of forming tentative and weak relationships, and tend to cope with anxiety by repression and withdrawal (Milkman and Frosch, 1973). They are not likely to be gang delinquents or to be overtly and physically aggressive. They lack security and a sense of belonging somewhere or to someone, and they use heroin as a solitary habit to escape the unpleasantness of the real world (Chapel and Taylor, 1972). Narcotic users are physically dependent on the drug and have habits that range in cost from as little as $10 to as much as $150 daily. Of course, this means that much of their waking energy is tied up in raising the necessary funds and in making a connection with a "pusher" to obtain a "fix." Most addicts are unable to accomplish this through legal channels and are forced to resort to criminal activities to satisfy their physical and psychological dependence. If stolen goods are involved, the items must be of considerable value inasmuch as their return through the black market will be less than their worth. Therefore, heroin users, out of their desperate need to feed their habit, are involved in such illegal acts as assault, mugging, robbery, burglary, prostitution, selling drugs, and even murder. There is a high incidence of hepatitis, tetanus, endocarditis (from bacterial infection of the heart), and suicide among heroin users (Eldefonso, 1972). Moreover, death from heroin usage occurs in twenty-five percent of these addicts. Cure in terms of long-term abstinence is expected to occur in only about one percent of the heroin users (Walker, 1973).

Heroin is the preferred drug for most narcotics addicts primarily because of its capacity to produce euphoric feelings quickly and to maintain the "high" over a prolonged period of time. Users rapidly develop a tolerance for heroin that requires them to continually increase the dosage to obtain the desired effect. Overdoses (ODs) resulting in fatalities can and do occur, because the quality of the drug is often so poorly controlled by the illegal seller. Although it is difficult to separate the physical from the psychological effects of heroin, withdrawal from the drug typically produces severe reactions that include cramps, muscle twitching, profuse sweating, nausea, anxiety, agitation, and sleep disruption (Bates and Crowther, 1973).

Data indicate that heroin use has sharply declined since the almost epidemic peak reached in this country in 1970, suggesting that stricter law enforcement, more treatment facilities, and increased public awareness of its dangers may have played an important role in stemming the tide for the time being (DuPont and Greene, 1973).

Marijuana is a wild plant that produces an active ingredient known as resin that is found in the leaves at the top of the plant. It is the most preferred drug of high-school and college-aged youngsters, and compared to most other drugs, it is probably the cheapest. Marijuana is readily available, and unlike the narcotics, its users often become suppliers to those who are without. It is a drug that is usually taken in a group or social setting in order to "share" experiences and to instruct the novice. Participants experience rapport and closeness with each other, although verbal interactions are often minimal (Chapel and Taylor, 1972). As might be expected, suburban high-school marijuana users were more likely to overestimate the percentage of peers using the drug, to believe that friends would not react negatively to marijuana use, to view its use as a positive expression rather than as a response to group pressure or personal difficulties, and to ascribe a positive rather than harmful effect to the drug (Tec, 1972).

Adolescents use marijuana as a means of being accepted by peers, as an act of rebellion against society and/or parents, or as a way of coping with personality problems. Peer relationships are extremely important during adolescence in giving the youngster a sense of belonging, adequacy, and self-worth. It is difficult for many adolescents to resist peer pressure and deny themselves the great satisfaction that comes from peer acceptance. Rebellion may be part of the group theme that is tacitly accepted by all of its members, or it may be a manifestation of family and personal adjustment problems. There are those who would suggest that the use of marijuana to deal with personality difficulties identifies the persons who are most likely to graduate to more serious and addictive drugs (Stanton, 1966). The recent results of a survey of middle- and high-school children showed that heavier consumers of alcohol reported more illicit drug use, delinquent activities, and alienation from their parents, and more frequent personal problems with their peers and school performance (Wechsler and Thum, 1973). There is also evidence that supports the relationship between maternal ideology and child-rearing practices and the adolescent's involvement in problem behaviors. Jessor and Jessor (1974) found that the more traditional the mother's ideology (nonpermissive), the less likely it would be that the adolescent would use alcohol and marijuana, behave promiscuously, or hold radical political beliefs. Some support was also found in the relationship between high maternal nurturance and control and the low incidence of these behavior problems.

As far as we now know, marijuana is neither addicting nor physically harmful, although more study is needed especially with respect to long-term effects before we can reach a definitive conclusion. "The real issue over marijuana appears to be not whether it causes mild physical damage but whether its use has already spread so widely that, as is true of alcohol, the social costs of efforts to prohibit it exceed the physical costs that would be incurred by eliminating criminal penalities for, or even legalizing, its use" (Wald and Hutt, 1972, p. 7).

LSD or lysergic acid diethylamide was first synthesized in 1938, but it wasn't until five years later that a chemist by the name

of Albert Hofmann discovered its potent hallucinogenic properties. Hofmann tested the drug on himself and experienced vivid fantasies of a bizarre and grotesque nature, visual hallucinations and illusions, vertigo, and uncontrollable incoherent speech, among other effects. During the 1950s, LSD was used experimentally by researchers who variously regarded it as a substance that produced psychosis (psychotogenic), mimicked psychosis (psychotomimetic), or expanded the mind (psychedelic). Some researchers ingested the drug themselves in the hopes that the experience might help them to be more empathic to their psychotic patients, while others gave it to their patients as a treatment adjunct to decrease their patients' defensiveness. But, LSD reached its popularity as a psychedelic in the mid- and late 1960s at the time of the hippie movement when it was faddish for young people to seek new pleasure experiences and to rebel against the establishment under the guise of "doing one's own thing."

LSD is tasteless and odorless and either can be injected or ingested in pill, powder, or liquid form (commonly a small drop is placed on a sugar cube). Small doses are capable of producing autonomic changes, vivid visual hallucinations, illusions, sensory distortions, and feelings of estrangement, depersonalization, and alterations of mood. It is nonaddicting, but because a tolerance for the drug builds up rapidly, it cannot be taken more than several times a week without losing the potency of its effects. The reaction of users to the drug is quite varied, depending on the personality of the person, the setting in which LSD is taken, and prior experience with the drug. Especially in those with pre-existing psychopathological conditions, psychotic reactions that require hospitalization have been reported in which the user is overwhelmed by fear, uncontrolled violent impulses, and intense auditory hallucinations.

During the height of its popularity when almost two million Americans had taken an LSD "trip," there were numerous frightening reports that suggested persistent and even irreversible adverse effects from LSD use (McGlothlin and Arnold, 1971). However, adequate support for the harmful claims of brain damage, chromosomal abnormalities, cancer, suicide, or enduring personality and behavior changes simply has not come forth as yet. Indeed, the results of the relatively few well-controlled studies on LSD indicate that when the drug was administered to psychologically normal subjects under secure circumstances, lasting adverse behavioral effects did not occur (McWilliams and Tuttle, 1973). The National Institute of Mental Health continues to study the biological, genetic, and psychological effects of LSD on animals and humans (*LSD, Some Questions and Answers*, 1970).

Reasons for using LSD were obtained from interviews with a sample of Harvard and Radcliffe undergraduates (Nicholi, 1974). They gave the following explanations for initially trying the drug: (1) a desire to improve poor interpersonal relationships, (2) extreme self-dissatisfaction, (3) alienation from and feelings of anger toward the adult world, (4) inadequacy feelings, and (5) strong feelings of moral worthlessness and a wish to have a religious experience. Most of these students discontinued using LSD after a few times because the drug failed to meet their expectations, and it did not consistently give them the desired mood alteration. However, many turned to other drugs (marijuana and barbiturates) to provide them with what they were looking for.

Amphetamines, popularly known as "pep pills," "speed," and "bennies," are drugs that stimulate the central nervous system. Often they are used to produce a state of euphoria, increase alertness, reduce fatigue and depression, and curb the appetite. They are taken orally in pill form, but they may also be injected to produce a quicker and more pronounced "high." Heavy doses can produce irritability, thought disturbances, and psychotic reactions. There is an increasing tolerance for amphetamines that requires the user to increase the dose to get the desired effect, but withdrawal of the drug produces profound depressive states and sometimes suicidal tendencies. Amphetamines are readily available either through the "black market" or medical prescriptions, where they are plentiful, in that twelve billion pills are legally produced by pharmaceutical houses each year in this country (Grinspoon and Hedblom, 1975). The heaviest abusers of amphetamines are adolescents who initially may take the drug to stay awake to complete an academic assignment or to aid in weight control. Although physical dependence is not known to occur, the user may develop the psychological need to be stimulated to the extent that he or she turns to the drug to achieve that effect. The personality style of amphetamine users has been found to be different from that of heroin addicts in that the addict reduces anxiety by withdrawal and repression, while the amphetamine user tries to maintain a posture of active confrontation with the environment (Milkman and Frosch, 1973).

The most extreme and disastrous abuse of amphetamines takes the form of intravenous injections of large doses of the drug where the user ("speed freak") administers the drug for several consecutive days. During this period (sometimes referred to as a "run"), the user experiences an intense "high" and euphoria, hyperactivity, tenseness, and paranoid ideas. Often, users go without eating or sleeping for two or three days before they "crash" in exhaustion and sleep without interruption for as many as two days.

Barbiturates are sedatives that act as central nervous system depressants to aid relaxation and sleep. They cause drowsiness, impaired motor coordination, mental confusion, slurred speech, irritability, and poor emotional control. Users develop a tolerance to the sedative effects of barbiturates, and some continue to take the drug until they ingest lethal doses. Overdoses can occur readily because the drug tends to blur time perception and produce mental confusion to the point where the user may erroneously take more than is intended. Consequently, the drug appears to be one of the most frequent causes of either suicide or accidental death (Eldefonso, 1972). The drug is physically addictive, and its withdrawal is particularly difficult and hazardous. Initially, the body becomes tremulous, followed by hypotension, fever, vomiting, uncontrolled tremors, and sometimes grand mal convulsions and delirium. Medical supervision is essential since withdrawal from barbiturates represents a real threat to life itself. Heavy doses of barbiturates may be fatal, and even more moderate doses are dangerous when used in combination with amphetamines, heroin, and alcohol.

Barbiturates such as amphetamines are easy to obtain either through medical prescriptions or the illegal drug market, with as many as thirty-four doses for each person over ten years of age being supplied each year by both legal and illegal channels (Bates and Crowther, 1973). Because they are relatively inexpensive and so accessible, adolescents of all socioeconomic levels find them useful as "downers" to promptly reduce uptightness and facilitate relaxation and sleep.

Alcohol is a psychoactive drug that has a depressant effect on the central nervous system. Generally, the drinker feels relaxed, less inhibited, and becomes more talkative (sometimes with slurred speech), impulsive, clumsy, and poorly coordinated with relatively small concentrations of alcohol in the blood. With increasing concentrations of alcohol, unsteadiness of gait, sensory distortions, impaired and disjointed speech, cognitive difficulties, drowsiness, and even stupor are apt to appear. Loss of consciousness and even death can occur with a large intake of alcohol in a brief period of time.

The consumption of alcohol is so prevalent in our society that we often tend to disregard it as a potentially dangerous drug. However, approximately one-third of the total arrests for youngsters under twenty-five years of age in 1973 involved some misuse of alcohol, such as violation of liquor laws, driving under the influence, and drunkedness (*Uniform Crime Reports,* 1973). Because alcohol is readily available in a variety of beverages and strengths, and because individuals differ greatly in alcohol tolerance and drinking patterns, its use and abuse are difficult to assess. Nevertheless, professionals who work with adolescents believe that alcohol consumption represents a serious and probably increasing problem of this age group.

During the 1960s when adolescents seemed extremely fascinated with illicit drugs, there appeared to be little concern about their drinking behavior. But, apparently young people have rediscovered alcohol as a cheaper, more accessible, and more socially sanctioned remedy for their discontent or pleasure. A recent survey of the drinking patterns of seventh to ninth, and tenth through twelfth graders in lower-middle, middle, and upper-middle class students living in a semi-industrial city and in a residential town showed the following: (1) no sex differences in drinking patterns between socioeconomic classes or places of residence, although at the lower grades (seventh through ninth) more boys were heavier drinkers (defined as distilled spirit users who reported having been drunk) than girls; (2) thirty-three percent of the lower graders from the city were heavy drinkers, while only eighteen percent from the town were so classified; and (3) among the upper grades (tenth through twelfth) sixty-six percent from the city were heavy drinkers in contrast to forty-four percent from the town (Wechsler and Thum, 1973). In addition to these alarmingly high estimates of excessive drinking, the survey found that heavy users also admitted to more illicit drug use, delinquent actions, alienation from their parents, interpersonal problems with peers, and poorer academic performance. It seems that alcohol isn't a substitute for illicit drugs, but for many youngsters it is an important companion in a combination of drugs (Freed, 1973). As a matter of fact, one study indicated that alcoholic beverages are almost always the first stage of adolescent involvement in illicit drug use (Kandel, 1975). Kandel employed two longitudinal surveys with a random sample of high-school students who were followed for a period of about six months in order to map their changes in drug use. He found four stages of involvement with drugs that were consistent for most of the youngsters sampled. They went from beer and/or wine to cigarettes and/or hard liquor, to marijuana, and finally to other illicit drugs. During the six-month period, thirty-six percent of non-drug users progressed to legal drugs (alcohol and tobacco) and then to marijuana where twenty-six percent escalated to other illicit drugs.

While we do not have an accurate estimate of how many adolescent drinkers go on to become alcoholics, we do know that uncontrollable alcohol consumption in adults is a major problem. It represents twenty-five percent of all admissions in a given year to state and county mental institutions, and it is a primary contributing factor to poor health (and even early death), unemployment, broken families, and to delinquency and crime (Page, 1975).

Etiological Considerations

Genetic and Biological Views

With the exception of alcoholism, at present there is no clear-cut evidence implicating either genetic or biological factors as causes of drug abuse. The fact that alcoholism runs in families has been taken by some as favoring a genetic view, although others contend that the evidence is reflective of social learning or imitation rather than hereditary influences (Winokur, Reich, Rimmer, and Pitts, 1970; Goodwin, Schulsinger, Hermansen, Guze, and Winokur, 1973; Tolor and Tamerin, 1973). Some years ago, Roe and her associates found that children from severely alcoholic parents showed no greater incidence of alcoholism after they were placed in a foster home than their controls (Roe, Burks, and Mittelmann, 1945). In addition, more recent findings showed that a family history of heavy drinking parents, especially fathers, was a good predictor of problem drinking in adult males (Cahalan and Room, 1974).

Taken together, these two sources argue for the importance of social learning in the etiology of alcoholism. However, in contrast to Roe's results, Goodwin et al. (1973) found that sons of alcoholics who were placed in foster homes early in their lives were much more likely (almost four times as much) to become alcoholics than their controls. Further analysis of these data showed high but not different rates of alcoholism between sons of alcoholics removed from the home in infancy and their brothers who remained at home (Goodwin, Schulsinger, Moller, Hermansen, Winokur, and Guze, 1974). These authors conclude that genetic factors play an etiological role in alcoholism since their study controlled for environmental forces and the impact of the family in social learning. The fact that their results indicate that the majority of sons did not turn out to be alcoholics (regardless of home placement) was interpreted to mean that there is a genetic predisposition for severe alcoholism but that psychogenic factors are more likely to be significant for heavy and all other degrees of drinking. Even if we assume that genetic factors contribute to the development of alcoholism, the large percentage of high risk (eighty-two percent) children who do not become alcoholics suggests that there is ample room for environmental and experiential influences to operate.

Biochemical factors also have been explored with respect to alcohol intake, but the results have been contradictory (Segovia-Riquelme, Varela, and Mardones, 1971). Various biochemical differences have been found between nonalcoholic and alcoholic individuals, although it has been virtually impossible to determine whether these differences are attributable to the drinking behavior or the biochemistry of the individuals prior to alcohol addiction.

Psychogenic Views

It has been known for a long time that sociocultural factors play a role in determining the extent, the incidence, and the patterns of drug use, especially alcohol (Bates, 1946). In cultures where alcohol is prohibited, such as the Moslems, the incidence of drinking is low, whereas the incidence of opiate use is high in a culture such as China that sanctions it. Both Italy and France have high rates of alcohol consumption, but differ in their rate of alcoholism. Alcoholism is low in Italy where drinking other than at mealtime is frowned upon, while the relatively high rate of alcoholism in France corresponds to their more permissive attitude toward drinking. Other sociocultural variables such as religious preference, socioeconomic status, and geographical area also are known to be related to alcohol consumption and patterns.

But beyond these broad variables, much has been written (especially about alcoholism) about the psychological forces that produce drug abuse. For many years, the literature has reflected a strong psychoanalytic influence that views addiction as a resolution to stress or conflict by which the addict gains pleasure from the drug and relief from intrapsychic pain and anxiety (Blum, 1966). For example, the alcoholic is viewed as an immature, dependent, and orally fixated person who substitutes "booze for boobs" (infantile feeding) and who derives pleasure from being taken care of and nurtured. Drug abusers, like other disturbed personalities, are viewed by psychoanalysts as wrestling with conflicts that are sexual or aggressive in nature. More specifically, alcoholics are seen as using alcohol as a maladaptive way of dealing with latent homosexual impulses or coping with internalized hostility and depression.

A more parsimonious and empirically based view of alcoholism and drug abuse centers around a tension reduction model of learning that was extremely popular during the late 1940s and in the 1950s. Simply stated, the model assumes that life stresses produce tension and that alcohol and other drugs are potent alleviators of the discomfort generated by the stress. In a matter of a few trials under stress conditions, drug use is reinforced because it promptly reduces the heightened tension state of the individual. In addition, the pleasurable effects of the drug increase its likelihood of occurring (in the presence of stress) and persisting, since immediate gratification tends to be more powerful than the long-term negative effects of drug abuse. With continued use and as the person becomes physically addicted to the drug, the drug response will become even stronger because its use will enable the person to avoid the very unpleasant reactions that come with withdrawal.

The evidence for this view came largely from several animal studies that are now classic. Masserman and Yum (1946) used an unsolvable approach-avoidance conflict situation wherein electric shock was given whenever hungry cats approached the food box. The animals reacted to this stressful condition by fear-related behaviors, which were referred to as *experimental neurosis.* After the neurotic-like reaction was established, the experimenters gave the animals a choice between plain milk and a solution of alcohol and milk. Under the stressful shock condition, cats who previously preferred the nonalcoholic fluid showed a greater preference for alcohol than their controls. In addition, their neurotic behaviors decreased while under the influence of alcohol. Similarly, it has been found that monkeys increase their alcohol consump-

tion under stress and decrease it under normal conditions (Clark and Polish, 1960).

Several years later, Conger (1951) did two experiments that showed that rats were less affected by the stress of an approach-avoidance conflict when given an injection of alcohol as compared to control rats who were given a placebo. More specifically, rats who were under the influence of alcohol made more approach responses than their controls in the shock stress situation. In addition, Conger demonstrated that alcohol inhibited or reduced the avoidance responses of the animals, while their approach tendency was not affected. More recent and similar experimental work indicated that rats in an approach-avoidance conflict increased their alcohol consumption, but only while they were in the conflict situation (vonWright, Pekanmaki, and Malin, 1971). An increase in alcohol intake was also noted for rats who were subjected to shock that was not contingent on their behavior, although under these conditions the increase only occurred after the stress periods. These findings imply that it is noncontingent stress that is more potent in producing a permanent increase in alcohol intake than specific conflict situations, although conflict seems to be responsible for a temporary increase in alcohol consumption.

Research with human subjects confirms the relationship between an increase in alcohol intake and stress, particularly when the nature of the stress concerned social frustrations and anxieties, that is, when subjects were angered and could not express their feelings, or when the subjects were being evaluated on personal attractiveness by peers of the opposite sex (Higgins and Marlatt, 1973; Marlatt, Demming, and Reid, 1973; Higgins and Marlatt, 1975).

The idea that drug use reduces tension and is a way for the individual to cope with interpersonal frustrations and anxieties (stressful situations) is certainly viable, although other possibilities exist. It may be that factors such as modeling of parental drug abuse, peer membership, and reinforcement for drinking or pill popping, and the opportunity to behave without inhibition while under the influence are operating in the acquisition of drug abuse. As a matter of fact, a review of the literature showed that parents of drug abusers as compared to controls tended to have a higher incidence of broken marriages, more evidence of emotional disturbance, and a higher frequency of drug abuse (Harbin and Maziar, 1975). In addition, student reports of their parents use of drugs was positively related to their own frequency of drug use suggesting the effects of modeling in the development of drug use patterns (Smart and Fejer, 1972). The jury may still be out with regard to the specific etiological factors involved in drug abuse, but as the evidence mounts it clearly suggests that the answer will be found in social learning variables.

Therapeutic Considerations

Before discussing the diverse treatment forms that have been used for alcoholism and drug abuse, it is important to note that while these forms of abnormal behavior may be regarded as homogeneous, the population manifesting them is, in fact, quite heterogeneous. Merely because we classify on the basis of a single common behavior such as excessive drinking, we cannot make the erroneous assumption that all alcoholics are alike. Indeed, drug abusers are very different, although their common behavior and diagnostic label lead us to talk about them as if they were the same. Studies that have attempted to identify a distinctive

alcoholic personality, for example, have failed, although the results generally show that there are more indications of maladjustment in alcoholics than there are in normal people (Goss and Morosko, 1969). Alcoholics and other drug abusers may be neurotic, psychotic, or even representative of a variety of personality disorders. The fact that we are dealing with such a diverse clinical population makes the choice and the evaluation of treatment methods much more difficult.

Biological Approaches

Hardly any professional working with alcoholics and other drug abusers would rely on a single remedial measure as an effective and total treatment program. Instead, favorable outcomes (and there are precious too few) most often occur when a combination of remedies is used. This is especially true of the biological approaches that attempt to restore some sort of physiological balance, and to provide some effect that makes the drug use either unnecessary or undesirable.

Almost all alcoholics and addicts (hard-drug users) need a *detoxification program* as a beginning phase of intervention and rehabilitation. Detoxification involves withdrawal from the addictive drug under medical management and the treatment of the unpleasant and severe behavioral and physiological reactions of withdrawal by means of tranquilizers and other drugs. In addition, vitamins and a high carbohydrate diet are given, especially to alcoholics, who are often poorly nourished. The "drying out" process requires a minimum of several days before the abuser can proceed with further treatment. At this point, some detoxification facilities begin alcoholics on daily doses of an emetic drug such as Antabuse that makes the person extremely nauseous and violently ill if alcohol is consumed. The object of giving Antabuse is to prevent the alcoholic from further drinking (aversive conditioning), but its effectiveness depends on the willingness and the ability of the abuser to take the drug daily.

A synthetic narcotic drug, called methadone, which was developed accidently in 1965, is now frequently used as a substitute for heroin in the treatment of these addicts (Dole and Nyswander, 1965). Methadone maintenance programs in which abusers are regularly given doses of methadone proportionate to their heroin habit have become so widespread that more than sixty percent of the estimated narcotic users in 1974 were coming to centers daily to take the drug (McGlothlin, 1975). Methadone has a number of advantages: it can be taken orally, it has a longer action than heroin, and it is less expensive and legally available. However, in a curative sense, it does no more than shift the addiction from one drug to another, and in the end the abuser is still addicted to a narcotic. In fact, as long as a person is on methadone maintenance, there is no motivation or need to "kick the habit" (Lennard, Epstein, and Rosenthal, 1972). At present, the major impact of methadone has been to cut down the crime-related activities of addicts who previously needed large sums of money daily to support their illegal habit.

Psychotherapeutic Approaches

Psychoanalytically oriented and other forms of individual psychotherapy aimed at providing insight and bringing about changes in basic personality have been widely used for drug abusers without much success (Hill and Blane, 1967). The method may have failed because it largely depends

on ingredients that are not usually present in drug abusers, that is, motivation to change and an ability to develop a mutually trusting relationship with the therapist. Moreover, psychotherapy on a once a week or even biweekly basis is severely hampered without strict drug control, since the immediate rewarding aspects of the addiction and the avoidance of the pain of withdrawal are both more potent than any talk sessions can be.

In contrast, group therapy, especially as one part of an overall treatment program, has enjoyed more success (Thomas, 1968; Zucker and Waksman, 1970/73). It provides abusers with an opportunity to recognize that others have the same problem, and to gain a better view of themselves by group affiliation and acceptance. With group support, the abuser can admit the truth about his or her problem and can gain courage for abstinence with the beginning and continued success of group members. During recent years, family therapy also has been used in the treatment of alcoholics and other drug abusers, but there are too few studies available to adequately assess this approach (Meeks and Kelly, 1970). While the assumption that drug abuse is a manifestation of or involves a family problem is unchallenged at present, one must question the feasibility of this approach with the chronic alcoholic or addict who frequently is irreparably separated from the family. However, family therapy seems more promising for adolescent drug abusers whose relationships with their family are likely to be strained but not irreconcilable.

A number of behavioral treatment approaches to drug abuse also have been reported in the literature, but most have been based on individual case reports in hospital settings, and they provide either no or inadequate follow-up measures (Callner,

1975). When long-term data are available we find, for example, that aversive conditioning in which the abused drug is paired with some noxious stimulus such as a nausea-inducing chemical or a strong electric shock results in only temporary abstinence in alcoholics and drug addicts (Droppa, 1973; Miller and Barlow, 1973). The ineffectiveness of behavioral methods in producing enduring changes, however, should not be the basis for discarding this approach, but perhaps should encourage therapists to include it in a multiform treatment regime.

Self-Help Organizations

Alcoholics Anonymous is probably the best known and most far-reaching organization in the world for helping any alcoholic who wishes to stop drinking. There are more than one half million members who maintain sobriety through their participation in A.A., and there are more than 16,000 A.A. groups in this country alone to which alcoholics can belong (Goldenberg, 1977). Membership is on a voluntary basis, and A.A. has no fees or complicated structure. The program was founded by laymen, and it continues to be run by laymen even today. Its twelve guiding principles include a heavy religious emphasis in which the individual is asked to believe in a greater Power who could restore sanity, to admit to God the nature of his or her wrongdoings, to gain a better understanding of God through prayer and meditation, and to turn his or her will and life over to God. The alcoholics are encouraged to admit their impotence with regard to alcohol and to recognize that they can never drink again. Regular meetings are held in which members publicly confess, and recovered alcoholics speak about their experiences. Each new member is paired with an ex-alcoholic who is available night and day to help the novice with the struggle over abstinence, and to provide strength and understanding when needed. Inasmuch as A.A. is not a research-oriented organization, there are little data concerning its effectiveness. However, its continued growth and popularity provide indirect evidence that it is a useful program for a substantial number of alcoholics.

A parallel self-help for drug addicts is Synanon, which was founded by a former alcoholic who developed a problem with hard drugs. Synanon is a residential center that is staffed by former addicts to provide a tightly controlled live-in environment. New members are required to carry out assigned jobs within the residence, although jobs get progressively better as the person complies with the expectations of the community, behaves maturely, and abstains from drug use. Members are encouraged to find new friends and life-styles that are quite different from their previous drug subculture. Participation in group therapy several times a week is required in which frank and sometimes painful verbal confrontations take place among the members. The idea behind these verbal attacks is to penetrate and strip away the common tendency of addicts to deceive themselves and rationalize their drug abuse. Other residential centers representing some variant of Synanon have since opened and are operating in various parts of the country. The effectiveness of these programs has been difficult to evaluate since few outcome studies are available. However, what little data we have indicate that relatively few addicts have been reached this way; the most favorable result has been obtained with those addicts who continue to live at Synanon and who are employed by the residence (Volkmann and Cressey, 1963; Yablonsky, 1967).

Prognosis

The overall outlook for drug abusers, especially chronic alcoholics and long-term narcotic addicts, is very poor. However, the extreme diversity in personality characteristics and in the type, duration, extent, and degree of drug abuse makes the issue of outcome virtually impossible to evaluate more specifically. In general, most observers agree that young drinkers and drug abusers who continue to function within their families and maintain employment have the most favorable prognosis. Chronic alcoholics of the Skid Row type and long-term narcotic addicts, in contrast, have the poorest chance of total abstinence and of achieving a good social adjustment. Moreover, outcome tends to vary with the type and degree of personality disorganization, that is, the more severe the disorganization the poorer the prognosis. The evaluation of outcome is also complicated by the criteria employed, in that the percentage of recoveries will depend on the definition one uses. For example, it stands to reason that one can obtain a higher rate of recovery for alcoholics if a sobriety period of three months is used as the criterion rather than insisting on a two year duration of sobriety. The matter becomes even more complex and pessimistic with regard to favorable outcomes when vocational, marital, and other aspects of social adjustment are included as criteria for recovery.

Summary

Three major areas of abnormal behavior of adolescence and youth were considered in this chaper—*delinquency, drug abuse,* and *runaway.*

Information about the incidence and a description of the types of delinquent behaviors have already been provided in Tables 12–1, 12–2, and 12–3; and Figure 12–1. A summary of the factors known to be related to delinquency, as well as its etiological considerations and therapeutic approaches follow on page 402.

We considered the growing problem of runaway children, their heterogeneity as a population, their diverse reasons for fleeing their family environments, and the need to carefully evaluate each runaway in order to construct effective treatment strategies.

Drug abuse (arrests for drug offenses) has increased by a staggering 4,673.3 percent for youngsters under eighteen as compared to an increase of 774.6 percent for persons over eighteen years between 1960 and 1970. Experimenting with drugs and the use of multiple drugs are common among high school and college students, with males showing a higher incidence than females by a ratio of about 2:1. For adolescents and college-aged youngsters the problem is sizeable and serious at all levels of the social scale. Excessive consumption of alcohol by adolescents was also discussed as an area of growing concern.

Other than some inconclusive evidence about alcoholism, there are no clear-cut data implicating either genetic or biological factors as causes of drug abuse. The weight of the present evidence points to cultural and social learning variables as playing the most significant role in the etiology of alcoholism and drug abuse. Psychoanalytic and tension reduction models of learning were discussed along with modeling, peer affiliation, and the opportunity to behave without inhibition while under the influence as possible etiological factors operating in the development of drug abuse.

Various therapeutic measures were presented in the context that alcoholism and drug abuse represent very heterogeneous

Related Factors

Delinquency is related to low socioeconomic background especially in urban areas. When unrecorded instances of delinquency are obtained, there is no difference in socioeconomic levels.

More delinquents come from broken homes. Both extreme permissiveness and strictness are associated with delinquency, although inconsistent discipline is most damaging. Parental rejection is also related.

Delinquents are poor academic performers and have high school drop out rates.

Mesomorph body type is related to delinquency, and positive EEG spike patterns are frequently noted.

Etiology Considerations

Sociological gangs.
1. Gangs arise from play groups as a result of conflict with other groups and as a means of banding individuals together.
2. Out of difficulties in successfully achieving middle-class goals, lower-class boys affiliate to legitimatize their aggression against middle-class institutions and to bolster self-esteem.
3. Different types of delinquent subcultures are formed by lower-class urban males as attempts to adapt to pressures created by the limited accessibility of middle-class channels.
4. Middle-class delinquency is gradual outgrowth of normal group activities in which deviant explorations become the group standard.

Psychological-personality problems are likely to be found in deficiencies of the ego or the superego.

Systematic research on aggression as an operant response that is maintained by reinforcements readily available in the environment.

Aggressive behavior is acquired through imitation or modeling.

Multi-factor views—mesomorphic body build with personality traits of aggressiveness, adventurousness, and acquisitiveness were found in delinquent youngsters. Also they disliked school, were scholastically retarded, pugnacious toward schoolmates, truant, and misbehaved at earlier age than nondelinquents.

Therapeutic Approaches

Juvenile judge may sentence to training or detention facilities, place on probation, or refer elsewhere for remedial measures.

Institutionalization offers poor programs and no more than twenty to thirty percent improve from them.

Community based programs involving individual and group therapy, vocational counseling, and supervision by probation officer are no more effective in reducing recidivism than incarceration.

Psychotherapy under court authority may be useful. Milieu-residential programs where group interaction and socialization are emphasized have been tried but without adequate evaluation.

Behavior modification in which positive reinforcement, punishment, and token systems were used to alter antisocial behavior and improve level of education have been successful.

However, more research to determine the long-term effects of behavior modification is necessary before a final verdict can be rendered about this treatment approach.

populations that one may erroneously view as homogeneous because of the way these common behaviors are classified. Biological approaches attempt to restore some sort of physiological balance and provide some effect that renders using the drug as either unnecessary or undesirable. These include detoxification programs, the use of Antabuse to make drinking aversive, and the substitution of maintenance doses of methadone for heroin. Individual psychotherapy, group and family therapy, and behavior therapies were discussed and evaluated in light of the available literature. Self-help organizations such as Alcoholics Anonymous and Synanon were described as widely known and popular treatment programs for alcoholism and drug abuse. Issues complicating the evaluation of outcome were also discussed.

Epilogue

In Defense of Youth

We call them wrong! God pity us, the blind,
Imputing evil as our grandsires did,
When we explored new realms with feet and mind,
Uncovering what old fogies damned and hid!
The dreams, the wanton fantasies are there,
As you and I once knew them loved them, till
We came to staleness and to foolish fear
Lest something change, be different, jolt our will!
'Tis life they seek, not sin, no sordid thing,
But joy in health and beauty, and in all
The urge of thrilling bodies that would sing
And freely dance with laughter at earth's call.
Let's laugh with them, full knowing that when tried
By Truth and Duty, Youth is on God's side!

BARSTOW

REFERENCES

AICHHORN, A. *Delinquency and Child Guidance.* New York: International Universities Press, 1969.

AMBROSINA, L. *Runaways.* Boston: Brown Press, 1971.

ANDERSON, R. E. "Where's Dad? Paternal Deprivation and Delinquency." *Archives of General Psychiatry,* 1968, *18,* 641–649.

BAER, D. J. and J. J. CORRADO. "Heroin Addict Relationships with Parents During Childhood and Early Adolescent Years." *Journal of Genetic Psychology,* 1974, *124,* 99–103.

BANDURA, A. *Principles of Behavior Modification.* New York: Holt, Rinehart, and Winston, 1969a.

BANDURA, A. "Social-Learning Theory of Identificatory Processes." In Goslin, D. A. (Ed.), *Handbook of Socialization Theory and Research.* Chicago: Rand McNally, 1969b, pp. 213–262.

BANDURA, A., Ross, D., and S. A. Ross. "Imitation of Film-Mediated Aggressive Models." *Journal of Abnormal and Social Psychology,* 1963, *66,* 3–11.

BANDURA, A. and R. H. WALTERS. *Adolescent Aggression:* A Study of the Influence of Child-Training Practices and Family Interrelationships. New York: Ronald Press, 1959.

BARSTOW, R. W. "In Defense of Youth." In Clark, T. C. and E. A. Gillespie (Eds.), *1000 Quotable Poems: An Anthology of Modern Verse.* New York: Willett, Clark, 1937, pp. 290–291.

BATES, R. F. "Cultural Differences in Rates of Alcoholism." *Quarterly Journal of Studies on Alcohol,* 1946, *6,* 480–499.

BATES, W. and B. CROWTHER. *Drugs: Causes, Circumstances, and Effects of Their Use.* Morristown, New Jersey: General Learning Press, 1973.

BLACKFORD, L. *Student Drug Use Surveys, San Mateo County, California.* Preliminary Report, County Department of Health and Welfare, San Mateo, 1974.

BLOCK, J. and B. MARTIN. "Predicting the Behavior of Children Under Frustration." *Journal of Abnormal and Social Psychology,* 1955, *51,* 281–285.

BLUM, E. M. "Psychoanalytic Views of Alcoholism: A Review." *Quarterly Journal of Studies on Alcohol,* 1966, *27,* 259–299.

BUSS, A. H. "Instrumentality of Aggression, Feedback, and Frustration as Determinants of Physical Aggression." *Journal of Personality and Social Psychology,* 1966, *3,* 153–162.

CALAHAN, D. and R. ROOM. *Problem Drinking among American Men.* New Haven, Connecticut: College and University Press, 1974.

CALLNER, D. A. "Behavioral Treatment Approaches to Drug Abuse: A Critical Review of the Research." *Psychological Bulletin,* 1975, *82,* 143–164.

CAVAN, R. S. and J. T. CAVAN. *Delinquency and Crime: Cross-Cultural Perspectives.* Philadelphia: Lippincott, 1968.

The Challenge of Crime in a Free Society. A Report by the President's Commission on Law Enforcement and Administration of Justice. Washington, D.C.: U.S. Government Printing Office, 1967.

CHANDLER, M. J. "Egocentrism and Antisocial Behavior: The Assessment and Training of Social Perspective-taking Skills." *Developmental Psychology,* 1973, *9,* 326–332.

CHAPEL, J. L. and D. W. TAYLOR. "Drugs for Kicks." In Reed, J. P. and F. Baali (Eds.), *Faces of Delinquency.* Englewood Cliffs, New Jersey: Prentice-Hall, 1972, pp. 64–65.

CLARK, J. and E. WENNINGER. "Socioeconomic Class and Area as Correlates of Illegal Behavior among Juveniles." *American Sociological Review,* 1962, *27,* 826–834.

CLARK, R. and E. POLISH. "Avoidance Conditioning and Alcohol Consumption in Rhesus Monkeys." *Science,* 1960, *132,* 223–224.

COHEN, A. K. *Delinquent Boys, the Culture of the Gang.* Glencoe, Illinois: The Free Press, 1955.

COHEN, H. L. and J. FILIPCZAK. *A New Learning Environment.* San Francisco: Jossey-Bass, 1971.

CONGER, J. J. "The Effects of Alcohol on Conflict Behavior in the Albino Rat." *Quarterly Journal of Studies on Alcohol,* 1951, *12,* 1–29.

CORTES, J. B. and F. M. GATTI. *Delinquency and Crime: A Biopsychosocial Approach: Empirical, Theoretical, and Practical Aspects of Clinical Behavior.* New York: Seminar Press, 1972.

"Current Views of College Students on Politics and Drugs." *Gallup Opinion Index,* Report No. 80. Princeton, New Jersey: Gallup International, February, 1972.

DAVIDSON, W. S. and E. SEIDMAN. "Studies of Behavior Modification and Juvenile Delinquency: A Review, Methodological Critique, and Social Perspective." *Psychological Bulletin,* 1974, *81,* 998–1011.

DOLE, V. P. and M. NYSWANDER. "A Medical Treatment for Diacetylmorphine (Heroin) Addiction: A Clinical Trial with Methadone Hydrochloride." *Journal of the American Medical Association,* 1965, *193,* No. 8, 646–650.

DOLLARD, J., DOOB, L. W., MILLER, N. E., MOWRER, O. H., and R. R. SEARS. *Frustration and Aggression.* New Haven: Yale University Press, 1939.

DROPPA, D. C. "Behavioral Treatment of Drug Addiction: A Review and Analysis." *International Journal of the Addictions,* 1973, *8,* 143–161.

DUPONT, R. L. and M. H. GREENE. "The Dynamics of a Heroin Addiction Epidemic." *Science,* 1973, *181,* 716–722.

ELDEFONSO, E. *Youth Problems and Law Enforcement.* Englewood Cliffs, New Jersey: Prentice-Hall, 1972.

ELLIOTT, D. S. "Delinquency, School Attendance and Dropout." *Social Problems,* 1966, *13,* 307–314.

ELLIOTT, D. S., Voss, H. L., and A. WENDLING. "Capable Dropouts and the Social Milieu of the High School." *Journal of Educational Research,* 1966, *60,* 180–186.

EMPEY, L. T. and M. L. ERICKSON. "Hidden Delinquency and Social Status." *Social Forces,* 1966, *44,* 546–554.

ENGLAND, R. W., JR. "A Theory of Middle-class Juvenile. Delinquency." In Reed, J. P. and F. Baali (Eds.), *Faces of Delinquency.* Englewood Cliffs, New Jersey: Prentice-Hall, 1972, pp. 270–277.

ERICKSON, M. L. and L. T. EMPEY. "Class Position, Peers, and Delinquency." *Sociology and Social Research,* 1965, *49,* 268–282.

ERON, L. D., HUSEMANN, L. R., LEFKOWITZ, M. M., and L. O. WALDER. "Does Television Violence Cause Aggression?" *American Psychologist,* 1972, *27,* 253–263.

FREED, E. X. "Drug Abuse by Alcoholics: A Review." *International Journal of the Addictions,* 1973, *8,* 451–473.

FREEMAN, B. and G. SAVASTONA. "The Affluent Youthful Offender." *Crime and Delinquency,* 1970, *16,* 264–272.

GERGEN, M. K., GERGEN, K. J., and S. J. MORSE. *Journal of Applied Social Psychology,* 1972, 2:1, 1–16.

GIBBENS, T. C. N. *Psychiatric Studies of Borstal Lads.* London and New York: Oxford University Press, 1963.

GIBBONS, D. C. *Delinquent Behavior.* Englewood Cliffs, New Jersey: Prentice-Hall, 1970.

GLUECK, E. *Unraveling Juvenile Delinquency.* New York: Commonwealth Fund, 1950.

GLUECK, S. and E. GLUECK. *Physique and Delinquency.* New York: Harper and Row, 1956.

GLUECK, S. and E. GLUECK. *Delinquents and Nondelinquents in Perspective.* Cambridge: Harvard University Press, 1968.

GOLDENBERG, H. *Abnormal Psychology: A Social/Community Approach.* Monterey, California: Brooks/Cole, 1977.

GOODWIN, D. W., SCHULSINGER, F., HERMANSEN, L., GUZE, S. B., and G. WINOKUR. "Alcohol Problems in Adoptees Raised Apart from Alcoholic Biological Parents." *Archives of General Psychiatry,* 1973, *28,* 238–243.

GOODWIN, D. W., SCHULSINGER, F., MOLLER, N., HERMANSEN, L., WINOKUR, G., and S. B. GUZE. "Drinking Problems in Adopted and Nonadopted Sons of Alcoholics." *Archives of General Psychiatry,* 1974, *31,* 164–169.

GOSS, A. and T. E. MOROSKO. "Alcoholism and Clinical Symptoms." *Journal of Abnormal and Social Psychology,* 1969, *74,* 682–684.

GRINSPOON, L. and P. HEDBLOM. *The Speed Culture: Amphetamine Use and Abuse in America.* Cambridge, Massachusetts: Harvard University Press, 1975.

HALIKAS, J. A. and J. D. RIMMER. "Predictions of Multiple Drug Abuse." *Archives of General Psychiatry,* 1974, *31,* 414–418.

HANEY, B. and M. GOLD. "The Juvenile Delinquent Nobody Knows." *Psychology Today*, 1973, *7*, 49–55.

HARBIN, H. T. and H. M. MAZIAR. "The Families of Drug Abusers: A Literature Review." *Family Process*, 1975, *14*, 411–432.

HATHAWAY, S. R. and E. D. MONACHESI. *Adolescent Personality and Behavior:* MMPI Patterns of Normal, Delinquent, Dropout, and other Outcomes. Minneapolis: University of Minnesota Press, 1963.

HERRICK, R. "To the Virgins, to Make Much of Time." In Allison, A. W., Barrows, H., Blake, C. R., Carr, A. J., Eastman, A. M., and H. M. English, Jr. (Eds.), *The Norton Anthology of Poetry*. New York: Norton, 1975, p. 111.

HIGGINS, R. L. and G. A. MARLATT. "The Effects of Anxiety Arousal on the Consumption of Alcohol by Alcoholics and Social Drinkers." *Journal of Consulting and Clinical Psychology*, 1973, *41*, 426–433.

HIGGINS, R. L. and G. A. MARLATT. "Fear of Interpersonal Evaluation as a Determinant of Alcohol Consumption in Male Social Drinkers." *Journal of Abnormal Psychology*, 1975, *84*, 644–651.

HILL, M. J. and H. T. BLANE. "Evaluation of Psychotherapy with Alcoholics: A Critical Review." *Quarterly Journal of Studies on Alcohol*, 1967, *28*, 76–104.

HOMER, L. E. "Community-based Resource for Runaway Girls." *Social Casework*, 1973, *54*, 473–479.

HOOK, E. B. "Behavioral Implications of the Human XYY Genotype." *Science*, 1973, *179*, 139–150.

HOWELL, M. C., EMMONS, E. B., and D. A. FRANK. "Reminiscences of Runaway Adolescents." *American Journal of Orthopsychiatry*, 1973, *43*, 840–853.

JEFFREY, C. R. and I. A. JEFFREY. "Delinquents and Dropouts. An Experimental Program in Behavior Change." *Canadian Journal of Corrections*, 1970, *12*, 47–58.

JENKINS, R. L. "Motivation and Frustration in Delinquency." *American Journal of Orthopsychiatry*, 1957, *27*, 528–537.

JENKINS, R. L. *Behavior Disorders of Childhood and Adolescence*. Springfield, Illinois: Charles C Thomas, 1973.

JENKINS, R. L. and A. BOYER. "Types of Delinquent Behavior and Background Factors." *International Journal of Social Psychiatry*, 1968, *14*, 65–76.

JENKINS, R. L. and L. HEWITT. "Types of Personality Structure Encountered in Child-Guidance Clinics." *American Journal of Orthopsychiatry*, 1944, *14*, 84–94.

JESSOR, S. L. and R. JESSOR. "Maternal Ideology and Adolescent Problem Behavior." *Developmental Psychology*, 1974, *10*, 246–254.

JOHNSON, A. M. "Sanctions for Superego Lacunae of Adolescents." In Eissler, K. R. (Ed.), *Searchlights on Delinquency*. New York: International University Press, 1949, pp. 225–245.

JOHNSTON, L. "Drugs and American Youth: A Report from the Youth in Transition Project." Ann Arbor, Michigan: Institute for Social Research, University of Michigan, 1973.

Juvenile Court Statistical Series, U.S. Department of Health, Education and Welfare. Washington, D.C.: U.S. Government Printing Office, 1970, p. 10.

KAHN, M. "The Physiology of Catharsis." *Journal of Personality and Social Psychology*, 1966, *3*, 278–286.

KAHN, M W. and J. McFARLAND. "A Demographic and Treatment Evaluation Study of Institutionalized Juvenile Offenders." *Journal of Community Psychology*, 1973, *1*, 282–284.

KANDEL, D. "Stages in Adolescent Involvement in Drug Use." *Science,* 1975, *190,* 912–914.

KAPLAN, M., RYAN, J. F., NATHAN, E., and M. BAIROS. "The Control of Acting-out in the Psychotherapy of Delinquents." In Szurek, S. A. and I. N. Berlin (Eds.), *The Antisocial Child: His Family and His Community.* Palo Alto, California: Science and Behavior Books, 1969, pp. 93–104.

KELLY, F. J. "The Effectiveness of Survival Camp Training with Delinquents." *American Journal of Orthopsychiatry,* 1971, *41,* 305–306.

KENISTON, K. "Prologue: Youth as a Stage of Life." In R. J. Havighurst and P. H. Dreyer (Eds.), *Youth.* The 74th Yearbook of the National Society for the Study of Education. Chicago: The University of Chicago Press, 1975, pp. 3–26.

LENNARD, H. L., EPSTEIN, L. J., and M. S. ROSENTHAL. "The Methadone llusion." *Science,* 1972, *176,* 881–884.

LIBERTOFF, K. *Perspectives on Runaway Youth: A Special Report.* Boston: Massachusetts Committee on Children and Youth, 1976.

LSD, Some Questions and Answers. U.S. Department of Health, Education and Welfare, Public Health Service Publications, No. 1828. Washington, D.C.: Government Printing Office, 1970.

MALLICK, S K. and B. R. MCCANDLESS. "A Study of Catharsis of Aggression." *Journal of Personality and Social Psychology,* 1966, *4,* 591–596.

Marijuana: A Signal of Misunderstanding. National Commission on Marijuana and Drug Abuse. New York: Signet, 1972.

MARLATT, G. A., DEMMING, B., and J. B. REID. "Loss of Control Drinking in Alcoholics: An Experimental Analogue." *Journal of Abnormal Psychology,* 1973, *81,* 233–241.

MASSERMAN, J. H. and K. S. YUM. "An Analysis of the Influence of Alcohol on Experimental Neurosis in Cats." *Psychomatic Medicine,* 1946, *8,* 36–52.

MCCORD, W. M., MCCORD, J., and I. K. ZOLA. *Origins of Crime: A New Evaluation of the Cambridge-Somerville Youth Study.* Montclair, New Jersey: Patterson, Smith, 1969.

MCGLOTHLIN, W. D. "Drug Use and Abuse." In Rosenzweig, M. F. and L. W. Porter (Eds.), *Annual Review of Psychology* (Vol. 26). Palo Alto, California: Annual Reviews, 1975, pp. 45–64.

MCGLOTHLIN, W. H. and D. O. ARNOLD. "LSD Revisited: A Ten-Year Follow-up of Medical LSD Use." *Archives of General Psychiatry,* 1971, *24,* 35–49.

MCWILLIAMS, S. and R. J. TUTTLE. "Long-term Psychological Effects of LSD." *Psychological Bulletin,* 1973, *79,* 341–351.

MEEKS, D. E. and C. KELLY. "Family Therapy with the Families of Recovering Alcoholics." *Quarterly Journal of Studies on Alcohol,* 1970, *31,* 399–413.

MILKMAN, H. and W. A. FROSCH. "On the Preferential Abuse of Heroin and Amphetamine." *Journal of Nervous and Mental Diseases,* 1973, *156,* 242–248.

MILLER, N. E. and J. DOLLARD. *Social Learning and Imitation.* New Haven: Yale University Press, 1941.

MILLER, P. M. and D. H. BARLOW. "Behavioral Approaches to the Treatment of Alcoholism." *Journal of Nervous and Mental Diseases,* 1973, *157,* 10–20.

MURRAY, J. P. "Television and Violence: Implications of the Surgeon General's Research Program." *American Psychologist,* 1973, *28,* 472–478.

NICHOLI, A. M. "Emotional Determinants of LSD Ingestion." *Journal of the American College Health Association,* 1974, *22,* 223–225.

Nir, Y. and R. Cutler. "The Therapeutic Utilization of the Juvenile Court." *American Journal of Psychiatry*, 1973, *130*, 1112–1117.

Ohlin, L. E. and R. A. Cloward. *Delinquency and Opportunity, A Theory of Delinquent Gangs*. Glencoe, Illinois: Free Press, 1960.

Page, J. D. *Psychopathology: The Science of Understanding Deviance*. Chicago: Aldine Publishing Company, 1975.

Parsons, B. V., Jr. and J. F. Alexander. "Short-term Family Intervention: A Therapy Outcome Study." *Journal of Consulting and Clinical Psychology*, 1973, *41*, 195–201.

Patterson, G. R. and J. A. Cobb. "A Dyadic Analysis of 'Aggressive Behaviors'." In Hill, J. P. (Ed.), *Minnesota Symposia on Child Psychology* (Vol. 5). Minneapolis: University of Minnesota Press, 1971, pp. 72–129.

Peterson, D. R., Quay, H. C., and T. L. Tiffany. "Personality Factors Related to Juvenile Delinquency." *Child Development*, 1961, *32*, 355–372.

Quay, H. C. "Dimensions of Personality in Delinquent Boys as Inferred from the Factor Analysis of Case History Data." *Child Development*, 1964, *35*, 479–484.

Quay, H. C. "Personality Dimensions in Preadolescent Delinquent Boys." *Educational and Psychological Measurement*, 1966, *26*, 99–110.

Redl, F. and D. Wineman. *Children Who Hate: The Disorganization and Breakdown of Behavior Controls*. Glencoe, Illinois: Free Press, 1951.

Reed, J. P. and F. Baali (Eds.). *Faces of Delinquency*. Englewood Cliffs, New Jersey: Prentice-Hall, 1972.

Roe, A., Burks, B. and B. Mittelmann. "Adult Adjustment of Foster Children of Alcoholic and Psychotic Parentage and the Influence of the Foster Home." *Memorial Section on Alcohol Studies*. No. 3. New Haven: Yale University Press, 1945.

Schreiber, D. "Juvenile Delinquency and the School Dropout Problem." *Federal Probation*, 1963, *27*, 15–19.

Schwitzgebel, R. K. *Streetcorner Research: An Experimental Approach to the Juvenile Delinquent*. Cambridge: Harvard University Press, 1964.

Segovia-Riquelme, N., Varela, A., and J. Mardones. "Appetite for Alcohol." In Israel, Y. and J. Mardones (Eds.), *Biological Basis for Alcoholism*. New York: Wiley-Interscience, 1971, pp. 299–334.

Sheldon, W. H., Hartl, E. M., and E. McDermott. "Varieties of Delinquent Youth: An Introduction to Constitutional Psychiatry." New York: Harper and Row, 1949.

Simmons, R. G., Rosenberg, F., and M. Rosenberg. "Disturbance in the Self-image at Adolescence." *American Sociological Review*, 1973, *38*, 553–568.

Smart, R. G. and D. Fejer. "Drug Use among Adolescents and Their Parents: Closing the Generation Gap in Mood Modification." *Journal of Abnormal Psychology*, 1972, *79*, 153–160.

Solomon, S. "The Neurological Evaluation." In Freedman, A. M. and H. I. Kaplan (Eds.), *Comprehensive Textbook of Psychiatry*. Baltimore: The Williams and Wilkins, 1967, pp. 420–443.

Stanton, A. H. "Drug Use among Adolescents." *American Journal of Psychiatry*, 1966, *122*, 1282–1283.

Tec, N. "Differential Involvement with Marijuana and Its Sociocultural Context: A Study of Suburban Youths." *International Journal of the Addictions*, 1972, *7*, 655–669.

THOMAS, M. "The Group Therapies." In Catanzaro, R. J. (Ed.). *Alcoholism: The Total Treatment Approach.* Springfield, Illinois: Charles C Thomas, 1968, pp. 127–145.

THRASHER, F. M. *The Gang.* Chicago: University of Chicago Press, 1936.

TOLOR, A. and J. S. TAMERIN. "The Question of a Genetic Basis for Alcoholism: Comment on the Study by Goodwin et al., and a Response." *Quarterly Journal of Studies on Alcohol,* 1973, *34,* 1341–1345.

TROJANOWICZ, R. C. *Juvenile Delinquency: Concepts and Control.* Englewood Cliffs, New Jersey: Prentice-Hall, 1973.

Uniform Crime Reports: 1968–1971 (U.S. Department of Justice, Federal Bureau of Investigation). Washington, D.C.: U.S. Government Printing Office, 1972.

Uniform Crime Reports, Federal Bureau of Investigation. Washington, D.C.: U.S. Government Printing Office, 1973, pp. 124–125.

VAZ, E. W. *Middle-class Juvenile Delinquency.* New York: Harper and Row, 1967.

VOLKMANN, R. and D. R. CRESSEY. "Differential Association and the Rehabilitation of Drug Addicts." *American Journal of Sociology,* 1963, *64,* 129–142.

VONWRIGHT, J. M., PEKANMÄKI, L., and S. MALIN. "Effects of Conflict and Stress on Alcohol Intake in Rats." *Quarterly Journal of Studies on Alcohol,* 1971, *32,* 420–433.

WALD, P. M. and P. B. HUTT. *Dealing with Drug Abuse: A Report to the Ford Foundation.* New York: Paeger, 1972.

WALKER, R. N. *Psychology of the Youthful Offender* (2nd ed.). Springfield, Illinois: Charles C Thomas, 1973.

WECHSLER, H. and D. THUM. "Teen-age Drinking, Drug Use, and Social Correlates." *Quarterly Journal of Studies on Alcohol,* 1973, *34,* 1220–1227.

WINOKUR, G., REICH, T., RIMMER, J., and F. N. PITTS. "Alcoholism III: Diagnosis and Familial Psychiatric Illness in 259 Alcoholic Probands." *Archives of General Psychiatry,* 1970, *23,* 104–111.

YABLONSKY, L. *The Tunnel Back: Synanon.* Baltimore: Penguin Books, 1967.

ZAX, M. and G. STRICKER. "Excerpts from Case Study, Thomas L. *Patterns of Psychopathology: Case Studies of Behavioral Dysfunction.* New York: Macmillan, 1963, pp. 238–239.

ZUCKER, A. H. and S. WAKSMAN. "Results of Group Therapy with Young Drug Addicts." *The International Journal of Social Psychiatry,* 1970/73, *17–18,* 267–279.

Adjustment Problems of Late Adolescence and the College Years

13

PROLOGUE

Susan was referred to the campus student counseling center while serving as a volunteer subject in an experiment that was associated with a course she was taking in personality development. During the experiment, she had trouble following directions and asked numerous questions that reflected her pre-occupation with personal problems. The experimenter wisely arranged for her to see a staff psychologist several hours later. She opened the interview with a gripping plea for help, saying, as she fought back the tears, "I don't know where to begin! Everything has gone sour, and no matter what I do, nothing seems to get better. I feel trapped and at my wits' end! My grades last semester were poor, but they are even worse now in spite of the extra hours I've put into studying. I haven't had much luck dating (becoming more tearful). . . . boys don't find me attractive. The girls in the dormitory never include me in what they are doing, except for my roommate . . . (a long pause) . . . Mary . . . she's a good friend but . . . she makes me feel funny and uncomfortable. I thought about leaving but I can't go home and face my parents . . . and I don't know anyone around here who could help me."

Susan, who recently turned eighteen, was the youngest of two children. Apparently, her twenty-year-old brother was doing well as a junior at another college. She had never before been away from her midwestern home without her parents, except for a few weeks of summer camp. Her father was the president of the town's largest bank, and her mother, a former schoolteacher, currently served as an elected member of the school board. Both parents were not only successful in their own right, but held high-achievement expectations for their children. Mother tended to be overprotective and doting, although she and her husband were strict disciplinarians, who rigidly imposed their conservative and moralistic values on their children. Both Susan and her brother were excellent students in elementary and high school, but Susan had to work hard to get good grades. In keeping with her parents' values she placed a premium on academic performance, and she regarded all else as secondary. Consequently, she had only a few close friends, went to an occasional party, and had formal dates with boys only for major social events sponsored by the school or the church.

Susan described both parents as orderly, perfectionistic, aloof, and distant in their relationships with each other and with her. She never could comfortably discuss her problems with either parent, although she noted that they were willing to help her with her school work, or with projects for which she could obtain special recognition. She spoke of being relatively happy at home in her "little world," but quite miserable since she arrived on campus. She has always enjoyed good health, although she has battled a tendency to be overweight since early childhood. Other than occasional masturbation for which she still feels guilt, Susan had no prior sexual experiences.

Additional interviews confirmed the initial impression that Susan was depressed, and revealed that she was struggling, unsuccessfully, to cope with her new-found freedom and independence, and to meet the high achievement expectations set by her parents, and now by herself. On campus she felt isolated, unadmired, unwanted, and unattractive to both boys and girls. With great hesitation, Susan also expressed the fear that she might be a lesbian, since she had become sexually attracted to her roommate when Mary tried late one night to physically comfort her and stop her from crying. In a desperate move to allay her mounting anxiety over her sexual feelings toward Mary, and to prove her heterosexuality, she decided to have intercourse with the next boy who asked her out. Fortuitously, her chance came the very next day before she could think things through or change her mind. But, she became so frightened and tense in bed that the sexual encounter was neither satisfying to her, or to her partner. Afterwards, she was overwhelmed with guilt and even more uncertain about her sexual orientation. Her condition worsened as she had difficulty sleeping, concentrating on her school work, and maintaining interest in any social contact with Mary and the other girls in her dormitory. The more she ruminated about herself and her problems, the further she fell behind in her course work and assignments.

One or more aspects of Susan's story has a ring of familiarity to most campus counseling services, or for that matter, to almost anyone who recently has lived in a college dormitory for any length of time. Her problems of coping with independence, meeting parental and self-expectations, managing peer and dating relationships, dealing with sexual impulses, and establishing a comfortable self-image and identification represent some of the most frequent and troublesome areas affecting the adjustment of many of our nation's college students.

All segments of American society now favorably regard education beyond high school as providing youngsters with opportunities to enhance their present and future lives. More specifically, the general hope is that the college experience will have a salutary effect on the student's physical and emotional health, social relationships, depth and diversity of knowledge and skills, and vocational alternatives that are both socially useful and personally gratifying. The importance of higher education to Americans is reflected in their willingness to pay escalating tuition fees, and to expend public funds to make this developmental opportunity available to students from all walks of life. In turn, young people tend to agree with this cultural emphasis by seeking admission to college in increasing numbers over the last seven decades. In fact, somewhere between seven and ten million youngsters representing more than half of our high-school graduates are presently enrolled in some college (Keniston, 1975).

From a developmental viewpoint, it has been argued that the college years are a significant stage of life, rather than an upward extension of adolescence, and that they enable:

. . . a more autonomous, more individuated position vis-à-vis the existing society and can permit the individual to achieve a degree of inner complexity, differentiation, and integration not vouchsafed (for) those whose development is foreshortened or foreclosed. Furthermore, the extension of human development means that we are creating—on a mass scale—a "new" breed of people whose psychological development not only inclines them to be critics of our own society, but might even make them potential members or architects of a better one than ours (Keniston, 1975, p. 4).

The decision to write a chapter dealing with the adjustment problems of the college years is admittedly unorthodox, inasmuch as similar textbooks as well as the traditional classification systems have virtually ignored this topic. Yet, we were persuaded that this phase of human development deserves special attention because of its potential impact on the lives of so many millions of our youth, and because of its special relevance to a college audience for whom texts such as this are primarily intended. The selection of the material to be included under this topic turned out to be more difficult than the decision to write about these important years, since much of the existing literature· is diverse, unsystematic, and limited both in terms of its quantity and quality. But, in the end, the choices were guided by two questions: What are the major factors likely to give rise to adjustment problems, and what are the serious behavioral consequences that arise during this period? With these questions in mind, we shall consider briefly the stress of (1) *dependence and independence*, (2) *academic pressures and career goals*, and (3) *peer relationships*, and more extensively the pervasive and serious problem areas of *sexuality* and *suicide*.

Dependence and Independence

Although widely used by lay people and professionals alike, the concept of dependence-independence is, at best, an imprecise one that refers to the extremes of a single personality continuum. In general, we think of the trait as a developmental progression from almost total dependence in infancy to greater maturity and independence in adulthood, thus conveying the value judgment that independence is better than dependence. Yet, few if any individuals are entirely dependent or completely independent, but, in fact, most evidence some elements of each. Where people fall with respect to this continuum depends on three interacting factors: (1) developmental norms, (2) the situation, and (3) how the personality trait is defined. In the early stages of life, developmental considerations far outweigh other variables in importance, since babies are dependent on others for almost every aspect of their existence. However, with increasing age, both situational variables and one's view of the continuum become more significant not only in describing these behaviors, but also in making judgments about whether they are abnormal or normal. For example, clinical observers would make little of a one-year-old clinging to his mother in the unfamiliar surroundings of a room full of strangers. But, the same behavior in a ten-year-old would be noteworthy since it is atypical for this age group and situation. In addition, dependent behaviors vary according to how they are defined. A youngster of ten who seeks the help of a parent in completing a school assignment evidences a different kind of dependent behavior from that of the child in the clinging illustration, although the difference might be obscured by the way these behaviors are construed.

Three different views of dependent behavior have been suggested in the literature: *emotional dependence, instrumental dependence,* and *passivity* (Ferguson, 1970; McCandless and Evans, 1973). Emotional dependence refers to behaviors that seek affection, protection, and emotional attachment from others—behaviors that are highly encouraged in young children in our society, but that are looked upon with less favor in adolescents and adults (especially males). Behaviors that seek help from others in completing a task that the person cannot do without assistance is seen as instrumental dependence. In this connection, the seeking of parental assistance by our ten-year-old might be regarded as

either emotional or instrumental dependence, both, or neither, depending on the view one adopts of this personality trait. The fact that everyone, at some time or other, needs some aid in completing a task may be taken as evidence that no one is completely independent, but it also may suggest that the behavior is so commonplace that classifying it as dependent serves no useful purpose. Finally, dependence may be interpreted as passivity, or inactivity involving a pervasive style of responding, in which others are set into motion to act in one's behalf. In this instance, dependent behaviors are inferred from the individual's unresponsiveness, which prompts others to take action if anything is to get done. Care must be taken in reaching this conclusion since other kinds of inactivity (the silence of anger or immobilization by fear, for example), also can move others to respond in similiar ways.

For Susan, and for many other entering freshmen, the shift to college involving the first prolonged separation from family, home, and familiar surroundings may have placed a major stress on the dependence-independence dimension of her personality. She found herself many miles away from home in a new setting without the people who had previously satisfied her emotional dependence. Quite often, college teachers, dorm advisors, or peers become quick and suitable substitutes for old ties, but Susan's failure to establish any replacement only heightened her anxiety and her sense of aloneness. Many youngsters experience this sort of anxiety in a milder form, commonly called *home sickness,* during the early days of a lengthy separation from family. However, it usually dissipates readily as they successfully manage on their own and as their needs for emotional dependence are met by others. Unfortunately, Susan's only source of gratification came from her roommate, who unintentionally became aversive when her actions aroused another conflict area.

In addition, the shift to the relatively unstructured confines of college life initially removes students from the people who primarily satisfied their instrumental dependency needs. Beginning students, like Susan, are free of close parental supervision and controls, and within broad limits, they are free to do as they please. But Susan functioned poorly when she had no one to prompt her (instrumental assistance) to do her homework, attend classes, keep regular hours, eat properly, or to aid her with the management of money, time, and personal affairs. In contrast, most students welcome and deal effectively with their new-found freedom, probably because they were encouraged long before going off to college to rely on their own resources and abilities, and because they had already achieved some measure of success in coping with problems on their own. While college life provides students with opportunities to gain further competence and greater independence through the emergence of response patterns that reflect their own interests, attitudes, and values, it also provides an additional stress that may lead to maladaptive behaviors for those in whom emotional and instrumental dependency needs are important.

Indeed, American colleges have shown their sensitivity to this problem for a long time by functioning *in loco parentis* or surrogate parents. Up until recently, most colleges imposed rather strict rules on students concerning class attendance, course requirements, dormitory curfew hours (especially for girls), dormitory visitation privileges, personal conduct, and the like. At present, colleges are in the unenviable position of trying to deal with the conflicting wishes of parents and students. On the one hand, parents of entering freshman support the *in loco parentis* policy, preferring that the schools be significantly involved in both the student's academic and extracurricula activities. On the other hand, beginning students voice strong opposition to this practice through their demands for more freedom with respect to housing rules and the use of alcohol and marijuana (Davis and Williams, 1974; Devine and Loesch, 1976). Too often, the ideas of freedom and independence are viewed as synonomous, when, in fact, they are more accurately thought of as related. Freedom merely provides the opportunity for people to act independently, but it doesn't guarantee that these behaviors will occur. For some students, the request for more freedom represents the wish to have their pleasure-seeking needs sanctioned and gratified, while others want to demonstrate their competence and learn additional ways of self-regulation without being unduly controlled by institutional constraints. The confusion between these ideas probably arises from the fact that most students evidence multiple motives in their quest for freedom, and more often than not they effectively use these opportunities to develop independent behaviors.

It may be too early to discern a trend but, in general, the changes that have occurred suggest that colleges are more responsive to student pressures than to parental wishes. Most dormitories have abandoned evening and weekend curfew hours, their stringent rules concerning visitation, and the requirement that students live in dormitories beyond their freshman year. Many colleges now provide some form of coed housing, a practice that seemed so radical just a few years ago. Apparently, colleges have made changes because they believe that the students' desire for more independence is valuable for their development and, secondarily, because it lightens the awesome responsibilities that accompany an *in loco parentis* policy. Except for self-report data obtained from students, there is little, if any, evidence concerning the effect of coed housing on students' performance or personal adjustment. Students claim that coed housing provides more opportunities for informal social interactions and emotional support, while unisex housing gives them greater privacy and independence (Moos and Otto, 1975). Moreover, these data suggest that both males and females in coed units showed drops in their levels of aspiration not shown by those living in unisex quarters. If anything, the findings argue against the students' view that coed housing is beneficial for the development of greater independence. Indeed, if college administrators are to make sound decisions about matters that could have important long-range effects on their students, they will need much more empirical data obtained from controlled studies using more reliable measures.

Academic Pressures and Career Goals

From the students' viewpoint, grades and the related problems of vocational choice, career planning, and personal unhappiness represent their primary concerns (Kramer, Berger, and Miller, 1974; Bishop and Snyder, 1976). This is understandable since students like Susan have learned the importance of meeting their own and parental expectations for high academic achievement and demanding professional careers

as an instrumental response pattern that has, in the past, satisfied so many of their basic needs (such as recognition, approval, affection, and self-esteem). However, students soon learn that the college setting presents a formidable challenge to successful performance. Its heavy academic demands in terms of course load, assignments, and competition for grades together with the impersonal nature of so many of the large classes are relatively new and potent stressors to most beginning students. Many find their sense of adequacy and self-esteem further jolted by the realization that their prior lofty academic ranking no longer applies, since a large number of their colleagues graduated with a similar distinction. The fact that academic success in high school is a very good predictor of college grades offers little reassurance to students troubled by this discovery since it is apparent that other students are just as good, if not more capable, than they are (Panos and Astin, 1968; Homstrom, 1973). In addition, the economic slow-down of the 1970s, the very tight post-college job market, and the scarcity of places in professional and graduate programs have markedly heightened the competition and the pressure to achieve academically.

The effects of these stressful circumstances are multiple and sometimes disastrous. There is ample experimental evidence indicating that stress increases anxiety levels and that high anxiety impairs one's ability to discriminate, and increases the probability of errors (competing responses) occurring in complex tasks such as verbal learning (Malmo and Amsel, 1948; Rosenbaum, 1953; Knopf, Worell, and Wolff, 1959; Knopf and Fager, 1959; Maher, 1966). Moreover, research findings bearing more directly on the relationship between anxiety and college achievement have shown that many students suffer from test anxiety that results in impaired academic performance and that this effect is particularly pronounced for students in whom the need to achieve is strong (McKeachie, Pollie, and Spiesman, 1955). Other studies have shown that a high level of anxiety interferes markedly with successful college performance (as evidenced by low grades) for those students who fall within the middle range of intellectual ability. In contrast, anxiety level has little effect on the academic performance of those students who are at either the lowest or highest groupings of scholastic aptitude (Spielberger, 1966). These results led to the conclusion that intellectually limited college students perform poorly regardless of their anxiety level, while the very bright ones are so capable that they are not adversely affected by anxiety, although in some instances anxiety facilitates their academic performance. It seems that the effect of high anxiety on the middle-range students is attributable to errors they make in interpreting complex or ambiguous test questions. According to Spielberger, these students can effectively reduce their anxiety levels through more careful preparation, and the acquisition of more factual information.

For Susan, poor academic achievement led to more anxiety and other dire consequences. Her sense of adequacy and worthiness was damaged, and she felt guilty and alienated from her parents and others whose approval she desperately needed. Many students in similar circumstances struggle to recover through temporary, but heroic, efforts at extra studying. Unfortunately, they often take this measure too late, because catching up in a college course is extremely difficult, and because an extra effort in one leaves less time for the others.

As noted in Chapter 12, some students turn to drug abuse, taking stimulants such as amphetamines to keep themselves awake for additional studying, but this solution, if continued over time, creates greater problems than it solves. Other students, like Susan, sink further into despair, become depressed, and withdraw as they have increasing difficulty in adequately coping with most areas of their lives.

Peer Relationships

From early adolescence, these relationships provide young people with a sense of community membership, personal acceptance, and group standards to which they can compare their own competence and frailties. This is especially important since during this period young people are in a state of limbo between childhood and adulthood, often at odds with the adult world, ambivalent about giving up the carefree pleasures of childhood, and uncertain about their identity and future directions. Anxiety and feelings of inadequacy commonly are reflected in concerns about being too fat, tall, short, skinny, shy, awkward, ugly, or otherwise unacceptable. Peer relationships often allay these anxieties by providing approval and confirmation from others that they are, in fact, "all right." Misery likes company, and one worries less about those glaring flaws in oneself if they also are found in others, especially when they elicit no adverse reactions from others.

For entering college students, peer relationships are potent sources of conflict and stress, largely because relocation severs ties with old friends and comfortable group affiliations without any assurance of suitable substitutes. Students arrive on campus with few, if any, social contacts to help ease their apprehensions about the academic and interpersonal aspects of their new environment. Typically, a series of social "mixers" are planned by the school to bring students together, and to help them overcome their initial anxieties. Yet, mixers seem to be most effective for those who need them least. Students who already have acquired social skills, poise, and competence usually have no difficulties in striking up relationships with others. However, the relatively shy and unaggressive student, like Susan, has problems in a large and impersonal social situation. Susan reported that she consciously avoided the first mixer by busying herself with unpacking and getting settled, but she was pressed into going to the second by her roommate. She remembered feeling tense, embarrassed, and uncomfortable as she slowly strolled the periphery of the social hall hoping that someone would stop to talk to her, but unable herself to take the initiative. After an hour of what seemed like an eternity, she quietly left and returned to her room feeling isolated and unattractive. This may have even been the beginning of a self-fulfilling prophecy for Susan, as she continued to isolate herself socially through the first semester. The extent to which her academic performance was related to her poor peer relationships is uncertain, although research data show that acceptance by a peer model can positively influence the scholastic performance of underachieving students (Engle, Davis, and Mazer, 1968).

We also know that students seek relationships with peers who are most similar to themselves and that this personal attraction is more effective in producing modeling behaviors than for those whom students see as dissimilar (Byrne and Griffitt, 1966; Byrne and Clore, 1967). The finding that

youngsters from low socioeconomic backgrounds and members of minority groups, more than other students, experience alienation and have greater difficulty in making friends may be related to the notion of personal attraction (Feldman and Newcomb, 1969; Jackson and DePuydt, 1974). If students look for similar characteristics in their friends, then it is possible that minority students have a harder time making friends at college, because of the fact that there are fewer who are similar to choose from.

Up to this point, our discussion of peer relationships has been restricted to friendships and group affiliations that are essentially nonsexual in nature. In the section to follow, we turn to the much more stressful area of human sexuality in which the impact of one's own sexual impulses, those of others and how these are managed, is especially profound for the adjustment of adolescents and college students.

Sexuality

Attitudes about Sex among Youth

Attitudes refer to mental positions that people take with regard to particular events and behaviors, although these positions should not be confused with overt behaviors, inasmuch as there is usually a discrepancy between a person's attitude and the action in question. The frequently heard admonition to "Do as I say, and not as I do" recognizes that inconsistencies of this sort actually exist. People smoke or drink while they strongly urge others not to because of its known harmful effects. In many instances, the difference between what people do and what people say is relatively easy to discern, since the pertinent behavior can be readily observed and noted. However, sexual practices are intimate, personal, and not typically open to public observations. What we know about sexual attitudes and behaviors comes from self-report data that do not include provisions to evaluate the accuracy of the reported behaviors. Therefore, the measurement of both sexual attitudes and behaviors are subject to those errors commonly associated with self-report data, such as social desirability, the anonymity of the responder, the perceived purpose of the study, the kinds of questions asked, or the characteristics of the experimenter, among others. To some extent, these errors can be lessened through using conditions that will encourage subjects to be truthful, standardized experimental procedures, large samples of subjects, and replication with similar populations.

Discrepancies between sexual attitudes and practices apparently do exist, as reflected in the finding that over ninety percent of sexually active adolescent delinquent girls believed that premarital intercourse is wrong (Ball and Logan, 1970). Yet, data reported by several recent sources indicate that the gap between sexual attitudes and behaviors has narrowed considerably over the years to the point where young people are more likely to be practicing what they believe (Christensen and Johnsen, 1971; Hutt and Sedlacek, 1974; McBride and Ender, 1977).

There seems to be little doubt that substantial changes in sexual attitudes have occurred in our society within recent years, as evidenced by our greater tolerance of pornography, homosexuality, and nudity, and the frequency with which implicit or explicit sex is depicted in TV and movie shows, or in commercial advertising. Almost every aspect of the contemporary scene suggests that sex is "in," and that we,

as a society, believe that more sexual freedom and gratification will cure almost all of our ills (Dreyer, 1975). The terms the *sexual revolution* or the *new morality* are widely used to describe these changes that are most pronounced among our youth, especially young women who now seem inclined to reject the double standard by becoming more similar to males in their approval of premarital sex (McCary, 1973). The available research findings indicate that the proportion of both college men and women approving of premarital sex has increased since the late 1950s, although the change has been more marked for women. Even during the two-year period between 1969 and 1971, students liberalized their attitudes toward premarital, extramarital and homosexual relationships (Christensen and Gregg, 1970; Yankelovich, 1972). In light of these more permissive attitudes, it is interesting to find that college men, in surprisingly large numbers (seventy-five percent), still strongly hold on to the double standard with regard to their preference to marry a virgin (Christensen and Gregg, 1970).

Factors such as race, age, strength of religious belief, socioeconomic level, and region of the country seem to be related to sexual attitudes. One study showed that older students from eastern, southern, or western colleges, with little religious conviction, were more permissive in their sexual attitudes than their more religious and younger counterparts attending midwestern colleges (Davis, 1971). Greater acceptance of premarital sex was found among black men and women as compared to whites, although significantly, more approval was evident in low socioeconomic blacks than in blacks from middle and upper-middle-class backgrounds (Reiss, 1970, 1971). In contrast, no socioeconomic difference was found among white men and women in terms of their attitudes toward premarital sex.

Perhaps a more important variable is the social context, or the extent of emotional involvement, associated with the sexual activity. In general, both sexes approve of either petting or having full sexual relations primarily when some degree of affection or personal commitment (engaged, or in love) is evident, although a small percent of the responders felt no affectional tie was necessary (Reiss, 1967). More recent data not only confirmed the need for some degree of personal commitment for both sexes, but also emphasized the greater importance of this variable for college women whose sexual attitudes tended to be strongly related to romantic and affectionate feelings (Davis, 1971; McBride and Ender, 1977). In this connection, Hunt wrote the following about contemporary young women as compared to those studied two decades earlier by Kinsey (Kinsey, Pomeroy, Martin, and Gebhard, 1953).

It is very likely that in absolute terms there are more single women today than formerly who are willing to have intercourse without any emotional ties, but in relative terms it remains true that most sexually liberated single girls feel liberated only within the context of affectionate or loving relationships (Hunt, 1974, p. 33).

While the evidence clearly reflects changing sexual attitudes among young people in the direction of more freedom and permissiveness, it by no means indicates (as some would suggest) wanton lust, promiscuity, or decadent morality ("Campus '65," 1965; Farnsworth, 1970; Masterson, 1971). To the contrary, it could be argued that these changes are no more liberal than society has generally become in so many other areas, and that the new attitudes remain quite similar to the sexual attitudes held by previous generations (Petras, 1973). Indeed, there is an old ring of familiarity in

the contemporary attitudes indicating that young men are more sexually liberated than young women, that they prefer to marry "good" girls and go to bed with "bad" ones, and that both sexes, but especially girls, are more likely to approve of sex when it occurs in the context of romantic commitment than as a frivolous thrill-seeking activity (McCary, 1973). What is new about these attitudes is the substantial shift that has occurred in the direction of greater openness, frankness, and freedom in discussing sexual matters and in exploring the limits of one's own sexuality. In addition, women have changed much more than men in that they now are inclined to claim the same sexual freedom that men have traditionally enjoyed (Rubin, 1971). Farnsworth has commented that these changes:

. . . have caused the great majority of people to become quite confused about older concepts of right and wrong, proper and improper, constructive and destructive as they apply to adolescent and early adult development (Farnsworth, 1974, p. 850).

Sexual Behaviors among Youth

Because petting for both sexes and masturbation in men are so commonplace and because these sexual behaviors pose no real threat to the adjustment of college students, they will not be discussed here. Instead we will focus on premarital sex, selected problems associated with coitis, and homosexuality.

Premarital Sex

In light of the increased congruence between self-report sexual attitudes and behaviors, it should not be surprising to learn that since the Kinsey volume appeared in 1953 (Kinsey et al., 1953), several sources have noted that premarital sex has increased slightly for men and dramatically for women (Cannon and Long, 1971; Kanter and Zelnick, 1973; Sorenson, 1973). The significant change for college men seems to be in the women with whom they have coition. Apparently the percentage of college men who have premarital sex with prostitutes has decreased considerably, while there has been a corresponding increase of sex with girls for whom they have some emotional attachment (Davis, 1971). For college women, the percentage of premarital sexual experience ranges anywhere from nineteen percent to fifty-five percent, depending on such factors as age, race,

strength of religious belief, region of the country, and so forth (Packard, 1968; Bell and Chaskes, 1970; Kaats and Davis, 1970; Bell, 1971; Walsh, 1972). More recent but unpublished data obtained from students enrolled in a course on human sexuality indicated that seventy-five percent of the females had had sexual intercourse at least once, and that this proportion had remained relatively stable for similar students over the last few years (Edwards, 1977). However, students who voluntarily enroll in a course in sexuality tend to have more permissive sexual attitudes and to be more sexually experienced than comparable controls (Zuckerman, Tushup, and Fin-

TABLE 13–1 *   Percentage of "Yes" Responses to Heterosexual Behavior Scale

Have you ever engaged in the following behavior with a member of the opposite sex?	Percentage of Males Saying "Yes"	Percentage of Females Saying "Yes"
1. One minute of continuous kissing on the lips?	86.4	89.2
2. Manual manipulation of clothed female breasts?	82.7	71.1
3. Manual manipulation of bare female breasts?	75.5	66.3
4. Manual manipulation of clothed female genitals?	76.4	67.5
5. Kissing nipples of female breast?	65.5	59.0
6. Manual manipulation of bare female genitals?	64.4	60.2
7. Manual manipulation of clothed male genitals?	57.3	51.8
8. Mutual manipulation of genitals?	55.5	50.6
9. Manual manipulation of bare male genitals?	50.0	51.8
10. Manual manipulation of female genitals until there were massive secretions?	49.1	50.6
11. Sexual intercourse, face to face?	43.6	37.3
12. Manual manipulation of male genitals to ejaculation?	37.3	41.0
13. Oral contact with female genitals?	31.8	42.2
14. Oral contact with male genitals?	30.9	42.2
15. Mutual manual manipulation of genitals to mutual orgasm?	30.9	26.5
16. Oral manipulation of male genitals?	30.0	38.6
17. Oral manipulation of female genitals?	30.0	41.0
18. Mutual oral-genital manipulation?	20.9	28.9
19. Sexual intercourse, entry from the rear?	14.5	22.9
20. Oral manipulation of male genitals to ejaculation?	22.7	26.5
21. Mutual oral manipulation of genitals to mutual orgasm?	13.6	12.0

When asked about their sexual experiences, male and female undergraduates in the 1970s tended to give quite similar responses. An interesting finding is that males are more likely than females to report having the milder or "less advanced" experiences, while this pattern reverses with respect to the stronger or "more advanced" types of sexual activity.

* From Curran, 1977, p. 197.

ner, 1976). Although the estimates of female sexual activity vary widely, the data consistently point to the conclusion that both sexes are now very similar to each other in their sexual behavior.

Perhaps more interesting are data obtained by Curran (1977) that showed a cumulative pattern of sexual experiences for both college men and women. The findings are included in Table 13-1, which gives the percentage of men and women who responded affirmatively to the items on the Heterosexual Behavior Scale. Note that men engaged in intercourse and mutual orgasm through manual manipulation earlier in their pattern of experience than women, but that women experienced both fellatio and cunnilingus earlier than men, suggesting to Curran that women, in contrast to men, participated in oral sex before sexual intercourse. This pattern provides women with the dual advantage of preserving their virginity while giving and receiving sexual gratification. Curran also interpreted the findings to support the idea that women are becoming more lax in their need for a personal commitment from men as a requisite to intercourse. Although they feel some emotional involvement is still important, college women are more willing to have coitus with men they are dating, or with whom they are going steady, than ever before (Bentler, 1968a, b; Bell and Chaskes, 1970; Curran, Neff, and Lippold, 1973). Indeed, college women seem to have achieved greater changes in their sexual practices than men, and they have demonstrated clearly that their sexual desires and responsiveness are equal to, if not in some instances greater, than male students. However:

Equality in sexuality can be a source of liberation for both men and women, but negative possibilities must be recognized. For example, the female who has successfully learned to suppress her sexual desires can suffer a blow to her self-esteem when she learns that other females are sexually active and enjoying multiorgasmic experiences. Analogously, the traditional male who has successfully learned that the initiation and total enjoyment of sexual interactions is a masculine prerogative can suffer an equal blow when he learns that females can be as sexually active and aggressive as he (Byrne and Byrne, 1977, p. 194).

Problems Associated with Coitus

Two areas of sexual inadequacy or dysfunction have been selected for discussion, *premature ejaculation* in the male, and *orgasmic dysfunction* in the female, because these seem to be the most frequent sources of anxiety and dissatisfaction for both sexual partners.

1. Premature ejaculation has been defined in various ways, although it refers to an orgasm that occurs in a male very quickly, resulting in his inability to satisfy his partner during coitus. Kinsey (Kinsey, Pomeroy, and Martin, 1948) characterized it by a time criterion in which ejaculation occurs either prior to, or within one minute after penetration, while Masters and Johnson (1970) prefer to define it as a man's failure to delay ejaculation long enough to enable his partner to reach climax in more than half of the occasions that intercourse takes place. The Cornell Medical Center group, in contrast, emphasizes the man's inability to achieve control over the ejaculatory reflex when intense sexual arousal occurs (Kaplan, Kohl, Pomeroy, Offit, and Hogan, 1974).

All of these definitions are arbitrary and limited in one way or another. The time criterion tends to ignore the requirements of different sexual partners and the variations of these needs from one occasion to another. If the female reaches her climax just as quickly as the man, or if she sometimes can be brought close to orgasmic release by intense foreplay to the point that she will later climax with a few thrusts of the penis, then both partners have been satisfied. Under these conditions, the time criterion would describe a problem that doesn't exist. Similarly, the Cornell definition emphasizes the man's inability to control the ejaculatory reflex, but overlooks the interpersonal context in which it occurs. Masters and Johnson, in fact, acknowledged that the inclusion of this consideration does not sufficiently take into account the man's sexual partner, since their definition becomes invalid if the female is unable to consistently reach orgasm for reasons other than the rapidity of the male's ejaculation. However premature ejaculation is defined, the important issue is that its occurrence poses a serious threat to a man's self-esteem and to his ability to sustain a harmonious relationship with a woman. This is especially true for men who have completed high school since it has been found that those with less education rarely are sufficiently concerned about the condition (Kinsey et al., 1948; Masters and Johnson, 1970).

The premature ejaculator is disappointed and anxious about his failure to be an adequate male, and he is even more debilitated when he learns from his partner that his incompetent bed performance fails to satisfy her sexually. As the condition persists, his situation worsens:

Time and again premature ejaculators of many years' standing not only lose confidence in their own sexual performance but also, unable to respond positively while questioning their own masculinity, terminate their sexual functioning with secondary impotence (Masters and Johnson, 1970, p. 100).

The early reaction of the woman is usually one of acceptance, compassion, and encouragement. Eventually, her feelings of frustration, irritation, and anger become evident and often are openly expressed in terms of his selfishness in using her as a sexual outlet without regard for her needs.

Except for rare cases of physical abnormalities or infections, premature ejaculation generally is considered a psychogenic condition (Kinsey et al., 1948; Masters and Johnson, 1970). Psychoanalytic thinking suggests unconscious conflicts and hostilities toward women as the underlying psychological basis of premature ejaculation (Kaplan et al., 1974), while others have implicated such factors as emotional tension, fatigue, low self-confidence, long period of abstinence before intercourse, extreme sensitivity, or too much sexual arousal during foreplay as possible causative factors (Thorne, 1943; McCary, 1973). However, Masters and Johnson's view, drawn from case history materials, seems to have received the most recent support, probably because it has led to a very effective treatment strategy. They suggested that ejaculation is a learned, conditioned response that is acquired during early sexual experiences that have been carried out and reinforced in hurried and tense circumstances. For example, they conjectured that men who are now over forty years of age frequently had their first few sexual experiences with prostitutes who encouraged men to reach orgasm quickly. The faster his performance, the better it was for her, and she rewarded him for it by her show of approval. In this way, the inexperienced man learned to release his sexual tension quickly and acquired a reinforced pattern of performance that was likely to persist throughout his life. Other circumstances that fostered hurried performance and the acquisition of premature ejaculation patterns included those initial sexual encounters that occurred in semiprivate surroundings in which there was the ever present danger of being caught, such as in parked cars, the back porch, or in the front parlor while the rest of the family was out seeing a movie.

The "squeeze technique" of Masters and Johnson has had a reported 97.8 percent success rate (only four failures out of 186 men treated), although other treatment methods ranging from home remedies, application of a local anesthetic to the penile glans, chemotherapy, psychoanalysis, to marital and behavior therapy have been tried, either with less effectiveness or without evaluative research data (Masters and Johnson, 1970; Kaplan et al., 1974).

2. Orgasmic dysfunction in women refers to either their failure to ever achieve a climax by any means of sexual stimulation (primary), or their present failure to achieve an orgasm, although they have reached at least one climax in the past (secondary or situational) (Masters and Johnson, 1970). That orgasmic dysfunction in women represents a sizeable problem is demonstrated in Kinsey's data (Kinsey et al., 1948) that showed that only sixty-seven percent of the women who engaged in premarital intercourse had experienced a climax, and that only seventeen percent of the orgasms had been reached in coitus. Moreover, these researchers found that between twenty-two to thirty-four percent of women in the first year of marriage failed to reach an orgasm during intercourse (depending on their educational level, that is, the higher the educational level the lower the percentage of failures). More recent data suggest that as many as twenty-nine percent of sexually active college women have never experienced an orgasm during premarital coitus (Edwards, 1977). Another large-scale study involving questionnaire responses of women ranging in age from fourteen to twenty-eight years indicated that thirty percent were considered nonorgasmic in intercourse (Hite, 1977). Although approximately ninety-five percent are capable of orgasm sometime during their life, and some of reaching multiple orgasms, the fact remains that women have more difficulty than men in achieving orgasm (McCary, 1973).

Our society has traditionally permitted males a great deal of freedom to develop and express their sexuality, while denying females similar opportunities. Females have been expected to grow up with repressed, inhibited, or curbed sexual appetites and responsiveness. To be a "good" girl, she was required to be chaste, unwilling to express interest in such base or dirty matters as sex, and unwavering in her resolve to avoid seduction. For her, sex was tied to romantic involvement, serious courtship, and marriage, as evidenced by Kinsey's data (Kinsey et al., 1948) indicating that most women who had premarital coitus did so after they were engaged to be married. In contrast, a man's macho image was bolstered and sometimes measured by the number and frequency of his sexual conquests and his perceived sexual prowess with women. These circumstances fostered the perception of women as sexual objects and denied women full understanding that they too needed sexual fulfillment. But, as the contemporary woman has become more liberal in her sexual attitudes and practices, she has broken with the old tradition and has given notice of her arrival as an equal, if not more responsive, sexual partner.

Since women who presently suffer from orgasmic dysfunction have in all likelihood grown up with these double standards, it is reasonable to expect that learning would play a substantial etiological role in the development of this form of sexual inadequacy. In fact, based on case history data, Masters and Johnson (1970) view orgasmic dysfunction as a learned response originating from numerous negative sources about sex from early childhood on. These include the withholding of information about sexual functioning by parents, the failure of the family to provide a model of sexual functioning that the girl could emulate, and the use of authority and fear (parental and/or religious) to communicate negative attitudes about either the admission or open expression of sexual impulses. In addition, these researchers attached a great deal of importance to the presence of strong repressive defenses by which the girl's strong sexual impulses are banished from, and kept out of her awareness. Other but related psychological factors implicated in orgasmic dysfunction have been identified as the emotional states of shame, guilt, and fear that serve to inhibit sexual expression (Ellis, 1961). Here, too, Ellis attributed the inhibition of nonorgasmic women to their learning of negative attitudes toward sex. Ellis also suggested that for some women failure begets failure, in that they become overly concerned and apprehensive about their orgasmic dysfunction to the point where they are too tense to reach a climax.

But learning and psychological variables are not the only causative factors involved in this condition. Orgasmic dysfunction (primary or secondary) may also be produced by organic and relational causes (Ellis, 1961; Coleman, 1972). The organic

bases may involve constitutional flaws and inadequacies of the sexual apparatus, damage brought about by injuries, hormonal deficiencies, impairment of the central nervous system, infection or tumors of the genitalia, alcohol and drug abuse, and physiological changes attributed to the aging process (McCary, 1973). In addition, factors that tend to disrupt the interpersonal relationships between sex partners, such as revenge, premature ejaculation on the part of male, or the insensitivity or physical unattractiveness of the male, may serve to reduce the female's sexual interest and responsiveness during coitus (McGovern, Stewart, and LoPiccolo, 1975).

Recent data from a five-year study on the sexual responsiveness of women tended to refute some of the widely held interpretations of female sexuality (Fisher, 1973). Interestingly enough, Fisher found no relationship between the woman's orgasmic responsiveness and the following factors: partner's sexual technique, her own sensitivity to stimulation, the source of her sex education, the attitudes of her parents toward sex, the strength of her religious belief, her sense of femininity, the absence or presence of prior sexual trauma, or the status of her mental health. The fact that his findings suggest that some of the factors associated with the learning of negative attitudes about sex were independent of the woman's orgasmic responsiveness weakens somewhat the etiological view proposed by Masters and Johnson, and by Ellis. Much more data from longitudinal studies like Fisher's are needed before we can obtain a clearer understanding of the causal factors of orgasmic dysfunction in women.

In general, there are some similarities among the various treatment methods used for orgasmic dysfunction in women in that the participation of both sexual partners is usually recommended, and most treatment regimes attempt to gradually increase the woman's sexual responsiveness through a variety of stimulative methods. Moreover, these treatments are best accomplished in the context of a relaxed, comfortable, and quiet environment where the woman feels no pressure to achieve an orgasm, and of cooperation and harmony between the partners. The treatment method suggested by Masters and Johnson (1970) claims a success rate of eighty-three percent for primary orgasmic dysfunction and seventy-seven percent for secondary cases. The therapy begins with a clinical discussion between the couple and the therapist to determine the areas and techniques of sexual arousal that are pleasurable and those that are repulsive to the woman, and to provide the couple with instructions about the sexual stimulation that is commensurate with the woman's needs. Practice sessions take place in the privacy of their bedroom and involve a progressive series of recommended bed positions for each partner, as well as steps for foreplay and intravaginal stimulation.

Variations of this method, especially with cases of secondary orgasmic dysfunction, have been reported in the literature in which the woman was taught new positions and techniques of masturbation that approximated coitus, sexual technique training was emphasized, or marital counseling was added to the regime (Annon, 1971; Lo Piccolo and Lobitz, 1972; McGovern et al., 1975; Snyder, Lo Piccolo, and LoPiccolo, 1975). However, it is difficult to assess these approaches at this time, since most of the favorable outcomes have been based on either a single or relatively few cases.

Homosexuality

In 1974, the American Psychiatric Association finally responded to a variety of internal and external pressures by withdrawing homosexuality as a category of psychopathology.[1] As salutary as the action might be for the future, it could not erase the significant untoward effects it has had on society for more than 100 years. According to one historian, the classification of homosexuality as a disease or illness:

. . . had the disadvantage of validating certain unproven assumptions, of giving a sort of scientific *imprimatur* to past prejudices, and this has proven to be disastrous in the field of sexuality —so disastrous in fact, that I would like to argue that it is not enough for the American Psychiatric Association to say that their previous categories of sexual pathology are inoperative, but they also must take cognizance of the damage they had done by their own erroneous assumptions, which in light of other scientific findings should long ago have been discarded (Bullough, 1977, p. 380).

In effect, the medical model of homosexuality perpetuated and gave scientific respectability to society's long-standing condemnation of this form of sexual behavior. Yet, homosexuality has been noted since the beginning of recorded history, and despite society's negative attitudes and its legal, social, and psychological prohibitions, homosexuality has not been eliminated as a sexual outlet (Freedman, 1971).

The term "homosexuality," as it is used here, refers to overt sexual relations between members of the same sex, although in broader contexts it may include not only

---

[1] DSM–III, however, still includes a category known as *dyshomophilia* (homosexuality) for those individuals who are distressed by their homosexual feelings, fantasies, or acts.

behavior, but also sexual feelings, desires, and attraction to persons of the same sex. It was Kinsey (Kinsey et al., 1948, 1953) who dispelled the notion that people can be classified as either homosexuals or heterosexuals, since his early findings for most men argued against such a dichotomy, and in favor of degrees of sexuality. Therefore, he and his co-workers constructed a seven-point rating scale ranging from exclusively heterosexual to entirely homosexual as a more accurate way of categorizing his subjects with respect to the relative frequencies of each kind of sexual response they experienced. Their findings were startling at the time, in that they showed that by the age of fifteen at least one homosexual act had occurred in sixty percent of the boys and thirty-three percent of the girls studied. In contrast, only about ten percent of the men and three percent of the women had been either primarily or exclusively homosexual at any given age period.

In the more than two decades since Kinsey, homosexuality among young people has not changed appreciably, although more liberal and permissive attitudes toward this sexual practice are evident (Hunt, 1974; Haynes and Oziel, 1976). To the extent that these findings are comparable to those reported by the Kinsey group, the fears generated by some segments of our society that homosexuality will increase with greater public permissiveness have not been supported by empirical evidence.

Almost every possible etiological variable has been suggested as contributing to homosexuality. Data by Kallmann (1952) strongly implicated genetic factors in that he found 100 percent concordance rates of homosexuality in male identical twins, but only about fourteen percent for fraternal twins. However, a more recent review of

the research literature indicated that later studies failed to confirm these concordance rates, or the conclusion that homosexuality is inherited (Rosenthal, 1970). Biochemical research, seeking to find hormonal imbalance as a causal link to homosexuality, has uncovered evidence indicating that urine or blood levels of testosterone, as well as sperm counts, were lower in male homosexuals than in heterosexual men. In addition, testosterone levels in the urine of female homosexuals were higher than for their heterosexual counterparts (Loraine, Adamopoulos, Kirkham, Ismail, and Dove, 1971; Kolodny, Masters, Hendryx, and Toro, 1971). However, several recent reviews of the research data suggest that no conclusion about the endocrine origin of homosexuality is warranted at this time, since the present evidence is largely correlational, and the possibility exists that the differences found in sex-related hormones could be the secondary result, rather than the cause, of the subjects' primary homosexuality (Money and Ehrhardt, 1972; Green, 1974; Acosta, 1975).

Although divergent, psychoanalytic interpretations of homosexuality have been among the most influential of the psychogenic views. At the risk of being too simplistic, most psychoanalytic notions about homosexuality can be reduced to the essential ingredient of *fear,* which causes the sexual interests (of both males and females) to be turned away from heterosexual objects (Fenichel, 1945; Bieber, Dain, Dince, Drellich, Grand, Gundlach, Kremer, Rifkin, Wilbur, and Bieber, 1962). The fear may be attributable to the anatomical differences between the sexes, in which the boy may fear that his penis will be cut off (castration) for engaging in sexual play or incestuous wishes (oedipal complex) and in which the female's genitals may become a phobic object, since she, too, may have been punished by castration. For the girl, psychoanalytic formulations are less clear, although the awareness of sex differences and the absence of a penis may lead her to feel inadequate and envious. Should her feelings be strongly aroused over her sexual inadequacy, she, too, will be diverted away from heterosexual objects, since the male genitalia reminds her of her own failings. In 1962, Bieber *et al.,* (1962) published the results of their extensive clinical study of 106 homosexual patients and 100 heterosexual controls that confirmed the psychoanalytic view that fear of heterosexuality is the underlying cause of homosexuality. They found disturbed relations between parents, mothers who were overprotective and seductive toward their sons and who communicated negative attitudes for this male role, and fathers who were weak, distant and resentful toward their sons. These family patterns were similar to what psychoanalytic theorists would describe as oedipal problems conducive to the development of homosexuality in males. Seven years later, using different subjects and different measures, Evans (1969) replicated many of the earlier findings, adding further credibility to the psychoanalytic view.

Social learning theory regards homosexuality as a learned sexual preference or orientation that stems from past experiences (direct or symbolic) in sexual arousal and satisfaction with members of the same sex. Although other factors may also contribute, the precondition for a homosexual orientation is either "positive attraction to, or experience with, members of one's own sex" (Freedman, 1971). If a male, for example, tends to avoid females because of repeated rejections, and he pairs this avoidance with sexual gratification from another

male, then the circumstances will likely foster a homosexual orientation.

Recently, some ethical questions about the treatment of homosexuality have been raised that focus on the division of opinion as to whether or not the behavior is abnormal, and the subsequent issue of whether or not the behavior should be treated (Bieber, 1976; Davison, 1976; Halleck, 1976). The most judicious and ethical position a therapist can take is one in which treatment goals are determined by the client and not the therapist. Whether the person either wants to move in the direction of heterosexual relations or wishes to be more comfortable with and accepting of his or her homosexuality, the facilitative role of the therapist must be the same for both alternatives. Obviously, homosexuals who are relatively free of anxiety, conflicts, and adjustment problems and who function effectively in their daily lives are no more in need of therapy than heterosexuals of the same description. Those who do voluntarily seek professional help are usually more troubled by the anxieties and difficulties of adjusting to two societies (gay and straight), the fear of discovery, the loss of a lover or a sex partner, or some unrelated problem, than they are about their overt homosexual behaviors. Fewer homosexuals want to change their sexual orientation, and for those who are truly motivated, only between one-fourth to one-third become exclusively heterosexual after several years of psychoanalysis or group psychotherapy (Bieber et al., 1962; Massett, 1969; Hadden, 1972). Even these few successes are probably exaggerated since they were based on reports of the clients and the therapist's clinical evaluation at the termination of treatment without follow-up and with clients who had previously engaged in some heterosexual activities.

Behavior therapy, especially aversive conditioning, has been used with subjects who wished to change from homosexuality to heterosexual behaviors with "good" success, although the numbers of treated cases are small and no follow-up data are available to assess the long-term effectiveness of the treatment (Lamberd, 1969; Mandel, 1970; McConaghy, 1971). Although we don't have any information about the treatment outcome for those homosexuals who entered therapy for problems other than their sexual orientation, there is no reason to suppose that their rate of therapeutic success is any different from that of heterosexual clients presenting similar difficulties.

Suicide

Problems of adolescents and college students that have been discussed so far, plus many others, may all play a role in the grim matter of suicide. There is always grief and tragedy surrounding death, but no death is so devastating, so puzzling, and so lamentable as that of the child who willingly takes his or her life. For most of us, life is precious and worth living, yet every half hour one American intentionally commits suicide. Self-destruction is the seventh leading cause of death among people of all ages in this country. But even more striking is the fact that it ranks fourth among adolescents between the ages of fifteen and nineteen, and it is assuming greater importance as deaths from other causes decline (Knott, 1973; McAnarney, 1975). In this age group, suicide is exceeded only by accidents, malignant neoplasms, and homicide, whereas among college students it is second to accidents and two times higher than in the same-aged youngsters who are not attending college (Knott, 1973; McAnarney,

1975). Moreover, studies have shown that students enrolled in the most prestigious universities (Yale, Harvard, Oxford, and Cambridge) have higher suicide rates than those attending lower ranked schools, although those who take their own lives tend to have better academic records than their peers (Ross, 1969; Seiden, 1969; McCulloch and Philip, 1972).

In 1972, the rate of suicides for those between the ages of fifteen and twenty-four was ten per 100,000, less than one per 100,000 for ten- to fourteen-year-olds, and almost nonexistent in children under ten *(Monthly Vital Statistics Report: Annual Summary for the United States, 1972,* published 1973). At all ages, more males take their own lives than females by a ratio of almost 3:1, although females greatly outnumber males in terms of suicidal attempts (Toolan, 1968). Self-destruction is not the exclusive behavior of any particular socioeconomic or educational level, religion, or occupation. However, the suicide rate seems to be higher in middle and upper classes than in the lower socioeconomic class, in urban rather than in rural dwellers, in Caucasians than in blacks, in the higher educated professional and student populations, and among Protestants as compared to Jews and Catholics. However, there is some recent indication that suicide is on the increase for young black males and females living in large urban centers as well as for divorced persons of both sexes (Morris, Kovacs, Beck, and Wolffe, 1974; Schneer, Perstein, and Brozovsky, 1975). Suicide among children aged eight to seventeen tends to occur most frequently during the spring, although this seasonal relationship is independent of temperature, humidity, wind or weather conditions (Mulcock, 1955; Porkorny, Davis, and Haberson, 1963).

For children between ten and fourteen

the preferred method of suicide is hanging and strangulation, while fifteen to nineteen year olds most often use firearms and explosives, followed in frequency by poisoning and strangulation. More girls in the older group used poison than boys (Bakwin and Bakwin, 1972), and this may, in part, explain the reversal of the sex ratio in attempted and actual suicides. Boys, who are more successful than girls in killing themselves, are inclined to use the more masculine firearms as their means of suicide. Consequently, they have less chance of survival or of being found before death occurs, whereas girls may have a higher attempted suicide rate than boys because they prefer poisons, which act slower and increase the possibility of their survival.

Most observers agree that suicide figures, particularly among children, are underestimated because the criteria used by coroners in reporting the official cause of death differ widely, and because families and others involved tend to protect the living (and the dead child) from the guilt and social stigma that such an event usually brings. In addition, self-destructive behavior may be expressed in ways that are not easily categorized as suicidal as may be the case with some car accidents by reckless drivers, overdose of drugs, or those homicide victims who have precipitated and provoked their own murder (Schuyler, 1973). When instances of attempted suicide are considered, the magnitude of the problem is even greater. It has been estimated that for every successful adult suicide there are approximately eight to ten unsuccessful attempts, while the ratio dramatically jumps to as high as 1:120 for teenagers (Finch, and Poznanski, 1971; Kreitman, 1972).

Apart from the essential condition of life or death, the difference between attempted and actual suicide is often a fortuitous matter that is dependent on the subject's lethal intent, and the care with which the self destruction is planned and carried out. The act of suicide is not as much a wish to die as it is a desperate response to the utter futility of life and its unalterable and intolerable circumstances. Were it only possible to find a solution to their problems, many would readily choose to live rather than die. In this connection, Coleman (1972) refers to an unpublished report by Farberow and Litman (1970) in which the following three types of suicidal behavior are described:

1. Those who use suicide as a way of communicating their distress to others, but not as an actual wish to die. This behavior represents about two thirds of the suicide population in which suicidal attempts are minor and arranged to be interrupted (although sometimes the plan backfires).
2. This group comprises another thirty percent of the suicide population, and it represents those who are ambivalent about death and who rely on chance or fate to determine the final outcome of their suicidal behavior. Dangerous but slow acting methods of suicide are characteristically used by these individuals.
3. This is the smallest group, consisting of about three to five percent of the suicide population and involving individuals who are intent on killing themselves. Little or no opportunity for interruption is left open, and the most certain and instant means of death are chosen such as shooting or jumping from tall buildings.

It is clear from Farberow and Litman's descriptive account that better than ninety-five percent of suicidal acts are committed with some wish to live. Many attempts are either interrupted or aborted, but among those who have attempted suicide, approximately ten percent eventually are successful (*Prevention of Suicide*, 1968).

Suicide and Abnormal Behavior

While it is true that suicide is more prevalent in those who manifest abnormal behavior, it should be noted that the two are separate and distinct entities (Wolfe and Cotler, 1973; Schneer et al., 1975). Suicides can and do occur in persons who otherwise show no evidence of classifiable psychopathology, and it is also apparent that not all those who have a diagnosable abnormal disorder evidence suicidal inclinations. Nevertheless, most of us are apt to explain acts of suicide as irrational, seemingly the product of a disordered and troubled mind.

For adults, the evidence indicates that former inmates of mental hospitals have a far greater risk of suicide than can be expected in the population at large, and that fifteen percent of those who have been diagnosed with one of the affective psychoses die by their own hand. Higher rates (but not as high as the affective disorders) are also found in schizophrenics, organics, alcoholics, sociopaths, and psychoneurotics (Osmond and Hoffer, 1967; *Prevention of Suicide,* 1968; Lester and Lester, 1971; Goodwin, 1973). As many as fifty percent of all actual suicides are committed by persons who are suffering from some form of depression (Choron, 1972). As a general rule, suicidal attempts are more likely to occur in neurotics, while completed suicides are more apt to be found among psychotic individuals (Lester and Lester, 1971).

In contrast, the relationship between suicide and abnormal disorders is less clear among children and adolescents than among adults. Except for psychotic youngsters, most adolescents who make suicidal attempts do not evidence discernible changes in behavior that would serve as a reliable warning to those around them (Otto, 1964; Sanborn, Sanborn, and Cimbolic, 1973). For that matter, there is nothing especially significant about the events or circumstances that precipitate the adolescent's suicide in that these are often stressors that are common during this age period, such as a quarrel with a parent, sibling, or friend, or the sudden dissolving of a romantic relationship. In addition, as noted in Chapter 11, depression in children and adolescents tends to be overlooked or undiagnosed because it represents a disorder that many do not expect to find in young people and because the clinical picture is less clear than it is with adults. The sharp and sudden mood swings and the emotional lability that characterize the adolescent often serves to mask depressive episodes to the point where only instances of the most profound symptoms of loss of appetite, sleep difficulties, and social withdrawal are readily recognized. Behavioral equivalents of depression in teenagers may be truancy, somatic preoccupation, restlessness, and antisocial acting out. Among those adolescents who have attempted suicide, approximately forty percent showed depressive symptoms (Mattsson, Seese, and Hawkins, 1969). Psychotic youngsters who attempt suicide are more apt to give no warning, use more serious lethal methods, and show the greatest risk during the first year of their disorder or during an acute psychotic episode. Probably the largest group of teenagers manifesting suicidal behavior are those impulse ridden, angry, and revengeful youngsters who are unable to adequately cope with a variety of psychological and social problems. They often are manipulative and when angry they threaten either homicide and/or suicide (Finch and Poznanski, 1971).

Etiological Considerations

Suicidal behavior is puzzling and difficult to explain. As noted above, some emphasize psychopathology as the primary and underlying cause, but surely this is not a sufficient explanation in that it neither accounts for those emotionally disturbed individuals who do not try to kill themselves nor for those who are not disordered but do attempt suicide. The popular idea that genetic factors are implicated in suicide has not been empirically supported (Kallmann, DePorte, DePorte, and Feingold, 1949), while the only biological variable found to be positively related to suicidal behavior, premenstrual and menstrual cycle, fails to provide an unequivocal interpretation (Mandell and Mandell, 1967; Tonks, Rack, and Rose, 1968). The relationship may be viewed as either implicating hormonal factors, or supportive of a psychogenic position in which premenstrual and menstrual tensions serve to heighten emotional stress.

In the main, investigators have focused their attention on psychological and social variables in their search to understand the etiology of suicide. Many psychological studies and clinical reports have been influenced by the Freudian notion that suicide represents repressed aggression that is turned inward either from the death instinct (thanatos), or from the loss of a love object for whom there are ambivalent feelings. To be sure, it can be argued that suicide is an act of aggression against oneself, but to do so in psychoanalytic terms is to make inferences about the unconscious motivation of the victim. This is not easily tested or demonstrated because data cannot be obtained from those who have been successful, and because of the more inherent difficulty in uncovering information that is presumed to be out of the awareness of the subject. Nevertheless, it is not surprising that studies have been undertaken within the psychoanalytic and later within a learning orientation that attend to the relationship between early childhood experiences and suicidal behavior. Parental loss either through death, separation, divorce, or desertion and its relationship to attempted and completed suicide has yielded conflicting results, although the data from recent studies of college students and adolescents strongly suggest that parental loss by age sixteen is an important factor in the development of suicidal tendencies and is a very important variable in producing suicide (Jacobs and Teicher, 1967; Jacobs, 1971; Lester, 1972; Wolfe and Cotler, 1973, Adams, Lohrenz, and Harper, 1973, Knott, 1973). Families of low socioeconomic adolescent boys who had attempted suicide were clinically studied by Margolin and Teicher (1968), who found that the boys were unwanted babies and that their mothers were angry, depressed, and withdrawn before and after pregnancy. Moreover, the boys were deprived of maternal affection and attention during the first year of life and experienced loss of father sometime before age four or five. Frequently the boys acted as heads of their households and as husbands to their mothers, but maternal love was not reciprocated. Attempt at suicide often came at a time when mother was depressed and withdrawn, and when the boy experienced maternal rejection or loss of her love. However, we must keep in mind that these findings exemplify much of the clinical literature where impressions are reported in the absence of adequate control groups and data analysis.

Another line of psychological research

has been attempts to determine personality correlates of suicidal behavior. Studies have shown that adolescents who attempt suicide are more irritable and impulsive, more negative about themselves, and more apt to be rigid thinkers, to be involved in conflict situations, and to have communication problems than their nonsuicidal counterparts (Jacobs, 1971; Lester and Lester, 1971; Levenson, 1974). In addition, these youngsters characteristically tend to use sleep as an escape from problems, although insomnia frequently appears as a presuicidal symptom (Lester and Lester, 1971).

Toolan (1968) studied a sample of 102 children (mostly adolescents) who were admitted to Bellevue Hospital in New York City for either suicide attempts or threats, and he found that most were immature and impulsive and diagnosed as having behavior and character disorders. On the basis of his clinical examination of these records, he arrived at the following five categories of causes: (1) internalized anger at another, (2) manipulative attempts either to gain love or to punish others, (3) a cry for help and a distress signal, (4) a psychotic-like reaction to inner disintegration, and (5) a wish to join a dead relative. More recently, Jacobs (1971) postulated a sequence of etiological steps regarding adolescent suicide, which includes a chronic history of problems throughout childhood to the beginning of adolescence, an increase in problems beyond that which is normally associated with the period of adolescence, progressive failure of the coping mechanisms to deal with the rise in problems, withdrawal and feelings of despair prior to the suicide attempt, and finally the rationalization (justification) of suicide to narrow the discrepancy between the suicidal thought and action.

Among college students, suicidal behavior has been attributed to a number of stressors that are particularly prominent during these years of schooling. Knight (1968) described fear of homosexuality, identity confusion, separation anxiety (resolving dependency while thrust into independent functioning), depression, fear of academic failure, and conflicts over the expression of aggressive feelings as potential determinants of suicidal acts in students. Knott (1973) found that students who attempted suicide reported feelings of rejection, hopelessness, self-blame, and evidenced more somatic complaints related to their emotional discomfort (headaches) than did control subjects. Suicidal students more frequently than nonsuicidal ones come from families in which there are a greater number of divorces, separations during childhood, and death of a parent, and their families are highly educated, suggesting the possibility that they are under more pressure to achieve academically (Blaine and Carmen, 1968; Adams et al., 1973). In addition, more suicide attempts are made by freshman than older students, and certain aspects of the college environment such as "impoverished interpersonal relationships, and intense, competitive atmosphere" are related to suicidal gestures (Wolfe and Cotler, 1973; Knott, 1973, p. 68).

Studies of the social variables involved in suicidal behavior have been influenced greatly by Durkheim's sociological view of suicide (Durkheim, 1951). Based on his analysis of suicide records obtained in different countries, Durkheim posited that suicidal behavior is common in societies where there is a high and a low degree of social integration and social regulation. Societies with a moderate degree of both social integration and regulation have the lowest incidence of suicide. For example, suicide is higher among divorced, widowed, and single individuals, and lower among those who are married, that is, higher for those who have a low degree of social integration than those who have maintained group ties. However, a high degree of group identification, such as evidenced by the Japanese during World War II and the Buddhist monks of Vietnam, is likely to heighten the suicide rate, as was the case of hari-kari and monks burning themselves in protest to the policies of the Vietnamese government. In addition, when group standards or norms decline in their social regulatory influence (anomie), such as in periods of economic depression or social revolution, the incidence of suicide is likely to be high. Using data from a sample of fifty-five societies, Rootman (1973) found that social integration may be more important than social regulation as a determinant of suicidal rates.

The major problem with Durkheim's theory is similar to the one encountered with other sociological views, namely, that it does not account for the different behaviors of individuals who have been exposed to the same demands and conditions of a given society. Nevertheless, the research dealing with the relationship between social variables and suicidal acts has shown that when group condemnation of suicide is high, the incidence is low (Catholics have a very low rate of suicide behavior). Moreover, unemployment carries a greater risk of completed suicides, and both low and high occupational status have a high incidence of suicide (Farber, 1968; Tuckman and Youngman, 1968; Ravensborg and Foss, 1969; Stengel, 1970). In addition, suicide seems to be negatively related to the state of the economy, and positively correlated to social disorganization as reflected in the instability introduced into the social system of a mental hospital by an in-

flux of new patients and staff (Kahne, 1968; Simon, 1968).

As research continues, it is clear that the data currently available do not provide any systematic or satisfactory answer to the perplexing question of why people try to kill themselves. Much emphasis is now placed on the matter of prevention.

Prevention Approaches

One obvious approach to prevention is to devise a method whereby individuals who are suicidal risks can be successfully identified. Psychologists have, in fact, addressed themselves to this issue in their attempts either to use existing tests such as the MMPI, the Rorschach, and the TAT, or to construct new instruments specifically designed for this purpose. Lester (1970) provides us with a good review of the literature in which he notes that many studies have methodological limitations, in addition to the more obvious problems of finding individuals to test prior to, rather than following their suicidal acts, and of securing adequate data from those who have been successful in their suicide attempts. Lester concludes that the TAT, Bender-Gestalt, Semantic Differential, and the Rosenzweig Picture-Frustration Test were of little or no value in identifying suicidal risks, whereas the use of the sign approach with the Rorschach and profile analysis with the MMPI showed promise. New and specially designed tests have not proved useful in identifying suicidal risks, or in discriminating those who have threatened from those who have attempted suicide. A more recent study by Resnik and Kendra (1973) found that the Scale for Assessing Suicidal Risk failed to identify suicide risk potential among hospitalized patients who attempted suicide.

The second major preventive thrust, the crisis intervention approach, is probably well known among laypersons in that almost every major community in the country operates such a program. In general, crisis intervention is not intended to provide long-term treatment for problems. Rather, its central focus is on intervention and referral. Crisis centers never close, and individuals may make contact either by phone or in person at any hour of the day or night, seven days a week. They usually are staffed by medical personnel who provide emergency medical treatment, and other trained personnel who deal with psychological problems. Counselors attempt to establish rapport with the client to maintain contact and obtain information about the specific nature of the current problem. At the same time, they assess the potential suicidal risk and the strengths of the client and other resources. To the extent possible, counselors and other members of the staff help formulate a constructive plan of action for the client, as well as try to mobilize the client to follow their recommendations.

Although there is both public and professional support for the value and effectiveness of crisis intervention centers, there is, in fact, little evaluative data available to date. The few studies that have attempted to compare suicide rates in communities with and without crisis programs have produced conflicting and not overly supportive results; and studies, that have tried to evaluate the effectiveness of some centers in reducing suicide, have shown increases in suicide or additional suicidal attempts in twenty percent of those intensely treated (Weiner, 1969; Bagley, 1971).

With respect to college students, Albert, Forman, and Masik (1973) suggest the following five steps by which the potential suicide might be identified and helped:

(1) assign every freshman to a faculty or older student advisor who would be responsible for helping the student with both academic and extra-academic matters, (2) provide special tutoring as a regular service to students in academic difficulties, (3) make available an ombudsman to help students on an individual basis with the complex impersonal aspects of the college, (4) sensitize the college medical facility (student health service) to the emotional components and needs of students with medical problems, and (5) make available competent counseling to all students wishing help on an immediate and anonymous basis. However, as untried as they are, these suggestions would move colleges back into an *in loco parentis* policy from which they are moving away, and it would add additional costs to an already financially strained student and family. Moreover, since some of these measures (if not all at some colleges) have been functional for years, it would be advisable to compare the suicide attempts and successes at schools with and without these services to obtain a more empirical view of what might be effective (if any of these services can be) in reducing these rates.

Summary

The college years were highlighted in this chapter as a period in which young people are exposed to certain stressful conditions that may affect their present and future adjustment. Three potential sources of stress were selected for discussion: those of dependence-independence, academic pressures and career goals, and peer relationships. In addition, even more extensive coverage was given to the areas of sexuality and suicide, because they represent either potential or real problems that are of special significance for this age group.

The nature of dependence-independence as a single personality continuum and the factors that determine where a person falls on the continuum were discussed. The extent to which college fosters independence and maturity or serves as stressful circumstances leading to maladaptive behavior, depends largely on the students' prior experiences and successes in independently managing their own affairs.

Academic pressures and career choice are primary concerns of students, who often struggle to meet parental and self-expectations for high academic achievement, and who are frustrated toward this end by heavy academic demands, a limited post-college job market, and a scarcity of places in professional and graduate programs. These stressful circumstances may adversely affect academic performance, especially in students for whom the need to achieve is strong. Poor or disappointing academic achievement may promote additional anxiety, feelings of inadequacy, guilt, and a sense of alienation from others which in turn may lead to temporary but extraordinary measures to recover. Failure to catch up may bring despair, despondency, withdrawal, and difficulty in coping adequately with other areas of one's life.

For entering college students, peer relationships are potent sources of stress. Research data show that acceptance by a peer model can influence positively the scholastic performance of underachieving students. Students also seek peer relationships with those who are most similar to themselves, and this personal attraction is more effective in producing modeling behaviors than those who are seen as dissimilar.

Sexual attitudes and behaviors among youth are discrepant, but less so at present than in the past. Substantial changes in sexual attitudes have occurred among youth and especially among young women who now seem to reject the double standard. Within the last two decades, both young men and women have become more liberal in their attitudes toward premarital, extramarital, and homosexual relationships, although large numbers of college men still hold on to their preference to marry a virgin. Sexual attitudes vary with age, race, strength of religious belief, socioeconomic level, and region of the country.

In terms of sexual behaviors, the findings since Kinsey's work show that premarital sex has increased slightly for men and dramatically for women. Premarital sex for college women has increased sharply over the last two decades to the point where both sexes are now very similar to each other in their sexual behaviors.

Two problems associated with coitus, premature ejaculation in the male and orgasmic dysfunction in the female, were discussed, because they represent the most frequent sources of anxiety and dissatisfaction for both sexual partners. Premature ejaculation was defined, described, and discussed in light of its devastating effects on the male's self-image and on his sexual partner. Etiological factors were noted, and the "squeeze technique" of Masters and Johnson, claiming a 97.8% success rate, was described as the most effective treatment for premature ejaculation.

Orgasmic dysfunction was defined and described as a common problem among women. Psychogenic factors as well as biological causes were discussed. A treatment method was described which claims a success rate of eighty-three percent for primary orgasmic dysfunction and seventy-seven percent for secondary cases.

Homosexuality (overt sexual relations between members of the same sex) has not changed appreciably since Kinsey's research, although more liberal and permissive attitudes toward this sexual practice are now evident. Genetic and biochemical factors do not seem to be major causal links to homosexuality. Psychogenic views including psychoanalytic interpretations and social learning postulates were discussed as more viable determinants of homosexuality. Treatment of homosexuality raises the ethical questions of whether or not the behavior is abnormal, and the subsequent issue of whether or not the behavior should be treated.

Suicide ranks fourth as a cause of death for adolescents between the ages of fifteen and nineteen, and only second to accidents among college students. It seems to be higher in the middle and upper classes, in urban dwellers, in Caucasians, in educated professional and student populations, and among Protestants. For children between ten and fourteen the preferred method of suicide is hanging and strangulation, while fifteen to nineteen year olds prefer guns. Boys have a higher incidence of completed suicides and girls have a higher attempted suicide rate.

Suicide is not always attributable to abnormal conditions, but in fact these are two separate and distinct entities. The relationship between suicide and abnormal disorders is less clear among children and adolescents than among adults. There is nothing discernible about the precipitating events and circumstances of adolescent suicide, and depression in youngsters tends to be overlooked and undiagnosed.

Genetic factors are not implicated as a cause of suicide, and other than a relationship between menstrual cycle and suicide, there are no significant biological variables as yet uncovered. The major emphasis has been on psychological and social variables in the search to understand the etiology of suicide.

Preventive approaches to suicide have taken two major courses: the construction of psychometric devices to identify those individuals who are suicidal risks, and the crisis intervention programs that aim to prevent suicide by providing support and assistance during times of personal crisis. Neither approach has, as yet, demonstrated effectiveness.

Epilogue

Susan's case illustrates the use of a multiple treatment plan that included environmental manipulation, individual psychotherapy, weight control, and group psychotherapy to help her achieve her goals of improving her academic performance, self-image, and social and interpersonal relationships. With the aid of the psychologists, she was permitted to withdraw (without penalty) from one academic course to lighten the stress of the scholastic demands that she could not realistically hope to meet. In addition, her therapist helped her to focus on what she needed to do for the remaining courses and showed her how she could budget her time to meet these requirements. Susan's level of anxiety promptly decreased as these initial steps were taken, probably because her previously thwarted dependency needs were at last being satisfied and because she was beginning to see that her high achievement aspirations could be realized. With reduced anxiety and a goal within her grasp, Susan felt freer to begin the process of looking at herself, of examining her feelings, and of resolving conflicts about herself and with members of her family.

In the course of individual psychotherapy, Susan became less dependent and more active and responsible for her own affairs. She managed to catch up with her academic assignments and diligently kept up with them on a daily basis. Her confidence grew as she successfully pulled all of her grades up to within the B to A range. She decided to lose weight and to join a Weight Watchers program to improve her appearance, which would enable her to pursue more effective relationships with boys and girls. At about this time, she and her therapist agreed that she was ready to participate in group therapy on a weekly basis, while continuing in psychotherapy biweekly.

Susan's program was rapid and remarkable in that she lost thirty pounds, bought new clothes, changed her hair-do, and transformed herself into an extremely attractive young girl. Boys were asking her out and her relationships with the girls in the dormitory has improved considerably. She became popular, friendly, more outgoing, and much more sensitive to the feelings and needs of others. Her academic performance by the end of the school year showed great improvement from borderline grades to almost a straight A average. Susan's self-confidence grew with every success. She came to recognize that she was not homosexual, but that it was all right for her to have deep affectionate feelings for her roommate. She went home at the end of the spring term feeling happy, self-assured, and eager to return in the fall.

REFERENCES

ACOSTA, F. Z. "Etiology and Treatment of Homosexuality: A Review." *Archives of Sexual Behavior,* 1975, *4,* 9–29.

ADAM, K. S., LOHRENZ, J. G., and D. HARPER. "Suicidal Ideation and Parental Loss: A Preliminary Research Report." *Canadian Psychiatric Association Journal,* 1973, *18,* 95–100.

ALBERT, G., FORMAN, N., and L. MASIK. "Attacking the College Suicide Problem." *Journal of Contemporary Psychotherapy,* 1973, *6,* 70–78.

ANNON, J. S. *The Therapeutic Use of Masturbation in the Treatment of Sexual Disorders.* Paper presented at the Fifth Annual Meeting of the Association for the Advancement of Behavior Therapy, Washington, D.C., 1971.

BAGLEY, C. "An Evaluation of Suicide Prevention Agencies." *Life Threatening Behavior,* 1971, *1,* 245–259.

BAKWIN, H. and R. M. BAKWIN. *Behavior Disorders in Children* (4th ed.). Philadelphia: Saunders, 1972.

BALL, J. C. and N. LOGAN. "Early Sexual Behavior of Lower-Class Delinquent Girls." In Shiloh, A. (Ed.), *Studies in Human Sexual Behavior: The American Scene.* Springfield, Illinois: Charles C Thomas, 1970, pp. 190–199.

BELL, R. R. *Marriage and Family Interaction.* Homewood, Illinois: Dorsey Press, 1971.

BELL, R. R. and J. B. CHASKES. "Premarital Sexual Experience among Coeds, 1958 and 1968." *Journal of Marriage and the Family,* 1970, *32,* 81–84.

BENTLER, P. M. "Heterosexual Behavior Assessment-I. Males." *Behavior Research and Therapy,* 1968a, *6,* 21–25.

BENTLER, P. M. "Heterosexual Behavior Assessment-II: Females." *Behavior Research and Therapy,* 1968b, *6,* 27–30.

BIEBER, I. "A Discussion of 'Homosexuality: The Ethical Challenge.' " *Journal of Consulting and Clinicial Psychology,* 1976, *44,* 163–166.

BIEBER, I., DAIN, H. J., DINCE, P. R., DRELLICH, M. G., GRAND, H. C., GUNDLACH, R. H., KREMER, M. H., RIFKIN, A. H., WILBUR, C. B., and T. B. BIEBER. *Homosexuality: A Psychoanalytic Study.* New York: Random House, 1962.

BISHOP, J. B. and G. S. SNYDER. "Commuters and Residents: Pressures, Helps, and Psychological Services." *Journal of College Student Personnel,* 1976, *17,* 232–235.

BLAINE, G. B., JR., and L. R. CARMEN. "Causal Factors in Suicidal Attempts by Male and Female College Students." *American Journal of Psychiatry,* 1968, *125,* 834–837.

BULLOUGH, V. L. "Sex and the Medical Model." In Byrne, D., and L. A. Byrne (Eds.), *Exploring Human Sexuality.* New York: Crowell, 1977, pp. 380–390.

BYRNE, D. and L. A. BYRNE (Eds.). *Exploring Human Sexuality.* New York: Crowell, 1977, p. 194.

BYRNE, D. and G. L. CLORE, JR. "Effectance Arousal and Attractions." *Journal of Personality and Social Psychology Monograph,* Part 2, 1967, *6,* 1–18.

BYRNE, D. and W. GRIFFITT. "A Developmental Investigation of the Law of Attraction." *Journal of Personality and Social Psychology,* 1966, *4,* 699–702.

"Campus '65." *Newsweek,* March 22, 1965, 43–54.

CANNON, K. L. and R. LONG. "Premarital Sexual Behavior in the Sixties." *Journal of Marriage and the Family,* 1971, *33,* 36–49.

CHORON, J. *Suicide.* New York: Scribner, 1972.

CHRISTENSEN, H. T., and C. F. GREGG. "Changing Sex Norms in America and Scandinavia." *Journal of Marriage and the Family,* 1970, *32,* 616–627.

CHRISTENSEN, H. T., and K. P. JOHNSEN. *Marriage and the Family.* New York: Ronald Press, 1971.

COLEMAN, J. C. *Abnormal Psychology and Modern Life* (4th ed.). Chicago: Scott, Foresman, 1972.

CURRAN, J. P. "Convergence Toward a Single Sexual Standard?" In D. Byrne and L. A. Byrne (Eds.), *Exploring Human Sexuality.* New York: Crowell, 1977, pp. 194–200.

CURRAN, J. P., NEFF, S., and S. LIPPOLD. "Correlates of Sexual Experience among University Students." *Journal of Sex Research,* 1973, *9,* 124–131.

DAVIS, J. F. and C. WILLIAMS. "Parents–Students: Split Heirs." *Journal of College Student Personnel,* 1974, *15,* 49–52.

DAVIS, K. E. "Sex on Campus: Is There a Revolution?" *Medical Aspects of Human Sexuality,* 1971, January, 128–142.

DAVISON, G. C. "Homosexuality: The Ethical Challenge." *Journal of Consulting and Clinical Psychology,* 1976, *44,* 157–162.

DEVINE, H. G. and L. C. LOESCH. "In Loco Parentis and the New Age of Majority: The Views of Freshman and Their Parents." *Journal of College Student Personnel,* 1976, *17,* 420–425.

DREYER, P. H. "Sex, Sex Roles, and Marriage among Youth in the 1970s." In Havighurst, R. J. and P. H. Dreyer (Eds.), *Youth.* Chicago: The National Society for the Study of Education, 1975, pp. 194–223.

DURKHEIM, E. *Le Suicide.* Paris: Librarie Felix Alcan (1897). Spaulding, J. A. and G. Simpson (Trs.). Glencoe, Illinois: Free Press, 1951.

EDWARDS, D. A. *Survey of Sexual Behavior of College Students Enrolled in a Course of Human Sexuality.* Unpublished survey, Emory University, Winter Quarter, 1977.

ELLIS, A. "Frigidity." In Ellis, A. and A. Abarbanel (Eds.), *The Encyclopedia of Sexual Behavior* (Vol. 1). New York: Hawthorn Books, 1961, 450–456.

ENGLE, K. B., DAVIS, D. A., and G. E. MAZER. "Interpersonal Effects on Underachievers." *Journal of Educational Research,* 1968, *61,* 208–210.

EVANS, R. B. "Childhood Parental Relationships of Homosexual Men." *Journal of Consulting and Clinical Psychology,* 1969, *33,* 129–135.

FARBER, M. L. *Theory of Suicide.* New York: Funk and Wagnalls, 1968.

FARBEROW, N. L. and R. E. LITMAN. *A Comprehensive Suicide Prevention Program.* Suicide Prevention Center of Los Angeles, 1958–1969, Unpublished final report, Department of Health, Education and Welfare, NIMH Grants No. MH 14946 and MH 00128. Los Angeles, 1970.

FARNSWORTH, D. L. "Sexual Morality and the Dilemma of the Colleges." *Medical Aspects of Human Sexuality,* 1970, October, 64–94.

FARNSWORTH, D. L. "The Young Adult: An Overview." *The American Journal of Psychiatry,* 1974, *131*:8, 845–851.

FELDMAN, K. A. and T. M. NEWCOMB. *The Impact of College Students: Volume I. An Analysis of Four Decades of Research.* San Francisco: Jossey-Bass, 1969.

FENICHEL, O. *The Psychoanalytic Theory of Neurosis.* New York: Norton, 1945.

FERGUSON, L. R. "Dependency Motivation in Socialization." In Hoppe, R. A., Milton, A. G. and E. C. Simmel (Eds.), *Early Experiences and the Processes of Socialization.* New York: Academic Press, 1970, 59–80.

FINCH, S. M. and E. O. POZNANSKI. *Adolescent Suicide.* Springfield, Illinois: Charles C Thomas, 1971.

FISHER, S. *The Female Orgasm: Psychology, Physiology, Fantasy.* New York: Basic Books, 1973.

FREEDMAN, M. *Homosexuality and Psychological Functioning.* Belmont, California: Brooks/Cole, 1971.

GOODWIN, D. W. "Alcohol in Suicide and Homicide." *Quarterly Journal of Studies on Alcohol,* 1973, *34,* 144–156.

GREEN, R. *Sexual Identity Conflict in Children and Adults.* New York: Basic Books, 1974.

HADDEN, S. B. "Group Psychotherapy with Homosexual Men." In Resnick, H. L. P. and M. E. Wolfgang (Eds.), *Sexual Behaviors; Social, Clinical, and Legal Aspects.* Boston: Little, Brown, 1972, 267–280.

HALLECK, S. L. "Another Response to 'Homosexuality: The Ethical Challenge.'" *Journal of Consulting and Clinical Psychology,* 1976, *44,* 167–170.

HAYNES, S. N. and L. J. OZIEL. "Homosexuality: Behavior and Attitudes." *Archives of Sexual Behavior,* 1976, *5,* 283–289.

HITE, S. *The Hite Report:* A Nationwide Study on Female Sexuality. New York: Dell, 1977.

HOMSTROM, E. I. "Low Achievers: Do They Differ from 'Typical' Undergraduates?" *American Council of Educators Research Reports,* 1973, *8,* No. 6, 1–44.

HUNT, M. M. *Sexual Behavior in the 1970s.* Chicago: Playboy Press, 1974, pp. 19–24, 31–38.

HUTT, R. L. and W. E. SEDLACEK. "Freshman Sexual Attitudes and Behavior." *Journal of College Student Personnel,* 1974, *15,* 346–351.

JACKSON, M. C. and D. DEPUYDT. "Community Service: An Adjustment Motif for Minority Students." *Journal of Non-White Concerns in Personnel and Guidance,* 1974, *2,* 94–97.

JACOBS, J. *Adolescent Suicide.* New York: Wiley-Interscience, 1971.

JACOBS, J. and J. D. TEICHER. "Broken Homes and Social Isolation in Attempted Suicides of Adolescents." *International Journal of Social Psychiatry,* 1967, *13,* 139–149.

KAATS, G. R. and K. E. DAVIS. "The Dynamics of Sexual Behavior of College Students." *Journal of Marriage and the Family,* 1970, *32,* 390–399.

KAHNE, M. J. "Suicides in Mental Hospitals: A Study of the Effects of Personnel and Patient Turnover." *Journal of Health and Social Behavior,* 1968, *9,* 255–266.

KALLMAN, F. J., DEPORTE, J., DEPORTE, E., and L. FEINGOLD. "Suicide in Twins and Only Children." *American Journal of Human Genetics,* 1949, *1,* 113–126.

KALLMANN, F. J. "Twin and Sibship Study of Overt Male Homosexuality." *American Journal of Human Genetics,* 1952, *4,* 136–146.

KANTNER, J. F. and M. ZELNICK. "Contraception and Pregnancy: Experience of Young Unmarried Women in the United States." *Family Planning Perspectives,* 1973, *5,* 21–35.

KAPLAN, H. S., KOHL, R. N., POMEROY, W. B., OFFIT, A. K., and B. HOGAN. "Group Treatment of Premature Ejaculation." *Archives of Sexual Behavior,* 1974, *3,* 443–452.

KENISTON, K. "Prologue: Youth as a Stage of Life." In Havighurst, R. J. and P. H. Dreyer (Eds.), *Youth:* The Seventy-fourth Yearbook of the National Society for the Study of Education. Chicago: University of Chicago Press, 1975, 3–26.

KINSEY, A. C., POMEROY, W. B., and C. E. MARTIN. *Sexual Behavior in the Human Male.* Philadelphia: Saunders, 1948.

KINSEY, A. C., POMEROY, W., MARTIN, C., and P. GEBHARD. *Sexual Behavior in the Human Female.* Philadelphia: Saunders, 1953.

KNIGHT, J. A. "Suicide among Students." In Resnik, H. L. P. (Ed.), *Suicidal Behaviors: Diagnosis and Management.* Boston: Little, Brown, 1968, pp. 228–240.

KNOPF, I. J. and R. E. FAGER. "Differences in Gradients of Stimulus Generalization as a Function of Psychiatric Disorder." *Journal of Abnormal and Social Psychology,* 1959, *59,* 73–76.

KNOPF, I. J., WORELL, J., and H. D. WOLFF. "Effect of Meprobamate on Stimulus Generalization under Experimental Stress." *Archives of General Psychiatry,* 1959, *1,* 630–633.

KNOTT, J. E. "Campus Suicide in America." *Omega: Journal of Death and Dying,* 1973, *4,* 65–71.

KOLODNY, R. C., MASTERS, W. H., HENDRYZ, J., and G. TORO. "Plasma Testosterone and the Semen Analysis in Male Homosexuals." *New England Journal of Medicine,* 1971, *285,* 1170–1174.

KRAMER, H. C., BERGER, F., and G. MILLER. "Student Concerns and Sources of Assistance." *Journal of College Student Personnel,* 1974, *15,* 389–393.

KREITMAN, N. "Aspects of the Epidemiology of Suicide and 'Attempted Suicide' (Parasuicide)." In Wadenstrom, J., Larsson, T. and N. Ljungstedt (Eds.), *Suicide and Attempted Suicide.* Stockholm: Nordiska Bokhandelns Forlag, 1972, pp. 45–46.

LAMBERD, W. G. "The Treatment of Homosexuality as a Monosymptomatic Phobia." *American Journal of Psychiatry,* 1969, *126,* 512–518.

LESTER, D. "Attempts to Predict Suicidal Risk Using Psychological Tests." *Psychological Bulletin,* 1970, *74,* 1–17.

LESTER, D. *Why People Kill Themselves: A Summary of Research Findings on Suicidal Behavior.* Springfield, Illinois: Charles C Thomas, 1972.

LESTER, G. and D. LESTER. *Suicide: The Gamble with Death.* Englewood Cliffs, New Jersey: Prentice-Hall, 1971.

LEVENSON, M. "Cognitive Correlates of Suicidal Risk." In Neuringer, C. (Ed.), *Psychological Assessment of Suicidal Risk.* Springfield, Illinois: Charles C Thomas, 1974, pp. 150–163.

LoPICCOLO, J., and W. C. LOBITZ. "The Role of Masturbation in the Treatment of Primary Orgasmic Dysfunction." *Archives of Sexual Behavior,* 1972, *2,* 163–171.

LORAINE, J. A., ADAMOPOULOS, D. A., KIRKHAM, K. E., ISMAIL, A. A. A., and G. A. DOVE. "Patterns of Hormone Excretion in Male and Female Homosexuals." *Nature,* 1971, *234,* 552–555.

MAHER, B. A. *Principles of Psychopathology: An Experimental Approach.* New York: McGraw-Hill, 1966.

MALMO, R. B. and P. AMSEL. "Anxiety-Produced Interference in Serial Rote Learning, with Observations on Rote Learning after Partial Frontal Lobectomy." *Journal of Experimental Psychology,* 1948, *38,* 440–454.

MANDEL, K. H. "Preliminary Report on a New Aversion Therapy for Male Homosexuals." *Behavior Research and Therapy,* 1970, *8,* 93–95.

MANDELL, A. J. and M. P. MANDELL. "Suicide and the Menstrual Cycle." *Journal of the American Medical Association,* 1967, *200,* 792–793.

MARGOLIN, N. L. and J. D. TEICHER. "Thirteen Adolescent Male Suicide Attemptors." *Journal of the American Academy of Child Psychiatry,* 1968, 7, 296–315.

MASSETT, L. "Homosexuality: Changes on the Way." *Science News,* 1969, *96*:24, 557–559.

MASTERS, W. H. and V. E. JOHNSON. *Human Sexual Inadequacy.* Boston: Little, Brown, 1970.

MASTERSON, J F. "Adolescents and the Sexual Evolution." *Sexual Behavior,* 1971, June, 3–9.

MATTSSON, A., SEESE, L. R., and J. W. HAWKINS. "Suicidal Behavior as a Child Psychiatric Emergency: Clinical Characteristics and Follow-Up Results." *Archives of General Psychiatry,* 1969, *20,* 100–109.

McANARNEY, E. R. "Suicidal Behavior of Children and Youth." *The Pediatric Clinics of North America,* 1975, *22*:3, 595–604.

McBRIDE, M. C. and K. L. ENDER. "Sexual Attitudes and Sexual Behavior among College Students." *Journal of College Student Personnel,* 1977, *18,* 183–187.

McCANDLESS, B. R. and E. D. EVANS. *Children and Youth: Psychosocial Development.* Hinsdale, Illinois: The Dryden Press, 1973.

McCARY, J. L. *Human Sexuality: Physiological, Psychological, and Sociological Factors* (2nd ed.). New York: Van Nostrand, 1973.

McCONAGHY, N. "Aversive Therapy of Homosexuality: Measure of Efficacy." *American Journal of Psychiatry,* 1971, *127,* 141–144.

McCULLOCH, J. W. and A. E. PHILIP. *Suicidal Behavior.* Oxford: Pergammon Press, 1972.

McGOVERN, K. B., STEWART, R., and J. LoPICCOLO. "Secondary Orgasmic Dysfunction. I. Analysis and Strategies for Treatment." *Archives of Sexual Behavior,* 1975, *4,* 265–275.

McKEACHIE, W. J., POLLIE, D., and J. SPIESMAN. "Relieving Anxiety in Classroom Examinations." *Journal of Abnormal and Social Psychology,* 1955, *50,* 93–100.

MONEY, J. and A. A. EHRHARDT. *Man and Woman, Boy and Girl: The Differentiation and Dimorphism of Gender Identity from Conception to Maturity.* Baltimore: John Hopkins University Press, 1972.

Monthly Vital Statistics Reports: Annual Summary for the United States, 1972. Washington, D.C.: U.S. Department of Health, *21*, June, 1973.

Moos, R. H. and J. Otto. "The Impact of Coed Living on Males and Females." *Journal of College Student Personnel*, 1975, *16*, 459–467.

Morris, J. B., Kovacs, M., Beck, A. T., and A. Wolffe. "Notes Toward an Epidemiology of Urban Suicide." *Comprehensive Psychiatry*, 1974, *15*, 537–547.

Mulcock, D. "Juvenile Suicide." *Medical Officer*, 1955, *94*, 155–160.

Osmond, H., and A. Hoffer. "Schizophrenia and Suicide." *Journal of Schizophrenia*, 1967, *1*, 54–64.

Otto, U. "Changes in the Behavior of Children and Adolescents Preceding Suicidal Attempts." *Acta Psychiatric Scandinavia*, 1964, *40*, 386–400.

Packard, V. O. *The Sexual Wilderness.* New York: McKay, 1968.

Panos, R. J. and A. W. Astin. "Attrition Among College Students." *American Education Research Journal*, 1968, *5*, 57–72.

Petras, J. W. *Sexuality in Society.* Boston: Allyn & Bacon, 1973.

Pokorny, A. D., Davis, F. and W. Harberson. "Suicide, Suicide Attempts and Weather." *American Journal of Psychiatry*, 1963, *120*, 377–381.

Prevention of Suicide. World Health Organization. Public Health Paper No. 35, Geneva, WHO, 1968.

Ravensborg, M. R. and A. Foss. "Suicide and Natural Death in a State Hospital Population: A Comparison of Admission Complaints, MMPI Profiles, and Social Competence Factors." *Journal of Consulting and Clinical Psychology*, 1969, *33*, 466–471.

Reiss, I. L. "The Influence of Contraceptive Knowledge on Premarital Sexuality." *Medical Aspects of Human Sexuality*, February, 1970, 71–86.

Reiss, I. L. "Premarital Sex Codes: The Old and the New." In Grummon, D. L. and A. M. Barclay (Eds.), *Sexuality: A Search for Perspective.* New York: Van Nostrand Reinhold, 1971, pp. 190–203.

Reiss, I. L. *The Social Context of Premarital Sexual Permissiveness.* New York: Holt, Rinehart and Winston, 1967.

Resnick, J. H. and J. M. Kendra. "Predictive Value of the 'Scale for Assessing Suicide Risk' (SASR) with Hospitalized Psychiatric Patients." *Journal of Clinical Psychology*, 1973, *29*, 187–190.

Rootman, I. "A Cross-cultural Note on Durkheim's Theory of Suicide." *Life Threatening Behavior*, 1973, *3*, 83–94.

Rosenbaum, G. "Stimulus Generalization as a Function of Level of Experimentally Induced Anxiety." *Journal of Experimental Psychology*, 1953, *45*, 35–43.

Rosenthal, D. *Genetic Theory and Abnormal Behavior.* New York: McGraw-Hill, 1970.

Ross, M. "Suicide among College Students." *American Journal of Psychiatry*, 1969, *126*, 220–225.

Rubin, I. "New Sex Findings: Some Trends and Implications." In Otto, H. A. (Ed.), *The New Sexuality.* Palo Alto: Science and Behavior Books, 1971, 26–43.

Sanborn, D. E. (III), Sanborn, C. J., and P. Cimbolic. "Two Years of Suicide: A Study of Adolescent Suicide in New Hampshire." *Child Psychiatry and Human Development*, 1973, *3*, 234–242.

SCHNEER, H. I., PERSTEIN, A., and M. BROZOVSKY. "Hospitalized Suicidal Adolescents: Two Generations." *Journal of the American Academy of Child Psychiatry*, 1975, *14*, 268–280.

SCHUYLER, D. "When Was the Last Time You Took a Suicidal Child to Lunch?" *Journal of School Health*, 1973, *43*, 504–506.

SEIDEN, R. H. *Suicide among Youth.* Bulletin of Suicidology Supplement. Washington, D.C.: U.S. Government Printing Office, 1969.

SIMON, J. L. "The Effect of Income on the Suicide Rate: A Paradox Resolved." *American Journal of Sociology*, 1968, *74*, 302–303.

SNYDER, A., LoPICCOLO, L., and J. LoPICCOLO. "Secondary Orgasmic Dysfunction: Case Study. *Archives of Sexual Behavior*, 1975, *4*, 277–283.

SORENSON, R. C. *Adolescent Sexuality in Contemporary America: The Sorenson Report.* Cleveland: World, 1973.

SPIELBERGER, C. D. "The Effects of Anxiety on Complex Learning and Academic Achievement." In Spielberger, C. D. (Ed.), *Anxiety and Behavior.* New York: Academic Press, 1966, 361–398.

STENGEL, E. *Suicide and Attempted Suicide.* Baltimore: Penguin Books (Rev. Ed.), 1970.

THORNE, F. C. "Ejaculata Praecox: Cause and Treatment." *Diseases of the Nervous System*, 1943, *4*, 273–275.

TONKS, C. M., RACK, P. H., and M. J. ROSE. "Attempted Suicide and the Menstrual Cycle." *Journal of Psychosomatic Research*, 1968, *11*, 319–323.

TOOLAN, J. M. "Suicide in Childhood and Adolescence." In Resnik, H. L. P. (Ed.), *Suicidal Behaviors: Diagnosis and Management.* Boston: Little, Brown, 1968, pp. 220–227.

TUCKMAN, J. and W. F. YOUNGMAN. "A Scale for Assessing Suicide Risk of Attempted Suicides." *Journal of Clinical Psychology*, 1968, *24*, 17–19.

WALSH, R. H. "The Generation Gap in Sexual Beliefs." *Sexual Behavior.* January, 1972, 4–10.

WEINER, I. W. "The Effectiveness of a Suicide Prevention Program." *Mental Hygiene*, 1969, *53*, 357–363.

WOLFE, R. and S. COTLER. "Undergraduates Who Attempt Suicide Compared with Normal and Psychiatric Controls." *Omega: Journal of Death and Dying*, 1973, *4*, 305–312.

YANKELOVICH, D. *The Changing Values on Campus: Political and Personal Attitudes of Today's College Students: A Survey for the JDR.* New York: Washington Square Press, 1972.

ZUCKERMAN, M., TUSHIP, R., and S. FINNER. "Sexual Attitudes and Experience: Attitude and Personality Correlates and Changes Produced by a Course in Sexuality." *Journal of Consulting and Clinical Psychology*, 1976, *44*, 7–19.

PART IV   Future Considerations

Outcome Implications
and Prevention

14

I am the Child.
All the world waits for my coming.
All the earth watches with interest to see
*   what I shall become.*
Civilization hangs in the balance,
For what I am, the world of tomorrow will
*   be.*

I am the Child.
I have come into your world, about which
*   I know nothing.*
Why I came I know not;
How I came I know not.
I am curious; I am interested.

I am the Child
You hold in your hand my destiny.
You determine, largely, whether I shall
*   succeed or fail.*
Give me, I pray you, those things that make
*   for happiness.*
Train me, I beg you, that I may be a blessing
*   to the world.*

COLE

Most Americans readily accept, in principle at least, the rather simple plea of the poet for the right of every child to succeed, to be happy, and to be a credit to society. In this land of opportunity, freedom, and vast riches, who among us would deny an innocent child his or her heritage? Because in a real sense children represent our future, we fondly think of them as our most treasured national resource, although in practice we have treated this valuable resource rather badly (Zigler, 1974; Keniston, 1975; Gordon, 1977). The infant mortality rate in the United States is almost twice as great for nonwhite as for white infants, and it is higher than in thirteen other countries in the world. Each year approximately one million children are physically abused by their parents to the extent that 1000 die and 100,000 require hospitalization. We continue to rely on a foster-care system that shifts children in and out of many different homes, as we espouse the contradictory belief that every child has a right to a stable home and "when we know that continuity, affection and solidity are what make for normal development" (Zigler, 1974, p. 25). There are more than 100,000 emotionally disturbed, handicapped, and minority children circulating in the foster-care market, whom nobody seems to want or who cannot be permanently adopted because our laws place more importance on the rights of biological parents than the basic needs of the child. Thousands more of our children are abandoned in public institutions for the retarded, or in back wards of mental hospitals with minimum care, stimulation, or hope for a better tomorrow.

Current statements on child advocacy affirm "the rights of children to be wanted, to be born healthy, to live in a healthy environment, to receive basic need satisfaction and continuous loving care, to ac-

quire optimal intellectual and emotional skills and appropriate treatment when required" (Williams, 1974, p. 45). To this, Williams adds the following commentary:

On the surface, child advocacy seems to fall within the limbo of those vacuously idealistic, hopelessly consensually validated concepts reflexly accepted by the zeitgeist. In actuality, however, advocacy refers to a radical social process which requires tremendous courage to implement and incisive examination to implement wisely. Child advocacy in action would challenge and work to change existing institutions which are inharmonious with the fullest development of the child. Implicit in the concept is recognition of the serious damage produced in children by many obsolete but entrenched social and political structures and of the necessity to oppose these structures. Without active intervention, child advocacy becomes dogooder lip service and the envisioned Child Development Councils little more than sites for grant hustlers (Williams, 1974, pp. 45–46).

In the spirit of child advocacy, it is only fitting that we devote our last chapter to the consideration of prevention of abnormal behaviors in children. Almost all discussions of this topic follow the public-health model, in which three levels of prevention are identified: (1) *primary prevention* referring to measures taken to ensure that abnormal behaviors will not occur in the first place, (2) *secondary prevention* dealing with the early identification of vulnerable or risk populations for the purpose of applying intervention measures (treatment) to abbreviate the duration and decrease the seriousness of the psychological disorder and, when all else fails (3) *tertiary prevention* referring to the rehabilitation of those who are emotionally disturbed and for whom treatment would increase their chances of a more satisfactory adjustment. For the most part, we shall focus on primary prevention, since the other levels already have been touched on in earlier chapters and since these are measures with the greatest potential pay-off for the elimination of childhood psychopathology. But first let us put the matter of prevention into perspective by reviewing some research findings and their implications with regard to the size of the current problem, and some of the variables associated with psychopathology that are relevant to prevention.

Relevant Research Findings

Current Incidence Estimates

Although noted in Chapter 2, it bears repeating that childhood psychological disorders represent a sizeable problem in our society, wherein approximately ten percent of all children enrolled in our public schools are affected (Bower, 1969). Other estimates indicate that there are more than two and one half million mentally retarded children, three million with speech impairments, and between five and ten million who are considered emotionally disturbed (Cowen, 1973; Huntington, 1974).

Incidence figures obtained either from longitudinal data on normal children studied from infancy to fourteen years or from middle childhood samples randomly selected from birth records reflect fewer instances of abnormal behavior and less frequent hospitalizations in children than adults (Macfarlane, Allen, and Honzik, 1954; Hagnell, 1966; Jonsson, 1967). These findings suggest that adjustment in childhood is not a good predictor of adult psychopathology, inasmuch as there are relatively more emotionally disturbed adults who were normal as children than maladjusted children who later as adults are

classified as disturbed (Clarizio and McCoy, 1976). Moreover, these hospitalization figures suggest that children's disorders are less severe than adults', since we know that families are more able to care for their emotionally disturbed youngsters at home and that fewer psychiatric hospital beds are needed for children than for adults. In fact, research data on the duration of childhood disorders indicate that most children are affected temporarily and that only less than one-third continue to be emotionally disturbed after a four-year follow-up (Glavin, 1967). However, for the specific conditions of delinquency, drug abuse, antisocial sociopathy, and psychosis, the estimates of persistence are considerably higher. For example, Glueck and Glueck (1940) followed up a group of 1000 juvenile delinquents in three five-year periods and found that after the first five years, as many as eighty percent were rearrested, while Roberts (1967) found a similarly high (eighty-two percent) recidivist rate for adolescent drug offenders. Other data indicate a poor prognosis for antisocial adolescents, no recovery in psychotic children after a five year follow-up, but recovery in ninety-one percent of children classified as neurotic (Masterson, 1967). However, a recent study involving the follow up of 255 male delinquents provided a much lower recidivist rate (only twenty-eight percent), but found that those with subsequent criminal records were twice as likely to require psychiatric care as those without further convictions (Koenigsberg, Balla, and Lewis, 1977). Thus, it seems clear that certain childhood disorders have the poorest prospects for the future and bear the greatest social and economic costs over the long haul unless effective preventive measures are found for them. It is important to note that these duration estimates do not include those youngsters who are more or less permanently disabled by mental retardation and brain damage, and for whom prevention is even more urgently needed.

Some Variables Related to Childhood Psychopathology

Research data tell us that low socioeconomic level is related to delinquency, to disruptive behaviors in school, and to poor academic achievement (Douglas, 1964, 1966). But even more powerful than socioeconomic status is the variable of parental influence, because antisocial parents or grandparents (regardless of socioeconomic condition) will have significantly more male offspring who drop out of school or who have police records than comparable groups of more adequate and stable parents (Robins and Lewis, 1966). In addition, a survey of the literature by Robins (1972) revealed that the presence of psychological disorders in parents increased the likelihood of their children having either the same or some other disturbance. The question arises as to whether the inadequate parenting reflects a genetic component or whether it represents faulty environmental influences that affect these children, or some combination of both. However, no definitive answer is available at this time, although in a pragmatic sense either interpretation would have similar implications for primary prevention at least with respect to the advisability of psychiatrically disordered adults having children. In this connection, it has been found that child abuse leads to serious psychological and physical problems in the abused children, and that those youngsters who were removed from the home showed significant physical and intellectual gains over those children who remained with their abusive

parents (Elmer and Gregg, 1967). More recently, suggestive findings from a study of ten infants who came from homes with poor mothering and who were placed into a day care program showed a subsequent salutary effect on I.Q. scores at age three (Resch, Lilleskow, Scheer, and Mihalov, 1977).

In general, abnormal behaviors of children tend to be age specific and are not likely to be evident some years later, although certain behaviors such as destructiveness, somberness, shyness, jealousy, and demanding of attention tend to persist into the teens if they appear at age six or seven (Robins, 1972). Prior to age six or seven, symptoms of psychological disorder are not good predictors of the child's later adjustment, but after that time more consistency and better forecasting can be expected. For example, children with many symptoms are likely to manifest multiple symptoms later and those who are poor academic performers, rebellious in school, and disliked by their peers are likely to be future delinquents in adolescence (Macfarlane et al., 1954; Mulligan, Douglas, Hammond, and Tizard, 1963; Rutter, Birch, Thomas, and Chess, 1964; Conger and Miller, 1966; Robins, 1972).

From the viewpoint of prevention, it is tempting to interpret these findings to support the idea that intervention should begin in the early years before certain behavioral patterns become more stable and difficult to modify (prior to age six or seven). However, as logical and appropriate as early intervention may be, the data are not interpretable beyond their forecasting value. The fact that early childhood problems tend to be age specific does no more than emphasize the particular importance of developmental factors during early childhood. At present, we know little about the frequency with which these young children develop new symptoms later on, and not enough about whether the behavioral signs of early problems are obscured by very limited response repertoires and restricted opportunities to perform outside of the home.

Prevention

Ideally, everyone favors prevention, but as a society we have invested little of our resources and energies in actively working toward this end, especially in the area of childhood psychopathology. We resist understanding prevention and its implementation, because the task is so enormous and extremely complex, and is one that potentially involves alterations in our basic attitudes and values, and perhaps in the restructuring of our society (Broskowski and Baker, 1974).

Eugenic Measures

The most obvious but controversial forms of primary prevention involve the control of procreation in certain at-risk individuals through sterilization, birth control practices, and therapeutic abortion. Involuntary sterilization for the improvement of the human race is quite unacceptable to Americans, because it strikes a fatal blow to our fundamental beliefs and our societal institutions. In a society such as ours where freedom and individual rights are highly regarded and protected, the idea of others determining who should or should not reproduce is repugnant and outrageous. However, we find voluntary measures of limiting conception or of aborting damaged or high-risk fetuses more palatable, and therefore more realistic, approaches to prevention since both individual and societal rights are more readily safeguarded.

Family Planning

Simplified surgical procedures for sterilization, the availability of new methods of contraception, and statutory changes in our abortion practices have helped promote this idea of family planning as an approach to aid parents limit and adequately space their families, and to reduce the number of defective children born. However, it has been estimated that of the more than five million medically indigent women who wanted assistance in family planning, only about one in ten actually received help, because of the limited number of available programs (*Crisis in Child Mental Health*, 1969). These women represent an important target population for family planning and prevention because of their high incidence of various types of morbidity, including offspring with mental retardation, neurological and sensory handicaps, learning disability, and emotional disorder. In a recent paper, Gordon (1977) noted that we live in an age in which it is acceptable for mature and healthy couples to decide not to have children, and in which it is no longer necessary or highly valued for married women to bear large numbers of children. Gordon argued strongly that the time is also right for an active national campaign to dispel the idea that every adult should be a parent and to discourage procreation for persons who are unable to take care of themselves. He asserted that "no couple has a right to bring a child into this world whom they cannot love and nurture" (Gordon, 1977, p. 8). Increased public focus on family planning and greater availability of these programs to target populations would be a large step forward in the prevention of childhood disorders.

Genetic Counseling

As substantial informational and technical gains are made in the field of genetics, and as an increasing number of pediatric disorders (twenty percent) are thought to be genetically based, genetic counseling is rapidly becoming a promising prevention measure (Day and Holmes, 1973). The process involves the assessment of the degree of genetic risk, as well as the social and psychological consequences of birth, followed by a discussion of this information with a couple to aid them in making their decision about conception (Headings, 1975; Nitowsky, 1976). Genetic risk is determined by family pedigree and chromosomal analysis in which the karyotype (arrangement of chromosome pairs by their length and other features of their appearance) made from one individual is compared to a standardized normal karyotype. In addition, statistical techniques are used to calculate and estimate probable genetic risk. While the effectiveness of genetic counseling services has not been adequately evaluated other than through subjective positive impressions, one group of investigators suggested the following as factors that influence people's response to counseling: (1) severity of the abnormal condition at-risk, (2) the existence of an effective therapy for the at-risk condition, (3) the statistical degree of risk, (4) the religious attitudes of the couple, (5) the socioeconomic level of the couple, and (6) their educational level (Leonard, Chase, and Childs, 1972; Coldwell, Say, and Jones, 1975).

Genetic counseling also includes *prenatal genetic diagnosis,* involving the use of a number of laboratory tests to detect chromosomal disorders, inherited metabolic disorders, X-linked disorders, as well as other fetal abnormalities (Littlefield, 1972; Goodner, 1976). The primary diagnostic tool for chromosomal problems is *amniocentesis,* a technique by which amniotic fluid is withdrawn for the purpose of examining through a chromosomal analysis those cells that grow on the culture medium. A relatively new radiologic procedure, called *ultrasonography,* uses ultrasound to diagnose neural tube defects, and other congenital malformations. Golbus (1976) and Young, Matson, and Jones (1976) emphasized that amniocentesis should be done only after careful recording of the family pedigree and appropriate genetic counseling, since the procedure itself is serious and many women who requested it did so for poor reasons. Apparently the probability of fetal loss by this procedure is no greater than the expected abortive rate in the general population, and its effectiveness is extremely good, in that as many as ninety-seven percent of the cases obtained the information they sought from the test (Young et al., 1976; Golbus, 1976). One group of investigators warned of a high incidence of depression (ninety-two percent among women and eighty-two percent among men) following abortion of the fetus for genetic reasons rather than psychosocial abortions or stillborns, although most of these families indicated that they would make the same decision given the same circumstances (Blumberg, Golbus, and Hanson, 1975).

As might be expected, considerable concern has been expressed in the literature about the legal and ethical issues associated with genetic counseling, diagnosis, and therapeutic abortions. These measures have raised many questions for which there are no clear-cut answers, although the need for adequate standards of practice is more apparent than ever before. A sample of these issues would include:

1. When does a couple have enough information to be able to decide on conception or give their consent to an abortion?
2. Is having children a right or a privilege?
3. Which member of a couple should have the final say when the mother and father disagree about an abortion?
4. When does the fetus become a living human who has a right to live?
5. Should the counselor be primarily concerned with the survival of the individual or the survival of the species?
6. What are the prospects of a "cure" becoming available in the near future?
7. Do counselors reflect their bias and thus influence the facts and the eventual decisions?
8. Should the heterozygote carrier have the privilege of confidentiality or should close relatives who may be at-risk have this information? (Kaback, 1972; Baumiller, 1974; Murray, 1974; Milunsky and Reilly, 1975; Hinman, 1976; Tormey, 1976).

Prenatal Care

Adequate medical, dietary, and emotional care can reduce birth complications and prematurity, which are conditions long known to be associated with neurological impairment resulting in intellectual and behavioral deficits in newborns (Birch, 1974). More specifically, a number of noxious factors during the course of pregnancy have been identified as contributing to miscarriages, congenital anomalies, premature births, and the subsequent abnor-

mal development of the child. These stress-agents include maternal infectious diseases (rubella, syphilis, diabetes), maternal malnutrition, large doses of radiation, ingestion of drugs (barbiturates, thalidomide, narcotics), blood-type incompatibility between mother and fetus, and possibly maternal emotional stress (Herbert, 1974). In addition to these sources of prenatal complications, we also know that premature birth is associated more frequently with congenital malformations, as well as with neurological, sensory, and behavioral disorders than are likely to occur in full-term births (Baumgartner, 1962; Pasamanick and Knobloch, 1966).

Complications during pregnancy, at delivery, and premature births are all much more common in lower socioeconomic and socially disadvantaged mothers in whom poor diet, physical status, and health, and lack of or inadequate obstetrical care are prevalent (Thomson and Billewicz, 1963; Donnelly, Flowers, Credick, Wells, Greenberg, and Surles, 1964; Drillien, 1964). It has been estimated that more than forty percent of medically indigent pregnant women deliver their babies either without any prenatal care or with only one visit sometime in the last trimester before birth. Mothers who received no prenatal care have fetal deaths at a rate that is four times greater than that which occurs for women who have one or more prenatal care visits (Hartman and Sayles, 1965). Although we know that comprehensive health care and adequate medical services significantly reduce infant mortality and premature births, especially for nonwhite females (Birch, 1974), we have been reluctant to make the social and economic commitment necessary for this form of prevention. In light of this paradox, the Joint Commission on Mental Health of Children (*Crisis in Child Mental Health*, 1969) strongly recommended programs of "early and systematic prenatal care for all pregnant women" together with ". . . reduced working hours, paid maternity leave, homemaking services, nutritional supplements, prepregnancy immunizations, extensive testing and strict control of drugs, and education aimed at teen-agers and young adults to emphasize the importance of good health and suitable timing of pregnancies" (p. 32), as preventative measures that could effectively improve the physical and mental health of both mother and child.

Neonatal Assessment and Care

Most hospitals routinely do an early evaluation of the neonate within minutes after birth as a means of alerting the pediatrician to potential problems of the infant that could lead to serious developmental problems later on. The Apgar method is regarded as the best way to quantitatively evaluate the infant's condition at birth (Tooley and Phibbs, 1975). A score of 0, 1, or 2 is given to the infant on each of five parameters, which include heart rate, respiratory effort, muscle tone, reflex irritability, and color. If the total score (sum of each score on each area) is between eight and ten within the first five minutes after the infant's birth, the baby is considered allright and not in need of special attention such as active resuscitation (which might prevent anoxia). Babies who receive scores of five or less require additional and immediate medical attention. In addition, pediatric neurologists have described the advantages of an early but thorough neurological assessment of the infant in order to detect possible signs of central nervous

system dysfunction (Volpe, 1975). This type of evaluation can provide early indications of later neurological disorders, as well as early intervention that can lessen the child's impairment and subsequent adjustment.

It is of interest to note that several pediatricians are in the process of constructing a system that will both record and analyze mother-infant interactions primarily for the purpose of assessing the mother's capacity to attend to the needs of her infant and also to evaluate the degree of pathology that might characterize their future relationship (Brazleton, Koslowski, and Main, 1974).

Child Care Programs

These are interventions aimed at supplementing deficiencies in the child's environment that are regarded as essential for normal and healthy development. Programs of this sort typically focus on providing infants and preschool children of working or disabled families adequate nutrition, health care, intellectual and social stimulation, and affection that otherwise may be absent, especially in low socioeconomic homes. For example, some of the consequences of faulty diet were noted in a recent study that found intellectual impairment, higher frequency of infections, and less social responsiveness in a group of chronically malnourished Philippine children ranging in age from six to thirty-six months (Guthrie, Masangkay, and Guthrie, 1976). The fear of interfering with and perhaps weakening the mother-infant bond by separating the infant from mother for long periods of time each day has kept many programs from accepting infants younger than six months of age. However, several carefully done studies have dispelled this concern by showing that the mother-child relationship was not adversely affected by attendance in an infant-care program (Caldwell, Wright, Honig, and Tannenbaum, 1970; Keister, 1970).

Infant day-care programs vary in terms of such variables as the program director's preferences, the service needs of the infants and mothers, the funds available, and the legal constraints (some states do not permit infant care outside of the home) (Honig, 1974). Honig described the advantages and disadvantages of tutorial programs where a trained specialist comes to the home to enhance the development and competence of the infant, of home-visit programs in which a specialist provides low income mothers aid in the nutrition and in the total development of the child, and of parent-group programs where parents are taught in a group ways to foster the development of older preschool children. She also noted that day-care center programs to which young children are brought for such services as baby sitting, proper nutrition, and pediatric care have demonstrated their effectiveness in producing significant developmental gains during the time the children were in attendance. While day care centers outside of the home provide youngsters with the benefits of pleasurable activities, adequate nutrition, good health, and the enhancement of their cognitive, social, and emotional development, they also bear the burden of high financial cost and the risk of decreasing already low parental involvement in the daily care of their children. With more than 4 million children below the age of six who have working mothers, and every prospect that this number will increase in the years ahead as more women choose careers outside of the home, the need for more day care and preschool

programs that are well planned and competently staffed is obvious and urgent (*Crisis in Child Mental Health,* 1969).

Early Identification (after birth)

Essentially these programs involve the assessment of children at critical transition times (such as when they leave the home to begin kindergarten, or when they are about to enter first grade) for the purpose of determining in advance which children are likely to have difficulties and what might be done to help them cope with the demands of the new situation more effectively. For example, one approach is to develop ways to screen preschool children who are about to enter into kindergarten. The Sumter Child Study Project (Newton and Brown, 1967) used psychological testing, structured observations, and interview data as the basis of dividing the children into two groups, the adjusted and maladjusted. Significant differences between the two groups were later found in such areas as absenteeism, initiative, number of completed reading assignments, and self-concept. The study also provided unverified clinical reports suggesting that specific remedial efforts by the professional staff successfully aided the subsequent adjustment of the children who were not then ready to enter school. Speech problems were helped through parent education and speech-skills programs, while others who needed peer experiences and the development of school related skills were either sent to a summer camp or directed to a community recreational program.

An interesting and consistent research finding concerning the optimal age at which children should be admitted to first grade has prevention implications that most school systems tend to ignore. Apparently, children who are younger than the mean age of their first-grade classmates are more likely to achieve less throughout all twelve years of schooling, to be viewed as emotionally disturbed, and to be referred more frequently for professional help than their older counterparts (Weinstein, 1968-1969). However, it was found that differences between entering younger and older first graders dissipated by the end of their second school year in a school program that grouped new students for the first four grades on criteria that included maturity level (Miller and Norris, 1967). In spite of the finding that it is inadvisable for children to begin first grade early, or (if this is done) to ignore maturity levels as a basis of assigning them to classes, school systems have not changed their admission or programming policies. Bower (1974) attributed the school's unresponsiveness partly to the "inertia of social institutions and all sorts of legislative and pseudolegislative (I'm sorry, Mrs. Einstein, but since your son Albert was born at 11 P.M. on December 31, he will have to start school this September, not next September) fol-de-rol" (p. 237). He optimistically maintains that appropriate changes can be brought about, although it would require enormous efforts from both parents and schools to alter legislative and administrative regulations.

Other attempts at early identification have focused on the development of screening programs for specific learning disabilities that typically consisted of the administration of a large battery of tests to kindergarten children. One such program failed to distinguish test patterns for high-risk learning disabled children (Haring and Rideway, 1967), while several others effectively identified children with learning problems, particularly with reading failures

(DeHirsch, Jansky, and Langford, 1966; Ferinden and Jacobson, 1970; Feshbach, Adelman, and Fuller, 1974). Interestingly enough, it was found that the subjective ratings of teachers proved surprisingly effective in identifying learning disabled children, and that a combination of teacher ratings and scores on the Metropolitan Readiness Test yielded an extremely high degree of accuracy (about ninety percent) (Maitland, Nadeau, and Nadeau, 1974).

In recent years, considerable attention has been focused on the health of children from poor families and culturally disadvantaged minorities. In 1967, the Early and Periodic Screening, Diagnosis, and Treatment Program (EPSDT) became a provision under the Medicaid Act to offer eligible children (which represented approximately 12,000,000 from birth to twenty-one years of age) a variety of services for early detection, assessment, and treatment of physical and mental defects (Moore, 1978). This program is still in the process of evaluation, and so far the data on the "developmental assessment component" (the assessment of mental defects) suggest that the EPSDT cannot adequately meet the urgency of the developmental needs of these children. The American Orthopsychiatric Association ("Developmental Assessment in EPSDT," 1978) proposed a series of regional, experimental pilot programs prior to implementation of EPSDT on a national level. These programs should be "aimed at determining and enhancing individual children's strengths to help offset developmental weaknesses and at defining structures of service useful to the Medicaid population" (p. 19).

In general, early identification programs are expensive and, as yet, unproven as a way of predicting poor adjustment years later, particularly in young children such as five- and six-year-olds (Bower, 1969; Bradley and Caldwell, 1978). Moreover, the belief that early identification readily results in the placement of the child into an effective remediation program is more mythical than real in that most school systems are not geared toward the special handling of emotional or learning problems, and most communities do not have the mental health resources to provide the needed services.

Educational Programs

Some investigators have been concerned about the paradox between educational goals and practices wherein our schools avow their interest in fostering the intellectual, social, and emotional development of children, but construct programs that primarily are designed for the restricted purpose of intellectual development. According to Dinkmeyer (1974), schools "are not as willing or ready to deal with the child's social immaturity, feelings of inadequacy, anger, joy, and excitement. They would really, in many instances, prefer to deal with 'an intellectual receptacle' in which they could place knowledge to be withdrawn and inspected at regular intervals" (p. 252). A number of innovative programs have been introduced into the schools for the purpose of enhancing the total development of the child, and on the grounds that this goal can be realized by educational programs aimed at teaching children and their teachers the motivational basis of human behavior, mental health principles, the understanding of self and others, and the like (Ojemann, 1967; Bessell and Palomares, 1967).

Special courses have been developed to teach school children basic behavioral science concepts such as learning theory, intelligence, Erikson's psychosocial stages of development, among others, and to teach them about emotional problems and mental health (described in Clarizio and McCoy, 1976). However, we do not know whether these courses have had a positive effect on the subsequent adjustment of the youngsters who were exposed to them. In contrast, Ojemann (1967) reported that the educational program developed by him and his colleagues produced favorable changes in his elementary-school students, but unfortunately, the findings are open to criticism on a number of methodological issues. Essentially, Ojemann's approach was founded on the idea that early instruction in understanding the underlying motivational components of situations and behaviors beyond their surface meaning lays the groundwork for children to be more sensitive to others and more effective in coping with their own problems. In many ways, Ojemann's program is too imprecise and therefore difficult for teachers to learn; perhaps so unspecific and cumbersome that it has not been widely used even though it has been known to educators since the early 1940s.

Sex education is one of the most controversial instructional programs that a school can offer, although its potential for decreasing ignorance about sex, reducing anxieties, unwanted pregnancies, venereal disease, and sexual hangups is apparent to many. Opponents of sex education in the school curriculum argue that it might lead to an increase in promiscuity, illegitimate births, homosexuality, rape, and venereal disease, or that some teachers are not trained or sufficiently stable to offer such a course. Some claim that sex is a natural phenomenon requiring no prior instruction, and that factual discussions will decrease its mystery and enjoyment later in life. While the opposition is usually vocal and sufficiently troublesome to create unnecessary problems for school administrators, the vast majority of American parents (about seventy percent) apparently favor sex education in the schools (Breasted, 1970). Perhaps this tells us something about the reluctance of many parents to assume the responsibility of educating their own children. Nevertheless, in spite of the fact that most youngsters prefer receiving sex instruction from their parents, friends rather than parents seem to be the primary source of their sexual information (Gagnon, 1965). Inasmuch as peers provide much of a youngster's sex education, it seems only reasonable that measures be taken to assure that what children learn and later communicate to others is sound and accurate.

Gordon (1974) suggests that sex education broadly conceived as encompassing biological and reproductive information as well as the interpersonal aspects associated with sexuality cannot be effectively taught as a separate course in the regular school curriculum. Instead, he favors the integration of human reproduction into an existing biology course where the topic of reproduction is ordinarily covered and the inclusion of information about venereal disease in health classes that typically discuss other communicable diseases. Additional sex education should ideally come from the parents, but since this is not likely to occur often enough, he advocates the development and utilization of community resources for sex information, counseling, birth planning, and so forth. At present, sex education programs in the schools vary considerably with respect to their goals and content, to the extent that their effect is extremely difficult to evaluate. Although much more systematic evaluation of its impact is sorely needed, "the contention is indisputable that the failure to receive a timely sex education makes children's and adolescents' growth into adequately functioning sexual adults considerably more difficult" (McCary, 1973, p. 22).

Educational programs outside of the school curriculum and aimed at young adults, expectant parents, or parents of young children have also enjoyed a measure of popularity as a prevention approach. Books, pamphlets, lectures, TV shows, magazine articles, and newspaper series are among the techniques used with the intent of increasing the sophistication level of the general population about such varied topics as birth control, prenatal care, proper nutrition, factors affecting normal and abnormal development, parent-child interactions, enhancing normal personality development, the effect of drugs on the developing child, family interactions, and a host of other pertinent areas. The fact that these efforts are frequently lucrative is but one indication of their large public appeal and the interest of so many in increasing their effectiveness as parents. However, too little is known about the impact of these mass communication approaches for bringing about enduring changes in behavior. Since these techniques are usually brief, general and superficial, easily misinterpreted to suit ones needs, and relatively unsupervised, it would seem doubtful that they alone could be powerful enough to alter existing habits and patterns.

Parent Effectiveness Training (PET) is an illustration of a more formal educational program designed to teach parents how to shift from either an authoritative or permissive stance to one of mutuality with the child in dealing with parent-child interactions and problems (Gordon, 1970). The idea is to eliminate power struggles between parent and child, to provide both opportunities for self-esteem, and to increase effective communication between parents and child. Lectures, group discussions, and role playing are used to train parents to be more effective, but evaluative data are needed to determine the benefits (if any) of the PET program.

Recently a government-created Follow-Through program has been developed for first and second graders to bolster and maintain the academic and social gains made by them while in the Head Start program (O'Leary and O'Leary, 1977). Workshops provided training to parents in behavioral methods which were aimed at maintaining and increasing desirable behaviors. It is the impression of O'Leary and O'Leary that "If teachers and parents are not taught to follow-through by reinforcing desired academic and social behaviors, the newly acquired academic and social behaviors will die" (O'Leary and O'Leary, 1977, p. 45).

Changing Roles of Female and Male Parents

From the beginning of recorded history, women have occupied a subservient, secondary, and devalued position in society. Their position has been tied to cultural, political, and economic influences and curiously enough to their unique biological ability to bear children. In primitive days, when paternity was often unknown and men were free to gather food without additional responsibilities, the burden of child care and survival fell almost entirely on women. The status of women and their children varied in terms of the economic conditions of the times, but almost always worsened when food was scarce and children (whom women brought into the world) were seen as unwanted competitors for these resources (Horton, 1974). The die

was cast for centuries as generation after generation expected women to function primarily as child bearers and caretakers, and later as wives and homemakers.

Within recent years, dramatic changes have taken place in the roles, functions, and status of women as old economic circumstances no longer apply, and as more and more women refuse to live vicariously through their children and husbands. Today women represent thirty-eight percent of the labor force and in increasing numbers they are preparing for vocational careers, although many are still exploited in salary and restricted in job opportunities and promotions (Horton, 1974). More than ever before, women are exercising reproductive control and are gaining society's sanctions for legal abortions. Women also have markedly changed their sexual attitudes and practices (see Chapter 13), reaching a parity with men and a sense of independence that carries with it implications for the joint sharing of child care. Motherhood with all of its nurturant and homemaking functions will in the future become even more obsolete as an exclusive responsibility of women.

Changes in the status of women and in their roles and functions also require alterations and new roles for men. The old role as the "breadwinner" and the historical idea of "fatherhood" are rapidly vanishing, giving way to *parenting* and sharing household jobs within the family that formerly were sex typed (Pickett, 1974). The importance of the male parent in fostering the normal development of the child was noted in Chapter 3. In making this transition, men will have to deal with and change their notions of masculinity to include as acceptable the performance of roles and functions that have been for so long assigned to women. Male parents and female parents will share in daily chores of home-making, provide warmth, nurturance and affection, as well as discipline to their children without regard for one's biological gender, but with consideration of the family's needs and particular circumstances. Whoever (male or female) is available to cook, take the child to school, listen to problems, run the vacuum cleaner, change the baby, or mow the yard will perform the function free of past exploitation and dominance that characterized our male oriented society. As Pickett so aptly stated:

Women have been the truly conservative force in society in that they have traditionally tended the hearth and nurtured the child while men have gone forth to procure food and make war. It is abundantly clear that these historic functions are in a state of rapid change, and that the social being known as the father will not return to past ways any more than the mother. If he would truly remove himself from the category of obsolescence, planned or otherwise, the man called Father, or the parent who happens to be male, will have to operate in future times as a conserving yet generative force in society.

To do so will mean to cease lamenting for lost glories and to seize the challenge of the hours and days ahead. The sole alternative is oblivion (Pickett, 1974, pp. 441–442).

Professional workers have recognized these changes and have tended to place increasing importance on joint parenting to enhance the child's development and to strengthen the family unit. In addition, the erosion of traditional sex-typed roles has not only brought the sexes into closer parity but more importantly has increased the opportunities for both boys and girls to develop and utilize fully their abilities and resources. In fact, Horton optimistically notes:

The liberation of women guarantees that each child will be wanted, not an accident; that every child will be cared for by two parents that love him/her, not by one in absentia and the other full of resentment; that every child can grow up to his/her fullest potential, not artificially stunted by inappropriate expectations; and that every child will have the chance to become a unique individual, and to be appreciated for what is, not what "should" be. When women are liberated, children can be liberated too (Horton, 1974, p. 436).

REFERENCES

BAUMGARTENER, L. "The Public Health Significance of Low Birth Weight in the U.S.A. with Special Reference to Varying Practices in Providing Special Care to Infants of Low Birth Weights." *Bulletin of the World Health Organization,* 1962, *26,* 175–182.

BAUMILLER, R. C. "Ethical Issues in Genetics." *Birth Defects,* 1974, *10,* 297–299.

BESSELL, H. and U. PALOMARES. *Methods in Human Development.* San Diego: Human Development Training Institute, 1967.

BIRCH, H. G. "Health and the Education of Socially Disadvantaged Children." In Williams, G. J. and S. Gordon (Eds.), *Clinical Child Psychology: Current Practices and Future Perspectives.* New York: Behavioral Publications, 1974, pp. 266–291.

BLUMBERG, B. D., GOLBUS, M. S., and K. H. HANSON. "The Psychological Sequelae of Abortion Performed for a Genetic Indication." *American Journal of Obstetrics and Gynecology,* 1975, *122,* 799–808.

BOWER, E. M. *The Early Identification of Emotionally Handicapped Children in School.* Springfield, Illinois: Charles C Thomas, 1969.

BOWER, E. M. "Mental Health." In Ebel, R. (Ed.), *Encyclopedia of Educational Research* (4th ed.). New York: Macmillan, 1969, pp. 811–828.

BOWER, E. M. "The Three-Pipe Problem: Promotion of Competent Human Beings Through a Preschool Kindergarten Program and Sundry Other Elementary Matters." In Williams, G. T. and S. Gordon (Eds.), *Clinical Child Psychology: Current Practices and Future Perspectives*. New York: Behavioral Publications, 1974. pp. 224–241.

BRADLEY, R. H., and CALDWELL, B. M. "Screening the Environment." *American Journal of Orthopsychiatry*, 1978, *48*, 114–130.

BRAZLETON, T. B., KOSLOWSKI, B., and M. MAIN. "The Origins of Reciprocity: The Early Mother–Infant Interaction." In Lewis, M. and L. A. Rosenblum (Eds.), *The Effect of the Infant on its Caregiver*. New York: Wiley, 1974, pp. 49–79.

BREASTED, M. *Oh! Sex Education!* New York: Praeger, 1970.

BROSKOWSKI, A. and F. BAKER. "Professional, Organizational, and Social Barriers to Primary Prevention." *American Journal of Orthopsychiatry*, 1974, *44*, 707–719.

CALDWELL, B. M., WRIGHT, C. M., HONIG, A. S., and J. TANNENBAUM. "Infant Day Care and Attachment." *American Journal of Orthopsychiatry*, 1970, *40*, 397–412.

CLARIZIO, H. F. and G. F. McCOY. *Behavior Disorders in Children*. New York: Crowell, 1976.

COLDWELL, J G., SAY, B., and K. JONES. "Community Genetics I." *Journal of the Oklahoma State Medical Association*, 1975, *68*, 299–302.

COLE, M. G. "The Child's Appeal." In Clark, T. C. and R. S. Gillespie (Eds.), *1000 Quotable Poems*. Chicago: Willett, Clark, 1937, 161–162.

CONGER, J. J. and W. C. MILLER. *Personality, Social Class, and Delinquency*. New York: Wiley, 1966.

COWEN, E. L. "Social and Community Interventions." *Annual Review of Psychology*, 1973, *24*, 423–472.

"Crisis in Child Mental Health: Challenge for the 1970s." *Report of the Joint Commission on Mental Health*. New York: Harper and Row, 1969.

DAY, N. and L. B. HOLMES. "The Incidence of Genetic Disease in a University Hospital Population." *American Journal of Human Genetics*, 1973, *25*, 237–246.

DEHIRSCH, K., JANSKY, J. J., and W. S. LANGFORD. *Predicting Reading Failure*. New York: Harper and Row, 1966.

"Developmental Assessment in EPSDT." *American Journal of Orthopsychiatry*, 1978, *48*, 7–21.

DINKMEYER, D. "Developing Understanding of Self and Others Is Central to the Educational Process." In Williams, G. J. and S. Gordon (Eds.), *Clinical Child Psychology: Current Practices and Future Perspectives*. New York: Behavioral Publications, 1974, 252–257.

DONNELLY, J. F., FLOWERS, C. E., CREADICK, R. N., WELLS, H. B., GREENBERG, B. G., and K. B. SURLES. "Maternal, Fetal and Environmental Factors in Prematurity." *American Journal of Obstetrics and Gynecology*, 1964, *88*, 918–931.

DOUGLAS, J. W. B. *The Home and the School*. London: Macgibbon and Kee, 1964.

DOUGLAS, J. W. B. "The School Progress of Nervous and Troublesome Children." *The British Journal of Psychiatry*, 1966, *112*, 1115–1116.

DRILLIEN, C. M. *The Growth and Development of Prematurely Born Children*. Baltimore: Williams and Wilkins, 1964.

ELMER, E. and G. S. GREGG. "Developmental Characteristics of Abused Children." *Pediatrics*, 1967, *40*, 595–602.

FERINDEN, W. E., and S. JACOBSON. "Early Identification of Learning Disabilities." *Journal of Learning Disabilities,* 1970, *3,* 589–593.

FESHBACH, S., ADELMAN, H., and W. W. FULLER. "Early Identification of Children with High Risk of Failure." *Journal of Learning Disabilities,* 1974, *7,* 639–644.

GAGNON, J. H. "Sexuality and Sexual Learning in the Child." *Psychiatry,* 1965, *28,* 212–228.

GLAVIN, J. P. *"Spontaneous" Improvement in Emotionally Disturbed Children.* George Peabody College for Teachers, Doctoral Dissertation, August 1967.

GLUECK, S. and E. GLUECK. *Juvenile Delinquents Grown Up.* New York: The Commonwealth Fund, 1940.

GOLBUS, M. S. "The Antenatal Detection of Genetic Disorders: Current Status and Future Prospects." *Obstetrics and Gynecology,* 1976, *48,* 497–506.

GOODNER, D. M. "Prenatal Genetic Diagnosis: Present and Future." *Clinical Obstetrics and Gynecology,* 1976, *19,* 973–980.

GORDON, S. "Is Parenting for Everybody?" *The Exceptional Parent,* 1977, 7, M8–M10.

GORDON, S. "Second Thoughts about Sex Education in the Schools." In Williams, G. J. and S. Gordon (Eds.), *Clinical Child Psychology: Current Practices and Future Perspectives.* New York: Behavioral Publications, 1974, pp. 453–460.

GORDON, T. *Parent Effectiveness Training.* New York: Wyden Press, 1970.

GUTHRIE, G. M., MASANGKAY, Z., and H. A. GUTHRIE. "Behavior, Malnutrition, and Mental Development." *Journal of Cross-Cultural Psychology,* 1976, *7,* 169–180.

HAGNELL, O. *A Prospective Study of the Incidence of Mental Disorders.* Stockholm: Svenska Bokforlaget, 1966.

HARING, N. G. and R. W. RIDEWAY. "Early Identification of Children with Learning Disabilities." *Exceptional Children,* 1967, *33,* 387–395.

HARTMAN, F. E., and E. B. SAYLES. "Some Reflections on Births and Infant Deaths among the Low Socio-Economic Groups." *Minnesota Medicine,* 1965, *48,* 1711–1718.

HEADINGS, V. E. "Alternative Models of Counseling for Genetic Disorders." *Social Biology,* 1975, *22,* 297–303.

HERBERT, M. *Emotional Problems of Development in Children.* London: Academic Press, 1974.

HINMAN, L. F. "Legal Considerations and Prenatal Genetic Diagnosis." *Clinical Obstetrics and Gynecology,* 1976, *19,* 965–972.

HONIG, A. S. "Infant Development Projects: Problems in Intervention." In Williams, G. J. and S. Gordon (Eds.), *Clinical Child Psychology: Current Practices and Future Perspectives.* New York: Behavioral Publications, 1974, pp. 142–167.

HORTON, M. M. "Liberated Women = Liberated Children." In Williams, G. J. and S. Gordon, *Clinical Child Psychology: Current Practices and Future Perspectives.* New York: Behavioral Publications, 1974, pp. 425–436.

HUNTINGTON, D. S. "Programs of Child Care: The United States Need and What Should Be Done." In Williams, G. J. and S. Gordon, *Clinical Child Psychology: Current Practices and Future Perspectives.* New York: Behavioral Publications, 1974, pp. 168–178.

JONSSON, G. "Delinquent Boys, Their Parents and Grandparents." *Acta Psychiatrica Scandinavia,* 1967, 43 (Suppl. 195), 264.

KABACK, M. M. "Perspectives in the Control of Human Genetic Disease." In *Genetics and the Perinatal Patient: Mead Johnson Symposium on Perinatal and Developmental Medicine,* 1972, *1,* 51–57.

KEISTER, M. E. *The Good Life for Infants and Toddlers: Group Care of Infants.* Washington, D.C.: National Association for the Education of Young Children, 1970.

KENISTON, K. *Do Americans Really Like Children?* Paper presented at the meeting of the 52nd Annual meeting of the American Orthopsychiatric Association, Washington, D.C., March 21–25, 1975. (Summary of Meeting Published in "The State of the Child: Highlights from the 52nd Annual Meeting of the American Orthopsychiatric Association," *Hospital and Community Psychiatry,* 1975, *26,* 518–527.)

KOENIGSBERG, D., BALLA, D. A., and D. O. LEWIS. "Juvenile Delinquent, Adult Criminality, and Adult Psychiatric Treatment: An Epidemiological Study." *Child Psychiatry and Human Development,* 1977, *7,* 141–146.

LEONARD, C. O., CHASE, G. A., and B. CHILDS. "Genetic Counseling: A Consumer's View." *New England Journal of Medicine,* 1972, *287,* 433–439.

LITTLEFIELD, J. W. "Recent Experience with Prenatal Genetic Diagnosis." In *Genetics and the Perinatal Patient.* Mead Johnson Symposium on Perinatal and Developmental Medicine, 1972, No. 1, 25–27.

MACFARLANE, J. W., ALLEN, L., and M. P. HONZIK. *A Developmental Study of the Behavior Problems of Normal Children between Twenty-one Months and Fourteen Years.* Berkeley, California: University of California Press, 1954.

MAITLAND, S., NADEAU, J. B., and G. NADEAU. "Early Screening Practices." *Journal of Learning Disabilities,* 1974, *7,* 645–649.

MASTERSON, J. F., Jr. "The Symptomatic Adolescent Five Years Later: He Didn't Grow Out of It." *American Journal of Psychiatry,* 1967, *123,* 1338–1345.

McCARY, J. L. *Human Sexuality.* New York: Van Nostrand, 1973.

MILLER, W. D. and R. C. NORRIS. "Entrance Age and School Success." *Journal of School Psychology,* 1967, *6,* 47–60.

MILUNSKY, A. and P. REILLY. "The 'New' Genetics: Emerging Medicolegal Issues in the Prenatal Diagnosis of Hereditary Disorders." *American Journal of Law and Medicine,* 1975, *1,* 71–88.

MOORE, B. D. "Implementing the Developmental Assessment Component of the EPSDT Program." *American Journal of Orthopsychiatry,* 1978, *48,* 22–31.

MULLIGAN, G., DOUGLAS, J. W. B., HAMMOND, W. A., and J. TIZARD. "Delinquency and Symptoms of Maladjustment: The Findings of a Longitudinal Study." *Proceedings of the Royal Society of Medicine,* 1963, *56,* 1083–1086.

MURRAY, R. F. "The Practitioner's View of the Values Involved in Genetic Screening and Counseling: Individual vs. Societal Imperatives." *Birth Defects,* 1974, *10,* 185–199.

NEWTON, R. and R. A. BROWN. "A Preventive Approach to Developmental Problems in School Children." In Bower, E. M. and W. G. Hollister (Eds.), *Behavioral Science Frontiers in Education.* New York: Wiley, 1967, pp. 499–528.

NITOWSKY, H. M. "Genetic Counseling: Objectives, Principles, and Procedures." *Clinical Obstetrics and Gynecology,* 1976, *19,* 919–940.

OJEMANN, R. H. "Incorporating Psychological Concepts in the School Curriculum." *Journal of School Psychology,* 1967, *5,* 195–204.

O'LEARY, K. D. and S. G. O'LEARY "Behavior Modification in Children." In O'Leary, K. D. and S. G. O'Leary (Eds.), *Classroom Management:* The Successful Use of Behavior Modification (2nd ed.). New York: Pergamon Press, 1977, pp. 1–56.

PASAMANICK, B. and H. KNOBLOCH. "Retrospective Studies on the Epidemiology of

Reproductive Casuality: Old and New." *Merrill-Palmer Quarterly*, 1966, *12*, 7–26.

PICKETT, R. S. "Children and Fathers." In Williams, G. J. and S. Gordon (Eds.), *Clinical Child Psychology: Current Practices and Future Perspectives*. New York: Behavioral Publications, 1974, pp. 437–442.

RESCH, R. C., LILLESKO, R. K., SCHEER, H. M., and MIHALOV, T. "Infant Day Care as a Treatment Intervention: A Follow-up Comparison Study." *Child Psychiatry and Human Development*, 1977, *7*, 147–155.

ROBERTS, C. F., Jr. *A Follow-up Study of the Juvenile Drug Offender*. Institute for the Study of Crime and Delinquency, Sacramento, California, October 1967.

ROBINS, L. N. "Follow-up Studies of Behavior Disorders in Children." In Quay, H. C. and J. S. Werry (Eds.), *Psychopathological Disorders of Childhood*. New York: Wiley, 1972, pp. 414–450.

ROBINS, L. N. and R. G. LEWIS. "The Role of the Antisocial Family in School Completion and Delinquency: A Three-Generation Study." *Sociological Quarterly*, 1966, *7*, 500–514.

RUTTER, M., BIRCH, H. G., THOMAS, A., and S. CHESS. "Temperamental Characteristics in Infancy and the Later Development of Behavioural Disorders." *British Journal of Psychiatry*, 1964, *110*, 651–661.

THOMSON, A. M., and W. Z. BILLEWICZ. "Nutritional Status, Maternal Physique and Reproductive Efficiency." *Proceedings of the Nutritional Society*, 1963, *22*, 55–60.

TOOLEY, W. H., and R. H. PHIBBS. "Delivery Room Management of the Newborn." In G. B. Avery (Ed.), *Neonatology*. Philadelphia: Lippincott, 1975, 111–126.

TORMEY, J. F. "Ethical Considerations of Prenatal Genetic Diagnosis." *Clinical Obstetrics and Gynecology*, 1976, *19*, 957–963.

VOLPE, J. J. "Neurological Disorders." In Avery, G. B. (Ed.), *Neonatology*. Philadelphia: J. B. Lippincott, 1975, pp. 729–795.

WEINSTEIN, L. "School Entrance Age and Adjustment." *Journal of School Psychology*, 1968–69, *7*, No. 3, 20–28.

WILLIAMS, G. J. "The Psychologist as Child Advocate: Reflections of a Devil's Advocate." In Williams, G. J. and S. Gordon (Eds.), *Clinical Child Psychology: Current Practices and Future Perspectives*. New York: Behavioral Publications, 1974, pp. 45–49.

YOUNG, P. E., MATSON, M. R., and O. W. JONES. "Amniocentesis for Antenatal Diagnosis: Review of Problems and Outcomes in a Large Series." *American Journal of Obstetrics and Gynecology*, 1976, *125*, 495–501.

ZIGLER, E. F. "Children's Needs in the Seventies: A Federal Perspective." In Williams, G. J. and S. Gordon (Eds.), *Clinical Child Psychology: Current Practices and Future Perspectives*. New York: Behavioral Publications, 1974, pp. 24–34.

Glossary

Activity Therapy. A group therapy designed for pre-pubescent youngsters in which play activities that are functionally related to the clinical needs of the children are used separately or as a group project.

Amniocentesis. A diagnostic tool for chromosomal problems in which amniotic fluid from a pregnant mother is withdrawn to permit a chromosomal analysis.

Anal Stage. The second phase of psychosexual development in which the anus becomes the site of sexual stimulation and gratification. The period extends from about eighteen months to approximately three years during which time the child seems to derive sensual pleasure from both retention and expulsion of fecal matter.

Animal Magnetism. Mesmer's belief that the stars influenced people through magnetic forces and that an imbalance of them within an individual could cause illness.

Anomie. A concept referring to a breakdown of society's regulatory machinery wherein the socially defined standards of conduct no longer serve as effective guidelines for behavior.

Anorexia. Refusal to eat, varying in severity from fussy appetites to rare life endangering self-starvation.

Anterograde Amnesia. Loss of memory for those matters that have occurred after the precipitant event.

Aphasia. A term used to designate an impairment of symbolic language (involving reception and/or expressive deficits) and in the comprehension of language.

Asynchronous Growth. A principle of development that states that different parts and subsystems of the human organism develop at different rates and times, and that the various parts of the organism do not grow equally or all at once.

Battered Child Syndrome (Child Abuse). A term referring to regular physical assaults of the child by the parents (usually one) with harmful objects that often result in serious injury and sometimes death to the child.

Behavior Therapy. A general term used to refer to treatment of abnormal behaviors by methods and techniques that have been derived from experimental psychology and the principles of learning.

Behavioral Assessment. Procedures that grew out of behavior therapy which focus on the measurement of target behaviors and the person's behavioral repertoire for the purpose of affecting behavior change in some desired direction.

Biofeedback. A therapeutic approach in which the client's physiological responses are monitored and fed back so that the client can learn to control them (sometimes with the aid of positive reinforcement).

Bronchial Asthma. A psychophysiologic disorder of the respiratory system in which the bronchial tube is restricted in air exchange producing frightening symptoms of wheezing and labored breathing.

Cephalocaudal Development. A directional flow of physical development in which growth and motor development generally proceed from the head to the tail end of the human body.

Child Welfare. A social and legislative movement that began late in the 19th century as a response to excessive child abuse, and which produced regulative legislation and the creation of special social agencies for the protection of children.

Classical Conditioning (Respondent Conditioning). A learning paradigm first introduced by Pavlov in which a neutral stimulus (CS), when repeatedly paired with a stimulus (UCS) that naturally elicits a response (UCR), will come to elicit by itself a response (CR) that is similar to the original one.

Client-Centered Therapy. A treatment strategy introduced by Carl Rogers in which the therapist provides the client with complete acceptance and warmth while being reflective of what the client says.

Colic. A condition that occurs within the first few weeks of life that is characterized by loud and persistent crying.

Conceptual Model. A frame of reference that provides a broad but cohesive way of understanding and explaining abnormal behavior.

Concordance Rate. The percent of cases in which both members of monozygotic and dizygotic twin pairs manifest the trait in question.

Conflict. Competing or opposing responses that tend to block or inhibit overt behavior.

Contingency Contract. An agreement reached by the therapist and the client concerning the behavioral goals and the reinforcement to be received when the goals are successfully met.

The Contingency or Family-Risk Method. The use of large samples of relatives of index cases (known carriers of the trait under investigation) to assess the degree to which the trait is related to blood ties and to hereditary factors.

Cont'ngent Negative Variation (CNV). A type of cortical response that has been associated with attention which is characterized by a slow rise in negative potential when the subject anticipates the presentation of a stimulus.

Cretinism (Hypothyroidism). A term used to designate several aberrant conditions of the thyroid that may be associated with mental retardation.

Criterion. A standard of functioning against which an assessment or treatment technique can be evaluated.

Cross-Fostering Method. A research approach to reflect the relative potency of hereditary and environmental factors. It provides for a comparison of children from biologically "normal" parents who are placed in foster homes in which one or both of the adopted parents are affected by a disorder with chidren from at least one biological parent evidencing the disorder and who are placed in "normal" foster homes.

Cultural Norms. Approved standards and expectations set by society for the behavior of its members.

Defense Mechanisms. A set of coping methods used to deal with conflict and anxiety that are unconscious but relatively fixed.

Delayed Speech. Failure to talk by the age of 30 months or very slow progress in the acquisition of new words and in the formation of sentences.

Delusion. A fixed belief that is based on a false premise and is discrepant with the person's cultural training.

Dementia Praecox. An obsolete term for Schizophrenia, originally used to describe a psychotic condition in adults that was characterized by unalterable and progressive deterioration of mental functioning beginning in adolescence.

Demonology. The ancient view that abnormal behaviors were caused by evil spirits that inhabited people.

Denial. The unconscious act of simply denying the existence of painful facts or feelings.

Detoxification. Procedure involving withdrawal from an addictive drug under medical management.

Developmental Norms. Expected age (expressed in range and average) for growth and behavioral patterns based on data obtained from large samples of normal children.

Diagnosis. The process of accumulating and discriminating data for the purpose of identifying (labeling) a pathological state.

Displacement. The transfer of instinctual emotions from one object to another, which permits the release of tensions in a manner that is less anxiety-producing.

Dissociation. The phenomenon described by Janet to reflect a separation between the systems of the personality (normal personality consisted of systems of organized ideas and actions that interacted with each other), and the isolation of certain systems from the rest of the personality.

DNA (Deoxyribonucleic acid). Complex chemical substance of genes responsible for genetic replication from one generation to another and for transferring genetic information.

Down's Syndrome (Mongolism). An autosomal syndrome associated with an extra Group-G chromosome resulting in distinctive physical features and mental retardation.

Drive. A motivational state that impels or energizes the organism to respond (without specific direction).

DSM-I, DSM-II, DSM-III. Diagnostic and Statistical Manual of Mental Disorder (and revisions) representing the diagnostic classification system officially adopted by the American Psychiatric Association.

Dyslexia. A term used to label those children of average intelligence who have a reading disability not attributable to deprived educational opportunities or gross sensory or neurological impairment.

Echopraxia. The unsolicited repetition and imitation of motor acts performed by another person.

Ego. A component of the personality postulated by Freud which emerges from the id to facilitate the aims of the id by the acquisition of skills that enable the child to achieve pleasure in ways that are within the bounds of objective reality. The ego controls cognitive and intellectual functioning and acts as a mediator between id impulses and the demands of reality, and between the id and the superego.

Electroencephalogram (EEG). An instrument used to record electrical activity of the brain by means of electrodes attached to the scalp.

Emotive Imagery. A modification of systematic desensitization that pairs imagery of pleasurable scenes (instead of relaxation) with a graded series of anxiety stimuli.

Encopresis. Involuntary defacation and withholding of feces not directly caused by physical disease occurring in children beyond the age of 3 years.

Enuresis. Involuntary passage of urine during sleep (nocturnal) or more infrequently during the day (diurnal) in children past the age of 3 or 4 in which the cause is not linked to any demonstrable organic pathology.

Evoked Potential. Cerebral responses evoked by sensory stimulation such as flashes of light or auditory clicks.

Expectancy Measure. The probability that a person will fall into a specific category of abnormal behavior sometime during his or her lifetime.

Extinction. The elimination of a learned response through the discontinuance of reinforcement.

Factor Analysis. A statistical method used to isolate empirically clusters of traits or characteristics derived from a series of intra-correlations of test scores.

Family Therapy. A therapeutic approach in which family members interact with each other and the therapist, and which is based on the idea that abnormal behaviors of a child represent expressions of family transactions and pathology.

Feeblemindedness (Mental Deficiency and Mental Retardation). Terms used interchangeably to characterize subnormal intelligence and retarded social development in individuals who have not been culturally or educationally deprived.

Filial Therapy. A variant of play therapy in which parents are trained to conduct non-directive play with their emotionally troubled children.

Free Association. A technique developed by Freud for releasing suppressed emotions and for revealing unconscious problems, in which the individual is asked to say whatever comes to mind without censuring his or her thoughts.

Galactosemia. An autosomal recessive metabolic condition which impairs the metabolism of galactose and usually results in mental retardation if not treated early.

Galvanic Skin Response (GSR). A measure of the change in skin resistance due to alterations in sweat gland activity which is thought to indicate arousal or emotionality.

General Paresis. A disease caused by syphilitic infection which involves irreversible and severe damage to the brain and produces the clinical picture involving loss of contact with reality, personality disorganization, delirium, paralysis, tremors, and locomotor ataxia.

Genital Stage. The last psychosexual stage of development occurring during adolescence and at a time when the sexual drive is heightened and the opposite sex becomes the sexual object for those who have developed normally.

Group Therapy. A therapeutic approach in which a number of unrelated clients are brought together at regular intervals to engage in psychologically planned interactions with each other and one or more therapists.

Hallucination. A sensory misperception experienced while awake and in the absence of any corresponding external stimuli.

Higher Order Conditioning. The successful pairing of a conditioned stimulus with a new conditioned stimulus which will elicit the same conditioned response as that produced from the initial classical conditioning.

High-Risk Children. Youngsters who have one biological parent manifesting the disorder but who have not themselves shown signs of the disturbance at the time of the initial study.

Homonculus. An ancient view of children in which a child was perceived as a little adult without a personality of his or her own.

Hyperamnesia. The unusual ability to recall minute and sometimes insignificant details learned in the distant past.

Hyperesthesia. Sensory difficulty characterized by heightened or extreme sensitivity.

Id. The inherited and original energy system of the personality posited by Freud as present at birth and from which the other two components of the personality (the ego and superego) are later energized and differentiated. The id represents the world of subjective reality and its activities are governed by the seeking of pleasure and the avoidance of pain.

Implosive Therapy (Flooding). A therapy based on maximal anxiety arousal by exposing the client to highly threatening stimuli to extinguish aversive reactions.

Incidence. The total number of new cases of a disorder that occurs within a specified population and a period of time.

Instincts. Inborn energy states and unconscious drives of the id that give rise to tension and which are reducible to the two fundamental ones of sex and aggression.

Intellectualization. The process of concealing threatening feelings by discussing them in an abstract, intellectual manner.

Intelligence Quotient (IQ). A quantitative term of intelligence reflecting the relationship between the child's mental age and chronological age.

Intelligence Tests. Standardized techniques for measuring intellectual functioning.

Intermittent Reinforcement. A schedule of reinforcement in which the wanted response is not always followed by a reinforcer.

Karyotype. Pictures pairs of normal chromosomes arranged in a prescribed order by which comparisons can be made in identifying chromosomal abnormalities.

Klinefelter's Syndrome. A disorder associated with an extra X chromosome in males that produces feminine secondary sex characteristics and sometimes mental retardation.

Latency Stage. The longest psychosexual stage of development extending from about 6 years of age through preadolescence. It is a stage where sexual tensions and activities are dormant, where the child can recover from the turmoil of the oedipal phase, and where further identification with the same sex parent occurs.

Learning. The process by which environmental forces bring about lasting changes in behavior through practice.

Libido. A psychoanalytic term used to reflect the energy of the sex drive.

Manic Depressive Psychosis. An affective disorder manifested in either alterations of emotional excitement and euphoria (mania) with periods of melancholia and depression, or episodes of mania or depression, or both.

Marasmus. A condition in which infants evidence progressive emaciation and possible death as a result of malnutrition or prolonged maternal separation and deprivation.

Maturation. Physical alterations in size, and qualitative changes in tissues or in anatomical and physiological organization that occur in the course of human development.

Mental Age. A measure of mental development derived from test results that were standardized according to chronological age.

Mental Retardation (Mental Deficiency, Feeblemindedness). Significantly subaverage intellectual functioning existing concurrently with deficits in adaptive behavior that is manifested during the developmental period prior to adulthood.

Milieu Therapy. A term used to refer to treatment methods involving ongoing experiences in which the daily environment is ordered, arranged, and planned as a therapeutic program.

Modeling (Imitation Learning). Learning that takes place by observing another person or a model making a response or a set of responses.

Negative Reinforcement. The strengthening of behavior through the removal of an unpleasant or aversive consequence.

Neologism. The coining of a new word.

Neuroticism. A statistically isolated dimension (by Eysenck) that is related to emotional instability and a poorly integrated personality.

Neurotransmitters. Chemical mediators of neural communication in the central nervous system.

Nightmare. A common fright reaction that occurs during the last third of the night in Stage 1-REM sleep.

Night Terror. A relatively rare fright reaction that occurs within the first two hours of the night in Stage 4-non REM sleep.

Oedipal Stage. A psychosexual stage of development between ages 4 and 6 in which the opposite sex parent becomes the object of libidinal pleasure. Also known as the phallic stage.

Operant Conditioning (Instrumental Learning). A learning paradigm in which S-R bonds are strengthened by making the reinforcement contingent on the emission of the proper response.

Oral Stage. The first stage of psychosexual development occurring during the initial eighteen to twenty-four months of the infant's life in which stimulation of the errogenous zones of the lips and mouth provide pleasure and relieve libidinal tension.

Orgasmic Dysfunction. Either a woman's failure to achieve a climax by any means of sexual stimulation (primary), or her present failure to achieve an orgasm after experiencing at least one climax in the past (secondary).

Paresthesia. A peculiar skin sensation without objective cause.

Pedigree Method. A research method that consists of tracing the incidence of a trait in all family members over several generations in order to make inferences about the genetic principle involved.

Perseveration. Repetition of one's prior response.

Phallic Stage. See Oedipal Stage.

Phenyketonuria (PKU). An autosomal recessive metabolic disorder in which phenylalanine is improperly utilized by the body, and its accumulation in the bloodstream causes brain damage and mental retardation.

Phobia. A persistent and irrational fear of an object or situation that the person is unable to dispel. The fear usually leads to the avoidance of the object or situation.

Phrenology. A theory proposed by Gall which proposed that character traits were localized in 37 different areas of the brain and that abnormal behavior was tied to the overdevelopment of these areas (which could be felt as bumps on the skull).

Pica. The craving and consumption of substances not ordinarily considered edible.

Play Therapy. A therapeutic approach for pre-adolescent children in which play activities are used to establish rapport and to facilitate communication.

Pleasure Principle. Psychoanalytic principle by which the id seeks immediate gratification of drives and desires and the avoidance of pain without regard for the consequences.

Positive Reinforcement. The strengthening of behavior through rewards that either meets the biological requirements or the learned needs of the individual.

Premature Ejaculation. An orgasm that occurs very quickly in a male resulting in his inability to satisfy his partner during coitus.

Prevalence. The total number of cases (old and new) present in a given population during a specified time interval.

Principle of Differentiation. Structural and functional development that progresses from the general to the specific or from the simple to the complex in patterns.

Projection. The unconscious act of blaming others or attributing one's faults to others.

Projective Tests. A class of personality tests consisting of a set of unstructured and ambiguous stimuli to which it is assumed that the respondent will reveal his/her basic personality.

Proximodistal Development. A directional flow of physical development in which growth and motor development proceed from the central axis to the periphery of the human body.

Psychic Determinism. The belief that every human act occurs as a function of prior mental events and not as a matter of happenstance. Previous events and experiences determine all facets of a person's behavior.

Psychoneuroses. A set of psychological disorders characterized by intense feelings of anxiety, personal discomfort and distress, and self directed reactions to the stress of conflicts.

Psychopathology. Abnormal behavior attributable to psychological and/or biological causes.

Psychophysiologic Disorders. Psychopathological conditions characterized by physical symptoms that arise from dysfunctioning and structural damage to a single organ system usually innervated by the autonomic nervous system which is primarily caused by prolonged psychological and social stress.

Psychosexual Stages of Development. The series of sequential and crucial developmental stages postulated by Freud that are associated with libidinal impulses (sexual) that play an important role in later personality formation.

Psychosocial Stages of Development. Sequential series of developmental stages postulated by Erikson that focus on important socialization conflicts at various points in a person's life span.

Psychosurgery. The removal or destruction of brain tissue as a therapeutic intervention for the elimination of abnormal behaviors.

Psychotherapy. A psychologically planned and ongoing interaction between a trained person, the therapist, and a client who has adjustment problems.

Punishment. A condition or event that is presented after a response occurs that will decrease the probability that the response will be emitted (weaken the S-R association).

Rationalization. The process of avoiding anxiety by finding justifiable excuses for doing something unacceptable.

Reaction Formation. The process by which the ego substitutes actions and feelings directly opposite to those that might be produced by sexual or aggressive impulses.

Reality Principle. Psychoanalytic principle governing the ego by which gratification of pleasure is deferred through the consideration of the demands of objective reality.

Reality Therapy. A therapeutic approach which focuses on the present and encourages the client to make value judgments about his or her behaviors, to make a plan that would achieve the desired goal, and to be committed to the plan.

Regression. A method of dealing with external or internal conflicts by retreating to an immature stage of development or by resorting to earlier modes of responding.

Reinforcement. Any event or condition which leads to the strengthening of a stimulus-response connection or to the increased probability that a response will be emitted.

Reliability. The extent to which a measure (test or rating) yields the same results each time it is used. The consistency of results may be derived from agreement between two or more observers (observer agreement), agreement between the same measure over points in time (consistency agreement), or agreement between two or more samples of the same population with regard to the expected frequency of occurrence of the measure (frequency agreement).

Repression. A basic and primary defense mechanism which actively banishes from consciousness unacceptable or anxiety arousing impulses, thoughts, or wishes.

Resistance. A psychoanalytic term that depicts the individual's opposition to therapeutic attempts to bring unconscious material to consciousness.

Retrograde Amnesia. Loss of memory for matters that took place prior to the precipitant event.

RNA (Ribonucleic acid). A single stranded molecule that receives the coded information in a DNA molecule. It acts as a messenger and initiates certain chemical reactions that eventually determine bodily structure and function.

Schizophrenia. Adult psychosis characterized by loss of contact with reality, ambivalence, disordered thinking, attentional deficits, and affective impairment.

Self Actualization. The realization of one's inherent potentials.

Shaping. A technique used by operant conditioners in which approximations of the wanted behavior is reinforced, followed by the reinforcement of responses that are increasingly similar to it until only the appropriate response is reinforced.

Shock Therapy. Somatic therapy in which drugs (Metrazol) or electricity are used to produce a convulsive reaction.

Somnambulism. A disruption of sleep characterized by sleep walking and occurring during the first two hours of the night in non-REM sleep.

Spontaneous Remission. Improvement that occurs over time without planned treatment intervention.

Stuttering. A term used to refer to a particular breakdown in speech fluency that is characterized by blocking, repetition, and prolongation of speech sounds.

Sublimation. A way of expressing unacceptable impulses in an acceptable manner by channeling ego-threatening drives into constructive outlets such as art and science.

Superego. Postulated by Freud as the moral and conscience component of the personality, it is recognized by its judicial functions in rendering judgments about right and wrong and in its strivings for perfection and the ideal.

Symptom. A biological, psychological, or behavioral manifestation of a disorder or illness.

Systematic Desensitization (Counter-Conditioning). A behavioral treatment method introduced by Wolpe in which the incompatible response of relaxation is paired with a graded series of anxiety stimuli to prevent the occurrence of a fear response and to allow anxiety to extinguish.

Tay-Sachs Disease. A recessive disorder of lipid metabolism found predominantly among children of eastern European Jewish ancestry. The disorder is progressive and death usually occurs before the age of four.

Temperament. A concept referring to individual differences in inborn potentials for action which are characterized by particular behavioral styles and which are significantly affected by the interplay of environmental forces.

Thought Disorder. Gross disruption and impairment of normal thought processes and content characterized by incoherence, disorganization, and inappropriate or bizarre content.

Tic. An involuntary spasmodic muscle twitching of the face or body parts that is repeated at frequent intervals.

Turner's Syndrome. An anomaly of the sex chromosome in females (XO) resulting in sexual infantilism, distinctive physical features, and mental retardation in about 20% of the cases.

Twin Study Method. A research method in which monozygotic twins and dizygotic twins are studied with respect to a particular trait to determine the influence of genetic factors.

Unconscious. Primarily but not exclusively a Freudian concept that refers to a state of unawareness in which certain unacceptable mental contents are inaccessible to consciousness under ordinary circumstanecs. The unconscious is also used to designate the storage of mental material banished from consciousness.

Validity. The extent to which a measure or an hypothesis verifies what it purports to measure or say.

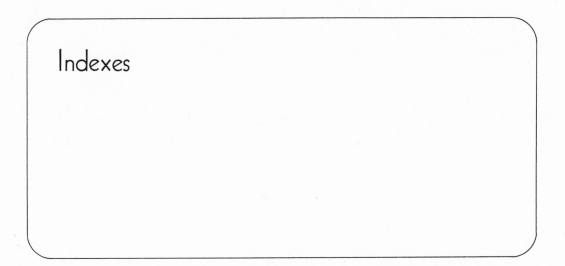

Indexes

AUTHOR INDEX

SUBJECT INDEX

ABAB design, 179
Abnormal behavior; *see* Childhood psychopathology
ABO incompatibility, 315, 327
Academic achievement, 39, 110, 183, 267, 272
  in adolescence, 367, 415–16
  and birth difficulties, 279–80
  and delinquency, 369, 377, 379–80, 386, 387, 402
  and drug abuse, 289–90, 395
  and hyperkinesis, 284, 285, 289, 295
  and I. Q. tests, 310
  and learning disabilities, 276, 280–81, 291, 293–94
  and reading difficulties, 277, 278
  in school-phobic children, 336–37
  and socioeconomic level, 318; *see also* Socioeconomic level
  and speech disorders, 272, 292
  tests of, 150–51
Accommodation (in Piaget's theory), 74
Acculturation, 109–10
Acting-out behavior; *see* Antisocial behaviors
Activity groups, 171
Activity level; *see also* Hyperactivity, Hyperkinetic syndrome
  in childhood schizophrenia, 231, 232
  in clinical assessment, 130

in early infantile autism, 242, 243, 256
in hyperkinesis, 283–85, 290
measurement of, 283
Adjustment problems, of late adolescence and college years, 410–43
  academic pressures, 415–16
  dependence-independence, 412–15
  peer relationships, 416–17
Adler, A., 107, 119
Adolescence (Adolescent)
  and academic achievement, 367, 415–16
  adjustment problems of, 415–43
  alienation in, 109
  and cognition, 75
  disorders, 34, 35–39, 42, 181, 367–408
    delinquency, 367, 368–87, 401
    drug abuse, 367, 389–401
    runaway, 367, 387–89, 401
    treatment of, 167, 168, 172, 179, 181, 184, 188, 385–87, 388–89, 398–401
  physical changes in 56, 367
  psychoanalytic views of, 72–73
Adoption studies, 97–98
Adult psychopathology, early views of, 10–12; *see also* Schizophrenia
Affective disturbances; *see* Emotional disturbances
Aggression (aggressive); *see also*

Antisocial behaviors, Delinquency
in childhood schizophernia, 236
control of, 179, 180
definition, 383–84
and drug abuse, 390
effect of punishment on, 84, 112, 114
from frustration, 383
increase of, by positive reinforcement, 84, 119
measure of, 147
from modeling, 84–85, 384, 401
relation to body type, 384
unconscious, 334, 336, 341, 342, 382, 383, 396
Alcoholics Anonymous, 400, 403
Alcoholism (alcoholic), 64–65, 114, 176, 190, 401
  clinical picture, 392, 394–95, 396
  etiology, 141, 394–95
  heterogeneous population, 398
  prognosis, 401
  self-help organizations, 400, 403
  treatment, 398–99, 401–2, 403
Amaurotic Idiocy, 312
American Association on Mental Deficiency (AAMD), 304, 305, 306, 317
American Orthopsychiatry Association, 453
American Psychiatric Association, 33, 34, 306
Amines, as antidepressants, 182, 184, 189

485